SEX CRIMES AND PARAPHILIA

Eric W. Hickey, Ph.D.

PEARSON

Prentice
Hall

Upper Saddle River, New Jersey 07458

Library of Congress Cataloging-in-Publication Data

Sex crimes and paraphilia / [edited by] Eric W. Hickey.
     p. cm.
   ISBN 0-13-170350-1
   1. Sex crimes.   2. Sexual deviation.   I. Hickey, Eric W.
   HQ71.S396 2006
   364.15'3—dc22

                                    2005014351

Executive Editor: Frank Mortimer, Jr.
Assistant Editor: Mayda Bosco
Editorial Assistant: Kelly Krug
Production Editor: Patty Donovan, Pine Tree Composition, Inc.
Production Liaison: Barbara Marttine Cappuccio
Director of Manufacturing and Production: Bruce Johnson
Managing Editor: Mary Carnis
Manufacturing Manager: Ilene Sanford
Manufacturing Buyer: Cathleen Petersen
Senior Design Coordinator: Mary Siener
Cover Designer: Michael Ginsberg
Cover Image: Lee Pettet/Stockphoto
Formatting and Interior Design: Pine Tree Composition, Inc.
Printer/Binder: Courier/Stoughton

10 9 8 7 6 5 4 3 2 1
ISBN 0-13-170350-1

This is a special dedication to Chad and Ben Buckarma, courageous Iraqi Freedom combat soldiers, serving their country in the distant battlegrounds of Iraq. These young men have come to learn that freedom always has a price. And to the hundreds of thousands of American, British and coalition forces who have served or will serve in Iraq, Afghanistan, or other combat zones. And to the thousands wounded and those who pay the ultimate price with their lives. Our debt is to them. Let us not ignore the personal battles many soldiers and their families will face long after the guns are silent.

Chad & Ben, you are heroes.

CONTENTS

PART I
UNDERSTANDING SEX CRIMES   1

PART II
PROSTITUTION, PORNOGRAPHY, AND OBSCENITY   33

PART III
PARAPHILIA   55

PART IV
BODY FLUIDS   109

PART V
FETISHES   153

PART VI

NONCONSENSUAL OR DANGEROUS PARAPHILIC INTERESTS   229

PART VII

HARMING CHILDREN   307

PART VIII
STALKING, RAPE, AND MURDER   369

PART IX
TREATING SEX OFFENDERS AND COMMUNITY ATTITUDES   449

PREFACE

Social science discourse is rife in unraveling the complexities of human behavior. None are more involved and convoluted than sorting out the motives, methods, and lives of sex offenders, those who imitate them, and those whose sexual interests rest on the cusp of the uncommon. Researching sex offenders and their victims is like removing a layer from an onion: There is always another layer to look at and decipher. Indeed, the ciphering of sex offending creates distractions even for the trained eye. Sex offenders are the poster-people for dysfunctioning humans and as such, we loathe them. Yet under their cloaks of criminal behavior lie tangled webs of childhood trauma that encompasses neglect, abuse, rejection, and abandonment. We are keen to dismiss such etiology as simplistic. After all, many people have suffered similar traumas in childhood and have matured into normal, productive adults. Unfortunately sex offending is far from being simplistic; otherwise we would understand it. Sex offenders follow many roads in their methods and answer to many whys in their motivations thus making them unique, each with their own stories, each with their own lies and self-deceptions. The rapist, the child molester, the pedophile, the lust killer, each has arrived at his destination of dysfunction via a series of events contingent upon cognition, perception, intellect, and skill. Psychopathology harbors its own unique density.

The chapters contained in this text are descriptive and informational. Their authors were challenged to provide not only well-researched material but also presentations that would distinguish them as thought-provoking and insightful. The 52 articles dispassionately examine a plethora of sex crimes ranging from nonviolent offenses such as exhibitionism, voyeurism, and obscene telephone calls, to serial rapes and lust murders. Although the pathway to violent sex crimes can be circuitous there are salient characteristics found among violent sex offending that have their roots in paraphilic fantasies and behaviors. Many paraphilia are not considered criminal activity yet they may serve as springboards for more deviant fantasies and behavior. Indeed, the term *sex crimes* can be a bit of a misnomer as some crime has more to do with the sexualization of crime than it has to do with a sex crime per se. For example, burglary is typically an *instrumental* crime because the primary purpose of the burglar is to steal property. They are usually not interested in confronting anyone but rely on stealth and expertise to gain undetected access to property. Sometimes burglars prefer "hot burglaries" in which residents are at home, often asleep. For some, this offers more excitement. For others, along with the thrill is the sense of power and control. These feelings can be sexualized through masturbatory conditioning. One offender noted that each time he climbed through an open window at night to carry out his burglaries, he always climaxed. This offender had sexualized a property crime. Another confided that he preferred hot burglaries because he liked the idea of being in the room with the victims while they slept. He said it made him feel powerful. He fantasized about touching the victim as she slept.

Sex offending is not just about men who rape women or molest children. Reported methods, motivations, and fantasies of these offenders tell us that American society has a pervasive problem with sex offending and the sexualization of criminality. Consider for a moment where you feel safest when you are away from your home. Offenders like to be where you feel safe because you become comfortable and let your guard down. The following are actual victim accounts:

- A woman entered a supermarket and was immediately noticed by a male wandering alone in the store. While she shopped he stalked her, watching and waiting. He knew that women become distracted in certain areas of stores. She arrived at the greeting card section and began browsing. Before beginning the search for just the right card, she glanced around. She barely noticed the man standing at the end of the aisle, staring in her direction. There were two other persons to her left reading cards. Oblivious to what was about to happen the woman began perusing the greeting cards. A moment later the other customers moved away. The aisle was now empty except for the man and the half-kneeling woman. A moment later she felt someone walk behind her so close that she could almost feel someone touching her. She read on, selected a card, and went to the check-out stand. As she reached back to get her purse that was on a strap over her shoulder, she discovered that her sweater and purse were covered in semen.

- A sixteen-year-old babysitter takes two 8-year-old girls to the local park. She had been instructed never to let them out of her sight. The sitter watched from a park bench as the girls played and soon began reading her novel. The girls wandered a bit over a small ridge of grass and down to the stream. They were only a few yards away but now out of view of the sitter. In a moment, a young man in his early twenties ran up to the girls and asked them to pull down their pants for $20. They refused, and before they could react he had exposed himself. The girls screamed and the man ran away.

- A father took his five-year-old daughter to a major department store to look at tools on sale. He became absorbed in the sale items on the table. The girl, wearing a dress that opened in the back, stood patiently by. A moment later a man approached the table and stood beside the little girl. Security had been tracking the man on video because he was only wearing shorts, tee shirt, and sandals. It was evident that he had no wallet and he seemed to be wandering aimlessly. But his search was not aimless at all. He was looking for his next victim. After a few seconds the man reached down and touched her bare back with his hand. The girl looked around perplexed, not knowing what had just touched her. She thought perhaps it was a fly. The man waited a few moments and resumed but this time he touched her buttocks. Confused, she again looked around and finally moved over to the other side of her father. The man moved away, stood behind a clothing rack, and waited. The girl moved back again beside her father and in a moment the man returned. This time he reached into his shorts and holding his penis leaned over and rubbed it up and down her bare back. It happened in just seconds, and he turned and exited the store. Neither the little girl nor the father knew what had just transpired. The predator was arrested as he left the store.

- A well-loved and respected youth minister was invited by a family to have dinner with them after church. The family offered him a ride to their home, and he accepted. He sat in the back seat with their young son who quickly fell asleep. The parents, both in the front seat and out of full view of their child had a discussion with the minister of plans for the new church soon to be built. During the discussion, the smiling minister molested the boy. Later the minister confessed to molesting dozens of children because it was so easy.

- A willing man was asked to become the scoutmaster at the church. He had been meeting with the boys for several months when a member of his church happened to be looking at the local sex offender registry and discovered the scoutmaster's photograph. The scoutmaster had been convicted several years before of molesting young boys and spent two years incarcerated in an institution for high-risk sex offenders. Boy Scouts of America had failed to run a background check, and thus another predator had slipped through the gates.

- An eleven-year-old boy walked into a public restroom in a local park only to be confronted by four men engaging in oral copulation. The men disbursed and no arrests were ever made in the case.

- A teenage girl was trying on new clothes in an exclusive shop unaware that she was standing in front of a video camera hidden behind a large mirror.

- A thirteen-year-old girl received an instant message on her computer. A nice man wanted to be friendly and offered her presents and a few pornographic pictures. She agreed to meet the man at a local shopping mall. The sixty-year-old doctor arrived at the mall in time to meet his prey who turned out to be a thirty-five-year-old police officer. The man was arrested.

These accounts of sex offending in our communities represent a small fraction of the types of incidents that occur across American communities on a regular basis. This text offers readers insight into the etiology of paraphilia, sex offending, sex offenders, and victims. The role of fantasy, paraphilia, and progression within sex crimes is explored along with intervention strategies. The information is disturbing but critical to a greater comprehension and treatment of these offenders.

Eric W Hickey, Ph.D.

ACKNOWLEDGMENTS

I wish to recognize and thank those who helped during the course of research and publication of *Sex Crimes & Paraphilia*. Many of my former students who have gone on to become clinical and forensic psychologists in prisons, psychiatric facilities, government agencies, and in private practice contributed articles for this textbook. I am so very proud of each and every one of them. I especially want to thank my project coordinator, Dr. Mila Green McGowan, a graduate of the California School of Professional Psychology's (now Alliant International University) Forensic Psychology program. Her dedication and organizational skills were critical to the production of this textbook. She also holds a master's degree in clinical psychology from Pepperdine University and a criminology degree from the University of Ottawa. Dr. Green McGowan specializes in criminal justice research and program development, and provides clinical services to both sex offenders and other specific forensic populations. Her interests lie in assessing and overcoming criminal stereotypes, developing new ways to understand sexual offending and obsessional harassment, improving forensic mental health service delivery, and encouraging offender-victim reconciliation efforts. After a post-doctoral position assessing and counseling paroled high-risk sex offenders, Dr. Green McGowan now treats mentally ill inmates within the California Department of Corrections system. Her past clinical experience also includes work with incest offenders, those living with HIV/AIDS, juvenile probationers, and victims and perpetrators of domestic violence and child abuse. She is a wonderful colleague who knows how to turn challenge into success.

I also want to thank Dawn Alley, a Scottish lass whose interests and scholarship involve developmental psychopathology with particular emphasis on attachment, trauma in early childhood, presexualization, and neurology development as a result of trauma. Dawn attended the University of California, Irvine, and the University of Birmingham, U.K., for her bachelor's, Pepperdine University for her master's, and Alliant International University for her Ph.D. She has worked for the Department of Justice in the CATIC program where she received extensive training on terrorism. Dawn is an adjunct professor of psychology at Fresno City College. She also worked with the Fresno Police Department in the Domestic Violence Unit, Child Abuse Unit, and Homicide to develop systemic improvements in the current juvenile justice system. Her interests are in developing methods to identify and intervene on behalf of high-risk children who might otherwise slip unnoticed through bureaucratic over-sights. I admire her passion. My appreciation is also extended to Jay Healey, a young Canadian from Newfoundland, for his passion and assistance in researching sex crimes, psychopathology, and serial murder. Jay is one of those "next-generation" re-searchers who will greatly advance the understanding of sex crimes and paraphilia. His reliability has been phenomenal.

A special thanks goes to California State University–Fresno. The sabbatical award afforded me time to finish developing the sex crimes and paraphilia manu-script. In addition, my appreciation goes to the entire Prentice Hall team, especially to my editor Frank Mortimer. I deeply appreciate their support and guidance in the production of this book. Never could an author expect to find a more competent, professional team of editors and staff than those at Prentice Hall.

Of course, every grandfather likes to dote upon his beautiful grandchildren. I have six of them: Joshua, Megan, Melissa, Lauren, Samantha, and Katie. As they journey through life might they know they are loved, deeply, and that being of serv-ice to others is the Higher Road. Travel it often. And in memory of my dear grand-parents, Paul and Annie Wakem, for the trips to the lake, the Carriage House, the haircuts, and that last steam engine ride. I miss their devotion, smiles, and hugs. And always to Holly, my wife, companion, and bestfriend.

Eric W. Hickey

LIST
OF CONTRIBUTORS

Dawn Alley, Ph.D.

James Alvarado, Ph.D.

Felicia Bloem, Ph.D.

Melinda Chau, Psy.D.

Lori Cluff, Psy.D.

Catherine Furtado, Psy.D.

Stephanie Gaudenti, Ph.D.

Mila Green McGowan, Ph.D.

James Healey, M.A.

Ainslie Heasman, Ph.D.

Eric Hickey, Ph.D.

Jeanne Johnson, Psy.D.

Elizabeth Jones, Psy.D.

Tamar Kenworthy, Psy.D.

Kerry Konrad-Torres, Psy.D.

Shay Litton, Psy.D.

Melissa McDonald-Witt, Psy.D.

Toyia McWilliams, Ph.D.

Deanna Monteith, Psy.D.

Stephanie Neumann, Psy.D.

Caleb Newman, Psy.D.

Katherine Nickchen, Psy.D.

Anne Marie Paclebar, Psy.D.

Matthew Peck, Ph.D.

Julie Penn, Psy.D.

Catherine Sanchez, Psy.D.

Brianna Satterthwaite, Psy.D.

Lisa Shaffer, Psy.D.

Corey Vitello, Ph.D.

ABOUT THE AUTHOR

Currently teaching criminal psychology at California State University, Fresno, Dr. Hickey has considerable field experience working with the criminally insane, psychopaths, sex offenders, and other habitual criminals. As an adjunct professor at Alliant University (California School of Professional Psychology), Dr. Hickey teaches courses and supervises dissertations in criminal personalities, sex crimes, homicide, and psychopathology. He has served as an adjunct instructor for the American Prosecutor's Research institute at the National Advocacy Center in Columbia, South Carolina profiling cyber-stalkers, criminal personalities, and sexual predators.

His expertise is regularly sought by the media including appearances on CNN, Larry King Live, 20/20, A&E Biography, Good Morning America, Court TV, Discovery, and TLC. A former consultant to the FBI's UNABOM Task Force, Dr. Hickey currently assists local, state, and federal law enforcement and private agencies and testifies as an expert witness in both criminal and civil cases. He conducts training seminars for agencies involving the profiling and investigating of sex crimes and paraphilia, arson, homicide, stalking, workplace violence, and psychopathology. Internationally recognized for his research on multiple homicide offenders, Dr. Hickey has conducted seminars in Canada, France, England, and trained VIP protection specialists in Israel in profiling stalkers and counter-terrorism. His research involving hundreds of victims of stalking examines the psychology and classification of stalkers, victim-offender relationships, intervention and threat assessment.

PART

UNDERSTANDING SEX CRIMES

I

CHAPTER

A LOOK AT TODAY'S SEX OFFENDER

MILA GREEN MCGOWAN

1

Sex offenders, compared to other serious offenders, have come to be treated differently by both the criminal justice system and the public alike. This differential treatment is rooted in society's prevailing beliefs about the nature of sex crimes and existing social norms about sexual behavior. It is informed by the public's heightened fear of sex crimes, the impact sex crimes have on victims, and the assumptions people make about the causes of sexual offending (Berliner, 1998). All these beliefs, coupled with a perceived increase in the number of sex crimes, have created feelings of antipathy and disdain in the public at large towards anyone accused of sexual misconduct or deviancy. Unfortunately, the pervasive public perception that sex crimes are on the rise may, in fact, be attributed only to increases in the awareness of sexual abuse and/or increases in the reporting of sexual victimization, rather than to an actual increase in prevalence (Peebles, 1999).

Regardless of the reasons behind any increase in sex crime rates or the number of sexual offenders and resulting victims, society has come to regard "[B]reaches of sexual prohibition as one of the more serious infractions an individual can commit" (Laws & O'Donahue, 1997, p. 1). Accordingly, researchers acknowledge that "[T]he sexual assault of women and children is a pernicious and distressingly prevalent social problem" (Hudson & Ward, 2000, p. 494) that has a high cost for victims, their families and society at large. It is thus an issue worthy of continued inquiry.

Sex offenses are different from other serious interpersonal or violent crimes as they involve a behavior that, when consensual and "appropriate" is associated with pleasure, intimacy and procreation by most, if not all, societies in the world. We have seen, however, when a sexual act becomes nonconsensual, coercive, or is considered "out of the ordinary," Western culture has generally defined it as criminal or deviant.

Though most would agree that sex offenders are different from other criminals in many ways, providing a definitive description of that difference is not possible as sex offenders make up a very heterogeneous group. While it is known that the majority of sex offenders are men and their victims women, different theories propose ways in which to incorporate this gender difference into explanations of sexual offending (e.g., evolutionary explanations, feminist theory, etc.). Research has shown that sex offenders as a group do not share a common set of psychological or behavioral characteristics, and not all sex offenders engage in deviant sexual practices, despite public beliefs to the contrary (Berliner, 1998). In reality, many sex offenders are similar to other criminals in many ways, and only a small group of sex offenders evidence sex offense–specific disorders (e.g., pedophilia).

To define sex offenders, Shaw (1999) suggested; "[A] sexual offender is an individual who has committed an act of sexual aggression that has breached societal norms and moral codes, violated federal, state and municipal law, statute or ordinance, and which usually but not necessarily results in physical or psychological harm to the victim" (p. 170).

SEX OFFENSES

The acts that sex offenders engage in that are defined as sexual offenses vary and cover a range of sexually coercive and deviant behaviors. For the researcher's purpose, a sexual assault or sex crime is defined as a criminal offense in which a victim is forced or coerced to participate in sexual activity (Douglas et al., 1992). Keeping this definition in mind, a plethora of sex offenses can be described, yet their exact definition depends on existing case law, federal and state statutes, and area-specific criminal justice practices. The most well-known sex crime, rape, is often categorized into gang, stranger, spouse-, or acquaintance-perpetrated rape. At the federal level, rape has been defined as any forced intercourse that may include psychological coercion and/or physical force. Acts of rape are not limited to intercourse, but also include attempted rapes, verbal threats of rape, and the assault of both men and women victims and hetero- and homosexual persons (Department of Justice, 2002). The Center for Sex Offender Management (CSOM, 2000) reported 43 percent of all rapes/sexual assaults occur between 6:00 P.M. and midnight and more than half take place in homes of the victim, family members, or friends.

Child sexual abuse or molestation includes incestuous/intrafamilial, acquaintance/extrafamilial, and stranger-perpetrated assaults against anyone under the age of eighteen. Adults or other youth can perpetrate these acts. Various paraphilias (which are psychiatric disorders involving a deviant erotic focus), such as voyeurism, exhibitionism, and necrophilia, are also considered sex offenses. The possession of certain types of pornography (e.g., child pornography, or "snuff films," in which, after sex, the actor is murdered on camera) or involvement in a child sex ring or sex-for-sale business are also considered sex offenses in some locales. Of most concern, though rare, are lust murders, which involve some form of sexual assault and murder (either before or after the sexual offense). The Diagnostic and Statistical Manual for Mental Disorders (APA, 2000) reports "[S]exual offenses against children make up a significant proportion of all reported criminal sex acts, and individuals with Exhibitionism, Pedophilia, and Voyeurism make up the majority of apprehended sex offenders" (p. 566).

State crime statistics further break down crimes of child molestation into lewd acts with a child, oral copulation, and sodomy. Oral copulation and sodomy can also be sex crimes perpetrated against adults. In any state, a rape charge may or may not include penetration with an object of one or more orifices.

SEX OFFENDER TYPOLOGIES

Classification systems have only been developed for certain sex offenses and offenders. Some of these typologies have been developed based on clinical descriptions (from various DSM editions) or "ideal types" of sex offenders that represent the prototypical features of a group. Other typologies have relied on demographic clusters of either the offender or the victim(s) (e.g., age, gender), while a third approach creates psychometric profiles of offenders derived from multivariate statistical analysis. Finally, specific psychological theories (e.g., social learning or object relations theory) have been enlisted to discriminate between sex offender types (Bickley & Beech, 2001). Prentky and Burgess (2000) explained, regardless of the intended mission or underlying design of sex offender classifications, the "clear purpose of most taxonomic efforts has been to increase the accuracy of predictions of dangerousness and reoffense risk" (p. 26).

RAPISTS

Rapists were first dichotomized in the 1960s by the nature of the offender's internal experience after the crime occurred. Thus, an "ego-syntonic" rapist was seen as an antisocial psychopath who experienced no guilt for his actions, while an "ego-dystonic" rapist committed the act as a result of a breakdown in mental defenses, often experiencing remorse afterwards (see Kopp, as cited by Prentky & Burgess, 2000). By the 1970s, rapist typologies began to diversify to include numerous types that better described both the internal motivations and post-rape experiences of rapists, such as "masculine identity conflict" rapist, "situation stress" rapist, "psychotic" rapist, etc. (see Rada, as cited by Prentky & Burgess, 2000).

Most recently, based on a study with convicted rapists that focused on the interaction of sexual and aggressive motivations, four rapist typologies were outlined by Groth, Burgess, and Holstrom (as cited by Douglas et al., 1992) in the late 1970s. Douglas et al. (1992) explained these prevailing four types as the power-reassurance rapist, the power-assertive rapist, the anger-retaliation rapist, and the anger-excitation rapist.

The power-reassurance rapist uses rape to express his sexual fantasies. He most often has a history of sexual preoccupation with a variety of perversions, high sexual arousal associated with a loss of control, a distorted perception of his relationship with the victim, and he feels acutely inadequate as a man. He uses the rape to convince himself the victim wants him and is enjoying the sexual act as if it was consensual and as the result of a preexisting intimate relationship. With the assertive rapist, the rape is an impulsive and predatory act. He has less fantasy life, and the actual rape act has less psychological meaning than with a power-reassurance rapist. The assault is often situational and results as the rapist prowls for women, though he is neither concerned with nor interested in the victim and wants only to satisfy his need for sex.

The anger-retaliation rapist uses the sexual attack as an expression of anger and rage. To this rapist, sex is primarily an aggressive urge that is directed towards the victim solely because he/she represents a hated individual. Despite the real feelings of rage and resentment, the rapist's perceived injustices may not be real. The excitation rapist uses rape as an expression of his aggressive and sadistic fantasies, in which sex and aggression are fused and increase together. Though this rapist's anger may not be readily apparent, other bizarre and intense behavior is, and sexual violence is often directed towards the victim's genitalia.

CHILD MOLESTERS AND PEDOPHILES

Initially, the clinical description classification method (based on the subjective impressions of interviewers) led to the conceptualization of child molesters into three subtypes: fixated, regressed, and aggressive (Cohen, Seghorn, & Clamas, 1969). Fixated offenders prefer the company of children and seek them out. They often assault children they know. Regressed molesters have some adult sexual interest, but because of feelings of inadequacy, they resort to children. The aggressive type of molester is sadistic and prefers children they do not know, especially boys.

More recently, another set of prototypical child molester types was detailed in the literature: preferential and situational (Quinsey, 1986). Preferential molesters, like fixated molesters, prefer children as both sexual and social companions, while situational molesters use children only as sexual surrogates when adults are unavailable or when they are under extreme stress. Preferential molesters are much like the true pedophile (to be discussed later), and situational offenders are traditionally incest perpetrators.

A most recent source (Holmes & Holmes, 2002) further subdivided preferential and situational molesters into smaller descriptive categories. Situational child molesters, described as having fewer victims than preferential offenders and no true sexual interest in children, were deemed as regressed, indiscriminant, or naïve. Preferential child molesters perpetrate more severe acts of sexual abuse and were divided into either mysoped or fixated subcategories. The regressed-situational offender feels a child is a temporary object for sexual gratification. They evidence low self-esteem and decreased self-image. Their victims are most often ones of opportunity and female gender. Indiscriminant-situational molesters will abuse anyone vulnerable; children are just another category of victim and are not preferred. This subtype of sex offender craves sexual experimentation of any kind. Finally the naïve (or inadequate)-situational molester is possibly mentally ill or developmentally delayed. They make poor distinctions between right and wrong, present as bizarre or strange, and are not capable of relationships with other adults. They will not physically harm a child, and few instances of sexual intercourse are found.

Mysoped-preferential molesters have formed a connection between sexual gratification and personal violence. This is commonly the sadistic pedophile who has an extreme desire to physically harm children. They may stalk a child prior to assault, and they make no attempt to seduce or "groom" their victim. Often death of the child results as their offenses are premeditated and can involve a weapon. The fixated-preferential molester exhibits little or no activity of any kind with adults. He is single, immature, and uncomfortable around adults, often appearing childlike. He has no interest in harming a child, so oral-genital sex is most common with intercourse occurring only after much time has elapsed. Holmes and Holmes (2002) sought to encapsulate the true range of pedophilic (or preferential molester) behavior with the following statement, "[T]he pedophile has developed a sexual interest in children that ranges from fondling to mutilation and murder. Not all pedophiles wish to harm children. Some wish only to hold and fondle them. To the other extreme, some sadistic pedophiles are only gratified with the death of their captive child" (p. 159).

INCEST PERPETRATORS

Though incest perpetrators are often adequately described by child molester typologies, additional subtype clarification is warranted. Cavallin (as cited by Studer, Clelland, Aylwin, Reddon, & Monro, 2000) outlined three categories of incestuous fathers. One, fathers with an indiscriminate promiscuity where incest is only a part of a pattern of sexual psychopathology; two, fathers with an intense craving for young children, which includes their daughter as a sexual object; and three, fathers who confine their sexual interests to family members (or endogamic incest). Studer and colleagues (2000) reported that while common knowledge has posited incest offenders are of least concern and least risk for reoffense when compared to other sex offenders, studies have tended to focus only on endogamic incest perpetrators when making this assertion. Their work with 328 incest perpetrators and 178 non-incestuous child molesters found this lack of concern dangerous. Their work uncovered many "cross-over" offenses; 23 percent of the incest sample reported additional incest victims, and 59 percent reported other non-incestuous child victims. This finding (and those of Rist; Summit & Kryso; as cited by Prentky & Burgess, 2000) refutes the premise that incest offenders are a discreet group who present a lower risk of re-offending and are only likely to commit one sex offense. Studer and colleagues (2000) concluded "many offenders who initially seem to be incestuous are, in fact, more pedophilic in their preferences and have acted on these preferences in the past" (p. 19).

CRITICISMS OF SEX OFFENDER TYPOLOGIES

It is important to keep in mind that none of the existing taxonomies for rapists, child molesters, or incest perpetrators have achieved universal acceptance. This lack of acceptance is based on numerous factors. Various researchers report the problem with categorizing sex offenders on anything other than their offense type is that as a group, these offenders are extremely heterogeneous in respect to their personal characteristics, as well as the process by which their sex crime(s) occur. "The childhood and developmental histories, adult competencies, and criminal histories of sexual offenders differ considerably. The motives and patterns . . . that characterize their criminal offenses differ considerably" (Prentky & Burgess, 2000, p. 27).

More specifically, Bickley and Beech (2001) remarked, "child molesters have been found to be an extremely diverse group in terms of personal characteristics, life experiences and criminal histories" (p. 51). Further, Holmes and Holmes (2002) warned, "[I]t would be a drastic mistake to assume that all pedophiles are the same" (p. 161), while, Prentky and Burgess (2000) opined "it would be misleading, not to mention erroneous, to suggest that there is a profile for all rapists or child molesters" (p. 27). The problem remains, as with any taxonomy system, that offenders with a sexual interest in children may fit into more than one category depending upon the offense in question, the relationship between offender and victim, victim type and gender, or physiologic sexual arousal test results (Bickley & Beech, 2001).

Bickley and Beech (2001) further maintained "[N]one of the theories to date have been able to adequately explain either the etiology and maintenance of sexually abusive behavior or provide a comprehensive description of the offense process itself" (p. 51). This criticism continues despite many researchers' hopes that classification systems could tell them "something about the course of life events that led to the onset of sexual offenses . . . [and that it may be possible] to discern the unique roots of each subtype" of offender (Prentky & Burgess, 2000, p. 29).

The misapplication of any classification system can bring about dire consequences; "careless or casual assignment of individuals to categories is far worse than no assignment at all" (Prentky & Burgess, 2000, p. 26). It has also been suggested that the basic fixated-regression dichotomy that underlies much of the existing child molester typologies today has evolved solely out of clinical experience and has not been supported by additional empirical studies. Some (see Prentky & Burgess, 2000) have gone on to say that all child molesters "manifest some degree of fixation" (p. 44) so trying to define an offender based on the fixation-regression dichotomy is both clinically impossible and misleading. Finally, it has been concluded that "classifications are inherently temporary and artificial, an a-priori structure serving a time-limited purpose . . . [that will] replace one another as our understanding of the real world changes" (Prentky & Burgess, 2000, p. 69).

THE PREVALENCE OF SEX CRIMES, SEXUAL DEVIANCY, AND SEX OFFENDERS

While Marshall and Williams (2001) asserted "the true prevalence of sexual offending can only be estimated" (p. 1), Krueger and Kaplan (1997) opined "[S]exual crimes are commanding more media attention in our society. Whether there is an increase in crime or an increase in reporting has not been empirically established. However, the focus on sexually 'deviant' interests has led to increased public interest in the paraphilias." (p. 131).

In 1987, Abel and colleagues found the paraphilic acts reported with most frequency among 561 subjects were masochism, frottage, transvestitism, exhibitionism, and voyeurism. Interestingly, child molestation was reported relatively infrequently in comparison, however those who targeted young boys outside their family committed the greatest number of crimes (Abel, Becker, Mittleman, Cunningham-Rathner, Rouleau, & Murphy, 1987). Later, in opposition to these earlier findings, in a nationwide study of over twenty-eight thousand American men suspected of a sexual offense, Abel and Harlow (2001) found among the possible deviant sexual behaviors an offender could engage in, child molestation was most common at 33 percent, then voyeurism at 17 percent, exhibitionism at 14 percent, and public masturbation at 11 percent. All other possible deviant interests, e.g., fetishism, frottage and telephone scatalogia, were reported by less than 10 percent of the sample.

Despite the assertion that "[S]exual assault is one of the fastest growing violent crimes in the Unites States" (Shaw, 1999, p. xi), it is difficult to ascertain the true rate of sex offenses as they are often underreported to the criminal justice system, and the rate of underreporting remains unquantifiable. One source, Lieb et al. (1998), reported rape underreporting rates range from 88 to 68 percent (per their studies in 1992 and 1995). This underreporting phenomenon is further complicated by that fact that sex offenders themselves often fail to report all their sexual offenses when arrested for a particular infraction. A study of 62 federally-charged sexual offenders found while the offenders only initially admitted to 52 crimes pre-trial; later, the same offenders revealed an additional 1,352 offenses posttreatment (Creager, 2003). Of these total 1,404 sexual crimes, only 30 percent involved no victim contact. Seventy percent of the 62 offenders reported 30+ victims over the course of their offending.

Throughout the 1940s to the 1970s, the national arrest rate for forcible rape remained stable, but in the early 1980s, it jumped up and has remained stable ever since. However, for every 1,000 persons in the United States over the age of twelve years, the Federal Bureau of Prisons (2001) reported rape rate decreases of more than 2.2 rapes between 1973 and 2001. In California, rape rates have been decreasing over the decades. In 1960, 2,859 rapes were recorded; in 1970, 7,005 rapes; in 1980, 3,411 rapes; in 1990, 3,553 rapes; and in 2000, 2,079 rapes (California Crime Rates, 1960–2000). For other sex crimes, there has been a steady and significant national rate increase from the 1940s until 1991, when the trend reversed (Lieb et al., 1998). In cases in which a sex crime ends up in murder, the FBI estimates that as of 1994 only 1.5 percent of murders involved a rape or other sexual offense.

The number of sentenced sex offenders sent to state prisons throughout the United States has only increased slightly since 1930 when compared to the rates of all other offender admissions (Lieb et al., 1998). In California in 2002, only 6.5 percent of new admissions to state prison had been convicted of a sex crime (California Department of Corrections, CDC, 2002a). As of June 2002, CDC reported 8.1 percent of its total state prison population was convicted sex offenders, with the largest group (7,143 inmates) serving time specifically for a lewd act on a child conviction. In 1997, the Federal Bureau of Prisons reported (as cited by CSOM, 2000) that on any given day, approximately 234,000 rape and sexual assault offenders were under the supervision of federal correctional agencies; 60 percent of these were being supervised through conditional release programs in the community. More recently, the same agency reported, as of May 2002, only 0.7 percent of its total inmate population (in federal facilities only) were incarcerated for sex offenses (Federal Bureau of Prisons, 2003). However, Helen Creager, of the U.S. Probation and Parole Department (2003), reported an increase in community supervision of federal sex offenders in the years spanning 1999 to 2002, a 40 percent increase in pre-trial supervision, and a 42 percent increase in probation supervision. As of December 2001, the CDC reported 5,538 sexual offenders of any type were on parole in the state, forming only 4.7 percent of the total parolee population (CDC, 2001a) and that California is home to about one-fourth of the nations' known sexual offenders (Tobin, 2003). In late 2000, California reported having 22,720 incarcerated sex offenders in its state institutions, representing 15 percent of its total inmate population (CDC, 2000).

SEXUAL RECIDIVISM

RESEARCH FINDINGS

Langstrom and Grann (2000) asserted "[B]ase rates for sexual recidivism among detected adult sex offenders are reportedly modest as compared to rates of general criminal recidivism. However, some studies suggest that sex offenders remain at continued risk for sexual recidivism for decades" (p. 855). Also, existing sex offenders are thought to be the most likely to commit new sexual offenses compared to other criminals (Berliner, 1998). Quinsey, Rice, and Harris (as cited by CSOM, 2000) found, in 1995, offenders who had extrafamilial female victims had a recidivism rate of 18 percent while those with extrafamilial male victims had a rate of 35 percent. Meanwhile incest perpetrators, regardless of victim gender, reoffended at about a rate of 9 percent.

Langstrom and Grann (2000) reported sexual reoffense base rates range from as low as 7.5 to 15 percent in some studies to as high as 37 percent in others. Meanwhile general criminal recidivism rates have been found consistently to be as high as 40 to 60 percent. Soothill and Gibbens (as cited by Prentky et al., 1997) reported a sexual recidivism rate of about 23 percent among their sample of sex offenders, with only half of the reconvictions occurring within the first five years of community release.

Hanson and Bussiere (1998) conducted a meta-analysis of recidivism studies and found a 12.7 percent sexual recidivism rate for child molesters and a 18.9 percent rate for rapists in an average four- to five-year follow-up period. Interestingly, they found incest perpetrators had very low risks of reoffense. Overall, when any type of reoffense (sexual, nonsexual, violent, nonviolent, etc.) was taken into consideration, reoffense rates rose for child molesters to 37 percent and 46 percent for rapists. From their work, Hanson and Bussiere complied a list of variables reliably associated with sexual recidivism. These included being young and single, having an antisocial personality disorder diagnosis, committing a high number of prior offenses (sexual or otherwise), demonstrating high amounts of sexual deviancy (or numerous paraphilias), and failing to comply with treatment.

Prentky et al. (1997) studied a sample of 136 rapists and 115 child molesters committed to a state treatment center. By relying on five different sources for recidivism information, the authors were able to follow participants for up to twenty-five years after their release into the community. They pointed out that, though most studies estimate recidivism by calculating the simple percentage of subjects who reoffend during the study period, this method underestimates true recidivism rates. Instead, they relied upon failure rate estimates instead so that the amount of time a sex offender had spent in the community, and was thus able to reoffend, was accounted for. For the rapists studied, the sexual reoffense rate after twenty-five years was 26 percent, with an average of 4.55 years before reoffense. For child molesters, the sexual reoffense rate was 32 percent, with an average of 3.64 years before reoffense. However, as expected, the failure rates of both groups for sexual reoffense (39 and 52 percent, respectively) were much higher than simple recidivism rates. The authors asserted that had they relied on the conventional one-year follow-up period of most recidivism inquiries, about 45 percent of all reoffenses would have been missed.

Prentky et al.'s (1997) work also illuminated patterns of reoffense between the two groups of offenders. Rapists demonstrated a stable 2 to 3 percent recidivism rate every year in the first five years after release with a rate drop to 1 percent from years six to twenty-five. Child molesters demonstrated a 4 percent recidivism rate in the first three years after release with a drop to 3 percent in the fourth and 2 percent in the fifth years. However, unlike the consistent decline in rapist reoffense rates, child molesters showed an "11% increase in sexual reoffenses between years 5 and 10, 9% between years 10 and 15, 7% between years 15 and 20 and 5% between years 20 and 25" (p. 650).

Abel et al. (1987) outlined their recidivism findings pertaining to the issue of same victim revictimization. When assessing 561 nonincarcerated sexual offenders, they found exhibitionists and rapists, by and large, only committed one act per victim and voyeurs only occasionally window-peeped on the same person on additional occasions. Only occasionally did extrafamilial pedophiles return to the same victim, but it was more likely if the victim was a young boy and the perpetrator an adult man. Incest perpetrators were the most likely to revictimize the same victim, with an average of thirty-six molests for boy victims and forty-five for girl victims.

OFFICIAL STATISTICS

The Federal Bureau of Prisons reported in 2001, 24 percent of rape offenders and 19 percent of other sexual assault offenders were on probation or parole for another crime at the time that they committed their sex offense. Unfortunately, the Bureau did not specify what types of offenses these sexual offenders committed previously to require supervision. The California Department of Corrections reported both one- and two-year recidivism rates for various types of sex offenders released from their institutions in 1999 (CDC, 2001c). After two years of follow-up, 47 percent of the released rapists had committed another felony and 36 percent of those convicted of a lewd act with a child had also reoffended. Forty-four percent (44 percent) of those convicted of oral copulation or penetration with an object had reoffended, while only 28 percent of released sodomists were known recidivists. Finally, under the "other sex crimes" category (which was left undefined by the CDC), 63 percent of the paroled felons had reoffended (CDC, 2001c). The CDC also reported (see CDC, 2001b) 2.3 percent of all parole violators returned to California's prisons in 2001 were former sex offenders. Unfortunately, in both CDC reports, the agency failed to specify if these incidents of felony reoffense were sexual in nature or otherwise.

As California now uses the "Three Strikes" rule as a way to enhance offender sentences, the CDC has also collected data on this select group of sex offenders. Regardless of what the first or second strike (felony convictions) were for, the data showed 1.5 percent of third-strikers and 4.5 percent of second-strikers in 2002 were serving time for a sex offense (CDC, 2002c).

CONCERNS ABOUT RECIDIVISM RESEARCH AND STATISTICS

Unfortunately, reported general criminal and sex offender recidivism rates vary depending upon the study cited and the type of offender studied. As sex offenders are not a homogeneous group, reoffense rates have been found to vary among offenders and relate to characteristics specific to the offender and the offense, such as victim gender and relationship to the offender (CSOM, 2000). Further, Prentky et al. (1997) asserted, "studies examining reoffense rates among sex offenders have varied in a number of critical dimensions; a) the study sample, b) the criterion for recidivism ... and c) the length and consistency of the follow-up period" (p. 636). They cautioned reported recidivism rates are obviously limited only to those criminal offenses that are detected in sample populations.

Marshall and Williams (2001) advised that recidivism studies suffer because they deal with low base rates of reoffending, regardless of treatment. This low base rate problem increases the chance of falsely endorsing treatment as ineffective. Many studies only count recidivism as a dichotomous variable (i.e., the sex offender has or has not engaged in another sexual offense), rather than counting the actual number of transgressions or victims that truly constitute the reoffending behavior (Marshall & Barbaree, as cited by Marshall & Williams, 2001). These researchers suggest that by counting victims as an index of failure, the base rate of recidivism may be a more useful comparison tool as analyses may become more statistically powerful.

Unfortunately, numerous authors (see CSOM, 2000; Studer et al., 2000) opined that official statistics regarding sexual recidivism are also woefully inadequate: "[T]he reliance on measures of recidivism as reflected through official criminal justice system data obviously omits offenses that are not cleared through arrest or those that are never reported to the police" (CSOM, 2000, p. 3). However, a researcher's sole reliance on self-reported recidivism when assessing known sex offenders also has numerous pitfalls. As Abel, Becker, Mittelman, Cunningham-Rather, Rouleau, and Murphy (1987) reported, "[I]ncarcerated sex offenders are likely to conceal the true scope and nature of their deviant interests and activities for fear of jeopardizing their hopes for parole" (p. 4). Sex offenders in postrelease treatment may also downplay their offending history or recidivism to avoid additional charges, "pass" treatment and finish their parole requirements, or avoid additional social stigma. Thus, self-report information should also be bolstered with collateral contacts, suggest Studer and colleagues (2000). Finally, Prentky et al. (1997) asserted trying to ascertain a single high-risk window for reoffense among sex offenders is impossible especially since "the decay process" (p. 652) is not similar for all types of sex offenses.

Regardless of published recidivism rates, many studies also "suggest that sex offenders remain at continual risk for sexual recidivism for decades" (Langstrom & Grann, 2000, p. 855). Many offenders may continue to reoffend for as long as thirty years, depending upon their choice of offending behavior and when they begin to offend (Berliner, 1998). Some research (e.g., Tracy, Donnelly, Morgenbesser, & MacDonald, as cited by Prentky et al., 1997) has found that certain factors inherent to each sex offender are important to recidivism risks, such as antisociality, psychopathy, lifestyle impulsivity, and the number of prior sexual offenses.

C H A P T E R

ATTACHMENT DISTURBANCES AND SEXUAL OFFENDING

2

A Progression from Victim to Offender

Dawn Alley

A nexus between attachment disturbances in childhood and sexual offending later in life appears to be intuitively viable yet seemingly too exigent to pursue. To date, no single link exists between being abused as a child (sexually, physically, or emotionally) and the implications for adult attachment disturbances, some resulting in subsequent sexual offending. In fact, the Department of Justice in their annual research report on violence suggests that most victims do not go on to abuse (U.S. Department of Justice, 1997). It would appear that the phenomenon of recapitulating generational violence is readily thought to be too complex to decipher the characteristics of the abuser and abused accompanied by the mediating factors that either influenced the abuser or protected the victim. Consequently, if a precise connection could be made or prevention established between insecure attachment and violence experienced in childhood and inveterately depicted in adulthood, it has thus far been elusive.

Perpetuating the imprecision are various robust theories of child abuse and the related morbidity factors inadequately littered in the literature as separate disorders. For example, in the annual publication for International Pediatrics (2001) conduct disorder, separation anxiety, substance abuse, antisocial behavior, and paraphilic disorders were purposed to be separate psychological diagnoses with common deficits of low self-esteem and social skills, stagnation, and poor intellectual functioning. However, it is suggested here that these disorders may not, in fact, be isolatory rather enduring symptoms of an attachment disturbance. Still, it is important to note that the objective is not to suggest a linear relationship between sexual offending and disturbances of attachment in childhood, nor to offer insecure attachment as an exhaustive explanation of the offending phenomenon. The intent here is to document the role of attachment in the development of sexual offending when correlated with presexualization and insecure attachment in childhood. Prevention is the motivation and the goal behind this exploratory connection and the base for future empirical pursuits.

ATTACHMENT THEORY

Ainsworth and Bowlby were the first to elaborate on the significance of early relationships between children and their caregivers (Ainsworth, 1967; Ainsworth, Blehar, Waters, & Wall, 1978; Bowlby 1969). Attachment theory postulates that infants are genetically predisposed to promote survival behaviors that enhance proximity to the caregiver in times of need. In view of that, attachment theory suggests that the interpersonal relationship between the child and caregiver contributes to the development of internal working models, which include mental representations of self, significant others, and the relationship between them (Manassis, and Bradley, 1994).

The attachment relationship has also been associated with various hallmarks in later development, far exceeding the confines of early childhood to include: development of personality (Bowlby 1969), learned interpersonal skills (Fonagy, 1997), the development of self (Sroufe, 1996), and the capacity for intimacy, (Ward, Hudson & Marshall, 1996).

Accordingly, the child-caregiver relationship serves as a prototype for attachment later in life whilst providing a foundation for the development of the child's sense of stability, controllability, predictability, and overall confidence in self and others (Bowlby, 1973). However, if the child cannot build from the attachment relationship a security based on the caregiver's sensitive and responsive care, the affective response of insecurity attenuates in intensity and so does the child's responsiveness to later attachments (Sroufe, 1996). Add parental maltreatment to the child's insecurity and the likelihood of significantly impacting attachment disturbances increases (Crittenden, Partridge, & Claussen, 1991).

ATTACHMENT PATTERNS AND RELATIONSHIPS

Initially, the observed patterns in the attachment relationships have been translated into three categories of attachment: secure, ambivalent, and avoidant (Ainsworth et al., 1978). Later, a fourth category of disorganized/disoriented was added to reflect the unpredictable patterns often exhibited in children considered to be high-risk (Main & Solomon, 1990). Attachment researchers have observed that when caregivers are consistently responsive in nurturance, are receptive, and are available to satisfy the child's need or desire for safety, the securely attached child learns self-worth, trust, and love. When caregivers oscillate between warmth/coldness and availability/rejecting, these ambivalently attached children learn to seek attention at any available opportunity; they tend to be impulsive, passive, and helpless. When caregivers are unnurturing, unresponsive, dismissive, and critical the avoidantly attached child learns to be emotionally distant, hostile, and restricted in empathy. Finally, when caregivers are punitive, threatening, and rejecting, the disorganized/disoriented attached child tends to be controlling, disregarding of rules, feelings, emotions, and they are afraid and rejecting of potentially genuine and loving relationships (Cassidy & Shaver, 1999).

ADULT ATTACHMENT CHARACTERISTICS

Studies have shown that insecure childhood attachments have a profound effect on relationships throughout the individual's life (e.g., Bogaert & Sadava, 2002). Accordingly, if these patterns are negative (e.g., insecure) and without intervention, the attachment patterns that emerge in adulthood can reflect childhood experiences and interpretations (e.g., Hazen & Shaver, 1987).

The secure adult pattern is reflected in confidence in self and others, trusting intimacy, and the tendency to feel close and stable in relationships. The ambivalent adult pattern resonates dependency and conflict, reluctant to view others as dependable or trustworthy, and consistently fearful of being unloved or abandoned, yet longing for a connection. They tend to show regressive and immature behaviors with their relationships based on manipulation. The avoidant adult pattern is emulated in emotional aloofness, untrusting toward self and others, avoiding intimacy by frequently employing hostility, whilst lacking empathy to hold self responsible for the emotional distance. They tend to engage in low-commitment relationships yet are vengefully isolated, blaming others for their distance. They exhibit high-risk behaviors and have a tendency to abuse substances. The disorganized/disoriented adult pattern ricochets between fearfully seeking comfort from the person whom they fear the most. Faced with these incompatible sources, they are caught in a cycle of disquietion while they frantically cling to anyone available; they have a tendency to destructively depress.

ATTACHMENT DISORDERS

The uniqueness of individual personalities corresponds to attachment patterns, which are the result of internal working models cumulated as a result of intimacies, interpersonal experiences, and events of childhood. Children who consistently receive insensitive and unresponsive care may develop, as a protective device from adversity, an insecure attachment to their caregivers (Bowlby, 1969; 1973). However, if the attachment that develops is chronically insecure, as a result of rejection or abuse, such children begin to see themselves as unlovable and unworthy of relationships.

Consequently, the child may fail to develop the necessary skills to form intimate relationships and instead develop superficial relationships characteristically and insidiously lacking trust, empathy, and/or compassion (van-Ijzendoorn, 1997).

Bowlby (1973) called this an "affectionless character," whereby the attachment disorder may be characterized by anxiety (see Manassis and Bradley, 1994; Sroufe, 1996; Turner et al., 1991; Warren et al., 1997), distrust of others (Cassidy & Shaver, 1999), and dysfunctional anger (Smallbone & Dadds, 2001; Sroufe, 1996). Furthermore, if the abuse inflicted upon the child was of a sexual nature, some suggest that affectionless psychopathology may possibly ensue (Alexander, 1992; Bowlby, 1973).

PRESEXUALIZATION

Principally destructive to the attachment relationship is the presexualization of the child, which is defined as the premature indoctrination into adult sexuality. If premature sexualization is incessantly integrated with insecure attachment, the child will experience a profound violation of trust. Presumably, the more meaningful the relationship between the assaulter and the child, the greater the subsequent psychological trauma (Prentky et al., 1989). The association of severity versus number of offenses in sexual offending was empirically confirmed to the sexual deviation, abuse, and insecurity of a caregiver in the childhood of the offender (Prentky et al., 1989). Furthermore, presexualization in conjunction with insecure attachment seems to suggest a model for hostility and violence in later offending. In other words, presexualization may provide a model for sexual aggression.

SEXUAL OFFENDERS: THE CONNECTION TO ATTACHMENT

The connection between childhood abuse and adult sexual offending is cautiously traced to this model and offered as a possible explanation of the reconstruction of abuse. Perhaps the once-victim, having felt some kind of emotional connection, albeit destructive and distorted, to their assaulter may be trying to recapture the "pleasure" and feelings of belonging and love from the presexualization encounters. However, because presexualization leaves behind confusion, vulnerability, and anger when the natural progression of age and sexual desire increases the individual is only equipped with uncertainty, naivety, and rage about sexuality. Coupled with lack of self-worth and self-esteem, the individual will likely ignite an impulsive, awkward, and inappropriate sexual or even relational advance. The inappropriateness of the gesture (not necessarily because of the individual himself or herself) may mean the respondent of the advance turns the individual down.

It is suggested that this may be interpreted as rejection, thus further reinforcing their feelings of inferiority and worthlessness. This perhaps leaves the person little choice availability (see Manassis & Bradley, 1994; Sroufe, 1996; Turner, et al., 1991; Warren, et al., 1997). These studies have shown that children with ambivalent/resistant attachments exhibit a consistent apprehension and uncertainty as to their attachment figure's care. These children lose their ability to tolerate separations and become fearful of even the smallest event.

Although at times the attachment figure does indeed care for the child, most of the time when the child signals for distress, the attachment figure is either inconsistent or unavailable. Still, the child hangs on to whatever safety may be there and exhibits clinging and demanding behaviors. In short, Bowlby believed that the actual experiences with caregivers influenced the ambivalently attached child to develop separation anxiety disorder. Furthermore, Cassidy (1995) concurred and felt that separations and even threats of separation by the caregiver leave the child at risk for later anxiety and depression. Ultimately, separation anxiety disorder may emerge from the neglected aspects of the child's experiences with his or her caregiver.

Klein (1994) analyzed the above findings and found that the symptoms of anxiety disorders follow a pattern, which parallels more familiar developmental milestones. In the first year of life, and with the development of cognition, comes object permanence and fear of strangers. In early childhood, fear of the dark and mysterious beasts and creatures come to haunt the child. In late childhood, concerns of performance are reported, and in adolescence, social and sexual anxiety is characteristic. The above findings taken alone are normal patterns of development, however, when combined, persistent, and intensified over time, *DSM-IV-TR* criteria for separation anxiety disorder are clearly visible (APA, 2000).

Bowlby (1973) showed that separation follows a three-part sequential emotional response of protest, despair, and detachment. The immediate response is protest typified by crying and thrashing in an attempt to prevent the caregiver from leaving; despair is the second response, which is marked by withdrawal and hopelessness; and finally, if the child remains separated from the caregiver, detachment occurs whereby there is indifference to the caregiver's return.

In the past, anxiety has been understood as a symptom of unconscious conflicts of sex and aggression (Freud, 1953). According to Freud, anxiety is activated by external events that initiate internal anxiety, which is connected to unconscious wishes that frequently combine libidinal and aggressive wishes. However, the notion that anxiety has internal origins and that it is the consequence of unconscious conflict has been discarded by other theorists (Klein, 1994).

Subsequently, Mahler, Pine, and Bergman's (1975) theory of separation-individuation suggests that separation anxiety may result when children fail to master and overcome the fear that comes when the child is separated from the caregiver and/or when the child becomes fused with the caregiver. If this developmental stage is not mastered, object constancy and autonomy in the child may not develop. Furthermore, the process of attainment can continue throughout late childhood and even into adulthood.

Bowlby (1973) noted that, "In the presence of a trusted companion fear of situations of every kind diminishes; when, by contrast, one is alone, fear of situations of every kind is magnified" (p. 201). Accordingly, children with ambivalent/resistant attachments have experienced inconsistent availability and comfort from their attachment figures (Ainsworth, Blehar, Waters, and Wall, 1978; Bowlby, 1973). Bids for attention have been frustrated and often met with indifference, inconsistency, or complete rebuffs from their caregivers. Because the caregivers cannot be relied upon to be accessible in times of need, ambivalently attached children are constantly concerned about the whereabouts of their caregiver, because of their fear of being left alone or being vulnerable to harm (Cassidy & Shaver, 1999). A history of unresponsiveness in childhood often results in the adult being unable to direct appropriate behaviors towards a potential partner or develop appropriate coping strategies. Instead, they may display clinging, demanding, or withdrawal behaviors, justified or not.

Mayseless and colleagues (1996) studied the unique ways in which anxiously attached young adults cope with the developmental task of leaving home (i.e., separation). Furthermore, they examined how these strategies related to children's internal representations. Findings indicate that while these young adults did leave home, they had few personal relations with peers and even fewer romantic relationships compared to securely attached young adults. Using the Separation Anxiety Test (Hansberg, cited in Mayseless et al., 1996), which depicts separations of varying severity, the ambivalent/resistant group reacted with more anxiety, feelings of rejection, and self-blame. Mayseless noted that, overall, this group perceived the separations as more emotionally upsetting and seemed impaired in their ability to offer coping strategies; instead, they suggested more self-harmful alternatives (e.g., staying close to someone who hurts them). The ambivalent/resistant group also reported more insecure attachment responses whilst giving the lowest number of self-reliant responses. This study showed that attachment behaviors correspond to attachment classifications and the internal working models to imagined separations. Warren et al. (1997) initiated the next logical step and monitored the childhood anxiety behaviors into adulthood.

If a child experiences inconsistent care, is classified as insecurely attached (specifically ambivalently attached), and is diagnosed with separation anxiety disorder in childhood, anxiety may continue into adulthood. Warren et al. (1997) showed in a longitudinal study spanning 17 years that this, indeed, could happen. Warren and her colleagues invited 172 children to participate in this extensive study. The children were assessed at birth for temperament and maternal anxiety. At 12 months of age, they were assessed using Ainsworth's Strange Situation. Finally, at 17.5 years of age, they were again assessed confirming that a relationship exists between ambivalent/resistant attachment, separation anxiety disorder in childhood, and later anxiety disorders in adulthood. Others confirm comorbidity and report findings of agoraphobia (Bowlby, 1973), panic disorder (de Ruiter & van Izendoorn 1992), general anxiety disorders (see Lipsitz et al., 1994 for a review) and sexual offending (Shear, 1996).

Accordingly, if presexualization enters the development of ambivalently attached children with separation anxiety, preoccupation with anxiety and dependency may now turn to identify with their offender in an attempt to hold onto the emotional relationship (Sawle & Kear-Colwell, 2001). However, presexualization is likely to predispose ambivalent individuals to perpetuate their lack of self-confidence, continually viewing themselves as unworthy and seeking constant approval from others;

they may seek a partner whom they can control and who admires them, such as children (Sawle & Kear-Colwell, 2001; Ward et al., 1995).

Ward et al. (1995) describes such men who are far more likely to offend children than females, as feeling more secure with and better able to relate to these needy children. However, Ward notes that not all ambivalent individuals become sexually involved with the children; some become a trusted and valuable friend. However, if they become emotionally dependant on the children, the dependency that results may confound adult relations making the child their sole emotional link.

At this point, the transformation of a relationship from an emotional one to a sexual one is not implausible and, in fact, may be aided if the man distorts the child's desire for emotional closeness to a sexual desire (Ward, Hudson, & Marshall 1995). This distortion will be facilitated through impulsive, awkward, and inappropriate conceptualization of sexuality, possibly resulting from the offender's own presexualization. However, because ambivalent individuals are emotionally dependant on others yet have difficulty obtaining intimacy in a satisfying adult relationship, it is likely that if the relationship between the adult and victim becomes sexualized, it is because of the ambivalent adult's desire for intimacy. Consequently, it is here that courtship and grooming behaviors take place for a period of time prior to engaging in sexual involvement (Ward, Hudson, & Marshall 1995). The sexual relationship is considered to be mutually satisfying by the offender. Consequently, the offender believes the child is enjoying the sexual behavior. To support this notion, Ward, Hudson, & Marshall (1995) found that those who are concerned with their victims' satisfaction and enjoyment tend to have ambivalently attached patterns. This possible connection to presexualization and sexual offending, specifically pedophilia would be reinforced with additional studies looking at pedophiles adult attachment relationships as they progressed from childhood. One possible connection is failure to develop intimacy in adult relationships.

INTIMACY

Bowlby (1969, 1973) suggested that if the bonds in childhood are insecure, it is likely these individuals have not learned the necessary skills needed to form and maintain close relationships. Instead these individuals grow up with a distorted view of intimacy. Some may even interpret early abusive sexual experiences as comforting regardless of the deviant nature, for them perhaps at least on some level it was intimate (Sawle & Kear-Colwell 2001), whereas others may fear and run from intimacy (Ward, Hudson, & Marshall 1995). Still, the interpretation that presexualization was intimate may be a protective justification so that at least some sense of being loved and desired is kept diffidently intact. Again, further probing is needed in this area of self-protection and justification and later identification with the assaulter's behaviors. What ensues is an emotional loneliness resulting when intimate relationships are unfulfilling.

EMOTIONAL LONELINESS

The construct of emotional loneliness is a state that arises from a lack of emotional intimacy in interpersonal relationships (Ward, Hudson, & Marshall 1995). It has been associated with hostility and aggressive behaviors (Diamant & Windholz, 1981) and acceptance of violence (Check, Perlman, & Malamuth 1985). Marshall (1989) has suggested that because of the lack of intimacy resulting in emotional loneliness, the offender may perceive emotional intimacy to be encapsulated in sex. Still, Ward cautions that the need for emotional intimacy coupled with a naive and immature sex drive can lead to sexual deviance as offenders progressively seek out a platform to fulfill an intimacy.

However, this kind of intimacy is virtually impossible to achieve because it is often distorted and based on aggression and suppression of the human spirit. Accordingly, it would be difficult indeed to find an individual who willingly and consistently surrendered his or her own sense of love and belonging in order to live up to a justification of a fantasy based on coercive sexual violations in childhood. Facilitating the distorted intimacy is a lack of empathy, which allows for easy disengagement of emotion. This is not to say however, that motivating the loneliness is a reactive formation to emotional intimacy. Each attachment is unique and specific to the individual, the different attachment patterns result in different offenses and various offending characteristics.

IMPLICATIONS

An attempt to document the role of attachment in the development of sexual offending has led to the development of a schematic suggesting a developmental pathway from insecure attachment to presexualization and later sexual offending (see Figure 2.1). This pathway indicates that without intervention, an insecure attachment in childhood when correlated with presexualization and emotional loneliness in adulthood increases the likelihood of offending when presexualization continues as natural sexual development and is replaced with distorted and confused notions of sexuality and intimacy. If this progression continues in isolation, shame, lack of empathy, and rage each adds fuel to the progression leading to sexual offending and revictimization. On the other hand, further exploration needs to be considered in antisexualism, that is, when sexuality is notably avoided and seen as an evil or wrong and the person may even be punished for healthy experimentation (e.g., masturbation). Thus, the child interprets the natural progression of sexuality as bad and, therefore, believes it should be repressed. Once again, without healthy intervention or alternative input, the child can develop a distorted view of sexuality.

However, much the way experiences can change or be reinterpreted, so too can patterns of attachment, which continually develop from personal experiences throughout the life span. And although the preliminary connections offered here cannot explain each offender or offense, a pathway has been forged allowing for further associations to be made and preventative measures to be accurately applied.

**Figure 2.1 Developmental Pathway from Insecure Attachment
to Presexualization and Later Offending**

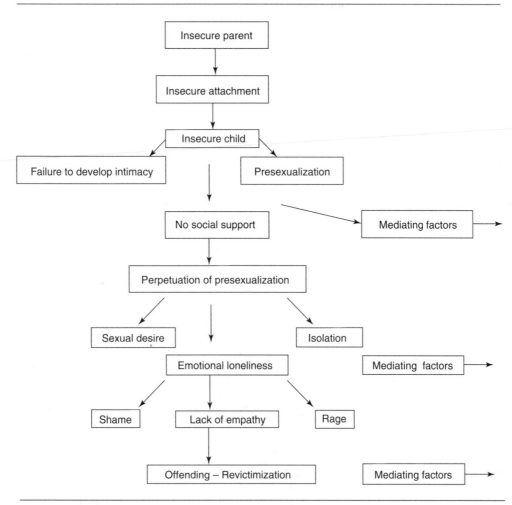

Concluding with a story of hope, it is suggested that it is never too late to form a secure healthy attachment. Paul Feyerabend, a seventy-year-old man, a known physicist and philosopher, in his biography, *Killing Time,* 1995 explained that the majority of his life he clung to an avoidant attachment firmly established in childhood. This attachment grew in the perpetual abuse inflicted on him by his father and depression and suicide of his mother, resulting in aggressive offending and coercive manipulation of others. He described his life as emotionally distressed and distant until he formed a deep and secure attachment to a woman. He explained that through her consistent and responsive love he became emotionally alive and reconnected to a childhood fraught with turmoil, facing it now with security he could let go and attach to a "... true love that is not a gift, it is an achievement ..."

PERSONALITY AND PSYCHIATRIC DISORDER COMORBIDITY IN SEX OFFENDERS

3

AINSLIE HEASMAN

Understanding the personality and psychiatric comorbidity of sex offenders is important for a number of reasons. First, there are many misconceptions of sex offenders. They are commonly lumped in to one category, irrespective of their offense or victim characteristics, or their personal background. This is important to understand when laws (e.g., Megan's Law) are being created based on one offender typology. Under Megan's Law in particular, all sexual offenders are treated equally. The desire to protect the public, and possible future victims is a top priority and should not be overlooked. However, classifying all sex offenders under the same umbrella may actually do more harm than good. Understanding the personality of sex offenders and their specific offense will help to understand the best methods of treatment for those groups of people. To help ensure that sex offenders do not reoffend, the characteristics of the offender and the offense should be carefully and fully taken into consideration to provide the best and most appropriate treatment and follow-up possible.

A second important reason for understanding the personality and psychiatric comorbidity of sex offenders is the impact it may have on the treatment process itself. Many sex offender programs, both inpatient and outpatient, are based on a cognitive-behavior model and often take the form of group therapy. Not all individuals will benefit from this type of treatment, at least not initially. Should the sex offender have an underlying psychiatric disorder, this may significantly interfere with treatment. For example, a severely depressed individual with low self-esteem may have difficulty withstanding, and benefiting, from the confrontational approach that is often used by other group members. Compliance with treatment may be difficult if the offender suffers from a more severe psychotic disorder. It may be necessary to establish a psychopharmacological intervention prior to, and during, another form of treatment.

In many sex offender treatment programs, offenders are taught how to cope with inappropriate sexual arousal and negative feelings. Lussier, Proulx, and McKibben (2001) classified offenders into two categories based on their scores on the Millon Clinical Multiaxial Inventory (MCMI-1): anxious and dramatic. Offenders with an anxious profile scored higher on the Schizoid, Avoidant, Passive-Aggressive, Schizotypal, and Borderline scales of the MCMI-1. In contrast, dramatic offenders scored higher on the Histrionic, Narcissistic, and Compulsive scales. The authors also found differences in the coping styles of these two groups of offenders. Anxious offenders more often distracted themselves in an effort to reduce their negative state, whereas dramatic offenders more often used rationalization to keep their self-esteem at a high level. The authors reason that it is important for treatment providers to understand these differences and to provide a variety of coping strategies to offenders, who will likely choose those strategies that best fit their personality. It is important to understand the difference in these strategies, as they can become maladaptive quite easily. Should an offender persistently distract himself from his inappropriate sexual arousal, he is doing little to recondition or extinguish that type of arousal, but is only "putting it off," until it appears again. Offenders who use rationalization to cope with negative states, often use this as a thinking error before, during, and after their offense. An offender who is able to make sense of the offense he is about to commit, or has committed, by providing himself with self-serving excuses and rationalizations is a dangerous individual. An offender may gravitate to the coping strategy that best fits his personality, and it may be similar to a thinking error employed around their offense. Therefore, understanding these subtle differences while the offender is in treatment will help address any concerns or issues before they arise. In contrast, adolescent sexual offenders are more likely to use interpersonal violence to resolve conflict. This maladaptive coping strategy is found more often among adolescent offenders than adolescents in general (Epps et al., White & Koss, as cited in Shaw, 1999).

Adolescents who sexually offend often have characteristics central to their offense, related to their self-image or view of others, that need to be addressed in treatment to ensure a more successful outcome. It is believed that adolescent child molesters, in comparison to nonoffending youth, have a lack of self-confidence, independence, assertiveness, and self-satisfaction. They are also more likely to be pessimistic and to blame themselves for negative events in their lives (Hunter Jr. & Figueredo, 2000). It is possible that, like adult male sex offenders, adolescents feel socially inept and unable to engage in healthy relationships with people their own age. Therefore, engaging in sexual activities with other children, often younger than the offender, is done in an attempt to satisfy whatever need or curiosity the adolescent has. It is essential that any treatment of the adolescent sex offender incorporate general life skills, including assertiveness, positive self-esteem, problem solving, and coping skills. Adolescent sex offenders often come from families that engage in poor role modeling, abuse (physical, verbal, or sexual), and/or a lack of communication. An adolescents' home environment is an important dimension to evaluate when planning treatment. Encouraging their families, when appropriate, to become active in treatment will often help the adolescent offender, especially if the offender is in an outpatient treatment program, because they often return home to their families where difficulties or dysfunction are central to that environment. Without adequate and appropriate family support, it makes it difficult for the offender to employ the skills they have learned in treatment.

Sex offenders often have stressors that are central to their offense cycle. Pithers, Kashima, Cumming, Beal, and Buell (as cited in Lussier, Proulx, & McKibben, 2001) found that in the hours proceeding their offense, 89 percent of adult sex offenders experienced a negative emotional state. Proulx, Perreau, and Ouimet (as cited in Lussier, Proulx, & McKibben, 2001) found that many child molesters and pedophiles experienced a stressor the year prior to their sexual offense. The researchers found that 63.6 percent experienced interpersonal problems, 50 percent low self-esteem, and 27.2 percent had work problems. Child molesters, compared to a community sample of adults, were found to have deficits in self-esteem, assertiveness, and empathy towards victims of sexual abuse. They were also found to be more emotionally lonely and have a higher level of personal distress than the comparison group (Fisher, Beech, & Browne, 1999).

Male offenders, whether adolescent or adult, often have difficulties with social competence. Their ability to engage in same-age peer relationships, whether romantic or platonic, is often hindered. They may resort to younger individuals in an effort to relate on a level that is closer to that of their own social competence level. Often an offender has low self-esteem that impacts his view of himself and his perceived ability to interact with others. When this outlook is developed in childhood or adolescence, and without effective intervention, it further compounds the difficulties offenders are likely to have as they become older.

Marshall and Barbaree (as cited in Hudson & Ward, 2000) believe that developmental adversity when young produces two negative consequences. This adversity does not enable the adolescent to develop self-confidence or a feeling of efficacy in their world. These experiences also create negative attitudes, feelings, and beliefs about and towards others. With these two factors combined, it makes it difficult for the adolescent to engage in socially appropriate relationships. The authors also hypothesize that the young male will not develop a separation between aggression and sexuality. Hudson and Ward (2000) suggest that deviant sexual activity on the part of male youth is done in order to compensate for the deficit they experience in interpersonal relationships and/or their isolation. Their negative feelings and attitudes may result in inappropriate sexual arousal. Hunter and Ward (2000) compared child molesters, rapists and a community control group on their level of assertiveness and anxiety. Child molesters were found to have the lowest capacity for assertiveness and the highest levels of anxiety. In contrast, the community control group had the highest level of assertiveness and lowest level of anxiety, while rapists were found to score between the two. What is interesting to note is not only the offenders' level of assertiveness, but also their interpretation of the assertiveness of others. In videotaped vignettes presented to offenders that included depictions of appropriate and inappropriate social interactions, rapists found the actor who was overassertive to be the most appropriate, and child molesters and a community control group found the actor who was underassertive to be the most appropriate (Marshall, Barbaree et al., as cited in Hudson & Ward, 2000). This finding may play a role in understanding an offender's victim selection. Howell (as cited in Hudson & Ward, 2000) found that child molesters preferred children because they were not threatening and are submissive.

Being caught for a sexual offense may significantly emotionally impact an offender, and may promote the development of a psychiatric disorder as a function of the arrest and subsequent consequences. Being caught and having to go through the legal process for a sexual offense often has a great impact on the offender, at least initially. They are often removed from their families, and those close to them are provided with often quite surprising information. This experience may be particularly traumatic to the offender, resulting in shame, guilt, and a reduction in self-esteem. The social relationships the offender has developed are often destroyed or severely damaged. Should these offenders end up in prison, they are considered to be very low in status on the inmate hierarchy and are often targeted for abuse of many kinds because of their offense. This type of social rejection may be difficult for the sexual offender (Hunter & Figueredo 2000).

Social competence and preoffending attitudes may play a significant role in treatment outcome for sex offenders. Beech (as cited in Fisher, Beech, & Browne, 1999) classified offenders into two categories based on the aforementioned variables of competence and attitude. Offenders with high levels of pro-offending attitudes and higher levels of social incompetence were classified as high-deviancy. Offenders with lower levels of pro-offending attitudes and more social competence were classified as low-deviancy. Deviancy was found to be associated with offense characteristics. High-deviant offenders were more likely to have been convicted for a previous sexual offense, more likely victimized males or both males and females, and had a victim or victims who were within the family, or both within and outside the family. Low-deviancy offenders were more likely to have one or more victims within their family. Not only did their personality characteristics affect their offenses, but it was found to influence their treatment as well. High-deviancy offenders required more hours of treatment than low-deviancy offenders to show a treatment effect (which was defined as a normal range of scores on several psychological measures as compared to when they began treatment).

Many sexual offenders have a psychiatric disorder that may often go undetected or untreated during treatment of the sexual offense. Palermo and Farkas (2001), however, contend that mental illness is rarely found in offenders, particularly in sexual offenders, except in "bizarre" offenses that are committed by schizophrenics. Raymond, Coleman, Ohkerking, Christenson, & Milner (1999), in a study of male adults diagnosed as pedophiles [according to the *Diagnostic and Statistical Manual of Mental Disorders–IV (DSM-IV)*] found that 93 percent were found to have a comorbid psychiatric disorder. An astonishing 56 percent met criteria for five or more diagnoses, aside from pedophilia. Most common among these men was a history of a mood disorder (67 percent), specifically major depression. Sixty-four percent had a history of an anxiety disorder, most commonly social phobia and posttraumatic stress disorder. In addition, 60 percent of the subjects indicated a history of substance abuse, with alcohol being most common. What was not indicated was whether these individuals suffered from a substance abuse problem prior to their first offense, or if alcohol or drugs was used as a coping mechanism to deal with the consequences or feelings surrounding the offense. More severe psychotic disorders may play a role in sexual offending. Smith and Taylor (1999, cited in Palermo & Farkas, 2001) found that 66 percent of the patients studied in a hospital, whose primary offense was for sexual aggression against women, met the criteria for schizophrenia. This study should be interpreted with caution however, since the patients case files were examined only, with no corroborating interview.

Antisocial personality disorder (ASPD) is often diagnosed among inmates in the prison population. It is likely that the general public feels that there is "something wrong" with an individual who commits a sexual offense. It could be argued that what the general public would define as this "something wrong" would be classified as an Axis II personality disorder. However, among the pedophiles studied by Raymond, Coleman, Ohkerking, Christenson, and Milner (1999), 77.5 percent did not meet the *DSM-IV* criteria for ASPD, and only 20 percent met the criteria for narcissistic personality disorder.

Working with adolescent sex offenders to address their attitudes and beliefs, as well as any existing psychiatric disorders is essential in preventing recidivism. It is believed that adolescent sex offenders often exhibit similar personality patterns to those of adult sex offenders. Limited social skills, deficits in assertiveness, and inappropriate sexual fantasies and beliefs (Abel, Mittelman, & Becker, as cited in Shaw, 1999) have been found in adult sexual offenders. Becker and Hunter (as cited in Shaw, 1999) have found certain factors common to adolescent sex offenders, including; a deficit in social and interpersonal skills, impulsivity, psychopathology, and delinquent behavior.

Adolescent sex offenders likely commit offenses for a number of reasons. As with adults, some adolescent offenders have very deviant arousal patterns and a level of psychopathy that is quite high. Hopefully, the minority of adolescent sex offenders fall into this category. Others, again like their adult counterparts, are limited in their social skills and emotional maturity and resort to younger children out of curiosity and a desire to experiment with their sexuality (Shaw, 1999). There are however, many emotionally immature adolescents who do not resort to sexually acting-out behaviors. The personality characteristics of juveniles who sexually offend are important to note at this point. Using the Millon Adolescent Personality Inventory

(MAPI), certain personality traits were found among adolescent sex offenders in a residential facility, including, "asociality, indifference to others, strong-willed traits, social uneasiness, tendency to dominate others, unkindness, impatience with the weakness of others, discontent, pessimism, and unpredictability and preference for unpredictable situations" (Shaw, p. 177). These adolescents also exhibited, "egocentricity, low self-esteem, poor self-concept, poor sexual acceptance, family discord, self-deprication, and a readiness to be influenced by others" (Shaw, p. 177). Emotional immaturity and the youths' personality characteristics may contribute to adolescents committing sexual offenses.

The severity of psychopathology among adolescents is important to note. In a study of seventeen violent sex offenders, Lewis, Shankik, and Pincus (as cited in Shaw, 1999) found that depression, auditory hallucinations, paranoid ideation, and disturbed thought processes were the most common features. The severity of psychiatric comorbidity may be a function of the juveniles' offense. Adolescents who find themselves incarcerated or in an inpatient hospital are likely to have more severe pathology than those adolescents who are routed to outpatient community treatment facilities. Kavoussi, Kaplan, and Becker (as cited in Shaw, 1999) studied outpatient adolescent sex offenders and found that 81 percent had a psychiatric diagnosis. The most frequent were "conduct disorder (48 percent), substance abuse (18.9 percent), adjustment disorder with depressed mood (8.6 percent), attention-deficit hyperactivity disorder (6.9 percent), and social phobia (5.2 percent)" (p. 175).

Believing that the adolescent sex offender does not have a pattern of sexually deviant behavior is a dangerous assumption. Abel, Mittelman, and Becker (as cited in Shaw, 1999) found that the average adolescent sex offender under the age of eighteen has committed 8 sexual offenses with an average of 6.7 victims. The relevance of psychiatric disorders to adolescent sexual offending should be noted. Shaw et al. (cited in Shaw, 1999) found that, "the younger the child when he committed his first sexual offense, the higher the number of coexisting psychiatric diagnoses" (p. 175).

The use of psychological measures has been employed to study sex offenders. Curnoe and Langevin (2002) found a significant difference on the validity and clinical scales of the Minnesota Muliphasic Personality Inventory (MMPI) between sex offenders with deviant sexual fantasies and those with nondeviant fantasies. Those with deviant fantasies had an elevated F (Infrequency) validity scale, and elevated Psychopathic Deviate (Pd), Masculinity-Femininity (Mf), Paranoia (Pa), and Schizophrenia (Sc) clinical scales. There are several possible interpretations of the elevated validity scale. It is possible that this group of sex offenders have significant psychopathology, which may be correlated with their level of deviant sexual fantasies. High scores on the Pa and Sc scales could reflect the social incompetence and uneasiness that has been described among sex offenders. Vaillant and Antonowicz (as cited in Vaillant & Blasutti, 1992) found that rapists were elevated on the Psychopathic Deviate and Schizophrenia scales of the MMPI, while child molesters were elevated on the Psychopathic Deviate and Depression scales. This suggests that both groups of sexual offenders experience similar levels of social alienation and have a tendency to come into conflict with other members of society.

Understanding the role mental illness plays in offending needs further study. Evaluating this connection needs to be done carefully, however. Understanding the influence of the mental illness on behavior is useful in treatment and prevention, however using the mental illness as an excuse for committing a sexual offense is dangerous ground. A common scientific adage would be useful here, "correlation does not imply causation."

Some adult sex offenders commit their first sexual offense while in adolescence. Their backgrounds are often ripe with early sexual experiences, whether the teenager engages in these activities himself or is exposed to them via family members or friends. For every adolescent sex offender who is apprehended, there is likely one who is not. Those that encounter the legal system are hopefully given an opportunity to learn and develop new skills and behaviors that will guide them the rest of their life. However, those whose deviant behaviors go unnoticed may grow up with the same inappropriate sexual behaviors and only as adults will they encounter the legal system. At that point, it may be too late to work with these offenders on restructuring their cognitions and attitudes, or the legal system may be less willing to give them the appropriate therapeutic treatment.

PART II

PROSTITUTION, PORNOGRAPHY, AND OBSCENITY

TRANSVESTISM AND PROSTITUTION

Caleb Newman

TRANSVESTISM

For many years, the notion of cross-dressing has been regarded as somewhat of a taboo in American society. Men are stereotypically depicted as the household provider, the master of the manor, the family protector. In order to uphold this image, men are expected to exhibit substantial amounts of bravado and machismo. The sight of a man dressed as a woman is, therefore, typically not viewed in a favorable light. Indeed, the mere image of a man in drag is enough to send shock waves through the heart of the stereotypical masculine heterosexual male. However, it should be noted that cross-dressing is an acceptable form of behavior in specific social contexts. For example, it is relatively common for men to dress as women for events in which costumes are required. Otherwise, cross-dressing is more or less frowned upon when undertaken in a public arena.

Movies such as *Tootsie* and *Mrs. Doubtfire* have created a pocket of acceptability for cross-dressing within American culture and, to an extent, popularized such behavior. However, these movies only present cross-dressing in a comedic light. As such, cross-dressing is most popular and accepted in our society only when it is used as a vehicle for comedy and entertainment (Bhugra, 2000). But what happens when cross-dressing is used in a manner that exceeds the boundaries deemed acceptable within our culture? What if men dress as women because they like it?

The term cross-dressing has become synonymous with transvestism. The notion of transvestism was first explored and developed by Hirschfeld, a German physician, in the early 1900s (Bullough & Bullough, 1997). Hirschfeld initially coined the term transvestitism to include any person that dressed as a member of the opposite sex. He published a book in 1910, entitled *The Transvestites: An Investigation of the Erotic Drive to Cross Dress,* which examined the lives of seventeen of his patients (Bullough & Bullough, 1997). Although the behavior was found to occur primarily in men, Hirschfeld examined at least one female patient who engaged in cross-dressing behavior. Ellis, another researcher interested in sexual practices in the early-twentieth century, concurred with many of Hirschfeld's conclusions. However, Ellis believed that cross-dressing represented a powerful set of cognitions and internal representations, rather than merely a behavior (Bullough & Bullough, 1997). As a result, Ellis regarded transvestism as a mental illness and treated it as such. He attempted to correct the "problem" with psychotherapy.

TRANSVESTITES, TRANSSEXUALS, AND TRANSGENDERISTS: A COMPARISON

Before any further examination of transvestism can occur, a clear distinction between transvestites, transsexuals, and transgenderists must first be made. These terms are loosely used in our society and often interchanged, although they do not have identical meanings. Transvestism is characterized by occasional cross-dressing characterized with accompanying sexual arousal. According to the *Diagnostic and Statistical Manual of Mental Disorders—Fourth Edition (DSM-IV)* (1994), transvestic fetishism is diagnosed "over a period of at least 6 months, in a heterosexual male, [involving] recurrent intense sexually arousing fantasies, sexual urges, or behaviors involving cross-dressing . . . [and when] the fantasies, sexual urges, or behaviors cause clinically significant distress or impairment in social, occupational, or other important areas of functioning" (American Psychiatric Association [APA], 1994, p. 575). The main component of the aforementioned definition is the sexual arousal that is associated with the act or notion of cross-dressing.

Contrary to transvestism, transsexualism is defined by an individual's desire to actually become a member of the opposite sex. Such individuals typically feel as though they are men trapped inside women's bodies, or women trapped inside men's bodies. "Transsexuals typically report a long-standing, intense experience of gender discordance—that is, of being cast into the wrong body relative to one's gender identity" (Docter & Fleming, 2001, p. 257). The most important element of transsexualism is the way in which individuals perceive their individual sexual identity. While there are transsexuals who attempt to alter their bodies surgically and hormonally, many transsexuals possess no such desire to undergo surgery. Therefore, the determining factor in transsexualism is not whether the individual has any plans of participating in a sex change operation, but rather whether the individual identifies primarily with his or her gender counterpart (de Silva, 1999).

The distinction between transvestism and transsexualism becomes confusing when transsexuals incorporate cross-dressing into their lives. Cross-dressing, in and of itself, does not necessarily equate with either transvestism or transsexualism.

Rather, cross-dressing may serve to solidify a transsexual's identification with the opposite sex. But if there is no accompanying sexual arousal, the individual cannot technically be considered a transvestite. Therefore, the motivation for cross-dressing is the key element in determining appropriate classification, if any such classification exists.

When the concept of transvestism was initially developed, it failed to account for individual beliefs regarding specific gender identification. Instead, it was developed as an attempt to classify those individuals who were readily observed to cross-dress. In response to this definition, the term "transgender" was introduced to include all individuals who choose to live continuously in the gender role opposite their genetic sex (Docter & Prince, 1997). The choice to live in an opposing gender identity entails more than simply dressing and looking like the opposite sex. It involved a specific lifestyle, beliefs, and attitudes. "Transgender is used to refer to the full spectrum of persons with nontraditional gender identities including pre- and post-transsexuals, transvestites, and intersex persons" (Carroll & Gilroy, 2002, p. 234). As such, although all transvestites and transsexuals are considered transgenderists, not all transgenderists are transvestites and transsexuals.

THE ORIGINS OF TRANSVESTISM

Because transvestism is often accompanied by feelings of shame and guilt, the act of cross-dressing is often done in private (Docter & Prince, 1997). Therefore, it is extremely difficult to estimate the existing number of transvestites in our society, and most likely a large number of transvestites are unaccounted for. Nevertheless, various studies have attempted to recruit large numbers of self-reported transvestites as participants. For example, Schott (1995) conducted a study that included eighty-five cross-dressing males. Aside from confirming that transvestites generally cross-dress in private settings, the study discovered the vast majority of participants never sought psychiatric help. It was surmised these subjects never engaged in therapy because they were too ashamed to take the first step to publicizing their inclinations or that the participants never considered the behavior a problem. Regardless, such findings explain why psychological literature on transvestism is relatively scarce.

Today there exists enormous pressure to fit the mold of the "normal" American. For example, "normal" men are attracted to women and exhibit stereotypical masculine traits. Homosexual men clearly do not fit this prototype and are, therefore, often reviled and shunned by society. Given the way that homosexuals are treated in our society, it begs the question, Why would anyone "choose" to be homosexual? Along a similar vein, given the way that transvestism is viewed and treated in American culture, why would anyone "choose" to be a transvestite? There has been continued speculation regarding the precursors or precipitating factors of cross-dressing. Some believe that transvestism is caused by a childhood history of abuse, whereas others believe it is fostered by a family environment in which the child is raised as the opposite gender. However, there is no consistent set of social or psychological factors that have been found to lead to the onset of transvestism.

CHILDHOOD FACTORS

In a self-report study by Schott (1995), many transvestites reportedly engaged in their first cross-dressing experience by the age of seven. However, the extent of their cross-dressing varied substantially: Some partially dressed as women, while others completely donned women's apparel and accessories. According to some of the participants, their first cross-dressing experience occurred in secret, while for other respondents, their first experience was being dressed as women by their mother or sister. Several participants admitted to being dressed in female attire as early as their first year of life, while another group did not begin engaging in cross-dressing until the age of twenty-five. The frequency with which the participants continued to engage in cross-dressing behavior was quite varied, ranging anywhere from once per year to multiple times daily (Schott, 1995).

It is unknown whether there were any significant differences between those who chose to cross-dress in private and those who were made to cross-dress by a family member. In either case, it was believed that their first experience of cross-dressing had powerful impacts on their internal frameworks (Schott, 1995). Perhaps some of the participants were secretly attracted to the thought of dressing as a female *prior* to their initial experience of cross-dressing or some of the participants were sexually aroused by the act of cross-dressing *after* their first experience. Regardless, at some point, the participants learned to pair sexual arousal with the act (or thought) of cross-dressing. It was common for the respondents in Schott's study to report being attracted to specific articles of feminine clothing associated with their first remembered cross-dressing experience. For example, participants who wore panties during their first cross-dressing episode continued to be particularly aroused by female panties, just as those who initially experimented with make-up continued to hold an affinity for such products.

Bullough and Bullough (1997) also conducted a survey of male cross-dressers. The results of the survey indicated that while the majority (56 percent) of the 372 participants were never caught as children while cross-dressing, an overwhelming majority (93 percent) feared being caught. According to the respondents, they were most fearful of being rejected by their family and peers for the deviant behavior. In addition, they also feared being labeled as "crazy" or "sissy," and a small percentage believed that cross-dressing was a sin. These findings seem to indicate that regardless of age, most children are at least partially aware of the negative social connotations associated with cross-dressing.

Although transvestites experience sexual arousal by the act or fantasy of cross-dressing, they do not always achieve orgasm (Bullough & Bullough, 1997). In fact, there are some transvestites who rarely (or never) reach orgasm through cross-dressing but still attain some degree of sexual pleasure. However, for others, the mere thought of cross-dressing or the sight of female clothing is enough to achieve an orgasm. This serves as further evidence that clothing and cognitive stimuli are extremely powerful secondary reinforcers that are often independent of orgasm (Schott, 1995).

According to the literature, the majority of transvestites are reportedly raised in two-parent households, in which the father provided a good masculine image and where they were raised as a boy (Docter & Prince, 1997). Nevertheless, Schott (1995) determined that a substantial number of participants in his study explained their cross-dressing tendencies as a result of their family environment. For some respondents, the mother was very domineering and controlling. For others, the father was not a significant presence within the family and, therefore, was unable to provide appropriate guidance and structure. Still others claimed to be heavily exposed to female figures (e.g., extended family) or overly attracted to women (termed "gender envy"). Furthermore, many of the participants reported having a stronger childhood attachment to their mother, relative to their father (Schott, 1995). Only a minority of respondents attributed their cross-dressing to genetic or internal factors such as: "I am really a woman," "I was born with it," or "It is the result of an inner drive" (Schott, 1995). This finding further supports the differentiation between transvestites and transsexuals. Specifically, the majority of transvestites dress as women because of the accompanying sexual arousal, rather than because of existing gender discordance.

ADULT FACTORS

The act of cross-dressing often carries with it a feminine and negative connotation for men. For example, many men who cross-dress in public (e.g., "drag queens") are viewed as homosexuals. Interestingly, the literature overwhelmingly cites transvestism as a heterosexual disorder, and by self-report, the vast majority of transvestites are heterosexual and married, many of whom have children (Bullough & Bullough, 1997). Further, according to the *DSM-IV,* transvestism is only seen in heterosexual men. However, the results of several studies seem to refute this assertion. Although many of the respondents in Bullough and Bullough's (1997) work were reportedly heterosexual, many of them reported having homosexual urges or fantasies. A number of participants (26 percent) reported having engaged in homosexual activity at some point during their lives. Thus, although a large percentage of transvestites are heterosexual, a significant portion are also bisexual or homosexual.

Because the majority of transvestites are married and self-proclaimed heterosexuals, it is no wonder that cross-dressing takes place in a private setting. In addition, the stigma that is attached to transvestism prevents many from venturing into public venues. However, a small percentage of transvestites cross-dress in public. In fact, there are clubs that specifically cater to public transvestism (Docter & Prince, 1997).

According to a study involving 1,032 cross-dressers (see Docter & Prince, 1997), a significant number of transvestites disclose their transvestic tendencies to their prospective wives before marriage. The majority (83 percent) of these wives were reportedly aware of their husband's cross-dressing behavior, although many discovered it accidentally. Of those wives who were privy to the cross-dressing, a substantial portion of them (28 percent) claimed to be completely accepting of the behavior. However, it was unclear whether the remaining 72 percent of wives were either nonaccepting or simply neutral about their husband's proclivities. Nevertheless, the prospect of having to disclose one's cross-dressing habits to a wife or family member can be incredibly daunting. On the one hand, disclosing such information might jeopardize relationships with both immediate and extended family members. The negative reactions of an unforgiving wife, judgmental sibling, or nonaccepting parents might lead to the destruction of a nuclear family. On the other hand, disclosing to loved ones could alleviate the lingering threat of being "caught" or discovered that many transvestites struggle with.

The potential impact of transvestism on a family is quite large. It would be understandably difficult for a wife to learn that her husband was more sexually aroused by cross-dressing than by her. Furthermore, children of transvestites may have tremendous difficulty accepting the behavior. If their father's cross-dressing became public knowledge, it would be extraordinarily challenging for the child(ren) to avoid taunting by their peers.

UNANSWERED QUESTIONS

The available psychological literature on transvestism tends to focus solely on male transvestites. The *DSM-IV* states that transvestism can only be found among the male population. Does that mean that women, by definition, are unable to be transvestites? It would seem improbable that there are no women that are sexually aroused by the act or fantasy of dressing as men. Clearly, there are women who identify themselves as men and choose to undergo sex reassignment surgery. Perhaps the hesitation surrounding the existence of female transvestites stems from society's inability to identify clothing that is male-specific, unlike delineating female-specific attire. It is not uncommon for women to wear slacks, button-down shirts, suits, ties, and suspenders. If there are women who are sexually aroused by wearing clothing that has been historically and traditionally viewed as male-specific, then maybe an argument could be made for including women in the diagnostic criteria. However, it would be extremely difficult, if not altogether impossible, to identify female transvestites because they can blend into society without being noticed, unlike male transvestites.

An interesting question arises when attempting to label or categorize individuals who choose to cross-dress. At what point is an individual considered a transvestite? If we solely examine both extremes of the spectrum, it is easier to make a distinction. On the one hand, suppose that a man dresses as a woman an average of four times per day, over a three-year time span. On each occasion, he achieves orgasm. According to diagnostic standards, it would be appropriate to diagnose this individual as a transvestite. On the other hand, suppose that a man dresses in female attire on one occasion at a costume party. He does not experience sexual satisfaction and he does not engage in cross-dressing behavior outside of the party. Therefore, it would be unreasonable to classify this man as a transvestite.

According to the definition in the *DSM-IV,* transvestism only occurs in heterosexual men, and it must involve cross-dressing behavior for upwards of six months. Furthermore, the behavior must cause an impairment in daily functioning (APA, 1994). The available literature suggests that many self-identified cross-dressers engage in such behavior anywhere from multiple times per day to once per year (Docter & Prince, 1997). According to diagnostic standards, those individuals who do not regularly engage in cross-dressing behavior are not considered transvestites. Yet studies on transvestism seem to indicate that there is significant variability in the extent and frequency of cross-dressing (Schott, 1995). In addition, the literature suggests that although many transvestites are heterosexual by self-report, many of them have fantasized or engaged in homosexual acts. A significant number of homosexual and bisexual men attain sexual arousal through cross-dressing. To discount them from the diagnostic category simply because of their sexual preference would seem unreasonable. Therefore, although the current definition of transvestism in the *DSM-IV* has considerably improved since the last edition, it would seem prudent to revisit the issue in the following years (Bullough & Bullough, 1997).

PROSTITUTION

Numerous theories have emerged over the years that attempt to explain the reasons for prostitution. It is well-known that the life of the average prostitute is not a glamorous one. Prostitution is an occupation that involves many risks, including physical and emotional abuse, rape, sexually transmitted diseases (STDs), and possibly murder. If these elements of danger associated with prostitution are common knowledge, then why do so many men and women choose to engage in this practice? Zatz (1997) reports,

> The experiences of [men and] women in prostitution will have quite a bit to do both with underlying features of their situation and with how they have learned to understand, interpret, and explain the world around them. Different theories of prostitution, linked as they are to particular understandings of sexuality, gender, commercial exchange, specific sexual acts, and so on . . . play a role in the production of experience as well (p. 279).

THE REASONS FOR PROSTITUTION

Perhaps the first and most obvious incentive for prostitution is financial. Prostitution is an extremely lucrative business, and there is a great deal of money to be made in the industry. Depending on the "quality" and services of the prostitute, it is possible to make thousands of dollars in a single evening. Money has always been effective lure for Americans, and prostitution is no exception.

There is also a common societal belief that individuals who engage in prostitution have been victims of childhood sexual abuse. The literature seems to support this notion, citing a variety of documented cases in which prostitutes have suffered some type of abuse during childhood (Dalla, 2000). While a past history of abuse does not necessarily cause people to turn to prostitution, it certainly contributes to the ways in which they perceive themselves and the world around them, and the ways they make important life decisions (Farley & Barkan, 1998). As victims of childhood abuse, many individuals are forced to utilize defense mechanisms in order to maintain appropriate daily functioning. Furthermore, defense mechanisms are often important during the actual act of abuse. For example, a child who is repeatedly raped by a family member over a multiyear time span might learn to detach from their emotions during the sexual episodes. As prostitutes, these same individuals are capable of engaging in sexual intercourse with numerous people by employing the same defense mechanisms—mainly, by separating the sex from their emotions (James & Meyerding, 1997).

It is believed by some that prostitution is a means of supporting a drug habit (Dalla, 2000). Drugs are an expensive habit, and the bulk of a single evening's profits can be easily spent on street drugs. It is not known, however, whether drug habits are typically precipitated by prostitution, or whether prostitution is facilitated through drug use (Maxwell & Maxwell, 2000). In either case, drugs can be used as an artificial defense mechanism, in the sense that it numbs affect, or at the very least, restricts it (Young, Boyd & Hubbell, 2000).

It is also hypothesized that many prostitutes are previously runaways. Children and adolescents run away from home for various reasons, including neglect, abuse, or general family dysfunction. After leaving home, many runaways often have no place to turn and are essentially forced to live on the streets. While living on the streets, these runaways often encounter drugs, violence, and poverty. These experiences serve to amplify and perpetuate the child's previous experience(s) of abuse and victimization (Nandon, Korerola & Schulderman, 1998) and set them up to resort to prostitution to survive. It is estimated that as many as 84 percent of prostitutes are homeless (Farley & Barkan, 1998). Because many prostitutes do not have adequate resources at their disposal, or appropriate support networks, they are often caught in a vicious cycle between stability and homelessness (Weiner, 1996).

Given the broad range of potential problems that are associated with prostitution, it is difficult to imagine the reasons anybody would remain in the profession, let alone enter into it in the first place. Research suggests that there are a number of obstacles that prevent prostitutes from leaving the business. For example, a significant number of prostitutes abuse drugs, and many of them need intense drug treatment. There are also many prostitutes that are homeless. However, it is extremely difficult for most prostitutes to access drug treatment programs or residential treatment services (Weiner, 1996).

Even if these services were more accessible, numerous factors may prevent a prostitute from trying to access any outreach services. First of all, some prostitutes fear they will be "discovered" by the outreach program and ultimately arrested for their illegal activity (Weiner, 1996). In addition, juvenile prostitutes who are runaways fear they will be identified and subsequently forced to return to a possibly abusive family. Furthermore, feelings of shame, guilt, and humiliation can be associated with outreach services.

While some prostitutes enter the business as a necessity or as a means of survival, there are also those who actively desire to become prostitutes and enjoy their work. Therefore, some prostitutes express no desire to change their lifestyle and appear perfectly content with their lives. Indeed, there are those that view themselves as "entrepreneurs with freedom of choice of where and when they work and the kind of services they offer to their client base" (Brewis & Linstead, 2000, p. 174).

THE RELATIONSHIP BETWEEN TRANSVESTISM AND PROSTITUTION

Given the information on both transvestism and prostitution, one must consider the possibility of a relationship between the two. Unfortunately, there is a dearth of research about such a relationship. Therefore, many of the following statements about prostitution and transvestites are inferred from the literature, rather than based on fact or study.

Because transvestites generally engage in cross-dressing behaviors in secret, and because prostitution typically involves public exposure, there is reason to believe that the number of transvestic prostitutes is rather small. However, this is not to say that transvestites never become prostitutes. It is reasonable to assume that transvestites choose prostitution for many of the same reasons that otherwise "normal" people do. Perhaps some transvestites are victims of childhood abuse and are products of dysfunctional family environments. Maybe others run away from home because of their transvestism and find no other reasonable options for survival. Further, it is possible that some transvestites are attracted to the business for monetary reasons or for sexual gratification purposes.

The notion of runaway children being at higher risk for prostitution may play a role in transvestic prostitution. As stated earlier, transvestism carries a very negative stigma. It is embarrassing and shameful for many individuals, especially children and adolescents, to admit that they are sexually aroused by wearing clothes of the opposite sex. Self-disclosure or discovery of cross-dressing tendencies is made easier by an accepting and nonjudgmental family. Unfortunately, most often this may not be the case. Family members are more likely to shame, humiliate, or simply alienate themselves from the child/adolescent. Ultimately, revealing one's cross-dressing may cause such tremendous discordance in the family, that the child or adolescent is forced to leave the home or runs away. Given that child or adolescent transvestites are at greater risk for experiencing family dysfunction, they are ultimately more prone to run away, and therefore are at higher risk of turning to prostitution.

As discussed earlier, prostitutes may use specific defense mechanisms, such as distancing their emotions from their behavior, to survive. This learned defense mechanism enables them to have sex with a large number of strangers frequently. Further, because of the negative label attached to transvestism, many transvestites might also learn to separate their emotions from their actions in order to cope. They may feel compelled to live their lives in shame and secrecy, suppressing their true feelings. As such, transvestic prostitutes might be capable of remaining in the industry for a relatively long period of time because of these well-developed defenses.

Over the years, increasing numbers of transvestic prostitutes have been murdered (Cramer, 1990). There is reason to believe that many of the murders are motivated by rage and revulsion, as it is not uncommon for transvestic prostitutes to refrain from revealing their true sexual identity to their customers. There are those clients who are aware of the true gender of the transvestic prostitute and choose them for that very reason. However, many transvestite prostitutes appear feminine enough in appearance to keep clients blissfully unaware of their gender. If and when the client discovers the actual gender of their partner, there may be overwhelming feelings of horror and disgust causing a few clients to react violently.

In San Diego, forty-two prostitutes were murdered within a five-year period, four of which were transvestites (Cramer, 1990). Approximately three dozen transvestites were known to continue prostituting themselves in the area, despite the surge in violence. One particular individual was shot twice in the ribs while soliciting sex. Nevertheless, he was back on the streets two weeks later with one of the bullets still lodged in his chest (Cramer, 1990). Many of the transvestites "[knew] that, by trying to pass as women, they may enrage customers who are surprised to find they have picked up a man . . . [t]hey can go into homophobic panic" (Cramer, 1990, p. 1). This act, continuing to prostitute oneself in the face of increasing violence, is testament to the power of prostitution. For some, "prostitution itself is addictive . . . it's a form of career that allows you to make money, and there's a very strong sense of family out there" (Chidley, 1996, p. 49).

CONCLUSIONS

There is no evidence to suggest that transvestites turn to prostitution for reasons different from other populations. Therefore, it is likely that many of the factors that contribute to prostitution in normal populations also exist in transvestic populations. Although all prostitutes experience risk within the profession, transvestites encounter increased risk by the very fact that their true gender is often concealed, thereby duping potential clients. Subsequently, transvestite prostitutes are more prone to being victims of violence.

CHAPTER

PORNOGRAPHY AND OBSCENE MATERIAL

5

FELICIA BLOEM

> I was 11 years old when I saw my first pornographic magazine. The image of a woman smiling invitingly at me has been burned in my brain ever since. Hormones danced inside my body and the chemistry of my brain was electrified. It was as if someone had injected heroin in my veins. That "high" wore off eventually and I found myself craving more. I began pursuing the next high and then the next high from pornography—a drive that lasted for the next 25 years.
>
> (Laaser, 1999, p. 1)

This man describes his contact with pornography as enticing, mesmerizing, and addictive with progressive qualities. Considering the implications of this scenario brings several questions to mind in understanding the use of pornography. Is pornography detrimental to the average consumer, or only to those who abuse it? What constitutes *normal* and abusive behavior in terms of pornographic consumption? Is pornography addictive? What type of persons use pornography? What do they use it for? What is classified as obscene material? What does research say regarding pornography? Despite seemingly apparent answers to these questions, complications, such as one's belief or value system, inhibit researchers and the general public alike from forming a consensus on the merits or destructive nature of pornography. In order to provide the reader with a clear understanding of the effects of pornography it is necessary to critically examine current research, the progressive attributes, and clinical characteristics of pornography and those who use it. Yet, before moving to an analytical discussion of pornography and its effects we must first provide the reader with a solid foundation of the concept of pornography.

DEFINITIONS

The Oxford Dictionary defines pornography as an "explicit description or exhibition of sexual activity in literature, films, etc." (Oxford, 2001, p. 641). Based on this definition alone, pornography can be thought of as any explicit depiction of sexuality. For example many classic works of art, such as those found in the Victorian Era, may be thought of as pornography. Yet modern-day conceptions of pornography are more closely related to obscenity. Obscene is defined as "offensively indecent, esp. by offending accepted sexual morality" (Oxford, 2001, p. 568). Obscene pornographic material ranges in diversity according to the belief system of the viewer and the legal laws of the state. For instance, many religious sects condemn any explicit depiction of sexuality and may consider it obscene, while other groups of individuals may use them as sexual aids. However, there are those explicit sexual depictions that the vast majority of the population find offensive and are sanctioned by various state and federal laws (e.g., child pornography). Judicially, obscene material is usually considered illegal. Yet despite the general distain for illicit material portraying coercion, violence, children, drugs, and animals, there is a large market for these materials which is fueled primarily by smugglers, the Internet, and illegal adult video stores. Although there are differences in the terms pornography and obscenity, because of their culturally/value-laden definitions, this chapter will consider any sexually explicit material as pornographic.

THE RESEARCH

Research indicates that the industries of pornography are some of the fastest-growing companies in our economy (Jones, Shainberg, & Byer, 1985, p. 628). Arising from this explosion are many questions including: Can we determine the effects of pornography on those who use it? Attempting to answer this question Malamuth, Addison, & Koss (2000) investigated the relationship between pornography and aggression and concluded "that not only are pornographic stimuli only one part of a larger corpus of mass media images, but the role of media stimuli cannot be fully appreciated in isolation from other variables" (p. 30). When considering cultural influences, family values, developmental years, substance abuse, genetics, academic opportunities, SAS, and outside occurring events, it becomes increasingly harder to determine the effects of one variable as opposed to any other. In spite of the difficulties in measuring such variables as family values, the Internet has provided researchers with reliable information concerning the amount of pornographic usage.

Griffiths (2001) states "the online pornography industry will reach $366 million by 2001 although other estimates suggest it is already worth $1 billion." (p. 1) The Internet has become a convenient, popular, fast, and free avenue to access a plethora of pornographic material. Griffiths, although unable to comment of the addictive nature of pornographic material on the Internet, concludes that the Internet has been used as a medium to engage in various addictive behaviors, (e.g., pornography) (p. 3).

Malamuth, Addison, and Koss (2000) claim "that exposure to both nonviolent pornography and violent pornography affects both aggressive attitudes and behaviors" (p. 14). Furthermore, the authors contend that violent pornography affects these attitudes more than nonviolent pornography. Similarly, they found that rapists were more aroused by violent pornography than nonrapists (Malamuth et al., 2000). Taken at face value, these findings may lead the reader to conclude that the viewing of violent pornography contributes not only to aggressive attitudes and behaviors but, in some incidents, criminality. Yet despite these findings, more research is needed to identify the influence of pornography in a variety of settings, which may be accomplished through testing cross-sectional populations, and with more effective measures.

REALITY OR FANTASY

Many researchers have focused on the use of pornography and its relationship to fantasy. People who choose to view or read sexual material may be doing so for the purpose of acting out their fantasies. In *Dimensions of Human Sexuality*, Jones, Shainberg, and Byer 1985 state, "Fantasy serves to expand, distort, and exaggerate reality, and is neither positive nor negative in and of itself. The way in which fantasy is used, however, determines whether its effect on our attitudes and behavior is positive or negative" (p. 629). Fantasy, when coupled with pornography, can produce a potentially dangerous situation: one in which intimacy can be superficially gained and wrongly substituted for actual intimate contact.

According to Leitenberg and Henning (1995), "In fantasy one can imagine anything one likes, however unrealistic, without experiencing embarrassment or rejection or societal and legal restrictions." (p. 2). Despite the safe harbor created by fantasy, certain risks are inherent to this process. Thinking distortions, or faulty perceptions about life, may become salient and self-perpetuating. Regarding the risk of pornographic fantasy, Leitenberg and Henning state,

> The male is not apt to share his pornographic experience with anyone else; he is not likely to check it out with friends to help determine where the lines between reality and fantasy are blurred. Such a check with reality usually is neither desired nor available. Self-perpetuating, the distortion stimulates a sexual response which, in turn, reinforces the enjoyment of the distortion. In sorting through the experiences, the consumer selects what to believe as reality and what to choose as fantasy (Leitenberg & Henning, 1995, p. 472). Balancing fantasy from reality, however, is not clear-cut and depends on the subjects personality, accountability, and physiological attributes of the person discerning the reality.

THE PROGRESSION OF ADDICTION

One of the most interesting questions involved in pornography is, why do some people choose to engage in pornography and others do not? At this point, this cannot be clearly answered. What is clear is there appears to be a progressive nature inherent to pornography, which is often compared to addiction. Griffiths describes this progression in specific terms identifying experiences attributed to explicit material. He defines Internet sex as "downloading pornography, cybersex relationships" (Griffiths, 2001, p. 2).

> Salience occurs when Internet sex becomes the most important activity in the person's life and dominates their thinking (preoccupations and cognitive distortions), feelings (cravings), and behavior (deterioration of socialized behavior). For instance, even if the person is not actually on their computer engaged in Internet sex they will be thinking about the next time they will be. Mood modification refers to the subjective experiences that people report as a consequence of engaging in Internet sex, and can be seen as a coping strategy (i.e., they experience an arousing "buzz" or a "high" or paradoxically tranquilizing feel of "escape" or "numbing"). Tolerance is the process whereby increasing amounts of Internet sex are required to achieve the former mood modifying effects (Griffiths, 2001, p. 2).

A major concern with the use of pornography is its progressive nature. Researchers believe that pornography may become increasingly addictive and cause the user to seek illegal material. Chronic pornography users, because of their progressive nature, have been likened to those with addictive personalities.

In Twerski and Nakken's (1997) book, *Addictive Thinking and the Addictive Personality,* they describe the clinical and treatment considerations of addicts. Their evaluation of addictive thinking starts with distorted thinking, which is described as having "a superficial logic that can be very seductive and misleading" (Twerski & Nakken, 1997, p. 6). The authors also describe characteristics of self-deception, low self-esteem, problematic concept of time ("I can quit anytime I want" (p. 27), confusing cause and effect "addictive thinkers turn logic around, they are absolutely convinced that their logic is valid" (Twerski & Nakken, 1997, p. 34). The authors also state that the three most common elements in addictive thinking are denial (denial of loss of control), rationalization (I can stop, it's not that bad), and projection (blaming external factors). Another attribute of an addictive thinker is hypersensitivity. This is described as "a stimulus that might not produce emotional pain in a nonaddict can produce great distress in an addict" (Twerski & Nakken, 1997, p. 58). This sensitivity can be focused on any perceived rejection from others. The next attribute is morbid expectations, meaning someone who has "a morbid feeling of being jinxed" (p. 61). This feeling of pessimism clouds the addict from looking beyond the circumstances of the present problematic situation. Addicts are also described as manipulators with problems admitting errors. They experience feelings such as guilt, shame, difficulties with expressing anger, and illusions of control (Twerski & Nakken, 1997, pp. 63–85). "Many addicts are self-described loners" (Twerski & Nakken, 1997, p. 87); this feeling of isolation from others is understandable considering the level of distress that accompanies the vicious circle of defeating thoughts, feelings, and behaviors. Understanding these personality characteristics as applied to a person addicted to pornography reveals vulnerabilities that perpetuate the addictive behavior. As someone becomes addicted to pornography it destroys daily functioning in work and interpersonal living.

DIAGNOSIS

Unfortunately the *Diagnostic Statistical Manual for Mental Disorders* does not stipulate pornography as an addiction. There are criteria for obsessive-compulsive disorder, substance abuse, and hyposexual disorder but nothing specifically for sexual addicts (*DSM-V-TR,* 2000). One article suggests implementing a hypersexual disorder category in the *DSM-V-TR* (Stein, Black, Shapira, & Spitzer, 2001). Another article from the Society for the Scientific Study of Sexuality refers to sexual addiction as compulsive sexual behavior or CSB (Coleman, 2001). This article also expressed the discussions of finding an appropriate term for sexual addicts stating, "disagreement exists as to whether CSB is an addiction, a psychosexual development disorder, an impulse control disorder, a mood disorder, or an obsessive-compulsive disorder" (Coleman, 2001, p. 4).

This controversy over terms suggests the need for one specific category of determination. There are identifying features of sexual addiction that effect daily functioning, personal resources, and work environment. There are several clinical symptoms including: withdrawal, low self-esteem, loss of control, characteristics of depression (guilt, shame, hypersensitivity, thinking distortions), and agitation. Defining the diagnostic term, establishing criteria, and testing effective empirical treatment interventions will continue to be the next phase in research.

CONCLUSION

> *Whether ever acted upon or not, the pornographic experience remains as part of one's experience and contributes toward defining values, molding personality, and shaping behavior* (Jones, Shainberg & Byer, 1987, p. 630).

There is a specific population of people who struggle with an addiction to pornography. This addiction controls their lives. The addiction to pornography affects each individual differently. Complex events, curiosity, loneliness, or even low self-esteem may all combine to affect someone uniquely. Some people get pulled into the seduction, instant gratification, false-intimacy, and fantasy, and become controlled by the sexual compulsions.

CHAPTER

SNUFF FILMS, PORNOGRAPHY, AND VIOLENT BEHAVIOR

LORI CLUFF

6

The way in which our global society interacts is becoming profoundly efficient, with communications and commodities exchanged oftentimes instantaneously. As the growth of individual and mass technology has exploded, societies have struggled to adequately regulate and monitor the type of mediums that are passing in and through homes, schools, communities, and society as a whole. As it is difficult to monitor or regulate the Internet effectively, surely difficulties will arise in our ability to accurately understand the negative impact that society will experience.

The benefits the technological advances have created would have been difficult to imagine one hundred years ago, so would have the perils. The rate at which perpetrators can victimize has been significantly increased with a wide variety of children, adolescents, and similarly vulnerable adults entering into the Internet highway. In addition, those with the potential for developing deviant interests and sexual addictions have access to more sexually explicit, violent, and even illegal materials without leaving their home (Mawhinney, 1998).

While society may appreciate the wealth of knowledge and opportunities given through the type of technology used each day, there are areas that will need to be monitored and policed to protect the mentally and emotionally impaired. Safeguards that may act as preventative measures, protecting potential victims, might be realized as the progression of illness is multiplied via Internet exposure.

The sexually addicted have a playground available to them through the Internet, anonymously soliciting and trading mass amounts of pornography. Addicts in this way can feed on each other's addiction without worrying about social inhibition that may have previously limited their involvement in illegal pornographic materials.

Increased anonymity has surely led to an increased demand, making various forms of violent pornography more lucrative and available than in past years.

An especially disturbing subtype of pornography is the creation, consumption, and trade of snuff films. Snuff films refer to video footage or feed in which a sexual aggressor ends the sexual act with the death of the victim. This is the ultimate conclusion for a sexual sadist.

For some the nature of pornography appears to be progressive. As one begins to examine pornographic materials readily available, obvious instances of violence are portrayed. Some viewers become desensitized to the violence and aggression, which initially may be caused by the representation of the violence as being pleasurable to the actor/actress or model. This is a denial that women have basic human emotions, and instead implies they enjoy their own degradation. Eventually an individual, by chance or by a sense of need, may be exposed to pornography with a greater degree of violence and pain.

An example of classical conditioning, violence, and sexual excitement become paired and reinforced. For some, humiliation, degradation, mutilation, rape, torture, and death can become the desired fantasy scenario required to achieve a sense of sexual gratification. For some, this can become a trend, with the levels of violence and pain ever increasing as an acceptable, if not essential, part of sexual arousal through desensitization (Fox & Levin, 1998; Malmuth & Donnerstein, 1984). The issue of what comes first is still a clouded issue—the preference for violence or exposure to pornography as a reinforcer for violent ideations. The violent ideations potentially lead to sexually violent behaviors or acting out (Fox & Levin, 1998). Ressler, Burgess, and Douglass (1988) found that a majority of sexual perpetrators partook of pornography with violent themes.

As previously noted, the ultimate end to the sadistic cycle is the scenario that incorporates images involving humiliation, rape, torture, mutilation, and finally death. While most pornographic viewers do not wish to have their fantasies end in death, the possibility for the demand to significantly increase is noteworthy. And while everyone may be entitled to fantasize about any situation they desire and find fulfilling personally, it is important to examine whether viewing these types of materials will ultimately lead to the actual victimizations of real persons by rape or sexual murder.

There appear to be many skeptics who do not believe that snuff films actually exist. While the effects of viewing pornography where the victim is murdered, feigned or not, may be immaterial to the question of the impact viewing such material can have, its existence is worth examining. The viewer's severity of psychopathology is not lessened if the material they are ingesting is the portrayal of a murder in place of an actual homicide.

Entering the term "snuff film" into an Internet search engine such as America Online or Yahoo will obviously not give results with a connection to the underground snuff market. Rather sites questioning the existence of actual snuff films are likely to be found. The consensus of the sites seems to purport snuff films as nothing more than an urban legend. Some report a belief that even the Federal Bureau of Investigations has never come across even one true snuff film. However, there is evidence to suggest that it is probable that such films do exist.

In *U.S. vs. Schmeltzer,* the defendant showed a video to the witness portraying the sexual abuse and torture of young girls who were either kidnapped or tricked into participating in the production of the video. Schmeltzer also showed a video that he described as a "snuff film." The film was of an Asian female being kidnapped, mutilated, and murdered. Schmeltzer indicated there were numerous snuff films available in Mexico. Schmeltzer was interested in having the witness contact individuals known to him in Mexico. The purpose of this was gaining access to young Mexican females. According to the witness, Schmeltzer wanted to gain access to the girls for the production of pornographic videos. Schmeltzer reported he could then sell the videos for approximately five thousand dollars each (960 F .2d 405; 1992 U.S. App. Lexis 7726).

The search of Schmeltzer's home resulted in the seizure of video equipment, sexual devices, several hundred magazines and videos. The videos contained footage of children and adolescents engaging in sexual intercourse and sexually deviant behavior. In the home was also a handwritten note Schmeltzer wrote describing sado-masochistic acts he wished to perform on children.

In another case, *U.S. vs. Depew,* the defendant was convicted of conspiracy to kidnap and sexually exploit a minor in a sexually explicit film. Depew and Lambey (codefendant) intended to seek out and kidnap a male approximately twelve years old for the purpose of creating a snuff video. They intended to sexually abuse, torture, and murder the intended victim (932 F.2d 324; 1991 U.S. App. Lexis 8272). Depew and Lambey were apprehended when they communicated to an undercover officer that they had found a boy who looked to be approximately thirteen years of age and were following him with the intent to kidnap him. They had developed detailed plans including the rental of a van and video equipment.

The individuals described were caught and apprehended before they could create additional victims, although it would seem naïve to believe that everyone who has conspired to create and sell snuff films has been caught before it was too late. In fact, Fox and Levin (1998) report that sexual serial killers Leonard Lake and Charles Ng created home videos with some of their victims.

Stone (2001) gives an historical outline of the first recorded sexually motivated homicides. The sexual murders date as far back as the first-century Roman emperors. Instances in which power was used to seduce, abuse, and kill victims are recorded. The first female sexual killer is Countess Erzsebet Bathory who lived in the sixteenth century. She would achieve sexual gratification through genital contact with other females who hung bleeding from hooks and eventually died (Penrose, 1970; Stone 2001).

Modern cases of serial sexual homicide are purported to have first been committed shortly after 1875 (Stone, 2001). One of the first notorious cases was Baker in 1867. Baker, while only having had one known victim, because of being apprehended, sexually assaulted, mutilated and murdered an eight-year-old female (Wilson, 2000). The sexual murderers of the first century were undoubtedly without the influence of violent pornography, thereby showing that the progression of an individual's violent sexual desires/fantasies into behaviors cannot necessarily be causally explained by the existence of violent pornography. There would likely be lust murders regardless of the existence of pornography. Yet, pornography may act as a vehicle in which occurrences of sexually violent acts are more frequent than would be otherwise.

That raises the question of whether the increase of lust murderers from the time of the first century is the result of violence in media or simply the result of an increasing population. So while the absolute number of perpetrators has increased, the rate of these offenders has not. Or have the chances of victims being discovered increased because of increased policing and improvements in forensic examinations? Does violence in pornography and the seeking out of extreme violence such as snuff films act to create additional sexual killers who would have not crossed the line otherwise? What factors can be identified that are static throughout time as motivating/precipitating factors in the reinforcement for violent images to be sexually exciting? Also troubling is predicting the potential impact on future generations, who as children now can access highly explicit images on the Internet at very young ages.

Conversely some professionals assert that there is not a significant pattern of violent themes incorporated in the majority of pornographic material and the rate of violence portrayed over time has not increased. Rather antipornography lobbyists are seen as extreme feminists whose beliefs are not based on fact (Mawhinney, 1998; Scott & Curvelier, 1993).

While it is difficult to identify psychosocial factors that led to the very first identified sexual murder in the first century, characteristics are identifiable in modern times. Family relationships and unhealthy sexual boundaries, personal victimization, sexual knowledge, social competence, patterns of disordered sexual arousal, cognitive distortions, exposure to violence in the home, and exposure to pornography as a child/adolescent are all factors that can play important roles in the development of deviant sexually aggressive patterns (Shaw, 1999).

Certain developmental factors are linked to later destructive paraphilia. Consumption of sexually violent material has been shown to affect male views about women and normalizes interpersonal violence (Shaw, 1999). Hickey (2006) illustrates a trauma control model that is helpful in understanding the complex series of variables and how they may interact in a way that leads to violent behavior.

Pornography as a business has been growing at substantial rates. From 1985 to 1996, the industry profit increased from $75 million to $665 million. There were 150 new films produced each week in 1996. During that same year, Americans spent $1 billion on phone sex. Playboy's Internet site had an average of five million hits per day. Sex performers who are in high demand earn an average of $100,000 per year. The companies who profit the most from the sale of pornographic materials are AT&T, Time Warner, Tele-Communications, Hyatt, Sheraton, Holiday Inn, and video rental stores. Their revenue comes from phone sex, pay-per-view, and adult video rentals (Mawhinney, 1998).

Pornography may be a facilitator by impairing healthy sexual functioning. As a professional community, research efforts need to be focused on the true impact of pornography, violent pornography and the proliferation of materials on the Internet.

PART III

PARAPHILIA

THE ETIOLOGY OF PARAPHILIA

A Dichotomous Model

JAMES HEALEY

7

Sexuality is an extremely important aspect of human life. Existing not only as means of procreation, human sexuality is seamlessly intertwined with our psychological and emotional well-being. It has the power to elicit such powerful feelings as love, envy, lust, and even aggression. Yet despite its potentially volatile nature, we know relatively little about our sexuality (with the exception of philological responses). For example, assuming, broadly, for a moment that sex exists for the sole purposes of procreation, then it would be likely to assume that the entire population would be heterosexual. Yet how do we explain homosexual behavior, if from a Darwinian perspective, such behavior is maladaptive? That is, homosexual behavior would not enable the species to procreate and survive. Additionally, there are many other *maladaptive* sexual behaviors, which taken on their own would not have any Darwinian benefit (e.g., fetishisms, sadomasochism, lust murder). The existence of such behaviors points to the development of a sexuality that does not exist in a vacuum; sexuality is influenced by its environment and possible biological factors, such as hormones or heredity. As varied as sexual behavior may be, this work will concern itself with aberrant sexual behavior or *paraphilias*. Defined as "the sexual arousal through deviant means," paraphilia run the gamut from seemingly harmless, such as *fetishisms*, to criminal, as in the case of *erotophonophilia* or *lust murder*.

Various etiological models, using behavioral and social learning theories, have been applied to paraphilias in an attempt to explain their development with limited success. Furthermore, researchers have grouped paraphilias into one homogenous group, claiming they exist on a continuum. This continuum places seemingly harmless (e.g., fetishisms) paraphilias on one end while placing some of the most complicated and horrendous human behavior on the other (i.e. erotophonophilia). Additionally, in regards to the continuum, no mention is made of how an individual acquires any given paraphilia, where he/she falls on the continuum, and whether or not an offender is able to progress or regress on this continuum.

This work will propose an etiological model in which paraphilias can be divided into two main groups: (a) those in which the paraphilia is a result of an introduction of deviant stimuli to a developing sexuality, and (b) those that are the result of psychological or physical "trauma" experienced during a developing sexuality (e.g., made to associate feelings of inadequacy, shame, guilt, hatred, fear, and aggression with sexuality). It is suggested that the former produces *harmless* (usually noncriminal) paraphilia as a result of physiological conditioning, whereas the latter can be thought to produce *deviant* paraphilia (e.g., intrusive, aggressive, or criminal,) as a result of negative feelings conditioned to be *associated* with sexuality.

In order to fully explain the current model, we will first operationalize paraphilia, its reliance on fantasy, and then provide several examples, which will be used to illustrate the proposed model. Second, we will examine current etiological models, including Purcell's Integrated Model, and their inability to effectively account for paraphilia. Third, we will provide the *Dichotomous Paraphiliac Model* based on a developing sexuality. Finally, psychopathy will be introduced to explain the progression from a potentially noncriminal paraphilia to a criminal paraphilia.

PARAPHILIA: DEFINITIONS

Atypical sexual behavior is any sexual behavior that does not adhere to any given societal or cultural concept of acceptable sexual conduct. Whether any sexual behavior is considered atypical depends on the culture in which it exists. Within North American culture, such behaviors are termed paraphilias. Paraphilia, according the *Diagnostic Statistical Manual of Mental Disorders* (4th ed.), is a mental disorder characterized by "recurrent intense sexual urges and sexually arousing fantasies" lasting at least six months and involving (1) nonhuman objects, (2) the suffering or humiliation of oneself or one's partner (not merely simulated), or (3) children or other nonconsenting peoples (American Psychiatric Association, 1994).

At this point, a distinction must be made between criminal and noncriminal paraphilia. Both criteria two and three of the *DSM-IV* clearly indicate criminality. This is demonstrated by various statutes, albeit unambiguous statutes in the penal code, which prohibit sexual violence directed towards nonconsenting adults or children. However, the initial criteria, which involves nonhuman objects is not necessarily criminal. Although this category may contain animals, it may also include inanimate objects such as shoes or lingerie. Therefore, despite our inclination to assume all paraphilias are criminal we must distinguish between those that carry criminal sanctions, and those that do not.

According to Levine 1997 (as cited in Strong & DeVault, 1997), males are most likely to engage in paraphilic behaviour between the ages of fifteen and twenty-five. Additionally, paraphiliacs generally have the following characteristics:

1. **A long-standing highly arousing and unusual erotic preoccupation.** Although they may begin as early as childhood, paraphiliac impulses usually manifest themselves in adolescence or early adulthood. Paraphiliac people find their erotic fantasies and masturbatory activities centering on unusual activities. These fantasies are usually aggressive, masochistic, and directed against the self.

2. **A need to act out the fantasy.** Paraphilic men and women feel a strong need to satisfy their unusual fantasies. They experience intense frustration and sexual dissatisfaction if they are unable to fulfill their fantasies.

3. **An inability to have a conventional sexual relationship.** Despite high rates of orgasm occurring when involved in unusual fantasies or activities, paraphiliac individuals are often dysfunctional with their partners under ordinary sexual conditions. Wives of paraphilacs typically complain that their husbands are uninterested in sex with them, never initiate, are unable to maintain an erection or have an orgasm. They do not seem to enjoy sex unless their wives act out their paraphiliac fantasy (pp. 329–330).

Eluded to in the previous paragraph is the paraphiliac's strong reliance on fantasy. Many researchers have pointed to the importance of fantasy in development of criminal paraphilias (Purcell, 2000; Arrigo & Purcell 2001; Hickey, 2001). Hickey (2001) states, "most psychosexual disorders are a result of an aberrant fantasy system fueled by a traumatic childhood and adolescent experiences (p. 23). This definition however confines the reliance of fantasy to criminal paraphilia. Moreover, it leads the reader to assume *all* paraphilias (psychosexual disorders) are a result of childhood trauma. Although the criminal paraphiliac's reliance on fantasy may be a function of avoiding capture, it is also likely that noncriminal paraphiliacs rely on fantasy to avoid social stigmatization. Similar to Hickey, many researchers assume that all paraphilias involve some sort of childhood trauma and because of this trauma retreat into a world of fantasy to satisfy their sexual urges. The current author does not dispute the importance of deviant fantasies in maintaining and perpetuating various paraphilia. Rather, the intention of the discussion is merely to separate three distinct concepts (fantasy, childhood trauma, and paraphilia), which have become effortlessly confused and assumed to be prerequisites of offending. The combination of these concepts, which peppers the criminological literature, contributes to the misconception that aberrant fantasy is a function of childhood trauma, which in turn leads to future offending.

Yet as Strong and DeVault (1997) point out, normal sexual fantasies have a number of important functions in maintaining our psychic equilibrium, which include: enabling us to plan or anticipate situations that may arise; a means of rehearsal, allowing us to practice in our minds how to act in various situations; and providing an escape from a dull or oppressive environment (p. 295). Finally, and perhaps more importantly the authors state, "even if our sexual lives are satisfactory, we may indulge in sexual fantasies to bring novelty and excitement into a relationship" (p. 295). Despite a paucity of research conducted on fantasy, the research points to the importance of fantasy not only to paraphiliacs but also to average citizens with *normal* sexual urges. Moreover, fantasies seem to stray away from mundane sexual activities, pointing not only to the potential for us to become desensitized with our own sexuality, but also the prevalence of deviation from *normal* fantasy. Unfortunately, we may never acquire a firm grasp of fantasies because of their personal nature and fear of disclosure. What we can establish is that sexuality, whether aberrant or *normal,* heavily depends on fantasy for its exploration, concealment, or expression.

PARAPHILIAS

Armed with a firm understanding of paraphilia and their reliance on fantasy it is implicit to provide the reader with several examples of common paraphilia in order to proverably "place a name to the face."

Fetishism is the sexual attraction to objects, which later become sexual symbols for the fetishist. Instead of relating to an actual person "the fetishist gains sexual gratification from kissing a shoe, caressing a glove, drawing a lock of hair against his or her cheek, or masturbating with a pair of underwear" (Strong & DeVault, 1997; p. 330). The *DSM-IV* characterizes a fetish as "sexual urges, or behaviors, which cause clinically significant distress or impairment in social, occupational, or other important areas" (p. 243).

Exhibitionism, according to the *DSM-IV,* must meet the following criteria: 1. be present for a period of at least 6 months. Involve, intense, recurrent sexually arousing fantasies of behaviors involving exposure of one's genitals to an unsuspecting stranger; or 2. the person has acted on these urges, or the fantasies cause marked distress or interpersonal difficulty (p. 569). Exhibitionism is a fairly common paraphilia and accounts for some one-third of all sexual offenders arrested (Strong & DeVault, 1997). Interestingly, when apprehended by authorities, most exhibitionists express an extreme sense of guilt, which seems to be superficial considering these offenders have an extremely high recidivism rate.

Voyeurism, also known as a *peeping tom,* is the sexual arousal through observing an unsuspecting person(s) undressing or engaging in sexual activity. In order to become aroused, the man must remain unseen, and the woman or couple must be unaware of his presence (Strong & DeVault, 1997; p. 334).

Telephone scatalogia is the making of obscene phone calls. According to Hickey (2001), "while callers seem to vary in their levels of sexual references, tone of voice and desire to shock frighten, the offender is often conditioning himself through masturbation to control his victims" (p. 28).

Frotteurism involves intense urges or fantasies, like all other paraphilias, to touch or rub against a nonconsenting person for the purpose of sexual arousal or gratification. The frotteur usually carries out his touching or rubbing in crowded subways, buses, or large public gatherings.

Necrophilia is sexual contact with corpses. According to Hickey (2001), necrophilia can be thought of as a process. Some necrophiles "use fantasy to experience sex with a corpse. Some prostitutes cater to paraphiliacs and for the right price will ice themselves down, dust on white powder, and lay motionless with eyes closed in a casket, while their 'john' acts out his fantasies" (p. 26). Additionally, there are those necrophiles who will actually seek out dead persons from funeral parlors, cemeteries, morgues, or hospitals. Finally, there are those necrophiles who will actually kill their victims just to have sexual relations with the corpse.

Biastophilia (rape), different from all other types of rape, biastophilia is when an offender becomes sexually aroused from the act of rape itself. Other rapists, such as the anger or compensatory rapists, use sex as a means of expressing pent-up aggression. The biastophiliac, conversely, has fused aggression and sexuality. He can only become sexually excited when he brutalizes, degrades, controls, and rapes his victim. This type of offender experiences uncontrollable outbursts of aggression. Because of the criminal nature of the crime, he relies heavily on fantasy.

Sexual sadism, involves sexual acts in which a victim is subjected to pain, humiliation, whether physical or psychological. According to Strong and DeVault (1997), "characteristic symptoms include obsessive and compelling sexual thoughts or fantasies involving acts centering around one's physical or mental harm" (p. 342).

Sexual masochism, the opposite of sexual sadism, involves masochistics who derive pleasure from being beaten, bound, humiliated, or made to otherwise suffer (Strong & DeVault, 1997; p. 342).

Erotophonophilia (Lust Murder) can be defined as: a paraphilic condition, in which the offender kills a victim in a sexual manner (e.g., mutilation of genitalia, or sadistically raping the victim while achieving orgasm at the time in which he kills her). Offenders experience an exhilarating feeling of sexual arousal and satisfaction from their actions (Purcell, 2000; p. 55). Additionally, the notion of a lust murder suggests not only the urge to kill but also to ravage the victim (Hickey, 2001).

ETIOLOGY

Despite the large amount of time dedicated to describing specific paraphilia, modern criminological and psychological literature has largely avoided the issue of etiology. Appearing to be working backwards, the literature has assumed that existing sociological, anthropological, criminological, physiological, and psychological paradigms can explain these complicated behaviors. That is, rather than beginning with etiology, the study of paraphilia has begun with describing these behaviors and placed etiology on the side. Yet, as we will see, these broad macro paradigms do not adequately account for paraphilic development. Although an inclusive discussion of all applicable paradigms is beyond the scope of this work, social learning and feminist models have been chosen to illuminate the shortcomings of contemporary etiological explanations.

Social learning models assume the culture in which offenders live is an important factor in the likelihood of offending. Maletzky (2002) contends that recent research has suggested that lack of parental care, physical punishment, and frequent or aggressive sexual activity within the family may all predispose the child to begin sexual offending in late childhood or early adolescence. Furthermore, proponents of this model have relied on anthropological and sociological literature and assume that societies that show high rates of "sexually aggressive behavior show high rates of nonsexual violence, greater male dominance and negative attitudes towards women" (Maletzky, 2002; p. 529).

Despite the importance of family functioning in the psychological, social, and sexual well-being of a child, the social learning model is too broad. There is no disputing the reality of learned behavior with respect to sexual offending. Countless studies cite high numbers of offenders who were sexually abused as children. Yet it seems unlikely that unique/specific behaviors such as sexual relations with corpses or the need to be urinated on are readily observable within many North American homes allowing them to fall into the realm of learned behavior. That is not to say that a small number of persons exhibiting these behaviors didn't observe them directly and become subsequently conditioned to become sexually excited. Rather, because of the amount of identifiable groupings of paraphilia, and how they reproduce over time, it seems plausible that, at the very least, those inflicted with the same paraphilia were subjected to similar, if not identical, processes.

Additionally, the behavioral model's dependence on cross-cultural studies and the suggestion that societies with high rates of sexual aggression also show high rates of nonsexual aggression, dominance of women, and negative attitudes of women provide only a partial explanation. Although such societies account for greater *rates* of sexual violence they do not account for incidents of sexual aggression worldwide. Moreover, different countries have various procedures for indexing crimes. Given that most crime statistics are generated from criminal justice agencies, it seems unlikely that researchers will be able to accurately obtain actual crime rates.

In adopting a feminist perspective, it is critical to make the distinction between the radical and contemporary movement. The contemporary feminist movement expects equal rights and nondiscrimination and should be differentiated from radical feminism. Assuming a radical feminist perspective, all men are potential aggressors and rape is driven by a man's desire to dominate women, even extending that desire over children. Researchers who subscribe to this etiological model assume offenders who commit sex crimes are not necessarily sexually driven but may be expressing latent aggressive impulses that many men harbor towards women.

Although this may be true of certain types of sexual criminals, specifically rapists, it does not account for all paraphiliacs. There is credence, however, in the idea that certain men harbor a great hatred for women. It is also true that some of these men manifest their aggression through an extreme sexuality. Yet it is no more conceivable to assume all men are potential aggressors than it is to assume that all women are incapable of duties outside of the home. That is not to say, that males are not the primary offenders of both aggressive and sexual offences, but rather to point out that not all males are biologically predisposed to be offenders.

As broad and as inconclusive as many etiological models may be, the work of Purcell (2000) has made considerable headway in attempting to explain the etiology paraphilias. Simply known as the Integrated Model, Purcell's model is a combination of the Federal Bureau of Investigation's Sexual Homicide Motivational Model and Hickey's Trauma Control Model. At this point, we will turn to a brief discussion concerning the Integrated Model. In fact, to date, Purcell provides the most inclusive and explanatory explanation to the development of paraphilias. At this point, we shall now turn to a discussion of the Integrated Model

PURCELL'S INTEGRATED MODEL

According to Arrigo and Purcell (2001), *formative development* is the foundation of the Integrated Model and where all paraphilic behaviors originate. Formative development "refers to early childhood adolescent experiences" (p. 19). Furthermore, "one's formative development significantly affects the manner in which one appropriately and successfully experiences psychosocial adjustment throughout the life course" (Arrigo and Purcell, 2001; p. 19).

Closely related to formative development and borrowed from Hickey's Trauma Control Model, *predispositional factors* refer to the idea that one's social environment cannot entirely account for an offender's paraphilia. Predispositional factors such as various psychological, biological, or sociological influences are partly responsible for an offender's disposition.

A sentiment echoed through much of the criminological, sociological, and psychological literature on offenders points to some sort of previous trauma experienced early in childhood. Arrigo and Purcell (2001) contend, "that paraphilias originate, in part, from largely unresolved or inappropriately addressed *traumatic life circumstances* occurring during the impressionable period of one's early adolescence" (p. 21). Combine these three aspects (formative development, predispositional factors, and traumatic events) and the child begins to experience low self-esteem. This sense of low self-esteem throws the child into a deep sense of personal failure, and, as a result, the child becomes less and less likely to form effective social bonds. Unable to develop meaningful relationships the child begins to "develop a genuine lack of regard for society and those who rejected him" (Purcell, 2000; p. 109). Daydreaming becomes a substitute for human contact and the child falls into the *Paraphilic Process.*

Initially, these daydreams are a way of filling a human void. However, over time "these images become more violent and erotic, incorporating assorted fetishes, rituals, and/or unusual and sexually charged objects as stimuli. The repetitive nature of the fantasy furnishes a sense of personal relief from the internal failures and experiences" (Arrigo & Purcell, 2001; p. 23). Because of the erotic nature of the fantasies, the child begins to masturbate to his fantasies. When masturbating to orgasm the offender becomes increasingly conditioned to his aberrant fantasies. Eventually he "loses all sense of normalcy and depends on the paraphilic fantasy for erotic satisfaction" (Arrigo & Purcell, 2001; p. 23).

Drugs and alcohol are used not only to further dehumanize a victim but also to muster the courage to commit the act itself. As with the case of paraphilia, the social stigma may be great, and the offender may need these stimulants to overcome the shame and/or embarrassment he feels as a result of his abnormal urges. *Pornography* has traditionally been thought to desensitize the offender and cause a progression in abnormal sexuality. Consistent with this notion, it has been found that many violent sexual offenders have extensively used drugs, alcohol, and pornography (Ressler et al., 1988; Hickey, 2001).

Purcell's Integrated Model proposes that triggering factors (e.g., rejection, isolation, or ridicule) are *stressors,* "constraining or thwarting one's capacity to cope adequately with everyday life" (Arrigo & Purcell, 2001; p. 25). Furthermore, "depending on the nature and severity of the triggering mechanism, the person may experience a momentary loss of control. Indeed the stressor activates childhood trauma and rekindles the negative and vile feelings associated with it within the individual" (Arrigo & Purcell, 2001; p. 25).

Purcell's model provides an excellent model of the underpinnings of paraphilia. Her work convincingly provides an explanation of the paraphilic process by providing the reader with a logical explanation of how once a paraphilia is acquired thought processes, feedback loops, and social relations combine to produce a cycle of thinking and behaving that is extremely difficult to break once established. Despite her great strides in producing a model to explain paraphilia, a concrete model of how paraphilias are acquired is not included. *Formative events, traumatic experiences, and predispositional factors* are undoubtedly important events in the construction of one's sexuality. Yet to date these three very important concepts have not been explored fully. Furthermore, much of the research has neglected or simply taken for granted the development of sexuality in terms of producing deviant sexual urges or behaviors. Considering numerous distinguishable paraphilia that reproduce consistently within North American culture, it seems more plausible that various *formative events, traumatic experiences, and predispositional factors* (whether cultural, social, psychological, or biological) are introduced (independently, in totality, or a combination thereof) to *a developing sexuality* to produce various paraphilias.

At this point, we turn our attention to a discussion of the current author's proposed model of paraphilic etiology. However, in order to fully explain the etiological model, it is first necessary to concisely describe a child's developing sexuality.

ETIOLOGY AND THE IMPORTANCE OF THE DEVELOPING SEXUALITY

A young child's psychosexual development lays the foundation for further stages of growth. Psychosexual maturity, including the ability to love begins to develop in infancy when babies are lovingly touched all over their bodies (Strong & DeVault, 1997; p. 158). Infants and very young children communicate through nonverbal cues (smiling, crying, etc.) because they are unable to speak. Before they understand words, they learn through body language and tone of voice (Strong & DeVault, 1997; p. 158). According to Renshaw (as cited in Strong & DeVault, 1997), during infancy:

...we begin to learn how we should "feel" about our bodies. If a parent frowns, speaks sharply, or spanks an exploring hand, the infant quickly learns that a particular activity—touching the genitals, for example—is not right. The infant may or may not continue the activity, but if he or she does, it will be in secret, probably accompanied by the beginnings of guilt and shame (pp. 158–159).

When children move into adolescence, they begin to learn an increasing amount of information from outside sources. As with other behaviors, much of what a child learns about his sexuality comes from observing and interacting with his respective parents. Strong and DeVault (1997) state,

...children create their own notion of what it means to be male or female by watching their parents and other important people in their lives or on television. They learn what activities, what attitudes, and what values are appropriate for one sex and not with the other. They observe how feelings and affections are expressed, or not, and by whom ... however the silence that surrounds sexuality in most families and in most communities carries its own messages. It communicates that some of the most important dimensions of life are secretive, off limits, bad to talk about or think about (p. 166).

Aside from incorporating verbal and nonverbal cues about sexuality from their parents, there are several other major influencing factors. Adolescents gather a great deal of information about sex from one another. Boys "encourage other boys to be sexually active even if they are unprepared or uninterested. They must camouflage their inexperience with bravado, which increases misinformation" (Strong & DeVault, 1997; p. 167). Sexual encounters, as opposed to relationships, function in large part to confer status among young boys (Strong and DeVault, 1997). Given the importance of one's peer group during the adolescent years, whether a positive or negative influence, it is a powerful force. Absence or complete immersion, without external controls, could prove to be disastrous. The child may develop misconstrued views of his/her sexuality based on the lack or flood of incorrect information.

THE PARAPHILIC DICHOTOMY

Given the importance of a child's developing sexuality it seems reasonable that future sexual deviations would stem from this particular period in life. The average age of the onset of puberty is thirteen, however, it is important to bear in mind that when puberty begins is not as important as is the physiological changes taking place. Regardless of age, adolescence is a period when children evolve into sexually mature adults. It is a time marked by turbulent hormonal changes, which often cause unfamiliar sexual feelings. It is also a period when masturbation begins to take place. Furthermore, masturbating to orgasm has also been touted as an extremely strong way of conditioning behavior often involving fantasy. Given the vulnerability and turbulent time period, the introduction of deviant stimuli may have a more powerful effect than once thought.

It is this author's contention that paraphilias can be divided into two broad categories: (a) those in which the paraphilia is a result of an introduction of deviant stimuli to a developing sexuality, and (b) those, that are the result of psychological "trauma" experienced during a developing sexuality (e.g., made to associate feelings of inadequacy, shame, guilt, hatred, fear, and aggression with sexuality).

TYPE A: INTRODUCTION OF DEVIANT STIMULI TO A DEVELOPING SEXUALITY

Examining how deviant stimuli may have an impact on a developing sexuality may provide clarity to this theory. For example, seemingly harmless paraphilia such as fetishisms or cyesolagnia (arousal from pregnant women) may be explained through the introduction of a particular stimulus during a child's sexuality. Take the preceding paraphilias as an example. A man (Jerry) who has a lingerie fetish may come from a very functional family, one that shows no sign of dysfunction (with the exception of mundane disagreements encountered by most all families). As a child, Jerry was shown affection and observed very typical behavior (both sexually and socially) from his parents. Yet unbeknown to others, Jerry developed a fetish for women's undergarments. Because women's lingerie carries such a powerful sexual connotation and is fairly observable, it is not unreasonable to conceive the development of lingerie fetishes. Jerry may have had several female influences in his household. By chance, he may have become exposed to lingerie during adolescence. Because of the sexual nature of the undergarments he may have become aroused and subsequently masturbated. Recognizing the erotic potential of the lingerie he may have begun to fantasize about them until finally he begins to get bored and seeks out actual underwear. Whether he desires to touch it, or buy it would depend largely on a number of factors (e.g., extent to which he desires the item or the presence of other paraphilia), yet this example was used to illustrate the conditionability of noncriminal paraphilia.

The introduction of the stimulus, in this case women's lingerie, is pivotal to the developing sexuality. Through masturbation and orgasm Jerry has become conditioned to become sexually aroused through the sight of women's underwear. However, there are variations in the degree to which a person may become aroused by the, inanimate object. Much as Jerry became bored with simply fantasizing about women's underwear other individuals may become sensitized by simply seeing the object. They may then resort to touching or rubbing the object on parts of their bodies.

Additionally, this conditioned behavior, coupled with our ability to become sensitized, may also account for other types of closely related noncriminal paraphilia. Cross-dressing, for example, has often been thought to be a product of some sort of issue with gender identity. Yet when cross-dressing is paraphilic and not an issue of gender identity it may be seen as a natural progression of a fetish. Those individuals who are paraphilic cross-dressers may have had simple fetishes for women's undergarments that inevitably tried them on. Becoming aroused by the feeling of women's clothing they may have progressed until finally donning an entire wardrobe of women's clothing.

TYPE B: RESULT OF *TRAUMA* EXPERIENCED DURING A DEVELOPING SEXUALITY

Unlike the conditioned paraphilia described previously, some paraphilia are the result of trauma. These paraphilia are the outcome of equating feelings of inadequacy, shame, guilt, fear, hatred, or aggression with sexuality. The trauma experienced to spawn these aberrant behaviors could either be experienced during the child's budding sexuality or, if experienced before adolescence, must leave a lasting impression so that it infiltrates the child's thoughts and fantasies, which subsequently become sexualized.

As stated previously, a child begins his/her psychosexual development in infancy. If a child incorporates feelings of inadequacy, fear, or aggression from a dysfunctional family at an early age, then by the time he hits puberty these feelings may well be established. Flooded by sexual feelings, the youth may be unable to distinguish between the pleasant and unpleasant. His sexuality may inevitably fuse. As simple as this may seem, there are conceivably thousands of different combinations of paraphilias and numerous variables which could affect the degree to which an individual possesses them. For instance: the amount of trauma the child was exposed to, how long was the child exposed, what type of trauma he/she was exposed (e.g., psychological, physical, sexual etc).

Those suffering from these paraphilia may have suffered *less trauma* than other paraphiliacs. Paraphilias such as telephone scatalogia, frotteurism, voyeurism, and exhibitionism point to sexual inadequacy. These individuals may have been made to feel inadequate by an overbearing and belittling parent or authority figure during his/her developing sexuality.

Sadism, erotophonophila, and biastophilia all point to issues of control. Someone suffering from anyone of these paraphilia may have been brutally abused as a child, whether it was sexually, physically, emotionally, or psychologically. In attempting to regain some sort of control, the individual has resorted to victimizing someone else in an ultimate display of power.

Despite these explanatory categorizations, the reader may be wondering how it is possible to have a variance in not only the type of paraphilia but also the degree to which a paraphilia is possessed and how, if at all, the paraphilia progresses. As mentioned previously, humans have a tendency to become sensitized and bored with their sexuality. This coupled with psychopathy, coping methods, and reinforced behavior may account for an individual's progression into violent paraphilia.

The degree of psychopathy may play an influential role in the progression of paraphilia, particularly the development of criminal paraphilia. Psychopaths "are social predators who charm, manipulate, and ruthlessly plow their way through life leaving a broad trail of broken hearts, shattered expectations, and empty wallets" (Hare, 1993; p. xi). Characterized by a glib and superficial exterior, Hare claims "psychopaths are often witty and articulate. They can be amusing and entertaining conversationalists, ready with a quick clever comeback and tell unlikely but convincing stories that cast themselves in a good light" (pp. 34–35). Moreover, these individuals lack empathy, feel little guilt or remorse for their actions, are extremely narcissistic, have shallow emotions, are impulsive, and have poor behavioral controls (Hare, 1993). Yet, as with other illnesses there are varying degrees of psychopathy.

The *Psychopathy Checklist* (PCL or the PCL-R [revised]) is a tool developed by Dr. Robert Hare to assess the degree to which a person has psychopathy. Just because someone has been diagnosed as possessing psychopathy does not mean they are a violent sexual predator. In fact, most psychopaths are not violent at all. They simply have little respect for others and are concerned with their own gain.

It is imperative to point out that psychopathy is not a prerequisite for either criminal or noncriminal paraphilia. Rather the presence and degree of psychopathy may be able to account for the progression into more violent paraphilic activity. Those who have combined issues of power and control with sexuality while concurrently having a severe degree of psychopathy are potentially dangerous individuals. Plausibly, these individuals, in light of their narcissistic personalities and sheer lack of remorse or guilt, would commit violent acts for their own pleasure.

CONCLUSION

Fundamentally, it is important that researchers make a clear distinction between those behaviors, that are paraphilic, and those, that are not. For instance, surely there are thousands of couples worldwide who enjoy watching other people have sex. This alone does not make them paraphiliacs. There must be a recognizable pattern to their behavior (at least six months) with recurrent fantasies and urges. Additionally, this must be the sole means by which the person(s) becomes sexually aroused. Simply because a couple enjoys watching others partake in sexual activity does mean they suffer from a paraphilia.

However, even after making a clear distinction between paraphilic and non-paraphilic behavior, there are many questions related to the etiology of paraphilia. For instance, would there be a difference in the type of paraphilia one acquired based on the type of abuse one suffered and how long it elapsed? Does an individual suffering mild forms of physical abuse have a lesser chance of developing a serious paraphilia as someone who suffers extensive sexual abuse? Does the degree of psychopathy actually contribute to the variance and progression in certain paraphilic clusters?

If we are to better understand and treat paraphilia, this author contends that researchers should begin by proposing and testing various etiological models. Only when solid models have been established can we begin to fully understand paraphilias. This can only be accomplished through the detailed examination of a developing sexuality and the variations experienced during this pivotal time.

CHAPTER

A COMPREHENSIVE PARAPHILIA CLASSIFICATION SYSTEM

8

LISA SHAFFER AND JULIE PENN

According to the *DSM-IV-TR,* paraphilia are mental disorders that consist of sexual urges, fantasies, and/or behaviors involving suffering or humiliation, nonhuman objects, children, and/or other nonconsenting person (American Psychiatric Association, 2000). Such activities or desires lie outside cultural norms and are, or have been crimes in certain jurisdictions (Wikipedia, 2002). What follows is the start of a comprehensive classification system of all of the paraphilia that currently exist and that have a verifiable population. The authors will also include paraphilia that either have a very small population or appear to be paraphilia-in-development, as it were. The authors assert there are five broad categories: (1) nonviolent, physical paraphilia; (2) nonviolent, nonphysical paraphilia; (3) sadistic paraphilia; (4) masochistic paraphilia; and (5) sadomasochistic paraphilia.

For the purposes of this work, physical paraphilia refers to any paraphilic behavior that is carried out on site within the general vicinity of another person or has direct physical contact with the paraphiliac. Nonphysical paraphilia are those behaviors where an individual obtains sexual gratification without physical contact or within view of another person(s).

NONVIOLENT, PHYSICAL PARAPHILIA

SWINGING

Criteria

Swinging is the common name for comarital sex, though singles can and do engage in swinging as well. Research into swinging thus far has been limited to couples (Jenks,

1998), thereby resulting in a "definition of swinging as married couples exchanging partners solely for sexual purposes" (Jenks, 1998, p. 1). Most areas of sexuality, including swinging, lack adequate and valid research, as it is quite difficult to obtain random samples. Studies also frequently fail to utilize control groups, and current research into percentages of married couples engaging in swinging also is lacking (Jenks, 1998).

Etiology

One of the most fundamental reasons couples get involved in swinging is for the variety of sexual experiences and partners. The second is for pleasure and/or excitement, including the notion of defying societal sexual norms. Third, couples find swinging a way to meet new people and increase their social lives. Other reasons have included ego boosts from learning one is attractive or desirable to someone other than one's spouse and recapturing one's youthfulness. Interestingly, though not surprising, voyeurism has also been linked with swinging. Watching others perform sexual acts has been reported as helping couples learn new techniques, overcome inhibitions, and add sexual excitement and thrills to the marriage (Jenks, 1998).

Several theories have linked autonomy from one's family and/or other social institutions, middle-class marginality, economic property, and sex being emphasized in male socialization as factors contributing to swinging. However, such theories fail to explain why all such people do not swing. Jenks (1998) asserts a social psychological model of swinging, whereby the first step entails an interest and/or early sexual involvement. Second, two personality characteristics are crucial: low degree of jealousy and liberal sexual predisposition. Last comes the initiation phases.

Initiation into the swinging world usually results from the husband learning of swinging first, as in 44 percent of the cases in Henshel's study (1973, as cited in Jenks, 1998). Wives learned of swinging first in only 16 percent of Henshel's cases. Upon initial discovery, a time lapse occurred before actual consideration, whereby a second time lapse occurred prior to finally deciding to become involved. Last, a third time lapse occurred before actually becoming involved. In a majority of cases, the husband makes the suggestion, as well as the final decision, to swing. In swinging situations, males tend to be the dominant forces, though the literature continues to debate this issue (Jenks, 1998).

Profile

Swingers tend to have above-average education and income, to hold management or other professional positions, and to fall in the middle- to upper-middle classes (Jenks, 1998; Gilmartin, 1975). They tend to be white, between the ages of twenty-eight and forty-five, politically moderate to conservative, and to associate with the Republican party (Jenks, 1998). Republican party affiliation, however, may be contributed to the fact that most swingers also have higher incomes and education, both of which are strongly indicative of Republican voting practices. Therefore, swingers may simply be voting according to social class interests.

A majority of swingers report no religious affiliation/identification (Jenks, 1998; Gilmartin, 1975), though similar percentages report having been raised in a religious home where church attendance was weekly. As for the American population as a whole, 92 percent report a religious preference, with only 4 percent reporting being completely nonreligious (Jenks, 1998). In addition, swingers tend to place personal values as a priority over more social ones.

EXHIBITIONISM

Criteria

The *DSM-IV-TR* classifies exhibitionism as a paraphilia whereby sexual fantasies, urges, and/or behaviors involve unexpected exposure of a person's genitals to another person or stranger. This must occur over at least a six-month period with the person either acting on the urges or else the urges cause marked interpersonal distress or difficulty (APA, 2000).

Etiology

Many different theories and beliefs exist regarding the causes of exhibitionism. Behaviorists theorize that exhibitionistic behavior develops because such an act has been linked with intense erotic pleasure over time, thus leading an individual to prefer such behavior. Psychoanalysts suggest that exhibitionistic behavior is a result of reverting to or repeating sexual habits that began early in life (Paraphilia, n.d.). Other theories suggest that exhibitionism is a type of pathological narcissism that also has obsessive-compulsive traits. Such theories assert that exhibitionists are motivated by attention and admiration needs and a desire to overcome feelings of shame and inadequacy, thereby making genital exhibitionism a sexualized type of countershame intended to create feelings of power and pride, ultimately leading to sexual arousal (Siverstein, 1996). And finally, it has also been suggested that exhibitionism is related to obsessive-compulsive disorder (OCD). This theory is a direct result of observations that exhibitionists treated with selective serotonin reuptake inhibitors (SSRI's), the type of psychotropic medication used to treat OCD, have been found to have a decrease in their thoughts, urges, and behavior (Abouesh & Clayton, 1999). Most studies done in the area of psychotropic medication, however, are limited to case studies. Also, correlation with OCD via SSRI-treatment does not indicate causation.

Profile

Exhibitionism has been found almost exclusively in males, with a peak occurrence age reported to be in the twenties. Many exhibitionists suffer from erectile difficulties in other areas of sexual activity and appear to have uncontrollable urges leading to their exhibitionistic behavior. They may have difficulty forming close, interpersonal relationships (Paraphilia, n.d.; Seidman, Marshall, Hudson, & Robertson 1994). Some individuals' primary goal is to shock or fear victims. Their sexual pleasure derives from watching visible victim reactions. Given that police tend to catch more exhibitionists than any other type of paraphiliac, the element of risk may play an important role in such behavior. Also, though the literature tends to agree that exhibitionists are unlikely to assault or rape their victims, this is not a hard-and-fast rule, especially if an exhibitionist is not satisfied with the response of his victim (Paraphilia, n.d.).

VOYEURISM

Criteria

Voyeurism, also known as scoptophilia, is defined as a paraphilia characterized by sexual behaviors, urges, and/or fantasies involving the observation of unknowing or nonconsenting individual(s), primarily unclothed and/or while engaged in sexual activity, in order to produce sexual excitement. Such intensely sexually arousing and recurrent fantasies, urges, and behaviors that involve observing a nonconsenting/ unknowing person in the process of engaging in sexual activity or disrobing must take place over a minimum period of 6 months. An individual must have either acted on their urges, or such urges/fantasies must have caused significant interpersonal difficulty or distress (APA, 2000; BehaviorNet, 2002). In most cultures, voyeurism is generally considered to be a deviant sexual act that may be tolerated at some level among certain societies given certain circumstances (Wikipedia, 2002, lists adolescent "peeping-toms" as an example).

Etiology

Voyeurism, like exhibitionism, has been linked with OCD because of voyeurist's responses to SSRI-treatment. However, once again, this does not imply causation. Voyeurists, themselves, report sexual thoughts, fantasies, and urges beginning in mid- to late childhood, with acting these out beginning in adolescence. They report an inability to decrease such fantasies or urges until they have acted on them.

Profile

Voyeurs are typically adult males in their twenties or thirties, but they may also be adolescent males, with no significant differences in frequency levels for adolescent and adult male sex offender populations. They appear to prefer observing women who are strangers and frequently are most sexually excited when risk of discovery is high. Voyeurs tend to limit their sexual activity to masturbation while actually peeping or while fantasizing about previous escapades (Paraphilia, n.d.).

NONVIOLENT, NONPHYSICAL PARAPHILIA

TELEPHONE SCATOLOGIA

Criteria

Telephone scatologia is a paraphilia in which sexual arousal and/or orgasms are achieved by exposing an unsuspecting victim to sexual or obscene material over the phone. The caller frequently will masturbate either while speaking to the victim or later while recalling the incident.

Etiology

Little research has been done in the area of telephone scatologia and, as such, it is still defined in the *DSM-IV* as Paraphilia, Not Otherwise Specified (NOS). It has been described as a verbal exhibitionism, as both telephone scatologia and exhibitionism involve sudden attempts to provoke shock and fear, and physical contact with the victim is not required for sexual gratification, thus the etiologies could be similar. However, there is not current understanding for the development of telephone scatologia.

TECHNOPHILIA

Criteria

Technophilia is a paraphilia in which an individual uses a computer to engage in sexual deviance. This typically involves cybersex with minors, but can include seeking out child pornography or chatting with minors under the guise of a same-age person. The individual will usually masturbate while conversing with the child.

Etiology

Technophilia is a relatively new paraphilia, as computer technology is fairly new and constantly improving. It is believed that many of the individuals who engage in this have other paraphilia that correspond well with technophilia (e.g., pedophilia, exhibitionism, and voyeurism with the use of Internet cameras).

Profile

Currently, there is no profile for a person who engages in technophilia. An increasing number of studies have been done to determine the etiology and profile of technophiliacs, however, no major characteristics stand out. It is believed that the individual is more socially isolated, as it involves more human-machine interaction. The deviance typically occurs when the Internet sex becomes the most important activity in the person's life. Young (1999) (as cited in Griffiths, 2001) classifies Internet addiction into five specific subtypes, with only two having sexual implications. The first is a cybersexual addiction, which involves the use of adult websites for cybersex and cyberporn. The second is a cyber-relationship addiction, which involves an excessive reliance on online relationships.

Based on a study conducted by Cooper, Putnam, Planchon, and Boies (1999) (as cited in Griffiths, 2001), a continuum model of people who use the Internet for sexual purposes has been offered. First are recreational users who access online sexual material mostly out of curiosity or for entertainment, but not for sexual behavior that is seen as deviant. Second are at-risk users. These individuals are identified as most likely not to have developed a problem were it not for the availability of the Internet. The last categories are sexually compulsive users. These individuals use the Internet as a means to express their pathological sexual fantasies, and rarely engage in sexual activities outside of the Internet forum.

SADISTIC PARAPHILIA

SADISM

Criteria

Sadism is a paraphilia in which sexual arousal and/or orgasms are achieved by inflicting pain and humiliation on another person and/or watching another suffer (Baumeister, 1989). Sadism may or may not be a consensual act. In consensual sadistic acts, a person who takes a dominant role in sexual intercourse with their partner is often referred to as the "top" (Stroller, 1991). Although a sadist may be reluctant at first to participate in such activities with their masochistic partners, they give consent in order to pleasure their partner (Baumeister, 1989; Stroller, 1991). Nonconsensual sadistic activity often involves a person becoming sexually aroused by humiliating or inflicting pain on a person without their consent. In fact, in some instances, this lack of consent may increase the amount of pleasure felt by the sadist.

Profile

Sadism appears to be a cross-cultural phenomenon that manifests itself in acts such as torture, public executions, and war (Baumeister, 1989). Most sadists began their sexual career as masochists who eventually progress into a dominant position (Baumeister, 1989; Phillips, 1998). Some sadists engage in dominating behavior at the request of their masochistic partner (Baumeister, 1989; Stroller, 1991). At some point these individuals begin to enjoy their dominating role (Baumeister, 1989; Phillips, 1991; Stroller, 1991). Some rare individuals desire to gain sexual gratification by inflicting pain and humiliation on partners whether or not they have established consent. These individuals usually commit sadistic acts such as rape and murder (Baumeister, 1989; Phillips, 1998).

PYROMANIA

Criteria

Pyromania involves the presence of several episodes of purposeful and deliberate fire setting. With more planning than most impulse control disorders, pyromaniacs tend to be more compulsive than impulsive (Pyromania, 2000). According to the *DSM-IV* and *DSM-IV-TR* (1994, 2000, respectively), it involves the following criteria:

- Deliberate and purposeful fire setting on more than one occasion.
- Tension or affective arousal before the act.
- Fascination with, interest in, curiosity about, or attraction to fire and its situational contexts (e.g., paraphernalia, uses, consequences).
- Pleasure, gratification, or relief when setting fires, or when witnessing or participating in their aftermath.

- The fire setting is not done for monetary gain, as an expression of sociopolitical ideology, to conceal criminal activity, to express anger or vengeance, to improve one's living circumstances, in response to a delusion or hallucination, or as a result of impaired judgment (e.g., in dementia, Mental Retardation, Substance Intoxication).

- The fire setting is not better accounted for by Conduct Disorder, a Manic Episode, or Antisocial Personality Disorder (Grohol, 2002, p. 1; American Psychiatric Association (APA), 1994; APA, 2000).

Etiology

Pyromania is a paraphilia involving the impulse to set fires. Developmentally, most children go through a phase or stage where they enjoy seeing fire. This is normal. Once taught about fire safety, children who are supervised can help adults around campfires. However, sometimes some children manage to sneak away to play with fire. Although frightening, this is not a psychiatric or psychological disorder (HBO & Company, 1998; Pyromania, 2000; Pyromania, 2001).

Individuals do not have pyromania if they deliberately set fires to cover up crimes, express anger, rage, or political beliefs, improve living circumstances, as a result of impaired judgment, or to collect insurance money, unless they also meet the criteria noted above. In order for a diagnosis of pyromania to occur, another diagnosis must not account for the fire-setting behavior (HBO & Company, 1998; Pyromania, 2000; Pyromania, 2001). Fires set in response to hallucinations or delusions are not pyromania. A person who sets fires as part of a bipolar disorder's manic phase or who has conduct disorder or antisocial personality disorder is also not a pyromaniac. True pyromaniacs just like fire—there is an attraction to it, even a sexual component in many cases. Individuals with pyromania frequently have emotional difficulties and poor learning skills. Most individuals who have pyromania in childhood improve or get better; however, if left untreated, adults (most sufferers of this disorder) don't. Children set roughly half of all arson fires (HBO & Company, 1998; Pyromania, 2000; Pyromania, 2001).

Profile

As noted above, individuals with pyromania are typically males who may have social skills deficits and/or learning problems. Pyromaniacs experience and display high levels of tension and/or affective arousal before and during firesetting. Their interest, curiosity, attraction, and/or fascination with fire and its situational contexts—such as the people, objects, and/or situations surrounding fire—goes beyond normal development or what an average individual experiences (HBO & Company, 1998; Pyromania, 2000; Pyromania, 2001). They experience intense pleasure, gratification, and/or relief from setting, witnessing, and/or participating in the aftermath of fires. Pyromaniacs make detailed plans in advance for starting fires. Many sufferers enjoy watching any fire they can, and they may enjoy setting off fire alarms. They may either be unconcerned or find satisfaction in the fire's results, including consequences to property, health, and/or life (HBO & Company, 1998; Pyromania, 2000; Pyromania, 2001).

Although it exists, childhood pyromania is rare. Though children also set a lot of fires, pyromania typically occurs in adolescence and/or adulthood. Typically, fire setting in juveniles is associated with other psychological or psychiatric disorders such as ADHD, adjustment disorder, or conduct disorder (HBO & Company, 1998; Pyromania, 2000; Pyromania, 2001).

MASOCHISTIC PARAPHILIA

MASOCHISM

Criteria
Sexual masochism refers to a paraphilia in which sexual arousal and/or orgasms are achieved by being controlled through bondage, regulations, or commands, having pain inflicted upon oneself, or experiencing embarrassment and/or humiliation (Baumeister, 1989; Stroller, 1991). In order for an activity to be considered masochistic, it must contain at least one of the following: physical pain, restraints, humiliation, or embarrassment (Baumeister, 1998). A person must engage in this behavior for his or her own consensual pleasure; s/he is not forced into this activity (Baumeister, 1989; Stroller, 1991). The person frequently assumes a submissive role in sexual relations with his or her partner, who is often referred to as the "bottom" (Stroller, 1991).

A Brief History of Sexual Masochism
Sexual masochism began to appear during the 1500s, but was not practiced regularly until the 1700s and 1800s (Baumeister, 1989). A researcher by the name of Krafft-Ebing invented the term masochism (gaining pleasure from pain and submission) based upon the writings of Leopold von Sacher-Masoch (Baumeister, 1989; Noyes, 1997). Sacher-Masoch wrote about attractive females humiliating and inflicting pain upon males (Baumeister, 1989; Noyes, 1997). This appeared to be an attempt to break gender barriers during his era (Noyes, 1997). Apparently Sacher-Masoch not only wrote about masochism, but also engaged in masochistic behavior himself (Baumeister, 1989; Noyes, 1997). According to Baumeister (1989), the writer continuously searched for women to partake in the dominating role to fulfill his own masochistic fantasies.

Profile
Baumeister (1989) estimated that approximately 5 to 10 percent of the general population engages in some variety of masochistic behavior. However, the percentage may have increased over the last thirteen years. Society has a tendency to perceive of women as masochists and men as sadists (Baumeister, 1989; Phillips, 1998). This makes it difficult to ascertain if there is a gender difference between sadomasochistic behavior. When a man admits he is masochistic, he is often perceived as having femi-

nine traits (Baumeister, 1989). According to Baumeister (1989), sexual masochism is not a universal phenomenon outside of the Western culture and appears limited to our society. However, one may be able to argue that sadistic behavior has been observed across cultures.

SADOMASOCHISTIC PARAPHILIA

SADOMASOCHISM

Criteria

Sadomasochism is defined as a paraphilia in which sexual pleasure is derived by inflicting pain on oneself or someone else, yet also exhibiting masochistic tendencies (Stroller, 1991). It is a term used to describe the behavior of sadists and masochists, since a sadist is needed to inflict pain upon a masochist.

Etiology

It is speculated that sadomasochistic behavior is an attempt to master childhood trauma (Stroller, 1991). For example, children who experienced a medical condition in which they had to receive intensive hospitalization and discomforting treatments might choose to participate in sadomasochistic behavior as an adult. Stroller (1991) believes that the more a child had to endure, the more likely he/she will seek out sadomasochism.

Profile

Sadomasochistic activities are used to create sexual pleasure as well as nonsexual pleasure such as relaxation (Stroller, 1991). Most sadomasochistic individuals participate in their fetish with a partner, but some individuals prefer to engage in solo activities (Phillips, 1989; Stroller, 1991). Prior to engaging in sadomasochistic behaviors with consenting partners, couples make a contract (Phillips, 1998). This contract contains the rules and regulations of the sadomasochism that is about to take place. It is the dominating partner's job to make sure that the "bottom" is safe, and that the rules are followed at all times (Phillips, 1998; Stroller, 1991). Some terms used in sadomasochism include S&M (sadism and masochism), B&D (bondage and discipline), and S&D (submission and dominance) (Stroller, 1991).

The following sadomasochistic techniques were taken from Stroller (1991, pages 10–14):

Whipping

- Whips (including long, short, thick, thin, rope, leather, cloth, braided, unbraided, with or without knots and studs). We also observed whips made out of horsehair and small metal beads.
  - Paddles
  - Canes
  - Hands (open, fisted, palm, dorsum)
  - Chains
  - Knouts
  - Belts

- Switches (single, bundles)
- Leather straps

- Riding crops

Piercing

- Nails (sharp, blunt)
- Needles
- Spears, arrows

- Jewelry
- Knives
- Crucifixion

Tattooing/Scarification Cutting

- Knives
- Razors
- Teeth

- Surgical instruments
- Scissors
- Nonsuicidal wrist and ankle slashing

Hanging

- Suspension of body
- Suspension of neck
- From limbs
- From wires
- From chains
- From instruments driven through the flesh
- Stretching on racks (machines are used to stretch different body parts)

- Mouth gagging
- Cloth
- Adhesive tape
- Ball-in-mouth
- Dildo
- Electric shocking (cattle prod, vibrator, medical machines, magneto)

Imprisonment

- In cages
- In pitch-black darkness (closets, blindfolds, diving bell)

- Masks
- Boxes, trunks, coffins, refrigerators, barrels, packing crates

Altered Consciousness

- Suffocation
- Anesthesia
- Hanging
- Drugs

- Prolonged suffering
- Alcohol
- Drowning

Mummification, Cocooning

- Loose leather bags
- Bandages

- Mesh fabric
- Head and/or body plaster casts

- Plastic
- Blankets

- Latex, rubber

Iron-maidened, Tickling

- Feathers
- Cloth

- Fingers

Hair Pulling or Shaving

- Scalp
- Eyebrows
- Eyelids

- Body
- Genitals

Bondage

- Rope, twine, cotton thread
- Wire
- Leather
- Cloth
- Chains
- Nylon stockings

- Handcuffs
- Steel shackles
- Rubber tubing
- Straitjackets
- In harness (such as pony game)

Excrement (expelled, retained, ingested, smelled, dirtied by)

- Urine
- Feces
- Sweat
- Semen
- Vaginal fluids

- Anus licking
- Enemas
- Catheters
- Other urinary and rectal foreign bodies

Burning

- Branding

- Dripped hot wax

Wrestling

- Two females

- Mud

Stomping

- High heels

- Bare feet

Amputees (desire for a person with amputated limbs) Infantilism

- Diapers
- Cuddling
- Feeding with milk or bottle

Bootlicking Asphyxiation

- Diving helmet
- Mask with air hose
- Rope
- Nylon stocking
- Hands
- Corseting, cinching

Clamping

- Surgical clamps (serrated or unserrated)
- Clothespins
- Nipple clamps

Fisting

- Anus
- Vagina

According to this list of techniques, the following paraphilia could be classified under sadomasochism:

Infantilism

- Autonepiophila

Excrement

- Klismaphilia
- Urophilia
- Coprophilia
- Catheterophilia
- Mysophilia
- Olfactophilia

Amputees

- Acrotomophilia

Asphyxiation

- Asphyxiophilia

Electric Shocking

- Electrocutophilia

APOTEMNOPHILIA

Criteria

Apotemnophilia is the classification designated to the desire and/or obsession with having a limb removed from the body (Dyer, 2000). It always involves the amputation of a specific limb, and patients are convinced they will only be normal once it is removed (Dyer, 2000). A New York City child psychologist who suffers from apotemnophilia, Gregg Furth, maintains that "the disorder revolves around feeling like a complete person" (Dotinga, n.d., p. 1). However, a second and larger piece of apotemnophilia involves the sexual arousal and sexual fantasies accompanying the desire to become an amputee. At Johns Hopkins University in Baltimore psychologist and sexuality expert, John Money, "gave the disorder its name in 1977 and declared that people with the disorder have a sexual fetish centered on amputated limbs" (Dotinga, n.d, p. 1).

Etiology

Cases of amputation obsession have been reported by medical experts since the 1860s, however the cause of apotemnophilia is still unclear. Very little research looks into apotemnophilia, with less than a handful of articles existing on the topic (Dyer, 2000). The Internet, however, has a wealth of information on apotemnophilia, albeit primarily personal testimony, chat rooms, message boards, and information on how and where to achieve what "wannabe" amputees desire. Individuals who visit these sites report very early onset of obsessive symptomology. In 1999, Greg Furth, a middle-aged man, informed a San Diego courtroom that he was four or five years old when his obsession with amputation first began (Dotinga, n.d., p. 1).

Apotemnophilia has also been associated with homosexuality and obsessive-compulsive disorder. One of the top U.S. medical ethicists and director of the University of Pennsylvania's Center for Bioethics, Arthur Caplan, stated, "apotemnophilia is clearly a medical disorder, and can't be cured by giving in to the disease" (Dotinga, n.d., p. 1). On the other hand, Richard Bruno, a New Jersey psychophysiologist specializing in brain-body disorders and one of a handful of people in the world who have studied apotemnophilia, asserts that people with this disorder are desperately seeking love and attention from others (Dotinga, n.d., p. 1). He maintains that such individuals frequently live hellish lives, feeling unlovable as they are, that all they really want is to be loved and accepted (Dotinga, n.d., p. 1).

However, there is still much more to be learned regarding ampotemnophilia and those who suffer from it. As Richard Bruno reportedly states, "There are just far more questions than answers about the disorder, and unfortunately, many of these questions may be unanswerable. We may never know why these guys want what they want" (Dotinga, n.d., p. 1).

Profile

Individuals with this classification feel an intense, desperate need to be amputees. They are not physically sick, and their limbs do not need to be amputated for any medical reasons. Rather, they have felt since childhood that they are not normal with a certain body part remaining attached. Though this aspect of the classification is important, another component involves the sexual arousal associated with the desire to become an amputee (Dyer, 2000; Elliot, 2000; Leo, 2001). Currently, no valid research exists on this particular aspect. Some apotemnophiliacs assert their obsession is not associated with sex; rather, they assert it's a disorder surrounding body image whereby the only cure is through amputation (Dotinga, n.d, p. 1). Such individuals also do not seek amputation for the blood or mutilation and pain associated with amputation. The desire is strictly to be an amputee (Elliot, 2000).

Often patients will attempt amputations of their own limbs through directly cutting them off, cutting off circulation in the hopes that gangrene will set in and surgeons will be forced to remove the limb, having "accidents" such as being run over by a train (by lying on the tracks) or shooting their limb off, as well as other forms of self-harm aimed at amputation (Dyer, 2000; Elliot, 2000; Leo, 2001).

CLASSIFICATION

What follows is a comprehensive listing of unique paraphilia based on the previous classification. Definitions have been provided to aid the reader in the better understanding of the classification. Additionally, a sixth section has been added which includes those paraphilia that contain behaviors which are both nonviolent physical and violent physical.

NONVIOLENT, PHYSICAL

Paraphilia in this category include physical contact with oneself or another person with the absence of violence. Classifier in this category is Desire, which includes paraphilia that are physical in nature but stipulate the presence of desire.

Definitions

Amomaxia—sex in a parked car
Aphephilia—deriving pleasure from being touched
Autoerotica—self-induced arousal
Axillism—the use of the armpit for sex
Basoexia—arousal from kissing
Chezolagnia—masturbation while defecating
Coitobalnism—sexual activity in a bathtub
Coitus a mammilla—penetration of penis between breasts
Coitus analis—anal sex
Coitus a unda—sex under water
Coitus intrafermoris—penetration between the legs
Fisting—inserting fist or hand into vagina or anus; considered lesbian paraphilia
Frottage—rubbing body against partner or object for arousal
Genuphallation—use of the knees for sex; insertion of penis between the knees of a partner
Gregomulcia—arousal from being fondled in a crowd
Gynotikolobomassophilia—sexual pleasure by nibbling on a woman's earlobe
Haptephilia—arousal by being touched
Hedonophilia—sexual arousal from engaging in pleasurable activities

Hyphephilia—arousal from touching skin, hair, leather, or fur
Knismolagnia—arousal from tickling
Naphephilia—arousal from touching or being touched
Nasolingus—arousal from sucking nose of partner
Nasophilia—arousal from the touch, licking, or sucking of a partner's nose; nose fetish
Normophilia—arousal by acts considered normal by one's religion or society
Osculocentric—arousal from kissing
Pantophilia—arousal from just about everything imaginable
Polyiterophilia—arousal only after having sex with a series of partners
Pteronophilia—sexual gratification from being tickled by feathers
Pygophilemania—arousal from kissing buttocks
Pygotripsis—arousal from rubbing buttocks
Sarmassophilia—arousal from kneading flesh
Somnophilia—arousal from fondling one's partner in their sleep
Tithiolagnia—sexual gratification from nursing
Titillagnia—arousal from tickling
Tripsolagnia—arousal from having hair shampooed
Tripsolagnophilia—arousal from being massaged
Tripsophilia—arousal from being massaged
Triolism—arousal by being the third party in a sexual scene; desire to share sexual partner with another person

Desire

Apodysophilia—feverish desire to undress
Hyperphilia—compulsive desire for sex
Nymphomania—an excessive, insatiable sexual appetite or drive in women
Satyriasis—an excessive, insatiable sexual appetite or drive in men

Partialism

Paraphilia in this category include an arousal or attraction to a body part or product from the body. Classifiers included in this category are Body Part, Fluid, or Odor.

Body Part

Acomoclitc—preference for hairless genitals
Alvinolagnia—stomach fetish
Amelotasis—attraction to the absence of a limb
Crurofact—leg fetish
Crurophilia—sexual arousal from legs
Dermaphilia—arousal from skin
Gomphipothic—arousal by the sight of teeth
Gynelophilous—arousal from pubic hair

Hirsutophilia—arousal from armpit hair
Lactaphilia—arousal from lactating breasts
Macrogenitalism—arousal from large genitals
Mammagymnophilia—arousal from female breasts
Maschalophilous—arousal from armpits
Mastofact—breast fetish
Mazophilia—breast fetish
Metopophilia—turned on by a person's face
Oculophilia—eye fetish
Organofact—fetish for some part of the body
Phallophilia—large penis fetish
Podophilia—arousal from feet; foot fetish
Pubephilia—arousal from pubic hair
Pygophilia—arousal from buttocks
Rhytiphilia—arousal from facial wrinkles
Strabimus—arousal from eyes of partner
Trichopathophilia—sexual attraction to hair
Trichophilia—sexual attraction to hair

Body Fluid

Hematigolagnia—arousal from bloody sanitary pads
Hygrophilia—arousal from body fluids or moisture
Molysmophilia—attraction to dirt, filth, or contamination
Mysophilia—arousal from soiled things, such as a dirty diaper or soiled undergarments
Salirophilia—arousal from ingesting saliva or sweat

Odor

Barosmia—arousal from smell
Bromidrophilia—arousal from bodily smells
Eprectolagnia/eproctophilia—fetish for farting
Idrophrodisia—arousal from the odor of perspiration, especially from the genitals
Olfactophilia—sexual gratification from smells
Osmophilia/Osmolagnia—arousal caused by bodily odors, such as sweat or menses
Osphresiophilia—an inordinate love of smells
Ozolagnia—arousal caused by bodily odors, such as sweat or menses

Pedophilia/Familial

A subcategory of nonviolent paraphilia, this category is associated with sexual contact involving a child and/or member of the family.

Definitions

Blastolagnia—arousal from young females
Corephallism—anal sex with a young girl
Ephebophilia—sexual arousal from adolescent sex partners
Fratrilagnia—arousal from having sex or imagining having sex with one's brother
Hebephilia—male arousal by male adolescent sexual partners
Nepiophilia/nepiolagnia—arousal by infants of the opposite sex
Nepirasty—arousal from handling an infant, often experienced by childless females
Novercamania—sexual attraction to one's stepmother
Nymphophilia—arousal of adult males who are attracted to young females
Matrilagnia—sexual arousal from real or imagined sex with one's mother
Patrolagnia—arousal from real or imagined sex with one's father
Pentheraphilia—sexual attraction to one's mother-in-law
Soceraphilia—arousal from one's parents-in-law
Sorophilia/sororilagnia—arousal from real or imagined sex with one's sister
Synegenesophilia—sexual attraction to one's relatives
Thygatrilagnia—a father's sexual love for his daughter
Vitricophilia—sexual attraction to one's stepfather

Transvestism

Paraphilia in this category are associated with dressing or playing out the role of a member of the opposite sex. Also known as autogynephilia, eonism, and transvestophilia.

Definitions

Adolescentilism—arousal from cross-dressing or playing the role of an adolescent
Andromimetophilia—arousal from a female partner who dresses like a male
Gynemimetophilia—sexual arousal from a male impersonating a female
Juvenilism—dressing or acting out in the role of a juvenile, sometimes sexually

Voyeurism

Paraphilia in this category include sexual arousal from watching others engage in various activities. Also known as scoptophilia.

Definitions

Allopellia—having orgasm from watching others engaging in sex
Candaulism—spouse who watches partner have sex with someone else
Capnolagnia—arousal from watching others smoke
Cryptoscopophilia—desire and arousal from seeing behavior of others in privacy of their home, not necessarily sexual
Ecouteurism—arousal from listening to others having sex without their consent

Mixoscopia—arousal and sexual gratification from watching one's own partner have sex with someone else

Exhibitionism

Paraphilia in this category include sexual arousal from exposing oneself to others. Also known as peodeiktophilia.

Definitions

Agoraphilia—arousal from open spaces or having sex in public
Autagonistophilia—sexual arousal and orgasm are contingent upon displaying one's self in a live show or while being photographed
Ecdyosis—arousal from removing clothes in front of others
Iantranudia—arousal from exposing yourself to your doctor, usually by faking an ailment

NONVIOLENT, NONPHYSICAL

Experiential, Nonphysical

Paraphilia in this category include arousal from experiences that do not include physical contact with others.

Definitions

Actirasty—arousal from exposure to the sun's rays
Allorgasmia—arousal from fantasizing about someone other than one's partner
Amaxophilia—attraction to riding in cars and motor vehicles
Antholagnia—arousal from smelling flowers
Choreophilia—sexual arousal from dancing
Claustrophilia—love of being confined in small places
Coproscopist—arousal from watching someone defecate
Ecdemolagnia—arousal from traveling or being away from home
Erythrophilia—becoming aroused by blushing
Flatuphilia—arousal from having partner pass gas
Furtling—the use of fingers underneath cut-outs in genital areas of photos for arousal
Hodophilia—arousal from traveling
Homilophilia—sexual arousal from hearing or giving sermons
Kainotophilia—getting pleasure from change
Neophilia—arousal from novelty or change
Ochlophilia—arousal to crowds or being in a crowd
Ombrophilia—turned on by rain or being rained upon
Phronemophilia—turned on by the act of thinking
Phygephilia—arousal from being a fugitive
Pluviophilia—sexual stimulation from rain or being rained upon
Scopophilia—arousal from being stared at
Sophophilia—sexual gratification from learning

Spectrophilia—arousal from looking at oneself in a mirror; arousal from image in mirrors; coitus with spirits

Sthenolagnia—arousal from displaying strength or muscles

Urolagnia—sexual pleasure from urinating

SADISTIC

Paraphilia in this category include arousal from inflicting pain and/or humiliation on others. Classifiers in this category are Direct and Indirect. Indirect paraphilia are naturally occurring (i.e., the individual does not directly inflict the pain and/or humiliation). Also included are paraphilia that cause emotional pain rather than physical pain. Direct paraphilia include acts of direct infliction of physical pain and/or humiliation.

Direct

Acarophilia—arousal from scratching

Acousticophilia—arousal from certain sounds, particularly someone screaming in agony

Agonophilia—person who is aroused by a partner pretending to struggle

Amokoscisia—arousal or sexual frenzy with desire to slash or mutilate women

Anophelorastia—arousal from defiling or ravaging a partner

Anthropophagolagnia—rape with cannibalism

Anthropophagy—pleasure derived from the ingestion of human flesh

Dacnolagnomania—sexually sadistic murder where sexual arousal and gratification are found in the act of killing, lust murder

Dippoldism—sexual arousal from abusing children

Erotophonophilia—sexual satisfaction from murdering complete strangers, lust murder

Leptosadism—mild form of sadism

Necrophilia—sexual gratification only by having sex with the dead

Necrosadism—arousal from mutilating a corpse

Odaxelagnia—arousal from biting

Phletbotomy—arousal from bloodletting

Pseudonecrophilia—arousal from having sex with someone pretending to be dead

Pseudozoophilia—arousal from partner who plays the role of an animal during sex play

Raptophilia—arousal only from raping a victim

Sapphosadism—lesbian sadism

Symphorophilia—arousal from arranging a disaster, crash, or explosion; arousal by accidents or catastrophes

Thlipsosis—arousal from pinching others

Indirect

Dacryphilia—arousal from seeing tears in the eyes of a partner

Frotteurism—sexual arousal from rubbing against of touching a non-consenting person

Harmatophilia—arousal from sexual incompetence or mistakes, usually in female partner
Kleptophilia/kleptolagnia—arousal from stealing things
Lyssophilia—sexual arousal from becoming angry or upset
Nosophilia/nosolagnia—arousal from knowing partner has a terminal illness
Pnigophilia—aroused from people choking
Psellismophilia—becoming aroused by stuttering
Scatologia/scatophilia—arousal from making obscene phone calls
Telephone scatologia—arousal from making obscene phone calls

Bestiality

Paraphilia in this category include sexual arousal or contact with animals. Also known as zoophilia. This category includes a classifier of bestialsadism, which indicates torture of animal during sexual contact. For this reason bestiality has been included within the sadistic category. Although there is only one identifiable paraphilia that is directly classified as bestialsadism, this modifier allows for classification of sexual contact with a specific animal with torture involved (e.g., sex with a dog while breaking its neck).

Definitions

Aelurophilia—deriving gratification from cats
Anolingus—arousal from licking lizards
Arachnephilia—arousal from spiders
Avisodomy—breaking the neck of a bird while penetrating it for sex
Batrachophilia—arousal or attraction to frogs
Bee stings—use of bees, such as to sting genitalia
Canophilia—arousal from dogs
Cynophilia—arousal from sex with dogs
Entomophilia/entomocism—arousal from insects or use of insects in sexual activity
Formicophilia—enjoyment of the use of ants or insects for sexual purposes
Melissophilia—arousal from bees
Musophilia—arousal from mice
Necrobestialism—arousal from having sex with dead animals
Ophidiophilia—arousal from snakes
Ornithophilia—arousal from birds
Phthiriophilia—attraction to lice

SADOMASOCHISM

Paraphilia in this category include arousal from both inflicting pain and/or humiliation, as well as receiving pain and/or humiliation. Also known as Algolagnia.

Definitions

Aichmophilia—arousal from needles or other pointed objects
Autonecrophilia—imagining oneself as a corpse or becoming sexually aroused by simulated corpses
Belonephilia—arousal from pins or needles
Biastophilia—arousal from raping someone or from the idea of being raped
Bondage—physical or mental restriction of partner
Coitus a cheval—couple having sex on the back of an animal or one acting out role of horse
Dystychiphilia—deriving pleasure from accidents
Kakorrhaphiophilia—arousal from failure
Pecattiphilia—arousal from sinning or having committed imaginary crime
Peniaphilia—erotic fascination with poverty
Phobophilia—arousal from fear or hate
Psychrophilia/psychrocism—arousal by being cold or watching others freeze

MASOCHISM

Paraphilia included in this category are associated with arousal from pain and/or humiliation inflicted on oneself. Also known as algophilia, asthenolagnia, mastigophilia, odynophilia, and poinephilia.

Definitions

Amychophilia—deriving sexual pleasure from being scratched
Apotemnophilia—person who has sexual fantasies about losing a limb
Asphyxiaphilia—arousal from lack of oxygen
Autoerotic asphyxiation—arousal from oxygen deprivation
Autoassassinophilia—arousal from putting oneself in a position in which s/he may be killed; arousal from orchestrating one's own death by the hands of another
Automasochism—inflicting intense sensations of pain on one's own body
Automysophilia—arousal from being dirty or defiled
Autonepiophilia—sexual attraction from being treated like an infant
Autopederasty—the insertion of one's own penis into one's anus
Catagelophilia—love of being ridiculed
Catheterophilia—arousal from use of catheters
Chrematistophilia—arousal from being charged for sex or having sex partner steal from them
Climacophilia—deriving pleasure from falling down stairs
Coprophilia—arousal from feces or being defecated on, "Brown shower," "scat"
Ederacinism—to tear out sex organs by the roots as in a frenzy or to punish oneself for sexual cravings

Electrophilia—arousal from electric stimulus
Emetophilia—arousal from vomit or vomiting, "Roman shower"
Harpaxophilia—getting pleasure by robbery or being robbed
Hypoxyphilia—sexual arousal from the deprivation of oxygen
Infantilism—attraction to childhood items; cross-dressing as a young child for sex play
Klismaphilia—sexual pleasure from enemas
Antiophilia—arousal from floods
Brontophilia—arousal from thunderstorms
Cheimaphilia—deriving pleasure from cold or winter
Cratolagnia—arousal from strength
Ergophilia—love of work and labor
Gymnophilia—arousal from nudity
Hypnophilia—turned on by the thought of sleeping
Keraunophilia—turned on by thunder and lightning
Kinesophilia—arousal from movement and exercise
Knissophilia—attraction to incense-burning
Ligyrophilia—arousal from loud noises
Lilapsophilia—arousal from tornadoes
Lygerastia—tendency to only be aroused by darkness
Lygophilia—love of darkness
Melolagnia—arousal from music
Metrophilia—arousal from poetry
Nebulophilia—arousal from fog
Nudomania—arousal from nudity
Nyctophilia—love of night
Oikophilia—attraction to one's home
Omolagnia—arousal from nudity
Psychrotentiginous—arousal from cold weather
Scotophilia—turned on by darkness
Taphophilia—love of funerals
Teleophilia—affinity for religious ceremonies
Thalpotentiginy—arousal from heat
Tocophilia—fondness for pregnancy and childbirth
Tonitrophilia—love of thunder
Toxophilia—love of archery
Uranophilia—sexual arousal by heavenly thoughts
Vicarphilia—arousal from other people's exciting experiences

Pornographic

Graphelagnia—maniacal interest in obscene pictures, arousal from photographs of nudity or sex
Iconolagny—arousal from pictures or statues of nude people

Ordune—arousal from photographs of nudes or sex
Pictophilia—arousal only from looking at erotic pictures
Teledildonics—arousal from computer sex games

Object

Agalmatophilia—attractions to statues or mannequins
Albutophilia—arousal from water
Altocalciphilia—high heel fetish
Anaclitism—arousal from items used as an infant
Androidism—arousal from robots with human features
Aulophilia—arousal from flutes
Chasmophilia—attraction to nooks, crannies, crevices, and chasms
Chionophilia—arousal from snow
Chrysophilia—arousal from gold or golden objects
Dendrophilia—arousal from trees, or fertility worship of them
Doraphilia—love of animal fur, leather, or skins
Exophilia—fetish for the bizarre or unusual
Galateism—arousal from statues or mannequins
Hematigolagnia—arousal from bloody sanitary pads
Hierophilia—arousal from sacred objects
Icolagnia—arousal from contemplation of, or contact with, sculptures or pictures
Kenophilia—attraction to empty or open spaces
Lithophilia—attraction to stones, gravel, or mud
Mechanophilia—turned on by machines
Megalophilia—arousal from large objects (not necessarily fat)
Nemophilia—arousal from forests
Pediophilia—attraction to dolls
Placophilia—arousal from tombstones
Potamophilia—arousal from streams and rivers
Pteridomania—an intense desire for ferns
Retifism—foot and shoe fetishism
Pygmalionism—falling in love with one's creation (a la "My Fair Lady")
Robotism—arousal by robots or the use of robots in sexual activity
Septophilia—sexual attraction to decaying matter
Siderodromophilia—arousal from trains
Sitophilia—arousal from food; use of food in sexual activity
Statuophilia—arousal from statues
Staurophilia—arousal from the cross or crucifix
Thalassophilia—love of the sea
Timophilia—arousal from gold or wealth
Undinism—arousal from water
Xylophilia—turned on by wooden objects
Ylophilia—arousal by forests

Character-type Preferential

Paraphilia in this category include a preference for a particular type of person or character.

Definitions

Acrotomophilia—sexual preference for amputees

Allotriorasty—arousal from partners of other nations or races

Alphamegamia—attraction to partners of another age group

Amaurophilia—preference for a blind or blindfolded sex partner

Anasteemaphilia—attraction to a person because of a difference in height

Anililagnia—sexual desire for older women

Chronophilia—arousal from the passage of time; arousal from an older partner

Cyesolagnia—pregnant woman fetish

Dysmorphophilia—arousal from deformed or physically impaired partners

Endytolagnia/endytophilia—arousal only from partners who are clothed

Erotomania—people who develop an unreasonable love of a stranger or person who is not interested in them

Gerontophilia—arousal from a partner from an older generation

Graophilia—arousal from an older female partner

Hermaphroditphilia—arousal from Hermaphrodites

Heterophilia—arousal from members of the opposite sex

Homophilia/homoeroticism—arousal from members of the same sex

Hybristophilia—sexual arousal due to the knowledge that one's partner has committed an act of violence

Iterandria—arousal from person of same sex

Macrophilia—attraction to giants or giant creatures

Maieusiophilia—arousal from childbirth or pregnant women

Maniaphilia—attraction to insane people

Matronolagnia—arousal from older female partner

Menophilist—arousal from menstruating women

Morphophilia—arousal from a person with a different physique

Nanophilia—sexual attraction to a short partner

Parthenophilia—attraction only to virgins

Pornolagnia—desire for prostitutes

Scelerophilia—attraction to bad guys or unsavory characters

Stigmatophilia—arousal from partner who is stigmatized (i.e. tattoos, piercings, scars)

Teratophilia—arousal from deformed or monstrous people

Threpterophilia—arousal from female nurses

Uranism—arousal from person of the same sex

Xenophilia—arousal from strangers; an attraction to foreign customs, traditions, and foreigners

Zenolimia—from strangers; an attraction to foreign customs, traditions, and foreigners

Verbal

Paraphilia in this category include sexual arousal associated with verbiage, both written and oral.

Direct
Coprolalia—arousal from using obscene language or writing
Erotographomania—arousal from writing love poems or letters
Laliophilia—arousal from public speaking
Moriaphilia—arousal from telling dirty jokes
Narratophilia—arousal from erotic conversations or discussing sex with others
Technophilia—arousal from computer sex (i.e. cybersex)
Telephonicophilia—arousal from using phone calls for sexual conversations

CHAPTER

PARAPHILIA AND SIGNATURES IN CRIME SCENE INVESTIGATION

9

ERIC W. HICKEY

Historically, crime scene analysis has been the purview of forensic experts, specifically crime lab personnel trained to gather and analyze physical evidence. Without a confession, law enforcement relied heavily upon results of crime scene investigations to gain convictions. Today *forensics* stands as a rubric for a multidisciplinary investigative approach that embraces psychology, criminology, victimology, as well as criminalistics: serology, toxicology, ballistics, DNA, fingerprints, and other physical evidence. Law enforcement personnel are now more active participants in crime scene analysis because of their ability to better interpret crime scene evidence. This redefining of forensics has part of its roots in criminal profiling where investigators and crime consultants piece together behavioral and physical characteristics of crime scenes. The results contribute to the creation of criminal profiles, or information that assists investigators in understanding the kind of person(s) committing such crimes. Since the 1940s when profiles of Adolf Hitler were created, profiling depicting personalities and behaviors of offenders have included the Mad Bomber, Son of Sam, the Unabomber, and many others. Profiling became entrenched in the 1970s and 1980s with the establishment of the FBI Behavioral Science Unit (BSU) at the FBI Academy in Quantico, Virginia. From their efforts and those of other law enforcement, practitioners, academicians, and media, profiling has drawn both public and governmental scrutiny.

Along with crime scene profiling several other types of profiling emerged including geographical, psychological, criminal, victim, and psychological autopsy. The original, dichotomous organized/disorganized crime scene profiling established by the FBI helped pave the way to more sophisticated profiling techniques. Each new type of profiling provides a new avenue to examine crimes and criminals especially where there is indication of mental, emotional, or personality abnormalities. Focus on *instrumental crimes* (crimes with primarily tangible, extrinsic value such as theft from stores and bank robberies) and *expressive crimes* (crimes that carry intangible, emotional, and psychologically laden characteristics such as hate crimes and domestic violence) has generated a plethora of criminal typologies. Profiling has been of particular interest in analyzing violent crimes, such as sexual assaults, arsons, and murder. Today, competent professionals utilize statistical analysis and scientific method in the creation of profiles. Inevitably such scientific focus impacts how we perceive violent criminals, their crimes and victims and guides us in our understanding.

The term *violent criminal* is a rubric for a host of offenders including an array of sexual predators. Etiological explanations for sex offending have led to classifications of sex crimes that can be confusing and unreliable when conducting crime scene analysis and criminal investigations. The purpose of this chapter is to examine behavioral patterns and motives of sex offenders in context with paraphilia and signatures found in crime scene investigations. Paraphilia are considered by the *Diagnostic Statistical Manual* to be sexual impulse disorders characterized by intensely arousing, recurrent sexual fantasies, urges, and behaviors. Paraphilic fantasies and behaviors often develop in early adolescence and differentially progress in intensity, duration, and frequency. While some paraphiliacs are not violent, others develop a pattern of paraphilic interests that can lead to violent sexual behaviors such as *erotophonophilia* or *dacnolagnomania* (lust murder), *amokoscisia* (arousal or sexual frenzy with desire to slash or mutilate women), *anthropophagolagnia* (rape with cannibalism), and *dippoldism* (sexual arousal from abusing children). The sexualization of violence is a construct of an offenders' development of specific paraphilic fantasies. Violent sex offenders such as lust killers, rapists, child molesters, and pedophiles engage in patterns of sexual behavior that suggest a progressiveness of sexual fantasy that enhances their psychopathology.

TRAUMA-CONTROL MODEL AND PARAPHILIA

Hickey, (2006) in his Trauma-Control model, provides a general framework (See Figure 9.1) for mapping out criminal pathways of serial killers from their formative years to the conclusion of their killing careers. These careers are influenced by genetic, environmental, and psychological conditioning from childhood to adult violent offending. Arndt, Hietpas, and Kim, (2005), in their empirical study of critical characteristics of male serial murderers, tested Hickey's Trauma-Control model and found it to be an acceptable framework in which to study serial killers, especially sex and lust murderers. The fact that the majority of serial killing has some intrinsic or extrinsic sexual component may enhance our understanding of sex crimes that are of a serial nature. Consider the life pathway of many serial sexual predators: childhood trauma, fantasies to suppress the trauma, masturbation to increasingly deviant and

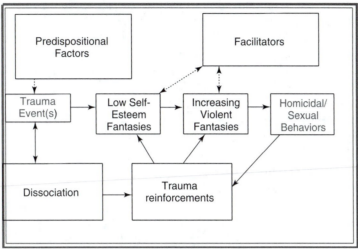

Trauma-Control Model for Serial Murder (Predispositional factors and facilitators may or may not influence the serial killing process.)

Figure 9.1   Hickey's Trauma-Control Model for Serial Murder

violent fantasies, sexual acting out (experimentation), and sexual violence. The pathway may be facilitated by drugs, alcohol, and/or pornography. As the offender develops into adolescence and adulthood, the childhood traumas are periodically reinforced by adult pain of rejection and loss. The offender's psychological need to subvert the trauma perpetuates the cycle of trauma-control. How common is this type of offender? McNamara and Morton (2004), in their ten-year study of serial sexual homicide in Virginia found that such cases represented only about .05 percent of all homicides in the state. Using the same protocol, they estimated the number of serial sexual homicides in the United States to be approximately 750 per year. This is by far a more accurate estimation of such crimes than original estimates of 5,000 or more per year. These estimates are in keeping with other researchers who have estimated the frequency of such crimes to be comparatively low (Hickey, 2005; Jenkins, 1988; Reiss & Roth, 1993).

PARAPHILIA AS A PROCESS OF CONDITIONING

Most important to this discussion of trauma-control is the *process* the offender experiences in his maladaptive, coping fantasies. Embracing certain paraphilia is far less by accident than by need. In concert with the Trauma-Control model, many developing serial sexual predators explore and condition themselves to clusters of paraphilia that are expressions of maladaptive control. Some serial rapists report histories of paraphilia, while others do not have any such histories. In histories of rapists where paraphilia is found, one might speculate that leaving a signature is an extension of his paraphilic behaviors and fantasies. For example, in a case where the serial rapist always carried a knife to force compliance, victims noted that the blade of the knife was pressed against his thumb rather than the blade facing toward the victim. In his fantasy, there was no weapon, but in order to have compliance he had to be armed. The conflict for the rapist was that he fantasized the meeting to be "consensual," that she wanted him and that they were having a consensual, intimate encounter. The attacker had no overt desire to harm the victim in any way, thus the knife was used more as a prop. Sometimes blood was found on the sheets. The attacker was so intense on wanting the victim to comply without force that he pressed hard on the blade with his thumb causing a bleeding wound. An investigator might conclude, without knowing the psychopathology, that the blood was proof of a signature. Although the blood was unintended, given the nature of masturbatory conditioning, the offender could easily have become conditioned to the sight of blood as he fantasized about the encounter. Jeffrey Dahmer collected carrion from road kills. He dissected the animals and, finding the glistening viscera arousing, masturbated to those images. Ultimately the sexual arousal from the organs of animals was transferred to humans, and Dahmer not only emerged as a serial lust killer but also an offender who sexualized the process of sexual violence.

Hickey (2006) points out that about half of serial killers in his study engaged in sexual activity with their victims. This does not account for the number of offenders who *sexualized* their criminal behavior without leaving evidence of some form of sexual assault. Sexualizing always involves fantasy development but may or may not involve sexual assault. This component can create difficulty in properly determining the motives and meanings of the attacks and methods used in those crimes. Pathways to sex offending can best be explored with emphasis on childhood development, fantasy, and masturbation. The process of developing paraphilia often begins with milder forms or *preparatory paraphilia* that can facilitate more violent forms or *attack paraphilia* (Hickey, 2006). The development process consists of interactive elements including paraphilic stimuli, fantasy, orgasmic conditioning, and facilitators such as drugs, alcohol, and pornography. The process of paraphilic fantasy may include stealing personal items such as underwear, toiletries, hair clippings, and photographs from victims. Other offenders have noted how they reach sexual climax each time that they burglarize a victim's home. For some sexual predators, the fantasy of burglarizing a home at night while the occupants are asleep is deeply eroticized, yet there is no sexual acting-out at the crime scene. Offenders who develop paraphilia may simultaneously engage in two to four different forms, often with one paraphilia more pervasive than the others. An offender is arrested, charged, and convicted of pedophilia, but unknown or ignored by authorities, he is also sexually self-gratifying through exhibitionism and collecting child pornography. These all provide him a modicum of relief and sense of control. Sexual predators, depending upon the type, often exhibit specific clusters of progressive paraphilic interests. For example, the most common type of stranger rapist, the compensatory or gentleman rapist, frequently engages in voyeurism, exhibitionism, and frotteurism. First these rapists want to see, then to be seen, then to touch.

Case studies and crime scenes demonstrate the pervasiveness and interconnectedness of paraphilia to violent crime. Understanding the role of paraphilia can facilitate crime scene investigations and contribute to effective classification, profiling, and apprehension of offenders. Failure to understand evidence of paraphilia involving sex crimes and specifically at crime scenes can hinder police investigations. For example, in one case, three female victims, a mother, a teenage daughter, and her friend were all murdered near a national park. The mother and friend were strangled in a hotel room and the daughter was found a few miles away in a wooded area, raped and nearly decapitated. Four men were eventually arrested based on the fact that a wallet belonging to one of the victims was found in the possession of the suspects. All four suspects had criminal records involving petty crimes and drugs. Convinced that the killers were in custody, law enforcement assured the public that the offenders had been caught. A few months later in the same vicinity, another young woman was found beheaded. Shortly thereafter, a man, who was an employee of the park, was arrested while hiding out in a nudist colony. He confessed to all the murders by providing incriminating evidence. The role of sexual fantasy and the behavioral characteristics of this lust killer were ignored in favor of a more obvious piece of physical evidence that appeared to tie the men to the crime. Later it was discovered that the killer had deliberately discarded the wallet in a neighboring town in hopes of thwarting law enforcement. The men had simply had found the wallet lying on the road. Had law enforcement evaluated the original crime scene as a serial sex crime and the purview of a solo predator, the focus of the investigation would have quickly shifted from the four suspects. In addition, there was nothing in the criminal histories of these young men to suggest a propensity or predilection toward violent serial sexual crimes.

The offender was known to be amiable, quiet, with a penchant for nudity. He frequented secluded lake areas to sunbathe. He was a loner who never dated and was not inclined to close friendships. He seldom used alcohol, smoked marijuana occasionally, and delved heavily into fantasy. He was artistic, and through his drawings, expressed his fantasies of murder and mutilation in graphic detail. They were always women, decapitated in the woods with monsters close by. Decapitations of his victims were sex acts by the offender, not just a method of killing. His fantasy was to be alone with them in a wooded area where he could totally dominate, terrorize, and act out his sexual fantasies. The offender was also suspected of being involved with the abduction, murders, and decapitations of at least three other women. Such an act of lust murder, in which the offender receives sexual arousal through the act of decapitation, is usually the purview of a solo sexual predator. The offender becomes sexually gratified by the fantasy of cutting into a victim's throat. The sense of sexual power gratifies and empowers the offender. Decapitation was his sexual signature linking him to other similar murders.

SEX CRIMES AND THE SEXUALIZED OFFENDER

Offenders who experience childhood trauma may sexualize those memories, a process described by Kaplan (1996) as *eroticization of childhood trauma.* A young child who witnesses the death of his brother as a result of playing with matches could easily be deeply traumatized by the event, especially if the trauma is reinforced by assertions from the family that had the boys not been playing with matches little Johnny would still be alive. To deal with this painful memory, a young male going through puberty might find that thinking about fire while masturbating brings a sense of relief and pleasure to the pain. He may also find the fire to be "magical" and finds himself drawn to setting fires. As he experiences puberty he may then masturbate to the thoughts of fire and may actually set fires and watches while he masturbates. Sexualized trauma may be produced by previous sexual abuse as well as from external sources. Seligman and Hardenburg (2000) noted that 25 percent of those found to have paraphilia were abused at one time. But many paraphilia do not generate from abuse, per se, but from conditioning to external stimuli that provides relief from fear, lack of intimacy, anger, guilt, loneliness, powerlessness, anxiety, rejection, and abandonment. Many developing offenders act out portions of their fantasies before embracing them completely. Westley Allan Dodd, killer of three young boys noted that he became bored with exposing himself. He then lured children into touching him. When that failed to satisfy him he escalated to molestation and then to murder (Fox & Levin, 2000, p. 36).

Exhibitionists, for example, who were sexually victimized in childhood, now sexualize the trauma of fear and violence through publicly exposing themselves, fantasizing and masturbating about the encounters. They seek attention to overcome feelings of low self-esteem, shame, and inadequacy. Exposing genitals is a sexualized form of *counter shame* that creates feelings of power, control, and sexual arousal (Silverstein, 1996). This is also demonstrated among some types of rapists. For example, a sadistic rapist may, through fantasies of violence, sexualize violent, ritualized acts that will ultimately be acted out. Thus, the *process of the aggression* that may include stalking, torture, bondage, beatings, and mutilations and other previously fantasized aggressions is sexualized in both form and content. Early trauma is compartmentalized and shrouded in compensatory fantasies involving violence and total domination (Carlisle, 2000). In a study by Neuwirth and Eher (2003), rapists who assaulted victims anally, or anally and vaginally were found to be more aggressive and demonstrate more sexualized behavior than offenders who raped vaginally.

SEXUAL SADISM

Crime scenes noted for signatures may have ties to *sexual sadism,* a DSM classified paraphilia involving, in most cases, real acts in which sexual excitement and gratification are derived from the psychological and/or physiological suffering of a victim, consenting or nonconsenting. These acts include intentionally harming animals; using objects to harm others such as whips and chains; *fantasy sadism* that involves sadistic fantasies without acts of sadism; *indirect sadism,* or indirect acts such as cutting off the hair of a victim without physical harm; *direct sadism;* direct injury to women such as stabbing, whippings, and beatings; mutilation of corpses, including necrophilia; and lust murder that includes anthropophagy (cannibalism) as evidenced in the cases of Jeffrey Dahmer, Edmund Kemper, and Gary Heidnik. Krafft-Ebing (1886/1965) noted that these forms of sexual sadism range from S&M (sadomasochism) consensual relationships to nonconsenting relationships that can produce injuries and death. In consensual relationships, sadism involves many forms of sadistic play including confinement, gags, bondage, role playing of dominant-submissive roles, humiliation, cross-dressing, urination/defecation, binding of genitals and breasts, flagellation, and other consensual acts. In nonconsensual sexual sadism, injury to the victim is common as well as the potential for death. These acts may include severe torture, rape, bludgeoning, vampirism, lust murder and necrophilia, genital mutilations, burning, and other injurious acts (*DSM-IV-TR,* 2000).

CRIME SCENES, CULTURE, AND SEXUAL MUTILATIONS

Consider murders with mutilation. Rajs et al. (1998) identified four types of motive based criminal mutilations: *Defensive mutilation* (dismemberment) is primary to dispose of a body and/or to make identification difficult to investigators. *Aggressive mutilation* stems from a rage killing in which the killer sometimes mutilates the victim's face and genitals following death. *Offensive mutilation* is often evident in lust murders and necro-sadistic murders. Offenders have necrophilic urges for post-mortem sexual activity with the victim, which may include pre- or postmutilation. Offender may also exhibit a sadistic desire to inflict severe pain, humiliation, or death while engaged in sexual activity that also involves pre- and/or postmortem mutilation. *Necromanic mutilation* involves sex acts with a corpse as seen in general necrophilia, along with a desire to mutilate and/or use body parts as trophies or to fulfill fetishes. Investigators examining victim mutilation must determine whether the degradations were part of the actual crime or secondary and inflicted to delay identification or to hide the corpse.

Now consider African *muti murder* that can appear to have the same elements of sexual mutilation yet have no merits of being a sex crime. These types of murders in Western culture would be considered to be sadistic, serial, or cult-related where criminal mutilation commonly occurs (Labuschagne, 2003). In truth, *muti* is a Zulu word meaning *medicine* and implies the intentional (although illegal) gathering of body parts for use in traditional African medicine. (Minaar, 2001). Muti murders are driven by greed for money, power, control, and prestige. Muti murders are not ritualized but rather culturally based murders done for the purpose of future good fortunes, and, for greatest effect, they must be carried out in a proscribed manner.

Human body parts removed from persons while still alive are considered to be exceptionally powerful for making strong muti. While a sadistic killer wants the victim to suffer and will use brutal force in such attacks, body parts in muti killings carry different meanings and functions for the person paying for the organ harvesting. Breasts are considered "mother luck" and are believed to attract women to businesses; genitals enhance virility; hands attract business and receive money; skulls protect members of a tribe from another; eyes provide better sight; Adams apple silences a witness intending to testify against a client; tongues smooth the way to a girl's heart (Labuschagne, 2003). Muti murders, although in appearance are sex crimes, are designed to be functional and only inflict wounds required to harvest the contracted body parts. The sadistic killer sexually degrades a victim through anal, oral, and vaginal rape, while the muti murder is fulfilling a contract and has no sexual theme. Serial killers who commit sex crimes or have sexualized their attacks have several victims while muti killings are not serial. Sadistic serial killers are fueled by fantasy and commonly leave distinctive patterns of mutilation on more than one victim, especially where lust murder is involved. Body parts sometimes are removed as trophies.

FORENSIC SIGNATURES

Signatures can be classified as *forensic* and *nonforensic*. Forensic investigations provide a multitude of investigative protocols that address signatures. Forensic signatures are those of a physical nature usually not intentionally left at crime scenes or other venues. For example, *heart-beat signatures* can now be filtered out of noise by use of sophisticated technology. Convicted criminals trying to escape from institutions or unwanted persons attempting entry into secure facilities can now be detected in vehicles passing through security checkpoints. Crime scenes are rife with signs of an offender's identity to the trained forensic eye. Crime scene analysis, for example, has developed methods for identifying *chemical signatures* in a victim's body that can be used to mark the exact time interval since death by examining chemical changes in decomposing organ tissue. Illegal drugs each have distinctive *synthetic signatures* that can be profiled and used in the detection of illicit drug manufacturing and "fingerprinting" street drugs to determine their origination. Through DNA, a criminal's *genetic signature* can be matched against past or future unsolved crimes. In crime labs, DNA offender profiles are developed and logged into computer data banks that systematically run cross checks with crime scene data banks. DNA from crime scene analysis can be gathered from blood, semen, skin left under nails during an attack, hair, and other physical material. Sometimes the forensic signature is part of the nonforensic signature created by the offender while committing the crime. A serial rapist who likes to ejaculate onto the breasts of his victims as part of his sexual fantasies leaves collectible DNA that can be matched to the offender. More and more offenders are being identified and convicted for crimes once believed to be unsolvable.

PSYCHOLOGICAL SIGNATURES

Signatures continue to be defined by those with experience investigating them and will vary from case to case. Crime scene signatures lack empirical, scientific research, and thus, much of what we know is based upon personal opinions. In comparing the opinions of two well-respected, experienced, American homicide investigators regarding signatures, the contrast was indeed startling. The first noted that signatures are extremely rare in cases of serial murder and almost never evident at crime scenes, while the other opined that they are very common in serial murder and always appear at crime scenes. The latter noted that in cases like Ted Bundy a signature was actually left at the crime scenes, but investigators failed to find it. The fact that the bodies were found months or years later and the crime scenes were subjected to the elements, wild animals and such, evidence of signatures had been permanently lost. The issue becomes even more clouded when these same experts cannot agree on a common definition for signatures. In fairness to these experienced investigators, there exists some truth to their findings. Indeed, signatures do exist; some are obvious, others obscure. In some cases, there is clear, physical evidence of signatures, and in others investigators note more psychologically driven signatures that require more than cursory inspections. Thus our knowledge base for signatures remains anecdotal until what we do know, what we think we know, and want we want to know is sorted out.

Part of the problem is arriving at consensus in definitions. The *method of operating,* or MO, is separate from motive and signature. MO includes techniques to commit crimes that may evolve as the offender becomes more skillful and confident in his crimes. *Signatures* are actions of the serial offender usually unnecessary in completing the murders. *Staging* refers to altering a crime scene to redirect an investigation away from the offender, while *posing* is deliberate placement of the victim or crime scene in order to draw the attention of investigators and/or to fulfill sexualized fantasies. While posing does occur in murder cases, the behavior is not common. *Personation*s are ritualized acts involving body positioning, mutilation, and symbolic gestures. *Undoing* is a form of personation. When the victim has particular meaning to the offender he may cover the face of his murdered victim with a towel or pillow, or turn the body face down. Crime scene signatures are distinctive marks or features that may indicate certain psychological characteristics in the offender. Thus, each sex crime scene may offer a unique look into the mind of a sexual predator. Signatures also referred to as *calling cards* or *trademarks* are not only the purview of serial killers. Kirby (2003) noted that signatures are also found in serial rapists and stalkers. Indeed, serial criminality is the foundation for signature development, as it becomes the personal marking of the offender. In cases of stalking, signatures may be fantasized and orchestrated through telephone calls, internet, fax, unwanted gifts, voice mail, following, workplace visits, home visits, vandalism, use of specific weaponry, or sending dangerous objects/devices to the victims.

Nonforensic signatures are considered to be a portion of an offender's behavior that extends beyond what is needed to commit the crime. Much of a signature suggests to investigators certain behavioral patterns and personality characteristics that are linked to his violent fantasies. With experimentation, serial sex offenders and/or offenders who sexualize their crimes can develop signatures that help the offender fulfill his fantasies. These crimes are not always the purview of physically violent offenders. They range from paraphiliacs such as voyeurs, exhibitionists, and scatologists who may develop sexualized signatures to violent serial offenders including offenders who are aroused by hurting children, men who slash and mutilate women, and lust murderers. Signatures may include crude or abusive language, necrophilia, use of foreign objects, bondage, mutilations, and many other tangible and intangible messages from the offender. As far as frequency of signatures is concerned, certain types of sex offenders and those who sexualize crimes will most likely vary depending upon degree of fantasy development, criminal maturity of offender, and paraphilic conditioning. Timing, or when the signature is created during a crime, will also depend upon the type of crime and criminal. For some, stalking and voyeurism become preparatory signatures that provide the offender with a greater sense of power and control before he attacks. Bodily degradation can be a manifestation of further psychological control. An offender may find that anal and/or vaginal insertion of foreign objects not only provides sexual arousal but also feelings of power and control.

Randy Woodfield, known as the I-5 Killer, followed his MO of finding women who were alone, binding them with duct tape, and forcing them to perform fellatio. Although he was physically far superior in brute strength and could easily have forced them to comply without using a weapon, Woodfield had sexualized the use of a weapon. By placing the barrel of a .38 on the forehead of his victim he became the immediate powerbroker. He reveled in watching the victims' fear, their submission, and their cries for mercy. Once he knew that he had totally dominated them he pulled the trigger. Like Cary Stayner who found sexual gratification while decapitating his helpless young victims, Woodfield fulfilled his sexual fantasies by shooting his victims when he felt most powerful because they were reduced to begging for their lives (four of his victims were not shot because they, like the others, did exactly what he ordered them to do, but were able to not act afraid. Consequently, his sexualized fantasies of total control were not realized, and he simply walked away from the victims). In this case, Woodfield did modify his MO in order to facilitate abductions, but his signature was always the intangible quest for ultimate and total domination of women.

The Trauma-Control Model suggests a progression in sexual fantasies of violence and control. Signature development is part of that process and will not exist in all cases, not even all cases of serial murder. Indeed, some cases of serial murder do not begin with any type of signature because the offender is still acquiring criminal skills and developing fantasies. When signatures are found in cases of serial murder, they are most likely to appear in later crime scenes.

Remember the progressive nature of serial sex crimes. Andre Chikatilo, the Russian Ripper, progressed in his violent fantasies from the point where he had first started luring children, stabbing them to death and masturbating onto their corpses to his final victims, whom he disemboweled and cannibalized their reproductive organs. Another serial killer who preyed upon gay men in Los Angeles developed a very distinctive MO. He lured unsuspecting gay men to motel rooms and while the victim was getting undressed for consensual sexual activity, the offender slipped a rope around his neck and strangled him to death. His signature was his rope, the same rope he used in each of his seven murders. During my interview with the killer, I asked him about his sexual interest in men. He denied such interests or having any sexual contact with the victims even though he admitted killing them all (in each crime scene, the victim was found nude and sodomized). The killer spoke almost affectionately about his rope, like it was an old friend. At least for some serial sexual predators, the weapon of choice has also been sexualized through conditioning and fantasies of violence.

A critical point to consider is that an MO may reveal well-concealed signatures that eventually surface as the fantasies of the offender develop. In one case, a victim was being stalked by her ex-husband who often visited her home and workplace. He was jealous that she was seeing other men even though they had been divorced for over two years. His harassments escalated, and she feared for her safety. During these encounters, the offender continued to profess his love for her. He left her candy hearts and cards with hearts. As the stalking progressed, so did the development of his signature hearts. At one point he came to her home and poured gasoline in the shape of a heart on her lawn. Later he poured acid on the hood of her car in a heart shape. Weeks later he returned one night, killed the family pet, cut out its heart and left it on the doorstep. His last visit became his climax when he arrived at her home on a Saturday afternoon, drove his vehicle onto her front lawn, and exited screaming and ranting about his love for her. Before police could arrive, the offender took out a knife, tore off his shirt and carved a large heart into his chest. The offender's MO was to stalk and harass his ex-wife at her home and workplace. His heart signature, developed in tandem with violent fantasies, became the focus of his rage. In this case, there was no indication that the heart or the stalking was sexualized, yet the development of signature was distinctive.

Bronswick (2001, pp. 85–89) lists the following as potential signature behaviors commonly found in serial murder investigations:

- Aberrant sex
- Attacks at the face
- Body disposal
- Cannibalism
- Decapitation
- Dismemberment
- Mutilation

- Necrophilia
- Penile/object penetration
- Picquerism (sexual arousal from repeated stabbing of a victim)
- Restraints
- Souvenirs (photos, clothing, jewelry, newspaper clippings)
- Torture
- Trophies (victim body parts used for sexual arousal)
- Weapons

Important to classifying these behaviors, many of which can be paraphilic, is to understand that some of these behaviors are *both* the mode of death, as well as the offenders' personal sexualized signature. One offender liked to surgically remove the eyeballs from his female victims while they were alive. Another cannibalized the sexual organs of his young victims, disemboweling them while still conscious, and yet another skinned his victims to make lampshades, eating utensils, and clothing. Signatures are helpful in profiling criminal behaviors and can link offenders to crimes. Besides the obvious ability of law enforcement to link signature crimes is the potential to determine the level of progression and sophistication of the predator. This often means that a first-time offender will not demonstrate the *savoir faire* found amongst experienced predators. A sexual predator will sometimes change his MO in order to elude police, but it is far more difficult for them to alter their fantasy-based signatures (Hickey, 2006). This does not mean that fantasy is so controlling that signatures cannot be changed. The fact that they evolve opens the door to change, especially if the offender is conditioned to more than one paraphilia.

Harvey Glatman liked to abduct women and take photographs of them before and after the sexual assaults and murders. Robert Keppel, an expert in serial murder cases and who was directly involved in the investigation and arrest of Ted Bundy, noted Glatman's desire to take photographs as his personal signature:

> His photos were more than souvenirs, because in Glatman's mind, they actually carried the power of his need for bondage and control. They showed the women in various poses: sitting up or lying down, hands always bound behind their backs, innocent looks on their faces, but with eyes wide with terror because they had guessed what was to come (Keppel & Birnes, 1997, p. 37).

In this particular case, Glatman had sexualized the photographs and most likely derived sexual gratification from viewing the photos. Glatman had sexualized the very process of taking photos, as well as having them as trophies of his control. This fantasized and conditioned behavior of Glatman became an integral part of his crimes. Customizing crime scenes was not part of his MO and thus provided uniqueness when compared to other cases of female abduction and murder.

CONCLUDING THOUGHTS

An FBI study of 128 elderly women who were murdered found that examination of the totality of the offenses, including detailed information regarding the sexual components of the killings, yielded far more insights into both the offenders and victims than simply concluding that the crime involved a rape and murder (Safarik, Jarvis, & Nussbaum, 2002). While this may seem obvious, such detailed information-gathering and analysis of crime scenes is relatively new protocol. Many of the over seventeen thousand law enforcement agencies in the United States lack the funding, manpower, and training to adequately carry out investigations at this level. Researchers and law enforcement must continue to collaborate in order to better understand the many nuances of crime scene investigations that involve sex crimes and sexualized behaviors. Understanding criminality requires an understanding of fantasy, sexual conditioning, and crime typologies. Application of criminal profiling can be especially helpful in "red flagging" specific physical and psychological crime scene behaviors (Douglas & Munn, 1992). Improved data analysis both within crime scenes and across crime scenes will greatly improve understanding of crimes, victimization, aggression, and sexual violence (Knight, Warren, Reboussin, & Soley, 1998).

THE SPECTRUM OF BLOOD-DRINKING BEHAVIORS

10

Mila Green McGowan

While some of the acts related to vampirism and blood-drinking are neither harmful nor problematic in a criminological sense, a portion of true vampiric acts can be classified as illegal and amoral. Therefore, it is important that the full gamut of vampiric behavior and blood-drinking pursuits be acknowledged, categorized, and understood. Many embrace vampirism as a way of spicing up their sex lives, especially since sadomasochism and fetishism are a big part of vampire culture. Today, communities of vampires appear to be growing throughout the world. However, these enthusiasts refer to their subculture as "vampyre" and not "vampire." In this alternative lifestyle, participants can have their darker sides accepted and celebrated. However, a select few are drawn to this community because vampirism is a true identity for them (Wolff, 1999). While most people just play at vampire, some consider it a religion, others do it to ingest human blood—and a few even kill for it.

EXISTING TYPOLOGIES

Out of the many myths and limited clinical vampirism studies, various typologies of vampiric behavior have developed. Generally, the versions vary according to the vampire's physical appearance, prey, motivations, gender, and means of victimization. However, nearly all have common themes of bloodsucking, killing, and possible deceit (Casey, 2000). As no vampire considers his or her behavior to be psychotic, bizarre, or abnormal, instead considering it solely an alternate lifestyle (Morse, 1993), large clinical samples with which to create reliable taxonomies are rare.

THE PREVAILING TYPOLOGY

In 1985, Herschel Prins created a four-category typology of vampirism that is still widely accepted today. The first type is *complete vampirism* in which sexual arousal in the vampire is related to blood, the death of the victim, the ingestion of their blood, and possible necrophilia and necrosadism. Others may refer to this vampirism as blood lust. The second type is *necrophilia* in which the death of the victim, sexual arousal, and the abuse of the corpse is present but no drinking of the blood occurs. Instead, sexual satisfaction comes from the death and not from blood or flesh ingestion. Third is the *blood-only* type of vampirism. Death is not important with these vampires, as only blood extraction and possible blood ingestion is. This type includes mutual vampirism, in which the death of either participant is not the goal and mutual blood exchange is a continual activity. The last type of vampirism is *auto-vampirism.* These vampires are sexually aroused at the ingestion or the sight of their own blood; no one else is involved.

THE AUTHOR'S PROPOSED TYPOLOGY

A more descriptive typology based on a compilation of numerous sources follows. It encompasses all forms of vampiric and blood-drinking behaviors.

The "Vampyre" Community

In this alternative lifestyle, vampirism is seen as a way to express oneself sexually. Actual blood ingestion in this group is not common, and many people who participate in the vampire culture "do not drink blood, many even find the notion unappealing, if not altogether unsafe" (Ramsland, 1998, p. 19). The vampyre persona provides participants with an erotic self-image and represents, to many, sexual freedom (Wolff, 1999). Ramsland (1988) found great "overlap between the vampire world and fetish culture—bondage and discipline, sadomasochism, dominance and submission" (p. 11). Vampyres report polygamy and jealousy are their two biggest "sins," not physical abuse, blood-drinking, or murder. To them, vampirism has become a lifestyle choice in which relatively young people (in their twenties and thirties), who merely enjoy biting and possibly drinking some blood, can interact (Morse, 1993). Drug use is commonplace. Most vampyre participants are intelligent, very spiritual and artistic, and would easily be considered free from mental illness.

The vampyre community itself categorizes members into two distinct groups: Role-players and Lifestylers. Role-players occasionally wear teeth implants and play with the whole vampire image but maintain traditional lives and jobs the bulk of the time. They often engage in role-playing board games or Internet vampire games fashioned after the original "Dungeons and Dragons" game design (Linedecker, 1998). Lifestylers wear permanent teeth and vampire-type clothing every day while working in vampire or Goth businesses, e.g., tattoo parlors and piercing shops, bondage and/or pornography stores. Within this group, some participants may drink blood, but because of the growing threats behind blood ingestion (e.g., HIV), feeding circles made up of medically-screened and willing donors and other vampires have been established as the common source of blood (Ramsland, 1998). Many Lifestylers report true vampires do not kill people but have the highest admiration for life; they must live by the laws around them as they are not superbeings (Linedecker, 1998).

Psychic and Psychological Vampires

Psychic vampires prey on the energy of their victims, feeding on aura and not blood. They leave victims feeling extremely weak and in need of nourishment but not drained of any actual fluid. Psychic vampirism is defined as "one person is drained of energy or life force by another" (Neil, 2000). Often this terminology is found in psychoanalytic literature. As such, in family contexts, the vampire theme relates to the psychodynamic aspects of a harmful early mother-child relationship, in which a voracious caregiver who is self-absorbed sucks energy from a developing child (Neil, 2000). This type of vampire may or may not be sexual in nature, as sexuality is not germane to the "sucking" of life.

Psychological vampires often engage in covert vampirism. They drain the emotional resources of another through their serious personality disorders. The psychological vampire is more a "vampire metaphor" than an actual vampire type, but this type of vampiric action tends to be the common idea underlying mistaken psychic vampire labels (Ramsland, 1998). All in all, such behavior is what forms the basis for codependent relationships.

Sexual Vampires

Many cultures associate sexuality with vampirism and see it as a means to obtain blood from others. In some cases, the methods by which modern vampires obtain blood sexually are achieved through either socially deviant or illegal methods and not mutual partner exchange or arranged donation. Many sexual vampires are thought to have undiagnosed psychological or psychiatric problems and come from dysfunctional homes (Morse, 1993).

A. **Nonconsensual, In-person Sexual Vampires.** This subtype of sexual vampire feed on blood obtained from biting activities and are most commonly associated with the normal perception of a vampire (see the Noseferatu myth). This traditional type of vampire sucks the blood of victims following or during sexual intercourse. These vampires gain energy in this way to prolong their life or fulfill their thirst for blood (Casey, 2000). Some who fall in this category of vampire may also have psychopathic tendencies (see Criminal vampires).

B. **Nonconsensual, Spiritual Sexual Vampires.** Spiritual vampires claim to be capable of taking on ghostly forms. These vampires then visit strangers at night, in their ghostly form, to have sex with the person and feed from them. When they leave, the victim may recall the event only as a dream because the blood sucking leaves them in a hypnotic state and completely lacking energy. This dream state provides the spiritual vampire with a vulnerable future victim for additional feedings. These vampires also claim to be capable of taking on the appearance of another person, making it relatively easy to enter homes of strangers. Spiritual vampires, though sexual, are more interested in sex as a means to acquire blood rather than the act of sex itself (Casey, 2000).

C. **Consensual Sexual Vampires.** It is thought that victims of consensual vampires must invite the vampire into their home before they engage in mutually beneficial vampirism. The drinking of blood during sex is seen by both partners as an act of intimate communication, but the exchange does give the vampire power over their partner and provides them with attention while making them feel important (Morse, 1993). Bourguignon (1983) believes that "sucking the blood of a living partner is more frequently practiced by women than by men and this practice is associated with an apparently normal sexual orientation" (p. 288). One female vampire remarked "I think the idea of draining the life force of another human being gives a sense of power, a sense that is overwhelmingly erotic, that is so intimate" (Ramsland, 1998, p. 265).

D. **Vampires who Prefer Sexually Energized Blood.** Some sexual vampires are those who draw power from the sensual ecstasy and heightened sexual tension of their partner during consensual sex. These sexual vampires feed on the flow of pleasure from their partner, generally just before the moment of orgasm (Casey, 2000). Though blood is still the focus, other body fluids may also be ingested, e.g., sperm and vaginal secretions, as they too are believed to be sexually energized. Such a sexual vampire claims the intercourse actually restores balance in their partners following the acquisition of their blood. They believe their partner is able to enjoy the raw pleasure of being fed upon when their blood is taken during an orgasmic state. Following the drinking act, the vampire enters their partner's body to perform the "healing act" of intercourse. This healing is deemed necessary as victims are believed to be a hypnotic state following the feeding.

Jon Bush, aged twenty-seven, exemplifies this type of vampire. In 1997, he was arrested in Virginia Beach, Virginia, after luring at least eight teens into joining his vampire community so that he could molest them (Linedecker, 1999). Bush told the girls they would become vampires if they had oral sex or intercourse with him and allowed him to bite them during sex as he need to drain the sexual energy from them to survive (Ramsland, 1998).

E. **Blood Fetishism.** Blood fetishists view blood drinking as an intimate, sexy turn-on that qualifies as foreplay to later sexual intercourse. Yet, this type of blood drinking is not always associated with being a vampire. Blood fetishists view sex as one-half of the means to achieve their erotic goal, while drinking or viewing blood is the other. For these vampires, blood is more orgasmic than sex could ever be. Sex tempts or manipulates the victim into providing blood fetishists with blood to drink or to view. But, the fetishist's erotic focus is on fresh flowing blood, or images of it, and involves their sexual partners but not the sex itself (Noll, 1992)

Clinical Vampirism

Clinical vampirism refers to the (sometimes periodic) psychological compulsion to drink blood; the irresistible urge for blood. Such a condition is rare and, when found, does not necessarily involve sexuality, though a strong sexual component has been found in many cases. Sufferers of clinical vampirism may exhibit an unusual affinity for the dead and display an uncertain identity: "I am a male with a great need for another's life force, blood cell to blood cell. Blood is the source of life and death, the price of preemptive sacrifice. I use blood in my ritual as a symbolic reconciliation with myself" (Ramsland, 1998, p. 23). Some clinical vampires drink blood for the purpose of increasing vitality and prolonging life without the problems associated with being a true vampire (Casey, 2000), as they have no expressed interest in sex. Other clinical vampires report blood ingestion brings them "mental relief without any ability to psychologically comprehend the experience or ascribe it any meaning" (Jaffe & DiCataldo, 1994, p. 536).

Actual blood ingestion quells the existing compulsion for blood, similar to the anxiety reduction reported by other patients who suffer from less deviant compulsions (such as those in obsessive compulsive disorder). Some clinical vampires report the blood-drinking urge has existed since childhood while other say it came on in puberty. Still others appear to only develop the blood compulsion once they are exposed to it by established vampires (Morse, 1993).

A. **Renfield's Syndrome and Mentally Ill Vampires.** Based on the beliefs that vampires hold regarding perpetual life and blood ingestion, Renfield's syndrome sufferers believe that by ingesting the life force of other living things, their own life force will be increased (Noll, 1992). The stages in this syndrome include the following. A pivotal event leads to some form of blood drinking for the first time (usually in childhood), and the experience of bleeding or tasting blood is found exciting; this excitement to blood can later be associated with blood after puberty and sexuality develops. Then, auto-vampiric activities occur; self-induced scrapes and cuts produce blood for the sufferer to ingest. Masturbation may or may not accompany these activities. Zoophagous activity comes next (the drinking of the blood of animals). This blood can be obtained legally, e.g., from slaughterhouses, or illegally, e.g., from the abuse of animals. Finally, true vampirism results as sufferers begin to procure and ingest the blood of humans either by stealing blood (from hospitals and blood banks), through consensual blood exchange activity, or by illegal and sadistic means.

Some scholars opine that "[V]ampirism as a single entity is extremely rare but, when present is often related to diagnoses of schizophrenia" (Jensen & Poulsen, 2002, p. 47), other schizophreniform disorders, severe psychopathic disorders, hysteria, mental retardation, or borderline and schizoid personality disorders. Others believe establishing a true relationship between diagnosed psychopathology and vampirism is hard to do as so few cases exist (Jaffe & DiCataldo, 1994), and in many cases of schizophrenia, other peculiar dietary habits are evidenced, aside from blood drinking.

In psychotic vampires, delusions of exsanguination and an all-consuming need to be provided with nourishment are common (Prins, 1985). Nevertheless, it has been concluded that "[V]ampirism is not a primary symptom of any psychiatric or psychopathic disorder, and its specific motive distinguishes it from other blood-related aberrations" (Hemphill & Zabow, 1992, p. 63). Richard Trenton Chase, dubbed the "Vampire of Sacramento" is one example of the interplay between mental illness and vampirism. Between 1977 and 1978, he shot and eviscerated two women and one infant, then drank their blood. He began by eating live animals and drinking the blood of dead ones in his teens. He went on to develop bizarre delusions and underwent treatment for mental illness. His delusions included beliefs that his own blood supply was dwindling, his pulmonary artery had been stolen, others were poisoning him, and UFOs and the Nazis were trying to kill him.

Another mentally ill vampire killed his grandmother and tried to drink her blood, because he believed she was stealing his blood. Previously, in prison, he attempted to kill a prison guard for his blood. He evidenced a history of delusions and fantasized about killing his mother. He reported a fascination with blood since age five and became preoccupied with witchcraft and horror stories. As a teen, he began to kill and eat animals, while developing a nocturnal lifestyle. He said he heard voices telling him vampires were trying to kill him, so he thought he could escape the voices if he could become a vampire himself and have eternal life. Once incarcerated, he was diagnosed as a paranoid schizophrenic (Mohandie, 2000).

B. **The Physiological Compulsion to Drink Blood without Mental Illness.** In these cases of clinical vampirism, the blood drinkers believe they must feed regularly to survive, but their ideas are not part of a larger delusional system. They often function normally in society. They report physical withdrawal symptoms without blood, e.g., night sweats and nightmares. Further, they feel that blood drinking helps them lead an actualized life and the blood takes on a mystical significance for them. The drinking is seen as a nutritious practice that increases their strength and immunity and prolongs their life (Morse, 1993). Some also believe the blood may make them clairvoyant and enhance their extra-sensory perceptions.

Cases of such vampires have been found throughout history. For example, in the 1600s, a Hungarian Countess, Erzsebet Bathory, killed six hundred peasant girls to either bathe in or drink their blood to retain her youth (Jaffe & DiCataldo, 1994). In Santa Cruz, California, in 1992, Deborah Finch murdered Brandon McMichaels by stabbing him twenty-seven times. She then drank his blood to keep his memory with her. In Florida in 1986, John Crutchley abducted and raped a nineteen-year-old female hitchhiker, keeping her hostage for twenty-two hours and draining and drinking nearly half her blood. He told her he was a vampire and needed her blood. He was also suspected in a series of unsolved homicides (Linedecker, 1998). In 1991 in Rio de Janeiro, Marvello de Andrade killed fourteen boys, sodomizing them and drinking their blood so that he could become as beautiful as they were. Both Crutchley and de Andrade's behaviors might also be categorized as criminally vampiric.

Autovampirism

Autovampirism has been defined as the sexual or emotional satisfaction gained from ingesting or seeing one's own blood. This type of vampirism is the rarest form of blood drinking. Jensen and Poulsen (2002) believe the existing anecdotal reports of auto-vampirism are from patients with severe mental illness only. Auto-vampires as a group are socially isolated and have limited sexual experience. They show an absence of schizophrenic process, a tendency towards depression, strong intellectual defenses, emotional and psychosexual underdevelopment, marked passivity and internalized conflicts between life and death (Bourguignon, 1983). This behavior is seen more often in females. Three subtypes have been described by the literature.

A. **Self-induced Ingestors.** These people bleed themselves and ingest the blood. Case studies have found when this behavior exists in a male, the act has a overwhelming sexual component and masturbation accompanies the blood letting. These males have reported they often fantasize about drinking another's blood while drinking their own, usually another male. Some people in this category hold psychotic beliefs, such as the ingestion of their own blood is life giving and part of a purification process. Further, they may have command delusions that order them to ingest their own blood or delusions that without drinking their own blood, they will disappear (Jensen & Poulsen, 2002).

B. **Voluntary Ingestors.** Voluntary ingestors do not induce their own bleeding, but when their blood becomes available for any number of reasons, e.g., while vomiting, or during a medical procedure, they ingest it.

C. **Auto-haemofetishism.** These autovampires bleed themselves but do not ingest their blood (Prins, 1985). As such, this last form of autovampirism often leads to severe hemorrhages and possibly, death. It is most common in women with similar life circumstances. For example, all of Prins's (1985) cases of haemofetishism evidenced "early affective deficiencies and disturbed family environments, and a history of medical and surgical interventions since childhood" (p. 292). These patients were found to have trouble forming trusting relationships so they used their "illness" to get attention and affection (like those suffering from Munchausen's syndrome might do).

Criminal Vampires: Lust Murderers and Psychopaths

Vampirism has been linked to several serial killings. Historically, it has been associated with the compulsive sexual presentations seen during bizarre killings. These blood drinkers are often diagnosed as psychopathic and evidence sadism, while there is also ample evidence of other perversions and a strong desire to control the victim (Hickey, 2002). "Vampirism may be the cause of unpredictable repeated assaults and murders and should be looked for in violent criminals who are self-mutilators" (Hemphill & Zabow, 1992, p. 62).

In the childhoods of these offenders, we see impulse control difficulties, undersocialization, early conduct disorders, histories of animal mutilations, and a lack of empathy. These criminals may have no allegiance to vampirism per se and are only psychopathic killers who merely use their teeth as a murder weapon. Morse (1993) believes extreme psychopathic and sadistic vampires will use their teeth or any other means to kill, withdraw, and swallow the blood of their victims. This last category of vampire is the most frightening: "[W]hen vampirism in embedded in a psychopathic personality disorder, the potential for extremely dangerous behavior seems compounded" (Jaffe & DiCataldo, 1994, p. 542). While some would argue that these criminal vampires are not necessarily interested in indulging in cruelty or self-punishment per se, but that their unprovoked violence while in a frenzy to obtain blood only appears to be a variant of sadomasochism (Hemphill & Zabow, 1992), others believe some repeat murderers and rapists who exhibit vampirism only do so as a secondary aspect of the killing and do not kill solely for blood (Noll, 1993).

Some cases of criminal vampirism are described below. In France, Eusebius Pieydagnelle, a butcher, became so obsessed with blood that he killed six women. He later admitted that the sight and smell of fresh human blood brought him to orgasm (Ramsland, 2002). The "Hannover Vampire," also a butcher, killed almost fifty male youth by luring them into his meat shop and biting their throats. He drained their blood and ate some of their bodies; using the rest for inexpensive meat in his butcher shop (Morse, 1993).

In 1872, Vincenz Verzeni killed several females and drank their blood by tearing off hunks of flesh with his teeth. As a boy, he was reported to enjoy decapitating chickens and watching the blood shoot out (Noll, 1993). Peter Kuerten stabbed and/or hammered to death several people. He then cut their throats post-mortem and drank their blood (Morse, 1993). In 1949, in United Kingdom, John Haigh clubbed nine boys to death, slit their throats, and drank their blood.

In Italy during the 1970s, Rantao Antonio Cirillo attacked more than forty women over a seven-year period. He tied them up, raped them, and bit them on the neck. In Poland, in 1982, Juan Koltrun killed two of his seven rape victims and drank their blood. In the Soviet Union between 1978 and 1990, Andrei Chikatilo was arrested for the murders of more than fifty people. He admitted to eating their body parts and drinking their blood. Reportedly the blood and fear of his victims gave him erotic excitement (Hickey, 2002).

SATANIC BELIEFS AND CRIMINAL VAMPIRISM

Some criminal vampires evidence and report allegiance to the devil or other demons as their reasons for killing and/or engaging in blood-drinking behaviors. Many of these persons may also qualify for delusional or obsessive disorder diagnoses. Recently, two such cases have emerged in Europe. In 2002, in Germany, a satanic worshipping couple stabbed a friend to death and drank his blood. They blamed their actions on orders from the devil (Cleaver, 2002). In 2001 in Britain, Mathew Hardman, aged seventeen, murdered an old women in her home and ripped out her heart so that he could drink her blood. The trial judge remarked to the boy that vampirism had become an obsession with him and that it was clear the boy thought the vampire myth was true; he would achieve immortality if he drank another's blood. The crime scene showed the attack was planned and deliberate despite the boy's obsessive and delusional beliefs in vampirism. Hardman also left satanic marking at the crime scene (Livingstone, 2002).

NECROPHILIA, CANNIBALISM, AND CRIMINAL VAMPIRISM

Vampirism as a condition has been used throughout the psychiatric literature to explain other pathologic behaviors such as the drinking of blood, sexual intercourse with deceased victims (necrophilia) and the eating of flesh (cannibalism). Vampirism is linked in some respects to cannibalism in that it fulfills a need of the vampire to become more completely a part of another person (by eating parts of them) or to build up additional energy stores. Necrophilic acts have been associated with vampirism as part of a person's need to confront death and discover its mysteries. Since vampires believe in the fusion of life and death, necrophilia seems to be a means by which certain vampires are capable of uniting the two and embracing them through copulation with corpses (Casey, 2000). Necrophilia itself is divided into three types: violent, fantasy, and romantic (Ramsland, 1998). Violent necrophiles have such overpowering urges to be near a corpse that they kill in order to have one. Fantasy necrophiles have fantasies in which death figures prominently in their erotic imagery so they may ask or hire sexual partners to act dead. The romantic necrophile feels such a strong emotional bond with their once-alive lovers, they keep the corpse around after death.

CHAPTER

VAMPIRISM

Mila Green McGowan
and Matthew Peck

PARAPHILIA AND VAMPIRISM

A paraphilia is defined by the presence of recurrent and intense sexual arousal through fantasies, urges and behaviors that generally involve animate or inanimate objects (*DSM-IV,* 1994). However, a paraphilic's sexual arousal is achieved predominantly through means that are generally not socially acceptable and may even be illegal because of the sometimes sadistic nature that underlies a paraphilic focus (e.g., sadomasochism) (Hickey, 2002). It is important for those practicing in the fields of mental health and law enforcement to gain a significant understanding of paraphilia generally and the crimes associated with them so that means can be developed to improve crime investigation and enforcement, deviancy deterrence, and treatment efforts for paraphiles.

Despite a lack of academic categorization, several paraphilia have been well researched and are fairly well understood. However, a vast number of paraphilia are abundant in practice and generally remain ignored in academic literature. One such paraphilia is vampirism.

For classification purposes, vampirism falls into the Paraphilia, not otherwise specified (NOS) category, with the erotic focus being on blood (see *DSM-IV-Tr,* 1994). Diagnosticians must consider the possible diagnostic overlap between a blood or vampirism paraphilia and a sexual sadism paraphilia, as the blood drinking may also involve inflicting pain on others. However, Milner and Dopke (1997) assert such an overlap does not exist in true vampirism as blood drinking and sadism are not the same aberrant behaviors; victim suffering does not always accompany the blood interest seen in those who practice vampirism.

DEFINING VAMPIRISM IN THE PAST AND TODAY

The name *vampire* originated in Slavic language as early as the sixth century (Jaffe & DiCataldo, 1994) and has several meanings, including flying being, drinking or sucking, and wolf (Gwennifer, 2000). It began to appear in English language at the beginning of eighteenth century and was used to refer to a corpse who left the grave to drink the blood of the living. The French later adapted the term vampirism to include acts of necrophilia, necrosadism (sadist impulses towards the dead), sadonecrophilia (sadistic sexual impulses towards the dead), and necrophagia (the eating of dead flesh). History tells us that Lucus Apuleius, a Roman writer and philosopher who lived from 125 to 180 A.D., was the first to give reference to vampirism in a novel he wrote about two wicked sisters who drank the blood of a man until his death.

By the nineteenth century, various perversions, including vampirism, were beginning to be discussed in the psychiatric literature as problematic and increasing in prevalence. An evolution in the ideas underlying vampirism came about at that time says Bourguinon (1983). He remarks, "a progression to more realistic and explicit relations of love and hate between the living and the dead (was evident), while mythological beliefs in demons, werewolves and sorcerers declined" (p. 280). Though vampirism has been more recently defined as sexual arousal resulting from blood extraction and refers mostly to behaviors directed towards the living, this definition is not the only one currently in use. Various scholars continue to put forth their own classifications and definitions of blood drinking, with or without overtly sexual behaviors.

Bourguinon (1983) defined vampirism as a "group of perversions that express a pathological relationship between death, blood and sexuality"(p. 278), while Morse (1993) specified that vampirism means blood-drinking that takes place during a sexual or lovemaking act. He concluded that biting and blood ingestion is always involved in his definition. However, Vandenbergh and Kelly (1992) defined vampirism as "the act of drawing blood from an object (usually a love object) and receiving resultant sexual excitement and pleasure" (p. 29). The sucking or drinking of the blood is an important part of the act, but not an essential one to their definition.

VAMPIRE MYTHS

THE FEMALE VAMPIRE AND HER VICTIMS

The original eastern vampire legends refer to the vampire as a female. Her motivation was fueled by anger and revenge for being the target of societal wrongdoing (Wilson, 2000). According to research by McNally and Florescu (1994), Eastern myths generally concur on belief in vampires, including such countries as China, Babylon, Egypt, and Greece. In 600 B.C., Chinese mythology told the story of a blood-sucking demon called Chiang-Shih who transformed into a wolf to attack victims. Similarly, the ancient Peruvians believed in a vampire called Canchus who gained energy from the life of sleeping babies by drinking their blood. Pellegrino (1994) argues that the Hebrew tradition tells of a female vampire called Lilith who was the first wife of Adam. According to legend, she was cast out of Eden prior to Eve. She had no knowledge of the difference between good and evil. She could live only at night and survived on the blood of children and wild beasts (Pellegrino, 1994).

Other ancient cultures believed vampires were female as well. In Mexico, the legend of Tlahuelpuchi has been told. This female vampire transformed into different animal forms to attack infants and suck their blood. Hebrew tradition tells of a female vampire called Lilith, who was the first wife of Adam (Morse, 1993). According to legend, she was cast out of Eden before Eve's creation. She had no knowledge of the difference between good and evil and she could live only at night and survived on the blood of children and wild beasts. Several countries believed vampires predominantly attacked other women's babies out of revenge for their own personal suffering (Wilson, 2000).

THE MALE VAMPIRE AND HIS VICTIMS

Around the nineteenth century, existing myths and legends about vampires were refocused onto males. This gender switch is largely attributed to the writings of Bram Stoker and his creation of Dracula. Stoker based his character on Vlad the Impaler, a cruel and sadistic Walchian warrior of the fifteenth century. Historians have uncovered Vlad often put his enemies', and sometimes friends', heads or entire bodies on stakes pre- and postmortem. The local populace also referred him to as Count Dracul (dragon or devil). Though he was not known to bite anyone, evidence now shows he did drink human blood and could thus be classified today as a clinical vampire. He dined among his impaled victims (McNally & Florescu, 1994) and dipped his bread into his victims' blood before eating it.

While Stoker incorporated many of the historical vampire myths into the now well-known vampire persona called Noseferatu or Dracula, he added some mythology of his own. This "new" vampire attacked predominantly female victims while they slept and engaged in sexual intercourse or acts with them during the blood sucking. These male vampires were thought to target innocent and pure women, sensually seducing them into illicit encounters with him.

Citizens of the Balkans believed male vampires turned into dogs and killed all the dogs of a village to make the village females more vulnerable. They characterized vampires as poor and rural people who had risen from the grave. The vampiric activity was thought to be mostly nocturnal, though in some cases, the recently dead (and now vampires) were seen during the day (Gomez, 1998).

THE PURPOSE AND ROOTS OF VAMPIRISM MYTHS

Most ancient cultures have myths that evoked "sadistic and masochistic relationships between the dead and the living" (Bourguinon, 1983, p. 279). According to Bourguinon, these myths served a purpose, to reveal and yet repress men's sexual interest in dead women, as most societies believed that fear and respect for the dead would limit necrophilic and necrosadistic tendencies.

Morse (1993) reported "beliefs in vampirism are based on basic human values and fears" (p. 183). These basic values include the following. First, uncertain beliefs about death and the future are involved. Second, questions about how deadly infections, such as the plague, are spread are important. Third, seeing blood as the essence of life, vitality, and strength is key. Finally, issues and discomfort with sexuality and male-female intimate relations are germane. Others believed vampires are only mythic creatures that reflect our dark human nature. For example, McCully (1992) suggested the vampire image represents the symbolic split between the animal and the social nature of man. As an archetype, vampires allow us to see the human condition in another realm (i.e., our mortality) and the vampyre culture allows youth to both express themselves uniquely and reflect the change between generations (Ramsland, 1998).

Myths also served another more sinister purpose in Western society—to further mark the distinction between majority and minority cultures. Activities such as blood drinking and cannibalism, either real or imagined, have often been ascribed to minority subgroups in a society to create a justification for mass executions, persecutions and "witch-hunts" of these out-groups (Noll, 1992). Periodic vampire scares in nineteenth century throughout Europe have influenced our present-day beliefs about vampires. Based on the "[P]revalent practice of premature burials during times of plague (and) by the large numbers of itinerants and beggars that abounded in such times and . . . that many took refuge in vaults and graveyards" (Prins, 1985, p. 666), vampiric myths are not surprising. These myths led to a "widespread folklore telling of a society of vampires that threatens humanity" in the seventeenth and eighteenth centuries (Noll, 1992, p. 5).

VAMPIRISM AND SEXUALITY

Vampirism has many definitions that can be found in literature. The methods by which blood and energy are obtained, and the reasoning for obtaining them may account for the variance among definitions. A vast culture associates sexuality with vampirism and uses it as a means to obtain blood and energy from others. Sexual vampires are those who draw power from sensual ecstasy and the heightened sexual tension of their partner. Sexual vampires feed on the flow of pleasure from their partner. This is generally achieved at the moment of orgasm through bodily fluids (Casey, 2000). In some cases, the methods by which vampires obtain energy and blood through sexuality are achieved through socially deviant methods, and in some cases illegal methods.

Specifically, spiritual vampires claim to be capable of taking on ghostly forms. These vampires claim to visit strangers at night, in the ghostly form, have sex with the person, then leave while the victim may recall the event only as a dream. Victims may not recall the event clearly because the blood sucking leaves them in a hypnotic state, completely lacking energy, providing the vampire with a completely vulnerable victim. The victim will only remember the experience of the vampire's visit as a dream. In one article, the author even joked that these vampires may be arrested for sex crimes such as attempted rape, then end up in a psychiatric institution when the vampire tries to explain him or herself to police. These spiritual vampires also claim to be capable of taking on the appearance of another person, making it relatively easy to enter homes of strangers uninvited. Often the vampire will visit the same victim repeatedly. Spiritual vampires are more interested in sex for the acquisition of blood rather than the act itself (Casey, 2000).

However, because of the varying types of vampires, several differing accounts explore how vampirism is associated with sexuality. Some vampires claim to feed on consensual victims. These consensual victims must invite the vampire into their home before they engage in mutually beneficial vampirism. These types of vampires claim to restore balance in their partners following the acquisition of their blood and/or energy. They believe that their partner is able to enjoy the raw pleasure of being fed upon, while the vampire takes their energy and/or blood. Following the act, the vampire enters their partner's body to perform a healing. This healing may be necessary as victims are believed to be a hypnotic state following the feeding (Anonymous, 2002). From the above, it is clear that in some cases victims participate in sexual relations, blood transfer, and release of energy willingly. Thus, some forms of vampirism would be considered deviant while remaining within the boundaries of the law.

Blood fetishism is associated with sexuality for those practicing vampirism. However, for the vampire the act of blood drinking is the turn-on while the sex is the turn on for the victim. Vampires view blood drinking as an intimate, sexy turn-on. It is often used as foreplay, or as a prelude to sexual intercourse. Also, blood drinking is not always associated with being a vampire. Some practitioners drink blood for the purpose of increasing vitality, and prolonging life without the problems associated with being a true vampire (Casey, 2000). However, some who practice vampirism view sex only as a tool for a means to achieve the goal of blood drinking. For these vampires sex blood is more orgasmic than sex could ever be. Sex is only used as a means to tempt or manipulate the victim into providing them with blood.

Another view on vampirism and sexuality is provided by Rucki (1997) in her article entitled *The Sexual Motivation Behind the Vampire*. She reports the blood associated with the loss of virginity during sex provided the vampire with the motivation to connect blood and sex. One particular vampire, called the Lamia, was a beautiful woman who seduced young men for the purpose of drinking their blood. During intercourse she would climax, at which point she would suck the victim's blood. She would utilize her sexuality to manipulate the men into vulnerability. Rucki further argues that the sucking of blood is connected in sexuality because of its roots in infancy through kissing. The drinking of blood gives the vampire sexual satisfaction through sexual means, and thus, the acts of vampirism are sexual in nature (Rucki, 1997).

THE PREVALENCE OF VAMPIRES

The practice of vampirism is not likely to be discovered readily except in criminal cases, by chance in psychiatric evaluations, or during treatment for self-induced injuries (e.g., autovampirism) (Hemphill & Zabow, 1992). It is highly unlikely anyone will report blood-drinking behavior openly, even in the most intimate settings, including therapy.

However, one study, completed in 1974 in France, reviewed fifty-three known cases of vampirism. The vampires were found to range in age from eleven to fifty-seven years old, while their victims were anywhere from seven months to seventy years old. No specific psychopathology was found, but the documented diagnoses were varied and plentiful: 19 percent were deemed mentally retarded, 4 percent psychotic, 5.5 percent depressed, and 13 percent neurotic (cited by Bourguignon, 1983). Recently, The American Vampire Research Center reported that some fifty to sixty true vampires exist in the United States, and there are some five hundred worldwide (Ramsland, 1998).

EXPLANATIONS FOR VAMPIRIC BEHAVIOR

PSYCHOLOGICAL AND DEVELOPMENTAL

Morse (1993) argues that vampirism may be explained in terms of anatomical and physiological stress reactions. He argues that vampirism may be created as a means for a temporary escape from the stresses of life, and in this way it may be considered healthy. However, he continues by addressing the sadistic, ritualistic, and cultic nature of vampirism and the dangers it presents. He concludes by recommending that future research be done to investigate extensive psychological and physiological testing for the purpose of determining whether or not there are patterns which could predispose a person to becoming a vampire (Morse, 1993). Other research has found massively disorganized oral sadistic regressions, feelings of depersonalization, a confused sexuality, and multiple concurrent delusions and thought disorders underlying vampirism (Jaffe & DiCataldo, 1994).

Vampirism has also been addressed from a psychoanalytic and Freudian perspective (See Neil, 2000; Wilson, 2000; Johnson, 2002). In his article, Johnson (2002) addresses the lectures of Laurence Rickels, who argued there is a strong link between vampirism and Freudian theory. He argues that when a loved one passes on, people tend to project their guilty feelings onto the corpse. Vampirism is a product of this projection and comes in the form of the corpse returning to life. This occurs when people are unable to properly grieve for the deceased. Consequently, grief-induced fears are projected onto the dead. In his analysis of psychic vampirism, Wilson (2000) explored the aspects of psychic vampirism and issues that arise in psychoanalytic treatment. He concludes that the vampire is a symbol of a transformed, horrific mother figure that promoted extreme anxiety in the child. He argues that changes in the transformed mother, who may be seen as draining the energy from the child, may in fact explain the development of the mythical vampire. Accordingly, since imperfect, inconsistent mothering is not rare, many people may be susceptible to vampirism.

Psychoanalysts also argue fixation at an early stage of development (the oral stage), coupled with very primitive mental and emotional functioning, are to blame (Prins, 1985). Arrest in the sado-oral stage of psychosexual development is thought to leave a child with the need to bite and a "[B]asic ambivalence and conflict between biting and being bitten." (Benezech, Bourgeois, Boukhabza, & Yesavage, 1981, p. 290). Social learning theorists hypothesize that a history of being bitten by care-givers teaches a child that pain, humiliation, and biting is effective means of control.

Finally, behavioral theorists look to the first reported innocent pairing of blood with pleasure, e.g., stopping a bleeding cut by sucking on it, as the beginnings of vampirism (Morse, 1993). Crossing the lines of social convention and breaching a cultural taboo by drinking blood marks the beginning of the disease of vampirism. By violating the taboo, excitement is experienced because the person engages in a forbidden act. This excitement only serves to reinforce the behavior and increases the likelihood that it will be repeatedly engaged in (Noll, 1992).

ENVIRONMENTAL

Vampirism concepts are ever-present in today's language and found in both verbal metaphors and colloquialisms (e.g., to devour someone with your eyes, don't bite the hand that feeds you, etc.). Vampire images can be found everywhere in our society: in food and snacks (e.g., cereal, pasta, candy bars, and sweets), used as spokespeople in TV commercials, on records/CDs and in music videos, in newspapers (real stories and political satires), as popular Halloween costumes, and on children's shows and cartoons (The Count on *Sesame Street,* Count Duckula) (Morse, 1993). All these images and semantics lower our inhibitions to actually blood-drinking or others who adopt the vampire persona.

The Internet has provided practitioners of vampirism with abundant means to unite, communicate, and fulfill acts associated with the paraphilia. Internet sites are common, where interested vampires can go to view erotic stories specifically focused on vampires, and view scenes associated with vampirism including graveyards, and cemeteries, view scenes of vampires engaged in erotic scenes, etc. There are also sites specifically dedicated to vampirism practices including bondage (associated with the power and control possessed by vampires), Goth and paranormal fetishes, blood fetishes, and many others. One of the major search engines, Yahoo!, provides a directory for those practicing vampirism, which contains over two thousand vampire groups. This paraphilia is easily accessible and seems to be practiced by many.

MEDICAL AND GENETIC

Historically, a number of rare medical conditions or diseases have been linked to vampiric presentations. Though today's medical community does not ascribe to the below explanations in many cases, our deeply-embedded cultural myths may have some factual basis in these disorders.

Porphyria and Hematodypsia

Congenital porphyria is a rare blood disease in which a person's blood lacks an essential iron component called haem or porphrin. Doctors do not believe drinking blood can curb the disease, but some sufferers do so to alleviate their painful symptoms (Maccaskill, 2001). This genetic disorder produces reddening of the eyes, skin and teeth, receding of the upper lip, cracking and bleeding of the skin, and photosensitivity (Jaffe & DiCataldo, 1994). Hematodypsia is a psychological, stress-related disease in which sufferers become blood addicts. They like the taste of blood and therefore crave it. They act just as other substance addicts do when given blood (e.g., they report sexually-related pleasure similar to a drug-induced euphoria) (Morse, 1993).

Anemia and Syphilis

Individuals with pernicious anemia lack the necessary vitamin B_{12} in their blood. They may drink blood hoping to gain the vitamin, even though evidence shows it does not alleviate the condition (Morse, 1993). Congenital syphilis sometimes causes children to be born with sharp and pointed anterior teeth called Hutchinson's teeth, that may appear vampire-like. Additional light-blindness and a pallid complexion associated with syphilis babies, could easily have been linked to vampirism in the past (Morse, 1993).

Rabies

The most likely disease to be historically associated with vampirism is rabies. It has one very important characteristic in common with vampirism; when a man or animal is bitten by someone or something with rabies, they become inclined to bite as well (although the transmission of rabies by human bite is very rare). In the eighteenth century, there were frequent reports of injuries due to bites by rabid dogs and wolves (Theodorides, 1998). Studies have proven the link between aggressiveness and various dysfunctions in the limbic region; symptoms common to both rabies and epileptic patients.

Other features attributed to vampires have also been associated with rabies or rare epilepsy diagnoses. Rabies symptoms commonly show up in humans two to eight weeks after being bitten. The general symptoms include loss of appetite, fever, disturbed sleep, anxiety, fatigue and pain, and abnormal sensations around the bite. Later, sufferers develop a form of encephalitis as the disease reaches the limbic system. They then begin wandering, are restless, exhibit feelings of terror, hypersensitivity to stimuli, insomnia, muscle spasms, and hydrophobia (fear of water). Many of these symptoms may look like vampirism as the muscle spasms cause facial grimaces (with teeth pressed outwards) and patients emit involuntary hoarse groans. Frothing at the mouth occurs from an excess of saliva. Hypersexuality may result and a predominance of violent behavior is observed. Rabies diagnoses are seen more frequently in the males of any species, including humans (Gomez, 1998).

CONCLUSIONS

Vampirism is deeply rooted in cultural mythology, and clearly apparent in today's society. Evidence provided in literature, crime history, and on the Internet clearly demonstrates the connection between vampirism, sexuality, and the possibility of it leading to extremely social deviance. The relative ignorance of vampirism in paraphilia classifications is indicative of the lack of academic research attention given to what seems to be a relatively significant paraphilia. Legal scholars, criminologists, law enforcement personnel, and mental health practitioners should address this paraphilia to further investigate the outcomes of vampirism. Identifying precursors, possible treatments, and preventative measures may lead to a decrease in the victimization from the paraphilia. And finally, criminal investigations, deterrence, and proactive policing may enable law enforcement and the courts to decrease future criminality committed by those associated this unrecognized paraphilia.

Vampirism, and its association with other paraphilia, presents possible dangers to society because of the deviant, and oftentimes sadistic, nature of the blood drinking. Although the prevalence seems to be undetermined, access and apparent activity of vampirism practices seem to be abundant. However, academic research is very limited on the topic and provides little insight into the development of interests in vampirism, and its potential effects on individual's pathology. Further research is clearly needed.

C H A P T E R

UROPHILIA

A Perversion of Humiliation and Control

COREY VITELLO

On his birthday, an old guy visits his physician for his annual exam. The guy says to his doctor, "I feel great but I have these weird spiritual experiences." The doctor says, "What do you mean"? The old guy says, "When I get up in the middle of the night to use the bathroom, I open the door and God turns the light ON for me. When I'm finished, I shut the door and God turns the light OFF for me." The doctor says, "I've seen this before in guys your age. You're not connecting with God . . . you're peeing in the fridge!!"

—taken from "Joy's Puddles Pages," www.weaselwerks.com/peebits.htm

Urophilia (or urolagnia) is a paraphilia associated with the sexual arousal from the sight of urine or the sight of someone urinating (Fedoroff, Fishell, & Fedoroff, 1999; Seligman & Hardenburg, 2000); psychoanalysts refer to it as *urethral eroticism* (Sigusch, 1998). The behaviors encompassing urophilia are commonly referred to as *golden showers* (urinating on another person as part of a sexual encounter) or *watersports* (erotic urination). Because urolagnia is referred to as a paraphilia (although it is not yet distinctly specified as such by the American Psychological Association [APA]), the conduct involves "intense sexually arousing fantasies, sexual urges, or behaviors generally involving . . . the suffering or humiliation of oneself or one's partner . . . that occur for over a period of at least 6 months . . . [which] cause significant distress or impairment in social, occupational, or other important areas of functioning" (American Psychiatric Association, 2000, pp. 522–523).

Urophilia can be classified as a sexually masochistic paraphilia. According to the DSM-IV (1994):

> The paraphiliac focus of Sexual Masochism involves the act (real, not simulated) of being hu-
> miliated, beaten, bound, or otherwise made to suffer . . . Masochistic acts that may be sought
> with a partner include restrain (physical bondage), blindfolding (sensory bondage), paddling,
> spanking, whipping, beating, electric shocks, cutting, "pinning and piercing" (infibulation), and
> humiliation (e.g., being urinated or defecated on, being forced to crawl and bark like a dog, or
> being subjected to verbal abuse)" (p. 529).

Some sadomasochistic behaviors that are often associated with urophilia are the acting out of fantasies. The conduct that is born from these twisted desires often provides an escape from internal psychological stress while at the same time it provides
immediate pleasure and satisfaction (Goodman, 1993).

According to ELYSA, (2002), there is no apparent erotic reasoning behind the
act of urinating on another, or being urinated upon. "The pleasure comes from seeing the person humiliated or wanting to be humiliated, all depending on who is urinating and who is receiving . . . The sadism comes from wanting to humiliate the
person by urinating on them, whereas masochism comes from wanting to be humiliated by someone urinating on them" (p. 1). According to Alison, Santtila,
Sandnabba, and Nordling (2001), urophilia can be classified in a cluster of hypermasculine behaviors because, as Weinberg, Williams, and Moser (1984) report, watersports was once common in the gay male leather scene as displays of manliness and
toughness. Interestingly, according to Alison et al. (2001), sadomasochism involving
behaviors meant to humiliate have recently been associated more with females and
straight men than with homosexuals.

Undoubtedly, urophilia is considered a socially deviant behavior, and consequently it is thought to be a paraphilia. However, perhaps there is a biological connection to explain why some humans desire to be urinated on or to drink urine.
Money (1981) suggests that humans have the same built-in biological drive to use
the mouth to clean urine and feces off their babies as do wild chimpanzees:

> Even though human primates have graduated from using the mother's snout end to keep the
> baby's tail end clean, it is safe to assume that, as a species, we still possess in the brain the same
> phyletic circuitry for infant hygiene as do the subhuman primates. Just as males and females
> have nipples, so also do both sexes have these pathways that, when they become associated with
> neighboring erotic/sexual pathways, produce urophilia and coprophilia [sexual arousal from
> feces] as paraphilias (Money, 1981, p. 98).

Conceivably, it stands then, that although the desire to be urinated on, to urinate on
others, or to even drink urine may be culturally and socially deviant, physiologically
humans may be wired to do the acts which most people find repulsive. As Money appropriately proposes, because urophilia is a paraphilia, and like other paraphilias,
once the deviant behavior is paired with something rewarding—in most cases sexual
arousal and climax—the urophiliac may become positively conditioned to the sight,
smell, feel, and taste of urine.

According to McCammon, Knox, and Schacht (1993) sexual masochistic paraphilias such as urophilia can sometimes be traced back to childhood associations

with punishment and sexual stimulation. Levine, Risen, and Althof (1990) suggest that paraphilias start early on in childhood and then continue into adolescence and adulthood. Although there is a paucity of literature as to the origins of urophilia specifically, one might propose that for many urophiliacs an association between frequent bedwetting, humiliation, punishment, and sexual gratification in childhood might provide some insight into their deviant sexual behaviors.

As a behavior, urophilia may appear quite disgusting and socially deviant. However, if the Internet might be used as an indicator of how many people are interested in watersports, the number of people who may be labeled urophiliac would be staggering. According to the Internet at the time of this writing, there are over a thousand sites dedicated to urophilia. One site in particular, "Joy's Puddles Page" (found at www.weaselwerks.com/peebits.htm) gives viewers and interested parties insight into watersports and the virtues of urine:

> Watersports is the sharing of something intimate and personal between individuals who are emotionally bonded and trust each other, and who seek to deepen their bond and their trust with this special token of their love. Urine is mostly water. Besides that, it contains the following: soluble minerals in excess of your body's needs, mostly salt, but with some magnesium, calcium, potassium, phosphate, and nitrogenous. Nitrogenous material, primarily urea. Also present is a more complex compound called creatinine . . . these substances are nontoxic. There is also a small amount of uric acid and even a smaller amount of ammonia. Neither of these [are] present in enough concentration to do any harm" (Joy, 2002, ¶ 2–3).

Several websites post pictures of men and women urinating—sometimes into toilets, sometimes in their own pants, and many times on one another—to be freely viewed by other urophiliacs (e.g., the site, www.peeing.com posts hundreds of these types of photographs boasting, "The web's wettest pee site! Great hidden pee cams!"). Many sites list classified advertisements that seek to connect urophiliacs with each other. Numerous ads contain pictures of individuals similar to those found on other, more socially acceptable Internet matchmaking sites. Examples of classifieds are taken from the thousands listed on the site.

It should be noted that, though many paraphilias are not criminal—urophilia is not—they can often be the gateway to behaviors that are indeed criminal, abusive, and deadly—especially if one's partner is not a consenting adult. Seligman & Hardenburg (2000) warn, and Perry & Orchard (1992) concur

> Paraphilias often change over time, escalating in frequency and severity and sometimes progressing from one paraphilia to another. A common pattern is for the disorder to begin with solitary behaviors such as frequent masturbation in conjunction with paraphilic fantasies, progress into behaviors such as exhibitionism and voyeurism that involve others but do not include physical contact, and then continue into more aggressive sexual behaviors (p. 109).

Urophilia is oftentimes just one sexual act in the repertoire available to individuals involved in sexual masochistic lifestyles. Santtila, Sandnabba, Alison, and Nordling (2002) investigated whether people who engage in multiple forms of sadomasochism, did so progressively. Specifically, they wanted to know whether there is an escalation in intensity of behaviors culminating in greater intensified experiences, as is the case for normal heterosexual sexual interactions. Gagnon (1990) and Simon and Gagnon (1986) refer to this escalation as an example of a sexual script: e.g., kissing leading to more intense foreplay leading to sexual intercourse. However, Santilla et al. (2002) were more interested in the progression of sadomasochistic behaviors over serial encounters. By questioning 184 members of two sadomasochistically oriented clubs, they found that individuals tend to purposefully begin by engaging in less intense behaviors and then graduate to more intense behaviors. For individuals involved in urolagnia, it appears they often begin with various urination themes and then often progress into themes in combination with enemas and coprophilia.

AN ANALYSIS OF UROPHILIA

Urophilia may be a means for people who lack self-esteem and self-worth to be humiliated; the way they believe they ought to be treated. Urophiliacs may have been traumatized as children. Currently, there is a dearth of research available correlating urophilia with childhood molestation, excessive and embarrassing bedwetting, or any other childhood misfortune. However, there is research associating a desire to engage in sadomasochism with childhood trauma; therefore, it stands that, because urophilia encompasses behaviors that are categorized by the APA as sadomasochistic, many, if not all, urophiliacs may have developmental issues worth exploring.

If the research by Santtila et al. (2002) is correct, then urophilia is often used as a measure of one's masculinity. Combine this with the desire to control and humiliate another person as well as derived sexual gratification, and one could readily see how violence could become the underlying motive of the behavior. Humiliation in and of itself is a form of violence. Both the humiliator and the humiliated must recognize the violence in their actions and yet both consent to this sadomasochistic ritual. There is a clear exploitation of even a willing partner. That is, when one person seeks out through classified advertising another human being to act as a target to urinate on, only self-doubting persons respond. In addition, those who respond to ads with people looking to be urinated on are expressing their need to control, violate, hurt, and humiliate another person. Either way, urophilia is a paraphilia that perpetuates harm to others regardless of consent.

Webmasters such as Joy from "Joy's Puddles Pages" might disagree. In fact, she endorses urolagnia and provides web surfers some suggestions on how to incorporate urine in lovemaking. Yet there are certainly violent undertones in her lovemaking suggestions, e.g., "pretending to be children again adds a fun twist to this game" of peeing on one another. Sexually exploitative individuals may progress from peeing on himself, to watching others pee, to acting "like children" during consensual sadomasochistic play, to actually finding a child to molest. Money (1981) suggests that humans might be evolutionarily wired to the desire to lick urine off children in order to keep them clean, as some primates do.

CONCLUSION

Urophiliacs become sexually aroused from the sight of urine or being urinated on which is not normal, socially acceptable behavior. The urophiliacs themselves might not find their behavior deviant or unhealthy. However, fascination with urine may serve as a beginning to more intense, potentially dangerous interests with other sexually deviant behaviors. Some urophiliacs may resort to child molestation, rape and degradation of children in their quest to humiliate, control, and defile another person. Although some wish to normalize urolagnia as a natural act, community standards maintain that such behavior contributes to an unhealthy and potentially dangerous lifestyle.

COPROPHILIA

Origins, Development, and Treatment

MELISSA MCDONALD-WITT

As long as humans have felt the desire for sexual relations there have been deviant ways of fulfilling those desires. Any given object or part of the body can be part of a deviant fantasy but some are more common than others. Common paraphilias involve human feet, inflicting and receiving pain, voyeurism, rubbing up against unsuspecting people, children focused, and exposing genitalia in public places. However, other paraphilias, albeit abnormal, do not have a victim involved but rather someone who is voluntarily involved in the activity. One such paraphilia, coprophilia, involves sexual arousal from defecating or being defecated on by another person. People who engage in coprophilia also become aroused from the smell, sight, and occasionally the taste of feces. Paraphilia, in general, is a topic that may receive much discussion but the research is limited, especially in terms of paraphilia that are not as common as others, including coprophilia.

PARAPHILIA

The need and desire to copulate is necessary in order for any species to survive, but in human beings the need to copulate goes beyond the physiological drive to keep the species alive. According to Kaplan (1996), sexual motivation is activated when the right amount of hormones are present and the external environment supports a feeling of safety and provides the individual with the opportunity for sexual activity. With human beings the power to imagine and fantasize about different people and situations while engaged in sexual activity is a strong motivator. Fantasy opens up a whole new world of possibilities when considering the type of sexual activity some-one may be engaging in, and it opens a door to a diverse world of deviant fantasies. According to Kaplan (1996), "Although they are seldom consciously aware of doing this, most normal men and women learn to manipulate the stimuli that regulate their sexual appetite. These unwitting tinkerings with our sexual desires can serve both healthy or pathological motives" (p. 41). The individualistic sexual manipulations then become very important when understanding the development of paraphilias and the importance of pornography in the development of a deviant sexual fantasy.

Mawhinney (1998) suggests that the occurrence of paraphilia have been on the rise, especially since the beginning of the twentieth century because of the increased production of pornography and the greater access to that pornography. According to Mawhinney, the number of x-rated video rentals has increased from 75 million in 1985 to 665 million in 1996, with the United States leading the world in the manufac-turing of x-rated videos. Along with the increased production of x-rated material, the advent of the Internet has further allowed the average person to have easy access to pornographic material that would otherwise have been difficult to gain access to be-fore the Internet. Mawhinney (1998) also stated that during the last three decades, the laws against pornography have become more lenient and more subjective, espe-cially in terms of defining the meaning of "community standards" in trying to prose-cute pornography that could be considered obscene.

Mawhinney's study (1998) suggests that with prolonged exposure to pornogra-phy comes greater acceptance of the material, thus creating a normalized view of the unusual sexual behavior. He also stated that the increased acculturation of pornogra-phy in the United States has lead to an increase in deviant sexual fantasies, behav-iors, and paraphilia. However, Langevin, Lang, and Curnoe (1998) found that the prevalence of deviant fantasies in sex offenders was not higher than that of the aver-age non–sex offender. They suggest that fantasies may not be a reliable measure for understanding the origin of paraphilia since there is no way of knowing if the behav-ior or the fantasy was first part of the sex offenders sexual world. To simply look at fantasies as a way to understand the origins of paraphilias is to naively look at the ear as the source of hearing, without looking at the brain as the main component in the ability to hear. One must look at the reason for the fantasies, beyond the avail-ability of pornography, because the next question would be to wonder why the per-son was drawn to pornography in the first place. Accordingly, the research on paraphilias must focus on the origin of the desire to view pornography. Although pornography may progress the paraphilia, it does not explain the initial draw a per-son holds toward viewing sexual material deemed deviant.

One must consider the importance of understanding childhood trauma that may be linked to the development of a paraphilia. Human sexual desire starts at a young age and usually involves the relationship between the mother and the child (Kaplan, 1996). A person's first sexual experiences often help form a map of the type of behaviors and feelings that are appropriate surrounding sexual desires. If a per-son's development is "normal," the sexual fantasies and behaviors that a person de-velops are based on interactions that are mutual and involve an age-appropriate, living human being. However, if a person's development is characterized by trauma then sexually inappropriate fantasies and behaviors may develop. Situations that may initiate paraphilia include inadequate mothering or neglect, sexual abuse, any other form of abuse, cruelty toward child by any adult or other children and the cultural or religious repression of normal developmental sexual exploration and desires (Kaplan, 1996).

Kaplan (1996) also found that under certain circumstances some painful childhood memories can be transformed into sexualized memories, a process that Kaplan described as "the eroticization of childhood trauma." The eroticization may begin because the child is trying to master or overcome the trauma and by changing the suffering into something pleasurable, the person then feels a sense of power and triumph. One study suggests that 25 percent of those who report a paraphilia have been abused at one time (Seligman & Hardenburg, 2000). This transformation can be from the trauma of previous sexual abuse, however, it is not limited to sexualized trauma (Kaplan, 1996). Family discord, culture, and religion will also play a part in a person's understanding of the world, sexual activity, self-worth, and appropriate behavior (Seligman & Hardenburg, 2000).

Seligman and Hardenburg (2000) suggest that paraphilias can provide immediate pleasure and/or an escape from some sort of internal uneasiness and anxiety surrounding sexuality. The person may likely experience a build-up of tension and a preoccupation with sexual behaviors and attempt to stop the sexual behaviors and fantasies. However, individuals who act on the paraphilic fantasies may perceive an initial sense of relief and release, followed by power and guilt. They likely wish for intimacy in relationships but fear rejection, and by focusing on the paraphilia they avoid feelings of loneliness, anxiety, anger, rejection, revenge, and powerlessness. Comorbid diagnoses are often common with people who have a paraphilia, including depression, anxiety disorders, obsessive-compulsive disorders, impulse disorders, and often other paraphilia-related diagnoses (Myers, 1995; Seligman & Hardenburg, 2000).

Although half of the people who have a paraphilia are married; a large majority of those who are married also suffer from sexual dysfunction with their partner (Seligman & Hardenburg, 2000). These people usually have a problem with social skills and a lack of self-esteem and thus resort to fantasy and the pursuit of the release of negative feelings through the paraphilia. A cycle develops that can reinforce the person's fantasies of pleasure derived from paraphilic sexual interaction, including a physical sexual gratification (orgasm) and an emotional release of negative thoughts (Seligman & Hardenburg, 2000). Added reinforcers to paraphilic sexualization can be the mystery and excitement of actively hiding fantasies and behavior, which may result in amplified paraphilic interests (Munroe & Gauvain, 2001).

According to Seligman and Hardenburg (2000), most people who suffer from paraphilia have specific personality characteristics. Most have low self-esteem, show little insight into their own behaviors and the needs of others, have little empathy, usually feel out of control in their lives, usually don't have a clear sense of who they are and do not handle stress in appropriate ways. In addition to the predisposition to develop paraphilia, the characteristics may also isolate the person from others so that deviant sexualization of objects and fantasies become easier than dealing with reciprocal sexual interactions with others.

Although under most circumstances development of paraphilia can be traced back to childhood trauma and the sexualization of that trauma and the progression of the paraphilia can be linked to the moderate use of pornography, paraphilias can have other organic origins. A study by Simpson, Tate, Ferry, Hodgkinson, and Blaszczynski (2001) found that sexually deviant behaviors increased after traumatic brain injury. They could not find any premorbid factors that influenced the likelihood of sexually deviant behavior after a traumatic brain injury, nor could they find any differences in brain damage between those who showed sexually deviant behavior and those who did not exhibit inappropriate behavior. The findings suggest that although brain damage could play a part in the acute onset of a paraphilia after head trauma, no reasons or patterns have been found as to why some develop sexually deviant behavior after head trauma and some do not (Simpson et al., 2001).

Although brain damage provides a small glimpse at a possible origin of sexually deviant behavior or paraphilia for some individuals, it is not the origin for all paraphilia. Only by looking at a person's history, background, parents, culture, religion, and childhood trauma, can understanding start to form as to why a person gravitates toward an object rather than a person for sexual gratification.

COPROPHILIA

Coprophilia is sexual arousal by the act of defecating, and/or viewing or smelling the odor of feces. It is a paraphilia that is considered to be a paraphilia not otherwise specified in the *Diagnostic and Statistical Manual of Mental Disorders IV-TR*. It is not considered common, and consequently research on this particular paraphilia is limited. Some research has been done on mentally handicapped people who engage in coprophilia or coprophagia (eating of fecal matter), but the origins of the paraphilia is seen as an organic developmental problem, not one that usually has its origins in childhood trauma.

One research article by Wise and Goldberg (1995) looked at a case study of a nonpsychotic man who practiced coprophilia and later coprophagia. This man was sexually aroused when he would defecate and then spread the feces on his body and genitals, while masturbating. He only partook in the activity when his wife was out of the house and admitted to having limited sexual contact with his wife during the marriage. The paraphilia became more severe when he started ingesting his own fecal matter after a period of marital problems.

According to Wise and Goldberg (1995), he was raised by a mother he described as cold since she and his father had divorced when he was two years old. At the age of eight, his father died allegedly from a car accident, but he later found out, when he was an adult, that his father had committed suicide. Around the age of nine, he started to have a fascination with and sexual arousal for fecal matter. He would often defecate in his underpants in public places because he found it arousing and during adolescence started to masturbate along with the defecation in his underwear.

The treatment that was given was antidepressants, psychotherapy, and Alcoholic's Anonymous. He suffered from depression and felt the paraphilia was something like an addiction. He was able to see that his wife was very much like his mother, that the sexualization of feces began soon after the death of his dad, and most of the desires to spread fecal matter on his body came after he would feel some sort of rejection, vulnerability, anger, or feeling of insignificance (Wise & Goldberg, 1995).

Themes of inadequate coping skills, low self-esteem, regression, and revenge all played a part in the case study but that does not provide an adequate look at the origins of coprophilia. An inherent part of smearing fecal matter on one's body is humiliation, and yet this case does not seem to address this probable part of the paraphilia (Santtila, Sandnabba, Alison, and Nordling, 2002). Comprehensive studies need to be conducted about the psychodevelopmental origins of this disorder in order to understand fully where the smearing of fecal matter becomes sexualized.

TREATMENT

Much as the research about the origins of specific paraphilia is limited, so is the research about efficacy of treatment of specific, less common paraphilia. According to Seligman and Hardenburg (2000), cognitive-behavioral techniques are used in the treatment of paraphilia, as well as group counseling. Through aversion therapy, reconditioning, cognitive restructuring, and thought stopping, cognitive-behavioral therapy tries to recondition the person into socially acceptable sexual fantasies and behaviors. Paraphilia, though, have a high recidivism rate, and so other forms of treatment have arisen from the need for better, more effective treatment.

A study done by Gijis and Gooren (1996) found that of all pharmacological options used to treat paraphilia, the anti-androgen cyproterone acetate (CPA) and medrozy progesterone acetate (MPA) appear to be successful at reducing paraphilic-related activity. However side effects can reduce the medication compliance. Some side effects include reduced erections, sleepiness, depression, weight gain, breast formation, hair loss, and reduced ejaculation. Fluoxetine has also been used to treat paraphilias with moderate success as well, but has much of the same side effects that CPA and MPA have on the body (Gijis & Gooren, 1996). The problem, though, with all pharmacological interventions, is that although the physiological problems may be solved, the psychological origins of the behaviors still exist and thus medications really only provide one part of the healing equation.

SOCIETY'S REACTION

Coprophilia, is difficult to research because the academic information on the subject is very limited beyond a basic definition of the paraphilia. Although the incidence rate of the paraphilia may not be high, it seems logical to assume that an interest would reside in the origins of behavior that can lead to sexual assault, rape, and murder.

Although coprophilia does not have an inherent victim, it does deserve some attention when one thinks in terms of severity and distortion of sexual activity. This paraphilia is closely related to that of urophilia and klismaphilia, both of which involve bodily functions and both fall into the category of an unhealthy obsession with bodily functions. It is not difficult to concede that after one experiences a desensitization of the sexualization of bodily functions other bodily functions, parts, or even the fascination follow. The focus of coprophilia could easily become a fascination with how the body works including a progression to strangulation, evisceration, and mutilation.

It has been suggested that the origins of the disorder stem from the childhood and the possible maladaptive relationship with the mother. However, exclusively relying on the mother/child relationship as a sole explanation would be an overgeneralized assumption. Other factors that could play into the development of coprophilia include low self-esteem, depression, inability to cope with stress, an addictive personality, and feelings of being socially unacceptable or dirty. One must think of the social norms that one is breaking when becoming sexually stimulated by fecal matter in order to understand a possible other part of coprophilia. A person must feel asocial, as if they are the waste of society and their families, or must think of themselves as socially unacceptable in order for this paraphilia to develop in a person.

The lack of research on coprophilia and many other less common paraphilia speaks to the lack of desire to study disorders that are not only hard to conceptualize but also are very socially unacceptable. Coprophilia does have the potential to become a serious problem and develop into something that could lead to the victimization of others and possibly sexual assault and murder. Treatment seems to be lacking in scope and efficacy; it seems that we are at the absolute beginning stages of understanding the development, course and treatment of all paraphilia, including coprophilia.

CHAPTER

PARTIALISM AND THE SEXUAL OFFENDER

The Fascination with Lactation

Toyia McWilliams

14

Throughout history, human sexuality has been both celebrated or repressed. In Ancient Rome, the expression of sexuality was prominent in that the people of Rome continually sought ways to satisfy their sexual needs and urges. During this time, paraphilia such as klismaphilia became widespread, as the use of enemas was a major source of sexual stimulation and gratification (although the Romans did not consider this deviant sexual behavior). As time went by, Western civilization began to set standards in regards to sexual norms and mores, which ultimately affected people's expression of sexuality.

In Puritanistic societies, sexuality was deemed inappropriate if done purely out of enjoyment and pleasure, as sex was intended for procreative purposes. In addition, the Victorian era also contributed to sexual inhibition in that expressions of sexuality were supposed to be repressed. Psychoanalyst Sigmund Freud, as a product of his environment, developed theories that essentially provided society with the notion that there is "perverted" sexual behavior. For Freud, having sex without love was considered a perversion. In addition, homosexual men were once considered abnormal or a perversion simply because they did not have the ability to procreate. Eventually, such theories continued to suggest that individuals have the capacity to engage in deviant or perverse sexual behavior; consequently, this lead to the development of paraphilia. According to Gardner (1993), paraphilia (or any form of atypical sexual behavior) are seen as "having species survival value" in that they increase the probability of procreation by enhancing the "general level of sexual excitation in society." That being said, Gardner (1993) asserted that some paraphilia (e.g., "breast fetishism") are a result of instinctual need for human survival.

BREASTS AND SEXUAL SYMBOLISM

According to historians and scholars, there is an innate fascination with breasts, which stems from ancestral experience. Although breasts are a part of the sexual anatomy, related to reproduction; there is a great deal of erotic allure and sexual symbolism associated with them. In American society, breasts are used in advertisements in order to sell products (e.g., beer, cars, and cologne) in an appeal to men's sexual desires. In doing so, the media has helped shape the perceptions of men pertaining to breasts and as a result, breasts have become associated with femininity, sexuality, and attractiveness.

As indicated by Bergman (1997), breasts assumed well-known places in mythology, especially, with the Amazons. According to legend, the Amazons (an all-woman society governed by a queen) removed their right breast in order to improve their ability to shoot an arrow against the male enemy, which strengthened the view of the Amazons as powerful women who elicited feelings of fear and respect. Writers and artists also idealized breasts by representing them in erotic poetry, statues, paintings, etc. By the twelfth century, breasts had become the object of courtly admiration and valued as sources of nourishment, as the ability to produce milk was seen as "womanly power." Throughout time, breasts have been viewed as sources of wonder, pleasure, sensual delight, humiliation, and anguish (Bergman, 1997).

In relation to paraphilia, breasts represent many psychological issues in that individuals attempt to use breasts to humiliate, dominate, and punish women. For some men this can be highly erotic and sexually arousing.

PARTIALISM AND BREAST MILK

Paraphilia are known to have social, biological, and psychological factors. Many paraphilia (e.g., fetishism, telephone scatologia, partialism, zoophilia, and necrophilia) develop in order to preclude intimacy (Gardner, 1993). Paraphilia such as partialism, could satiate one's need for closeness and relatedness with others without the investment of a romantic relationship. Some men attempt to bond with women through consuming or rubbing breast milk all over oneself.

Before further discussion in partialism and breast milk, it is necessary to differentiate between partialism and fetishism, as laymen generally tend to confuse these two sexual disorders. Partialism is sexual interest in specific body parts (e.g., feet, breasts), whereas fetishism is a sexual interest to objects (e.g., heels, bras). Such terms, "foot fetish" or "breast fetish," give the impression that partialism and fetishism are the same. Dictionaries also contribute to this confusion in that they tend to combine the two disorders. According to Agnes, (1996) fetishism is an "abnormal condition in which erotic feelings are excited by a nonsexual object, as a *foot, glove, etc*" (p. 501). For the purpose of this chapter, fetishism and partialism will be used interchangeably in an effort to use the vernacular used by those who are sexually aroused by breast milk or lactation.

There has been a recent trend with respect to the fascination with breast milk and lactation. Typically referred to as "breast milk fetish," some men enjoy drinking and playing with breast milk. In fact, there are clubs that cater to this sexual interest, as well as websites that depict pictures and videos of women "squirting" and "milking" their fans (refer to http://seemilk.com/beauties.htm, along with a great number of other websites). In an HBO special, the women who work in these clubs reported that they generally tend to "keep getting pregnant" in order to have a supply of breast milk at all times. The women appeared to enjoy providing breast milk to the men, while the men appeared to enjoy the experience of drinking breast milk, which was supplied in a cup (the men were not allowed to suck on the nipples). It appeared that the men received intense sexual gratification in drinking breast milk and had conditioned themselves to respond sexually when engaging in such behavior.

Although this phenomenon has not been fully explored by scholars and researchers, it is believed that the individual becomes highly aroused with breast milk as it ultimately becomes the primary source of sexual gratification (Gardner, 1993). Some scholars do not perceive men's fascination with breasts to be a form of fetishism or partialism because "all men engage in it to a certain degree" (Gardner, 1993). Additionally, the preoccupation with the breast originates from the idea that breasts are the first "sex object" of the male, which is further explored in Freudian theory.

THE PSYCHODYNAMIC PERSPECTIVE

Freud asserted that breasts were the first "erotogenic" zone (Bergman, 1997). Furthermore, Freud theorized that sexuality emerges from the moment one engages in suckling, as the breasts are assumed to contribute a great deal to the development of the child's psyche. Accordingly, "men's erotic craving for women's breasts is tied up with longing for the mother" (Bergman, 1997), as there is ongoing stress placed on the female breast as a source of nourishment because breast milk is a bodily fluid that is associated with the maternal bond. As indicated by Gardner (1993), a woman derives pleasure in breast-feeding by identifying with the breast-feeding infant in addition to the gratifying sensation that she receives in having her nipples sucked. This pleasure purportedly sexually arouses men. For the infant, being held against the mother is quite comforting in that she is seen as his/her shelter and refuge. In relation to men who have the partialistic interest in digesting breast milk, the same feeling could be applied because the woman virtually becomes a source of protection, as well as the symbol of kindness and abundance. Freud's stages of psychosexual development further explain this phenomenon.

Although there are four stages to this Freudian developmental theory, the most important is the Oral Stage in which the individual is preoccupied with nursing him/herself because of the pleasure of sucking and accepting things into his/her mouth. Additionally, the woman's breast becomes the sole source of food and drink, as well as love and nurturance. Given that, scarce and forceful feeding can cause an individual to become fixated on this stage, which is generally established by the mother's response to the hungry child. The development of the oral character begins as the mother refuses to nurse the child on demand or suddenly ceases breast-feeding. Consequently, pessimism, envy, suspicion, and sarcasm develop in this individual. The overindulged oral character, however, is formed when the mother greatly satisfies the hunger needs of the child. Contrary to the oral character, this individual tends to be more optimistic, gullible, and full of admiration for others around him. In connection to partialism, psychoanalytic theory suggests that there is a severe castration complex in some men, which is triggered by relational reactions of women. For some men, breast milk fetishism operates as a defensive function in that it increases the competency of the penis.

PARTIALISM AND THE SEXUAL OFFENDER

The etiology for partialism in relation to breast milk fetishism is unknown. There appears to be substantial parental and social influence that contributes to the development of this specific sexual disorder. Possibly the offender develops a deep-seated hatred and resentment toward women as a result of his upbringing. To overcompensate for this bitterness, the sexual offender displaces his anger by striking against any representation of women.

Although most men who have a partialistic interest with breast milk are not dangerous or harmful to others, some serial murderers have fetishisms or partialisms. In fact, some serial murderers have actually removed the breasts of their victims in order to keep them as tokens, which are later used for masturbation and violent sexual fantasies. Other offenders find satisfaction in consuming the bodily fluids or body parts of their victims in an attempt to "keep" the victim with them. The progression of violence tends to increase when the sexual offender or serial murderer desires to "own" his/her victim, through urges to dominate and overpower their victims. Thus fetishism and partialism continue to be an area of concern for law enforcement agents because of their association to criminal activity.

KLISMAPHILIA
Enema Love

KERRY KONRAD AND
STEPHANIE GAUDENTI

Should one wish to explore the world of sexual deviance and paraphilia, one need only spend five minutes on the Internet, and via any decent search engine, the possibilities appear to be endless. With the increased ease in which such information is now available, it is easy to forget that many of the well-documented paraphilia have been in existence for centuries. According to the *Diagnostic and Statistical Manual of Mental Disorders (DSM-IV),* paraphilia are characterized by recurrent, intense sexually arousing fantasies, sexual urges, or behaviors that generally involve nonhuman or unusual objects, the suffering or humiliation of oneself or one's partner, or nonconsenting persons or children. Associated symptoms must be present over a period of at least six months, and must cause significant distress or impairment in important areas of functioning (American Psychiatric Association [APA], 1994). Currently, the *DSM-IV* (APA, 1994) formally recognizes the following paraphilias: exhibitionism, fetishism, frotteurism, pedophilia, sexual masochism, sexual sadism, transvestic fetishism, voyeurism, and paraphilia not otherwise specified (NOS) for less frequently encountered deviances. One such sexual deviance is klismaphilia.

DEFINITION AND BRIEF HISTORY OF KLISMAPHILIA

As explained by Denko (1973), who named the phenomenon, the term klismaphilia is derived from the Greek *klysma* (enema) and *philia* (to love). Klismaphilia involves sexual stimulation through the use of enemas, either taking, or giving, or both (Denko, 1976; Hickey, 2006). Agnew (1982) points out that enemas have been used for an array of purposes dating as far back as the Egyptians, Sumerians, and Mesopotamians. In the sixteenth century, enemas were used on "hysterical" women as a way of exorcising the devils responsible for their condition. During the seventeenth and eighteenth centuries, enemas were used for sexual arousal as is evident through references in plays, paintings, and literature of that period. However, by the nineteenth century, the enema fad appeared to fade somewhat.

In recent years, there appears to be a renewed erotic interest in enemas. Agnew (1982; 1986) suggests that because of society's increased tolerance of what was once considered taboo, new methods of sexual stimulation have been explored, including anal sexual activity. Accordingly, a more in-depth exploration of the mechanics of this paraphilia, as well as reports from klismaphiliacs, will help to further investigate this phenomenon.

PHYSIOLOGICAL EXPLANATIONS

Agnew (1982) in exploring the physiological aspects of klismaphilia, describes the process by which an enema is given, and offers some explanation as to nature of the sexual stimulation. He explains that "the insertion of the nozzle or tube provides stimulation of the anal sphincter, and the muscles and the nerves of the peripheral mucosa. Injection of the enema solution, though not directly felt by the rectum, stimulates interoceptive and stretch receptors in the colonic walls, due to distention created by the increasing pressure" (p. 560). The author further specifies that for women, the "pressure on the back of the vagina can stimulate the same set of nerves and produce the same erotic experience as deep penetration of the rectum" (p. 560). In men, filling and dilating the rectum with enema solution causes direct pressure on the prostate and seminal vesicles resulting in sexual stimulation. However, considering that not all people experience sexual arousal from enemas, it is likely that psychological factors also play a key role, beyond the biological.

PSYCHOLOGICAL EXPLANATIONS

Unlike the majority of paraphiliacs, who are male, many of those who engage in klismaphilia, are women (Denko, 1976). Also, a large percentage appear to be married or involved in relationships. In addition, klismaphilia often coexists with normal sexual relations. It is a sexual deviation that does not generally involve a victim, but has occasionally been used in an aggressive manner by some sex offenders.

Seligman and Hardenburg (2000) explain that paraphilia are often driven by nonsexual motivations. The behavior of some sexual deviants may represent an attempt to defend against anxiety, depression, or loneliness. It appears that klismaphiliacs will often turn to an enema when under pressure or feeling tired, finding it a quick method to achieve sexual gratification and relieve tension. In addition, Denko (1973) suggests that it provides the person absolute control in this one area, in which he or she is both the giver and taker. Enemas may also allow men a mode for passive sexual gratification not ordinarily available to them. However, these points do not offer a complete explanation of the manifestation and maintenance of this paraphilia.

Researchers have explored the childhood experiences of klismaphiliacs in hopes of identifying factors that contribute to the emergence of this sexual deviance. Based on the works of Denko (1973; 1976) and Agnew (1982), it appears that many of these people received enemas as children for constipation or as routine health maintenance. Though many indicated that they did not initially enjoy them, many reported that they reacted with pleasure at some point. Therefore, it is possible that the sexual response may be learned, and that a pleasurable rectal reaction becomes conditioned when paired with sexual arousal or orgasm. However, this explanation does not account for all who engage in klismaphilia, and others experiencing an enema for the first time with the expectation of having an erotic response, after having experimented with a variety of genital and extragenital forms of sexual stimulation (Denko, 1976). There is no clear or obvious answer to the question of what causes klismaphilia, but certain salient characteristics can be identified amongst klismaphiliacs.

TYPOLOGY OF KLISMAPHILIACS

In her 1976 study, Denko developed three categories that group klismaphiliacs possessing certain similarities, depending upon the way in which their disorders manifest: (1) those who view their deviance as ego-dystonic, whether it occurs independently or with other paraphilias; (2) those who have come to accept the sexual deviance so that it does not cause them internal conflict, and is accompanied by normal sex; and (3) those with additional paraphilia who perceive their atypical sexual behaviors as ego-syntonic.

Denko (1976) named the first category the ego-alien, compartmentalized type. Within this group, an enema is not a substitute for sex, but an additional arousal. However, they view their klismaphilia as shameful and abnormal and would prefer to be rid of the habit if it were not so pleasurable. Most of these people perform their enemas alone and are unaware that the behavior exists in others. In the majority of these cases, enemas were administered in childhood. It is not unusual for klismaphiliacs in this category to be homosexual, and there is often an additional mild, but coexisting paraphilia, such as mild masochism, coprophilia, fetishism, or bondage. Overall, by keeping their deviance compartmentalized, the klismaphilia has little effect on the rest of their lives.

The second group, as described by Denko (1976) is the ego-syntonic, pervasive type, monodeviant. People in this category tend to be more open regarding their klismaphilia because they have accepted it as part of who they are. Many share their sexual preference with their partners, and incorporate it into normal sexual relations. Similar to the above group, their klismaphilia does not interfere with the rest of their lives.

The final category, titled ego-syntonic, pervasive type, polydeviant by Denko (1976) is considerably different in that the klismaphilia permeates their lives and relationships. Most of the people in this group recall enjoying enemas at any early age. These klismaphiliacs tend to associate with others who have similar sexual interests, and take enemas with them. In addition, people in this group engage in a variety of paraphilia, including transvestism, masochism, bondage and discipline, fetishism, and urophilia.

Interestingly, one participant in Denko's 1976 study conducted some research of his own, and reported "that 50 percent of klismaphiliacs used other masochistic devices, such as spankings, bondage, and compelled retention, while 20 percent combined the enemas with urine and/or excrement fetishes" (p. 244). The reporting of these coexisting paraphilia is not surprising when considering the masochistic nature of enemas that utilize painful solutions or force retention, as well as the humbling nature in which they are often administered. Seligman and Hardenburg (2000) also indicate that it is not uncommon to find comorbid mental disorders in people with paraphilia, particularly personality disorders.

CYBERSPACE ENEMAS

Due to the sparse and dated research available in academic journals, it is relevant to utilize the Internet in order to gauge the present interest and participation in klismaphilia. An abundance of websites are dedicated to clubs, bulletin boards, chat rooms, and enema paraphernalia. Online bookstores educate about klismaphilia and the history of enemas. Many references to pornography based on klismaphilia also exist, including video quests such as *Dump Site, Drainman, Enemagic, Enemasters,* and *Waterworld.* In addition, many sites post instructions on administering enemas to oneself or to another, and supply detailed information regarding positions, expulsion, retention, and temperature.

Not surprisingly, types of enemas are also described and recipes listed, particularly for coffee enemas, which are reported to be efficient in cleansing the large intestine and the liver. One website described the golden enema, which consists of a man inserting his penis into his partner's anus and urinating (Anal Ecstasy, 2002). The Society for Human Sexuality (2002) also posted an unusual enema solution consisting of beer or wine, which results in the receiver becoming intoxicated when the alcohol is absorbed into the bloodstream through the intestines, and corroborates with similar findings by Agnew (1986). Another site outlined numerous different substances used in enemas, including coffee, wine, urine, enema water from a previous enema, egg yolk, turpentine, ice-cold club soda, mineral oil, and tomato juice (Speculum Pages, 2002). The potential for death exists with some of the ingredients used, such as laundry detergent. However, it seems that for some the possibility of some "good cramping" outweighs the risk of dying. In general, there is no lack of enema enthusiasts on the Internet.

CONCLUSION

Despite the fact that engaging in enemas to obtain sexual arousal has been prevalent for ages, it is shocking to recognize how little organized research has been conducted on this paraphilia. It would be extremely interesting to explore the current origins of klismaphilia in light of changing parenting practices across generations, especially with regards to administering enemas to children. In particular, it would be interesting to note if there has been an increase in people becoming klismaphiliacs at an older age because of less inhibited sexual practices and fewer people exposed to enemas at young ages. Paraphilia are understudied phenomena that warrant closer attention, particularly when considering the frequency with which paraphilia co-exist.

CHAPTER

FETISHISM

Development, Personality Characteristics, Theories, and Treatment Indicators for the Fetishist

16

TAMAR KENWORTHY AND SHAY LITTON

The term fetishism implies "the worship of inanimate objects . . . given a sexual connotation" (Brown, 1983). Throughout the last several decades, sex has become more accepted and socialized into mainstream society. In fact, sexual behaviors that were once considered too "taboo" to discuss openly are now popular topics in magazines, movies, and on television. Society has become increasingly desensitized to sexuality and the question now becomes, what classifies as "abnormal" sexual behavior. The "abnormality" of certain sexual behaviors was considered in an article by Brown (1983):

> Clinicians only study those who come to see them and many factors, some unknown, define who comes and who does not from a population sharing a certain disorder . . . There is no satisfactory epidemiology of sexual deviance and representative samples are particularly hard to find for obvious reasons. The social climate, which has much to do with the definition of deviance, also influences the presentation of deviant people in clinics (p. 227).

Therefore, what constitutes "abnormal" or deviant sexual behaviors may change with one's social environment and culture. What we define as taboo depends on society's opinion of what sexual acts should be acceptable. The sexual activity of fetishism has been categorized as a sexual disorder by the American Psychiatric Association (APA, 1994). Researchers have proposed several different theories as to why individuals develop fetishes. Some of these theories include the classical conditioning theory, the operant conditioning theory, and the attachment theory. This chapter will attempt to define fetishism, list the personality characteristics of someone with a fetish, and list possible theories as to how individuals acquire their fetishes.

The way in which society condemns or praises sexual behaviors will determine what sexual activities are accepted by the majority of cultures (Bhugra, 2000). Sexual desires and behaviors that deviate from the mainstream may be listed as sexual disorders or paraphilias. A sexual fetish is one of several types of paraphilias. Psychologist Alfred Binet was the first to define fetishism. Binet described fetishism as a sole sexual desire or intense interest for an object or part of the human body (Freund, Seto & Kuban, 1996). The term fetishism was first listed in the *DSM* in 1987. Some common fetishes include women's undergarments, leather, shoes, and feet. These objects are typically required or preferred for sexual excitement, and without these objects present individuals may experience sexual dysfunction. Many fetishisms do not typically come to clinical attention unless within the context of another paraphilia. This is partially because many fetishes do not result in criminal behavior, and because most individuals who have a sexual fetish do not perceive it as problematic. Those that do cause impairment in functioning are classified as fetishism by the *DSM-IV-TR* (2000).

To meet the diagnostic criteria of fetishism, a person must meet the following criteria as listed in the *DSM-IV-TR* (2000):

A. Over a period of at least 6 months, recurrent, intense sexually arousing fantasies, sexual urges, or behaviors involving the use of nonliving objects (e.g., female undergarments).

B. The fantasies, sexual urges, or behaviors cause clinically significant distress or impairment in social, occupational, or other important areas of functioning.

C. The fetish objects are not limited to articles of female clothing used in cross-dressing (as in Transvestic Fetishism) or devices designed for the purpose of tactile genital stimulation (e.g., a vibrator) (p. 570).

The development of this disorder will typically occur in early adolescence and the disorder is usually chronic in nature (APA, 1994). Some of the other popular fetishes involve women's clothing such as bras, underwear and shoes (Money, 1988). Criminologist Eric Hickey (2006) noted that some serial killers and rapists have also been known to have fetishes, which can include body parts of their victims. However, Gerbhard (1965) suggested that a fetish should only be categorized if the inanimate object or body part is absolutely necessary for sexual stimulation in an individual.

ASSESSMENT

Several different assessment tools can be utilized to assess a paraphilic disorder, specifically fetishism. The personality assessments that can be used in accordance with other materials for diagnosis included the Millon Clinical Multiaxial Inventory-III (MCMI-III) and the Minnesota Multiphasic Personality Inventory-II (MMPI-II) (Seligman & Hardenberg, 2000). Seligman and Hardenberg (2000) further suggest administering other assessment tools when diagnosing some one with a paraphilia or fetish. Examples include the Beck Depression Inventory, the Beck Anxiety Inventory (Psychological Corporation), Aggressive Sexual Behavior Inventory (Mosher &

Anderson, 1986), the Sexual Outlet Inventory (Kafka, 1994) and the State-Trait Anxiety Inventory (Consulting Psychologists Press) (Seligman & Hardenberg, 2000). Another diagnostic tool that can be administered to children (twelve and older) and adults is the Abel Assessment for Sexual Interest (Abel Screening, Inc., 1995). However, these assessment tools do not allow for a definitive diagnosis of fetishism. Rather, these instruments should be used in conjunction with a thorough, structured interview.

PERSONALITY CHARACTERISTICS

There has been a collective amount of research on the personality characteristics of a typical fetishist. One study by Gosselin (1979) investigated different personality types and the developmental age of individuals with a rubber fetish. Approximately half of Gosselin's study participants reported their first attraction to rubber occurred between the ages of eight and thirteen (1979). The typical fetishist is usually described as someone who has not developed appropriate social skills and is emotionally estranged. Nagler (1957) described the typical fetishist as "insecure, passive, dependent, and inadequate male" (p. 737). He further described a fetishist as depressed, reserved, and inhibited individual who may have crushing feelings of being inadequate for the typical male, social role (Nagler, 1957). In addition, Carrera (1981) described a fetishist as lacking in ability to develop or maintain intimacy with others. Carrera further listed inadequate social skills as another characteristic of fetishists, which may further encourage them to isolate from others (1981). This isolation can lead the fetishist to develop sexually deviant behaviors to compensate for their lacking social relationships. Storr (1964) additionally described the personality characteristics of fetishists as introverts who are unaware of the realism of the world. Thus, Storr additionally noted, fetishists will lead lives that are secluded from others. These encompassing characteristics can lead to feelings of overall inadequacy in life and aid in the development of self-esteem problems (Weinberg, Williams, & Calhan, 1995).

DEVELOPMENT OF THE FETISH

Some fetishists are attracted to inanimate objects, while others are attracted to certain body parts of humans (Seligman & Hardenburg, 2000). Foot or feet fetishes are one of the most common fetishes. One of the largest-scale studies conducted on foot fetishism was performed by Weinberg, Williams, and Calhan (1995). They attempted to determine if foot fetishes were a learned or acquired behavior. Weinberg, Williams and Calhan surveyed over 260 men who were members of the Foot Fraternity. The Foot Fraternity is a large-scale mail organization for foot fetishists in the United States. Members of the Foot Fraternity can mail order several different foot fetish items, such as photographs of feet, videos of feet, and books about feet. Over 80 percent of the respondents were working in white-collar jobs. A large majority of the respondents (89 percent) were white. Approximately 88 percent of the respondents reported being homosexual. The remaining 12 percent listed themselves as bisexual. The respondents who had received therapy for their disorder was less than 10 percent of this specific population. Weinberg, Williams, and Calhan (1995) found that over 80 percent of the participants denied having negative events in childhood that lead them to the development of their fetish. Approximately 45 percent of the respondents listed pleasurable childhood memories or events leading them to develop a foot fetish. The average reported age for developing the foot fetish for this study was twelve years of age. Almost 30 percent of the respondents reported that they masturbated during adolescence to feet or footwear. Over half of the respondents reported not having as many friends during their childhoods. Twenty percent of the respondents that answered open-ended questions regarding how they developed their fetishes listed their father's feet as an object of arousal for them. One of these responses is as follows:

> At 6 or 7 I had my stocking feet worshipped by a 30-year-old uncle. He would massage my feet and either masturbate on them or sodomize me. I began finding men in their stocking feet sexually exciting. My primary fantasy that permeates all my sexual activities is a male with socks on (Weinberg, Williams, & Calhan, 1995).

This study was different from previous research regarding foot fetishes since the respondents were not clinical patients with diagnoses. Additionally, this study provided a deeper investigation into the development of a foot fetish and the behavioral practice associated with the fetish (Weinberg, Williams, & Calhan, 1995).

FETISHISM COMORBIDITY

Those categorized as having a paraphilia are likely to have 2–3 paraphilias at one time (Hickey, 2006). Researchers Kafka and Prentky (1994) performed a study on men with paraphilias and the comorbidity of other diagnostic disorders. Kafka and Prentky found that the participants in their study averaged having 1.8 paraphilias at one time (1994). Additionally, Bradford (1996) found that paraphilics are more likely to have comorbid diagnoses of obsessive-compulsive and impulse control disorders. Kafka and Prentky (1994) further suggest that individuals with paraphilias are estimated to have more occurrences of disorders such as substance abuse and mood disorders. Perry and Orchard (1992) additionally found the antisocial personality disorder is more likely to occur in adolescents with paraphilias. Similarly, fetishism is many times paired with other paraphilias such as body art, body piercing, and sadomasochism.

Body art is many times viewed as a deviant form of self-expression involving things such as tattoos and body piercing. While body piercing is a rather common form of self-expression in today's society, erotic body piercing seems to take on a different meaning for some individuals. A study conducted on males by Buhrich (1983) found a connection between erotic body piercing and sadomasochism, bondage, fetishism, and homosexuality. This study also found cases of sadomasochism to include fetishism; "the link between fetishism and sadomasochism was so close that it was often difficult to tell the difference" (p. 170). Fetishisms associated with sadomasochism typically included leather, boots, and jeans.

One may ask, how do these different paraphilias become entwined? While it is difficult to determine which paraphilia came into existence first, it may not be difficult to ascertain how these different paraphilias became part of a sexually arousing combination. For example, in the case of body piercing one may have begun by enjoying the sight of piercings on other people. If this was perceived as being sexually arousing, the individual may have begun experimenting with piercing his or her own body. Eventually, it is possible that the act of piercing itself produced sexual pleasure for the individual with the piercing fetish. This pairing of pain with their particular fetish may even have heightened their sexual pleasure, which induces the paraphilia of masochism and can lead to sadism. According to Brown (1983):

> Sadism may be defined as the obtaining of sexual satisfaction from causing pain, injury or humiliation to others and masochism as obtaining satisfaction from being the recipient of these . . . Because sadism and masochism usually occur together in the same individual, it is convenient to join the two as sadomasochism (p. 228).

Therefore, an individual who has a piercing fetish and is considered to be a sadomasochist may find a very profitable career both monetarily and sexually in the area of body art. This, too, can be found on websites designed for individuals with piercing and tattoo fetishisms. The experience of a particular fetish can lead an individual into other various forms of paraphilia when their fetish is paired with pleasure. The question now remains, what causes one to experience sexual pleasure from an object?

FETISHISM THEORIES

Numerous theories exist pertaining to why individuals participate in paraphilias "ranging from psychoanalytic theories describing unresolved earlier conflicts, to endocrinological and brain abnormalities, to sociological and cultural factors" (Pa, 2001, p. 5). According to psychoanalysts, "fetishism is the result of a developmental disturbance leading to sexual interest in symbolic objects rather than real people" (Brown, 1983). Psychoanalysts believe that early childhood conflicts revolving around the Oedipal and Electra complexes, that have not been resolved properly, carry over into adulthood and manifest themselves in the form of fetishisms. Freud "described the fetish as a substitute for the maternal phallus which the subject does not want to renounce because of the intensity of his castration fears" (Chasseguet-Smirgel, 1981, p. 516). In fact, the very existence of fetishisms and other paraphilias seem to give rather strong support for psychoanalyst theories because of their focus on sexuality and how sexual conflicts lead to adult disorders. However, according to a study by Furnham and Haraldsen (1998) on the etiology of factors associated with fetishism and other paraphilias, sexual conflicts in childhood are not the primary motivating factors for individuals who develop a paraphilia:

> Interestingly, the items that the participants thought most important in the etiology of the paraphilias were fearing the opposite sex, being abused as a child, having strict and dominant parents, and possessing repressed sexual feelings . . . Less emphasis was placed on biological factors, religious and moral education, and parental guidance (p. 697).

Causal factors for fetishism and other paraphilias may very well develop in childhood, but it appears that more than just psychoanalytical conflicts fuel these "abnormal" sexual behaviors.

Researchers have proposed several other theories as to how paraphilics develop their foot or feet fetishes. One theory proposed by Rachman and Hodgson (1968) is based on the classical conditioning theory. The classical conditioning theory is defined by Gleitman (1996) as the following:

> In *classical conditioning,* first studied by I. P. Pavlov, one learns about the *association* between one stimulus and another. Prior to conditioning, an *unconditioned stimulus* or *US* (such as food) elicits an *unconditioned response* or *UR* (such as salivation). After repeated pairings of the US with a *conditioned stimulus* or *CS* (such as a buzzer), this CS alone will evoke a *conditioned response* or *CR* (here again, salivation) that is often similar to the UR (p. 118).

Rachman and Hodgson applied this theory to an experiment involving slides of a sexual nature with women's boots. They found after several pairings of the stimuli, their participants had an increase in sexual arousal when they were shown boots that were not paired with sexual seductive items (Rachman & Hodgson, 1968), thus showing the behaviors of paraphilics with foot fetishes can be conditioned by early experiences in their adolescences leading to the development of the disorder (Weinberg, Williams, & Calhan, 1995).

An additional theory on the development of a fetish involves the operant conditioning theory. The operant conditioning theory suggests that "behavior is learned and developed through interaction with the environment. If behavior is reinforced in some way, it will continue, while behavior that is punished or not reinforced will be diminished" (Plante, 1999, p. 61). An article by McGuire, Carlisle, and Young (1965) applied the operant conditioning theory to fetishes, describing the experience in using the fetish for masturbation with an end result of an orgasm. The individual's desire for the object or body part is reinforced through the sexual release of an orgasm (McGuire, Carlisle, & Young, 1965).

An additional approach suggests the individual develops the fetish as a behavior to make up for the adolescent's lacking social network. These individuals do not have many friends during their adolescent years, so they develop a desire for an inanimate object or body part to compensate for their lack of social connectedness.

Some theorists propose that individuals suffering from paraphilias experienced difficulty in engaging in intimate relationships as children (Hudson & Ward, 1997), while other theorists suggest the inability to develop appropriate attachment bonds with their caregivers as the main cause of their diagnosis (Marshall, 1989). Palermo (2001) further stated his theory as follows:

> It is my belief that under the intense stress due to inner conflicts and frustrated sexual desires, and because of their ego weakness and the sudden resurfacing of the above-mentioned ambivalence, they are unconsciously driven into a state of cognitive deconstruction. Then they are unable to properly assess their behavior, control themselves, and be positively influenced by their higher moral self. They become disinhibited, pursue their desires, and are only interested in the concreteness of the situation they are in-the here and now of their sexual predatory act (p. 4).

The inner conflicts and sexual desires, when studied developmentally, may be explained by previous childhood victimization experienced by the pedophiles themselves.

Feeney (1995) studied the relationship between early attachment and coping styles in adults. Feeney found if inadequate attachments were made with the child's primary caretaker, the child would have ineffective coping styles in stressful situations. A significant part of the adolescent and child's growth involves the development of bonds and social skills. The methods the parents use to interact with their children can affect their future relationships with other adults. Flinker, Englund, and Sroufe (1992) found "children who form secure attachments to their primary caregivers (usually mothers) develop an internal working model and a sense of self that leads to positive experiences in their relationships with others" (p. 81). Developmental theorists have found that when adolescents did not have strong attachments with their parents, their likelihood of delinquency was increased (Baer, 1999). Researchers have also found that weak attachment bonds between adolescents and their parents lead to other detrimental effects such as low self-esteem, poor social performances, and decreased positive interactions with peers (Engles, Dekovic, & Meeus, 2002). Gosselin (1979) further supports this view by suggesting that children that have a more problematic emotional relationship with their parents are more likely to develop fetishes. Gosselin describes his theory of fetishism as an unconscious process and further suggests that previous psychological problems experienced can encourage the fetish development.

CRIMINALITY OF FETISHISM

While it does not appear that worshiping of feet could be construed as criminal behavior, the methods to which individuals go to experience their fetish may well fall under the criminal umbrella of a sexual offense. "The term sex offense broadly connotes any illegal conduct of a sexual nature . . . other sex offenses include gross sexual imposition, voyeurism, importuning, public indecency, pandering obscenity, and corruption of a minor" (Noffsinger & Resnick, 2000, p. 2). Thus, benign fetishes may still fall within the classification of a sex offense if the fetish is acted upon in a criminal fashion. Many times, a rather benign fetish such as body piercing may become entangled with other paraphilias that lead to more risky and deviant behaviors. Social scientists have researched the evolution of the paraphilic or fetish behaviors in offenders.

Zolondek, Abel, Northey Jr., and Jordan (2001) demonstrated the importance of studying the causes of fetishisms in their study on juvenile sex offenders. This study found that more than a quarter of their sample of juvenile sex offenders reported fetishism, and that the proportion of juvenile sex offenders engaging in fetishism and other paraphilias was higher than that of their adult counterparts. These paraphilias tend to go undetected and do not typically surface unless a juvenile is arrested on a sex offense charge. This study further reported that it is important for clinicians and researchers to go back to preadolescent years when investigating the age of onset of sexual behaviors because "deviant sexual patterns exhibited in preadolescent boys must be taken seriously to prevent later sexual offending and to understand the etiology of paraphilic behavior" (p. 7). Therefore, while many sexual behaviors such as fetishisms may appear to be harmless on the surface, the reasons behind the sexual arousal to the fetish object can lead to errors in judgment and criminal offending if not detected early. However, early detection does not guarantee the cessation of the paraphilia because treating paraphilic behaviors such as fetishism is still an area that needs further exploration. Typically, paraphilias that lead to criminal behavior are given more treatment demand, but many times the "benign" paraphilias can be causal indicators of future criminality.

TREATMENT

The treatment of paraphilias, in particular fetishism, is an area full of hypotheses and many varied techniques. Most treatment methods correspond to the theoretical orientation of the therapist. Those who subscribe to psychoanalysis see great utility in resolving early childhood conflicts through the use of psychotherapy. Different methods may include the use of hypnosis and regressing an individual back into their earlier childhood so that they may first acknowledge or remember the conflict and then find a resolution. This form of treatment typically takes many years of intense psychoanalysis aimed at uncovering childhood Oedipal and Electra complexes that were never resolved. Psychoanalysts believe that by working through these unresolved conflicts, the fetish will lose its sexual significance for the individual because the individuals will be able to reclaim their sexual arousal through their genitals.

Treatment methods aimed at correcting faulty cognitions or biological abnormalities typically rely on cognitive-behavioral treatment techniques. These techniques are aimed at changing faulty thought patterns and pairing healthy thought patterns with healthy sexual behavior. Therapists subscribing to these treatment methods believe that individuals with paraphilias were not taught the proper way to think about sex and sexual arousal. This then led to inappropriate sexual behaviors based on these faulty learning patterns. So for the individual with fetishism, an object was mistakenly paired with sexual arousal because the proper manner of sexual arousal was not learned early on. Changing these faulty thought patterns requires re-learning of healthy and adaptive ways to achieve sexual arousal. This method also explores with the individual the reasons why fetishism is an inappropriate means of sexual arousal. When cognitive-behavioral methods fail and it is still assumed that brain function plays a role in the paraphilia, more aggressive techniques such as electroconvulsive therapy may be employed. These methods pair pain with the sexual arousal of the fetish object; however, as discussed previously, many fetishes can lead to further paraphilias such as sadomasochism. The pairing of pain with the fetish object may only serve to further enforce its sexual significance.

While all of these treatment methods may aid individuals in overcoming their paraphilia, the crucial variable for determining treatment success lies in the relationship between the etiology of the paraphilia and the corresponding cure. According to a study conducted by Furnham and Haraldsen (1998):

> The majority of the factors were significantly correlated, suggesting a clear relationship between etiology and cure. One of the most important relationships was considered to be between early childhood relationships and therapy of some sort . . . Both the factors involving lack of religious and moral guidance and the one involving biological issues were highly correlated with external control as cure (p. 698).

Therefore, the best form of treatment may lie within the individual and their experience of what led to their paraphilia. In the case of most paraphilias, and in particular fetishism, the failure of treatment methods is commonplace due to the fact that many individuals do not perceive their fetishism to be problematic and therefore no "cure" is needed.

SUMMARY

Fetishisms can originate from a myriad of factors that seem to take hold in early childhood. It seems likely that an object being paired with sexual arousal is fulfilling a need for the individual. The need may lie in that the fetish object does not offer rejection if the fetish object is inanimate. The fetish object also may symbolize a need that went unmet in childhood, either because of abuse or lack of love and attention. For example, a man who was sexually aroused by dog training discovered he linked his desire for affection from his father, who was a veterinarian, with his desire to be a dog "because he wanted his father's attention" (Pa, 2001, p. 5). Once this connection was made, his deviant sexual behavior ceased. Another possibility is that the fetish object provides a suppressed desire in the individual. Individuals with a foot fetish may have an inner desire to be dominated or "walked" all over. Similarly, those with a piercing fetish may have an inner desire to inflict pain upon themselves or to punish themselves by disfiguring their body appearance.

Overall, the experience and the etiology of the fetish lie within the individual. It seems unlikely to believe that individuals with the same fetish object developed their desire in exactly the same manner. There are several different proposed theories as to why and how individuals develop fetishes. Most of these theories suggest the individual had a deviant or delusional development of the disorder, further finding the individual as having a sexual disorder. Most of the research on fetishes describes only the behaviors that lead to criminal sanctions, such as panty thefts. In contrast, the practice of fetishism may be practiced far more often than the public is aware. Therefore, it appears that unresolved childhood experiences, the pairing of the fetish object with some type of reinforcement, and an individual's perception of these experiences, plays a large role in the development of "abnormal" sexual behaviors.

CHAPTER

FOOT FETISHISM

Podophilia and Retifism

KERRY KONRAD-TORRES AND
KATHERINE NICKCHEN

Concerns have increased over the last several decades regarding deviant sexual behavior. Evidence of this can be readily observed in the overwhelming amount of media attention dedicated to the topics of sex and violence, whether through television, movies, or literature. As a result, the general public is more frequently exposed to details of such behavior, regardless of whether the information is accurate. Fortunately, increased social concern often leads to funding, which ultimately enables researchers to initiate studies pertaining to these issues.

Little is understood about many sexually deviant behaviors, also referred to as paraphilia. As a result of the lack of knowledge, a great deal of fear exists about these behaviors and, in some cases, rightly so. However, a number of paraphilia involve consenting individuals and consist of nonviolent activity. Such is most often the case regarding the behaviors that comprise fetishism.

Fetishism has been classified by the American Psychiatric Association (1994) as a paraphilia. According to the *Diagnostic and Statistical Manual of Mental Disorders (DSM-IV)*, paraphilias are characterized by recurrent, intense sexually arousing fantasies, sexual urges, or behaviors that generally involve nonhuman or unusual objects, the suffering or humiliation of oneself or one's partner, or unconsenting persons or children. Associated symptoms must be present over a period of at least six months, and must cause significant distress or impairment in important areas of functioning (American Psychiatric Association [APA], 1994). However, *Weinberg, Williams, and Calhan* (1995) explain that fetishism should only be considered a paraphilia when the interest is so profound that the object must be present for sexual gratification. According to Nagler (1957), fetishism, in general, can be defined as the adoring or worshipping of something that acts as a substitute for the original object. More specifically, for the purpose of this discussion, fetishism refers to sexual arousal involving nonliving objects, such as female undergarments or specific parts of the body.

Weinberg et al. (1995) indicate that the French psychologist, Binet, introduced the term fetishism in 1887. Research suggests that it is a condition that is found almost exclusively among men and is quite common in its milder forms (Seligman, 2000; Weinberg et al., 1995). However, the study of fetishists and their characteristics has been problematic because the majority of subjects have come from case studies and clinical settings, such as sex offender treatment programs. While paraphilia research with sex offenders is important, the information obtained is not generalizable to the overall population of those with paraphilias. Accordingly, Weinberg, Williams, and Calhan (1994) suggest that fetishists who have not come into contact with the law or mental health services are an unknown majority. An additional concern regarding the research is the paucity of studies conducted on specific fetishes.

This chapter will present an overview of the literature available on foot fetishism, including podophilia and retifism. As outlined by Kippen (2002), podophilia is a pronounced sexual interest in the lower extremities or anything that covers portions of them. In general, the response of the fetishist to the foot is the same as a conventional person's arousal at seeing genitals. In contrast, shoe fetishists or retifists, while similar in principal to foot fetishists, are stimulated by the shoe, which becomes the total focus for arousal. In fact, some retifists need only the shoe and not the person to be satisfied, while others will incorporate a shoe into their normal sexual habits. However, amongst true shoe fetishists complete satisfaction is impossible unless a shoe is involved (Kippen, 2002).

CHARACTERISTICS OF FOOT FETISHISTS

In a study by Weinberg et al. (1994), 262 homosexual and bisexual foot fetishists belonging to an organization called the Foot Fraternity, provided information regarding their interests and practices. The subjects were comprised of men between the ages of 21 and 65. The majority of the respondents (81 percent) were employed in white-collar jobs, and only 2 percent were unemployed. Also, approximately 69 percent indicated that they had a college or graduate degree, whereas 2 percent did not complete high school. Eighty-nine percent of the subjects were Caucasian, and most (88 percent) were homosexual. In addition, less than 10 percent reported having received treatment related to their fetish.

Observations revealed that the main interest of the respondents was male feet and footwear. However, the range of what was actually considered arousing was quite varied. For example, 60 percent of the subjects found clean feet to be exciting, followed by boots at 52 percent, shoes at 49 percent, sneakers at 47 percent, and smelly socks at 45 percent. In addition, almost half of the fetishists were turned on by clothing and leather. Even more interesting was that the specific style of shoe was very important to almost three-quarters of the respondents, and 60 percent indicated that the same was true about the type of feet. However, it also appears that for many, the specific interests change over time or become more generalized to include a wider range of arousing fetish interests (Weinburg et al., 1994).

Another intriguing finding from the Weinberg et al. (1994) study was that 58 percent of the fetishists stated that footwear that had never been worn by anyone was not exciting at all. Several respondents indicated that they were especially aroused by footwear that had been worn by an attractive person. Some subjects were most aroused by footwear purchased at a thrift store because they could fantasize about the looks of the previous owner in any way they desired. Also, two-thirds of the men reported that it did not matter to them whether the footwear was worn by a heterosexual or homosexual male. Another important finding was that respondents linked styles of footwear to particular types of men. For example, one subject linked docksiders with preppies, sneakers with young punks, and boots with dominant men.

Considering these responses, Weinberg et al. (1994) suggest that it is not simply the object itself that is arousing, but the object's connection with a living person that is more important. Accordingly, they caution that definitions of fetishism that place too much emphasis on inanimate objects may lose perspective regarding this more personalized dimension.

AROUSING ASPECTS OF FEET AND FOOTWEAR

In exploring the phenomenon of foot fetishism, Weinberg et al. (1994) inquired about the sexual attraction to feet and footwear. Almost 20 percent of the respondents were unable to explain their arousal. However, 50 percent made a reference to one of the senses when describing the sensual aspects of the fetish object. The sense most frequently mentioned was that of smell and the odors specific to feet and footwear. Pleasure derived from sight or touch was mentioned with about equal frequency. Two subjects indicated that taste was most important, and only one man mentioned arousal derived through hearing. However, it was not uncommon for more than one sense to be mentioned when describing the pleasure derived from feet or footwear.

Finally, the remaining 30 percent of respondents indicated that symbolism was the basis for the appeal of the fetish object. In addition, several of the subjects who emphasized the sensual aspects of the object also referred to the symbolic as well. Weinberg et al. (1994) explain that "sensual aspects are made exciting through their associations and these meanings clearly evoke cultural scripts relating to masculinity" (p. 618). The researchers expand further in suggesting that homosexual foot fetishism evokes the theme of masculinity, much in the same manner that heterosexual foot fetishism symbolizes femininity. Interestingly, it appears that fetishism works by signifying gender and that "culturally constructed gender differences seem to lay at the base of sexual arousal in general" (Weinberg et al., 1994, p. 618).

PREFERENCE VS. PARAPHILIA

Paraphilic research is difficult not only because of concerns regarding generalizability, but also because of the ambiguous nature of criteria used to determine the existence of a disorder. How does one draw the line between normal sexual fantasies or behaviors and pathological sexual behavior? This distinction remains subjective, even within the *DSM-IV*. Though there is debate amongst researchers regarding what constitutes true fetishism, it is generally accepted that paraphilias can be considered to lie on a continuum between preference and paraphilia (Weinberg et al., 1994).

The aforementioned study examined the importance of the fetish object in order to gain a better understanding of the point at which the fetish becomes a substitute for a partner. Eighty-three percent of the respondents indicated that at least once a week they self-masturbate while fantasizing about feet or footwear. Also, the majority (92 percent) of the subjects read or look at pornography involving feet or footwear, 53 percent collect footwear advertisements, and 38 percent subscribe to footwear magazines. Based on these responses, clearly foot fantasy during masturbation plays a significant role in their sex lives.

Further inquiry into the importance of the foot fetish in the respondents' sexual repertoires revealed that 77 percent had engaged in foot play with a sexual partner within the last year. Foot play consists of any number of activities including foot licking, foot masturbation, foot sucking, foot bondage, foot tickling, foot worship (caressing and kissing of the feet), shoe worship, foot tonguing, and foot eating (Society for Human Sexuality, 2002; Weinberg et al., 1995). Also, 35 percent of the subjects indicated that feet and footwear were usually the main focus of their sexual activity with others, and another 38 percent stated that the fetish was an important part, but not the main focus, of their sexual activity. Contrary to much research on fetishism, it appears that most of the respondents were able to integrate their foot fetish into their sex life with partners, which is an important distinction. As indicated by Kippen (2002), most shoe and foot fetishists are relieved to learn their partner will usually accommodate foot-loving into normal intimacies. It is likely that this is the case because foot fetishism is usually considered nonpathological and a variation of normal intimacy.

Consistent with prior research regarding paraphilias, it appears that fetishism often exists in conjunction with other paraphilias. Weinberg et al. (1994, 1995) found that it was not uncommon for the fetish interest to be integrated into sadomasochistic (SM) play, bondage and discipline, humiliation play, or dominant/submissive play. In fact, two-thirds of the men had interest in some type of SM behavior, and between 15 and 30 percent reported that they engage in SM activity often or always during foot play.

ORIGINS OF FOOT FETISHISM

As indicated by Weinberg et al. (1995), much of the research suggests that fetishism is a learned response and that under the right conditions anyone can become a fetishist. It is speculated that such conditioning most likely occurs at puberty, because it is a critical period in sexual development. However, studies have disagreed in terms of the type of conditioning involved.

Some investigators suggest that fetishism stems from classical conditioning, when the fetish object is paired with sexual arousal. Other researchers advocate that operant conditioning is at work in the development of fetishism. The latter argue that "initial experiences with a fetish object can be used in masturbatory fantasies, and that the ensuing orgasm acts as an operant conditioning reinforcer" (Weinberg et al., 1995, p. 18). Still other studies focus on the role of the family in the development of fetishism, especially with regards to households that are highly restrictive sexually, as is illustrated by Cautela (1986).

In exploring further clarification, Seligman (2000) suggests that individuals with paraphilia typically have nonsexual, as well as sexual, motivations and drives that are important in influencing their behaviors. Research indicates that the rituals of fetishists may provide a sense of self, feelings of power, and direction or meaning to their lives. In addition, such behavior may serve to stave off anxiety, depression, and loneliness, or may be used to express anger, rage, and revenge (Seligman, 2000).

A corresponding explanation found in the literature examines the fetishist as a type of person in which the fetishism is only one aspect of underlying psychological problems, and a personality profile typical of this kind of person is often made reference to. Nagler (1957) describes the fetishist as "an insecure, passive, dependent, and inadequate male" (p. 737) who fears the male social role. Nagler (1957) further suggests that this personality pattern is the result of early childhood experiences with an overprotecting, restrictive mother and a critical, disapproving father. This explanation is also illustrated by Bemporad, Dunton, and Spady (1976) in their case study of a childhood foot fetishist who was raised in such an environment.

Though the results of the study by Weinberg et al. (1994, 1995) primarily provide support to the roles of operant conditioning, as well as classical conditioning, in the development of fetishism, there was some evidence of the influence of other factors as well. Those respondents who reported a higher level of psychological difficulties seemed to engage in fetishism that would meet the criteria for a paraphilia, and appeared to have characteristics that fit the personality profile described in the above literature. Therefore, it seems likely that a number of factors are at work in determining one's likelihood of developing a fetish, as well as the level of functional impairment, if any, that will occur as a result of the fetish.

DISCUSSION

In reviewing the available literature on fetishism, and podophilia and retifism in particular, it seems abundantly clear that additional research is essential for a better understanding of these behaviors. Though some recent literature was available, its focus was solely on foot fetishism in homosexual males, which was limiting to a certain degree. Surprisingly, very little information was located addressing heterosexual foot fetishism, making it difficult to comment on similarities and differences between the groups. The outdated literature dealt primarily with case studies and psychodynamic explanations of the fetish object, and is therefore difficult to generalize to the greater population.

After becoming familiar with the available research, a number of questions arose. First, it would be interesting to determine the prevalence of foot fetishism in the general population. Also, very little research is devoted to the study of women and fetishism. A more general study by Fedoroff et al. (1999) addresses the topic of women and paraphilia, but virtually nothing is known about the frequency with which women participate in podophilia or retifism. Finally, while foot fetishists appear to be nonviolent and similar in many ways to the "average" member of society, it seems that a better understanding of foot fetishes, and fetishism in general, could be established by exploring the possibility of creating a typology based on the severity of the behavior and corresponding origin of development. As previously stated, paraphilia in general are an understudied phenomena that warrant closer attention from the academic and professional communities.

CHAPTER
TRANSVESTIC FETISHISM

18

AINSLIE HEASMAN,
JEANNE JOHNSON,
AND MELINDA CHAU

Magnus Hirschfield first described transvestism in the early 1900s. In fact, he coined the term while studying sixteen men and one woman in their cross-dressing habits. He believed that transvestites were predominately male and heterosexual in their orientation. He felt this type of behavior began in childhood, continued and increased in frequency during adolescence, and changed little as individuals moved in to adulthood (Bullough & Bullough, 1997). It appears, however, that cross-dressing (in some form or another) existed before the twentieth century. Ellis (as cited in Bullough & Bullough, 1997) indicated that women were, in fact, the most frequent cross-dressers prior to the 1900s. Their motivation was likely different from that of cross-dressers today. Rather than sexual gratification or fantasy being an influence on their dress, it was for economic benefit and a wish for freedom. In the early-twentieth century, research on transvestism was done by treatment-oriented psychiatrists who characterized transvestism as an illness and sought to treat it with psychotherapy. These psychiatrists searched for key elements in childhood history, such as castration anxiety or homosexual panic that would help them understand and treat their clients (Bullough, & Bullough, 1997).

No formal study on the incidence or prevalence of transvestic fetishism has been undertaken (Zucker & Blanchard, 1997), yet it has been included in all editions of the *Diagnostic and Statistical Manual (DSM)* since 1952 (Zucker & Blanchard, 1997). The definition of transvestic fetishism, according to the *Diagnostic and Statistical Manual for Mental Disorders DSM-VI-Tr* (American Psychiatric Association, 2000), involves the explicit behavior of cross-dressing. Usually the male with transvestic fetishism keeps a collection of feminine clothes that he intermittently uses to cross-dress. While cross-dressed, he usually masturbates, imagining himself to be both the male subject and the female object of his sexual fantasy.

Despite the confusion that may arise as a result of cross-dressing, research suggests that transvestites are not necessarily homosexual (Bullough & Bullough, 1997). Most transvestic fetishists acknowledge their cross-dressing began in early childhood, that it increased during puberty, and remained almost unchanged after that point (Bullough & Bullough, 1997). The age at which most transvestites first cross-dressed ranged from six to nine years of age (Bullough & Bullough, 1997; Buhrich & McConaghy, 1977; Buhrich & McConaghy, 1979). Most transvestites' predominant sexual urge is focused on themselves dressed in women's clothing rather than focused on thoughts of others of the same or opposite sex (Bullough & Bullough, 1997). Others have suggested that transvestites simply feel more comfortable and relaxed while dressing as the opposite gender, and it is not necessarily done to provide sexual gratification (Freund, Steiner, & Chan, 1982).

Docter & Prince (1997) identified two subgroups of cross-dressers based on differences in cross-gender identity. One group is characterized by higher sexual arousal, lower cross-gender identity, propensity for heterosexual orientation, less propensity to feminize the body, and less motivation to live entirely as a woman. The other group is associated with cross-dressing, a propensity for sexual relationships with males, and transsexual inclinations, including plans for living entirely as a woman. The distinction is also made for men who dress in women's clothing for the purpose of alleviating the anxiety, pressure, and strain related to being a male, which is not paraphilic and is known as non-fetishistic transvestism (Buhrich & McConaghy, 1979).

Blanchard (as cited in Zucker & Blanchard, 1997) coined the term *autogynephilia* to describe any cross-dressing behaviors or fantasies that are sexually arousing. The term is derived from Greek roots meaning, "love of oneself as a woman" (Zucker & Blanchard, 1997, p. 258). Zucker and Blanchard (1997) outline four main types of autogynephilia. Their descriptions illustrate an approach focused more on the behavior and characteristics of these individuals, versus a specific diagnosis.

1. **Physiologic Autogynephilia:** this involves men who masturbate while concurrently fantasizing about being pregnant or giving birth.

2. **Behavioral Autogynephilia:** the thought of taking part in activities that symbolize femininity. The most common fantasy is to think of oneself as a woman participating in sexual or erotic activities.

3. **Anatomic Autogynephilia:** Fantasies about having a female body.

4. **Transvestic Autogynephilia:** Fantasies or actual behavior of making oneself more like a female.

Zucker and Blanchard's (1997) studies have found men with transvestic fetishism were no more effeminate in childhood than other men (Zucker and Blanchard, 1997). Langevin, Wright, & Handy (as cited in Adshead, 1997) found that heterosexual transvestites and homosexual men have similar scores on the Masculine-Feminine (MF) scale of the Minnesota Multiphasic Personality Inventory (MMPI), suggesting they both identify with feminine behaviors and attitudes. What is curious is if these heterosexual men have always identified with feminine attitudes and behaviors, or if the socialization they encounter as a result of cross-dressing influences these behaviors and beliefs.

The difference between transvestic fetishism and transexualism should be noted as they are not the same. It is believed that among transvestic fetishists, the sex organs are sources of pleasure, while in transsexualism they are sources of disgust (Buhrich & McConaghy, 1977). It is believed that transvestic fetishism does not exist in transsexuals because transsexuals desire to be the opposite sex, are not happy with their gender, and desire to change both their gender and sex, while transvestites are happy with their sex yet gain sexual pleasure from dressing as the opposite sex (Buhrich & McConaghy, 1977). In a study of 516 biological males (88 percent were self-described transvestites and 12 percent were transsexuals), it was found that transvestites and transsexuals live quite different lifestyles; however, their erotic motives have similarities. Common experiences include very intense feminine gender identity, actual transgender role behavior or conduct, and an intensity of erotic attraction or affectionate, and/or sexual expression towards another male (Docter & Fleming, 2001). Although theses experiences are similar, the transvestites in this study reported preferring a female partner or were married to a female.

Neurobiological explanations have also been used to understand transvestic fetishism. Hoenig (as cited in Zucker & Blanchard, 1997) found a relationship between transsexualism and electroencephalogram (EEG) abnormalities. In this study, some participants were also transvestic fetishists. Epstein (as cited in Zucker & Blanchard, 1997) indicates that some fetishism is the, "result of inhibition or release of limbic regions with seizure activity" (Zucker & Blanchard, 1997, p. 268). There has also been a suggestion that some fetishism is a result of head injury. A number of cases were documented in which an individual's fetishism was reduced or eliminated with surgery to remove the area of the brain that was the focus of the head injury. Medication to control seizures resulting from a head injury has also been documented to reduce fetishism (Zucker & Blanchard, 1997). While this is a promising lead to explain a relatively few number of cases, it appears at this point to not be generalizable to all forms of fetishism, particularly that of transvestic fetishism, that appears to contain a component of socialization and reinforcement in its etiology. Removing any amount of brain tissue will likely result in changes in the behavior and/or personality of the patient, which may account for the reduction or diminution of a fetish.

There are several theories as to the cause of transvestism among men. Zucker & Blanchard (1997) cite several psychoanalytic authors who believe the "illusion" of being a woman with a penis is sexually arousing. Some theorize that as children, transvestites were humiliated or punished by women and forced to dress in female attire (Seligman & Hardenburg, 2000). Others theorize there is an unconscious desire to cross-dress, for example being sexually attracted to one's mother as a young child and attempting to identify with the mother as a way to relieve the fear of castration anxiety (Peabody et al., 1954). Other authors cite behavioral reinforcement as a main cause (Zucker & Blanchard, 1997). Masturbation is highly reinforcing and when coupled with a stimulus, that stimulus may eventually be conditioned to be sexually arousing. For example, if a man were to masturbate or become sexually aroused while holding women's undergarments or while being dressed in them, that item (or others like them) may eventually become what is associated with being sexually aroused. Schott (1995) found that 78 percent of men studied found certain items of feminine clothing sexually arousing as children. Docter (as cited in Schott, 1995) believes that a high number of boys are exposed to factors that may affect their sexual attraction to women's clothes, but that most of these boys do not become cross-dressers. He believes that males who do begin cross-dressing are faced with unique social learning experiences and reinforcements resulting in the development of transvestic tendencies between the ages of eight and eighteen.

Many of these men who do cross-dress proceed to full transvestic fetishism. While in childhood, and at the beginning stages of cross-dressing, a favored article of clothing may become erotic and may be used habitually, first in masturbation and later in intercourse. Over time, the occurrence of cross-dressing may change from occasional to continuous, however, the sexual arousal of those experiences may diminish or disappear altogether. When this happens, cross-dressing becomes an antidote to anxiety or depression, or it may contribute to a sense of peace and calmness. This may especially happen when the individual is under situational stress with or without symptoms of depression. When gender dysphoria emerges, many individuals will seek treatment (APA, 2000; Buhrich & McConaghy, 1977; Person & Ovesey, 1978).

The diagnosis of a paraphilia can only be made if the symptoms are present for at least six months (Seligman & Hardenburg, 2000). Schott (1995) hypothesizes that only or eldest male children are more likely to become transvestites than males in other positions along the birth order. He believes these men were subject to significant, direct exposure to feminine influences (i.e., by their mother) without the mediating effects of an older male sibling. The exclusion of fathers as a "mediating" influence was not explored in this study. The reason for initial cross-dressing may result from a feeling of sexual excitement or gratification, however this may not forever remain the case. In a survey of 1,032 cross-dressers (Docter & Prince, 1997), it was found that 72 percent of the sample indicated their cross-dressing was associated with sexual arousal, namely orgasm. The sexual excitement that some transvestites feel from wearing women's clothing may diminish as the individual grows older. This does not mean, however, that the desire to cross-dress is diminished as well. In fact, for some, the desire to wear women's clothing becomes stronger, but it is no longer associated with arousal, but of comfort and a sense of well being (Zucker & Blanchard, 1997).

A strong area of interest related to the understanding of transvestic fetishism is the individual's childhood and family environment. Schott (1995) found that 97 percent of his sample had their first experience with cross-dressing prior to age thirteen.

Half of those indicated their initial exposure to cross-dressing in some form (having their nails polished, or hair tied back, trying on women's shoes in secret, or being dressed in women's clothing by family members) occurred before age seven. Almost half (45 percent) of the males that were dressed in women's clothing by their mother, or by choice, indicated that it happened infrequently, however 13 percent indicated it was a regular or daily occurrence.

As with homosexuality, there has been a move to look at the different styles of parenting that were had by transvestites in an effort to understand the etiology. Schott (1995) found that 86 percent of transvestites reported a neutral or very positive relationship with their mothers. Conversely, 68 percent reported neutral or very negative relationships with their fathers. In the comparison/control group, however, the men rated their mothers and fathers higher in the quality of their relationships. As noted earlier, a significant portion of cross-dressing occurs at a young age for men who become adult transvestites. It is difficult to say if the poor relationship some of these men experienced with their fathers contributes to their cross-dressing, or if their tendencies, demonstrated early on, were difficult for their fathers to handle, thus putting a strain on their relationship. On the other hand, Zucker & Blanchard (1997) indicated there is some antidotal clinical evidence to suggest that a mother-son relationship characterized as hostile and rejecting may influence the development of transvestic fetishism. There is a need for more systematic research, as evidenced by conflicting studies related to maternal attachment and its role in the psychology of those with transvestic fetishism.

Individuals with paraphilias often grew up in turbulent environments. Many grew up with fathers who were emotionally unavailable and indifferent, or had a mother who was unaffectionate and belittling. Others had loving parents and as a way to connect with their parent would dress in clothing that their parent used to wear (Seligman & Hardenburg, 2000). It has also been found that many people with paraphilias have been abused themselves, although they are reluctant to admit that this has anything to do with their paraphilia. It was also found that the abuse is more physical in nature than sexual (Seligman & Hardenburg, 2000). People with paraphilias often feel out of control but are reluctant to acknowledge this, and they also vacillate between devaluing and idealizing themselves, between punishing themselves and having a sense of entitlement (Seligman & Hardenburg, 2000). It should be noted that characteristics of individuals with paraphilia might not be generalizable to those with transvestic fetishism.

It is rare for adolescents to cross-dress and to pass themselves off as women. This tendency is more common among adults (Zucker & Blanchard, 1997). It has been found that some adolescents, in addition to masturbating in the presence of women's clothing, cut, urinate, or defecate on the garments (Zucker & Blanchard, 1997). It may be that the adolescent's feelings of pleasure are mixed with feelings of shame or guilt for their behaviors and thus feel the need to "destroy" the object that provides them with sexual excitement.

Zucker & Blanchard (1997) has found that there is an association between transvestic fetishism and other paraphilias, such as masochism. These authors believe that some men are often forced by a more dominant woman to cross-dress and wear cosmetics. Strong masochistic fantasies (e.g., whipping, bondage), they believe, are present in a minority of cases. There is also evidence that autoerotic asphyxia is more common in men who have a fetishistic component to their cross-dressing (Zucker & Blanchard, 1997).

It appears that although transvestic men may possess feminine attitudes and behaviors, their career choices are not stereotypical feminine occupations. According to Brierley (as cited in Adshead, 1997), in nonclinical samples, most of the transvestic fetishists surveyed were employed in professional or managerial roles. Men who are in stereotypical masculine, high-powered, stressful occupations may feel a sense of "relief" in dressing in women's clothing, especially if these men wear women's undergarments beneath their own attire so they may gain a sense of internal satisfaction from the "contradiction" of these two roles.

Blanchard (as cited in Zucker & Blanchard, 1997) indicates that transvestites have some difficulty developing and maintaining intimate relationships. He cites two main reasons for this: 1) Male cross-dressers are often more interested in the nonhuman features of women (e.g., clothing), and 2) they receive most of their sexual excitement from themselves (dressed in women's clothing) than from others. However, Brierley (as cited in Zucker & Blanchard, 1997) found that over 50 percent of transvestites in a nonclinical population were married. This does not however, speak to the quality of the marital relationships however. In a study of women in relationships (Brown, 1994) with transvestic men, 40 percent of women were aware of their partner's cross-dressing before their relationship became serious and committed. Forty-eight percent of women in the study indicated their partner cross-dressed in some capacity for at least one sexual encounter. Of those, 39 percent indicated being sexually aroused occasionally by their partner's cross-dressing. The level of acceptance, or desire to accept their partners' behavior is intriguing. Of the women, 22 percent would support their partner's desire to undergo treatment to be increasingly feminine (e.g., estrogen treatment or sex reassignment surgery). Another 44 percent believed they should be more accepting of their partner's cross-dressing. It appears common for some transvestites to cease their cross-dressing when they initially fall in love with a woman (Zucker & Blanchard, 1997). It often, however, reappears later and would be evidence to support a biological component to transvestic fetishism.

There is a great deal of discomfort associated with cross-dressing in public or sharing this particular part of one's life with family or friends. It was found that the most common fear among transvestic fetishists was that of rejection as well as being considered weak, crazy, or gay (Bullough, & Bullough, 1997). However, most people with a paraphilia will not seek treatment as they receive some amount of pleasure from their fantasies and behaviors and by seeking treatment they may be stigmatized (Seligman & Hardenburg, 2000).

There are now in existence transvestic clubs, organizations, and societies where transvestites can meet and socialize with one another without the fear of rejection (Denny, 1999). Some organizations limit their acceptance of members based on their sexual orientation. For example, Tri-Ess, the Society for the Second Self, will not accept members who identify as homosexual, bisexual, or transsexual (Denny, 1999). Paraphilia have been compared to impulse-control disorders such as bulimia nervosa, substance use disorders, and pathological gambling (Seligman & Hardenburg, 2000). A person with a paraphilia will often experience tension before initiating the paraphilic behavior, and become preoccupied with those behaviors associated with the paraphilia and the activities leading up to the behavior. These individuals may repeatedly try in vain to decrease their performance of the behaviors, yet continue despite evidence of the harm that it may cause in their lives (Seligman & Hardenburg, 2000). Furthermore people with paraphilia may develop a tolerance or feel a need to increase the behavior in order to achieve the level of pleasure that was once achieved prior to the tolerance (Seligman & Hardenburg, 2000). Some may experience an increase in the behaviors as a way to relieve situational stress (Buhrich & McConaghy, 1977; Seligman & Hardenburg, 2000) while others deny that situational stress is related to the frequency of their transvestic behaviors (Buhrich & McConaghy, 1979).

Although, as noted earlier, autoerotic asphyxiation and other negative consequences related to relationships are more common among transvestites, there are plenty of reasons to suggest that transvestites are men who enjoy the physical, as well as internal satisfaction of dressing as women. While transvestic fetishism is classified as a mental disorder, implying that it causes significant impairment in at least one area of functioning, there appear to be many men in which anxiety does not result from this behavior.

CHAPTER
APOTEMNOPHILIA

Deanna Monteith
and Melinda Chau

19

Apotemnophilia is a specific paraphilia involving the achievement of sexual fulfillment by fantasizing about being or becoming an amputee (Bruno, 1997). The paraphilia goes by many names, including amputeeism, and the Ugly Duckling Syndrome (Anonymous, Surgical Questions, 2002). It is estimated that as much as one in five-hundred persons are afflicted with apotemnophilia (Anonymous, Surgical Questions, 2002), but due to its private nature it may be often underreported.

There are three defined forms of apotemnophilia: devotees, pretenders, and wannabes. Dr. Richard Bruno differentiates between the three forms by the way the paraphilia is acted out. Devotees are persons who are perfectly healthy and have full use of all four limbs but are sexually drawn to disabled persons. Pretenders are also fully mobile but they find sexual gratification in pretending to be disabled (Bruno, 1997). They go so far as to tape their ankles to the back of their thighs and rent wheelchairs, then go out in public and act as though they are disabled. Wannabes are the "true" apotemnophiliacs. People with this form of the paraphilia have a compulsion to become amputees. They often go to great and extraordinary lengths in order to remove the offending limb.

Documentation of this paraphilia is rare, because there has been little to no true scientific research regarding it. Less than half a dozen research articles exist that focus on apotemnophilia (Koa, 2001), and those are dated back to the 1970s. There are no shortages of theories by doctors who have encountered cases of it. Some believe that apotemnophilia is a paraphilia that involves an attraction that is truly individualistic. The apotemnophiliac is essentially attracted to the self, not to someone or something else (Elliot, 2000, sec. 2, p. 4). It is a desire that is not discussed with or observed by others, as other paraphilia generally are. John Money first coined the term apotemnophilia to describe a paraphilia that involves the desire to cut off ones limb(s) in order to perform better sexually (Dotinga, 2000).

Others see apotemnophilia as a rare form of body dysmorphic disorder in which there is no sexual component at all. In this theory, apotemnophiliacs are convinced that they are not complete or whole with all of their limbs intact (Dyer, 2000). They become obsessed with becoming whole by removing the limb they feel is not a true part of their body.

A third theory attempting to explain the rare desires of the apotemnophiliac strives to bridge the gap between a sexual fetish and a misinterpretation of one's own body and self. It relates the paraphilia to transvestism, indicating that sufferers are not at home in their body sexually or cognitively (Dotinga, 2000). They do not feel like someone with two arms and two legs and therefore can not feel completely comfortable sexually or in every day activities.

According to the *Diagnostic and Statistical Manual of Mental Disorders-IV* APA, 1994), paraphilias are characterized by recurrent, intense sexual urges, fantasies, or behaviors that involve unusual objects, activities, or situations and cause clinically significant distress or impairment in social, occupational, or other important areas of functioning. The editor of the *Diagnostic and Statistical Manual,* is faced now with the decision of including apotemnophilia in the *DSM-V.* If current research being conducted concludes that apotemnophilia is in fact a paraphilia it will simply be subsumed into that existing category (Elliot, 2000, sec. 3, p. 4). The real question becomes, does the possibility of a psychological diagnosis of a disorder encourage increased development of that particular affliction, or does it simply increase awareness and treatment of existing cases?

An example of this particular diagnostic fear would be gender-identity disorder. The increase in gender reassignment surgeries has become more visible with the development and acceptance of the procedure. This does not mean that people have suddenly decided to surgically become a person of the opposite sex. What it does indicate is that persons with the preexisting condition feel more comfortable and able to seek help because of the social and technological advances (Elliot, 2000, sec. 3, p. 3).

The same idea could be true for persons afflicted with apotemnophilia. This disorder, like transvestism, is a private disorder. It may even be more so a personal struggle because it completely excludes the participation of anyone else, even a partner. So were it to be diagnosable and, in that light, treatable, the scenario would likely be that more persons afflicted could seek aid, not that more people would become intrigued with the idea and "develop" the disorder.

Recent cases of apotemnophilia have made it into the media because surgeons are now recognizing and treating the disorder. A British surgeon, Dr. Robert Smith, amputated the healthy legs of two patients. The surgeries were not brought to the media's attentions until Gregg Furth, an American psychologist, decided to sign up and have his healthy leg amputated. The hospital where the amputations were performed changed their guidelines for surgical procedures (Anonymous, Surgical

Questions, 2002), and the Furth's amputation was subsequently canceled. Dr. Smith noted that regarding the surgeries, that he had both patients thoroughly evaluated and saw no other option but to help them (Surgical Questions, 2002).

The alternative to surgical amputation was brought brutally into the public's eye when a friend of Furth's and fellow apotemnophiliac died because of gangrene caused by an underground leg amputation performed in Tijuana. Philip Bondy, eighty, felt he was going to finally fulfill a lifelong dream of having his leg amputated above the knee when he found John Brown, an ex-con and ex-surgeon performing underground sex changes in Mexico. Brown, known as a fringe doctor, performed the surgery for ten thousand dollars in a clinic in Tijuana then left Bondy in a motel outside San Diego. Bondy called his old friend Furth who promptly flew to California to watch over him. The next morning Furth found Bondy dead in his hotel room (Dotinga, 1999).

In this case, Brown received fifteen years in prison for his participation in Bondy's death. But what about the cases when people perform self-amputations? For instance, one man used a homemade guillotine to sever his arm, and a woman attempted to amputate both her legs by fashioning tourniquets around her upper thighs and packing them in ice (Elliot, 2000). Another man succeeded in amputating his leg by using a log splitter. Other reported self-amputation methods that are utilized by apotemnophiliacs include industrial "accidents," gunshot/shotgun wounds, self-inflicted gangrene, dry ice, cigar cutters, chainsaw "slips," wood chippers, and laying on train tracks (Elliot, 2000, sec. 2, p. 1).

Returning to the two men who each had a leg surgically amputated, the results of doctor assistance can be seen. Both men report to be happier and more complete than they were prior to their amputations (Elliot, 2000), and they are both alive and healthy. If they had been unable to seek professional help they may have both resorted to alternate means which possibly could have resulted in their deaths. (Elliot, 2000, p. 2).

Apotemnophilia is fed by the combination of two distinct feelings: that of not feeling whole and that of being sexually gratified by the idea of being an amputee. Furth described the feelings as having an alien body connected to you that you need to rid yourself of (Dotinga, 2000). Other apotemnophiliacs describe their paraphilia as the desire to physically be whom they feel they are inside. Staying true to that perception one could suspect that apotemnophilia is not a "philia" at all, but is a problem with body image (Elliot, 2000). The desire to be an amputee could simply be described as a longing to be comfortable with who the apotemnophiliac feels they truly are.

An argument against relating apotemnophilia in general to body dysmorphic disorder is that, although there is a similar quest for self-improvement, it is not based in a similar belief system. Unlike sufferers of body dysmorphic disorder, apotemnophiliacs do not feel that others see them as incomplete, defective, or unattractive (Elliot, 2000).

In contrast to Furth, another male apotemnophiliac described his experience as very sexually based. He described how as an overweight child he would pretend to be an amputee and fantasize being an amputee because he felt that if he were legitimately handicapped he would not have to join in his physical education class. He related his negative feelings toward physical education to his fear of being nude after a childhood circumcision that left him scarred. He realized at one point that he could reach orgasm by pretending to be a leg amputee (Money, 1990).

Like this man, most reported cases of apotemnophilia begin in early childhood, usually prior to the age of six or seven (Elliot, 2000). Some therapists and apotemnophiliacs relate the paraphilia to childhood trauma (Elliot, 2000, sec. 3, p. 3). Although currently there is little scientific research supporting this claim, one study found that 51 percent of apotemnophiliacs were so because a traumatic childhood experience left them believing that the only way they could be deserving of love or sexual gratification is if they were disabled (Bruno, 1997). This is further explained as an association in childhood to a disability-related stimulus, such as an amputee's stump or leg braces, with a powerful emotional state. Money (1990), suggested that one apotemnophile's childhood fear of amputation may have been replaced by the eroticization of the stump, transforming a terror into a joy. A more intuitively appealing mechanism would be the pairing in childhood of a disability-related stimulus with sexual arousal. For example, one plaster cast devotee had his first sexual experience with a girl who was wearing a leg cast. However, only 19 percent of respondents of Dixon (1983) related their interest in amputees to any kind of direct contact with a disabled person, and the overwhelming majority of devotees have reported their interest in disabled persons began long before puberty.

Additionally, attraction to disabled persons has also been related to homosexuality, sadism, and bondage (Elman, 1997). Researchers have suggested that the desires of devotees, pretenders, and wannabes develop from a combination of a strict antisexual attitude in the child's household, deprivation of maternal love, and parental rejection in early childhood that creates a fear for survival and a self-generated fantasy for security (Bruno, 1997; Dixon, 1983; Everaerd, 1983). An example of this triggering event may be a comment of sympathetic concern by the mother regarding an amputee. The child rationalizes that he would be loveable if only he were an amputee like the person his mother spoke so sympathetically about (Everaerd, 1983).

With the onset of puberty, this individual's emotional turmoil is repeated and that same solution is applied to the new problem (Bruno, 1997). This time the solution is applied to the person to whom the adolescent feels he is expected to be sexually attracted to. From out of his subconscious, the thought evolves that to be loveable, the person must be an amputee (Bruno, 1997; Dixon, 1983; Elliott, 2000). During puberty, these individuals develop daydreams and fantasies that revolve around being an amputee and these fantasies and behaviors often lead to masturbation (Elliott, 2000). Other behaviors included the collecting of amputee's materials or self-bondage for fabrication of the illusion to be an amputee.

In addition, devotees may attempt to fulfill their own unmet need for love and attention by projecting themselves onto persons with disabilities (Bruno, 1997).

Childhood experiences of pretenders and wannabes may have rendered them unable to meet their own needs and caused them to conclude that disability is the only socially acceptable reason or even the only possible reason for one to be worthy of love and attention (Dixon, 1983).

For some forms of apotemnophilia, the sexual attraction lies not only with the amputation itself, but also in the form of the amputation. Most apotemnophiliacs will attempt to amputate as much of the offending limb as they can, purportedly in an attempt to end with a stump in close proximity to genitalia. For instance, a woman will try to amputate her arm at a point that would result in a stump that rests near her breast, and a man will attempt to amputate his leg at a point that will place the stump near his genitalia (Wenig, 2002). A unique aspect of apotemnophilia is its entirely masturbatory nature. There is not an attraction to an object or another person, it is self-attraction. The act of amputating a limb increases the attraction to the self (Elliot, 2000, sec. 2, p. 4).

Typically there is no desire for pain in attainment of sexual gratification, by the apotemnophiliac. The testimony and amputative behaviors of apotemnophiliacs suggest that pain, in fact, is something to be avoided. One man who self-amputated his leg with a wood chipper researched anesthesia and wound control prior to attempting and completing the act (Elliot, 2000, sec. 2, p. 1). Another man drank himself unconscious while lying on railroad tracks in an attempt to avoid experiencing the pain (Gregson, 2002). The pain that is reportedly associated with apotemnophilia is more of the emotional variety: a desperation and emotional longing that combines with sexual fantasies to feed a rare form of gratification.

The true cause of apotemnophilia may never be pinpointed. There are likely many factors feeding into its manifestation. It has been claimed that persons who are afflicted with it are commonly also afflicted with other psychiatric disorders, such as depression, obsessive-compulsive disorder, eating disorders, and forms of transvestism (Elliot, 2000, sec. 2, p. 2).

Some researchers indicate that individuals afflicted with apotemnophilia may prefer a disabled or disfigured individual because they might be perceived as less threatening, more attainable, easily dominated, or represent a "love object" (Bruno, 1997). However, it does not explain the some times obsessive and compulsive attraction to disabled persons or the powerful desire to appear or to become disabled.

According to the Dixon (1983) study, only 13 percent of apotemnophiles have had a long-term relationship with an amputee. An actual relationship would cause the disabled individual to become a "real person," making projection of the devotee's own needs difficult or even impossible, and eliminating this indirect means for experiencing love and attention (Money, 1990). Researchers suggest that apotemnophiliacs need only one medical intervention that leaves them with an indelible and obvious stigma of disability that they believe will permanently satisfy their need and attention (Money, 1990; Dixon, 1983).

Apotemnophiliacs are involved in a deviant effort to be loved, and to them that means receiving. They receive economic benefits perhaps, maybe a handicapped parking sticker for their car, but more importantly, sympathy (Bruno, 1997). As victims, apotemnophiliacs feel justified in receiving help from others, and they feel justified in not assisting others. (Cheaney, 2001). One way to look at apotemnophilia is to see it as a form of attention seeking. There are self-reports expressing a need to be in a position to do something extraordinary, namely be able to display exceptional coping skills, the ability to rise above a disability and still master tasks of the nondisabled person (Elliot, 2000). This as well could stem from childhood experience or perceptions. The inability to attain greatness as you are, but in the face of adversity (i.e., being disabled), the ability to complete seemingly normal tasks successfully is just as heroic as a soldier in war or a star football player. It is interesting to note that perceived heroes in the western cultures are commonly sexualized, a plus for the apotemnophiliac.

With the advent of the Internet and other media sources, apotemnophiliacs have moved toward a more public domain. There are many websites and chat rooms devoted to amputeeism including compact discs with the voices of amputees (cyberblastrecords.com).

The newly fostered connections and friendships between apotemnophiliacs may form a support system, sharing techniques for home amputations. As the nature of the paraphilia is not currently harmful to others, it rarely even comes to the attention of others. However, the sympathy given to accidental amputee victims is quite possibly what the apotemnophiliacs are in search of. Others, like Philip Bondy, may be so ashamed of their desires that they would rather live with the obsession or die trying to secretly satisfy it. As one apotemnophiliac stated, "As a psychology major, I have analyzed and reanalyzed, and rereanalyzed just why I want this. I have no clear idea" (Elliot, 2000, sec. 3, p. 6).

C H A P T E R

HYPOXYPHILIA, ASPHYXIOPHILIA, AND AUTOEROTIC ASPHYXIA

20

MILA GREEN MCGOWAN
AND DEANNA MONTEITH

In today's society, oddities are capitalized on, including unique sexual preferences. Various mainstream films have portrayed sexual variations or paraphilia. *American Pie,* a teen comedy, is well known for depicting a young man sexually experimenting with an apple pie. *Boxing Helen* chronicles the fantasy story of a man's progressive dismembering of his female lover to satisfy his sexual attraction to amputees (a paraphilia called apotemnophilia). The worldwide web is rife with articles and stories about adolescents and adults found dead from an assortment of compromising sexual endeavors. For example, a young man was reported to employ a cow's heart as a masturbatory aid. The youth hooked the dead heart up to an electrical outlet to cause it to beat to stimulate him sexually. This activity resulted in his electrocution. Stories like this only serve to distort public knowledge and understanding about paraphilia and sexual variations. Further, such stories result in public misinterpretation of the actual level of dangerousness and pervasiveness of these sexual deviations.

HYPOXYPHILIA AND ASPHYXIOPHILIA

Hundreds, of paraphilia are practiced by thousands of people each year. One particular paraphilia which has become increasingly more recognized is hypoxyphilia or asphyxiophilia (de Silva, 1999). Asphyxiophilia is defined as "a paraphilia in which sexual arousal and the attainment of gratification depends on hypoxia induced through strangulation, smothering, chest compressions and/or inhalation of volatile substances" (Book & Perumal, 1993, p. 687). While Quinn and Twomey (1998) would

185

agree with this definition, they clarify that the induction of cerebral hypoxia to produce or enhance sexual excitement is *deliberate,* thus implying a directed and active approach to oxygen deprivation in this paraphilia. This particular paraphilia reportedly has origins in the 1600s, stemming from treatment for erectile dysfunction and impotency (de Silva, 1999).

Other researchers have referred to this paraphilia as sexually-motivated smothering (www.studioja.com), sexual asphyxia, terminal sex, "scarfing" (Hickey, 2006), or Kotzwarrism (Kotzwarra, a famous musician, is believed to have died in 1791 when a prostitute agreed to hang him briefly as part of their sexual encounter; Milner & Dopke, 1997). The term hypoxyphilia comes from a blending of the Greek words *hupo* (meaning under), *oxus* meaning oxygen, and *philia* meaning love. Though no distinct clinical diagnosis exists for this paraphilia in the *DSM-IV-Tr,* such pursuits would fall under the Paraphilia Not Otherwise Specified category, atypical focus involving human objects—self or others (Milner & Dopke, 1997). While some people engage in mutual or nonconsensual partner asphyxiophilia during sexual relations, and would qualify for an Asphyxiophilic or paraphilic label, the bulk of sexual asphyxia cases involve autoerotic practices.

AUTOEROTIC ASPHYXIATION DEMOGRAPHICS

The term autoerotic asphyxiation (AEA) implies the solitary practice of asphyxiophilia; thus it is referred to as an "autoerotic" activity. This practice involves self-applied means that deprive the brain of oxygen while masturbating. The literature maintains autoerotic asphyxiation practices are most commonly found among adolescents and young adult males aged fifteen to twenty-five (Clark, 1996; Levay, 2000). However, some anecdotal evidence shows a few women do participate in this activity, but usually in the context of dominant/submissive role-playing with a partner (Levay, 2000). Only a few cases of true female autoerotic asphyxia have been detailed in criminological literature (Douglas, Burgess, Burgess, & Ressler, 1992; Holmes & Holmes, 2002). These scholars believe the identification of AEA activity in lone females in complicated by the fact that in the few female AEA deaths that do occur, common autoerotic fatality death scene indicators are usually absent (e.g., props, cross-dressing items) (Milner & Dopke, 1997). Overwhelmingly, practitioners of AEA appear to be white, but this belief is predicated solely on the fact that accidental asphyxia fatalities are almost exclusively white (Holmes & Holmes, 2002).

Holmes and Holmes (2002) have found certain psychological traits common among those who die of AEA. For example, loved ones of the victims often report the person was shy, introverted, possibly socially isolated, and had few interests or hobbies. Further, they lacked the necessary social skills to interact adequately with those of romantic interest to them. Many have been described as overachievers in all aspects of their lives, including physical health and grooming. A middle-class upbringing and parents who are or were professionals is not uncommon. Finally, and most ironically, many AEA practitioners are avid churchgoers and seen by others as devout. This may explain why the "aberrant" sexual activity of masturbation is further bastardized and hidden, becoming the foremost outlet for otherwise unwelcome sexual urges.

ASPHYXIATION METHODS

STRANGULATION OR SMOTHERING

This type of autoerotic asphyxia practice often involves hanging, as this method effectively constricts the blood flow to the brain (Levay, 2000), thus deoxygenating the brain, by exerting pressure on the carotid arteries in the neck (Holmes & Holmes, 2002). Hanging is the most dangerous form of AEA, as it is too easy for victims to accidentally restrict their ability to pull themselves out of an ill-fashioned noose before they lose consciousness. Suffocation, another AEA method, may be achieved when plastic bags are placed around the head or by the use of gas masks or surgical masks to cause loss of consciousness.

INHALANTS OR "INTERFERENCE WITH BREATHING" APPARATUS

This form of hypoxia involves the use of chemical inhalants or narcotics to cause euphoria and near loss of consciousness (because of constricted breathing passages). For example, tetrachloroethylene, a component in Fix-a-flat tire repair aerosol cans (Isenschmid, Cassin, Bradford, & Sawait, 1998), or freon (an air conditioning chemical) (Holmes & Holmes, 2002) have reportedly been used during sexual "huffing" practices. In two-person asphyxiation practices (or with one very creative person), chest compression allows only a little air to get through into the lungs. In other instances, the nose and mouth of the person may be blocked with clothing or material so that the desired affect is achieved.

OTHER PARAPHILIA ASSOCIATED WITH AUTOEROTIC ASPHYXIA

TRANSVESTITISM

Male victims of autoerotic fatalities are often been found dressed in women's clothes, holding some piece of women's clothing, wearing make-up, or with shaved legs (Levay, 2000). Zucker and Blanchard (1997) found the practice of AEA is associated with fantasies of being a woman engaging in sexual intercourse or other erotic activities. These authors discovered a significant correlation between the presence of dildos at the death scene and feminine attire on the deceased in 117 cases of autoerotic fatalities. A study by Hazelwood, Dietz and Burgess (1983), cited in Adshead

(1997), found 13 percent of autoerotic fatalities were reported, posthumously, to be cross-dressers and another 20 percent were found cross-dressed at the time of death.

PORNOGRAPHY

Sadomasochistic literature and other pornography, including stories, videos, and photos, have often been found in the vicinity of the deceased at autoerotic fatality scenes. Many researchers believe that such literature is one unfortunate way that young men discover AEA practices to begin with. In many autoerotic fatalities, investigators also find a mirror (of varying size) within the visual field of the deceased as the person had attempted to view themselves during masturbation, especially if they were cross-dressed, to enhance their fantasy (Holmes & Holmes, 2002).

BONDAGE AND SADOMASOCHISM

Often self-binding and other bondage activities are used in AEA pursuits. Practitioners may dress up in tight forms of dress, latex or leather hoods, rain boots, blindfolds or gags, use masochistic nipple clips, or engage in genital branding (www.studioja .com); all of which may increase pain and/or the chance of fatal strangulation.

Hypoxyphilia and autoerotic asphyxia are thought of as forms of sexual masochism, a recognized chronic disorder which involves sexual arousal related to being humiliated, caused to suffer, or bound in some form (Seligman & Hardenburg 2000). Though it is not currently recognized as the most pervasive form of sexual masochism, it is one of the most dangerous forms. However, many forensic professionals believe that people who engage in autoerotic asphyxiation do not meet the diagnostic criteria for sexual masochism per se, as asphyxiophilia enthusiasts do not usually enjoy pain and may more often attempt to diminish discomfort by padding ligatures or placing soft cloths between restraints and skin. The erotic focus of asphyxiophilia is not on the suffering caused by the hypoxia methods, nor on the methods themselves, but on the increased arousal resulting from a lack of oxygen.

The *DSM-IV-Tr* suggests that sadomasochistic disorders like hypoxyphilia and autoerotic asphyxiation typically become apparent in childhood and then overt in early adulthood (p. 152). For some persons with these disorders the nature of the behaviors does not escalate with time, but others increase the severity of their sadomasochistic behaviors, which, in turn, increases their chances of their actions resulting in accidental death (p. 152).

A study conducted by Alison, Santilla, Sandnabba, and Nordling (2001) found that sadomasochistic behaviors are often preferentially divided among male participants and female participants. Results indicated that females most preferred sadomasochistic activities revolving around humiliation (symbolic pain), whereas males more often practiced sadomasochistic behaviors that were related to hypermasculinity (literal pain) (Alison et al., 2001). The study further showed that, among others, hypoxyphilia was related to hypermasculinity, not humiliation. This finding could explain why more males are interested in or practice hypoxyphilia than females.

THEORIES REGARDING AUTOEROTIC ASPHYXIA DEVELOPMENT

PSYCHOLOGICAL

For some individuals, literal pain is not the central attraction of sadomasochistic behaviors. Califia (1979) suggested that sadomasochism's attraction for some who engage in it is more related to power than to pain (cited by Alison et al., 2001). This suggestion more clearly explains asphyxiophilia, as pain is not the focus of this paraphilic pursuit. Other research has indicated that the element of self-endangerment and the life-threatening nature of hypoxyphilia, when combined with the physiological aspects or cerebral anoxia heightens the sexual arousal. Others have postulated that the loss of voluntary control over one's freedom of movement or ability to breathe is psychologically connected with the arousal in sexual asphyxia. Many believe the fear and risk of injury or death is the arousing component. Additionally, fantasies of death are thought to figure prominently into some AEA practitioners' sexual enjoyment (www.studioja.com). Practitioners who believe masturbation is wrong may attempt to punish themselves with near death for engaging in it (Milner & Dopke, 1997). The practice of autoerotic asphyxia may hold symbolic meanings about death, even though practitioners are by no means suicidal. The process of ejaculation under such intense and dangerous conditions is equated in these individuals with "a symbolic death as in each orgasmic experience, one loses a part of the self" (Resnick, 1983, p. 243). People who feel weak and helpless may simulate death, and the "escape" from it, through AEA activities to gain a sense of power and control in their lives.

Psychoanalysts deconstruct autoerotic asphyxia to the basic sexual and aggressive drives they report all men hold towards the incestuous object, their mothers. Men thus resort to AEA behavior as punishment for these incestuous feelings. Others in this theoretical paradigm purport AEA behavior is driven by a desire to assume a passive role in the family by hanging—the hanging represents castration and reduces the castration fears they hold that stem from an Oedipal complex (Milner & Dopke, 1997). Unfortunately, these postulations do not adequately explain all AEA activity, especially that of females.

Social learning theorists report that autoerotic asphyxia practitioners must have experienced strict and punitive punishment as a child, so they begin to somehow associate punishment with sexuality and love. Meanwhile, behaviorists say the act of producing sexual asphyxia is acquired like any other behavior and is thus incorporated into a "paraphilic masturbatory ritual" because of how good it makes a person feel (Milner & Dopke, 1997, p. 412). As such, Thornton and Mann (1997) report "many people who engage in sexual masochism, including AEA, report a diminished capacity for non-masochistic sexual practices" overtime (p. 249). Their obsession with AEA behavior ends up undermining their ability to develop emotionally intimate relationships with others as they focus only on autoerotic stimulation.

PHYSIOLOGICAL

Historically, numerous cases have been documented in which men executed by hanging had visible erections and orgasms right before death. This phenomenon and the known physiologic reactions to brain hypoxia are believed to have contributed to the creation of AEA behavior at some point. The "high" of asphyxiation produces dizziness, shivering, goose skin, heart palpitation, breathlessness, and sometimes pain; all contribute to the orgasmic response (www.studioja.com). During asphyxiation, "the cerebral cortex is partially knocked out and its normal inhibitory influences on the thalamus and the hypothalamus (areas that stimulate sensations of pleasure) is removed" (Levay, 2000, p. 1).

DEVELOPMENTAL

The few existing studies of living AEA practitioners demonstrate that such practices typically begin experimentally in adolescence (Levay, 2000). Inconclusive studies have proposed that possible sexual abuse in childhood provokes the behavior (Clark, 1996), However, the profiles of both teen and adult AE fatalities show little drug or alcohol use, no homosexual inclinations (despite the cross-dressing), little depression, intact parental relationships, and few conduct disorder or antisocial personality diagnoses. Therefore, issues of previous abuse, neglect or family dysfunction may not figure prominently into all cases of AEA.

Studies have shown that older practitioners of AEA are more likely to engage in both transvestite fetishism and bondage (Zucker & Blanchard, 1997), suggesting as interest in and reliance on autoerotic activities for gratification advances, the need for additional stimulation grows as well. However, most documented autoerotic fatalities occur in adolescents and persons in their early twenty's. Thus, maturation may decrease the lethality of such practices, not because less time is spent engaging in autoeroticism, but safer and more intricate methods of hypoxia have been concocted by older enthusiasts.

NEUROCHEMICAL

Some documented cases of autoerotic asphyxia provide evidence of an underlying neurochemical component to AEA. Quinn and Twomey (1998) present a case of AEA occurring in a man with a history of mild mental handicap, epilepsy, and schizophrenia. His autoerotic behavior reemerged only after his neuroleptic medication was reduced and his sexual urges returned. Another psychiatric patient, when prescribed lithium carbonate, was able to extinguish his very dangerous AEA practices according to a case study by Cesnik and Coleman (1989).

PREVALENCE OF AUTOEROTIC ASPHYXIA AND RESULTING FATALITIES

Individuals who enjoy such pursuits (e.g., autoerotic asphyxia) rarely seek professional advice (Quinn & Twomey, 1998). As such, this sexual practice is normally only discovered when some harm (Holmes & Holmes, 2002) or an accidental death results from an act of asphyxiophilia. Even then, accurate statistics are difficult to amass because many of these accidents are misidentified as accidental deaths or suicides (Holmes & Holmes, 2002; Levay, 2000). The *DSM-IV-Tr,* reports, "due to the relatively unrecognized nature of the paraphilia only one or two of these accidental deaths are actually recognized yearly" (p. 152). However, it is suggested that hypoxyphilia can be credited with hundreds of deaths each year (Hickey, 2006).

One Scandinavian study estimated a frequency of up to two autoerotic asphyxia deaths per one million inhabitants (as reported in Denmark, Sweden, and Norway by Innala, Goeteborgs & Ernulf, 1989). Canadian researchers estimated ten autoerotic fatalities per year in Ontario and Alberta combined (Hucker & Stermac, 1992), while Clark (1996) surmised five-hundred to one-thousand young men die in the United States annually from AEA. Clark further estimates as much as 30 percent of all adolescent hanging fatalities can be attributed to failed attempts at autoerotic stimulation. Hypoxyphilia has reportedly been responsible for 6.5 percent of adolescent deaths and 31 percent of adolescent hanging deaths spanning ten years (*The Auto-erotic Asphyxiation Syndrome*).

MISINTERPRETATING AUTOEROTIC ASPHYXIA ACTIVITIES

In many cases, the discovery of AEA behavior is misinterpreted, especially among the mentally ill, as parasuicide activity or a suicidal gesture. Further, as many AEA practitioners are not discovered until they accidentally kill themselves, the ruling out of either a homicidal or suicidal act must occur before concluding the death is the result of failed autoeroticism.

Families and survivors of those who die because of AEA are often puzzled and troubled by this bizarre behavior in someone they believed to be free of any "abnormal" sexuality (Clark, 1996). As such, "it is widely documented that families alter the scene of victim's death in such cases in order to mislead investigators and avoid embarrassment" (Turvey, 1995) or out of pure ignorance. Loved ones may reposition or re-clothe the body or replace feminine attire with male dress (Douglas et al., 1992) prior to calling the police. They may also remove key AEA indictors, such as pornography and sex toys or ropes and bindings from the scene, thus complicating the work of investigators. Finally, they may go so far as to write a suicide note to make the accident appear a suicide (Douglas et al., 1992).

SHOULD WE BE CONCERNED ABOUT AUTOEROTIC ASPHYXIA?

Many people have issues with autoerotic asphyxia because of their moral beliefs surrounding sexuality, especially fetishism and masturbation. The subject of AEA is often seen as taboo and not discussed, as it should be. This lack of open discussion is of concern for two reasons:

First, the risks involved in the pursuit of autoerotic asphyxia behavior are not well publicized and people, especially youth, are attempting such bizarre activities without fully understanding the dangers. Regardless of the method employed, it is clear that any attempt to deprive the brain of oxygen to achieve certain physiological effects is dangerous. It not only increases the risk of death caused by a direct lack of oxygen or unconsciousness, but it can also trigger heart irregularities and heart attacks (www.studioja.com). As young men and women often learn about AEA either through peers, pornographic material, the media, or accidental self-discovery (Resnick, 1983), they are not educated about how risky such a pursuit can be. Open discussion and a proper understanding of autoerotic asphyxia practices could lead to a better classification of the high "suicide" rates among youth (Milner & Dopke, 1997) and could prevent future accidental fatalities and the deaths of children as young as eight and nine years old (Douglas et al., 1992).

Second, some researchers (Hucker, 1997) have hypothesized that a link between asphyxiophilia, and AEA specifically, and lust murders exists, based on clinical interviews with forensic inpatients and criminal defendants. Hickey (2006) concurs as he writes "a few serial offenders have reported engaging in a variety of autoerotic activities" (p. 24). If this is the case, a greater understanding of autoerotic asphyxia is clearly warranted. One wonders if initially autoerotic forms of asphyxiophilia in adolescence can in fact progress to partner asphyxiophilia and then coerced hypoxia. If this is the case, as we have seen that some AEA practitioners become dependant on hypoxia for a true sexual high (see Thornton & Mann, 1997), a sexual predator's reliance on nonconsensual asphyxiophilia is not any stretch of the imagination (especially in cases where the offender believes their victim will actually enjoy the sex e.g., power reassurance rapists or pedophiles). If autoerotic asphyxia can result so easily in accidental death, so, too, can partner asphyxia, consensual or otherwise. Further, sadistic sexual offenders have also been known to used coercive asphyxia on their victims to enhance their own sexual pleasure, not by seeing the victim enjoy the assault, but for the control they exert over the victim's existence and the pain and suffering it causes.

C H A P T E R

NYMPHOMANIA
Historical Foundations

CATHERINE SANCHEZ

21

Society has been uncomfortable acknowledging that women can be sexual beings, but that attitude has begun to change recently. When exhibited openly by males, normal sexual behavior is seen as an integral part of their character. Any time females have exhibited sexual behavior that is similar to that of a male, it is seen as more serious and an issue that must generate greater concern.

Starting in the 1960s, women began to experience an atmosphere in which they were afforded opportunities to explore their sexuality. For over the past forty years, women have been able to explore parts of their personalities related to sexuality that have been historically off limits. With this freedom to express themselves, women have been taking back and owning those terms that have come to depict women in a derogatory light. Terms such as "bitch" and "nympho" that are used to demean women are now being used by women as a way of removing the stigma from the words.

This examination of the history of nymphomania is to assist readers in understanding how it came to be viewed so negatively by society. Females are rarely diagnosed with or seen as having paraphilia or other sexual perversions. Paraphilia are often seen as afflictions for men only and are described in terms of their effects on men and how men deal with them. However nymphomania is a specific paraphilia/sexual perversion that is associated with females.

DEFINITION AND SYMPTOMATOLOGY

Nymphomania has been defined as " a female disorder consisting of an excessive or insatiable desire for sexual stimulation and gratification (Corsini, 1999, p. 653). This was a diagnosis that gained popularity in the eighteenth century and was seen as a disease with a biological basis that could be treated like any other biological condition. It appears that true nymphomania is a rare condition, society was seemingly so uncomfortable with the notion of a woman displaying her sexuality that the behaviors had to be defined as deviant in some way for society to accept that the behaviors could occur (Ellis & Sagarin, 1964). Other characteristics of nymphomania can include multiple encounters with multiple partners, an inability to achieve sexual satisfaction, an internal conflict regarding their behavior, and an inability to see potential partners as humans rather than sex objects (www.medfriendly.com). The clinical diagnosis of nymphomania no longer exists; it has not been included in the *Diagnostic and Statistical Manual of Mental Disorders (DSM)* for over twenty years.

Historically, a clear-cut list of specific symptoms defined nymphomania. The determination and diagnosis of nymphomania was also based on the behaviors of the female and how "out of the ordinary" the female's behavior was viewed to be by the physician (Groneman, 1994). Some of the symptoms of nymphomania included speaking obscenities, vulgar body gyrations, extreme restlessness, erotic dreams, an enlarged uterus, and a long clitoris (Groneman, 2000).

The nonsexual symptoms of nymphomania, such as convulsions, paralysis, blindness, and the appearance of strangulation, could be associated with the diagnosis of hysteria. A diagnosis of nymphomania was made when a physician determined the sexual symptoms displayed by an individual were more excessive than they should have been for society's norms (Groneman, 1994).

Differentiating nymphomania from promiscuity is an important part of understanding the paraphilia. There is often confusion between the two because for some it may be difficult to believe that a woman would want to have multiple sexual partners. Some key differences are that nymphomanics lack control, possess a continuous need for sexual activity, and are compulsive (Ellis & Sagarin, 1964). According to Ellis and Sagarin (1964), true nymphomaniacs are unable to control their desires for sexual contact and the urges become so intense they must be filled immediately, no matter what the cost. These urges appear to be insatiable (Ellis & Sagarin, 1964). Even though nymphomaniacs usually have the ability to achieve orgasm, it is not enough to satisfy their urges, so they search for more partners in order to satisfy their needs.

The course of nymphomania is compulsive by nature. Ellis and Sagarin (1964) state that a nymphomaniac will be driven to satisfy her urges even though she may try in vain to change her behavior. A final defining characteristic of nymphomania is personal contempt (Ellis & Sagarin, 1964). Because the nature of the behavior is sexual, they could be seen as dirty and less human than their peers. They are more likely to be judged by society for their behaviors, and this is likely to promote a negative self-image that results in personal contempt (Ellis & Sagarin, 1964).

EARLY TREATMENT

The treatments developed for nymphomania were fairly standard for the time period. Women were treated with a variety of methods, including caustics being applied to the genitals in order to diminish their erotic feelings, being bled with leeches, being subjected to cold-water douches, cooling baths, and a moderate diet (Groneman, 1994). These were very common treatment methods for the eighteenth century and were widely accepted as being helpful in treating and curing nymphomania. The treatments were picked depending on the symptoms being exhibited by the patient and the severity of each of the symptoms. For example, in a mild case of nymphomania, restricting a female's diet and frequent cooling baths may have been enough to resolve the symptoms. In the case of severe symptoms, it may have been necessary for caustics, cold-water douches, and bleeding with leeches to be used frequently to resolve the symptoms.

CAUSES OF NYMPHOMANIA

The causes of nymphomania have been widely speculated, but no consensus has been reached. Some research suggests that nymphomania results from a psychic disintegration that is a product of some trauma or meaningful life event (Krafft-Ebing, 1906). In his book *Psychopathia Sexualis* (1906), Krafft-Ebing recounted several case studies of women who were affected by life events and deteriorated into nymphomania, including one woman who began to demonstrate nymphomaniacal symptoms after being left by her betrothed. Krafft-Ebing (1906) also stated that a woman's menstrual cycle or another medical condition, such as dementia or psychosis, could have an effect on the presence and progression of nymphomania.

Other research suggests that nymphomania is the result of frequent masturbation and participation in other illicit sexual acts (Abbey, 1882). Abbey (1882) and his colleagues believed that nymphomania could occur in any social class and could eventually progress into complete insanity and madness if left untreated. Abbey also stated the presence of nymphomania could lead to a variety of other diseases, such as hysteria or epilepsy, and in the most extreme untreated cases, death.

PHYSICIANS' PERCEPTIONS

Once the diagnosis of nymphomania became popular, it was diagnosed in a wide variety of situations. The diagnosis essentially became a catchall for any symptomatology that involved a sexual component. Nymphomania was diagnosed in cases relating to childbirth, malaria, homosexuality, consumption, and opium use (Groneman, 1994). It may be likely that when physicians could not make a definitive diagnosis based on their skill and knowledge, a diagnosis of nymphomania would be made in order to explain any type of behavior that was out of character for the individual.

In the eighteenth century, women were supposed to be seen as moral and decent. They were to uphold the values of society and act as role models for others. During the course of diagnosing nymphomania, one of the criteria would be evaluating the loss of decency and morality the individual exhibited (Groneman, 1994; Krafft-Ebing, 1906). Physicians felt it was their duty to return women suffering from nymphomania to their previous positions of decency and morality.

SOCIETY'S VIEW

In the eighteenth century, women were thought to be passive, modest, and the bastions of domesticity (Groneman, 1994). They were not seen as sexual beings, and society shunned those women who did express themselves in that manner. This passive and domestic attitude towards women has persisted to the present day. During the height of the sexual revolution, it became common for women with high sex drives who expressed themselves openly to be called "sluts" and "whores."

The term "nympho" has come to be a pejorative term to describe a woman. It is likely that many men who are unable to reconcile the openness of a woman who is comfortable with her sexuality must degrade her in some way in order to feel better about themselves. It is also likely that men who need to degrade women are dealing with their own sexual dysfunction and may accuse others of being hypersexual in order to conceal their own deficiencies. Even though women have made great strides in terms of becoming independent and self-sufficient, double standards still exist when sexuality is the topic. Men who have multiple sexual partners and openly demonstrated their virility are admired by some for their conquests, but women who demonstrate the same attitude and behavior may be viewed as "sluts," "whores," or "nymphos" as a way of putting them down and discounting them (www.ensexlopedia .com).

CONCLUSION

Nymphomania is rare, but the connotations associated with the word are not. The term and its derivatives have come to be used to describe any female who exhibits any type of overt sexual behavior. This term has become outdated, but the attitudes and beliefs regarding women who exhibit their sexuality remains. Perhaps when society can accept women on equal terms with men the negative terms used to describe women will lose their meaning.

CHAPTER

HYBRISTOPHILIA

The Love of Criminals

COREY VITELLO

22

Charlene Gallego, a well-off suburban girl with a high IQ, seemed to be totally submissive to husband Gerald. She called him "Daddy," tiptoed around his slaps and elbow-jabs, and catered to him in any way she could, even sharing him with other women when she had to. When he developed erection trouble, Charlene suggested that they pick up sex slaves—but only to make her man happy, mind you, not because she was, herself, an admitted raging sex addict who liked little girls. Gerald gave Charlene the excuse she needed to indulge her own sick appetites. They raped and killed eight young women in pursuit of Gerald's erection and Charlene's orgasm.

(Erlbaum, 1999, *Heinous as Hell*).

Hybristophilia is a paraphilia of the predatory type in which sexual arousal, facilitation, and attainment of orgasm are responsive to and contingent upon being with a partner known to have committed an outrage or crime, such as rape, murder, or armed robbery (Money, 1989). Although many times actual sexual contact between the hybristophile and his/her paraphilic object are frustrated by prison rules and iron bars, a segment of the population is turned on by inmates nonetheless. These individuals are known as *prison groupies* (Linedecker, 1993). Most infamous prisoners have their paraphilic fan clubs; some eventually marry their admirers despite the implausibility that the partners will ever consummate the nuptials "and such normal pleasures of married life as sharing a home and parenthood will clearly be beyond reach" (Linedecker, 1993, p. 15).

According to Money (1989), hybristophilia comes from the Greek word *hybridzein* meaning "to commit an outrage against someone" and *philo* meaning "having a strong affinity or preference for." As a paraphilia recognized more often in women than in men, hybristophiles are attracted to those who commit outrages and criminal acts (Money, 1999). Erlbaum (1999) states

> Hybristophiles may idolize whichever roughneck cretin is currently terrorizing the town on their favorite soap. Or they might write fan letters to convicts, professing their admiration and support. Maybe they found a passive guy to carry out their vicious self-hating desires by proxy.

Many female hybristophiles have mastermind criminal plans and coaxed their boyfriends into participating in order to achieve sexual arousal (Erlbaum, 1999). Hybristophiles may even instigate a partner to commit a crime in order to be convicted and sent to prison (Money, 1989). This "Bonnie and Clyde Syndrome" ranges from mildly criminal to deadly: "It may manifest itself merely as an attraction to sneering pop stars. Or, for [many] women . . . it may result in an irresistible compulsion to seek out and partner with heinous sexual sadists in crimes against other women" (Erlbaum, 1999).

THE DEVELOPMENT OF HYBRISTOPHILIA

Hybristophiles are often the past and present victims of physical and sexual abuse resulting in low self-esteem and insecurity, making them particularly vulnerable to deviant sexual preferences and criminality. "Many come from abusive backgrounds, some continue to suffer at their partners' hands, and a few wind up dead when their partners run out of handy objects for their rage" (Erlbaum, 1999). On the other hand, many are not victims at all; they merely want to sublimate their violent tendencies by collaborating with a perpetrator of violence. Worse still, they may enjoy taking part in a brutal sex crime (Erlbaum, 1999). Whatever the case may be, the "compulsive attraction to criminals [for hybristophiles] varies in disposition and degree. The results of these attractions vary as well" (Erlbaum, 1999).

Money (1999) theorizes that hybristophiles partake in the "opponent process learning" (p. 128). This process turns the accepted principles of operant conditioning upside down;

> [The] opponent process converts negative into positive, tragedy into triumph, and aversion into addiction. Two recreational examples of opponent process reversals are bungee jumping and riding a gravity defying roller coaster. The novice whose apprehension amounts to sheer terror at first may, after very few trials, discover that terror transmogrifies into exhilaration and ecstasy as if the brain had released a flood of its own opiate-like endorphins. Thereafter, the thrill returns with each repeat, totally replacing terror (p. 128).

Money believes this process is evident in all paraphilic behaviors; "The ideation and imagery that other people disapprove of and punish if translated into action reasserts itself repetitiously and insistently demands a live performance, consequences notwithstanding" (p. 128). This process can be seen clearly in hybristophilia, manifested in the paraphilic fixation on partners known to have committed violent crimes or committed other socially unacceptable outrages. According to Money (1999), this process takes place even if one's own life is at stake. "In its most malignant form, the woman subtly precipitates a rage attack in her partner, and then she has him arrested and imprisoned for domestic violence. Subsequently, she visits him in prison and sexually frustrates him by her unavailability" (p. 128). For the hybristophile, this scenario would be exciting and sexually arousing.

THE BAD-BOY PHENOMENON AND THE MEDIA

Women, teens especially, have the unfortunate reputation for wanting to find a partner who fits the "bad boy image" (Erlbaum, 1999). "The sexy bad boy is a staple American icon. He embodies machismo, individualism and all that other . . . potent ideals of the U.S" (Erlbaum, 1999). Bad boys come in differing degrees, and most women would confess to having a minor crush on at least one at the end of the spectrum (Bruce, 2002).

This hybristophilic phenomenon is proliferated and seemingly encouraged on television, in movies, and in magazines. According to Erlbaum (1999), the media sensationalizes criminals to the point that many women crave to be associated with them and their deviant lifestyles. From made-for-television movies to books to websites to music, crime is eroticized for the viewing and listening pleasure of youth across the United States.

Criminals are portrayed as sympathetic and the stars that play them on TV are almost always hunky, teen idol types. ". . . The media doesn't just reward celebrity impersonations of criminals. The media will be happy to reverse the formula and bring you the actual criminals, celebritized for your vicarious pleasure" (Erlbaum, 1999). The network that gets the big exclusive with the latest serial killer is certain to score large with the ratings—especially if that serial killer is good-looking and charismatic.

Cara Bruce (2002), author of *The Thrill of the Killer,* recounts her fascination with the bad-boy icon:

> . . . when I was 18, I liked the excitement. I had a fetish for bad boys—crazy, violent, dangerous—the more insane, the better. Reality wasn't cutting it for me and drugs weren't always available. And besides, there was something sexy about a total f**king nutcase, about the uncertainty of what he might do next."

Perhaps the James Dean rebel character represented an alternative to growing old and responsible. Maybe, women fall for the bad boys because they are forbidden— "[P]erhaps it's the ultimate taboo, thus, the ultimate aphrodisiac" (Bruce, 2002). Consequently, those women who do not grow out of the bad-boy fixation become a hybristophile because the image is so strongly paired with sexual arousal; they need to be with a notorious partner to achieve sexual pleasure.

Erlbaum (1999) suggests that the development of this "bad boy" attraction is greatest among teenaged girls.

> For teenaged girls, the appeal of the 'bad boy' is often twice as strong. When rebellion mixes with the first flushes of hormonal attraction, the chemistry can become explosive. This is, especially true when the young lady in question has parents who object to her new swain. Her romance, once forbidden, becomes even more attractive than before, and woe to the parents who get in their way (Erlbaum, 1999).

THE BONNIE AND CLYDE SYNDROME

Although research into hybristophilia is scant, some experts believe that childhood abuse might be partly to blame. Teens who have been abused oftentimes adopt a masochistic perception of life. Perhaps they feel that they deserve to be punished (similar to victims of domestic abuse), or they believe that love can only be found in partners who are violent.

When a person becomes sexually aroused by the thought of being with a violent partner, that person has developed a paraphilia. This development may start early. "If a girl has suffered abuse in the home since childhood, she's usually been waiting for the onset of puberty to bring her new powers and better options. Now she can seduce someone, find love, and marry out of the family" (Erlbaum, 1999). However, most abused women are not destined to become infatuated with criminal partners.

PRISON GROUPIES

The literature on women who fall in love with men incarcerated for violent and often murderous crimes is limited. The seminal writing on this subject is Clifford Linedecker's 1993 work, *Prison Groupies: The Shocking True Story of the Women who Love America's Deadliest Criminals.* In his book, Linedecker exposes the love affairs of many of the most notorious convicts and their hybristophile devotees. Through his research into hybristophilia, Linedecker (1993) found that the women amorously involved with incarcerated murderers and the like come from all walks of life: "Sophisticated European beauties, college coeds, models, lawyers, corrections officers, television reporters, artists, a Hollywood actress, a best-selling author—even a judge—have succumbed to the dubious romantic charms of long-term prison inmates and serial killers" (p. 15). Even a juror became lovesick for the rapist-murderer she helped to convict; "after sitting through the grisly testimony of a grueling six-month trial . . . [Sandra Wix] married the convicted killer [Steven Erickson]. Then she asked the California Supreme Court of Appeal to overturn the conviction, claiming undue jury pressure on her" (Linedecker, 1993, p. 16).

Linedecker (1993) believes that hybristophiles are individuals who have difficulty forming normal social relationships or they harbor tremendous guilt about

---

CASE EXAMPLE

Charles Starkweather and Caril Ann Fugate

Spree killer, Charles Starkweather and hybristophile, Caril Ann Fugate terrorized the mid-west in the 1950s. The true story of their killing saga has become the basis for popular movies like *Badlands* and *Natural Born Killers*. "In 1958, 14-year-old Fugate's family forbade her to marry 19-year-old Starkweather, a bow-legged, ne'er-do-well punk with a history of violent assault. So her mother, stepfather and infant sister were all summarily murdered as the couple kicked off an infamous eight-day killing spree" (Erlbaum, 1999).

Caril Ann was an attractive young girl with a wild streak and an itch for rebellion (Bardsley, 2002). Although she was not a very good student, Charles thought very highly of her intelligence. "He treated her like a goddess. And, probably because she was so young, she thought he was really cool . . ." (Bardsley, 2002).

A true hybristophile, Caril claimed that she was an innocent victim in Starkweather's murderous rampage. "Though Caril Ann aided and abetted Starkweather, collecting newspaper clippings of their adventures as they ran from police and racked up bodies, she claimed to have been forced against her will to stay with him. She witnessed her family's death, and then stayed in the house with Starkweather for five days afterwards . . . while keeping relatives at bay. She guarded some of their captives while [Starkweather] napped, and she held a loaded gun on others, but swore that she was a hostage and not an accomplice" (Erlbaum, 1999).

Fortunately, the jury did not buy Caril Ann's claim. She received a life term, although Starkweather was executed for the pair's heinous crimes. According to Erlbaum (1999), on his way to the electric chair, Starkweather attested to the power of the hybristophile Caril Ann Fugate: "[Caril Ann was] something worth killing for . . . She put the spark and thrill into the killing" (Erlbaum, 1999).

---

something in their past and must redress. No one knows exactly why a person becomes a prison groupie, but several explanations are possible:

> [Such explanations] range from everything from poor self-esteem, a need to control others, and Florence Nightingale or savior complexes, to sadomasochism and a personal desire for attention . . . One psychiatrist has described prison groupies as often being the type who adopts stray puppies. They have a pathological or abnormal need to assist or help someone else (Linedecker, 1993, p. 18).

A PRISON GROUPIE/HYBRISTOPHILE TYPOLOGY

As a preface to Linedecker's work, Densen-Gerber (1993) provided a typology of the thousands of women who engage in hybristophilia. She described fourteen types of hybristophiles who pursue a relationship with a violent prisoner.

The Rescuer

These women feel they must nurture and rescue the little boys who have done bad things. "Often men are seen as perpetual little boys whose mommies kiss the 'boo-boos' of life and make them all better" (p. 11).

The Controller

These women long to be in control. They are aroused by the restrictiveness of the prison; that is, they are free to do as they please while their lover is safely locked away. "Many of these women came from families in which control issues were paramount, usually with the female being subjugated and submissive" (p. 11).

The Celebrity

These women are attention seekers or exhibitionists. They are bored, insecure, and long to be recognized. "A subset of this type of woman is one who has achieved some success, but not enough to fill her craving to be noticed. . . . In her interactions with men such as these, no one can miss her (i.e., walking together to the conjugal trailer)" (pp. 11–12). Fully aware that the social deviancy of her affection along with the likelihood of receiving media attention because of it only further arouses this celebrity-seeking hybristophile.

The Rule Breaker

These women have had it all. Spoiled but unsatisfied, they become involved with a rule-breaker. These hybristophiles want to take a risk without jeopardizing their livelihood, or social standing. "Frequently, a woman like this had had everything in life but caring. Her relationships have been materialistically satisfying, but distant and sterile. She feels empty and deficient" (p. 12).

The Starved

This type of hybristophile has experienced little more than pain and emptiness in her life. Although she has often been the one to look after those close to her, no one has ever returned the sentiment. "In aligning herself with this type of man, she knows she is needed. She finally *matters* and for that feeling, she may eventually die" [italics in original] (p. 12).

The Russian Roulette Player

Out of insecurity and boredom, these women need to prove to themselves that they are destined to survive despite any risks that are taken. "She tempts fate through these alliances [with convicted killers]" (p. 12).

The Already and Always Guilty

These women have been considered bad seeds all their lives. They feel persecuted and are often blamed for conduct they may or may not have committed. Because they feel as though they are always expected to do wrong, they choose to become romantically involved with someone who has committed an outrage to "really stand out" (p. 12).

The Atoner

These women truly feel guilty and want to be punished by society in order to atone and be forgiven. "Her sins may be real or not, but she perceives them real and needs authorities to make the final determination; much like patients who want to die but need to be assisted" (p. 13).

The Team Player

These women are loners. They have never had a real social connection at any point in their lives. Thus, they seek out a relationship with a convicted criminal in order to satisfy a desire to belong. "She seldom acts out her fantasies by actually becoming involved with a man, but she lives vicariously through letters, etc." (p. 13).

The Rager

This type of hybristophile has been physically or sexually abused or otherwise victimized. Similar to many victims, she has begun to identify with the perpetrator. "Through her relationship with the criminal she becomes the strong one. She can rage at the world for its injustice and often considers her partner innocent" (p. 13).

The Already Wedded

These women have a learned attachment to depraved men. "[These women] . . . may have, as a child, killed for cults, committed other crimes, worshipped evil and became bonded to the dark side" (p. 13).

The Juror

These women are prior victims of crime. Yet, they see their imprisoned partners as mere victims of an unjust society. "Similar to the rescuer, she is the righter of injustice, the avenger of the miserable. She becomes judge, jury and the Supreme Court" (p. 13).

The Deviant/The Identifier

These women identify with the criminality of their chosen convict partner, yet to avoid repercussions, they choose to live vicariously through his deviance. "She is usually more careful in her interactions with the criminal, but usually treats him like the freak she feels she is but has carefully hidden" (p. 14).

The Savior

This final type of hybristophile feels that she alone is the only one capable of saving the criminal by teaching him to love acceptably. ". . . and through saving him she herself can be saved" (p. 14).

UNDERLYING MOTIVATIONS

Although the underlying theme of any paraphilia is sex, and the definition of hybristophilia asserts that sexual arousal is contingent upon partnering with a person who has committed an outrage, Densen-Gerber (1993) believes that sex is not the sole drive for most prison groupies:

... the glue here is not sex, but power; not romance, but abuse; and finally not love, but self-hate.... [Hybristophiles] are drugged, so to say, by the dance, the music, the evil, and the need to prove they could either perish or survive it—thereby being omnipotent and meaningful (p. 14).

CONVICT ROMEOS

Linedecker (1993) refers to prisoners who have love-struck admirers as *convict Romeos*. These convicts are often the most brutal, deadly, and notorious the United States has ever seen. The fact that these inmates are so repulsive to most others means little to the women who long to be with them. "Most experts who have studied the phenomenon are convinced that the guilt or innocence of the convict is irrelevant" (Linedecker, 1993, p. 18). In fact, the hybristophile routinely cites excuses like, "... the purported lack of a fair trial, media prejudice, an unhappy childhood, or say simply that their man is now a different person than he was when he shot down a half-dozen innocent people in robberies, or raped and dismembered a couple of teenagers because he was bored" (Linedecker, 1993, p. 18).

There are many benefits for the prisoner who takes up with a devoted hybristophile. The one obvious benefit is the conjugal visitation. But for the numerous states that prohibit such encounters, there are still advantages for the inmate. "[The prison groupie] may provide [the convict] with spending money, lobby for his early release, or work closely with his attorneys on appeals. She becomes his voice, and body,

---

CASE EXAMPLE

Erik Menendez

On March 20, 1996, Lyle and Erik Menendez were convicted of savagely murdering their parents in Beverly Hills, California. They were sentenced to two consecutive life terms without the possibility of parole. Prosecutors maintain that the motive of the brothers' action was pure greed—the duo wanted the family's fortune (www.ABCNews.com).

In June of 1999, Erik Menendez married his hybristophile admirer, Tammi. According to an interview with *20/20*'s Barbara Walters, Tammi Menendez states, "I am very much in love with him and he is very much in love with me and it's a love that I have never known" (www.etonline.com). Tammi and Erik met after writing to one another. Tammi moved from Minnesota to Florida to be closer to Erik. She visits him three to four times a week and they talk to each other every day on the phone. Despite not being able to consummate the marriage, Tammi is aroused by the relationship nonetheless. "We can hug and kiss on the way out, and hold hands during the visit. The holding of hands during the visit is everything" (www.etonline.com).

Richard Ramirez

Known as the "Night Stalker", Richard Ramirez is one of California's most notorious and heinous serial killers and as such, he is the perfect mate for any hybristophile.

> He broke into homes, raping and killing while playing AC/DC tapes on his victims' stereos. He [would] stay all night at his victims' homes, raiding the fridges and spray painting pentagrams and satanic messages on the walls. He also carved a pentagram into one of his victim's thighs. He gouged out the eyes of a woman with a spoon and mailed them back to the crime scene the next day (www.geocities.com/mistrssdarkness/horror/ranirez.html).

Even though Ramirez was convicted of thirteen murders, he receives a tremendous amount of fan-mail from love-sick prison groupies. ". . . the menacing, gap-toothed Ramirez with an appetite for heavy metal music, cocaine, rape, and murder was barely behind bars before he was acquiring a perplexing harem of beautiful women and girls who were outspokenly devoted to him" (Linedecker, 1993, p. 233).

Richard Ramirez provides the fame and notoriety so many hybristophiles seek. He is a man accused of such disturbing crimes that the media and his fans cannot resist becoming completely infatuated with him. According to Linedecker (1993):

> During Ramirez's grueling fifteen-month marathon trial in Los Angeles for thirteen murders and a host of other felonies, a bevy of pretty cheerleaders quickly formed and scrambled for seats as near to the front of the courtroom as they could get. . . . Some claimed to be college students conducting research. Others, like Bernadette Brazelle, were more honest. The dark-haired college student admitted she was in love with the accused killer. . . . Bernadette described the curly-haired killer as movie star handsome, and talked of his need for someone caring to steer him on the right path (pp. 233–234).

In 1996, Doreen Lioy, a middle-aged magazine editor, married Ramirez. "She was first attracted to Ramirez when she saw his picture in the newspaper, and wrote him regularly for months before they met. . . . With no chance of conjugal visits for the lifer and his wife, [one] can only speculate as to the nature of the unique bond they share" (Erlbaum, 1999).

---

on the outside" (Linedecker, 1993, p. 20). The most frightening fact of all is that hybristophiles often irreparably ruin their lives and can die trying to please their men.

> Prison groupies have hijacked helicopters, attempted murder, and died in dramatic attempts to free pen pal lovers from maximum-security prisons. They have thrown away promising careers by smuggling guns to killers behind bars, and they have abandoned

heartbroken families and friends perplexed by their bizarre obsession with some of the nation's most universally hated violent criminals (Linedecker, 1993, p. 16).

HOW WOMEN MEET THEIR CONVICT ROMEOS

Hybristophiles meet their partners most often through letters of adoration sent to the prisons that house the criminals (Linedecker, 1993). However, there are many other methods these women use to garner the attention and affection of their convict Romeo.

> Women also meet convicts as volunteer visitors through religious ministries or other programs, after introductions by relatives or friends, or through their work as lawyers, prison guards or news reporters . . . [and many hybristophiles] begin their courtship during trials (Linedecker, 1993, p. 16).

The prisoners are not always mere passive objects of the affections of paraphilic fans. In fact, many place ads in local tabloids seeking a sympathetic female admirer to partner with. "And it's not unusual for a convict to be corresponding with as many as from ten to thirty or forty women at the same time while judiciously juggling their visits" (Linedecker, 1993, p. 16).

HYBRISTOPHILIC LOVE ON THE INTERNET

The Internet is a large resource for men and women seeking love with those individuals who have committed outrageous crimes. A sampling of the websites available to the hybristophile include http://www.meet-an-inmate.com, http://www.prisonerlife .com, http://www.pennmates.com, http://www.penpals-n-prison.com, and http://www .capturedhearts.com.

One site, http://jailbabes.com, and its companion site, http://jaildudes.com, attempts to match hybristophiles who share an "interest in starting a pen-pal friendship that could lead to a lifetime relationship with the right man or woman." For a mere $7 per address, a hybristophile can find love in the corrections system. "Thousands of people, men and women alike, after many years of searching for the right woman [or man], have finally discovered Jail Babes [and Jail Dudes]. This has led them to the kind of happiness and intimacy they have been looking for" (www.jailbabes.com). It has never been easier to become a prison groupie.

C H A P T E R

EXTREMES
Modern Genital Modification
LORI CLUFF

The human body has been described as a temple, a house for the soul, and a vessel through which our humanity is achieved. Throughout the centuries, various beliefs have been expressed in regards to physical alteration of the body. Some cultures and religions do not condone any form of modification while certain subcultures are sans any limits on the extremes that are performed.

With the resurgence of tattooing and piercing, extreme body modification has become of increased interest in some modern social circles. Extreme body modification has deep roots in history, although currently there is debate over whether it is pathological self-mutilation or rather a means of self-expression for those who are so inclined. Many individuals engaging in extreme body modification assert modification of their genitals is an expression of themselves sexually, spiritually and sensually.

The term *body modification* holds various definitions and encompasses a variety of acts from the relatively minor (ear piercing) to the most extreme (e.g., castration). The purpose of this chapter is to identify the various forms of genital body modification and examine the meaning in expressing oneself through genital body modification.

Atkinson and Young (2001) identify several motivations for body modification. The first is subculture membership and resistance. Modified persons are able to make themselves distinct and separate from the larger social culture. They are socially disenfranchised and therefore readily accept the social stigma they receive because of their altered appearance. The modified form their own community socially and feel they have a group to which they belong.

Body modifications can be used as a tool of self-expression. The individual is able to make themselves unique and unlike other persons. Body modifications are also a strong statement condemning conformity and limitations socially placed on personal expression.

Another and more traditional motivation is modifications as a means of personal status passage. The act of receiving modifications can be cathartic for some individuals. Through their procedure they are able to create themselves anew and release suppressed emotional pain and trauma. The modification then becomes symbolic of their passage from one stage to another. Some individuals enjoy pushing themselves to tolerate pain and demonstrate their ability to physically endure painful procedures. These individuals are likely to see pain endurance as a measure of personal growth. The re-creation of themselves through modification is also seen by this subculture as a means to transform their bodies into works of art. Instead of painting or sculpting or typical artistic mediums, the body is used as the expression of art.

Lastly, Atkinson and Young (2001) identified modifications as being a spiritual practice. For example, the Neo Primitives of Canada are thought to be reclaiming the spiritual practices of their tribal ancestors through modern practices of modification. Atkinson and Young (2001) did not address the issue of enhanced sexual sensitivity or modifications as a means to deal with gender identity issues. However, as expressed in interviews found in Larratt (2002), sexuality has a great influence in the motivation for many of the extreme modifications.

In order to examine the body modification subculture, one must become familiar with vocabulary that is basic to genital body modification:

Ampallang—horizontal male glans piercing
Anal fold—area that can be pierced
Apadravya—vertical male glans piercing
Ball stretching—weights to stretch and titillate the scrotum
BDD—body dysmorphic disorder, fear of one's own body
Beading—see pearling
Bifurcation or bisection—genital splitting
Body play—ritual application of body art and body modification
Breadboard—board used to present the male genitals for CBT
Burdizzo—a castration device which crushes the testicular cords
Castration—removal of the testicles
Catheter—hollow tube inserted into the bladder during genital healing
CBT—play piercing of the male genitals
Cenobites—experimenters in the higher realms of sensation
Chastity—piercings and devices intended to force chastity
Christina—female pubic mound piercing
Circumcision—removal of all or part of the foreskin or penile shaft skin
Cleopatra—Reverse Prince Albert
Clitoris piercing—piercing through the clitoris itself
Cock and ball torture—see CBT

Cultural appropriation—theft of rituals and behavior from one culture by another
Cutter—an underground castration practitioner
Deep PA—deep urethral piercing
Deep shaft piercing—see shaft ampallang
Diy—do it yourself
Dolphin—a single piece of jewelry adjoining two PA's
Dydoe—glans ridge piercing
Elastrator—a castration device that strangle the testicles
Eu—short for eunuch, a castrated man
Female circumcision—removal or splitting of the hood or labia
Female guiche—female perineal piercing
Flesh tube—a healed tunnel of flesh
Foreskin restoration—recreation of foreskin through via stretching and other means
Fourchette—rear labial piercing
Frenum ladder—a series of frenum piercings forming a ladder
Gauging—slang for stretching a piercing
Gelding—a castrated male, eunuch
Genital beads—see pearling
Genital splitting—see bisection
Glans—head of the penis
Glansectomy—removal of the glans of the penis
Guiche—piercing behind the scrotum, in front of the anus
Guiche weight—stimulating weights attached to the guiche piercing
Hafada—side scrotal piercing
Hood splitting—see female circumcision
Horizontal hood—horizontal piercing through clitoral hood
Hymen piercing—piercing of the hymen
Implant—implantation of three-dimensional objects under the skin
Industrial—two piercing connected by a single barbell
Infibulation—temporary nullification or "closure" of the genitals
Inner labia—piercing through labia minora
Inversion—genital splitting with the glans left intact
Isabella—deep clitoral shaft piercing
Jack Yount—grandfather of heavy body modification
Jacob's ladder—frenum ladder
Jon Cobb—piercer responsible for many extreme piercing innovations
Labiaectomy—female circumcision
Lorum—is a low frenum
Magic cross—combination apadravya and ampallang piercing
Meatotomy—splitting of the lower half of the glans
Nailing—CBT play involving hammering nails through the genitals
Nipple shield—decorative nipple accessory
Nullification—voluntary removal of body parts
Orbital—two piercings connected by a ring
Outer labia—piercing through the labia majora

Pearling—insertion of small beads under the skin
Penectomy—removal of the penis itself
Play piercing—piercing for the sake of piercing
Prince Albert—male urethral piercing exiting below the glans
Princess Albertina—female urethral piercing
Pubic—male piercing at the base of the shaft
Queen Victoria—Reverse Prince Albert
Reverse prince albert (PA)—urethral piercing exiting the top of the glans
Saline injection—inflation of the scrotum and other body parts using saline solution
Scrotal implants—implants inside the scrotum itself
Scrotal ladder—scrotal piercings arranged in a linear configuration
Scrotal stretching—gradual lengthening of the scrotum through stretching
Scrunnel—transscrotal
Shaft ampallang—an ampallang passing through the penis shaft
Shaft apadravya—apadravya pierced through the shaft of the penis
Shakki—term referring to the sound when needles puncture skin
Smoothy—a penectomized eunuch
Sounding—urethral stimulation
Sounds—tool used for urethral stimulation and stretching
Subincision—splitting of the lower half of the penis/urethra
Superincision—splitting of the upper half of the penis
Tara Klamp—low-tech, low maintenance circumcision device
Tongue splitting—splitting of the tongue to achieve a forked effect
Tran scrotal—piercing passing from the front to the back of the scrotum
Triangle—piercing passing underneath the clitoral shaft
Trophy hunter—a body part (usually testicle) collector
Urethral flaring—surgical widening of the urethral opening
Vertical hood—vertical clitoral hood piercing

(Bmezine, 2002)

Body modification has existed in many cultures stretching across time. Themes of castration can be found in Greek mythology, and castration is thought to have began some five thousand years ago with animals to achieve the desired effects of reducing aggression and increasing size and taste (Favazza, 1996). The occurrence of castration of humans has traditionally been to punish, prevent sexual misconduct, bring a higher sense of spirituality or as part of institutionalized eunuchism (Favazza, 1996).

Favazza (1996) gives an historical accounting of the origin and existence of castration practices over the centuries. Indians in the Caribbean are the first known group to castrate their prisoners, and would later engage in cannibalism with the killing of the same individuals. The Babylonian Code of Hammurabi dates back to 2000 B.C. and is a written code of laws that describe castration as a form of punishment for sexual misconduct. Also noted is the adaptation of castration in the West, as well as other countries such as Denmark and Norway, as a means to attempt control over serious sexual offenders. Men are also documented as having castrated themselves.

Attis, 5000 B.C., castrated himself because of his infidelity and later festivals were held in his honor. The festivals were called the Day of Blood and consisted of cult priests castrating themselves. Pleased with their sacrifice, they ran through the streets displaying their severed genitals. Rome in 204 B.C. carried on the same rituals, and in both times, the priests would then live out the rest of their lives as women (Favazza, 1996). The Eastern Roman Empire chose eunuchs for important political appointments with the exception of emperor. There were three types: one who had their testicles crushed, another who had their testicles cut, and those with both penis and testicles severed.

Traditionally in the psychiatric community, self-castration and/or penis removal has been seen as an act of a person suffering from acute psychosis (Favazza, 1996; Walsh & Rosen, 1988). Larratt (2002), notes several cases in which men cut or had their testical and/or penises removed. The procedure was sometimes done themselves. In an interview with one of these men, Tomas, he describes the personal motivation for his castration and his desire for a penectomy. Tomas is a heterosexual male who has had the desire to become emasculinated. For him, the act itself is not part of an erotic fantasy as it can be for others; his drive is to achieve the end result. In addressing sexuality, he states, "you are assuming that sexual acts involving one's genitals are the only valid or pleasurable ones. A persons largest sexual organ is their skin . . ." (Larratt, 2002, p. 33).

Favazza (1996) also identifies the diverse motivations that lead to cutting off of the penis. Reasons can include, "sanitation, substitution for human sacrifice, symbolic castration, desire to be like women, elevation to the status of manhood, sexual differentiation, enhanced fertility, contraception, resolution of identity conflict, permanent incorporation into a social group, control of sexual urges, a mark of caste, a test of endurance, a covenant with God, and so on" (Favazza, 1996, p. 184). When looking at a penis that has been cut, known as subincision today, it does resemble the genitals of a woman.

Subincision had been thought by Favazza (1996) to be mainly isolated to aborigines in Australia and a few other remote areas of the world. However, in researching the practices among those in modern body modification circles, subincision is not uncommon nor is it the most extreme of the procedures being performed today. Subincision is believed by some to encompass a feminization process (Favazza, 1996; Roheim, 1949) and is also performed in order to expose the inner areas that are said to be highly sensitive to sexual stimulation (Larratt, 2002). Among the Australian aborigines, the subincision is one of a series of steps of the initiation process, as a boy becomes an adult. The subincised penis is also wider and is believed in modern circles as well as aboriginal tribes to enhance the sexual pleasure for the female (Larratt, 2002; Favazza, 1996).

Male infibulation is quite different today when compared to Roman times. In Roman times, the foreskin was sewn together to make erection painful or impossible (Dingwall, 1925). This was done in order to preserve strength of the gladiators and the vitality of men in general. In the 1800s, infibulation was used to treat illness and epileptic disorders thought to be caused by excessive masturbation. Today infibulation is usually achieved through the use of glue, piercing, or sewing. This is oftentimes part of a chastity fetish, although it may be pleasing for preoperation transsexuals (Bmezine, 2002). Some males have recreated their genitals into a hermaphrodite presentation. This is done by leaving the penis intact and creating new openings for the purposes of urination and intercourse. The penis is purely for sexual pleasure and the individual can experience penetration similar to that of vaginal intercourse.

One area of great controversy has been that of female genital mutilation. *Introcism* is the enlargement of the vaginal opening by an instrument or by the hand of the practitioner (Favazza, 1996). The Australian aborigines had practiced introcisim until 1938. Immediately following the procedure the young female was required to have intercourse with several young males. Blood and semen were then collected and consumed by the sick and old members of the tribe. Some Muslims have drawn negative public attention because of their practice of female circumcision, where in some cases complete removal of the clitoris and labia are performed. The vaginal opening is typically sewn almost completely closed until the time of marriage.

After childbirth, a Muslim woman may undergo recircumcision in order to tighten the vaginal opening to increase the male's pleasure during intercourse. In certain countries such as Sudan, Hosken (1978) found that most girls are infibulated by age twelve and circumcision is performed on 40 to 80 percent of girls. It seems that these practices have remained common because of the high importance placed on virginity and the guarantee that these procedures purport to offer (Morgan & Steinem, 1980).

Modern practices of female genital modification in the western culture are varied. Extreme female genital modifications are not as common as in males, however Larratt (2002) states that this is changing. The structural differences of the female have limited the progression of some of the more radical procedures seen in males.

Females may become circumcised in different ways including vertical and horizontal clitoral hood piercing, as well as piercing through the clitoris itself. Women also can pierce their labia minora and majora, and the skin between the vagina and anus, called a female guiche. Piercings through the labia can be locked, thus forming a similar chastity function of infibulation.

Some body modification procedures are temporary. Cock and ball torture (CBT) uses various methods for inserting needles into genital tissue. In some instances the scrotum is cut open, exposing the testicles, which are then inserted with needles (Larratt, 2002). The objective achieved through this varies, however it appears to be a demonstration of physical endurance and personal catharsis through the pain that is experienced.

Among the modification community, implants using various mediums are done to visually alter the appearance of the skin. A silicone shape or ball may be inserted under the skin to create a new look and texture. This has also been done in the genital area, primarily in males. The process is known as beading or pearling. The implants change the overall appearance of the genitals and sexually enhance sensation for the individual and his or her partner (Bmezine, 2002; Larratt, 2002).

The acts of extreme body modification are an intriguing and at times perplexing method of human self-expression. As a group, these individuals are becoming more connected and more formally organized in part through Internet communication. As this subculture continues to grow, the once extreme becomes more common. Boundaries are crossed in order to reinvent what will be considered the new extreme.

C H A P T E R

SADOMASOCHISM

Practices, Behaviors, and Culture in American Society

ANNE MARIE PACLEBAR,
CATHERINE FURTADO,
AND MELISSA MCDONALD-WITT

24

Once thought to be a localized and veiled sexual practice, sadomasochism has been thrust onto view of the general public and exploited out of proportion by television, art, movies, and the media in general. Sadomasochism, also termed S&M, is a subsection of what those in the mental health community consider a paraphilia. A paraphilia can be identified as an aberrant sexual activity. This sexual practice is difficult to define precisely because of the wide range of activities involved. According to the American Psychiatric Association (1994), sadomasochism refers to actions that include sadism (gratification through inflicting pain or humiliation on others), and masochism (gratification by receiving pain or humiliation) (Mawhinney, 1998).

Sadomasochism is a type of paraphilia that involves the eroticizing of pain. The practice of sadomasochism typically involves two or more individuals, some playing the role of sadist, some playing the role of masochist. The sadist is the individual who inflicts the pain, punishment, or humiliation on his or her partner. The masochist receives the pain from the other. Those who take part in sadomasochistic behaviors often follow scenarios in which one individual has power or control over the other. These scenarios may include teacher and student, master and slave, or parent and child (Sexual Health, 2002).

These scenarios or role-playing activities are not necessarily deviant forms of sexual activity. What allows these scenarios to fall into the category of sadomasochism is the pervasive theme of control. In all of these scenarios, one individual is playing the role of controller and the other of submissive. This control is the underlying stimulation for many of those who enjoy and participate in sadomasochistic activities.

Sadomasochism has developed into a subculture and a way of thinking not only about sex but also about social roles and life. This development into an established subculture and community has the potential to become dangerous, not only because it normalizes the behaviors that the sadomasochistic community participates in but it also has the potential to devalue life, women, sex, and the human body. In a society where hedonism is becoming more embraced, most measures to increase pleasure, especially sexual pleasure, are welcomed. Therefore, with sadomasochism's origins founded in pain, submission, humiliation, power and control, it is a dangerous and possibly deadly paraphilia that is becoming all too accepted.

SADOMASOCHISTIC INDIVIDUALS AT PLAY

Analysts have observed five features generally present in a sadomasochistic encounter (Green, 2001):

1. **Dominance and submission**—the appearance of control of one partner over the other

2. **Role-playing**—the participants assume roles that they recognize are not reality

3. **Consensuality**—a voluntary agreement to enter into SM "play" and to honor certain "limits"

4. **Sexual context**—the presumption that the activities have a sexual or erotic meaning

5. **Mutual definition**—participants must agree on the parameters of what they are doing, whether they call it SM or not.

Sadomasochistic play is reportedly a highly negotiated and mutually satisfying event. "The credo of S/M sex is Safe, Sane and Consensual. 'Safe' refers to physical safety and acknowledging the potential risk of inflicting harm or 'extreme stimulus' on a participant" (Green, 2001). Therefore, caution is taken so as not to inflict any irreversible damage. In order to maintain safety while engaging in risky behaviors, a "safe word" is often selected before the action begins. When this safe word is uttered, the dominant person must cease all activity and the sex act ends.

The "sane" aspect of S/M is based on the principle that SM sex is done for the pleasure of everyone involved. According to Green (2001), "Erotic play should not cause emotional anguish; it should not abuse the submissive's vulnerability or subject a submissive to unreasonable risk." It is the responsibility for the dominant person to know when and where the fantasy stops.

Lastly, "consent" is considered the "first law" of SM sex, the moral dividing line between SM and brutality. Consent is required to be voluntary, knowing, explicit, and with full understanding of the previously agreed parameters. The ongoing consent of the participants is required, and constructive consent is never sufficient (Green, 2001).

Alison, Santtila, Sandnabba, and Nordling (2001) attempted to classify some of the behaviors associated with sadomasochism in terms of their purpose. They identified four clusters of behaviors falling into the categories of hypermasculinity, the administration of and reception of pain, physical restriction, and psychological humiliation. Falling into the category of hypermasculinity were such behaviors as the use of dildos, fisting, and the use of catheters. Cockbinding was also included in this category, however it differed from the others in that it involved more pain being applied to the penis. They classified the use of a catheter as representing the highest level of hypermasculinity and the use of dildos as the lowest level of hypermasculinity. Included under the category of pain was what may seem like a wide variety of behaviors. These behaviors included spanking, caning, the use of clothespins, weights, and electric stimulation. It was found that the use of clothespins was most common. Clothespins are much easier to obtain than the necessary equipment to administer electric shocks. Five behaviors were included in the category classified as humiliation. These behaviors included flagellation, the use of knives, face slapping, verbal humiliation, and gagging. Verbal humiliation was found to be the most common behavior in this category.

Six behaviors were classified as restraint behaviors. These include bondage, the use of chains, handcuffs, slings, straightjackets, and hypoxyphilia. A seventh behavior, wrestling, was also included in the restraint category but did not have the same characteristics as the other behaviors in this category. Wrestling is one behavior that does not require one partner to be the dominant partner and the other the submissive partner. This is probably the only sadomasochistic behavior not containing an element of control or power (Alison et al., 2001).

SADOMASOCHISTIC BEHAVIORS AND GENDER DIFFERENCES

Not all sexual activities that involve dominance, submission, bondage, and role-playing are defined as being sadomasochistic. According to Ernulf and Innala (1995), there are differences between sadomasochism (S&M), dominance and submission (D&S), and bondage and discipline (B&D). Dominance and submission, as used in the subculture, is used as an all-encompassing term to describe both S&M and B&D, but the term also describes other paraphilias and sexual behaviors like transvestitism and role-playing (e.g., teacher-student, officer-prisoner, boss-employee). This term is used when any sort of exchange of power is used between consensual sexual partners and can be verbal, tactile, or physical. Since the term D&S encompasses a wide range of sexual acts and sexual fantasies, a significant amount of people in the general population may have participated in some sort of dominance and submission (Ernulf & Innala, 1995).

Bondage and discipline (B&D) usually refers to use of physically restraining devices and/or the use of verbal commands to restrict someone else's behaviors (Ernulf & Innala, 1995). This sort of sexual behavior usually manifests itself in acts of servitude and obedience by the submissive and enslavement by the dominator. Bondage and discipline can also be used to describe specific articles of clothing that are worn for the purpose of binding or restricting in order to gain sexual gratification. Historic examples of such articles of clothing are foot binding and corsets. This form of sexual activity is not done with the intention of inducing physical or psychological pain for sexual gratification but may involve punishment of the submissive if orders given by the dominator are not followed (Ernulf & Innala, 1995; Alison, Santtila, Sandnabba, & Nordling, 2001).

Sadomasochism, specifically, refers to the use of pain as the means of sexual stimulation and excitation of both partners (Ernulf & Innala, 1995). A person who derives sexual pleasure from inflicting pain on his/her partner is referred to as the sadist or the dominant in the scenario. The person who derives sexual pleasure and satisfaction from pain is known as the masochist or the submissive. Studies have established that 61 percent of college students have admitted to being aroused by some form of sadomasochistic act or pornography (Donnelly & Fraser, 1998).

Sadomasochism may have developed into a subculture and may even be destructive enough in a person's life to warrant a psychological diagnosis. However, one must realize that S&M behavior is likely to have originated differently in a person's life, as well as have different effects on men and women. A study by Donnelly and Fraser (1998) found that not only are there differences in men and women's sexual fantasies, with men fantasizing more about dominating women and women fantasizing more about being rescued from danger by their lover, but also males are more aroused than females, by fantasies about and participating in activities that are considered to be sadomasochistic. Hence, more men than women fantasize and actually participate in sadomasochistic behaviors. There could be many explanations for these findings, including societal roles, repression, fear of sexual violence, and biology.

Another study looking at gender and S&M practices, conducted by Levitt, Moser, and Jamison (1994), found that of all the women who were in the study, college women had 50 percent more sadomasochistic behaviors than those who were not college-educated. Women who were not married also had 70 percent more S&M encounters than their married counterparts, and of those who were part of the subculture of S&M, most had an idea about their paraphilia at a young age. Of those women active in the subculture, most preferred to be submissive, a considerable minority described a liking for both roles, and a small minority stated their preference was to play the dominant role (Levitt, Moser, & Jamison, 1994).

Similar findings by Alison et al. (2001) established that women were significantly more likely to prefer the submissive role, not only in the practice of S&M

behaviors but in fantasy as well. This study found that humiliation was preferred by women and to a lesser extent by heterosexual males, with a small amount of homosexuals and an even lesser number of heterosexuals having a preference for the role of the dominate, a hypermasculine role. Other studies have also found that the higher the socioeconomic status, the more likely one is to be involved in sadomasochistic behaviors. Additionally, women are more likely to become involved in the S&M culture while in a relationship with a partner who prefers sadomasochistic sexual activities (Ernulf & Innala, 1995).

THEORIES ABOUT THE ORIGINS OF SADOMASOCHISM

Leading theories for the development of any paraphilia are those that have their roots in childhood. Since childhood is usually seen as the precursor to many mental health difficulties in adulthood, a problem in childhood or a trauma suffered at a young age may lead to the development of a paraphilia (Alison, Santtila, Sandnabba, & Nordling, 2001; Donnelly & Fraser, 1998; Kaplan, 1996).

Traumas that children may suffer during childhood can become sexualized during adulthood as a way of gaining control of a memory in which they felt out of control and/or victimized. By turning a situation in which they felt victimized into something sexually pleasurable, adults may feel they have overcome that childhood trauma and feel a sense of power (Kaplan, 1996). Forms of discipline, such as spanking and physical abuse, may also become eroticized in the mind of the child and as an adult in order to not only gain control over their environment, but to also internalize the discipline of the parent. This idea then means that as an adult, the person may seek sadomasochistic behavior for sexual stimulation and relief. However, it also serves to internalize their parent or authority figure, punishing the adult for bad behavior (Donnelly & Fraser, 1998). Kaplan (1996) also notes that any form of abuse such as neglect, cruelty toward a child and cultural or religious repression of sexual desires, can all lay the foundation for an adult paraphilia, especially sadomasochism. However, it is important to remember that the sexualization of a childhood trauma or a form of discipline does not develop without the continuing process of adult socialization to the sexualized acts (Alison et al., 2001).

Other explanations for the development of sadomasochism in adults include the beliefs of such psychologists as Freud, who view women as innately masochistic, thus always taking on the submissive role (Donnelly & Fraser, 1998). Along the same lines, theorists have argued that since women are marginalized in society and have cultural limits and roles placed on them, they may feel a need to punish themselves for their inability to live up to those roles or the inability to mold themselves into the perfect wife and mother. However, focusing only on females when looking at the origins of sadomasochism limits the possible origins of the paraphilia. It can be misconstrued as a masochistic "myth used to justify and reinforce male dominance in women" (Donnelly & Fraser, 1998, p. 393).

Another theory for the origin of sadomasochism lies in upper-class society. More affluent and well-educated individuals are noted to partake in sadomasochistic behaviors than any other group. This has been deemed a result of persons feeling they are not worthy of their status and possessions, both financially and intellectually. Therefore, they may feel a need to punish themselves for acquiring something they do not deserve, thus turning toward sadomasochistic behavior (Donnelly & Fraser, 1998).

Sadomasochism has also been looked upon as an escape from one's self, as well as an escape from the responsibility of one's thoughts and behaviors (Alison et al., 2001). Since the role of a submissive is intrinsically passive and obedient, it is easy for someone to feel they are not responsible for their own behavior when instructed to commit a certain act. This then allows the submissive to feel that their behavior is not a reflection of who they are, and so become even more likely to act in ways they would normally not consider engaging in. These individuals are able to escape the responsibility of their actions and identity when they put themselves in the role of the submissive, both of which are highly reinforcing to those who do not feel comfortable with themselves (Alison et al., 2001).

PROPONENTS OF SADOMASOCHISTIC BEHAVIOR

There are many views in support of those who engage in sadomasochistic behavior. One such view holds that sadomasochism is not the actual acting out of aggressive sexual behavior but rather the symbolic reenactment of their love and pain (Alison et al., 2001; Hopkins, 1994). Hopkins (1994) refutes the idea that sadomasochistic behavior perpetuates patriarchal society and relationships because he feels that sadomasochistic practices do not replicate patriarchal relationships, it simulates it. He argues that the difference between replication and simulation is one of great degree. Hopkins (1994) states,

> Replication implies that SM encounters merely reproduce patriarchal activity in a different physical area. Simulation implies that SM selectively replays surface patriarchal behaviors onto a different contextual field. That contextual field makes a profound difference (p. 123).

His argument focuses around the acting out of violence, not the actual use of violence in a sexual way. He feels that there is a difference between acting out a rape scene for sexual pleasure and actually raping someone for sexual pleasure. He focuses on the fact that the submissive's orgasm rests entirely in the hands of the dominant and since orgasm is always the goal in the activities, violence, pain, nonconsent, and hierarchy are only being symbolically acted out by the players and have nothing to do with violence and power (Hopkins, 1994).

Despite the common belief that those who take part in sadomasochistic activities are mentally ill, research has found that many of these individuals are socially well-adjusted (Sandnabba, Santtila, & Nordling, 1999). Many people interested in participating in sadomasochism are part of a subculture in which this behavior is looked upon favorably. During the day, they are the businesspersons and blue collar workers seen everywhere. At night, they are the master or the slave receiving sexual gratification from enduring or inflicting physical or emotional pain. In their study examining the behavior and attitudes of individuals participating in sadomasochism, Sandnabba et al. (1999) found that two-thirds of their sample held leading positions at work or performed services in the community.

Sandnabba and colleagues (1999) also looked at differences between homosexual and heterosexual sadomasochists. They found that most individuals admitting to sadomasochistic desires or behaviors fell between the ages of twenty-one to thirty years old. Most claimed they first became aware of their sadomasochistic desires around the age of eighteen. However, their first experience did not occur until years later. It was discovered that those who described themselves as exclusively heterosexual became aware of their sadomasochistic sexual preference at a younger age than those describing themselves as bisexual or exclusively homosexual (Sandnabba et al., 1999). This could be attributed to the common confusion over sexual identity experienced by bisexuals and homosexuals as they develop. These individuals often undergo criticism and discrimination as they are coming to terms with their own sexuality. It may take them longer to discover they prefer sadomasochistic activities to traditional sexual activity because of the time it takes for them to come to terms with being homosexual.

Various behaviors are included in the category of sadomasochism. Sandnabba and colleagues (1999) found that the most common activities were oral sex, bondage, and the wearing of leather outfits. The least common involved the use of knives, razor blades, catheters, and the practice of zoophilia. This demonstrates that the focus of sadomasochism may not be torture or the infliction of serious pain, but rather the playing out of a scenario. It was found that the homosexual participants preferred leather outfits, anal intercourse, rimming, dildos, wrestling, special equipment, and uniform scenes. The heterosexuals tended to prefer verbal humiliation, masks and blindfolds, gags, rubber outfits, cane whipping, vaginal intercourse, cross dressing, and straightjackets. It is interesting that these two groups had different preferences (Sandnabba et al., 1999). This could be attributed to the various subcultures they may belong to involving sadomasochism. Homosexual individuals interested in participating in sadomasochistic activities may surround themselves with other homosexuals with similar interests. The same may be true for the subcultures to which heterosexuals belong.

This study (Sandnabba et al., 1999) demonstrates that individuals participating in sadomasochistic activities are not necessarily different from individuals who enjoy conventional sex. The participants had average to above-average levels of education and maintained steady, upstanding occupations. A majority of the participants also reported a high-income level. However, one issue that posed a problem for many of the sadomasochists in this study was the development and maintenance of permanent relationships (Sandnabba et al., 1999). This may be the result of their sexual preferences.

It is difficult enough to maintain relationships based upon differing personalities. It is also difficult to imagine the complications arising in trying to find someone to connect with on a personal and sexual level when one enjoys and participates in what many consider deviant, unthinkable sexual acts. The reason many of these individuals find themselves involved in sadomasochistic subcultures may be because of the difficulties in finding a sexually compatible mate.

This type of relationship or activity, reinforces the difficulty of finding a permanent partner with which to have a healthy relationship. Whether or not this power difference is acted out in the bedroom is irrelevant when discussing significant relationships. There is a strong chance that the roles of one partner always being in control and withholding love from the other in order to maintain that control will carry over into a relationship beyond the bedroom. Paraphilias have a way of expanding and progressing, becoming more and more important in relation to the way an individual lives their life.

For the heterosexual majority in Western countries, sexual interaction usually follows a relatively fixed sequence of behaviors (Santtila, Sandnabba, Alison, & Nordling 2002). According to Simon & Gagnon (1986) as cited in Santtila et al. (2002), these sequences are sexual scripts that suggest, "to a large degree, that sexual interaction conforms to a premeditated sequence of intentional actions. Script theory has mainly been used for describing conventional heterosexual activities." However, the authors conclude that very little is known about the "scripting" of more unusual sexual activities, including sadomasochistic sexual behavior.

Because sadomasochism tends to involve ritualistic patterns of behavior in which partners are often assigned roles and are expected to enact particular sequences of behavior, it can be hypothesized that those who engage in sadomasochistic acts learn sequenced patterns of behavior that facilitate the enactment of complicated SM sexual scenarios (Santtila et al., 2002). It can also be stated that the combination of behavioral structures is theoretically meaningful. Thus the existence of progressions of SM behaviors are similar to the existence of partially cumulative structures that can be likened to sexual scripts for ordinary heterosexual sexual behavior (Santtila et al., 2002). This is important to the understanding and conceptualization of sadomasochism as a "sexual phenomenon." We can understand that individuals who engage in sadomasochistic practices possess different scripts and behaviors that develop according to their own practices, culture, and experiences. However, the process itself by which individuals engage in sex is probably shared in most expressions of human sexuality and not truly abnormal.

SADOMASOCHISM AND THE WORKPLACE

Williams (2002) takes the view that sexual harassment can be another form of sadomasochism. The author proposes that "any woman who purports to enjoy (hetero)sexualized interactions, especially in work organizations controlled by men, is suspected of being a victim of false consciousness." Williams (2002) states that those who practice sadomasochistic acts are engaging in the psychological defense of "splitting." Instead of accepting that there are good and bad qualities in all people, we sometimes divide the social world into "good guys" and "bad guys," which assures our uncomfortable ambivalent feelings (Williams, 2002). Sadomasochism is a form of splitting in which the partners agree that the masochist is "all good" and the sadist is "all bad." This is an example of splitting called "false differentiation." Alternative to false differentiation, true differentiation, occurs when mutual recognition is achieved and the partners accept both the shortcomings and the virtues of each other.

Because sadomasochism is psychologically "easier" to achieve than mutual recognition, sexual relationships are always vulnerable to breaking down into subordinating and dominating roles. Therefore, sadomasochistic dynamics is more common in societies than originally thought. "It is commonplace to find sadistic bosses who seem to enjoy harassing workers and sycophantic employees who cater to their bosses' arbitrary whims" Williams (2002). These dynamics can also be seen in colleges and universities, among the relationship between professor and student. According to Williams (2002), this potential is there because in colleges and universities professors are more powerful than students, their opinions are considered more valuable, and their demands more credible and reasonable. In return, students often idealize their professors and seek recognition from them, sometimes in sexual ways. Likewise, some male professors seek confirmation of their power and omniscience, including sometimes their sexual virility, from their students. These conditions make sexual relationships between students and professors vulnerable to developing sadomasochistic dynamics, especially if the student's needs and desires are not considered on a par with the professor's demands.

SADOMASOCHISM AND PORNOGRAPHY

A study by Mawhinney (1998) found that the number of x-rated video rentals has increased from 75 million in 1985 to 665 million in 1996. The study also found evidence that prolonged exposure to pornography increased that likelihood of someone assuming that others are involved in atypical sexual activities. In the mid-1980s, the pornography industry started to become very specialized, and the advent of pornographic videos and pictures that dealt specifically with S&M themes were developed and marketed to consumers (Shortes, 1998). This specialization of pornography does not imply that up until the mid-1980s sadomasochism was not part of the pornography business, that the demand for S&M pornography was absent or that there were not people practicing S&M behaviors. The division came from the development of the home video and consequently the increased demand for specialized pornography based on an individual's personal "tastes" (Shortes, 1998).

With this division of pornography came an explosion of pornographic materials that were geared toward the S&M consumers. Consequently increasingly violent content in this genre of pornography became available. Lo and Wei (2002) found that S&M themes are pervasive in all pornography, not simply that geared toward the S&M subculture. The study determined that in nonspecialized pornographic videos and books, the main themes were hierarchy, objectification of women, submission and violence toward women. Ernulf and Innala (1995) found that in sexually explicit magazines men were dominant in 71 percent of pictures and submissive in 29 percent of the pictures. These findings suggest that sadomasochistic themes are not only prevalent in specialized S&M pornography but in general pornography as well. The pervasive themes of dominance over females, the acceptance of violence and pain as part of sexual activity in all pornography, and the establishment of an S&M culture has begun to normalize deviant sexual practices. Considering that this paraphilia is one involved with pain, suffering, and dominance, the acculturation of its beliefs and activities could lead people down a road of psychological dysfunction and tolerance of sexually dangerous activities that could result in death.

SADOMASOCHISM AND AMERICAN CULTURE

According to popular literature and the explosion of sadomasochism, it can be stated that sadomasochism, has established a distinct presence in modern American culture. Sadomasochistic iconography can be seen in television, Internet, read in books and magazines, and displayed as art or used to sell clothing. From such experiences as body piercing, tattoos, the proliferation of sex toys and S/M tools, to theme restaurants or bed and breakfast inns, sadomasochism can be found anywhere. "The imagery of kink has proliferated through the emergence of an astounding variety of niche markets" (Green, 2001). As cited in Green (2001), "an S/M French Restaurant named La Nouvelle Justine, decorated with a prison cell, 'slave' busboys and 'dominant' waitresses, birthday spankings and leather wrist cuffs, operates on Manhattan's 23rd Street and is so popular that dinner is by reservation only."

Body modification in the form of tattooing and body piercing is becoming increasingly common and well accepted in western society. Ten to 13 percent of adolescents age twelve to eighteen have tattoos, and 3 to 8 percent of the general population have tattoos. Body piercing at locations other than the ear lobes has also been increasing in frequency and acceptance (Carroll, Riffenburgh, Roberts, & Myhre, 2002). The majority of medical literature on tattooing and body piercing has focused on the risks and complications of these procedures, however, behavioral surveys have suggested that increases in homosexuality, sexual risk-taking, and sadomasochism are associated with body piercing (Carroll et al., 2002).

Sex sells, and the media is doing its best to glorify and scorn it. Through this constant media attention, as can also be depicted in the movie *Basic Instinct,* in which the film opened with a man being tied to a bed by a woman, sensationalistic stories corroborate presumptions that sadomasochism is a violent sexual pathology.

SADOMASOCHISM AND THE LAW

Within the last few years, a notable shift in SM prosecutions has been in charging SM sex as both assault and rape. Therefore, there has been an upsurge by sadomasochists to have a more culturally informed legislative inquiry into the dynamics of SM relationships.

> Regulating sex is incredibly complicated because sex is complicated. However, sex laws should be shaped by social realities based on an honest assessment of what is actually occurring in private society, rather than romanticized conceptions of coquettish procreative love which fictionalizes carnal pleasures as fitting within some logical order (Green, 2001).

Questions surrounding the notion of any paraphilia, such as sadomasochism, include the issue of legality. Is it in fact legal for one person to torture another, even though the act is completely consensual? Consequently, can an individual fully consent to participate in such an act? Many individuals have been brought to court for partaking in sadomasochistic activities. In most cases, they are not charged for the actual act of sadomasochism but rather the act of assault. When the charge is assault, an individual cannot use the defense of a consensual act. In the *Commonwealth of Massachusetts v. Appleby,* Appleby was charged with battery for beating his homosexual partner with a riding crop while engaging in sadomasochistic behaviors. Appleby was sentenced to ten years in prison for this act despite the fact that both had consented to this sexual activity. The court held that, "because assault is a general intent crime, the only intent required is an intent to do the act causing the injury; a showing of hostile purpose or motive is not required" (Pa, 2001, p. 55).

John Ward, the defense lawyer in the Appleby case, disagrees with prosecuting consensual sadomasochistic behavior between adults. In discussing a woman who was recently arrested for being involved in a sadomasochistic party, Ward stated that if we permit boxing in our society, "it's hard to see how the law could interfere in this case. I think the only reason the police are interested is because this case is about sex" (Goldstein, 2002, p. 1). Is society trying to punish people for being sexually different or are they truly trying to protect individuals from being physically harmed? A number of sexual advocacy groups such as the National Coalition for Sexual Freedom strive to protect people from being prosecuted for nontraditional sexual acts as long as they are consensual. However, how does one know that consent was truly given? In cases of child molestation, a child may consent but out of fear or deceit.

The *Commonwealth of Massachusetts v. Appleby* is not the only case in which the question of whether sadomasochism should be considered abuse or assault has risen. The city of London has also debated this question. In 1987, English police recovered videotapes of sadomasochistic activities. The videos consisted of such activities as ritualistic beatings and the infliction of pain on the genitals with needles, hooks, hot wax, and sandpaper. These activities were clearly consensual, and all participants were required to follow certain rules. The videos were distributed only to those who participated in the filming. Several of the individuals involved in the sadomasochistic activities were prosecuted and found guilty. Similar to *Commonwealth v. Appleby,* the courts believed that, despite the clear consent to these activities, the acts were unlawful. The defendants were convicted of violating the Offenses Against the Person Act of 1861. This act states, "whoever shall unlawfully and maliciously wound or inflict any grievous bodily harm on any other person, either with or without any weapon or instrument, shall be liable to imprisonment" (Green, 2001, p. 543).

Cases brought before other courts involving sadomasochistic behaviors have resulted in the judge or jury finding that because the act was consensual it could not be deemed criminal. This has been the court ruling in cases involving husbands and wives. In a 1996 case, *R. v. Wilson,* a husband was prosecuted for branding his initials on his wife's "buttocks" with her consent. The court stated that any consensual activity between husbands and wives is not a matter of concern for the courts (Green, 2001). Is it appropriate for courts to hold a double standard in cases involving sadomasochistic behaviors? The courts, as well as society, must decide if these sexual acts are truly damaging and should remain an issue for the courts or if it should remain a matter of personal choice.

CONCLUSION

There remain varying arguments in support of as well as in complete outrage for the practices involved with the paraphilia, sadomasochism. One side holds that paraphilia, in general, cause much confusion and leave many questions unanswered. Why do some people enjoy sadomasochistic activities? Why is the participation in these behaviors necessary for some to achieve sexual satisfaction? Does society have a right to punish individuals for being involved in consensual sexual activities because they are not traditional? If the act is consensual and is not hurting others beyond the level they desire, then should society intrude on the freedom for individuals to practice a particular sexual activity? Sadomasochistic activities may involve physical, emotional, and psychological pain, but those who participate in such activities desire this pain. It does not involve one individual harming another for his or her own sexual pleasure against the will of the other. Consent is key to this phenomenon. Because the behaviors are consensual, these activities are simply a matter of personal choice.

Consequently, the opposing view holds that sadomasochism is a paraphilia that has become an established counterculture in our nation, one with its own terms, groups, clubs, and toys. This paraphilia is based on control, power, violence, and pain, yet people embrace it as if it were a new psychologically healthy sexual lifestyle. Few individuals in the S&M community truly desire to discover the basis for their need to be dominated, humiliated, and punished in order to become aroused. Many in the S&M community would rather justify their actions by using words like safe play, simulation (not replication), love, and roles, rather than confront the harm such behaviors cause. The truth of the matter is that there are people who die each year during S&M activities; moreover, there are significant long-term problems associated with the role-playing (e.g., rape scene), as well as with being verbally and physically humiliated and abused (Hopkins, 1994).

This paraphilia is one of violence and pain, not one of love and pleasure. This is a paraphilia that can escalate into the practice of increasing violent activities. As persons become accustomed to being humiliated and degraded they will often search for more extreme forms of sadism or masochism for sexual pleasure, ultimately leading to death. Sadomasochism may have its origins in childhood, but it is in adulthood that the taste for pain and dominance is cultivated and developed into a lifestyle that is based upon brutality and cruelty.

Has pornography, the media, and the Internet contributed to sadomasochistic tendencies? Or, did the practices of sadomasochism lead to its explicit images and influence in today's society? There are many arguments in support of as well as in complete abomination of such a sexual practice. However, whatever the reason for a particular point of view, it is important for individuals in society to become aware of the practices and behaviors of sadomasochism, and to become aware of the mental, physical, and emotional dangers of engaging in such activities.

C H A P T E R

VOYEURISM

Stephanie Neumann

25

Voyeurism is one of the main paraphilias recognized by the American Psychiatric Association. This chapter focuses on a description of voyeurism, frequent disorders that are comorbid with voyeurism, and various treatment strategies for voyeurism and other similarly categorized sex offenses. Some important aspects that are addressed include: (a) the type of offender who most frequently engages in voyeuristic acts; (b) women and voyeurism; (c) juvenile sex offenders and voyeurism; (d) voyeurism and the legal system; and (e) treatment concerns.

THE PARAPHILIA

According to the American Psychiatric Association (2000), voyeurism involves, "the act of observing unsuspecting individuals, usually strangers, who are naked, in the process of disrobing, or engaging in sexual activity" (p. 575). A more intense form of voyeurism involves the exclusive observation of individuals engaging in sexual activity. A voyeur typically achieves orgasm through masturbation during the voyeuristic act or following the act, in response to a memory of the voyeuristic act. While masturbating, the voyeur fantasizes about a sexual experience with the individual he or she observed. (American Psychiatric Association, 2000). Voyeurism is generally identified by the age of fifteen. Therefore, it is not uncommon for adolescent sex offenders to engage in voyeurism or have a diagnosis of voyeurism.

According to the American Psychiatric Association (2000) the criteria required for a diagnosis of voyeurism are:

(a) Over a period of at least 6 months, recurrent, intense sexually arousing fantasies, sexual urges, or behaviors involving the act of observing an unsuspecting person who is naked, in the process of disrobing, or engaging in sexual activity; (b) the person has acted on these sexual urges, or the sexual urges or fantasies cause marked distress or interpersonal difficulty (p. 570).

VOYEURISTIC OFFENDER TYPOLOGY

The onset of voyeurism is typically before the age of fifteen. Therefore, the course of voyeurism is chronic. Unlike many paraphiliacs, voyeurs can be either male or female. There is little research concerning the demographics of voyeurs. There is however, research examining the demographics of individuals who engage in online sexual activities, including computer voyeurism.

A study conducted by Cooper, Morahan-Martin, Mathy, and Maheu (2002) examined the demographics of individuals who engage in online sexual activity (OSA). OSA is "the use of the Internet for any activity (text, audio, or graphics) that involves sexuality" (p. 106). This includes looking at or watching "cybercams" while masturbating. Although this is not a conventional form of voyeurism, it is rapidly growing with the expansion of the Internet. Cooper et al. report that individuals who typically engage in OSA are adult, married males who are in their early thirties. The most common reason reported for engaging in OSA was distraction or the need to "take a break" (Cooper et al., 2002, p. 113). Cooper et al. report that individuals who tend to engage in OSA participate in such behavior weekly for less than one hour. Although this study appears to be valid, it is necessary to consider that all of the data collected was self-reported. In self-reported data individuals can either overreport or underreport, which would skew the current data.

McCarthy (1994) suggests that sexual compulsivity, such as voyeurism, is predominantly associated with males. Furthermore, the sexual compulsivity associated with voyeurism is caused by "anxiety, fears of intimacy, low self-esteem, obsessive-compulsiveness, and poor interpersonal relations" (Rinehart & McCabe, 1998, p. 370). Rinehart and McCabe found that individuals who engaged frequently in voyeurism were significantly more depressed than individuals who less frequently engaged in voyeurism.

Studies suggest that some voyeuristic individuals develop into more serious sex offenders who become sexually aggressive with women. This is not to say that all voyeurs become sexually aggressive, however individuals who are sexually aggressive with women tend to have a history of voyeurism and exhibitionism (Abel et al., 1987; Guay, Proulx, Cusson, & Quimet, 2001). A study conducted by Raymond, Coleman, Ohlerking, Christenson, and Miner (1999) found that 33 percent of pedophilic individuals in their study also engaged in exhibitionism, frotteurism, and voyeurism. Overall, these studies suggest that voyeurism is often comorbid with other paraphilias. If not comorbid with other paraphilias, voyeurism may be a precursor to more extreme sexually inappropriate or deviant behavior.

It has been suggested that individuals who engage in voyeurism have experienced childhood trauma such as sexual abuse that manifests in exhibitionistic behaviors such as voyeurism (The Virtual Psychology Classroom, 2002). Kafka and Prentky (1994) found that a history of sexual abuse was present in 25 to 35 percent of men with paraphilias.

WOMEN AND VOYEURISM

A majority of research conducted with convicted sex offenders examines male perpetrators. This suggests that there is bias within the research and within diagnoses, excluding female sex offenders. A study conducted by Federoff, Fishell, and Fedoroff (1999) found that women in their sample were more likely to have multiple paraphilias than the men in the sample. In general the women who presented with paraphilias such as voyeurism were: single, employed, heterosexual, high school graduates, with a family history of alcoholism (Fedoroff et al., 1999).

Paraphilia diagnoses are based on self-report criterion, therefore paraphilias are easily misdiagnosed. Similarly, paraphilic disorders can be easily malingered in order to achieve a desired outcome. Fedoroff et al. (1999) give a case example of a female voyeur and pedophile who simulated paraphilias and used her diagnosis to avoid being reunited with her children. The case presentation is as follows:

> This heterosexual woman was assessed at the request of her lawyer, responding to a request from Children's Aid concerning the question of whether she could care for her children. Concerns had arisen after she self-disclosed in a treatment group for women who had themselves been sexually abused, that she herself had once sexually assaulted a "ten to twelve-year-old boy." She proceeded to report the event to the police and Children's Aid Society. She said she had met the boy in a park, become sexually aroused, and lured him to an abandoned apartment where she had sex with him against his will . . . In the past, she had worked as a prostitute which she claimed was for the purpose of "improving my self esteem" rather than for financial reasons. She had also worked as an "exotic dancer" which she found very sexually arousing. Although she admitted having fantasies of spying on unsuspecting males she had never actually done so (p. 135).

This case example illustrates how self-report data regarding voyeurism can be malingered, and ultimately lead to a misdiagnosis of voyeurism or other paraphilic disorders.

JUVENILE SEX OFFENDERS AND VOYEURISM

A study conducted by Zolondek, Abel, Northey, and Jordan (2001) found that 17 percent of juvenile sexual offenders reported engaging in voyeuristic acts. The mean age of onset of this type of behavior was reported to be 11.0 years old. Furthermore, the average number of victims reported by these juvenile voyeurs was 8.8. Although the number of victims was only 8.8, the mean number of voyeuristic acts engaged in by adolescents was 16.9. The number of juveniles that reported engaging in voyeurism did not differ from the number of reporting adults.

Zolondek et al. (2001) also found that individuals with low social desirability reported engaging in more paraphilic behaviors, including voyeurism. Juveniles reporting the highest level of social desirability reported the lowest frequency of paraphilic behaviors. Zolondek et al. report that 25.7 percent of juveniles with a low social desirability level engage in voyeurism; 20.0 percent with a medium social desirability level engage in voyeurism; and 8.9 percent with a high social desirability level engage in voyeurism. This suggests that as a juvenile's desire to be socially accepted increases, their tendency to engage in voyeurism will decrease. Similarly, if a juvenile's desire to be socially accepted is low, his or her tendency to engage in voyeurism will increase.

Overall, Zolondek et al. (2001) found that between 10 and 20 percent of paraphilic juveniles report engaging in voyeurism. Furthermore, nontactile offenses, such as voyeurism, had a higher mean number of acts committed than tactile offenses such as molestation. Juvenile sex offenders who engage in voyeurism, exhibitionism, and frotteurism also tend to have a greater number of victims than juveniles engaging in molestation. Zolondek et al. (2001) conclude that "deviant sexual patterns exhibited in preadolescent boys must be taken seriously to prevent later sexual offending and to understand the etiology of paraphilic behavior" (p. 83). This suggests that although voyeurism is not a tactile sexual offense, it can lead to more serious and chronic sexually inappropriate behavior if not addressed at an early age.

VOYEURISM AND THE LEGAL SYSTEM

According to Frost (2002), "the law does not preclude or punish voyeurism" (p. 209). Contradictory to Frost's statement, Slobogin (2002) states that at least twenty-five states prohibit voyeurism. Statutes in these states criminalize the act of looking into a home under the terms "voyeurism," "criminal surveillance," "criminal trespass," or "disorderly conduct." Most laws prohibiting voyeurism require, however, that trespassing is part of the offense. Typically, voyeurism convictions are affirmed under "Peeping Tom" statutes or disorderly conduct statutes. There is no evidence however of the illegality of observing other people from areas that are not considered trespassing. For example, watching a nonconsenting individual from your own home may not be legally seen as voyeurism. However, watching the same individual engaging in the same act while standing on their property may legally be considered voyeurism because in addition to the act of voyeurism, the perpetrator is also trespassing.

TREATMENT FOR VOYEURISTIC SEX OFFENDERS

Three treatment modalities used in the treatment of paraphilic sex offenders are: (a) surgical castration, (b) psychotherapy, and (c) pharmacotherapy. However, the literature focuses mainly on psychotherapy, pharmacotherapy, and a combination of these two modalities for voyeurs. The most effective treatment for pedophilia, exhibitionism, and voyeurism is a combination of psychotherapy with long-acting gonadotropin-releasing hormone (GnRH) (Rösler & Witztum, 2000). In order for treatment to be effective with voyeurs, it is necessary to employ long-term treatment, relapse prevention, and monitoring (Seligman & Hardenburg, 2000).

When psychotherapy is the selected form of treatment with a voyeur, it is important to implement psychodynamic techniques, cognitive-behavioral techniques, and group counseling (Seligman & Hardenburg, 2000). These approaches attempt to exert control over impulsivity. Psychotherapy also assists the voyeur in developing interpersonal skills with the expectation of creating healthier methods of sexual gratification and more adept social relationships.

When seeking a pharmacological treatment for voyeurism, it is suggested that treatment start with specific serotonin reuptake inhibitors (SSRIs). However, if the voyeur has a comorbid diagnosis, more intense treatment may be necessary (McDonald & Bradford, 2000). The use of SSRIs in the treatment of voyeurism and other similar paraphilias suggests that the compulsive nature of the voyeur can be likened to individuals with obsessive compulsive disorder (OCD) (Abouesh & Clayton, 1999).

One pharmacological treatment that has decreased the intensity and frequency of voyeuristic acts in sex offenders is paroxetine. This SSRI not only decreases the frequency of voyeuristic thoughts but improves impulse control as well. Other frequently used pharmacological treatments include fluoxetine, sertraline, fluoxamine, and clomipramine (Abouesh & Clayton, 1999). The effectiveness of these treatments depends on the correlation between the paraphilia and OCD. If an individual's voyeuristic behavior is not in the realm of obsessive compulsive disorders, it is likely that the use of SSRIs will not be as effective as with individuals whose behavior stems from OCD. One case report on the use of paroxetine to treat voyeurism is as follows:

> Mr. A, a 50-year-old divorced white male and the father of two, was self-referred for the evaluation and management of his voyeuristic behavior. He reported long-standing erotic compulsions to look up women's skirts using a mirror in public places. He did not remember the first time he did this, but remembers episodes during his teen years, involving his sisters. He also spent several hours a day watching naked women in pornographic movies while masturbating 4–7 times a day. He continued his erotic behavior during his early adulthood, describing feeling flushed and aroused by his voyeuristic behavior . . . He went home drunk one night and attempted to videotape his daughter in the shower . . . He noted a sense of relief of his urges afterward, associated with frustration over his inability to control his behavior. . . . His dose was increased to 20 mg at bedtime. There was a noticeable decrease in his voyeuristic behavior with a decrease in the frequency as well as a reduction in the intensity of his urges and thoughts. . . . He then opted to discontinue his medication and continues to do well (for the past 4 months) (Abouesh & Clayton, 1999, p. 24).

PERSPECTIVES ON VOYEURISM

Voyeurism can be a compulsive disorder with severe lack of impulse control (Abouesh & Clayton, 1999). Therefore, it should be treated like obsessive compulsive disorder (OCD) or similar illnesses. However, if a voyeur is not motivated by a lack of impulse control and compulsive behavior, is it fair to attempt to medicate this person the same way individuals with OCD would be medicated? To what extent does a voyeur have to engage in voyeuristic activity in order to substantiate treatment, such as therapy or medication? The responses to these questions are often left to the treating psychologist and/or psychiatrist.

If a voyeur does not seek treatment, it seems unlikely that he or she will be mandated to therapy. If voyeurism was not a precursor to other more aggressive sexually deviant behaviors, would it be necessary to treat voyeurism? It does not seem appropriate to treat a voyeur who is not motivated for treatment or who does not have the desire to alter his or her sexual behaviors. Therefore, for treatment to be effective with a voyeur it seems reasonable that the voyeur must have a vested interest in change.

Is voyeurism transforming into a more socially acceptable form of deviant sexual behavior as a result of the revolution of the computer and the Internet Age? The direction in which voyeurism appears to be traveling seems to be less harmful to its victims. A question to consider is whether the prevalence of computer-based voyeurism will decrease the likelihood of voyeurs becoming more aggressive sexual predators. If so, will voyeurism eventually be eliminated as a paraphilia?

CONCLUSION

In summary, voyeurism is the act of watching a nonconsenting individual who is naked, disrobing, or engaging in sexual activity. In order to be diagnosed with voyeurism, it is necessary for the acts to cause the voyeur marked impairment or interpersonal difficulty. For some individuals, voyeuristic behavior will become uncontrollable and may be associated with features similar to obsessive compulsive disorder. Most voyeuristic behavior has an onset before the age of fifteen. Individuals who engage in acts of voyeurism seek therapy only when their behavior becomes distressful and impairing. If their behavior is not distressful, a voyeur will not seek therapy, which could lead to the exacerbation of sexually deviant behaviors.

When a voyeur's interest in voyeurism decreases, he or she may seek alternative behaviors to achieve a similar sexual release. This suggests that voyeurism is a precursor to more aggressive sexual deviancies. Therefore, it seems necessary for the voyeur to obtain psychological treatment to reduce the likelihood of the occurrence of further, more aggressive sexually deviant acts. The literature suggests that the most effective approach to the treatment of a voyeur is a combination of psychotherapy with pharmacotherapy. More specifically, psychotherapy in conjunction with SSRIs has been evidenced to significantly reduce the prevalence of voyeuristic behaviors and impulse control problems that may accompany the voyeuristic behavior. Voyeurism has been criminalized in twenty-five states, however, to be considered a crime, voyeurism often must be accompanied by the offense of trespassing. Most acts of voyeurism remain undetected and are not penalized by law.

FROTTEURISM, PIQUERISM, AND OTHER RELATED PARAPHILIAS

26

STEPHANIE NEUMANN, DAWN ALLEY,
ANNE MARIE PACLEBAR, CATHERINE SANCHEZ,
AND BRIANNA SATTERTHWAITE

FROTTEURISM

The word frotteurism is derived from the French word *frotteur*, which means to brush or to rub. Frotteurism, or the "recurrent, intense sexually arousing fantasies, sexual urges or behaviors involving touching and rubbing against a nonconsenting person" (American Psychiatric Association, 2000, p. 570), is a specific class of paraphilias that involve aberrant sexual practices. Frotteurism is distinguished from molestation by the brief, public nature of the assault. Incidents usually occur in crowded, public places that enable the frotteur to be less easily detected and can help to ensure his getaway with little detection. Usually this contact occurs on places such as subways, busses, or busy sidewalks where there are many potential victims, as well as a good deal of anonymity which both benefit the perpetrator in his act (American Psychiatric Association, 2000).

Like many other sex offenders, the frotteuristic perpetrator is able to recognize the inappropriateness of the act and successful completion of the act ends in escape without detection. This inappropriate sexual behavior generally begins in adolescence and persists until early adulthood. It is evidenced there is a decrease in the frequency of acts of frottage after the age of twenty-five (American Psychiatric Association, 2000).

Frotteurism, as described by the *Diagnostic and Statistical Manual of Mental Disorders, Fourth Edition, Text Revision* (DSM-IV-TR) (2000),

> involves touching and rubbing against a non-consenting person. The behavior usually occurs in crowded places from which the individual can more easily escape arrest (e.g., on busy sidewalks or in public transportation vehicles). He rubs his genitals against the victim's thighs and buttocks or fondles her genitalia or breasts with his hands. While doing this he usually fantasizes an exclusive, caring relationship with the victim. However, he recognizes that to avoid possible prosecution, he must escape detection after touching his victim. Usually the paraphilia begins by adolescence. Most acts of frottage occur when the person is ages 15-25 years, after which there is a gradual decline in frequency (p. 570).

According to the *DSM-IV-TR* (2000), the sexual urges and fantasies and the touching and rubbing behaviors have to occur during a six-month time period and the urges, fantasies, and/or physical behaviors must cause some psychic distress or cause difficulties in the individual's relationships.

COMORBIDITY WITH OTHER PARAPHILIAS

Paraphilias are often comorbid with other paraphilias (Price, Gutheil, Commons, Kafka, and Dodd-Kimmey, 2001). A study by Abel, Becker, Cunningham-Rathner, Mittleman, and Rouleau (1988) demonstrated comorbidity between telephone scatologia, exhibitionism, voyeurism, and frotteurism, while a study by Bradford, Boulet, and Pawlak (1992) showed comorbidity between voyeurism, exhibitionism, frotteurism, telephone scatologia, pedophilia, hebephilia, and cross-dressing. This demonstrates that those individuals who are diagnosed with one paraphilia need to be assessed for the presence of other paraphilias.

Statistics on the disorder demonstrate the prevalence of the paraphilia and also highlight the fact that many offenses occur before the perpetrator is ever arrested. According to one source the typical frotteur may commit up to 850 acts of frotteurism before getting arrested. The typical frotteur (if such a distinction exists) may also be engaging in four or five other deviant sexual behaviors while at the same time experiencing the urges to frotteur. Though some of the statistics noted that frotteurs may have a history of rape, the majority of the comorbid deviances fall along similar lines such as exhibitionism and voyeurism (sexual deviancy).

THEORIES OF ETIOLOGY

Most reported cases of frotteurism involve males as the perpetrator. Reasoning for the overwhelming prevalence of frotteurism within the male population is that frotteurism is often defined as, "pressing the penis against the buttocks of an unsuspecting female stranger" (Freund, Scher, & Hucker, 1983). Therefore, frotteurism is rarely diagnosed in females (American Psychiatric Association, 2000).

Many theories have tried to discover the causes of paraphilia. Several of these theories are examined to determine how much each theory can explain the etiology of paraphilias and why there are low numbers of women diagnosed with paraphilias.

The theories include psychoanalytic theory, courtship disorder theory, Money's lovemap theory, learning theory, and the monoamine hypothesis.

Psychoanalytic Theory

One psychoanalytic theory looks to an individual's childhood for events or traumas that turn into significant markers for future behaviors (Doermann, 1999). According to some theorists, any monumental events that occur in an individual's life will have repercussions for the rest of their behaviors regarding certain aspects of their lives. It is likely that the individual with the paraphilia is reliving the significant event or trauma while committing the behavior in an attempt to change the traumatic event. A second psychoanalytic theory suggests that the paraphilia is a hostile reaction to the event or trauma that occurs in childhood (Doermann, 1999). When individuals act out the paraphilic behavior, they are reacting against whatever caused the trauma and punishing those who initially caused the trauma. Based on this theory, someone who develops frotteurism may have been touched or rubbed against inappropriately at a younger age and reacts to dealing with this trauma by acting out in a similar manner by touching or rubbing against someone without their consent.

Based on this theory, there does not seem to be any specific piece of evidence that would exclude women from being diagnosed with frotteurism. Psychoanalytic theory is based on Freud's work with female patients and his conclusions that both men and women deal with their own unique crises (Mitchell & Black, 1995). He allows for women to have traumas in their lives, and it seems logical that women would respond to crises in a similar manner as men, by developing some type of behavior to deal with similar situations as that of the initial crisis. Using this reasoning, it seems that more women might be diagnosed as paraphilics.

Courtship Disorder Theory

Freund 1984 suggests that several paraphilia are on a continuum. He specifically notes that telephone scatologia, frotteurism, exhibitionism, voyeurism, and preferential rape could be seen as behaviors that represent different stages of a courtship relationship (Freund, Scher, & Hucker, 1984). Freund et al. (1984) describes four stages of courtship that make up his theory, the finding phase, a pretactile phase, a tactile phase, and a copulatory phase. According to Freund et al. (1984), an individual's behavior escalates the more invested the individual becomes in a relationship, either reality-based or perceived. By fitting the paraphilias into a model, voyeurism occurs in the finding phase, telephone scatologia and exhibitionism occur in the pretactile phase, frotteurism occurs in the tactile phase, and preferential rape occurs in the copulatory phase. The paraphilias would become more severe with the increased contact with the subject. To Freund et al. (1984), the paraphilias stem from one another and escalate in seriousness from no contact to forcible rape.

While they speculate on a specific cause for the development of the paraphilias, the preference for certain types of stimuli, they do not demonstrate how the paraphilias can influence one another and evolve into other paraphilias. An individual who develops frotteurism is likely to be escalating from telephone scatologia or exhibitionism, according to this theory (Freund et al., 1984). Another study, conducted by Price, Gutheil, Commons, Kafta, and Dodd-Kimmey (2001) found a relatively high comorbidity rate between telephone scatologia and frotteurism. Research has found that 21 percent of individuals who engage in telephone scatologia also engage in frotteurism (Abel, Becker, Cunningham-Rathner, Mittleman, & Rouleau, 1988). Therefore, it should be expected that frotteurs engage not only in frotteurism but other sexually deviant behaviors as well.

In general, the paraphilic individual will have experienced some type of trauma or experienced an event that directs their path towards needing deviant sexual gratification. If individuals are not receiving enough stimulation from the paraphilia they are currently practicing, they may seek a new way to seek sexual pleasure by experimenting or escalating their paraphilia.

Courtship disorder theory does not directly address the issue of female paraphilics. The theory does not discount the possibility that a female could fall into the behavior patterns typical of paraphilics. The theory states that initial sexual contact is governed by a set of circumstances that uses erotic cues to condition the individual to the paraphilia. It is likely that this could occur for women as well as men.

Money's Lovemap Theory

The Lovemap theory likens the paraphilias to the phenomena of sexual addictions. Various types of deviant sexually-arousing stimuli become inappropriately linked with sexual intercourse as an appropriate way to express one's feelings (Money, 1984). Money (1984) speculated that these links between the deviant stimuli and sexual intercourse represent their ideal love relationship. The theory states that paraphilias occur when an individual develops an "all or nothing" thinking pattern towards love; thinking that love and lust cannot coexist within a single individual at the same time without causing some type of psychic distress (Money, 1984). This theory posits that early exposure to the "all or nothing" thinking pattern promotes the development of paraphilias. Those who develop frotteurism have committed thinking errors causing them to believe they cannot develop normal sexual relationships and can only receive gratification through sexual acts that are nonconsensual.

Money's theory does not address the issue of prevalence of paraphilias among females. While the theory does not specifically address the issue of women, it also does not discount that women could develop paraphilias. The thinking error (all-or-nothing thinking) that Money (1984) discusses in relation to his theory is universal; it can be committed by anyone and has been committed by both men and women. Based on theory alone, according to Money, it is possible that females could develop and be diagnosed with paraphilias.

Learning Theory

Learning theory suggests a very basic explanation for the development of paraphilias in individuals; that behaviors are learned because they are unintentionally and conditionally linked to specific, deviant stimuli (McGuire, Carlisle, & Young, 1965).

In terms of developing paraphilias, the first time a pairing occurs is when the deviant sexual behavior is accidentally linked with sexual arousal and gratification. Each time after the original pairing, needing the deviant sexual behavior in order to achieve sexual arousal and gratification reinforces the paraphilia. Every time the paraphilic engages in his or her deviant behavior, the person is self-reinforcing the paraphilia. Frotteurism is developed through an individual pairing sexual gratification with touching or rubbing an unwilling, and sometimes unknowing, victim. This usually occurs accidentally at first and can become the only way the paraphilic can achieve sexual gratification.

Learning theory has been applied to both males and females in regards to many different issues. This theory has shown that everyone can be influenced and is susceptible to being affected by the conditioning and reinforcement process. This is another theory that does not adequately demonstrate why females are not diagnosed with paraphilias. It does not provide an adequate explanation why a theory that explains much of normal female behavior fails to extend to possible deviant sexual behaviors that females could commit.

The Monoamine Hypothesis

The monoamine hypothesis is a biological explanation for the development of paraphilias. Kafka (1997a, 1997b) hypothesized that a disruption in the distribution process of the monoamine neurotransmitters (norepinephrine, dopamine, and serotonin) was a primary cause for the development of paraphilias. Research by Kafka (1997a, 1997b) has supported the position that changes in the levels of the monoamine neurotransmitters, through medication or physical changes, has an effect on paraphilic behavior. Further study is needed to test this hypothesis in order to determine if this process is one of the actual causes of paraphilias or if the changes in the monoamine neurotransmitters is a by-product of changes that occur in the body that cause the paraphilias. Further research is needed to determine how frotteurism would develop using the monoamine hypothesis. This theory also does not mention gender differences and assumes that the majority of offenders will be male.

The Timid Rapist

It has been argued that although the frotteur has been elusive as a research subject, including apprehension, and incarceration, this should not minimize the crime (Horley, 2001). Instead, Horley suggests that it is possible the frotteur is a timid rapist and just as paraphilias can progress so, too, can a frotteur. In other words, the frotteur may lack the assertiveness and confidence to follow through with the act of rubbing and often flees before the act is complete only to later fantasize about the completion of the act. This does not mean he lacks aggression, desire, or intent to go further. The reinforcement of masturbating and fantasizing can strengthen desire and coupled with aggression, the once timid frotteur may now progress to other sexual assaults, including rape.

According to this view, the frotteur tends to be relationally ineffectual, inexperienced, and would rather retreat than be confronted with his own passivity.

However, given the right set of circumstances, this could change (Horley, 2001). Our understanding of frotteurism thus far comes from confusion in the diagnostic criteria, which may facilitate the frotteur in eluding detection, receiving minimal sentencing, and avoiding psychological treatment.

PIQUERISM

Another paraphilic disorder that involves the unsuspecting victim is that of piquerism. This is qualified as one who engages in the "act of obtaining sexual satisfaction from stabbing, piercing, cutting flesh and shedding blood" (Glossary.Sex.Com). Piquerism is obscure enough that it does not yet appear in the *Diagnostic and Statistical Manual* (American Psychiatric Association). This crime is incredibly invasive and may be seen as far more drastic of an assault than frotteurism. Piquerism is not commonly seen in clinical settings but has been noted to be prevalent in countercultures. Piquerism extends beyond the surprise attack on a subway or crowded sidewalk; couples are engaging in ritualistic piercing, tattooing, and carving with their partner in an effort to gain sexual arousal and gratification. This appears to be similar to the element of escalation seen in other paraphilias. Presumably the piquerist does not initially engage in mutual carving but begins with small stabs or piercings and eventually intensifies his/her acts to encompass carving for sexual gratification.

Though most activities involved in piqueristic actions are deemed extreme just by the nature of the offense on a continuum some acts are less destructive. Generally, piquerism is manifested in two ways. One, the offender may pierce (pierce is differentiated from stab because the object used is usually less than a knife in these situations) an unsuspecting victim. A second type of piquerist is one who uses the piercing as part of the pre- or post-mortem torture of a murder victim (Geberth, 1996).

UNDERSTANDING BOTH FROTTEURISM AND PIQUERISM

The element of fantasy has become increasingly important in understanding such paraphilias as frotteurism and piquerism. A fantasy world exists for the frotteur and the piquerist who believe they are engaging in some form of meaningful relationship (Mental Health and Psychology Directory, 1998). This fantasy may have been created for a number of different reasons, and since most paraphilias are found to originate prior to the age of eighteen, childhood and adolescence appears to be the most logical place to begin exploring (Shaw, 1999). Specific cognitive distortions exist central to sexual offending; offenders must find a way to justify what they are doing in order to make the offense tolerable in their mind (psychopaths excluded). These distortions originate from a variety of places in childhood: childhood victimization, faulty family relationships, poor social adjustment, and general distress in psychological functioning.

Frotteurs and piquerists present themselves as disconnected and impersonal, common to avoidant personality characteristics that are consistent with these paraphilias (American Psychiatric Association, 2000). Both primarily act out with strangers, though as previously discussed, there is some component of consent when piquerism develops into carving. Fantasy replaces normal interpersonal contact. Fundamental to those with avoidant personality disorder is the desire for relationships but are unable to obtain them. Much of the anxiety caused by the idea of real personal contact is rooted in faulty cognition that they may be rejected because they are unworthy, inadequate, and unappealing. The possibility of rejection precludes them from developing a healthy, intimate relationship.

Failure in intimacy may well evoke a proxy form of sexual contact for frotteurs and piquerists. Both types of paraphiliacs desire contact with another person, but their intense lack of confidence and fear of being rejected thwarts such relationships (American Psychiatric Association, 2000). In these persons' fantasies, they can overcome any sort of self-esteem problem, any discomfort they feel in potentially intimate situations, and they are able to be as powerful and in control of their world as they choose. It is easy to become lost in such fantasies.

LEGAL CONSIDERATIONS

"Fantasies can be reinforced by powerful sex drives that, in turn, facilitate some unusual behaviors" (Hickey, 2002). Some individuals will go to great lengths to fulfill their deviant sexual fantasies. Some individuals may think that an anonymous pat on the back end or a pinch is harmless, since many victims do not even realize they are targets. Los Angeles is one city that assigns undercover officers to hunt for frotteurists or "gropers," on buses and trains. These officers arrest suspects ranging in age from seventeen to eighty-two, and have included day laborers, businessmen, a chemical engineer, a teacher's aide, a gynecologist, and a pastor. An estimated 80 percent are married with children (*There's a word,* 2002). "Going up and down a bus aisle, left and right, an offender may leave several victims in his wake in a single ride" (*There's a word,* 2002).

When in court, offenders who have been diagnosed with a mental illness may claim insanity. However, it has been established that an offender who has been diagnosed as a frotteur cannot plea insanity because acts of frottage are voluntary and intentional and, like psychopaths, frotteurs have no internal coercion that affects their will (Winick, 1995). According to much of the literature, frotteurism is essentially an impulse control problem. Frotteurs do not have a compulsion to engage in such behavior, rather an impulse and lack of restraint allows the engagement in acts of frottage. The extensive commentaries by Winick (1995) on the topic of frotteurism are peculiar because frotteurism, although punishable by the law, is rarely seen in court.

A question that remains unanswered by the literature regarding sex offenses and frotteurism is whether a frotteur is a danger to society. It remains questionable whether acts of frottage are beginning behaviors that may lead to further more

serious sex offenses. Acts of frottage may also be overlooked symptoms of more serious offenses, as seen in the literature regarding courtship disorders.

However, according to some research, it has also been hypothesized that not
only have rapists engaged in acts of frottage but that frotteurs and toucheurs sometimes engage in sexual assault and other sexually aggressive acts. Frotteurs and
toucheurs are often monitored for potential rape behavior rather than merely frotteuristic behavior. Authorities often classify a frotteurism attempt in a secluded
space "attempted rape"; frotteuristic charges of this type are often subject to more
severe charges than frotteurism in a crowded area (Open Love Christian Community, 2000).

ARE PARAPHILIC DISORDERS A FORM OF ADDICTION?

The term sex offense broadly connotes any illegal conduct of a sexual nature. Sexual
battery is defined as touching of an erogenous zone of another person for the purpose of sexual arousal or gratification, using force or coercion. Other sex offenses include frotteurism, gross sexual imposition, voyeurism, importuning, public indecency,
pandering obscenity, and corruption of a minor (Noffsinger & Resnick, 2000). According to the *DSM-IV-TR* (American Psychiatric Association, 2000), in addition to
the many other sexual disorders, those previously listed would be considered paraphilias. Because the diagnostic criteria and clinical features of paraphilias are similar
to that of substance abuse, can paraphilias be considered as addictions?

Paraphilias by definition, involve recurrent and intense sexually arousing fantasies, urges, or behaviors causing clinically significant distress or impairment in social, occupational, or other important areas of functioning. Many individuals with a
paraphilia report an escalation of their paraphilic behavior over the course of time,
which may be described as a form of tolerance to its effects. Just as substance users
often abuse more than one type of substance, paraphilic experience is not one-
dimensional; most sex offenders with a paraphilia had significant experience with as
many as ten different types of sexual behaviors, without regard to gender, age, and
familial relationship to the victim (Noffsinger & Resnick, 2000). Furthermore, some
individuals with paraphilias respond to treatment with twelve-step programs mod-
eled after Alcoholics Anonymous. This is consistent with the model that both substance abuse and sexual addiction are forms of pleasure seeking that have become
habitual and self-destructive (Noffsinger & Resnick, 2000). Based on these factors,
an argument can be made that paraphilias may have some of the characteristics common to addiction. Conversely, paraphilic disorders lack the physiological qualities of
withdrawal inherent in an addiction, and the clear presence of psychodynamic factors in most paraphilias argues against classifying them as addictions. Viewed in this
manner, it can be argued that paraphilias are better classified as sexual compulsions,
not sexual addictions.

Regardless of whether paraphilias are viewed as an addiction, it is clear that society views individuals with a paraphilia as having some element of voluntary control

over their compulsions. Just as a person who is clearly addicted to alcohol is viewed as having an element of control over the decision to drink or not to drink, individuals with paraphilias are viewed by society as having some measure of control over whether to act on their urges. However, this is still open to much debate.

TREATMENT

According to Noffsinger and Resnick (2000), treatment of sex offenders and paraphilias involves a multimodal approach. Each person undergoing treatment should receive careful assessment and individualized treatment tailored to his or her specific symptoms. The main goal of treatment is to block the offender's interest in deviant sexual behavior. Most individuals with paraphilias do not seek treatment voluntarily, but are ordered into treatment by the court after conviction of a sex offense. Clinicians should realize that they may be "fighting" an uphill battle in treating sex offenders with little insight or only external (court) motivation to change their behaviors. Individual motivation to change greatly reduces recidivism rates (Noffsinger & Resnick, 2000).

Lothstein (2001) suggests that a psychodynamic-focused group therapy model has a significant impact in the treatment of sex offenders. Psychodynamic-focused group therapy tended to have an impact on the relapse and recidivism rates of sex offenders. Lothstein (2001) based this trend on the notion that, "when empathic relationships are established in the immediacy of the group, genuine empathy can be learned and generalized toward others outside the group" (p. 567). When working with the different sex offenders, it is important to keep in mind the goal of the therapy. With frotteurs, it is important that they are able to recognize their inappropriate behavior and replace the acts of frottage with more acceptable behaviors.

Most group therapy takes place in prison utilizing a cognitive-behavioral psychoeducational model of care. Given that over 250,000 sex offenders are in non-incarcerated treatment, newer models of care need to address their specific needs. Lothstein (2001) created a naturalistic outpatient study involving his private practice of 109 consecutive sex offenders treated over a ten-year period. He outlined a multimodal model of care that is framed in psychodynamic theory. Individuals treated in his study appeared to have benefited from an integrated, psychodynamic, biopsychological, and multimodal approach to treatment that addressed deficits in early object relations and the affective component of their sexual victimization. Lothstein (2001) noted that when empathic relationships are established in the immediacy of the group, genuine empathy can be learned and generalized toward others outside the group. Therefore, the author concluded that an integrated approach to the treatment of sex offenders may have a significant impact on relapse and recidivism of sex offenders (Lothstein, 2001).

Serber (1970) suggests that another effective mode of treatment for individuals who engage in deviant sexual acts is shame aversion therapy. However, for this type of therapy to be effective offenders must be ashamed of the act of frottage. Shame aversion therapy requires that the offender engage in an act of frottage in front of a group of individuals. Embarrassment and shame felt by the offender should reduce recidivism (Serber, 1970). In Serber's (1970) study, he found that approximately 63 percent of paraphiles remained free from recidivism during a six-month follow-up period after engaging in shame aversion therapy.

Another method of treatment involves the use of medications such as antiandrogens and antidepressants. Antiandrogens reduce paraphilic behaviors by lowering testosterone levels. Rather than reducing testosterone levels, antidepressants reduce the frequency and severity of fantasies and urges in which paraphilic offenders engage (Seligman & Hardenburg, 2000). Winick (1995) reports that paraphilias such as frotteurism are not organic in nature, therefore, frotteurs do not respond to organic treatments such as psychotropic medications. Winick explains that with frotteurs psychotherapy or behavior therapy would prove to be more effective than psychotropic medications.

Although research has been conducted on the treatment of paraphilias in general, there is a dearth of research examining the treatment of frotteuristic behavior. The limited research in this area is most likely from frotteurs not seeking clinical help. When frotteurs are seen in the clinical realm, they are likely there for the presence of other sexually deviant behaviors. Successful treatment with frotteurs only occurs when individuals are able to "recognize that they have a problem and wish to bring about change . . . without the cooperation and willingness of the individual, these treatments do not seem to bring about any lasting change" (Winick, 1995, p. 575).

CASE STUDIES

To augment the above discussion, two case studies are presented highlighting the frotteurs' insecurities and ineffectualness, and how these factors collide with the desire for a loving relationship. The first comes from Dr. Wayne Myer's clinical interactions with a patient called "Mr. A" (Myers, 1991). The second comes directly from the California court system, dealing with a perpetual offender who was released on probation; this individual will be referred to as Mr. G (Findlaw.com, 2002).

MR. A

Mr. A is married and has a son. He came to see Dr. Myers at the request of his wife who stated that she was fearful of the abuse Mr. A inflicted on her when he drank too much. Mr. A stated that he only drank when he felt less of a man according to what he deemed himself to be. Initially, Dr. Myers reports that Mr. A was inchoate as to the onset of his insecurities. However, as therapy progressed and trust developed Mr. A began discussing his persistent sense of declining masculinity. He disclosed that although his marriage was troubled he still desired to be close to women, a closeness he felt his wife could not provide. This desire evoked in him a compulsive urge that was soon actualized by his first frotteuristic incident, which occurred on the way to work in the subway. He recalled that he was jolted into a women, stating that his groin area braised the woman's buttocks and from this he felt aroused and alive. He wanted to reach out to her yet was fearful of his inability to carry out the act. Doubting his masculinity he dashed off the subway only later to ruminate on the incident and begin a three-year span of frotteurism (1991).

From that incident, he began to relate the story of his childhood. He recalled that he was never able to keep up with his older brother, who was known to be a "jock" and a ladies man. When Mr. A was moved into his big brother's bedroom after the birth of another brother, he was elated at the opportunity to learn how to be "a real man." It was that same euphoric feeling he felt on the subway. Perhaps this is where the connection was first made between sexuality and security. Instead, Mr. A developed shame and guilt from the "night games" that his bother taught him. Mr. A described his brother's anal play and how he would allow his brother to penetrate him. Mr. A explained that he felt somehow more like his brother, a real man because a part of his brother's manliness was in him. However, he soon began to feel victimized by his brother. Still, he did not want to admit his brother meant to hurt him, and instead began his own victimization process of replicating the vulnerableness and passivity into active identification with his brother (1991).

Mr. A explained that initially he would play the same "night games" with his male friends, however, as they matured the boys halted the games to protect their masculinity. For Mr. A the longing and desire to feel loved and assured was continually taunted by his shame and doubt. Although he eventually married, his wife was dominant, aloof, and provided no loving stability. Therefore, when the incident occurred on the subway he felt this was the only way to gain back his manliness. Mr. A saw these women as helpless and felt that he was giving to them what his brother tried to do. Ultimately, he realized that he gave nothing to the women but fear and realized that he identified more with the women than his brother. The connection was eventually unlearned between the feelings of helplessness and passivity and how he was trying to identify with his brother in order to diminish the sexual overstimulation. He was then able to overcome some of his insecurities and end the justification of the nocturnal childhood incidents with his brother onto women he frotteurized in the subway (1991).

MR. G

Mr. G is a practicing orthodontist of twenty-seven years. In 1990, he was arrested after being accused of inappropriate and lewd sexual conduct with his young female patients. After reviewing the case, several factors emerged, which seemed to have influenced the court's decision: (a) Mr. G was a respected doctor; (b) he sought treatment at the time of his arrest; (c) he was diagnosed with frotteurism; (d) Mr. G. claimed to have a reasonable amount of control over his behavior (i.e., he selected his victims, thus indicating "some control" of his disorder); and (e) he had practiced for, at the time, twenty years with discretion (i.e., he did not frotteur men or older women). After being arrested for one of the offenses, he pled guilty and was given a four-year probation. His license was also suspended for five-years with a stipulation that he could still practice with supervision and have limited access to patients (Find-law.com). Mr. G. is an example of how the courts treat "less severe" infractions of sexual misconduct.

TELEPHONE SCATOLOGIA

27

Catherine Furtado
and Caleb Newman

OBSCENE PHONE CALLS

In 1989, approximately 22,000 complaints of obscene telephone calls were filed in the Washington area alone (Price, Gutheil, Commons, Kafta, & Dodd-Kimmey, 2001). It was estimated that those complaints represented anywhere between 7 to 20 percent of the actual number of obscene phone calls that were placed in that area. Given that the large majority of victims were women, many of whom lived alone, it should be no surprise that these calls were often perceived as violent and threatening by recipients. Victims of these calls frequently reported feeling vulnerable and exposed (Price et al., 2001).

TELEPHONE SCATOLOGIA

When an individual participates in telephone scatologia, he or she is exposing call recipients (the victim) to sexual and obscene material in an effort to seek sexual gratification. The victim is unsuspecting, having no idea what awaits him or her on the other end of the telephone line. The caller will frequently masturbate while on the phone with the victim, or after the call is complete, the perpetrator fantasizes about the telephone call (Price et al., 2001).

Telephone scatologia is considered a paraphilia as it is characterized by "a pattern of sexual arousal associated with exposing an unsuspecting victim to sexual and obscene material over the phone" (Price et al., 2001, p. 226). According to the *DSM-IV* (APA, 2000), this behavior is considered a diagnosable disorder when it significantly impairs daily functioning and has been occurring for at least six months. Making an occasional obscene telephone call does not qualify one as a telephone scatologist because he or she does not routinely engage in the behavior nor rely on it as their sole means of sexual gratification.

Fantasies and urges that accompany obscene calls are as important as the phone calls themselves. Since this particular paraphilia is inherently reflective of verbal confrontation rather than physical confrontation, the victim is rarely prone to physical harm. Evidence suggests that the telephone scatologist is primarily aroused by the real or imaged reaction of the victim, rather than the physical attractiveness of the victim (Price et al., 2001). In fact, many scatologists report feelings of anxiety and stress when asked to imagine confronting the victim in person (Moergen, Merkel, & Brown, 1990). Therefore, the disorder is commonly deemed to be one of the more harmless of the paraphilias (Price, Kafka, Commons, Gutheil, & Simpson, 2002). However, ensuing psychological and emotional victim damage can be significant.

THE SCATOLOGIST AND HIS/HER TARGETS

A 1994 study conducted by Smith and Morra attempted to discern more specific qualities of obscene telephone calls, including what types of women are targeted, a profile of callers, and the prevalence of reporting and subsequent apprehension of callers. Sixty-six percent of the women surveyed in this study reported having received obscene or threatening phone calls at some point in their lifetime. Another 64 percent reported having received silent calls in their lifetime. This group reported that, although these silent calls did not include threats or obscene material, they still felt uneasy after the telephone call. Most of the women who reported being victimized by either obscene or silent calls reported being victimized frequently. Smith and Morra (1994) found that divorced or separated women, young women, women who live in a major metropolitan area, and those who are "independent" are more often victimized by such calls. The researchers also investigated which calls were perceived as most disturbing by female victims. Seventy-eight percent of the disturbing calls were of the obscene or threatening nature, whereas only 22 percent of the disturbing calls were of the silent nature.

The average caller, based on the reported phone calls, was profiled as an adult male whom the victim did not know personally. In the majority of cases, the caller was also not a work colleague. Surprisingly, out of 1,600 women who reported receiving disturbing obscene phone calls, only 218 women reported the calls to the police whereas 314 reported the calls to the telephone company. Out of those calls reported to authorities, a very small percentage of the perpetrators were identified (Smith & Morra, 1994).

THE SCATOLOGIST'S MOTIVATIONS

The obscene telephone caller aims to increase his self-esteem by creating awe and fear in his victim. He has more of an advantage, however, than an exhibitionist, as there is less risk to exposing oneself over the phone than exposing oneself in person. This type of individual has a heightened ability for fantasy, a necessary component in order for callers to gain sexual gratification while maintaining a safe distance. The fantasy victim and scenario created by the obscene caller is more important to arousal than the actual victim. Physical contact with the victim is not necessary and is often avoided so that the fantasy is not ruined (Price et al., 2001).

An obscene phone call may not include just sexual innuendoes. Often these calls also have an air of anger and hostility to them. Through these calls, a scatologist releases not only sexual tension but also pent-up aggression and hostility towards women. The distance through the telephone provides the caller with protection from any type of retaliation, something callers often fear. Further, the distance allows the victim to be viewed by the perpetrator as helpless and inferior (Price et al., 2001).

SCATOLOGIST TYPOLOGIES

Theorists have attempted to classify the types of telephone scatologists. For example, Mead (1975) developed a classification system with three types of obscene callers: the shock caller, the ingratiating seducer, and the trickster. The shock caller is believed to enjoy the shock or angry reaction of the victim. He will likely continue to make obscene phone calls as long as he or she is obtaining the desired reaction. Juveniles largely constitute this type of caller. The ingratiating seducer is typically classified as one who initially utilizes a false pretense to gain the victim's trust. Once this has been established, the perpetrator uses obscenity to elicit a desired reaction. The third and final type of obscene caller, according to Mead, is the trickster. Similar to the ingratiating seducer, the trickster uses a guise in order to establish trust. From there, the trickster's goal is to have the victim reveal personal information, preferably in the form of sexual information (Price et al., 2001). For example, the trickster scatalogist might pose as a family gynecologist and attempt to convince the victims to remove their clothing and touch their genitalia.

Masters, Johnson, and Kolodny (1982) proposed a different classification system. They suggested that there are four different types of obscene callers. The first and most frequent caller is one who boasts significantly about his genitalia and then describes in detail his masturbatory behavior while on the phone. The second type is one who explicitly threatens the victim in a sexual fashion, although he rarely follows through with his threats. Similar to Mead's depiction of the trickster, the third type of caller in Masters et al.'s classification system is one who attempts to gain personal information about the victim without revealing his own identity. In many ways, this type of caller is akin to a voyeur, because he is more of an observer than an active participant (Price et al., 2001). The fourth and final type of obscene caller is the phone masturbator who calls phone crisis centers. Although he may call with a legitimate concern, he is typically masturbating in secret for the duration of the call; he usually does not reveal this information until the end of the phone encounter.

THE RELATIONSHIP BETWEEN TELEPHONE SCATOLOGIA AND OTHER PARAPHILIAS

It was originally believed that telephone scatologia was a rare paraphilia that occurred independently and in isolation from other paraphilias. On the contrary, it is now estimated that the majority of telephone scatologists have comorbid paraphilias such as voyeurism, exhibitionism, and sadomasochism (Alford, Webster, & Sanders, 1980). Some psychologists have theorized that telephone scatologia is actually a form of verbal or non-visual exhibitionism as the caller exposes the victim to obscene, sexual material but does not expose himself. According to Price and colleagues (2001), "both exhibitionism and telephone scatologia involve sudden attempts to provoke fear, shock, or aversion in strangers, and physical contact with the victim is not required for the sexual gratification of the perpetrator" (p. 226).

Numerous parallels can be drawn between the traditional exhibitionist and the telephone scatologist. Both paraphiles are characterized by low self-esteem, feelings of inadequacy, deficits in social skills, difficulty in normal heterosexual functioning, and feelings of powerlessness (Moergen, Merken, & Brown, 1991). Acting out such deviant sexual behaviors is a means of attaining power, self-esteem, and adequacy. The primary goal of each is to elicit a reaction from the victim, rather than establish any real interpersonal relationship.

A 1988 study conducted by Abel, Becker, Cunningham, Mittleman, and Rouleau found that, out of 561 male non-incarcerated paraphilics, 3 percent admitted to engaging in obscene telephone calls. The majority of these men admitted to engaging in other paraphilic behaviors: 63 percent—exhibitionism; 47 percent—voyeurism; and 21 percent—frotteurism. Many of these men also admitted to being pedophiles. Thirty-seven percent reported having committed rape. Transvestism and sadism also came up as comorbid paraphilias. Only one of the men who admitted to making obscene telephone calls had no other paraphilias (Abel et al., 1988).

HOW DANGEROUS ARE SCATOLOGISTS?

Telephone scatologia has often been characterized as a harmless behavior. While it may make the victim uncomfortable for a few minutes, once the telephone call is over, the victim is assumed to be fine. However, because scatologists often suffer from multiple paraphilias, they may be more dangerous than they appear to be from the phone calls alone. Ressler, Burgess, Hartman, Douglas, and McCormick (1986) examined murderers who had raped and mutilated their victims. Of the thirty-six murderers involved in the study, 22 percent reported having made obscene telephone calls in the past. These individuals made obscene phone calls and later went on to rape, kill, and mutilate victims. This progression is obviously not harmless.

However, does this mean that a fifth of all telephone scatologists are murderers? Of course not. But the fact that obscene telephone calls appear commonly associated with various more dangerous paraphilias (and apparently among a significant portion of murderers) suggests that there is probably some connection. As such, courts have begun to realize the danger obscene telephone callers pose to the public. For example, an individual who makes an obscene phone call to a child, whether intentional or not, can now be charged with child molestation. In a recent court case, *State v. Vines,* the court held that, "a sexually explicit telephone call to a child, conducted with the intent to arouse or satisfy sexual desires, was sufficient to support the charge of child molestation" (1997). The court opined that the actual presence of the child was not necessary for the offense to be considered child molestation. Though an obscene telephone call to an adult is also considered an offense punishable in a court of law, the caller will, usually, not face as stern a punishment as if the call was directed at a child.

SCATOLOGIA CAUSATION

PSYCHODYNAMIC THEORY

Various case studies have used psychodynamic theory to formulate hypotheses about the root of this paraphilia. In one case study, a married man reportedly achieved sexual arousal by making obscene phone calls to men and attempting to engage them in conversation while simultaneously masturbating (Goldberg & Wise, 1985). He admitted to having a history of homosexual fantasies, but never directly participated in homosexual activities. Goldberg and Wise (1985) proposed that this telephone scatologist suffered from castration anxiety, which ultimately stemmed from an erotic form of hatred toward his mother or maternal object. A low self-esteem and hidden self-rage contributed to his major dependency needs.

Alford et al. (1980) describe a second case study involving a married man diagnosed with telephone scatologia and exhibitionism. His exhibitionism began at age sixteen, while the obscene calling began at age twenty. He would locate women through a telephone directory and then crudely proposition them over the phone. He would attempt to keep them on the line as long as it would take to reach orgasm. They theorized both his paraphilias were inherently intertwined because each represented attempts to achieve sexual gratification through the reactions of strangers. In addition, neither paraphilia involved direct physical contact with the victim (Alford et al., 1980).

Psychodynamic theory provides an interesting, albeit far-fetched, explanation for the etiology of telephone scatologia and exhibitionism. According to the theory, the "obscene phone call is understood as an act that is essentially exhibitionistic. The exhibitionist seeks reassurance against castration . . . [and] conveys two messages to his victims: 'Reassure me that I have a penis by reacting to the sight of it and reassure me that you are afraid of my penis'" (Price et al., 2001, p. 229). Unfortunately, this theory fails to accurately encapsulate the etiology of telephone scatologia alone. Supposing that there are actually female telephone scatologists, how would castration anxiety play a role in their behavior? Do they exhibit penis envy instead?

COURTSHIP DISORDER THEORY

Telephone scatologia, along with exhibitionism and voyeurism, are considered disorders pertaining to courtship behavior. The normal courtship sequence includes four phases:

1. the finding phase, consisting of locating and appraising a potential partner;
2. an affiliative or pretactile phase characterized by nonverbal and verbal overtones such as looking, smiling, talking to a potential partner;
3. a tactile phase in which physical contact such as embracing and petting is made;
4. a copulatory phase in which sexual intercourse occurs (Price et al., 2001, p. 231).

Exhibitionism and telephone scatologia are considered disorders pertaining to the second phase in which nonverbal and verbal cues are sent to a prospective partner. Normal cues could include a smile or a compliment. However, deviant cues include flashing or exposing oneself to another individual or making sexual suggestions.

While it appears that many telephone scatologists are married or otherwise involved in heterosexual relationships, this in no way confirms that sexual orientation is a determinant of this paraphilia. Instead, the most common similarity among telephone scatologists appears to be their lack of appropriate social skills. They tend to have general difficulties effectively relating to other people.

LEARNING THEORY

Learning theory is perhaps the most pertinent when addressing paraphilia development. Basically, learning theory purports the infant mind is a blank slate, so to speak, which is imprinted upon by experience. Proponents of learning theory believe that even though the capacity for deviance is inborn and that many biological factors create the preconditions necessary for deviant behavior, the ways in which people manifest any deviant behavior are learned (Wrightsman, Neitzel & Fortune, 1998). In addition, the concepts of normal and deviant behavior are based on societal norms and values and thus the evaluation of any deviant behavior is based on one's learning what is acceptable within a given culture.

Learning theory posits the content of what is learned, and the process by which that learning takes place is important to paraphilia (Vold, Bernard, & Snipes, 1998). The content refers to those techniques or methods that are learned and ultimately used to act deviantly, and the process relates to those experiences that help shape one's view of society. The key element in determining deviancy is the way that a person relates to the surrounding environment; "people have a tendency to generalize the meanings of certain experiences, and then apply those generalizations to other situations" (Vold et al., 1998, p.186).

LOVEMAP THEORY

This theory holds that every individual has a cognitive representation of his or her idealized lover and idealized romantic or erotic relationship. Whereas most individuals try to make these fantasies a reality by meeting and beginning relationships, telephone scatologists prefer to maintain these fantasies internally by using women's reactions to their sexual comments (Price et al., 2001).

THE ACCEPTANCE OF SCATOLOGIA

Interestingly, while telephone sex operators provide a relatively safe environment for people to express their sexuality in an anonymous fashion over the phone, telephone scatologists do not often call these hotlines to obtain sexual gratification. To the scatologist, such hotlines remove the caller's ability to elicit a desired reaction of surprise, disgust, or embarrassment, a key component to their sexual arousal. Instead, by making obscene phone calls to unsuspecting victims, scatologists are able to fulfill this craving, while simultaneously remaining anonymous and maintaining a safe distance from the victim.

Most telephone scatologists are cognizant that making obscene phone calls is an unacceptable, socially unsanctioned form of sexual behavior. Given that many perpetrators are married or otherwise involved in a relationship, they may go to great lengths to conceal their paraphilia. The combination of these two factors no doubt strengthens the sexual satisfaction of the behavior. In other words, the fear of getting caught by their wife, combined with the thrill of engaging in a socially inappropriate behavior, elevates the excitement that is experienced by a telephone scatologist. The level of excitement and sexual arousal that accompanies the first obscene phone call can be likened to a drug user's first experience with cocaine, for example. However, just as a drug user may continue to use cocaine in an attempt to achieve the same level of euphoria experienced with the first use of cocaine, telephone scatologists may never again achieve that same level of sexual arousal that they experienced with their first obscene phone call.

PROGNOSIS AND TREATMENT

Are all telephone scatologists doomed to an eternity of obscene phone calls, masturbating in secret while propositioning unsuspecting victims? Fortunately, there are ways to treat this paraphilia. Gutheil, Price, Commons, Kafka, and Dodd-Kimmey (2001) suggest that, "the early confrontation of denial is an important ingredient of successful psychoanalytic treatment for the obscene telephone caller" (p. 282). Following the confrontation of the individual's denial of his problem, the therapist must examine the hostility and aggression this individual feels towards women. Ideally, once this hostility and anger has been worked through, the behavior will dissipate (Gutheil et al., 2001).

Covert sensitization is a common form of treatment for scatologists (Moergan, Merkel, & Brown, 1991). For example, the patient is presented with a series of audiotapes depicting various obscene phone calls. Immediately following the presentation of each audiotape, clients are shown aversive scenes. The goal is to have the patient begin to pair the obscene call with an aversive situation, thereby decreasing their sexual arousal. Pairing covert sensitization with social skills training has also proven extremely effective. The covert sensitization helps diminish the sexual arousal while the social skills training decreases social anxiety and increases social behavior (Alford et al., 1980).

To continually assess a client's interest in scatologia, the penile strain gauge, which assesses the percentage of full erection, can be used (Alford et al, 1980). In this way, clinicians are able to determine the level of client arousal associated with obscene phone calls, with the hope that the percentage of erection will decrease over time as therapy continues. The penile strain gauge is connected to a Grass Model 7B polygraph in order to obtain accurate data.

Cognitive-behavioral therapy has also proven successful in decreasing obscene telephone calls in scatologists. In this type of therapy, fantasy is seen as the motivation for maintaining the deviant behavior. The therapist works to reduce the intensity of the conscious sexual fantasies that motivate the phone calls.

Psychotropic or hormonal drugs are another form of treatment for paraphilias. Although the literature does not indicate specific pharmacological agents for telephone scatologia, there are drugs that are commonly used to treat sexual deviation in general. For example, serotonin reuptake inhibitors, hormonal drugs, and anti-androgens are some of the more popular types of drugs (McDonald & Bradford, 2000). While hormonal therapy has also been used to treat a number of paraphilias, this type of therapy is normally reserved for more aggressive paraphilias than telephone scatologia. Hormonal therapy attempts to suppress sexual fantasies and arousal, however, it does have many side effects. This therapy would not be the first course of action for telephone scatologists but may be used if absolutely necessary (Gutheil et al., 2001).

CONCLUSION

Many obscene calls are misconstrued as disturbing but harmless by victims. However, the dangerousness of obscene telephone callers should not be underestimated as individuals suffering from telephone scatologia also often suffer from other paraphilias, or such deviancy may progress to more concerning behaviors. The reality is very few paraphiles participate only in obscene telephone calling. As discussed above, some paraphilias, such as telephone scatologia, exhibitionism, and voyeurism, can escalate into more dangerous pursuits such as stalking and rape. Therefore, victims must learn to report these calls more often to the police or the phone company.

One of the benefits of making obscene calls for a scatologist is that they cannot be seen and are not known by the victim. In the same way, many of these same individuals receive as much pleasure through exposing themselves in less anonymous ways. Both acts aim to invoke fear and surprise in their victims for the sole purpose of sexual gratification.

C H A P T E R

EXHIBITIONISM

Development and Treatment

TAMAR KENWORTHY
AND FELICIA BLOEM

28

Exhibitionism can be defined as including "fantasies, urges, or behaviors involving exposure of one's genitals to strangers" (Seligman & Hardenburg, 2000, p. 107). While this generally elicits images of the "flasher," the exhibitionistic who wears a long trench coat with nothing underneath and who opens his or her coat to expose him or herself to others, not all exhibitionists fall within this category. In fact, exhibitionism has become a widely sanctioned form of sexuality and sexual expression within modern-day society. This chapter will explore some of society's sanctions of exhibitionism, a case example of exhibitionism, etiology and "cures" for this paraphilia, and what the future holds for the exhibitionist.

EXHIBITIONISM DEFINED

Hickey defines exhibitionism as "deliberate exposing of one's genitals (usually male) to an unsuspecting stranger" (Hickey, 2002, p. 24). Rickles defines it as ". . . a pathological condition characterized by a compulsion to expose the male genitalia periodically for the relief of inner tension—an act which is seemingly incongruous with the rest of the individuals personality" (Rickles, 1950, p. 1). According to the *Diagnostic and Statistical Manual of Mental Disorder-Fourth Edition-Text Revision* (*APA*, 2000), exhibitionism can only be diagnosed if it occurs over a period of six months and involves recurrent, sexually arousing fantasies, behaviors, or urges involving exposing one's genitals to strangers. Furthermore, the person must have acted on these urges, or the fantasies or urges must have caused marked distress in the person's daily or interpersonal functioning (p. 569). While the range of distress is not outlined, the *DSM-IV-TR* does provide other guidelines for determining exhibitionistic behaviors. For example, if persons do act on their exhibitionistic urge to expose their genitals, there is typically no initiation of sexual activity with the stranger. However, others may engage in exhibitionism because of sexually arousing fantasies in which the stranger becomes sexually aroused by observing the exhibitionist expose him or herself (p. 569). The exhibitionist, therefore, does not expose his or her genitals in order to initiate a relationship with the other person. Rather, it is the idea of exposure or the fantasy associated with the exposure that drives this deviant activity.

In American society, a growing population of people enjoy nudity and the expression of human sexuality. This is commonly seen in places where people with similar appreciation for sexual expression unite, engaging in activities such as nudist retreats, beaches, or clubs that display nudity of males and females for consenting adults. The factor that separates the exhibitionist from populations that market sexuality is described in this excerpt from Kenneth Jones. "The vice of exhibitionism lies partly in the fact that the element of choice is taken away from the victim. Looking at another's genitals is not offensive if that is what a person wants to do. But with exhibitionism, the victim is unwillingly used for the sexual excitement of the offender." (Jones, et al., 1985, p. 603).

Labeling this activity as deviant, though, precludes it from society's realm of acceptability, and this is not the case. Many exhibitionistic activities are sanctioned within society such as prostitution in Nevada, exotic dancing businesses, and pornography. These individuals within these industries could certainly fall under the diagnosis of exhibitionism if they have been in their line of work for six months or more, but many of these exhibitionists do not perform their job because they receive sexual gratification from it. Exhibitionists who cannot become sexually aroused unless others are watching them as inactive participants, or those who get a sexual "thrill" from exposing themselves publicly tend to be the focus of clinical attention. It is this category of exhibitionist that may be a danger to others, or that may participate in other deviant forms of sexual gratification (e.g., molestation).

Exhibitionism has been found to begin before adulthood and to decline as the individual ages; few arrests are made of individuals over the age of forty. This behavior also has been found to increase in severity during times of stress or disappointment (Seligman & Hardenburg, 2000, p. 107). A study by Marie-Josephe and Chopin-Marce (2001) found three common characteristics in their group of exhibitionists. These included: "psychosocial immaturity, presence of previously repressed psychological conflicts, and a tendency to feelings of humiliation and violent antisocial reaction when experiencing humiliating situations" (p. 627). These common variables allowed these individuals to act out on their sexual urges, which typically included fantasies of violence. Exhibitionists, however, are not a homogenous group (Marie-Josephe & Chopin-Marce, 2001). Just as sex offenders differ in terms of child molesters, rapists, and pedophiles, so do the typologies of exhibitionists. For example, some exhibitionists find ways of fulfilling their fantasies and urges of exposing themselves publicly in a lawful manner (e.g., exotic dancers, and prostitutes) while other exhibitionists expose themselves in public areas such as restrooms, in crowds, or in front of children. Understanding what drives the exhibitionistic activity is important in implementing treatment techniques.

CHARACTERISTICS OF THE EXHIBITIONIST

Most research concludes exhibitionists are primarily male although there are reports of female exhibitionism (Tollison & Adams, 1979, p. 240). One interesting suggestion in rebuttal of the few reported female exhibitionists is that the nude female body is generally more of an accepted or pleasurable witnessed sight then the male genitals (Tollison & Adams, 1979, p. 240). Additionally, male exhibitionists are visually stimulated and visually aroused therefore increasing public disturbance and reportable incidents.

"Few exhibitionists are dangerous or a menace. More of a nuisance, they rarely become involved with more serious crimes, except for those few who also molest children. The child molester is much more likely to become an exhibitionist than the exhibitionist is likely to become a molester." (Jones et al., 1985, p. 603) This quote distinguishes between two types of exhibitionists. Exhibitionists who are solely interested in exposing themselves and additionally, those who act in a series of sexually related crimes where exhibitionism is a symptom of numerous mental and criminal concerns.

VICTIMS

Usually the perpetrator's victims are of the opposite sex although reports of indecency towards children are also recorded. This information on sexual preference does not necessarily determine sexual orientation of the offender. One author discusses research supporting the premise that frequent exhibitionist acts have a relationship in determining at-risk criminal behavior stating, "the more often a man was convicted of indecent exposure, the greater the likelihood he also had convictions for other crimes" (Rosen, 1996, p. 177). Considering the dangerous implications of repeat offenders in this area of sexual paraphilia it is important to understand stages of development of the exhibitionist.

ETIOLOGY

Individuals who exhibit exhibitionistic tendencies are not always employed in professions that involve the exposure of their genitals such as prostitution or exotic dancing. Many of these individuals may be involved with these professions simply for their lucrative nature. The true exhibitionist's primary motivation is fulfilling the sexual urge or fantasy. According to Marie-Josephe and Chopin-Marce (2001):

> The population of sexual delinquents, similar to other criminals, is not homogeneous. At times, they suffer from personality disorders, neurosis, or psychosis. . . . Exhibitionists,

similar to other sexual criminals, tell us that they do not know why they act the way they do. They describe being pushed internally by a force that they cannot control. They claim that they are driven by an urge that is obsessive-compulsive in nature. That is obviously due to unconscious psychological conflicts (p. 627).

These urges are sometimes so demanding that they interfere with the individual's normal everyday life. This is many times demonstrated in a lack of friends or close family members, lack of employment or independent employment, and a lack of a healthy social life. Uncovering the root of these deviant sexual urges is important in understanding the underlying cause of this exhibitionistic activity.

Some research has linked exhibitionistic fantasies to early childhood trauma, in particular emotional abuse (Meston, Heiman, & Trapnell, 1999). The lack of stability and predictability in these early relationships appear to damage healthy future relationships. In fact, it has been a long-standing hypothesis that the origination of sexually deviant behaviors can be found in early childhood experiences. Psychoanalytic theory relates male exhibitionism to early childhood libidinal experiences; "he acts out his ancient castration anxieties in a ritual of reassurance through invited audience reaction" (Allen, 1974, p. 36). According to this theory, the male partakes in exhibitionism as a result of his castration complex, and therefore the female is not likely to develop an exhibitionist paraphilia:

> The person who exposes his genitals is reassured that he possesses a penis by the reaction to the sight of it, often fear, by the person to whom the exhibitionistic act is directed . . . The very fact that the woman has no penis and feels this as a narcissistic mortification makes her replace the infantile desire to expose her genitalia by the desire to expose all other parts of the body with the exception of the genitalia. Since displaced exhibitionism cannot reassure against castration fear, it cannot develop into an actual perversion (Zavitzianos, 1971, p. 300).

Cases of female exhibitionism do tend to be rather rare, but they also appear to surface in other more acceptable forms, such as pornography. While pornography is a lucrative business, it does leave the female exhibitionist relatively unexplored. In fact, female exhibitionists are more likely to be seen in therapeutic settings under the diagnosis of Histrionic Personality Disorder. In contrast, males are typically court-ordered or legally referred to seek treatment for their exhibitionistic tendencies. The nature of their referral does not often come under the guise of a personality defect. In general, both males and females who are "careful" in their exhibitionist activity are seldom referred for treatment and continue to partake in their deviant sexual fantasies without the knowledge of others around them.

DEVELOPMENT OF THE DISORDER

The stage of development in exhibitionism starts with a critique of the "personality of the offender" or how an exhibitionist arrives at the arousal of public indecency. First, there is one general similarity that all exhibitionists share and that is a strong or active sexual drive. Also, each exhibitionist has a diverse background of influences and personality characteristics that have influenced their initial arousal to exposing themselves. No exhibitionist can be explained in one catchall theory because of the vast uniqueness of perceptions and thinking templates each offender possesses, although there are some psychological explanations that describe the etiology of exhibitionists convincingly.

Of all the approaches, addictive thinking makes the most sense considering the constructs of the dysfunction. "As addiction develops, it becomes a way of life. Rather than being rigid, addiction is continually changing. As it changes, it inflicts changes on the person suffering from the addiction. . . . Addiction, like other major illnesses, changes people in permanent ways. In Stage One, a personality will be permanently altered. Addiction is so powerful that it can permanently alter a person's personality" (Twerski & Nakken, 1997, pp. 19, 20). As exhibitionists fantasize about sexual encounters and scenarios, their concept of reality is altered to a new perception of thought. This new perception of thought involves scenarios of exposing one's genitals to another in an act of sexual arousal. The excitement and the stimulation received from the visualized encounter of exposure reinforce anticipation of the event, escalating to acting out the image for increased sensory stimulation. The victim, in the mind of the exhibitionist, is initially an actor in the scenario that becomes played out in the mind. When the perpetrator acts out this scenario in reality, the person is again an actor, although this time the victim responds to the event. Mohr states regarding the expected act of the victim by the offender that "although all authors agree that some reaction is sought, it is not clear what this reaction actually is . . ." (Mohr et al., 1964, p. 120). What reaction is the offender seeking from the victim, if any?

Exhibitionism is a series of progressions in thought. Thoughts that precede actions going beyond the limitations of accepted behavior in society. The reinforcing intensity of the sexual climax is the reinforcing factor altering each stage of progression. The thoughts stimulate hormone release (sexual arousal), that builds with anticipation as the scenario plays out in the mind of the exhibitionist. This addictive quality of arousal is described in the following:

"Both arousal and satiation are attractive, cunning, baffling, and powerful highs. Arousal comes from . . . sexual acting out . . . Arousal causes sensations of intense, raw, unchecked power and gives feelings of being untouchable and all-powerful. It speaks directly to the drive for power. Arousal makes addicts believe they can achieve happiness, safety, and fulfillment. Arousal gives the addict the feeling of omnipotence while it subtly drains away all power. To get more power, addicts return to the object or event that provides the arousal and eventually becomes dependent on it" (Twerski & Nakken, 1997, p. 3).

POWER, CONTROL, AND THE ROLE OF FANTASY

This is a powerful explanation of the control that obsessive fantasies have over exhibitionists. The power and control felt in arousal is a large part in the progressive sexually deviant behavior. As the exhibitionist progresses from fantasy to action, so does the addiction progress in strength and control. Losing power of one's "life" to the addiction drains resources (emotional, financial, physical, and mental) from the person's "real" personality construct. The feelings of power found in the arousal build narcissistic characteristics that cover up deep feelings of personal inadequacy and low self-esteem. These desperate feelings become momentarily satisfied in the false power and control gained in arousal, although disappears when the reality of the fantasy is uncovered. The offender is often embarrassed when charged with the offense as one author states, "exhibitionists who are caught often express sincere embarrassment and remorse for their crimes but on release quickly recidivate" (Hickey, 2002, p. 24). This "sincere embarrassment" or shame reveals another side of the exhibitionist's personality. This shamed side of the personality is not in control of the addictive compulsions that are acted out.

"The impulsive–compulsive nature of the act has been observed by most investigators . . . describe the offender as experiencing an urge which so overcomes him that he can no longer control his behaviour, in spite of the fact that on some occasions that act may appear to be premeditated and carefully planned. Compulsive characteristics and a diminished ability to tolerate stress also appear in other areas of the lives of offenders . . ." (Mohr et al., 1964, p. 120). This strong compulsion dictates control over the offender's life and consumes the offender into obsessive thoughts and perceptions that are filtered through the compulsion to act until fulfilled arousal.

TREATMENT

Considering the addictive and compulsive behaviors discussed in the previous sections, some recommended treatment alternatives include medications, group therapy, longer convictions or legal consequences, community provisions, and individual therapy. One writer states "many sex offenders appreciate the wrongfulness of their conduct and intensely desire to reform themselves" (Lotke, 1996, p. 3).

Searching for the "cure" for the exhibitionist is not a fruitful endeavor. Those that subscribe to the biological approach to treatment endorse the use of medications. Typically these medications have fallen within the spectrum of anti-androgens that were designed to inhibit the sex drive of the patient. While these drugs proved useful in lowering or inhibiting physical signs of sexual arousal, fantasies still remained. More recently, treatment providers have viewed exhibitionism and other paraphilias as being related to obsessive-compulsive disorder:

> Based primarily upon case reports as well as studies indicating the effectiveness of serotonin reuptake inhibitors in the treatment of sexual paraphilias, it has been speculated that sexual paraphilias lie within the obsessive-compulsive spectrum. Redefining sexual paraphilias as a component of the obsessive-compulsive spectrum might encourage further use of SSRIs by the average psychiatrist, who might find it less threatening than antiandrogens. This would result in a much larger role being played in the treatment of paraphilias.
>
> (Abouesh & Clayton, 1999, p. 23).

These studies have demonstrated some effectiveness in the treatment of exhibitionism with serotonergic drugs such as Paroxetine. These drugs work to suppress the sexual appetite of the patient. In one study, patients showed a decrease in the intensity and frequency of their deviant sexual thoughts, and they were able to demonstrate marked improvement of their impulse control (Abouesh & Clayton, 1999).

Pharmaceutical research indicates successful treatment of exhibitionism with a medication called Fluvoxamine. This research viewed exhibitionism as a compulsive disorder and "eliminated the undesired impulse or behavior without affecting sexual desire" (Zohar, Kaplan, & Benjamin, 1994, p. 1). This is an interesting study because most medications that are prescribed for sexual deviate behavior eliminate the sexual desire and neglect the compulsive component of the disorder. This particular study focuses on the obsessive-compulsive tendencies in exhibitionists and works within this treatment strategy. While this form of treatment may prove effective in many cases of exhibitionism, another avenue of treatment centers on psychotherapy.

Psychotherapy is often used in the treatment of sexual paraphilias, such as exhibitionism. The focus of the treatment is on breaking down faulty patterns of cognition and exploring with the client possible reasons for their behavior. These reasons, according to psychoanalysts, lie within the client's childhood. Uncovering traumatic childhood experiences, unresolved conflicts, or suppressed memories is thought to aid the individual in discovering the root of their current malfunctioning. Therefore, by exploring with these individuals the possible reasons behind their current behavior the therapist is able to help them understand where these deviant thoughts, urges, or fantasies originated. Through realization that they do not have a character flaw or something inherently wrong inside of them, clients are able to better understand themselves and can work toward changing their behaviors. Whichever treatment framework takes place, it is important to recognize the cognitive limitations of the client, their current environment, and how deeply entrenched they are in their deviant sexual urges. All of these aspects aid in the probability of helping the clients to not offend or reoffend by understanding their system of relating to the world around them. How exhibitionism is viewed by society also is important when conceptualizing the client, and whether society's values play a role in the perpetuation or cessation of these deviant fantasies or desires.

SOCIETY AND FUTURE TRENDS

Exhibitionism has been around for centuries. In Ancient Rome, public bathhouses were fixtures of everyday life. While the intent of the bathhouse was not to participate in sexually arousing activities, the sanctioning of public exposure was evident and carried through to many generations. However, as society became more modernized, the appeal of public bath facilities quickly declined and was replaced with a sense of privacy in regards to bathing. Similarly, prostitution has followed a similar form. In eighteenth-century Europe, prostitution often occurred within public view on the streets rather than behind closed doors. This, too, engendered a sort of sanction to public exposure, which also ended within the last century. While these factors may not have a direct influence on the modern-day exhibitionist, they have set up a framework in which public exposure has been viewed by society over the centuries.

Currently, not all forms of exhibitionism are viewed as unlawful. While society does not outright sanction certain behaviors such as prostitution and exotic dancing, these forms of exhibitionism are typically overlooked. It appears that society has become more and more lenient in regards to sexual activity within the public sphere. Similarly, exhibitionism is often referred to as a sexually exciting activity and many popular magazines go so far as to give suggestions and ideas for exploring public pleasure:

> How else can you expand your erotic repertoire? Think outside the bedroom. Whether it's an alfresco fling on your balcony or some action on an airplane, exploring a bit of exhibitionism could be in order. . . . Forbidden trysts invite an element of outrageousness that can give your union a boost (O'Rourke, 2002, p. 156).

Articles such as this demonstrate society's growing acceptance and exploration of exhibitionism. While exhibitionism remains illegal in public places, legal restrictions do not apply within the privacy of one's own home, or computer.

The use of web cams has become increasingly popular within modern-day society. These devices allow individuals to broadcast their life, or pieces of it, across the Internet for anyone to view. The majority of these sites focus on sexual interests and take exhibitionism to another level. The ability of exhibitionists to videotape their sexual exploits is many times a satisfying way in which to explore and act out on their fantasies. With the Internet, they can legally videotape themselves and then correspond with individuals viewing their website regarding their reaction. This can further feed into their sexual gratification of knowing others are viewing them as well as any fantasy they have regarding how the other person feels about seeing them exposing their genitalia or other body parts. The future for exhibitionists appears to be more victim accessible and legalized.

SUMMARY

Overall, exhibitionism is a paraphilic disorder that can be expressed in a socially acceptable manner. Exhibitionists can range from individuals who simply enjoy knowing others are watching them in legal activities (e.g., modeling nude, web cams) to individuals who act out their sexually deviant urges by exposing themselves in public or exposing themselves to children. This behavior may stem from a faulty thought pattern, childhood trauma such as abuse, or biological imbalances. Whatever the cause of the behavior, the intent of the exhibitionist is always one driven by pleasure and control.

> Part of the attractiveness of an addictive lifestyle is believing one has control over one's world. Ironically, it is the addict's search for control that causes him or her to have less of it. In a world of objects and events, the addict's increased search for control, increased loss of control, and increased shame all lead to more emotional isolation and produce tremendous emotional and psychological stress (Twerski & Nakken, 1997, p. 53).

When attempting to understand the exhibitionist and how these deviant sexual fantasies developed, it is important to obtain a complete picture of the individual. In trying to comprehend the mind of an exhibitionist, it becomes simplified in applying the concept of addictive thinking. A low self-esteem, problems with expressing intimacy with those close to them, and a lack of power or control contribute to compulsive acts and thinking. Exhibitionism is a paraphilia based on sexual expression, but it crosses the boundary of healthy sexual expression in its intensity and propensity for leading the individual into further deviant sexual interests or even sexual offenses.

Clearly, there is validity to the treatment of sexual offenders. There is a loss of control that needs to be successfully regained and modified. Effective treatment would decrease recidivism and provide methods of change for those who struggle with sexual addiction. Individual therapy, group therapy, and accountability to family and community start the process to break the cycle of addiction. In Gold and Heffner's research they state "... it seems clear that aggressive and extensive empirical exploration of the phenomena that are alleged to constitute sexual addiction is urgently needed if we are to ultimately design effective interventions for those suffering from its potentially life-threatening consequences" (1998, p. 380). It is evident that further research is needed in the area of sexual addiction. This will determine the future intervention of therapeutic services in community-based support and legal settings.

SOMNOPHILIA

A Paraphilia Sleeping in Social Science Research

MATTHEW PECK

29

DEFINITIONS AND INCLUSIONS

As with all paraphilias, somnophilia may be associated with crime, may be danger-ous, and even lead to homicide. Therefore, it is important that social science re-searchers lend more attention to the etiology of somnophilia and its potential association to criminal behavior. Paraphilias are commonly misunderstood and lack comprehensive research.

Somnophilia is defined as a desire to partake in a sexual act with a sleeping person, whether the subject is a willing partner or unwilling victim (Hekma, 2001). As it pertains to paraphilia, the sexual act with the sleeping person results in sexual arousal through deviant or bizarre activities (Hickey, 2002). Sexual arousal may be achieved through intercourse, fondling, or any act of intimacy with the sleeping vic-tim. Somnophilia is also referred to as the "sleeping princess syndrome," or the "sleeping beauty syndrome," and may also be associated with other paraphilias or deviant sexual fetishes. Specifically, persons with this paraphilia are stimulated through sexual acts or intimacy with a sleeping victim. As with many paraphilias, stimulation may be achieved in association with other paraphilias, such as frot-teurism, toucheurism, pedophilia, raptophilia, and asphyxiation (Kippen, 2002).

For the purposes of the present chapter, it is also important to note that the definition of a sleeping partner or victim is not limited to the basic understanding of sleep. In a study of characteristics of sexual assaults, Stermac, Du Mont & Dunn (1998) note that offenders may sedate their victims through the use of drugs or alcohol. Somnophilia may include victims or partners that are sleeping, but also include those who are sedated, drugged, or otherwise unconscious. These inclusions are made because the desire of the somnophilic is to achieve stimulation by means of a victim or partner who is, or appears to be, asleep (Roche, 2000). Though criminal acts associated with somnophilia are rare, instances of physical violence, rape, and even murder have been associated with the paraphilia (Stermac et al., 1998). Therefore, it is important that somnophilia is understood for the purpose of improving law enforcement investigations, mental health treatment, and development of interventions.

CURRENT RESEARCH

In a study by Fedoroff et al. (1997), the researchers investigated the attributes of men who sexually assaulted sleeping victims. The study reports that those accused of sex crimes do not always have paraphilias. In fact, the researchers found that some offenders were simply opportunistic, while others were suffering from severe mental disorders, commit their crimes while they were intoxicated, or a combination of the above. Finally, the authors argue that some offenders are either falsely accused of their crimes, or their crimes are not paraphilias at the time, but may lead to paraphilia in the future. Overall the implications of this research demonstrate that somnophilia and some other paraphilias may be a result of crimes, rather than the crimes being results of the paraphilias (Fedoroff, Brunet, Woods, Granger, Collins & Shapiro, 1997; Fedoroff, Hanson, McGuire, Malin & Berlin, 1992).

In a study by Stermac et al. (1998) the researchers examined 1,162 cases of women who were victims of sexual assault. The researchers found that 96.9 percent of the cases involved sexual assaults resulting from coercion by the offender. Coercion was in the form of physical aggression, confinement, restraint, verbal threats, use of drugs or alcohol, and those commited while the victim was sleeping. The researchers concluded that assaults committed on sleeping victims were rare, and were usually committed by offenders who were known by the victims for greater than twenty-four hours (Stermac et al., 1998).

THE LAW AND SOMNOPHILIA

Congress has acted to deter and prevent sex crimes associated with somnophilia through the enactment of legislation that functions to increase penalties for those acting on their somnophilic desires. Federal guidelines provide sentencing enhancements for violations against victims who were sleeping at the time the act was committed. The increased penalty is applied to the vulnerable victim adjustment provided by section 3A1.1 of the United States Sentencing Guidelines (Anonymous, 2000). For the purposes of this law, victims who are sleeping are assumed to be in a position in which they are considered to be vulnerable, which is classified under the section of the vulnerable victim law with victims who are physically helpless, mentally incapacitated, or mentally defective (*State v. Dionne,* 2002). In *State v. Dionne,* the offender entered the room of a twelve year old and sexually battered the victim while she was sleeping. The defense argued that the twelve year old could not testify as to what happened during the battery because she was sleeping, and therefore her testimony would be strictly speculation. However, the court ruled that her testimony was admissible. Overall, the criminal justice system has demonstrated an interest and dedication to protecting vulnerable victims under the federal sentencing guidelines, including those who are sleeping during the commission of the crime (Anonymous, 2000; *State v. Dionne,* 2002).

The implications for the legislation protecting vulnerable victims are significant. By addressing the vulnerable state victims are in when they are sleeping, Congress is essentially functioning to take the control and power away from the sex offender. The sex offender often acts with the understanding that the victim is not in a conscious state and therefore will most likely have little recollection of the assault or battery. Furthermore, by ruling the testimony of the sleeping victim to be admissible, the court is further limiting the power the offender possesses during the commission of the crime. Consider the consequences if the testimony of sleeping victims was not admissible in court hearings. Offenders with somnophilia would have complete power and control over their victims with the knowledge that their crimes would likely not result in conviction because of the lack of testimony and evidence to prove the occurrence of the offense.

SERIAL KILLING, MURDER, AND SOMNOPHILIA

Cases of serial rape provide evidence for the importance of laws protecting victims of somnophilics. Unfortunately, these laws do not provide aid for victims of serial murder. The case of Carroll "Eddie" Cole is an example of a serial killer with somnophilia. Cole grew up in San Diego where he experienced an apparently terrible childhood. Cole blamed his string of murders on an extreme hatred toward his mother and in 1971 he strangled Elsie Louie Buck in San Diego. Following this murder he was detained by police and questioned. However, he was released and continued his murderous rampage in Las Vegas strangling Kathlyn Blum and Marnie Cushman in 1979. Cole proceeded to murder Bonnie O'Neal in San Diego, then Dorothy King and Wanda Fay Roberts in Dallas in 1980. Cole was apprehended while performing necrophilia on his last victim, Sally Thompson. Most of Cole's victims were strangled in parking lots before he took them home to sleep with their corpses. After nine years as a serial murderer Cole was convicted and sentenced to death by lethal injection. He thanked the judge ("Male Serial Killers," 2002).

The Orange County California Sheriff's department continues to seek a serial killer/rapist dubbed the "East Area Rapist." Between 1976 and 1979, he committed at least fifty sexual assaults, attacking women while they were sleeping. In 2001, DNA traced the rapist to six murders between 1980 to 1986 in southern California. Initially the suspect would stake out homes and enter at night, attacking single women in their sleep. However, the rapist/murderer evolved to attacking male and female couples. He would wake the victims, then brutally rape them, sometimes for several hours. Eventually the rapist evolved into a killer. He bludgeoned victims with blunt objects and sometimes shot those whom he could not control. (Anonymous, 2002).

In 1993, a serial killer is Spring Hill, Florida, struck four times during a two-month killing spree. The killer, named the "Granny Killer," attacked seniors in the community while they were sleeping. The killer would set fires to aid in his escape (Sharp, 1993). In London, England, Abbas Dadgarnejad, thirty-eight, was charged with raping his sleepwalking tenant in October, 2001. The victim, a nineteen-year-old barmaid, apparently was a chronic sleepwalker and had wandered into her landlord's room. She awoke in the arms of her landlord, naked, and engaged in intercourse with him (*Landlord Jailed,* 2001).

THE DEVELOPMENT OF SOMNOPHILIA; THE SUBCONSCIOUS PARAPHILIA

Development of somnophilia has not been addressed in research. However, this chapter poses possible environmental links to somnophilia. First, the acts associated with somnophilia are linked with victims who are, or appear to be, completely helpless. This perception of helplessness gives the offender a sense of power and control over the victim. Therefore, it is theorized that the offender may have lost some sense of control in life, especially in relationships with persons of the opposite sex. This provides the offender with a way to control the victim without being rejected. In cases of violent acts perpetrated on the sleeping victim, in addition to satisfying a need for power and control, the offender may have some sense of envy toward the victim. Therefore, it is possible that associating sexual pleasure with sleep may be a result of insomnia or some type of sleep disorder together with a predisposition for violence or aggression. Lastly, studies have found that sexual abuse is directly related to offending (Araji, 1997; English & Ray, 1991; Fedoroff, Fishell, & Fedoroff, 1999; Pithers & Gray, 1997). In a study by Araji (1997), the researcher found that, in instances of female sex offenders, 100 percent of the offending females reported a history of sexual abuse (Araji, 1997). Therefore, it is theorized that somnophilia may be a result of a loss of power and control, poor relationships, sleep disturbance or disorder, and a history of sexual abuse.

Though few research studies have focused on somnophilia and it's development, several studies have been done to investigate a similar phenomenon referred to in research as sleep sex (Mangan, 2002; Rosenfeld & Elhajjar, 1998; Shapiro, Fedoroff, & Trajanovic, 1996). Michael Mangan, Ph.D., authors a monthly newsletter that appears online at sleepsex.org. The site provides professional advice, academic research and resources for people who interested in sleep sex. As defined by research, sleep sex is a phenomenon where people engage in sexual acts while sleeping (Mangan, 2002; Shapiro, Fedoroff, and Trajanovic, 1996). Medical reports indicate that approximately 18 percent of the general population are prone to sleepwalking. Sleepwalking (somnambulism) is said to have a genetic component, with onset prior to puberty continuing into adulthood (Mangan, 2002), and research indicates it is generally the result of several complex neurological factors (Shapiro, Federoff and Trajanovic, 1996).

A possible association may exist between sleep sex and somnophilia. That is, those engaging in sleep sex may be satisfying an unconscious paraphilia. During one experiment, researchers recorded a session in which a man and his wife (both sleepwalkers) actually had sexual intercourse. (Shapiro; Federoff & Trajanovic, 1996). If somnophilia is related to sleepwalking, what are the implications?

Consider the case of Scott Falater, a forty-three-year-old engineer. Falater killed his wife of twenty years, Yarmila, by stabbing her forty-four times with a hunting knife and drowning her in the family pool. He, then attempted to conceal all the evidence. When the police arrived and arrested Falater he acted as though he was completely confused and distraught. He claimed that he had been sleepwalking and had no recollection of the events. He acted devastated after learning his wife had died (Stryker, 1999). Falater was eventually convicted of murdering his wife. Consider also a case in Pleasantville, New Jersey. Richard Overton, known for his extreme instances of somnambulism, awoke in his girlfriend's house, naked, on top of her seven-year-old daughter. A Superior Court judge ruled that Overton was guilty and would spend three years in state prison (Colin, 1999). Further research to investigate whether sleepwalking is a form of somnophilia is warranted.

SIMILAR PARAPHILIAS

Similarities can be drawn between somnophilia and other paraphilias. First, recall that somnophilics derive sexual pleasure from sexual acts with sleeping partners or victims. Similarly, necrophiliacs derive pleasure from sexual acts with the dead, who appear to be sleeping (Roche, 2000). Though there are differences, the basic idea is similar. That is, both paraphilias provide offenders with sexual arousal through a victim that is, or is perceived to be, sleeping. Second, somnophilia has similarities with asphyxia. Asphyxia may result in an unconscious, or nearly unconscious victim, who may appear to be sleeping. Furthermore, both paraphilias are associated with total control over the victim. Lastly, somnophilia is closely related to frottage in that somnophilia often involves the act of sexual contact through rubbing. In cases of somnophilia, the rubbing may involve fondling of a stranger while the victim is sleeping. Overall, somnophilia is a very unique paraphilia.

THE MEDIA

As with many paraphilias, somnophilia is prevalent on the internet. An abundance of Internet sites offer chat rooms, pictures, information, videos, correspondence, and stories related to somnophilia. Some of the sites include ways to make your partner appear to be sleeping, ways to sedate your partner, and even videos demonstrating the use of gas to put your partner to sleep. The Internet and the media provide substantial access to sites promoting somnophilia.

CONCLUSIONS

Somnophilia is a paraphilia that lacks attention from social science research. Somnophilics may resort to nothing more than mutually pleasurable acts with their spouse. However, individuals who are unable to control their sexual urges toward sleeping victims have been serial rapists and serial murderers. Federal guidelines provide sentencing enhancements for those found guilty of crimes against vulnerable victims, including sleeping victims, but this does not provide protection from murder, or sexual assault. Future research needs to investigate possible correlations between sleepwalking and somnophilia as well as treatment strategies.

CHAPTER

NECROPHILIA

Ainslie Heasman
and Elizabeth Jones

30

Sexual contact with a corpse, commonly known as necrophilia, is an abhorrent practice to most in Western society. Understandably, this practice, whether it is touching or stroking a corpse for sexual gratification, or in its most extreme form, sexual intercourse with a corpse is perceived by most individuals in Western society as one of the most abhorrent of the identified paraphilias.

Necrophilia is often believed to be rare and not often studied from a theoretical or scientific point of view. According to Burg (1982), there is a substantial amount of research and scholarly discourse on the topic. He concludes that the reason it appears that there is such limited knowledge is because few cases have been brought to the attention of researchers and scholars. Burg posits that the number of individuals with necrophiliac preferences and those who fantasize about the act, but do not carry it out, is larger than believed. Most research, formal and informal, has been conducted by interviewing sexual serial killers that act out necrophilia as a part of the act of homicide. There is a high level of interest in these offenders, most notably Jeffery Dahmer, who murdered and in some instances performed sexual acts and cannibalized his young male victims.

NECROPHILIA DEFINED

The general definition of necrophilia is "having sexual relations with a corpse" (Hickey, 2002, p. 25). Although this is the basic understanding of necrophilia, perhaps the definition can be clarified by additionally recognizing related necrophilic behavior. Necrophilia, to the general public, is sexual intercourse with a dead person. Necrophilic behaviors can range from touching or stroking a corpse, masturbating on or in the vicinity of a corpse, rubbing body parts including genitalia on the corpse or the act of sexual intercourse with a corpse. Latent necrophilia is defined as having fantasies of sexual contact with a corpse (Anonymous author, 2002).

The first known discussion of necrophilia is found in 1850 by Joseph Guislain. According to Nobus (2002) the Belgian alienist coined the term in his "*Lecons orales sur les Phrenopathies,*" indicating he first used the term in a lecture. It is widely believed that the first known case of necrophilia was by Sergeant Francois Bertrand, a sergeant in Napoleon's army. He eviscerated and dismembered both men and women he retrieved from graveyards. Still, it is suggested that Bertrand's case is not true necrophilia, as the mutilation of corpses was central to his offense, and his sexual gratification was secondary (Nobus, 2002).

One of the first to scientifically study necrophilia was Richard von Krafft-Ebing. He began his exploration by studying the cases of Francois Bertrand and Victor Ardisson. He expressed difficulty in determining the origins of necrophilia, but indicated it may be the result of heredity or an acquired perversity. He believed that senility or a mental weakness had to be present to account for acquiring such an unusual perversity (Burg, 1982).

OTHER RELATED PARAPHILIAS

Necrofetishism is the term that defines having a fetish for corpses. This can be documented by those individuals who keep cadavers in their homes or other locations (Hickey, 2006). These cadavers, while being attractive to the individual who keeps them, are not necessarily kept for sexual gratification. The individual may enjoy having the dead around them, preferring to eat dinner with cadavers as their dinner guest, as companions while watching television, or dancing with the dead. It should also be noted necrofetishism, as well as necrophilia, can extend to other paraphilias, such as partialism, where individuals keep body parts rather than complete corpses in their possession. Again the individual can view these as objects of beauty or it may progress into using the body parts for sexual gratification.

Another deviation of necrophilia is pygmalionism. This practice is defined as "lust for statues" (Anonymous author, 2002). This behavior can range from stroking various portions of statues, masturbating near or on a statue as well as sexual intercourse utilizing a statue as an inanimate sexual object. This paraphilia, although perhaps not a formally recognized one, can also involve partialism. The individual who practices pygmalionism may find only specific portions of statues, such as hands, feet, lips, or hair sexually arousing to the touch.

Other practices related, although somewhat loosely to necrophilia, are that of vampirism and cannibalism. Vampirism is the drinking of blood, most often but not exclusive to human (Prins, 1985). Cannibalism is the eating of human flesh (Prins; Hickey, 2006). Cannibalism is most frequently noted in the behaviors of serial killers, such as Jeffery Dahmer (Stone, 2001; Hickey, 2006). Often it is not seen as a sexual act, but rather the final act of a sexual homicide. Vampirism is typically used as a mode of sexual expression for some and is practiced between consenting individuals during the act of sexual intercourse. Unfortunately, these two paraphilic practices can be the cause of death, whether intentional or unintentional, to some participants.

UNDERSTANDING PARAPHILIAS

Paraphilias, in which necrophilia is a part, have been recognized as mental disorders since 1905 (Levine, Risen, & Althof, as cited in Seligman & Hardenburg, 2000). Seligman & Hardenburg (2000) explain that the term paraphilia is derived from the Greek word *para,* meaning deviation, and *philia* meaning attraction. The *Diagnostic and Statistical Manual of Mental Disorders,* text revision (APA, 2000) includes paraphilias among the diagnoses. While some disorders in the manual are more frequent among certain genders or ethnic groups, paraphilias are an exception. Aside from gender, with most paraphilias occurring in men, they occur in all ethnicities, socioeconomic statuses, levels of intelligence and sexual orientation (Seligman & Hardenburg, 2000). This finding supports a social process theory in helping to understand the etiology of paraphilias. A review of the literature suggests that the effect of an individual's family and early life experiences, including trauma and abuse—particularly sexual abuse, contribute to an individuals' exploration of paraphilias (Seligman & Hardenburg, 2000; Klaf & Brown, 1958).

O'Brien and Bera (as cited in Seligman & Hardenburg, 2000) developed a typology of adolescent sex offenders. These authors believe the typologies are useful in describing and understanding individuals with paraphilias:

1. Naïve experimenter: limited number of exploratory paraphilic behaviors, uses no force or threats.

2. Undersocialized exploiter: sexually isolated, unskilled; seeks self-aggrandizement, intimacy; behaviors are long-standing.

3. Pseudosocialized exploiter: has good social skills, often suffered abuse, rationalizes behaviors, feels little guilt or remorse, and seeks sexual pleasure.

4. Sexually aggressive: angry and aggressive, wants to dominate and humiliate others, often has coexisting problems with substances, has poor impulse control, and the disorder endures over time.

5. Sexual compulsive: repressed and enmeshed family background, engages in repetitive and compulsive behaviors for anxiety reduction, and no direct physical contact with victims.

6. Disturbed impulsive: severely troubled family, emotional and cognitive difficulties, often misuses substances, and impulsive.

7. Group-influenced: motivated by peer pressure and a desire for approval and admiration.

With the exception of one, the pseudosocialized exploiter, these types of offender all have limited social competence. An offender's difficulty connecting in interpersonal relationships may contribute to their exploration of paraphilias. Most paraphilias, including necrophilia, do not involve the direct, consenting participation of others. An individual's limited ability to engage others in an interpersonal relationship may contribute to their seeking out of other means in which to gratify their sexual desires. What is important to consider, however, similar to the "chicken and the egg" dilemma—is which comes first. Do individuals with paraphilias engage in their behaviors as a result of under-socialization, or do their paraphilic tendencies marginalize them and force them to withdraw from interactions with others? In all likelihood, it is a combination of both of these factors.

Some paraphilias appear to be progressive in nature. Some individuals tend to escalate in their practice of a paraphilia, in both frequency and severity. They also tend to increase the number of paraphilias they have at one time (Seligman & Herdenburg, 2000). Kafka and Prentky's study (as cited in Seligman & Hardenburg, 2000), indicate that the men they studied had an average of 1.8 paraphilias. O'Brien and Bera's typologies may not necessarily be distinct, separate categories, but may reflect a progression in the offenders personality.

Paraphilias are often comorbid with other mental disorders. Goodman's research (as cited in Seligman & Herdenburg, 2000) indicates that personality disorders often accompany the more severe paraphilias. Marshall (as cited in Seligman & Herdenburg, 2000) described individuals with paraphilias as vulnerable, lacking empathy and insight, and having impaired self-esteem and social skills. Fisher and Howells (as cited in Seligman & Herdenburg, 2000) identified people with paraphilias as angry, lonely, and self-centered. Goodman, (as cited in Seligman & Herdenburg, 2000) found them to oscillate between "devaluing and idealizing themselves and between punishing themselves and feeling entitlement." This tendency is referred to as splitting, in which individuals see things, others and themselves as either all good or all bad. It is a common feature of Borderline Personality Disorder. The research just described is characteristic of several different personality disorders in the *DSM-IV-TR* (American Psychiatric Association, 2000). More specifically they are characteristic of Cluster B personality disorders (Antisocial Personality Disorder, Borderline Personality Disorder, Histrionic Personality Disorder, and Narcissistic Personality Disorder). Individuals with features of one of the above-mentioned disorders often exhibit features of the other personality disorders in that cluster as well.

UNDERSTANDING NECROPHILIA

A variation of necrophilia is a "Sleeping Beauty"-type preference (Calef & Weinshel, 1972) in which individuals are sexually attracted to others who are or appear to be sleeping. This has also been characterized as "sleepy-sex" on Internet websites (Anonymous author, 2002). This practice often involves a female partner who is sleeping or otherwise not fully conscious and a male partner performing the sexual act. It was further stated the male who performs the sexual act is aroused by the struggle of the female who is placed into a state of unconsciousness through use of substances (chloroform, alcohol, or other depressant substances.) Calef and Wein-shel (1972) take a very psychoanalytic approach to the "sleeping beauty" phenome-non. They feel that patients they have treated who express frustration with their spouses going to sleep before sexual contact can be initiated, are in truth expressing their attraction towards the sleeping "sexual object" and a desire to have sexual in-tercourse with them. The degrees of necrophilia are important to consider as well. Some individuals fantasize of sex with deceased individuals or those pretending to be deceased. As mentioned above, there are individuals who exhume corpses from graveyards to fulfill their sexual needs. Others still, murder in order to obtain an ob-ject for their gratification. Considering paraphilias have a tendency to escalate, it is not unreasonable to assume that some offenders start off only fantasizing, later pro-gressing to finding sexual partners (often prostitutes) who are willing to fulfill their "clients" fantasy of playing dead. A further escalation may be seen when a "pretend" corpse is no longer sufficient. Gaining employment in areas where access to the de-ceased is common (for example, hospitals and mortuaries) or resorting to disinter-ring the deceased may result. In a minority of these cases, the offenders may progress to murder in order to satisfy their needs. It is possible that more serious pathology exists in an individual who will kill in order to have an object for gratification.

A study by Rosman and Resnick (as cited in Jynxed's Realm) indicated that in their analysis of 122 necrophiliacs, 57.1 percent of them were employed in profes-sions that allowed them access to corpses. Do individuals choose these professions in order to satisfy their sexual need or does their sexual interest in the deceased arise out of the continued work and daily contact with the dead? While many individuals are uneasy around and sometimes disgusted by the deceased, people in these profes-sions are likely to lose their uneasiness and uncomfortabless around the dead. Mor-ton (as cited in Nobus, 2002) describes how Karen Greelee, a necrophiliac working in a funeral home, removed the body of a thirty-three-year old man in order to perform sexual acts with him. When interviewed, she indicated that there is a lot of sexual ac-tivity with corpses in that profession and that it often goes unnoticed. She further in-dicated that if individuals are caught engaging in these behaviors, employers often do nothing about it for fear of bad publicity for their business. Ms. Greenlee received sexual gratification from the aura of death, the coldness of the body, the smell of death and funeral surroundings (Morton, 1990).

The development of necrophilia is difficult to explain. Much of the theoretical viewpoints on necrophilia stem from the psychodynamic approaches, believing that individuals turned to necrophilia to cope with the loss of a love object (Rappaport, as cited in Klaf & Brown, 1958), through an unconscious death wish (Jones, as cited in Burg, 1982), or the fantasy of submission, but fear of engulfment by another (Alvin & Rivera, 1995). Marie Bonaparte (as cited in Klaf & Brown, 1958) attributed necrophilia to the individual, as an infant, witnessing a sexual act between his mother and father in which the child interprets as a sadistic act. Presumably Bonaparte is suggesting that the child sees the father engaging in missionary-style intercourse with the mother, while he "dominates" her sexually. The child is likely to perceive that the mother is helpless and passive in the act, and takes that away as one of his first sexual experiences. Early explanations attributed a more biological and hereditary component of a reduced cognitive capacity in order to explain necrophilia (Burg, 1982). Moll (as cited in Burg, 1982) believed that "patients in cases of necrophilia who after being rejected by women seek corpses for gratification were engaging in a form of masturbation" (p. 244).

Franzini and Grossberg (as cited in Nobus, 2002) concisely summarized several necrophiliacs' experiences engaging in that particular behavior:

> They (necrophiliacs) frequently mention the desirability of a partner who is helpless, unresistant, and completely at their mercy. The dead lover never rejects caresses and is always available when required; makes no demands, is never unfaithful, and never rejects you. This lover does not compare your love-making skills with others', will go along with any sort of kinky sex, and, if things go too far, cannot be harmed and will never file a complaint against you (p. 178).

Control of a sexual partner is experienced and enacted by many necrophiles. The control is complete when sexual contact or intercourse occurs when the partner is deceased. Necrophilia allows individuals to engage in a "relationship" with another human being, a relationship they perhaps crave but have not been able to satisfy with living humans. Necrophiliacs can exercise complete control over their relationship, never having to answer to their "mate."

Alvin and Rivera (1995) explored the issue of control in examining a Thematic Apperception Test (TAT) protocol of a seventeen-year-old male who was admitted to a state hospital after a suicide attempt involving injection of roach poison. This assessment technique is thought to elicit projective detail from the client. The following is an excerpt of a response from one card and suggests a collection of paraphilias. It should be noted this young man's other TAT responses involved several paraphilias, including pedophilia and gerontophilia, seeking out elderly persons for sexual purposes (Hickey, 2002).

> . . . Then in a flash I heard a man's voice talking. He said, "I believe in Satan. I worship Satan. Satan is my God and my Lord. The way to put your wife to death is using witchcraft. Now go out and find a grasshopper and green herbs and pull a strand of hair and put it in the bowl and grind it up. Then give your wife sleeping pills or something to put her in a deep sleep. . . . And when the lighting flashed for a final time, my wife's heart stopped. . . . I saw some black widow spiders in the corner and raped my wife, her dead corpse.

NECROPHILIA ONLINE

The Internet is rife with information on necrophilia, including academic descriptions, tips on how to find corpses, the benefits of necrophilia to society, and a movement to legalize its performance. One website (Jynxed's Realm) describes the principles to which necrophiliacs should abide by. These include the right to engage in whatever sexual acts they desire with a corpse, comparing a necrophiliac's relationship to that of a "normal" couple. That attendance at funeral homes (during visiting hours, of course) should be encouraged as an "outlet" for necrophiliacs. One interesting yet controversial point, is that deceased individuals lose all their rights the moment they pass away. The website claims, that at worst, erotic acts with the deceased are the "destruction of physical matter."

In evaluating the criteria from the *DSM-IV* for paraphilias, Nobus (2002) suggested an argument could be made that necrophilia may not appropriately fit to the diagnosis of a paraphilia. The first feature of a paraphilia requires that it involve, ". . . 1) nonhuman objects, 2) the suffering or humiliation of oneself or one's partner, or 3) children or other nonconsenting persons that occur over a period of at least 6 months," and that it ". . . causes clinically significant distress or impairment in social, occupational, or other important area of functioning" (APA, 2000, pp. 566–567). Nobus (2002) suggests that it is difficult to determine if a deceased person is able to give consent or not, and if inflicting humiliation and suffering on a dead body is even possible.

In several years, is it possible that necrophilia might no longer be considered a sexual disorder, but a sexual preference? Nobus (2002) postulates that because of the status we, as a society, place on the deceased, it is unlikely that necrophilia will become accepted into the mainstream. He believes that, "the sociocultural and religious status (of the dead) is exceedingly complex, as reflected in the sophisticated arrangements of funeral rites and death cults" (p. 184).

RESEARCH

As formal research on necrophilia is sparse, there are several areas that are in need of exploration. One area is that of death preference in individuals who participate in pseudo-necrophilia. This practice is when two consenting individuals participate in acting out of necrophilic fantasy by one individual pretending to be deceased, usually the female, while the other individual, most often male, performs sexual acts upon the other. Sometimes, the female will choose the mode of death, most often strangulation. Other modes of death include stabbing, gutting, gunshot to the belly, impalement, drowning, and public execution by any of the aforementioned methods of death. What is it about the mode of death that the individual finds sexually arousing? Is there symbolism that the person is aware of, or for some it is an unconscious experience? For the males who chose the mode of death, is this another method of exerting ultimate control? Is the mode of death more gentle, such as suffocation or does the death involve blood and gore? Does the violence of the death chosen provide any indication of future violence potential?

Another area that could be explored is that of using projective techniques, including the Rorschach Inkblot Method, Thematic Apperception Test and Projective Drawing Battery to explore fantasy material. These methods, which do not involve the subject answering objective questions with either an affirmative or a negative, instead require the subject to respond to more ambiguous stimuli. This often provides insight into material that may be repressed or suppressed by the individual, perhaps as a method of protecting necrophilic or other paraphilic fantasy from judgment by others.

Victim selection by those who practice necrophilia is another area to explore. Topics include how those who practice necrophilia view the body used for sexual activity. Are these bodies seen as purely sexual objects or do the bodies have something more than a physical shell? Another area is that of poses for the dead bodies chosen by the living partners. What can these poses tell mental health professionals about necrophilic behaviors?

Finally, psychological underpinnings could be explored to ascertain what psychological needs are being met by participating in necrophilic behaviors. Is there a fear of rejection, which cannot be experienced when the sexual partner is deceased? Is it, as was previously stated, an issue of control, which can be experienced in its ultimate sense when having sexual intercourse with a corpse? These are all relevant questions that can be answered to assist in furthering the understanding of this paraphilia.

Surely, the practices and fantasies associated with necrophilic behaviors are only understood on the most surface of levels. This makes necrophilia particularly interesting for future study. The psychological aspects, including fantasy, control and actual sexual acts can be examined more thoroughly through use of psychological instruments as well as by nonjudgmental mental health and other professionals. Necrophilia is not only an act practiced by serial killers, it is a paraphilia that has a multitude of different individuals participating at various levels. In understanding human sexuality, necrophilia will need to be better understood in order to have a more complete understanding of human sexual behavior.

C H A P T E R

PYROPHILIA

Crimes Sparked by a Fire-setting Paraphilia

Matthew Peck

31

Abnormal sexual behavior, or paraphilia, may lead to significant criminal offending (Hickey, 2002; Wrightsman, 2001). According to Wrightsman (2001), paraphilia may even result in such serious sexual deviance as serial murder, as was the case with Jeffrey Dahmer. Dahmer butchered seventeen young men and kept their body parts in an effort to maintain a sexual intimacy with them (Wrightsman, 2001). Though most paraphilias will not inevitably lead to murder or even criminality, there is a significant probability that extreme deviance may lead to some form of offending or criminal pattern. When these abnormal sexual deviances are paired with troubled childhood environments, the chance of paraphilia leading to offending is at its peak (Hickey, 2002). With consideration for the potential harm resulting from deviant sexual behavior, it is important for law enforcement investigators, social science researchers and other behavioral specialists to have a significant understanding of paraphilias and the dangers they present to society. Fire setting is a paraphilia that presents significant potential for harm on society and must be given increased attention in social science research.

PYROPHILIA VERSUS PYROMANIA

Pyrophilia is the designation for the paraphilia commonly associated with deliberate fire setting. However, this term is rarely used because of its more recent development in literature. The term pyromania may be used throughout this chapter because of its extensive usage in past literature to describe the relevant behaviors of fire setters. A variety of definitions for pyromania have been offered in past literature. According to Reinhardt (1957), pyromania comes from the Greek combination of fire and madness. The author uses the term sex pyromaniac to "refer[s] to an individual who experiences a sex delight, that is definitely associated with fire, and who for that conscious reason has a compelling interest in starting conflagrations" (Reinhardt, 1957). The pyromaniac has also been defined as a person who receives some direct satisfaction from an association with fire (Morneau & Rockwell, 1980). More current definitions recognize pyromania as a psychological disorder. For example, Davis and Palladino (2000) refer to pyromania as an impulse control disorder that refers to a compelling and intense desire to observe, prepare, or start fires (Davis & Palladino, 2000). Put in much simpler terms, the Texas Commission on Law Enforcement Officer Standards and Education (2001) describes pyromania as eroticized arson ("Texas Commission," 2001).

The *Diagnostic and Statistical Manual of Mental Disorders,* fourth edition (DSM-IV) published by the American Psychiatric Association (2000), offers a much more detailed definition of pyromania. According to the DSM-IV, there must be a deliberate and purposeful fire setting that occurs more than one time, there must be arousal prior to the act, the offender must have a fascination, interest, curiosity or attraction to fire, the offender must take pleasure in the act or when witnessing its' aftermath, and the fire must not be done for pleasure rather than other personal gain (e.g., revenge, economic gain, political reasons, etc.) (APA, 2000). From this definition, it can be assumed that sexually motivated arson would be considered a form of pyromania. Overall the definitions of pyromania differ. However, all encompass the act of fire setting based on sexual motivation.

PYROMANIA: A SEX CRIME OR NOT?

There has been significant debate over whether arson should be considered a sex crime (Lewis & Yarnell, 1951, cited in Reinhardt, 1957; Quinsey, Chaplin, & Upfold, 1989; Rothenberg, 2002; Soltys, 1992). Quinsey et al. (1989) presented fire setters, and non–fire setters (control group) with narrated audiotapes which described fires, sexual incidents, and neutral incidents. The researchers found no differences in the degree of sexual arousal when comparing the fire setters with the control group (Quinsey et al., 1989). Further, Soltys (1992) notes that despite early arguments by psychoanalytic studies linking sexuality with fire setting, few studies have found psychosexual motives for fire setting. However, these arguments are limited. Quinsey and researchers (1989) simply read narratives describing fire setting scenarios to the subject, leaving out the significant factors of watching the fire burn, and actually committing the act and being responsible for the destruction it creates. These contexts are significant motives for arousal in fire setters, yet were not accounted for in the study led by Quinsey (Morneau & Rockwell, 1980; Reinhardt, 1957). Overall, the studies arguing no connection between sexual motives and fire setting are limited, and contain serious methodological flaws.

Conversely, there is vast research demonstrating crimes of arson are sexual in nature (Davis & Palladino, 2000; Lewis, 1965; Lewis & Yarnell, 1951, cited in Reinhardt, 1957; Morneau & Rockwell, 1980; Reinhardt, 1957; Rothenberg, 2002). Davis and Palladino (2000) argue that little research has been done to explore the link between sexuality and arson, but the authors assert that fire setting has been associated with paraphilia. The authors also note that David Berkowitz, the New York City serial killer named the Son of Sam, set more that two thousand fires during the 1970s (Davis & Palladino, 2000). Nolan Lewis (1965) argues that fire setting is a crime of sexuality by citing folklore, legends and case histories that will be described further in the chapter (Lewis, 1965). Additionally, some of the earliest systematic research on pathological fire setters found subjects commonly had a history of psychosis in the family, displayed abnormal sexual behavior, had borderline intelligence, and came from disrupted family backgrounds (Lewis & Yarnell, 1951 *cited in* Reinhardt, 1957). In the authors' article addressing the role of fantasy, as it pertains to violent crime, Rothenberg asserts that arsonists live in a fantasy world. She argues that arson is often a sexually-based crime that allows the offender to gain a sense of control through the knowledge that he is responsible for the destruction resulting from the fire he set (Rothenberg, 2002). Overall, there is an abundance of research arguing pyromania is a sex crime.

THE HISTORY OF PYROMANIA

In his article, Nolan Lewis (1965) presents a historical overview of the association between sexuality and fire. Early accounts of pyromania attribute the behavior to an insanity coupled with an irresistible impulse to set fires. The author argues that fire was thought to represent magical power, which some men believed they could use to exert control and display power. This served to provide arsonists with satisfaction in lives that, for most arsonists of this time, were characterized by impotence, shame, depression, jealousy and failure. The fire would serve as an outlet for the purpose of dealing with problems that the pyromaniac could not deal with in a normal way. Lewis also explains that sexually motivated fire setters gain a perverted sexual pleasure from their acts, which are phallic in nature (Lewis, 1965).

Lewis continues by explaining folklore and ancient symbols that link sex and fire. The color of fire, red, is the universal symbol for sexual excitement, murder, and blood. In Chinese folklore, homes and shop walls were printed with men and women engaged in sexual intercourse for the purpose of protecting the buildings from destruction by fire. Fire was believed to represent the male principle, while water was the female principle. Together the male and female principles protected against the destruction of fire. Fire was thought to be second in worship only to the sun, was identified in sex worship and was used in many religious ceremonies (Lewis, 1965).

Lewis continues his explanation of sexuality and fire relatedness by citing ancient folklore from around the world. Two similar legends come out of New Guinea's Milne Bay and Southeast British Guiana. The two tribes from these areas, the Wagawaga people and the Tarumas, respectively, believed that the owner of fire is an old woman. This old woman holds the flame hidden from everyone in her vagina, only producing it when she needs it. Other Guiana tribes believed that this woman only produced fire when she spat or defecated. Lewis argues that this indicates and oral and anal relationship between fire and sexuality. Folklore from Malaysia and Indonesia say that fire is the representation indicating that a beautiful woman is present. In these cultures, women were said to be the protectors of fire. The Wunambal people of Northwest Australia believed that fire originated from one of their most important ancestors who discovered fire during an operation known to them as subincision of the penis. These people say that when this ancestor split his penis during the operation, a bright flash of lightning was let out. The fire was released when the man exposed the red color from inside his wound (Lewis, 1965).

Lewis also explains that fire is represented through sex constantly in the unconscious minds of arsonists and even in the conscious minds of normal people. He claims that mentally ill people have frequent dreams and delusions associated to fire and that they are unable to concentrate because of fantasies of fire. The author explains that pyromaniacs often have dreams of fire the night before setting their fires. The symbolism of fire and sex can be found in such terms as the fire of passion and the fire of love. Further symbolism between fire and sex can be found in the relationship between urination and fire. Children in many modern cultures are warned that if they play with fire, then they will wet their bed during the night while they are sleeping (Lewis, 1965).

Freud argued that man has an instinctual drive that motivates him to extinguish fire through urination. Freud's theory speculated that following the capture of fire by prehistoric man, he gave woman the responsibility of guarding the fire. Freud believed women were given this duty because their female anatomy kept them from the temptation to extinguish the fire by urinating on it, and this duty for women seemed fit since fire was difficult for primitive man to produce. Also in regards to fire setting and sexuality, Freud theorized that repression occurs when an individual desires something, but when rationalizing, finds that the act is wrong. Thus, when an act of arson is committed and the motive is disguised or unclear, this may be a direct result of repressing the sexual urges to set fires. Freud argued that this was the case when arsonists were caught and claimed that their only motive was gaining some kind of satisfaction from watching the fire burn (Freud, 1934).

Overall, history provides insight into the roots of the relationship between fire and sexuality. Though some of the early explanations may seem farfetched, they may be relevant to our current understanding of fire setting and paraphilia.

CLASSIFYING PYROMANIACS

The classification of pyromaniacs is most commonly addressed concerning their motivations for setting the fires (Douglas, Burgess, Burgess, & Ressler, 1997; Inciardi, 1970; Lewis, 1965; O'Connor, 2001; Soltys, 1992). Lewis (1965) argues that fire setters are mentally ill psychotics and psychopaths that set fires for one of the following motives: 1) to protest social order, 2) to exact revenge against an employer, 3) as an act of revenge towards someone who may have injured the offender's personal image, 4) in reaction to a jealous rage, 5) to create an opportunity for the offender to appear as a hero by extinguishing the fire on their own, 6) to achieve sexual gratification, or for the purpose of satisfying some sexual perversion. The author also notes that these pyromaniacs often possess the following characteristics: alcoholism, maladjustment, rejection of social order, sexual deviance, and pleasure seeking in performing acts related to extinguishing fires (Lewis, 1965).

Douglas and researchers (1997) studied incarcerated arson offenders. The study consisted of four groups of fire setters grouped by stated motivation including: thrill seeking, attention seeking, wanting recognition, or achieving some form of sexual satisfaction from the fire setting. The researchers found that offenders most commonly tended to target residential property and public buildings. In most cases, the targets for the fires were selected because they offered safe surrounding areas from which the offender could secretly watch the fire burn and watch emergency response personnel fight the destruction. The researchers concluded that serial offending is common among these groups of fire setters (e.g., thrill and attention seeking, and sexually motivated) and the offenders are likely to have prior convictions for arson and a fair history of petty offenses (Douglas et al, 1997).

Some of the earliest systematic research performed on fire setters concluded there were sexual elements to these crimes (Lewis & Yarnell, 1951 cited in Reinhardt, 1957). Lewis and Yarnell (1951) studied a group of 1,145 fire setters. The researchers reviewed case summaries from files on arsonists obtained from the National Board of Fire Underwriters. They found that approximately 8 percent (91 of the 1,145) of the offenders were identified to be acting on some form of sexual motive. The researchers reported a general profile of these sexually motivated pyromaniacs, which included the following characteristics: borderline intelligence, poor socioeconomic status (hereafter SES), tended to be middle aged ($M = 39$ years), exposed to immorality in childhood, 75 percent had been married, were characterized as having repeated spousal problems, sexually promiscuity, alcoholism, history of past criminal behavior, and high instances of organic diseases (e.g., organic brain diseases, general paresis, epilepsy, etc.). Notably, the sexually motivated pyromaniacs tended to have difficult in adjustment, had feelings of inferiority and insecurity, and were considered by the researchers to be unstable individuals (Lewis & Yarnell, 1951).

Inciardi (1970) gathered a sample of 138 cases of sentenced arson offenders through the New York State Division of Parole for the purpose of developing a typology of the adult fire setter. From analysis of these case summaries, the researcher categorized the offenders into six behavioral categories of fire setters based on motivational patterns. The six categories include: revenge fire setters, excitement fire setters, institutionalized fire setters, insurance claim fire setters, vandalism fire setters, and fire setters whose motive was to cover up another crime (Inciardi, 1970). It will be argued here, for reasons that follow, that sexually motivated arsonists fall into the category of excitement fire setters as described by Inciardi. Recall that sexually motivated fire setters gain some form of excitement by watching the fire burn or watching emergency crews work to extinguish the fire (Davis & Palladino, 2000; Lewis, 1965; Lewis & Yarnell, 1951 cited in Reinhardt, 1957; Morneau & Rockwell, 1980; Reinhardt, 1957; Rothenberg, 2002). Also, as Reinhardt (1957) argues, although sexual motives may not immediately be obvious, they frequently exist. Similar to the above-mentioned research, Inciardi (1970) explains the excitement fire setter as one who acts because he or she finds excitement in watching the fire burn or watching the conflagration of fire personnel and equipment working on the scene. Based on this evidence, it is reasonable to assume that sexually motivated pyromaniacs fall under Inciardi's category of the excitement fire setter. The author reports that this type of fire setter represents 18 percent of his sample (24 of 138 cases). He reports the following characteristics were found in this type of offender: generally single, Caucasian, males, median age of twenty-three years, of average intelligence, working in unskilled labor, from urban communities, coming from intact homes, with a history of criminal behavior usually beginning prior to their eighteenth birthday, and a history of alcohol abuse. Notably, sexual perversion was identified in 18 percent of the cases. Also, recall that Lewis and Yarnell (1951) reported high instances of organic disease (Lewis & Yarnell, 1951 cited in Reinhardt, 1957). It is important to note that Inciardi reported evidence of organic disease in only eleven cases (8 percent). Though there is some disagreement with other research, Inciardi's description of the excitement fire setter is generally consistent with other research on pyromaniacs.

In a similar study, McKerracher and Dacre (1966) did not attempt to create a typology of arsonists; rather they differentiated fire-setter characteristics from other criminal offenders. The researchers reviewed extensive case histories of 177 patients at a special security hospital for criminal offenders. The data revealed that arsonists had a greater tendency to mutilate themselves, greater frequency of suicide attempts, had higher instances of emotional instability, and were more prone to depression than the non-arsonist offender sample. Notably, the researchers concluded that arsonists were found to have committed fewer sexual offenses that the non-arsonist group (30 to 56 percent, respectively) and the authors report that they were surprised to find that arsonists were no more likely to commit acts of aggression against another person than the non-arsonist group (McKerracher & Dacre, 1966). This study contributed to research knowledge of pyromaniac characteristics by reporting findings that had not been discussed in detail in past research.

More recently, O'Connor (2001) developed a profile of arsonists. According to the author, the typical arsonist is a white, male, under the age of eighteen, from a low SES background, with less than average intelligence, coming from a disrupted family background, having low social skills, lacks remorse, and has a history of juvenile offending. The author classifies arsonists into the following categories; arson for revenge, arson for excitement (encompasses sexually motivated arsonists), arson for vandalism, arson for profit, and arson committed for the purpose of concealing another crime. The author notes that motivations of revenge and excitement are the most common (41 and 30 percent, respectively). The stated precipitating factors for excitement arsonists are boredom, sexual thrill cycle or the need for attention. Targets of these arsonists are generally parks, construction sites, arenas and residential areas. The characteristics, categories and motivations asserted by the author are generally consistent with past research (O'Connor, 2001).

GENDER- AND AGE-SPECIFIC FIRE SETTING

Research addressing child fire setting is limited (Stewart & Culver, 1982). According to a study by Stewart and Culver (1982), past research generally indicates that child fire setters commonly possess the following features; "fighting, disobedience and destructiveness; most of them set fires at home and on their own; boys greatly out number girls; and a high proportion of the children come from disrupted homes" (Stewart & Culver, 1982, p. 357). The researchers studied a sample of forty-six children who had set at least one fire and who were admitted to a psychiatric ward. They results of the study show that the most common referral problems were identified to be: fighting, resistance to discipline, disruptive behaviors in school and theft. A majority of the children in the sample experienced parents fighting in the home, divorce, desertion, and many experienced abuse. The researchers also found that children who had fathers who were either antisocial or alcoholic began setting fires at an earlier age compared to those who did not. Upon a follow-up review of the subjects in the study, the researchers found "[t]he following types of behaviors had occurred in more than 20 percent of the children . . . ; never admitting guilt, going with bad friends, persistent lying, stealing from family members, truancy, drinking without parents' permission and precocious or excessive interest in sex." (Stewart & Culver, 1982, p. 361). Reinhardt (1957) adds that juvenile fire setters are motivated by sexuality and, therefore, as they age into adulthood and establish normal sexual outlets, fire setting may decrease or even stop completely (Reinhardt, 1957).

There is currently very little literature concerning female arsonists. Again, Lewis and Yarnell (1951) analyzed two hundred cases of female fire setters in their study. Of these cases, only sixteen were separately considered as juvenile types. The researchers came to several notable findings in their analysis of the female cases. First, sixty-four females were considered to be psychotic. Second, the location of the fires differed significantly from the fires set by male offenders in the study. Females tended to light fires on their own property and of an employer. Also, women tend to be classified as arsonists, as opposed to pyromaniacs. In other words, half of the women in the study set only one fire, whereas men tended to light numerous fires. Additionally, women were less likely to offend in a group. In general, the findings of this study suggest that female arsonists are significantly different from male arsonists (Lewis & Yarnell, 1951, cited in Reinhardt, 1957).

Tennent, McQuaid, Loughnane, and Hands (1971) arrived at conclusions similar to those found by Lewis and Yarnell (Tennent et al., 1971). The researchers examined fifty-six female arsonist patients at three Special Hospitals. In their review of past research, the authors recognize the underlying sexual roots that have been asserted as motivations for fire setting by female offenders. Case notes were obtained and analyzed for the purpose of comparing prior histories in terms of psychiatry, criminal involvement and social history. Results indicated that the female arsonist group had more problems with their sexual relationships than the control group. It is also important to note that the researchers concluded that the arson group was not found to be more aggressive than the control group. However, consistent with past research, female arsonists were frequently involved in disruptive family structures in childhood. The researchers also report that, despite promiscuity among the female arsonist group, the subjects report little satisfaction in their sexual activities (Tennent et al., 1971). Recall that Lewis (1965) argued that fire setting served as a substitute for lack of sexual excitement (Slovenko, 1965). Therefore, it may be assumed that the female arsonists in the Tennent et al. study were striving to substitute lack of sexual excitement by attempting to achieve sexual excitement through the setting of fires.

In general, from the literature reviewed, it appears that female fire setters are significantly different from their male counterparts. Women tend not to be serial arsonists, tended to have more problems with sexual relationships, and tended to select different targets than male arsonists (Lewis & Yarnell, 1951 cited in Reinhardt, 1957; Tennent et al., 1971).

THE MOTIVATIONS OF PYROMANIACS

Recall that, in the majority of past literature, fire setters have been classified according to motivations (Douglas et al., 1997; Inciardi, 1970; Lewis, 1965; O'Connor, 2001; Soltys, 1992). Sexual motivations have been stressed (Tennent et al., 1971). In support of this contention, Morneau and Rockwell (1980) argue that the pyromaniac receives direct sexual excitement from fires. The authors argue and provide evidence for a strong relationship between fire and water, which begins in childhood with what Abrahamsen (1960) describes as urethral eroticism. This concept describes a sexual relationship between urination (water) and fire (Abrahamsen, 1960). Morneau and Rockwell (1980) explain the sexual motivation of the pyromaniac:

> He may be thrilled by the sound of large pumping equipment thundering through an intersection or by the sight of leaping flames and the smell of smoke. On the other hand, it could be general excitement present at a fire scene with people scurrying around from place to place, new equipment arriving with sirens and red lights that provides satisfaction (p. 125).

Additionally, Hoyek (1951) points out that the pyromaniac may attempt to avoid suspicion from police by helping extinguish the fire. The fire setter may appear at the scene of the fire they set, and likely will appear out of place at the scene (Hoyek, 1951). Emergency personnel may notice the offender getting some thrill from the fire or some other aspect of the scene (Morneau & Rockwell, 1980).

Another significant motivation of the pyromaniac is that they gain a sense of power and control from knowing the destruction they have caused (Reinhardt,

1957). Psychoanalytic theory suggests that these aspects of fire setting provide pleasure for the ego of the offender. The author further asserts that the excitement and sexually motivated fire setters may be similar in that both receive pleasure in the power and control provided by the destruction of the fire, and also, neither are inhibited by the possible consequences of the act (Reinhardt, 1957). Kirk (1969) contributes that consequences for pyromaniacs are often not seen. Arson investigations involving fire and police personnel are sometimes uncoordinated and, therefore, offenders are often difficult to identify and prosecute, which contributes to the already strong motivations of power and control that pyromaniacs often enjoy in carrying out their crimes (Kirk, 1969; Morneau & Rockwell, 1980).

The Texas Commission on Law Enforcement Officer Standards and Education (2001) supports the contention that sexually motivated arsonists seek power and control. The Commission suggests that pyromaniacs may achieve these goals either through sexual fetish, by burning a sexual related object, or by watching their fires spread and observing the destruction they have caused. Notably, the authors argue for the importance of pyromaniac offender profiles for use as a tool by law enforcement to aid in the capture of arson suspects (Texas Commission on Law Enforcement Officer Standards and Education, 2001).

Law enforcement personnel investigating crimes of arson should also consider observing scenes both during and after the fire. Recall that pyromaniacs often gain pleasure from watching the fire and emergency response (Morneau & Rockwell, 1980). Additionally, Brown (2002) notes that arsonists are sometimes associated with fire service agencies. In fact, an eighteen-year U.S. Forest Service veteran was charged with setting fires beginning on June 8, 2002, which burned more than 135,000 acres and 22 homes in Colorado representing the largest fire in the state's history and the largest fire in the United States this year. Further, in Sacramento, California a former military firefighter allegedly set fire to two fields and may be responsible for nine other fires in the area the same day. In a similar case, two men, one of whom was a volunteer firefighter, and another who was just accepted to the Los Angeles City Fire Academy, deliberately set a fire that spread over 185,000 acres, killed three people and caused over $375 million in damage (Brown, 2002). John Orr, California's most prolific arsonist and pyromaniac was responsible for the deaths of at least 6 people and hundreds of millions of dollars in property loss. Clearly, destruction is yet another motive of the pyromaniac.

Hall, Jr. (1998) illustrates the amount of damage done by arsonists in his article addressing current trends in fire research. The author reports that arsonists are responsible for nearly 40 percent of the economic loss associated with residential structural fires and are the leading cause of fires in homes, automobiles, and outdoor properties. Brown (2002) further notes that arsonists were responsible for nearly four hundred fires in each of the last five years, which burned an average of twenty-one thousand acres per year according to forestry department statistics. Also, as Brown makes clear, arsonists tend to be extremely destructive. For example, in 1992 arsonists set only 13 percent of California's forest fires, but caused 67 percent of the damage, which totaled $114 million (Brown, 2002).

CASE SUMMARIES

For the purpose of demonstrating the sexual motivations and dangerousness associated with some of the most prominent pyromaniacs, the following case summaries are offered.

Robert Dale Segree's violent criminal offending began at the age of eight when he killed a small girl with a rock. He continued to set many fires and also strangled three people. Finally, on July 17, 1950 Segree was caught after torching the Ringling Brothers Barnum and Bailey Circus in Hartford, Connecticut. The blaze killed 169 spectators in less than six minutes. In court Segree testified that his motivation for his crimes was to burn out unpleasant sexual memories that haunted him. He also claimed to have recurring nightmares about a flaming rider on a blazing horse (Reinhardt, 1957).

David Berkowitz, also known as the Son of Sam serial killer, wrote in his diary that he had set more than two thousand fires in the New York City area over a period of several years. Following the end of his fire setting, Berkowitz began his serial killing, possibly suggesting pyromania may lead to even more serious offending (Morneau & Rockwell, 1980).

A boy, unidentified in the case summary, was with a group of friends smoking cigarettes when carelessness led to a fire in the barn where they were smoking. The subject stayed behind to watch the fire burn and watch the fire crews arrive. The boy realized that the fire provided him with some kind of sexual gratification. In the newspaper the following day, police and fire crews acknowledged that they were searching for the arsonist responsible. The boy claimed that he got more excitement from reading the account of the fire. He began to light more and more fires all the while gaining excitement from the accounts in the newspaper the day following his blazes. Beginning with the boy's fourth fire setting, he began to identify an intense sexual gratification from the fire and admitted to masturbating while watching one building he set on fire. The boy also received immense satisfaction from reading the newspapers, knowing that the police were searching for the offender, but he was the only one who knew what he had done (Reinhardt, 1957).

Schmid (1914) was the first to provide the description of a pyromaniac who masturbated to orgasm while watching the fires he set. The man, a twenty-seven-year-old farmer, set fire to five homes. The offender was present at each scene following the blazes and was reportedly participating in peculiar behavior (Schmid, 1914 cited in Slovenko, 1965).

Morneau and Rockwell (1980) describe the case of a male prostitute who was questioned by police following the death of one of his long-time customers. The prostitute told police that the deceased male would hire him to come to his home where he would have the prostitute sprinkle lighter fluid on his penis, scrotum, and abdominal area. The man would then light the fluid on fire. The prostitute claimed to have never lit the fires, but described the man's pubic region to be a mass of scar tissue. The prostitute claimed the man would contact him to participate whenever pubic hair grew in this region of his body (Morneau & Rockwell, 1980).

An unknown author (2001) describes the crimes of serial killer Peter Kurten. Beginning in the summer of 1929 Kurten began murdering men, women, and children in Düsseldorf, Germany. Corpses were found almost weekly, most bludgeoned, slashed and sexually assaulted. His murders continued for fifteen months, totaling more than thirty murders. He was arrested in May of 1930 for assault at which time he confessed to his serial killings. He told police that he loved to kill, and the more people, the better. He stalked his victims at night and claimed to gain sexual gratification from his killings. At nine years old, he killed two of his childhood playmates by drowning them in a river. In his mid-teens, he strangled a young girl in the woods. At the young age of sixteen he was sentenced to prison for seventeen years for crimes including arson and theft. In 1929 Kurten killed an eight-year-old girl, stabbing her thirteen times. He also covered her in kerosene and set her on fire. The related paraphilias listed by his psychiatrist after his apprehension included sadism, masochism, fetishism, and pyromania (Unknown, 2001).

Finally, Litman (1999) describes the case of a nursing assistant whom he provided treatment for. The author argued that his case was the first to be what he considered one of pyrophilia. The author argues that the patient qualified for the criterion described in the *DSM-IV* as pyromania and also met the criterion for paraphilia. However, pyromania does not include the criterion for sexual arousal, and therefore the author claimed to coin the term pyrophilia. The following behaviors were noted in the twenty-five-year-old white male patient: watched fires in the neighborhood, set off false fire alarms, gained pleasure from watching emergency personnel arrive at the scene, spent time at the local fire department, set fires for the purpose of being associated with the fire department, showed no remorse for death and destruction he caused, had irresistible compulsions to set fires, was sexually aroused by talking about the fires or having his wife talk about burning things, reported getting penile erections from listening to audiotaped scenarios of fires, reported sexual arousal from fantasizing about fire and heat, and reported sexual arousal to fantasies of being set on fire by a heterosexual partner (Litman, 1999).

THE TREATMENT OF PYROMANIACS

Treatment of pyromaniacs, also referred to as pyrophiliacs, varies. Dr. Litman (1999) reported that, in the process of treatment of his patient, he responded to a medication called clomipramine hydrochloride, which is generally prescribed for treatment of depression and obsessiveness. The patient reported that this medication reduced the amount of time he spend ruminating about fire by about 75 percent. Recall that psychoanalytic theory asserts that fire setting is commonly associated with repressed sexual drives, commonly oedipal in nature (Reinhardt, 1957; Soltys, 1992). Litman concurs with this assertion and therefore recommends long term psychoanalytic treatment as his intervention of choice for pyrophilia. However, the author notes that treatment of such patients is not often successful. Evidence for this contention can be found in the fact that this patient underwent intensive medical and psychotherapeutic treatment without success, including antidepressant medication, sodium amytol interview, group psychotherapy, and marathon group therapy with sleep deprivation (Litman, 1999).

Though treatment interventions seem to be difficult in deterring adult fire setters, treatment for juvenile offenders appear to be an option worthy of aspiration (Hall, Jr., 1998; Soltys, 1992). Hall, Jr. (1998) argues that a necessary task for mental health practitioners working with juvenile fire setters is to become more aware of the many types of offenders, assess the particulars of each case and match it with the best fitting treatment (Hall, Jr., 1998). Soltys (1992) reviewed the relevant literature and suggests the following treatment techniques for rehabilitation of juvenile fire setters: parenting training, behavior contracting with token reinforcement, special problem solving skills training, relaxation training, overt sensitization, fire safety and prevention education programs, individual and family therapy to deal with family dysfunction and medications for underlying psychiatric or medical disorders (Soltys, 1992).

INSIGHTS AND CONCLUSIONS

From the available literature, research and case summaries, it is clear that the following conclusions can be made with regards to pyromaniacs; they generally experience disruptive family situations, abuse, drug addiction, psychopathology, personal struggle, adjustment problems, seek attention, impulsivity, sexual frustration and promiscuity, and have a history of criminal behaviors. In many cases, a diagnosis of conduct disorder may be evident (Bassarath, 2001). It is also clear, from the literature, that pyromaniacs or pyrophiliacs are extremely dangerous in that they have the potential to cause a massive amount of destruction and death. Systematic research regarding pyrophilia is limited and, in most cases, dated. Further academic research is needed to establish a more clear determination of motives, typologies, associated psychological disorders, backgrounds, investigative tools, and possible treatments for pyrophilia.

C H A P T E R
PYROLAGNIA
Sexual Pyromania
CATHERINE SANCHEZ

32

As long as the concept of human sexuality has existed, people have chosen to express themselves in deviant ways. For some individuals, the only way to receive sexual gratification is through deviant sexual behaviors known as paraphilias. One known paraphilia is pyrolagnia, which is receiving sexual arousal or gratification from fire. Many issues surround the distinction between a fire setter who is in need of sexual gratification and those who set fires for other reasons.

This discussion will review the etiology of paraphilias in a brief overview; examine the distinction between those who set fires for sexual gratification and those who set fires for other reasons. Developmental issues in children and adolescents will be considered, as well as treatment programs. Due to the lack of treatment program for adult fire setters, a program will be suggested and areas of further research will be identified.

PARAPHILIAS

Paraphilias have been defined by the *Diagnostic and Statistical Manual of Mental Disorders,* Fourth Edition, Text Revision (*DSM-IV-TR*) (2000) as "recurrent, intense sexually arousing fantasies, sexual urges, or behaviors generally involving 1) nonhuman objects, 2) the suffering or humiliation of oneself or one's partner, or 3) children or other non-consenting persons that occur over a period of 6 months" (American Psychiatric Association, 2000, p. 566).

The *DSM-IV-TR* also states that for some individuals the deviant fantasies, urges, or behaviors must be necessary for sexual arousal and must be a part of the individual's sexual activity. For other individuals, the behaviors, fantasies, and urges can occur intermittently, possibly during periods of intense stress or anxiety, and the individual is able to maintain a period of normal sexuality. One of the primary characteristics necessary for a diagnosis of a paraphilia is the discomfort the presence of the paraphilia brings to the individual's interpersonal, occupational, and social functioning (American Psychiatric Association, 2000).

An individual with a paraphilic disorder may not have developed the social skills necessary to forge appropriate relationships with others (Palermo & Farkas, 2001). Palermo and Farkas (2001) hypothesize that the paraphilics social ineptitude reinforces their isolation and in turn their deviant behaviors. It is possible the paraphilic attempts to engage others in relationships through their deviant behaviors.

PYROMANIA, INCENDIARISM, AND PYROLAGNIA

Many names have been used to describe those individuals who engage in fire-setting behavior. Fire-setting behavior has generally been defined as setting fires to express a negative emotion, a symptom of mental illness, or a behavior that is used to conceal another crime (Corsini, 1999). Some individuals seek sexual arousal and/or gratification from fire, by either setting a fire, watching a fire, or extinguishing a fire. The term pyromania has been used to describe a love of fire and those individuals who compulsively set fires (Corsini, 1999). Within the category of pyromania, two different subcategories exist: incendiarism and pyrolagnia.

Incendiarism is when an individual will either compulsively set fires or will set a fire as a primary or secondary crime without receiving any type of sexual arousal and/or gratification (Corsini, 1999). This is the individual who will set fires for no reason, or will use fire to conceal another crime, such as burglary, vandalism, or homicide.

Pyrolagnia, also known as pyrophilia, is the act of gaining sexual arousal and/or gratification from fire (Corsini, 1999). This is the individual who will gain pleasure from setting a fire, watching it burn, or watching the fire being extinguished by fire personnel.

DEVELOPMENT OF PYROMANIA

Pyromania was once considered a developmental disorder (Stekel, 1943). For many years the sexual component of the disorder was overlooked by criminal investigators who seemed to be more interested in solving crimes than discovering why they were perpetrated.

However, there are several representational characteristics that should not be overlooked when examining individuals who develop fire setting behaviors. These characteristics include the fact that children like playing with fire, children dream of water and fire more often than adults, and the connection between the fireman's hose and the human bladder, in regards to the fire and water games of childhood (Stekel, 1943).

It has been suggested that when children were warned not to wet the bed for fear of starting fire, the fire and water association was made. Stekel (1943) further hypothesized that enuresis progressed into a symbol of sexuality. Still, for some individuals fire was associated with and came to represent love (1943).

> To be in love is to be on fire . . . We speak of the fire of passion, of stifling the flame of love, which, like fire, dies down; one is afire for a girl. In the dream fire and water often represent the love passion, the raw craving (Stekel, 1943, p. 126).

The connection between fire and water is an internal one. Stekel's research has also shown that fire-setting behaviors frequently begin as children enter puberty or following a traumatic life event.

THEORIES OF PYROMANIA

PSYCHOANALYTIC THEORY

Freud (1932) speculated that the pairing of fire and sexual arousal was symbolic of the conflict between the libidinal and phallic-urethral drives. He also speculated that for males a connection was made between the power of a fire hose and the penis. Freud (1932) also hypothesized a homosexual conflict through the desire of men to extinguish fires with their own urine. Other theorists have conducted research that supports the hypothesis that fire setting is a possible regression to the urethral-phallic phase of development and that the act of fire setting is a possible substitute for masturbation or the individuals only way of achieving sexual arousal (Kaufman, Heins, & Reiser, 1961).

Observational data does exist to support this theory of fire setting, including the occurrence of masturbation and orgasm during the act of fire setting (Stekel, 1943). A link between enuresis and fire setting has also been made to the presence of sexual dysfunctions (Lewis & Yarnell, 1951). It has been hypothesized that individuals who are unable to control their bladders would seek some type of control thus, connecting fire setting with possessing the power to extinguish them (1951).

Some flaws have been noted in this theory, with the main objection being that every case of sexual conflict does not correlate with a case of fire setting (Gold, 1962). It appears to be evident that a causal relationship does not exist, but this does not discount the possibility of some type of relationship. It is possible that the act of fire setting may be a pathological behavior related to sexual conflict, but not necessarily a direct result of sexual conflict (Gaynor & Hatcher, 1987).

LEARNING THEORY

Learning theorists posit that sexual conflict is the main factor for fire setting behavior. These theorists argue that fire setters need an outlet for their negative emotions and use fire setting as a means of expression (McKenacher & Dacre, 1966). It is possible that these individuals are uncomfortable with expressing their emotions to themselves and others and seek any type of expression to relieve themselves of the distress emotion is causing them (Gaynor & Hatcher, 1987).

The major thrust of this theory is that the fire setter is socially and/or interpersonally inept and is unable to find another outlet for their emotions. The act of fire setting becomes a way for the individual to control their environment and to become skilled in an area; an experience the individual may not have had before (Gaynor & Hatcher, 1987).

There is agreement in the field that this theory is easily applicable to adult fire setters who are unable to act appropriately on the sexual and aggressive impulses they are trying to manage (Federal Bureau of Investigation, 1982). According to this theory, it is more likely for individuals to act out against inanimate objects rather than people because of their intense social deficits (Wolford, 1980).

Learning theory may be an adequate explanation for pyromania still, no research has been conducted to test the applicability of the theory (Gaynor & Hatcher, 1987). Further research is necessary to determine how family and environmental factors have an impact on the individual's personality development.

DYNAMIC-BEHAVIORAL THEORY

Fineman (1980) suggested an alternative to the psychoanalytic and learning theories that takes into account more societal, environmental, and personality characteristics. The concept, dynamic-behavioral theory, places more of an emphasis on factors other than those that are emotionally based. However, historical and constitutional factors are emphasized, such as family history, school functioning, previously acted-out behaviors, organic problems, and physical problems. The theory also emphasizes those environmental conditions that encourage children to play with fire, including modeling, imitation, and inconsistent parenting. Stress, peer pressure, and emotional distress are also major factors in creating the desire to set fires. Fineman points out major flaws to his theory in that the majority of research conducted in a clinical based environment and as such, suffers from design flaws such as sampling errors and recording bias. Consequently, Fineman's theory does not explain how the varying factors would lead an individual to start setting fires. Fineman recognizes that taking the theory a step further to show how and why the various factors would result in someone developing a pathological paraphilia would be helpful. Further research is necessary for the theory to be validated in the research community.

TREATMENT

Only a small amount of literature on the treatment of fire setters and pyrolagniacs exists. The majority of the literature on treatment speaks to children and adolescents. Within the research, three main categories seem to have developed as current methods of treatment: case study examples of programs designed for individual children, assessment and intervention services that are based in a community multidisciplinary system, and programs based within existing mental health services (Stadolnik, 2000).

Previous research has indicated that prior to the late 1970s, a majority of the behavioral research interventions revolved around electrical aversion therapy (McGrath, Marshall, & Prior, 1979). However, individualized treatment plans would be ideal due to the unique circumstances that exist and contributes to the development of an individual considered to be a fire setter.

Some behavioral researchers (e.g., Carstens, 1982) have taken an opposite approach with acts of fire setting by promoting behavioral alternatives that emphasize hard labor. Other researchers promoted controlled fire setting interventions, employing interventions that are strictly supervised by a therapist (Jones, 1981).

One of the main components of treatment is a psychoeducational class to teach about fire safety and prevention (Stadolnik, 2000). These fire education classes would benefit greatly from the involvement of members of the community, such as fire and police officials who are responsible for investigating fires. An example of this type of community involvement is the "Firehawks" program. This program includes a mentoring component that pairs an experienced firefighter with a child or adolescent who has a history of fire-setting behaviors (Stadolnik, 2000).

Several intervention programs were developed in the 1980s by the Federal Emergency Management Agency (FEMA) and were based on the Firehawks programs. These programs took the stance of looking at a more inclusive way of approaching the life and environment of juvenile fire setters. The components of the program included empirically supported interventions, an examination of family variables associated with fire setting, a psychoeducational program, and a program evaluation including outcome data (Kolko, 1988). The goal was to provide services to the juvenile exploring family dynamics. Correspondingly, individualized intervention and plans could be developed for each juvenile. Outcome data regarding these programs is not available to determine their effectiveness. Based upon available data from the current literature on treatment, programs and mental health professionals working with fire setters report a 10 percent recidivism rate (Kolko, 1985; Stadolnik, 1999).

TREATMENT PROGRAMS FOR ADULTS

Because of the lack of known adult treatments, this section explores a possible treatment program. Unfortunately, most adult pyromaniacs are not discovered until they are already a part of the criminal justice system. They are likely to have a lengthy history of setting fires and may be entrenched in their behavioral patterns. It is also likely that many of the adult fire setters will be unwilling to change. The suggested model for an adult treatment program would incorporate the aspects of the juvenile multidisciplinary treatment programs.

PSYCHOEDUCATIONAL CLASSES

The first component of the treatment program would be psychoeducational. The participants would be required to attend a twelve-week class that would teach about fire safety and prevention. This class would also focus on the actual human cost of fires and what arson means to the community.

Several classes would focus on fire safety and what the appropriate uses of fire are. The prevention part of the class would focus on how to properly set and attend to fires and under what conditions fires are appropriate. The class would consist of fire department personnel teaching for several classes about what is necessary for them to fight fires and the danger they are in when they respond to calls.

The class would also be visited by police officers who assist in fire investigations to learn more about the criminal justice system consequences of their fire-setting behaviors. Finally, the class would be visited by insurance adjusters so participants would be able to learn about the financial impact of their behaviors and learn about the devastating effects their actions have on innocent people.

VICTIM OFFENDER REHABILITATION PROGRAM (VORP)

The offenders enrolled in the program would be required to attend meetings with willing victims in order to learn and understand the impact of their crime on the victims and their families. During the meetings, the offender would be required to listen to the victim's recounting their experiences of crime and how it has impacted their lives. The offender would also be afforded the opportunity to explain to the victim their motivation for the crime. At this time, the victim and the offender would negotiate an agreement for the offender to pay restitution for their crimes.

INDIVIDUAL PSYCHOTHERAPY

The participants in the program would be required to attend individual psychotherapy for one year. This is necessary in order to examine the issues that are at the root of their fire-setting behavior. Ideally the psychotherapy would be individualized and each offender would progress at his or her own rate. For some participants, it will be easier to talk about those issues than for other participants. These issues will take time to emerge and will be difficult to deal with in therapy. Hopefully, therapy will be helpful and a positive experience for the participants.

GROUP PSYCHOTHERAPY

Participants will be required to participate in one year of group psychotherapy with other offenders in the program. This will give the offenders the opportunity to speak with others that have similar problems and will show them that they are not alone. Group therapy will provide the offenders the place to share their feelings with their peers and to be in an environment in which they will not be judged. It will also give the participants the opportunity to work on skills that will help them when they leave therapy and will teach them strategies to prevent relapse.

COMMUNITY SERVICE

The participants would be required to perform one hundred hours of community service in order to complete the program. The duties of community services would include the participants speaking to children and adolescents who have been deemed to be at risk for future fire-setting behavior. The purpose of this is to give the juveniles a glimpse at the life that they would have if they continue on the path of fire setting. Community services would also be working for a local organization that assists the victims of fires, so the participants will be able to help those who have been disadvantaged by someone else's reckless act of fire setting.

AREAS FOR FURTHER RESEARCH

Additional research is needed in the areas of adult fire setters. Literature on the adult population is scarce, perhaps indicating that the adult population has been discarded or deemed untreatable. Pilot studies could target the adult population to determine the individual's capacity to be successfully treated. Additional research is also necessary in the area of juvenile treatment programs. Specific base strategies need to be developed in order to maximize the efficacy of the programs. More clinical research into existing programs needs to occur so that strategies that work can be optimally utilized, while those strategies that do not have an impact on outcome can be discarded.

Identifying those individuals who are pyromaniacs is a difficult process. It is important not to ostracize and label those individuals, but to seek them out so they can be treated. Ideally, it is more likely that interventions will be successful if implemented early in the individual's development. Placing the individual into an appropriate program is also a necessary component to successful treatment. A more complete understanding of the etiology of paraphilias, as well as the development of pyromania is necessary for any treatment program to be successful. Further research is necessary to understand the theories of etiology and these theories need to be consulted when treatment programs and the guidelines for entry into treatment programs are developed.

Pyromania is one of the more difficult paraphilias to treat. Only with a complete understanding of the paraphilias and their development can psychology make a difference in how they affect the lives of those who are afflicted with the paraphilic disorder.

CHAPTER

ZOOPHILIA AND BESTIALITY

KATHERINE NICKCHEN AND
JEANNE JOHNSON

33

Zoophilia or bestiality is considered a diagnosable disorder within the DSM-IV that is used for sexual fantasies, urges, and behaviors that meet the general criteria for paraphilias (Seligman and Hardenburg, 2000). Examples of this include telephone scatologia, necrophilia, zoophilia, etc. A zoophile is a "person who has a profound emotional and/or physical attraction to animals" (Fetish Information Exchange, 2002). This person has an emotional attraction for their animal partner. Zoophilists (zoos) or animal-lovers, as they prefer to be called, prefer animals as their sex partners, often forming deep emotional relationships with them. Bestialists are usually only interested in the sexual aspects of such practices. In fact, many zoos do not like the term bestiality as it implies the coercion, degradation, and sexual abuse of animals (Taormino, 2002).

ROOTS OF ZOOPHILIA

Zoophilia has a strong taboo in Western Society and most people feel disturbed by the mere thought of it (Linzey, 2000). Issues of moral or religious underpinnings vary much upon the individual. The main argument that is supported within the legal community is the issue of consent. Those who are for restriction of zoophilia argue the animal cannot give consent. A domesticated animal is subjected to human control and domination, automatically negating the ability for the animal to consent. This parallels the molestation of children. This is considered animal abuse and Animal Rights' groups are petitioning states to maintain stricter laws for zoophilia/

bestiality. Those who are against restriction of zoophilia argue consent was given and their actions are just a way of displaying their love and affection. Interestingly, this argument also parallels the arguments given to legalizing sex with children by pedophiles.

The two sides of the debate on bestiality are interesting. One side claims the animal enjoys the sexual intercourse and is doing the animal a favor by having sex with them by releasing their tension. Arguments have even gone so far as to say that it keeps the animal healthier. The other side states their main concern is that of consent, the animal cannot give full consent, like a child cannot give full consent. Some authors state that bestiality should be legal as long as no animals are harmed or mistreated in the event (Dekkers, 1994). However, one needs to ask how one can tell if an animal is harmed or traumatized?

Other authors question why bestiality is illegal. If one can obtain consent from their animals/sex partners, then legality should not be an issue. Of course the question is raised of how to obtain consent from their animal. While zoophilists argue that consent is received and their animals actually enjoy the sexual encounter, others feel that this is a form of self-deception in order to feel more accepted (Linzey, 2000). The argument is made that domestic animals are subject to human control and domination, therefore they depend upon their owner. Following this line of thought, they are not able to give consent as their entire existence depends upon their owners' happiness and approval (Linzey, 2000). Pedophiles have also made this claim about the children they molest, in that the children give consent. These children's entire existence also depends upon the happiness and approval of their molester. Therefore, all sexual contact is coercive, as consent cannot be given (Linzey, 2000).

Bestiality discussions spur controversy just about everywhere they are held. For example, in Stanwood, Washington, an article was published in a high school newspaper on the occurrences of bestiality (Stein, 1996). This article was about "farm boys having sex with animals" and was quite disturbing to the farming community in which it was published. So much so that it caused the school to reprimand the teacher who approved its publication, and the school board held a school-parent conference to discuss it. The article was actually based on a scholarly publication from the 1940s that researched and found that one in five boys who lived on farms regularly had sex with animals. The article went on to ask the opinion of the readers on how they felt about one-fifth of the adolescent male population having sex with farm animals. One adolescent was quoted as saying, "I don't believe it's morally wrong because I read it in a book that is 2,000 years old" (Stein, 1996).

Stories of bestiality have been circulating since Biblical times. "Whosoever lieth with beasts shall surely be put to death" (Exodus cited by Dekkers, 1994). There is also a great deal of bestiality in Greek mythology, from menotaurs, to other mythic creatures that are half animal/half human. Other examples of how bestiality has been portrayed in myths, story-telling, and urban legends is that of the typical Tarzan story. Essentially, an animal raises a child who has been left in the wilderness (Doniger, 1995). In this process, the child is treated like an animal and is considered one of the species. It is not a far leap to assume that the child eventually grows up and starts a family of their own to fit into the pack.

Other links between bestiality and mythology or story-telling are not as far reaching. Some suggest that myths have a connection to sexual fantasy and practice. This is also suggested as a way for men to exert their power over women. Most mythology is that of a women having sex with an animal rather than men (Leach, 1998). In actuality, most of the actual acts of bestiality were with men, not women.

LAW, CONSENT AND ZOOPHILIA

Since 1533, bestiality has been outlawed and anyone caught performing the offense would be put to death or stripped of all their possessions. Actually, married men were more severely punished than single men (Fudge, 2000). The offense of bestiality, then known as buggery, was considered so detestable that Christians would not name it. They called it a "sin against God, Nature, and the Law." The offense was considered not only immoral, but also a pollution of the species, in that it was believed to be reproduction across species boundaries (Fudge, 2000). The fear of the pollution of the species was so great that animals born with deformities were considered to have been produced from a bestial relationship. These animals were then killed and displayed in front of the Church as a symbol of God's warning of what was to come (Fudge, 2000).

Many zoophilists want legislation that will legalize "zoo couples" or human/nonhuman relationships and marriages (Steyn, 2001). Zoos claim that they are a misunderstood minority who are born with a true love for animals and have a lifelong commitment to their care. They also make the claim that if it is legal for two animals to have sex and two humans to have sex, why is it illegal for animals to have sex with humans (Steyn, 2001). In actuality, some states still outlaw sodomy, therefore, it is not legal for all humans to have sex with all other humans.

Many zoos believe that they have entered into a consentual relationship with their partner, often going so far as to be wed by an actual licensed minister. In fact, recently *The First Church of Zoophilia (Observant)* was established in order to protect Zoophiles under the guise of being protected by the Constitutional right to freedom of religion. This church is devoted to praising animals and the practice of making the animal one with their owner. This church website includes a licensed minister who is a zoophile himself, preferring dogs but enjoys horses as well (see www.thoughtshop.com/fcz/RevLykaon.htm for the minister's license), and connections to pornographic stories of those "praising" their "sacred animals." The language this church uses are such that they appear to be trying to legitimize their bestial practices. Some examples of the language used are: "Adoration and Administration of Sacred Duties to the Holy Animal," "Marriage Ceremonies between Adherents of the Church and their Loved Ones," and "The proper procedures in how to extract the maximum amount of Sacramental Wine from the Sacred Animal in question, while providing the Sacred Animal with as many blessings as possible at the same time."

The church patrons consider themselves an "oppressed minority" (much as the Christians were approximately two-thousand years ago). An interesting side note is this church attempts to sell their members on their eternal salvation. For example, the benefits they can offer their followers are: 1) official membership certificates, complete with an address; 2) "Security in the knowledge that, provided you Truly Believe and Have the Utmost Faith, and follow our tenants, you shall be doing a great service to your Sacred Animal, for which I am certain *they* shall most definitely be eternally grateful, and happier and healthier to boot"; and 3) "An assurance that you shall achieve eternal salvation upon your death: anyone who does NOT receive eternal salvation upon their death, please email us *immediately* at the address listed above . . . simply email us after your fleshly demise, and We promise to set things aright for you in the Eternal Hereafter."

Connected to the First Church of Zoophilia, Observant, is a web page that provides the basics on how to become connected with other zoos (Zoophilia for Beginners, 2002). These are not pornographic basics, but rather how to meet like-minded people, tips on how to receive homemade pornographic pictures, and how to stay away from the pornographic sites that are "profit-greedy." This site also advises to check if there were any laws that would be broken before downloading the material.

ETIOLOGY

Studies researching sadomasochism, juvenile sexual offenders, serial killers, paraphilias, women with sexual disorders, etc. have included zoophilia in their studies. While the focus of the study may have been on some other form of sexual disorder, zoophilia may be included in their sexual history. It is interesting that people with paraphilias often suffer from more than one. The research has indicated that within studies on paraphilias or sexual disorders, approximately 5 percent or less have zoophilic tendencies (Fedoroff et al., 1999). For sadists or psychopaths it could be a form of animal abuse. For the person who finds submission sexually appealing, the animal is a lower life form and can be easily controlled. A person with masochistic tendencies may have sex with animals as a way of being "degraded." The person with Antisocial Personality Disorder and who may be a sexually violent perpetrator may find violent sex with animals as a beginning or practice session to fulfill sexual fantasies. In an article evaluating women with paraphilic sexual disorders, several of the subjects included a history of zoophilic tendencies. Out of fourteen subjects, three had zoophilic tendencies (Fedoroff et al., 1999). This is a much higher rate than in other studies on bestiality. Are women more likely to have zoophilic tendencies or are men? These are all questions that need to be researched further.

Seligman and Hardenburg (2000) noted paraphilias often have similarities to impulse-control disorders and sexual addictions. Sometimes paraphilias occur in the context of other symptoms relating to substance abuse, psychosis, or mania. Developmentally delayed individuals, as well as those with dementia or a general medical condition, may engage in unusual sexual behavior. This is where the background information becomes important because if the behaviors are comorbid, are egosyntonic, and these sexual behaviors are infrequent, a paraphilia may not actually exist (Seligman and Hardenburg, 2000).

It is important to obtain a thorough sexual history to determine the etiology of the paraphilia. The nature, time of onset, duration, frequency, and the progression of symptoms is important to either facilitate change in therapy or for research purposes. It is also important to determine how the zoophilic tendencies manifests over time including fantasies, urges, and behaviors (Seligman and Hardenburg, 2000). This is an area of research that needs to be further considered.

To understand the origins and dynamics of how zoophilia developed, one must understand the individual's background. This includes familial upbringing, cultural motives, and experiential information (Seligman and Hardenburg, 2000). A dysfunctional home environment is often common. Seligman and Hardenburg (2000) describe a father who is emotionally distant, indifferent, and uninvolved with family, and a mother who is unaffectionate, demanding, intrusive, and belittling. These problems can lead to inadequacies, low self-esteem, and problems in social skills (Seligman and Hardenburg, 2000). Many individuals have experienced physical and sexual abuse, and for some zoophilia may be a way to obtain love and closeness or to perpetuate the abusive cycle.

In a report by Yiffy Raptor (2002), he indicates zoophilia usually arises from childhood trauma. The inability to form appropriate emotional attachments to other humans leads these people to look elsewhere.

Information obtained on the Fetish Information Exchange had a different perspective on the development of zoophilia. While this may be totally unsubstantiated, it is interesting to note. The special connection to animals, for some, is a result of humans being animals as well. Animals and humans are similar in both physical and sexual proclivities (Fetish Information Exchange, 2002). Beyond these similarities is a far more unusual explanation. According to MacLean (1990) in his book *The Triune Brain in Evolution* the human brain is comprised of two animal brains and one human brain. As a result of evolution, newer forms of the brain were built upon older forms of the brain and the older forms of the brain are retained inside. MacLean argues that every human brain holds a reptilian brain, an older mammal brain found in dogs or horses and a human thinking mammal brain (Maclean, 1990).

In all of our daily activities, all three brains are making contributions to our thoughts, behaviors, emotions, and feelings. Consequently a desire to engage in sex with animals is natural (Maclean, 1990). The Fetish Information Exchange (2002) and *The Triune Brain in Evolution* (1990) suggest that bestiality enhances these three interacting brains and promotes harmony. They also suggest that to have sex with animals will reduce aggressive feelings and tendencies because it will release pent up or blocked animal drives in the human brain (MacLean, 1990). In an effort to normalize zoophilia the argument is made that such behavior is healthy and promotes inner peace (MacLean, 1990).

A diagnosable paraphilia must affect the daily functioning of the individual. Some individuals use paraphilic behaviors as a way to experiment or bring excitement into their lives. Their behavior, however, is kept under control and does not inhibit daily functioning, relationships, or conventional sexual behavior. Those with severe paraphilias can have impairment in several areas. There may be difficulties in marriage and in conventional sexual behavior. According to Seligman and Hardenburg (2000), some lack sexual understanding and confidence and therefore fail to establish healthy sexual relationships. The focus of their time and energy may be invested in the continuation of their paraphilic behavior.

CONCLUSION

For zoophiles, not only will there be deficits in daily functioning, but the stigmatizing quality of their particular paraphilic choice may create societal and familial upheaval that creates further negative repercussions for the individual. Individuals facing treatment may experience a lowering of their self-esteem prior to improvement. This would need to be addressed in therapy. With some paraphilias group therapy would need to be paraphilic specific, meaning a group especially for zoophiles, a group for necrophiles, etc. The greater picture is to understand the development and motivations of a zoophile.

Zoophilists, zoos, animal-lovers, or those who participate in bestial acts search for ways to have their sexual choices accepted by society. One must ask, if we legalize bestiality, then are children next? After all, if we allow interspecies sexual practices to be legalized, what is to stop us from legalizing those who wish to have sex with our children? The leap is not far to make, the arguments for having sex with an animal has already been equated with the same arguments that pedophiles make about children.

PART VII

HARMING CHILDREN

C H A P T E R

PEDOPHILIA

S HAY L ITTON

34

In order to be labeled as a pedophile, one must meet the criteria of pedophilia. Pedophilia is one of several paraphilias or sexual disorders listed in the *Diagnostic and Statistical Manual of Mental Disorders* (4th ed.) *Text Revision (DSM-IV-TR)* (2000). The term pedophile can be confused with other sex offenders. However, pedophiles are differentiated from other sexual predators such as child molesters and hebephiles by distinguishing characteristics. Some of these characteristics include the sex and ages of the victims or the level of aggressiveness used with the victims. Research in the area of pedophiles suggests several different theories regarding the development of pedophilic behavior. Several researchers have explored the relationship between attachment and sexual abuse and its influential effect on the development of pedophilic behaviors (Marshall, 1989). While other researchers have analyzed the comorbid diagnoses in pedophiles (Raymond, Coleman, Ohlerking, Christenson, and Miner, 1999), given the previous research, therapy with pedophiles has not focused on inadequate attachments or comorbid diagnoses (Raymond et al., 1999). If the focus of therapy were to incorporate the offenders' previous background, the effectiveness of the therapeutic process would be likely to increase.

The term pedophilia was first listed in the *Diagnostic and Statistical Manual of Mental Disorders* (3rd ed.) in 1987. Pedophilia is one of several types of paraphilias. In the most recent *(DSM-IV-TR)* (2000), published by the American Psychiatric Association, paraphilias are categorized as a diagnosable sexual disorder. Paraphilia is defined as the following:

> recurrent, intense sexually arousing fantasies, sexual urges, or behaviors generally involving 1) nonhuman objects, 2) the suffering or humiliation of oneself or one's partner, or 3)

children or other nonconsenting persons that occur over a period of at least 6 months (Criterion A) . . . the diagnosis is made if the behavior, sexual urges, or fantasies cause clinically significant distress or impairment in social, occupational, or other important areas of functioning (Criterion B) (p. 566).

Numerous types of paraphilias include autoeroticism, anthropophagy, coprophilia, exhibitionism, fetishism, gerontophilia, klismaphilia, infibulation, lust murder, necrophilia, pedophilia, pederasty, pyromania scatophilia, scoptophilia/voyeurism, and sadomasochism (Hickey, 2002). One of the more common and well-known paraphilias is pedophilia. To further meet the diagnostic criteria of pedophilia, a person must meet the following criteria as listed in the *DSM-IV-TR* (2000):

A. Over a period of at least 6 months, recurrent, intense sexually arousing fantasies, sexual urges, or behaviors involving sexual activity with a prepubescent child or children (generally age 13 years or younger).

B. The person has acted on these sexual urges, or the sexual urges or fantasies caused marked distress or interpersonal difficulty.

C. The person is at least 16 years and at least 5 years older than the child or children in Criterion A (p. 572).

Pedophiles are typically men and many times are often family members or acquaintances of the victims (Murray, 2000). According to Fontana-Rosa (2001) pedophiles are likely to have immediate access to children and are more often single. Pedophiles are mostly male and are at least twenty-five years old. Pedophiles typically live with their parents or by themselves. Pedophiles' behaviors tend to be habitual and their likelihood of repeating the act is increased if the offender is homosexual (Murray, 2000).

Those categorized as having a paraphilia are likely to have several paraphilias at one time (Hickey, 2002). Price, Gutheil, Commons, Kafta and Dodd-Kimmey (2001) researched telephone scatologia and it's comorbidity with other disorders. They reported, "[F]orty-two percent of the scatologists admitted to female non-incestuous pedophilia, 16% to male non-incestuous pedophilia, and 26% to female incestuous pedophilia" (Price et al., 2001, p. 226). A study by Raymond, Coleman, Ohlerking, Christenson, and Miner (1999) found, in their sample of forty-five men meeting the *DSM-IV-TR* (2000) criteria for pedophilia, that over 30 percent of their participants met the criteria for another paraphilia. Many pedophiles may also develop fetishes or sexual pleasure from objects related or connected to their sexual partner preference (Hickey, 2002).

The public may confuse pedophiles with other child predators such as child molesters and hebephiles. Child molesters, in contrast to pedophiles, are more likely to have irregular employment histories and have recurrently been arrested (Fontana-Rosa, 2001). Furthermore, child molesters are not diagnosed in the *DSM-IV-TR* (2000), thereby not requiring a specific time period of offending. Adolescent offenders may be classified as child molesters instead of pedophiles to avoid being stigmatized by a mental illness diagnosis (Fontana-Rosa, 2001). Others may confuse pedophiles with hebephiles because of the closeness in the age range required for the diagnosis of a pedophile. The pedophile is attracted to children aged from pubescent to thirteen, while hebephiles victims' ages range from thirteen to sixteen (Hickey, 2002).

When pedophiles approach their victims, they may attempt to become the child's friend or companion. Pedophiles may work in schools or in other areas involving children to be closer to their victims. They are not likely to force sexual intercourse with their victims and are more likely to engage in fellatio or cunnilingus with children. Other pedophiles prefer fondling or touching their victims. In cases where the pedophile does engage in intercourse, the victim is more likely to be older (Murray, 2000). Pedophiles usually prefer female rather than male victims. Researchers Bogaert, Bezeau, Kuban, and Blanchard (1997) suggest that females are favored rather than male victims over 60 percent of the time. If the victim is a female, the offender is more likely to be a relative, and the offense will probably occur in the victim's residence. In contrast, if the pedophile chooses a male victim, the perpetrator is more likely to be a stranger and the offense occurs outside of the residence (Murray, 2000). Another study by Ames and Houston (1990) reported that many pedophiles are attracted to both male and female children. Murray (2000) suggests that pedophiles that target females prefer these victims in the age range of eight to ten years old, in contrast with the pedophiles preferring older male victims. A study by Greenberg, Bradford, and Curry (1995) found that pedophiles that targeted infant victims were on average younger in age themselves. Murray further reported that if the victim is older than nine years old at the time of their offense, the pedophiles are more likely to have lower self-esteem.

Most pedophiles will only engage in sexual assaults on their victims. However, a small percentage of pedophiles murder their victims. Researchers have tried to differentiate between these two groups to determine any prevalent characteristics. One study by Firestone, Bradford, Greenberg, and Nunes (2000) analyzed the predictive ability of phallometry for homicidal and nonhomicidal child molesters. Using a phallometric assessment method, the researchers noted any changes in penile circumference while the subjects were viewing vignettes. The vignettes in the study had varied ages, sexes, coercion, sexual experiences and levels of violence. Although several findings suggests little if any difference between the nonhomicidal and homicidal child molesters one index was statistically elevated for homicidal child molesters. Homicidal child molesters scored significantly higher on the pedophile assault index. The researchers reported that "men who have committed nonviolent sexual offenses against children may derive little sexual pleasure from depictions of clearly assaultive acts against children . . . homicidal child molesters seem to be equally aroused by assaultive and nonassaultive depictions in which children are victims."(Firestone et al., 2000, p. 1849).

Social scientists have researched the evolution of the paraphilic, more specifically the pedophilic, behavior in offenders. Some theorists propose that pedophiles experienced difficulty in engaging in intimate relationships as children (Hudson & Ward, 1997), while other theorists suggest the inability to develop appropriate attachment bonds with their caregivers as the main cause of their diagnosis (Marshall, 1989). Researcher Palermo (2001) suggests that offenders are acting out inner conflicts when engaging in pedophilic behavior. Palermo further stated his theory as follows:

> It is my belief that under the intense stress due to inner conflicts and frustrated sexual desires, and because of their ego weakness and the sudden resurfacing of the above-mentioned ambivalence, they are unconsciously driven into a state of cognitive deconstruction. Then they are unable to properly assess their behavior, control themselves, and be positively influenced by their higher moral self. They become disinhibited, pursue their desires, and are only interested in the concreteness of the situation they are in-the here and now of their sexual predatory act (p. 4).

The inner conflicts and sexual desires, when studied developmentally, may be explained by previous childhood victimization experienced by the pedophiles themselves.

Feeney (1995) studied the relationship between early attachment and coping styles in adults. Feeney found if inadequate attachments were made with the child's primary caretaker, the child would have ineffective coping styles in stressful situations. A significant part of the adolescent and child's growth involves the development of bonds and social skills. The methods the parents use to interact with their children can affect their future relationships with other adults. Flinker, Englund, and Srouge (1992) found "children who form secure attachments to their primary caregivers (usually mothers) develop an internal working model and a sense of self that leads to positive experiences in their relationships with others" (p. 81). Developmental theorists have found that when adolescents did not have strong attachments with their parents, their likelihood of delinquency was increased (Baer, 1999). Researchers have also found that weak attachment bonds between adolescents and their parents lead to other detrimental effects such as low self-esteem, poor social performances, and decreased positive interactions with peers (Engles, Dekovic, & Meeus, 2002).

A recent study by Sawle and Kear-Colwell (2001) analyzed the effect of attachment and sexual abuse. Their sample consisted of three male groups: pedophiles who have been convicted; university students–control group; and nonoffending victims of sexual assault. The participants were given the Attachment Style Questionnaire (ASQ) and the Child Abuse and Trauma Scale (CAT). The results of this study showed that both the victims of sexual assault and convicted pedophiles were both found to be "more insecurely attached than the controls" (Sawle & Kear-Colwell, 2001, p. 40). They further found "the nonoffending victims do have issues with insecure attachments, but at the same time are securely attached; there is a different pattern of attachments in the victims when compared with pedophiles" (p. 40). Another finding of this study showed that over 80 percent of pedophiles reported sexual abuse by a family member. In contrast, the victim of sexual assault group reported less than 38 percent had experienced sexual abuse by a family member. Sawle and Kear-Colwell concluded:

the current study has produced evidence that secure attachment is salient to breaking the link between being abused and progressing to sexually offending against children. The current findings provide some explanation as to why some victims become offenders and some do not (p. 47).

The previous research has shown the possible impact of insufficient attachments on children's future behaviors. Other recent research explored the prevalence of other listed disorders in pedophiles. Researchers Raymond et al. (1999) administered a semi-structured interview to forty-five men who met the *DSM-IV* diagnosis criteria for pedophilia. Their results found that over 90 percent of the participants had comorbid Axis I and Axis II disorders. Their findings were as follows:

> Fifty-six percent of the subjects met the criteria for five or more comorbid diagnosis in addition to pedophilia. Sixty-seven percent of the subjects were diagnosed as having a history of mood disorder. The most common was major depression, with over half of the group reporting a history of this disorder. Sixty-four percent of the subjects were diagnosed with a history of anxiety disorder. Social phobia and posttraumatic stress disorder were the most common anxiety disorders. Sixty percent of the populations reported a history of substance abuse (Raymond et al., 1999, p. 787).

Less than 25 percent of the participants met the criteria for narcissistic or antisocial personality disorder. These findings contrast the popular beliefs that most pedophiles have a personality disorder, mostly consisting of antisocial personality disorder (Raymond et al., 1999). These findings may influence future treatment methods for psychologists and other professionals treating pedophiles.

An area of increasing research involves the effectiveness of treatment for pedophiles. A chief problem in finding a consistent treatment for pedophiles may result from the varied explanations for their behaviors. One theory of pedophilic behavior is improper sexual stimulation. When analyzing this theory, researchers have used numerous methods and different standards. Without consistent methods, no precise conclusions have been produced to offer empirical support for this theory (Kear-Colwell & Boer, 2000). Other theorists, Oberholser and Beck (1986), propose that pedophiles choose children as victims because of easy access and their lack of social abilities. According to this theory, pedophiles prefer that the children are vulnerable and not as assertive as their adult counterparts. Another theory discusses the previous reported childhood sexual abuse of pedophiles. This theory has lead to recent research regarding childhood sexual abuse and the lasting effects it has on sex offenders (Murray, 2000). Kear-Colwell and Boer (2000) reported on the consistency of characteristics of pedophiles: "[T]he majority of pedophilic offenders come from abusive backgrounds, display evidence of personality damage, and have insecure attachments" (p. 601).

Researchers have also surveyed pedophiles and analyzed self reports in attempt to discover the motivation for their acts. Pollock and Hashmall (1991) attempted to investigate the offenders' reasoning behind their behavior by collected statements of 250 child molesters. They analyzed their reported explanations for their behavior and found that almost 30 percent of the sample insisted that the victim consented to the behavior. Another result found that over 20 percent of the offenders stated that the victim made the first move. Intoxication was also given as a primary reason for the sexual behaviors by over 20 percent of the participants. These results when paired with other professionals explanations for pedophilic behavior may impact future treatment options for therapists.

Most pedophiles do not fit the "dirty old man" stereotype. Pedophiles have varying characteristics, such as their age and preference of victims. Some pedophiles prefer young, female victims, while others prefer older, male victims. Several researchers have tried to develop a theory to explain the pedophilic behavior. Because of the differing levels of abuse and other motivating factors of the offenders, they have been unable to come to a consensus. Therapists attempt to treat clients with pedophilia with the same types of therapy. Most pedophiles' comorbid diagnosis and previous history of abuse are not a focus of therapy (Fontana-Rosa, 2001). This may be the missing link to effective and preventative treatment for pedophiles. If therapists and other professionals began to look at the core of the pedophile instead of the stereotypical perception, everyone would benefit.

C H A P T E R

PEDOPHILE ORGANIZATIONS

LORI CLUFF

35

One of the most valuable and precious gifts to the world, societies, communities and families are children. Children represent the possibility for cultures, traditions, and namesakes to be passed on and for humanity to continue advancing. Children also represent innocence and are free from moral corruption. There are many ways that children in societies throughout the world are sexually initiated into their respective societies. Some of these are culturally sanctioned while others are not.

While children throughout the world negotiate the course of sexual development differently as they mature into adolescence and finally into adulthood, sexual acts imposed on children by adults are generally looked upon with revulsion. Pedophilia is one sexual disorder that is widely looked upon as legally, socially, and morally wrong. However it remains a significant problem that has long-lasting negative affects on victims and families. Pedophilia, pedophiles, and the opportunities that are afforded this sexually perverse group via the Internet are examined in this chapter. Unfortunately the Internet has become a vast playground for opportunistic pedophiles to contact and befriend children in order to meet their desires for emotional and sexual contact.

The *DSM-IV-TR* defines pedophilia using the following three criteria:

A. Over a period of at least 6 months, recurrent, intense sexually arousing fantasies, sexual urges, or behaviors involving sexual activity with a prepubescent child or children (generally age 13 years or younger).

B. The fantasies, sexual urges, or behaviors cause clinically significant distress or impairment in social, occupational, or other important areas of functioning.

C. The person is at least age 16 years and at least 5 years older than the child or children in Criterion A.

Specify if:
    Sexually Attracted to Males
    Sexually Attracted to Females
    Sexually Attracted to Both

Specify if:
    Limited to Incest

Specify type:
    Exclusive Type (attracted only to children)
    Nonexclusive Type

Important to note is that there is a difference in criterion B when comparing the *DSM-IV* and the *DSM-IV-TR*. The *DSM-IV* erroneously implied that the diagnosis of pedophilia could only be made if the individual was distressed by their fantasies, sexual urges, or behaviors. This would prohibit the diagnosis of many pedophiles who believe they are providing educational experiences to the children they abuse.

Pedophilic behavior typically begins during the offender's teenage years, although some resist acting on their fantasies until later in life (Murray, 2000). Some offenders have experienced sexual abuse themselves as children, although this is not always a prerequisite in the development of a pedophile (Freund, Watson, & Dickey, 1990).

There has been great controversy regarding the understanding of pedophiles and the subsequent treatment. Pedophiles are seen as difficult clients due to their unwillingness to honestly discuss behaviors they have engaged in with children and usually defend their actions with a myriad of cognitive distortions that excuse them from acknowledging any wrongdoing. A study by Kear-Colwell & Sawle (2001) attempts to understand pedophiliac behavior as motivated by problems with attachment styles in these offenders.

The pedophile is thought to be an individual who is so afraid of rejection and emotional pain therefore they are unable to engage in age appropriate relationships. The pedophile seeks to engage in relationships that are void of intimacy and emotional involvement. This reduces the demand for them to self-disclose and allows them to remain distant emotionally. With children, sexually they are able to meet their needs in an impersonal and therefore emotionally safe manner (Kear-Colwell & Sawle, 2001). This rationale is also used to explain why they are so often treatment failures and are seen as difficult clients. Pedophiles have difficulty developing the interpersonal trust and bond that is necessary to create a therapeutic relationship they are invested in (Kear-Colwell & Sawle, 2001).

The opportunities presented to pedophiles via the Internet are practically infinite. Initially the pedophile is anonymous and able to seek out wayward children whose activities on the Internet are not closely monitored by adults. A friendship can then be created and eventually a meeting of the two may be arranged or the pedophile may glean enough information for them to ascertain where the child can be found (Anonymous, 2002).

Another advantage of the Internet for the pedophile is the ability for them to organize worldwide to advance their philosophy and create networks. The largest Internet organization that can be found on the web is NAMBLA, which stands for the North American Man-Boy Love Association. The Association raises money through their website by collecting membership dues and selling literature/books. The website is very thorough, highlighting mission statement, testimonials of children, a news page and a prisoner pen pal program: "[C]onsensual intergenerational experiences of younger people are often quite positive and beneficial for the participants, regardless of their ages. In contrast, non-consensual experiences, when the wishes of the youngster are disregarded, can be very damaging." NAMBLA even cites a study that examined over eight thousand victims of sexual abuse, which purported to find that none of the children were harmed. The study results were also purported to be achieved using interviews and psychological testing profiles.

The NAMBLA prisoner program is also quite unique. In order to help their brothers out and provide moral support while in prison, a pen pal program is organized. An individual may mail a request to NAMBLA and will then be connected with an incarcerated pedophile. The site highlights that pedophiles are the lowest in the prison pecking order, even when compared to murderers. Prison and parole therapy programs are also discussed, "these programs have never been shown to have any lasting value for the prisoner or for society" (www.nambla1.de/prisoner .htm, p. 2).

One of the top news stories for NAMBLA is a discussion about web filters. This group sees these filters as a form of wrongful censorship. Children are being blocked from websites that are seen by this group as nonpornographic and are not harmful to children. NAMBLA also takes an anti–death penalty position in their news section and are "especially offended by the execution of children" (www.nambla1.de/ new.htm, p. 1)

Americans for a Society Free from Age Restrictions (ASFAR) is another highly organized web group. Their site focuses primarily on legal issues. The mission statement is as follows:

> We, the Americans for a Society Free from Age Restrictions believe that in a free society, government should allow its citizens the greatest degree of freedom as possible without placing the public safety in jeopardy. We believe that the spirit of the Constitution of the United States calls for such a policy. However, we believe that age-restrictive laws legislated by federal, state, and local governments in the United States violate such principles. Therefore, all laws that are based on age should be repealed, and all government policies that discriminate by age should be reversed (www.asfar.org/declaration/, p. 1).

The position of this group is children and adolescents should not be restricted from any form of free speech (e.g., movies, music), driving, voting, drinking, the right to bear arms, as well as the legal right to consent to sexual relationships.

An organization that appears to have more international roots is that of the Pedophile Liberation Front (PLF). Languages available on this website are Suomeksi, Italian, Deutsch, Slovensky, Spanish, French, and Nederlaandse. Their site has four main components: articles supporting a reassessment of pedophilia, links to additional resources and organizations, news, and member pages (www.childlove.org/plf/home.html). This site states it has two purposes. One in being a "lighthouse in the dark for all the pedophiles in the world, who may thus feel they are not alone," and second to spread the ideals of the PLF (www.childlove.org/plf/intro-faq.html, p. 1). This site lists twenty-seven other organizations throughout the world and gives links to most.

The Internet serves many beneficial functions in our global society, and while the proportion of traffic that exploits the innocence of children may be small it is significant. Free speech is a precious concept that should be protected, however not at the price of a child's right to be protected. Children are unable to protect themselves and adults are too often incapable of monitoring all the various activities they participate in. Pedophiles, with their complex and perverted ideals, values, and philosophies are able to reinforce their cognitive distortions in part through the Internet community.

C H A P T E R

CHARACTERISTICS OF CHILD MOLESTERS

36

SHAY LITTON

STUDIES ON ADULT CHILD MOLESTERS

The topic of child molesters is a sensitive subject for many Americans. Reports of high recidivism rates, multiple victims, and heinous methods mean the public has a right to fear the leering stranger. But are most child molesters strangers, or are they family members of the victims? This among other considerations will be examined in the following literature review on child molesters and their characteristics.

A consensus on the definition for sexual abuse of children has not been developed. Some of the behaviors from differing definitions include acts such as fondling, kissing or sexual penetration of a child under the age of eighteen (Murray, 2000). Nevertheless, there have been several studies on the characteristics of child molesters and their victims. One of the earlier studies by DeFrancis (1969) found that approximately half of the child molesters in his study reported using physical force to coerce their victims. However, in a study by Stermac and Segal (1989), child molesters were likely to report that they were the victims of the child's coercion or manipulations.

The public may confuse pedophiles with other child predators such as child molesters and hebephiles (adult males sexually attracted to post-pubertal adolescents, 14–17). Child molesters, in contrast to pedophiles, are more likely to have irregular employment histories and have recurrently been arrested (Fontana-Rosa, 2001). Furthermore, child molesters are not diagnosed in the *DSM-IV-TR* (American Psychiatric Association, 2000), thereby not requiring a specific time period of offending. Adolescent offenders may be classified as child molesters instead of pedophiles to avoid being stigmatized by a mental illness diagnosis (Fontana-Rosa, 2001). Others may confuse child molesters with hebephiles because of the closeness in the age range required for the diagnosis of a pedophile.

A study conducted by Dube and Hebert (1988) analyzed over five-hundred childhood sexual abuse cases. The age of child victims ranged from two years to twelve years of age. The majority of the victims in the study were females (85 percent). The perpetrator was acquainted with the victim in some way in most of the cases reviewed. If the child was sexually abused by a stranger, the event was more likely to be violent and involve only one incident. (Dube & Hebert, 1988).

Finkelhor, Williams, and Burns (1989) conducted a large-scale study to examine the prevalence of child sexual abuse in over 200,000 day-cares in the United States. Of the day-care facilities researched, Finkelhor et al. (1989) found over 2,500 child victims of sexual abuse. Although men were the majority of the offenders in the cases, women were found to be perpetrators in the offenses involving teachers or other day-care facility employees. Approximately two-thirds of the women that committed the offenses had children of their own. Additionally, they were more likely to be married and considered socially outgoing. When examining the sexual offense, Finkelhor et al. (1989) found the female perpetrators were more likely to have more victims than the men, and had more girl victims than boys. Another unexpected finding from this study found the women used more coercion and threats than the male child molesters. The findings of this study suggest that female perpetrators may account for more offenses of childhood sexual abuse than previously thought. Because of society's view of women as primary care-givers and mothers, and children's subsequent attachment with females, the offenses perpetrated by women may be highly underreported.

Additionally, Finkelhor, Hotaling, Lewis, and Smith (1990) conducted a telephone survey with both male and female study participants ($N = 2,626$). The participants were questioned about possible childhood sexual abuse. The results of the study found that 16 percent of the male participants reported having been a victim of sexual abuse during their childhood. Of the male participants that were victimized, the majority of the perpetrators were male (83 percent). Approximately 26 percent of the women participants reported being previous victims of childhood sexual abuse. As for the male victims, the perpetrators of the female victims were mostly male (90 percent). The majority of both the female and male victims reported being abused only once by their perpetrator (Finkelhor et al., 1990).

Hanson, Scott, and Steffy (1995) conducted a study examining characteristics and recidivism rates of child molesters and nonsexual criminals. The participants for this study were comprised of 191 convicted child molesters and 137 offenders that had no history of sexual offenses. The study participants were followed up for an estimated 15 to 30-year time period. Approximately 42 percent of the child molester sample had histories of previous sexual charges, with an additional 40 percent having a history of property offenses. Eighty-seven percent of the nonsexual offender group was sentenced for property offenses, with 83 percent having prior convictions for similar charges. The nonsexual offenders were more likely than child molesters to be single, younger in age, and to have more current criminal charges. During the follow-up period, the nonsexual offender group produced a higher recidivism rate (83.2 percent) than the child molester group (61.8 percent). For the child molesters that recidivated, 41.1 percent of the convictions were for nonviolent offenses, followed by 35.1 percent for sexual offenses, and 12.6 percent for nonspecific violent offenses. The nonsexual offenders were more likely to recidivate in the nonviolent offense category (79.6 percent), followed by the nonspecific violent offenses (38.7 percent), and the nonsexual violent offenses (32.8 percent). The child molester group was found to be 9.21 times more likely than the nonsexual offender group to be convicted of a subsequent sexual offense. The child molester group was also "83 percent less likely to recidivate with a violent offense, 47.8 percent less likely to recidivate with a nonviolent offense, and 41.7 percent less likely to recidivate with any offense" (p. 333). When comparing the recidivism rate for sexual abuse for both groups, child molesters comprised 97 percent of the sexual offenses. As a result of their findings, Hanson et al. suggest that child molesters should be studied separately as criminal offenders due to the differences in their recidivism. Furthermore, this type of offender is more likely to recommit sexual offenses than other groups, thereby suggesting a difference in their motivational factors for their offenses.

A study conducted by Stermac, Hall and Henskens (1989) attempted to examine the levels of aggression and violence committed by child molesters. The sample for this study was comprised of 66 male inpatients that were participating in treatment at the Clarke Institute of Psychiatry in Toronto. Thirty-seven of the participants were nonfamilial sex offenders, followed by twenty-nine familial or incest sex offenders. Approximately 88 percent of the study participants were referred to participate in a pre-trial assessment for their sexual offense charge. Information regarding the patients' demographical and personal histories was collected from police reports, medical records and social service agency reports. The results of the study found when comparing the nonfamilial to incestuous offenders, 16.2 percent of the nonfamilial offenders and 58.6 percent of the incestuous offenders were married. Furthermore, the nonfamilial offenders were more likely to be younger and unemployed than the incestuous group. Although many of the offenders from both groups did not complete high school, 83 percent of the nonfamilial offenders and 77 percent of the incest offenders were listed as having at least an average intelligence level. When reviewing the criminal histories of the study participants, 59.4 percent of the nonfamilial and 34.5 percent of the incest offenders had prior convictions for sex offenses. Additionally, the nonfamilial offenders had a higher mean number of victims than the incest offenders (3.50 compared to 1.79, respectively). When comparing the victims from both groups of offenders, most of the offenders had molested female children (77.3 percent). The incest offender group was more likely to use physical violence and have more reports of injuries by their victims than the nonfamilial group. However, a majority of the nonfamilial offenses (78 percent) were assessed as violent. Over 62 percent of the incest offenders and 48.6 percent of the nonfamilial offenders had penetrated their victims vaginally, anally, or orally. The results of this study found that incestuous offenders had fewer victims, were more likely to use

physical force and aggression with their victims and were more likely to have penetration with their child victims. However, the majority of nonfamilial offenders'
methods of coercion were considered violent. Although the sample for this study
consisted mainly of offenders that were referred to be assessed in an inpatient setting, suggesting they may have committed severe offenses, the findings suggest the
offenses committed by both the offender groups can have significant damage on the
childhood victims.

Marshall and Christie (1981) conducted an analysis of the sexual behavior characteristics of 41 correctional files of convicted child molesters. The results of their
analysis found that even though all of the perpetrators denied having any intercourse with their child victims, there was prominent evidence of penetration in at
least 30 percent of the cases. Approximately 71 percent of the offenders used some
form of violence or threats of violence during their offense.

Additionally, Erickson, Walbeck, and Seely (1988), also found evidence of penetration with child victims during their review of 299 child molesters. The results of
their study found that approximately 42 percent of the female victims were vaginally
penetrated by their offenders. Additionally, 33 percent of the male victims were
anally penetrated.

STUDIES INVOLVING PHALLOMETRIC
TESTING ON CHILD MOLESTERS

Chaplin, Rice, & Harris (1995) performed a study on the effects of audiovisual stimuli of children on male offenders. The sample was comprised of fifteen child molesters: eleven had one or more sexual assault charges, and the remaining four
offenders were charged with performing one of the following acts, with a female victim fourteen years of age or younger—indecent assault, sexual interference, sexual
exploitation, or sexual intercourse. The samples' demographic characteristics are as
follows: average age was 37.9 years old, average education was listed as 10.2 years,
and an average of 3.27 sexual offenses. Over half (8) of the study participants committed offenses only within their families (i.e., familial), followed by 3 participants
that chose victims outside of their families (nonfamilial) and 3 participants with both
nonfamilial and familial victims. A comparison group consisted of 15 men that had
an average of 12.1 years of education and were for the most part, unemployed. The
study participants were required to watch audiovisual stimuli of a female child's and
a male's testimony of their sexual interactions. The participants' responses and reactions to the stimuli were recorded from phallometric testing and questionnaires. The
results of the study found that child molesters responded more to stories of sexual
activity, particularly when told by the child. Although there were distinguishable differences among the child molester and control group in the phallometric testing responses, the differences further increased when violent and aggressive stimuli were
used. Child molesters produced higher responses than the control group when presented with more sadistic stimuli. Additionally, the nonfamilial child molesters pro-

duced higher deviant scores than the familial offenders. Child molesters also scored lower than the control group on the Hogan Empathy Scale. Furthermore, the child molesters endorse more items diminishing the criminality of sexual activity between an adult and child on the Child Sexuality Survey, than the control group. These findings suggest the child molesters were more enticed when they perceived children were being harmed (Chaplin, Rice, & Harris, 1995). These findings show that although familial offenders appear to use more violent methods with their victims, they were not as enticed by the violent stimuli as nonfamilial. Familial offenders may fear their victims will tell another member of the family, therefore, they may use more force or coercion to scare the child or children.

A subsequent study by Firestone, Bradford, Greenberg, and Nunes (2000) analyzed the predictive ability of phallometry for homicidal and nonhomicidal child molesters. Using a phallometric assessment method, the researchers noted any changes in penile circumference while the subjects were viewing vignettes. The vignettes in the study had varied ages, sexes, coercion, sexual experiences and levels of violence. Although several findings suggest little, if any, difference between the nonhomicidal and homicidal child molesters, one index was statistically elevated for homicidal child molesters. Homicidal child molesters scored significantly higher on the pedophile assault index. The researchers reported that "men who have committed nonviolent sexual offenses against children may derive little sexual pleasure from depictions of clearly assaultive acts against children . . . homicidal child molesters seem to be equally aroused by assaultive and nonassaultive depictions in which children are victims"(Firestone et al., 2000).

STUDY ON RECIDIVISM RATES OF CHILD MOLESTERS

Hanson conducted a large-scale study to assess the recidivism rates of different categories of sex offenders. The sample for this study was comprised of 4,673 convicted sex offenders. The offenders were divided into three categories based on their victims' characteristics: rapists ($N = 1,133$), incest offenders ($N = 1,207$), child molesters who victimized extrafamilial children ($N = 1,411$). When comparing the average ages among the groups, incest offenders were the oldest (38.9), followed by extrafamilial child molesters (37.1), and rapists (32.1). The results of this study found an approximate recidivism rate of 17.5 percent for all three of the sample groups. However, as the offenders' age increased, the rate of recidivism decreased. When comparing the recidivism rates of the sample groups separately, the incest group had the lowest recidivism rate (8.4 percent). The rapists sample's recidivism rate (17.1 percent) was more than double the rate of the incest group. The extrafamilial child molester sample produced the highest recidivism rate (19.5 percent) of the three groups. Additionally, "the highest risk age period for extrafamilial child molesters was between the ages of 25 and 35 (not 18 to 24). The recidivism rate of the extrafamilial child molesters showed relatively little decline until after age 50" (Hanson, 2002, p. 1054).

Hanson suggested the decrease in recidivism as the offenders get older can be explained by a loss of sex drive and/or deviant interests, an increase in self-control, and more limited opportunities with children.

ADOLESCENT CHILD MOLESTERS

Ford and Linney (1995) conducted a study to examine the similarities and differences between juvenile sex offenders, violent nonsexual offenders, and status offenders. The sample for the study was comprised of 82 juveniles residing in residential facilities. The juveniles selected for the study were categorized into the following groups:

A. juveniles who sexually assaulted peer-age victims or adult persons (juvenile rapists);

B. juveniles who sexually assaulted a child 5 or more years younger than the offender (child molesters);

C. youths adjudicated on charges of assault . . . (violent nonsex offenders);

D. youth adjudicated on charges of incorrigibility, runaway, or truancy without other nonstatus offenses (status offenders) (p. 61).

Most of the juveniles lived in single family homes and were found to have an average or below average intelligence. The results of the study found that child molesters were more likely than the other groups, including rapists, to have been victimized by their family members and/or witnessed violence or aggression in their homes.

Furthermore, child molesters were more likely to have been sexually abused. When assessing the juveniles' self-concept, child molesters differed from the other groups by reporting more difficulties with "displays of problematic behavior, attitudes toward their physical appearance, dysphoric mood and anxiety, and popularity with peers" (Ford & Linney, 1995, p. 68). Additionally, child molesters were more likely to display a need to be in charge of situations with others by methods such as demanding others to obey them. Ford and Linney suggest that "[t]his early victimization experience may contribute to their reported desire for control in interpersonal relationships and their need to initiate relationships" (p. 69). They further propose the early experience of sexual abuse by the child molesters may have set an example for future behavior and aided in their need to dominate situations with others.

POSSIBLE DEVELOPMENT EXPLANATIONS
FOR ADOLESCENT CHILD MOLESTERS

Research on developmental theories of adolescence has shown that parent's participation in their child's life has a significant impact on their behaviors (Baer, 1999). The time of adolescent development can be a confusing and frustrating period for a child. The adolescent is learning and developing supporting relationships with their families and peers (Updegraff, Madden-Derdich, Estrada, Sales, & Leonard, 2002). Adolescents are acquiring socialization skills and developing strong attachment bonds through interaction with family members and friends (Baer, 1999). A significant part of the adolescent's development of bonds and social skills involves the influence of the parent's method of interacting with their child. However, an overwhelming majority of the adolescent participants in the previous studies come from single-parent homes. Most of the adolescents were residing with only their mothers. Awad, Saunders, and Levene (1984) provided additional support for this theory in their study of male adolescent sex offenders. The results of their study found that an absence of a positive relationship with a male figure was consistent among the group of adolescent sex offenders.

A subsequent study by O'Brien and Bera (1985), on adolescent sex offenders, provided similar support to the previous research regarding the family characteristics of child molesters. The majority of their study participants also reported having limited, positive contact with their fathers or other male role models. The lack of support and guidance from the adolescents' parents can adversely affect the child's relationship with others.

When comparing delinquent juveniles to their adolescent counterparts, significant differences were noted in formal decision-making abilities. Researcher Redding (1997) found that "juvenile delinquents generally are less cognitively capable than their peers and, therefore, less likely to be among those exceptional individuals who might be considered fully responsible for their actions prior to the age of 18, despite their lack of experience upon which judgment depends" (Redding, 1997, p. 728).

During adolescence, children are seeking autonomy and reach their developmental milestones at different rates. Delinquency for many juveniles is a normative expectation during their adolescent growth and development. Studies have shown that most adolescents do not become adult criminals (Redding, 1997). Researchers have proposed that the developmental levels of maturity for adolescent children relate to their competency.

> A different perspective on the question of age differences in risky decision-making has been suggested by several writers, including the present authors, who have argued that there may be developmental differences between adolescents and adults in non-cognitive (or psychosocial) realms that account for age differences in behavior and that may have implications for assessments of adjudicative competence as well as culpability. (Cauffman, Woolard, & Reppucci, 1999, p. 411).

A recent study by Engels, Dekovic, and Meeus (2002) analyzed the effect of social skills on parenting practices, parental attachment and peer relations. Their sample consisted of 508 adolescents ranging from twelve to eighteen years old. The adolescents filled out batteries of questionnaires about their mothers and fathers separately. The questionnaires measured affection levels regarding how their parents' reacted to their needs and how they felt in social situations. The results of this study showed that the parenting variables were compellingly correlated with attachment levels. "Adolescents with parents who were warm and responsive without harsh discipline, stimulated them to act on their own but at the same time, knew what their children were doing and had more satisfying friendships indicated by higher levels of attachment," (Engels et al., 2002, p. 6). Another finding of the study showed that when parents were aware of where their children were, the adolescents had decreased levels of anxiety and maintained positive social behaviors (Engels et al., 2002). Single mothers may have a more difficult time keeping track of where their children are. Other developmental theorists, Hill and Holmbeck (1986) proposed that adolescents who have steady and consistent emotional bonds with their parents will be confident enough to positively explore their surroundings.

Another prominent study in the area of adolescent parenting practices and the attachment bonds between parent and the child was conducted by Hirschi (1969). The main premise behind Hirschi's theory was that parental supervision and family bonding will constrict the juvenile's tendency to behave in a deviant manner. Hirschi proposed that juveniles are hypersensitive to their parents' opinions of them. If the juvenile has a strong emotional bond with the parent, they will restrain from behaving in a deviant manner. Researcher Baer (1999) furthered Hirschi's work on family relationships, parenting behaviors and adolescent deviance. Baer devised a study using over seven thousand adolescents in seventh, eighth, and ninth grade that resided in large metropolitan areas. Baer sampled three ethnic groups, Mexican Americans, African Americans and Euro-Americans, in her study. The students were given multiple-choice questionnaires that assessed a variety of constructs. Some of the constructs in Baer's study measured attachment between the parent and juvenile, parental monitoring levels, parental encouragement for independence, and frequency of deviant behavior. The findings showed that parental monitoring was significantly related to deviant behavior. Baer's research supported Hirschi by showing the positive effects of parental control or monitoring on juvenile's decisions to engage in deviant behavior.

SUMMARY OF RESEARCH FINDINGS FOR CHILD MOLESTERS

Although most of the research on lack of appropriate attachment bonds was performed on adolescents, the research findings may also be relevant to their adult counterparts. Both the adolescent and adult child molesters choose child victims, a majority of them female. Researchers have found that child molesters use more force, especially intrafamilial molesters, with their victims. Although there is evidence that not all child molesters penetrate their victims, most offenders do use some form of violence or forceful methods during their offense (DeFrancis, 1969). Child molesters are also more likely to report that the child was sexually coming on to them and they were coerced and/or manipulated into the sexual act (Pollock & Hashmall, 1991; Stermac & Segal, 1989). Additionally, child molesters will deny that they engaged in any form of intercourse (either anal or vaginally) with the victim, even when there is evidence of such penetration (Marshall & Christie, 1981). Child molesters are likely to be married, especially intrafamilial offenders, and unemployed (Stermac, Hall & Henskens, 1989).

CHILD MOLESTER TYPOLOGY

After a review of the literature, the following typology was created by the present author, to distinguish child molesters from pedophiles:

CHILD MOLESTER CHARACTERISTICS

- Perpetrators: Mostly male, but studies have found female perpetrators in day-care facilities
- Irregular employment, with previous arrest histories, more likely to be married
- Are more likely to engage in intercourse with their victims than pedophiles
- In nonfamilial cases, the perpetrator is not likely to know their victim
- In familial or incest cases, the victim may experience more severe forms of violence and aggression
- Their behavior is categorized as chronic, but many commit their offense only once with each victim, they average more victims per offender than pedophiles
- Older victims suffer more brutal forms of violence
- Overall, they will use more force during their offenses, and may use substances such as alcohol to coerce their victims
- More influenced by how others see them, they worry about "negative evaluations," they are unassertive

PEDOPHILE CHARACTERISTICS

- Mostly male, choosing a majority of female victims
- Usually live with their parents or alone
- Will more likely have steady employment histories and will work where they can be close to children such as schools or athletic clubs
- They commit their offenses due to their need for affection and affirmation, they want to be a friend to the child
- Not likely to force sexual intercourse with the victim, they are more likely to fondle and touch their victims
- Report seeing themselves as shy, introverted, sensitive, and depressed

CHAPTER

CHILD MOLESTATION AND INCEST

BRIANNA SATTERTHWAITE

37

Incest is the perpetration of child sexual abuse by a member who is either biologically or societally perceived to be within the victims family; this includes all step relations, live-in partners of parents, and those who have taken a role of close family member in the child's life (Courtois, 1988; Maltz & Holman, 1987). The rates of child sexual abuse overall is astounding; the numbers range from 114,000 to 300,000 cases of child abuse per year (Sheinberg & Fraenkel, 2001). In a related study, up to 90 percent of offenders of child sexual abuse (CSA) were either parents or other family members, making the incidence of incest a national problem (Sheinberg & Fraenkel, 2001). These numbers are debated as both being too high and too conservative because of either false memory recovery or underreporting by certain demographic categories, so interpretation of such statistics must be taken cautiously.

ETIOLOGY

From an anthropological view, humans have an aversion to incest for three reasons: social structural, biosocial and psychoanalytic (Meigs & Barlow, 2002). The first addresses the fact that incest is detrimental to the social design of procreating strong, capable beings. Meigs and Barlow (2002) demonstrate that in history, the strength and solidarity of cultures require individuals to go beyond their family of origin.

The biosocial view highlights the seminal work by Westermark, which proposes that those raised in proximity to one another will have a sexual aversion to each other. This accounts for siblings, close relatives and even parents and children among other inhibitors. Meigs and Barlow (2002) outline research on kibbutzim marriages, and Lebanese and Taiwanese marriages, which found "lessened sexual attraction, lower birth rates and higher divorce rates among partners who were raised close together such as in arranged marriages where the people grow up together. This points out that both anthropologically and biologically, incest is taboo.

The psychoanalytic view of incest is highlighted by Freud's Oedipal complex; not that there is the innate desire to mate with one's parent, but when that desire cannot be squelched, Oedipus was willing to gouge out his own eyes as a result. This drama is indicative of the taboo by showing how much shame and guilt Oedipus felt when he realized his attraction (Meigs & Barlow, 2002).

Sexually abusive behaviors can include fondling, oral sex, anal sex, and intercourse, among a few (Maltz & Holman, 1987). These acts may occur only once, but in most cases, the incestual relationship continues on repeatedly. This occurs for a number of reasons: victims are scared, confused, and hurt and may be too young to stand up for their personal rights; victims know they should say something but feel that they may be seen negatively for acquiescing to the sexual activity; the perpetrator has intimidated the victim to such a degree that the victim feels as though he or she has no one to confide in; or finally the sexual abuse may be a family-sanctioned act (Maltz & Holman, 1987).

Some survivors of incest report that they were unaware of what was happening to them, but they knew it was wrong (Maltz & Holman, 1987). In their cases, they also reported feeling ashamed to be a part of whatever they were experiencing and therefore felt frightened to confide in anyone, even their parents, or in the other parent in the case of parental incest. Some perpetrators of incest will rely on blackmail or intimidation to continue their assaults (Maltz & Holman, 1987). Another dilemma faced by the victims of incest is whether they are able to participate in the abuse physically to avoid other punishments, but remove themselves emotionally (Sheinberg & Fraenkel, 2001). Unfortunately in some cases, children may feel that they are not able to stop the physical abuse and therefore must continue to endure the trauma. The last bit of control they have over their bodies is to dissociate from the experience. This carries a number of implications later in life for the victims who separate themselves from the trauma by splitting off somewhere in their consciousness in an effort to deal with their pain. Such implications will be discussed later.

Incest is further convoluted by those parents who are aware of the abuse their partner is perpetuating against their children and do not intervene (Author's notes). This dynamic is particularly horrific because the abuse of a child within the family is being overlooked or blatantly supported. From this author's work with one woman in particular who had been a victim of an incestual relationship with her father, it was apparent that the victim felt she had no safe place to turn and no one to turn to because her abuse had been sanctioned by her mother as well as by her father; this ultimately means that both parents are offending against their child and the child may feel equally as lost because of this dynamic. In working with this particular individual, she made it clear that her mother's blind eye was the ultimate betrayal of love sometimes surpassing the betrayal her father expressed through the actual assaults.

In Canada, the law maintains that incest exists only when it is between first- or second-degree blood relatives and also includes adopted children. Otherwise the offense is considered extrafamilial. Colloquially, incest can be attributed to any relation that is socially perceived to be a family member, but it is not supported in the letter of the law (Rice & Harris, 2002). A general understanding of incest includes the surrogate caregiver as well as the biological one.

TYPES OF INCEST

Inherent differences exist within the variety of perpetrators of incest. One category of incest is with a father perpetrator and a daughter as the victim. According to Rice and Harris (2002), men who molest their daughters or stepdaughters are among the most prevalent type of incest offenders. They attempted to outline reasons in the literature for the molest behaviors within a family through four explanations. The first explanation is that possibly the perpetrators are pedophiles (Rice & Harris, 2002). They determined that pedophiles, are those who have clear differences in their sexual preferences for arousal from children. This hypothesis does not cover the full gamut of pedophilia particularly if the father-daughter incest is the offender's only act of sexual deviance. Therefore, the researchers continued to look into other explanations for the incest.

The next hypothesis is that humans have a genetic disposition against incest because of the potential genetic problems that could arise (Rice & Harris, 2002). Those who then do engage in incest as the aggressor may have a defective genetic makeup that does not keep them from engaging in sexual behavior with family members. The researchers posed that this may have been because of a genetic line of ancestors who "are less reproductively successful" (p. 329). Another supporting hypothesis of a genetic problem is the Westermark hypothesis which states that those individuals who are raised together will have an aversion to sexual activity with each other. This is generalized to those who are placed in caregiver roles with a child to inhibit paternal incest (Rice & Harris, 2002). With this theory in mind, those that defy the social norms and seek incestual relationships may then, as the hypothesis goes, have a malformed genetic response to those they either grew up with (in terms of brother-sister incest,) or parent-child incest.

The third hypothesis constructed by Rice and Harris (2002), suggests that the perpetrators are deprived sexually by their spouse and, therefore, out of a perceived necessity move to the next most preferred gender-age category of potential relationships. With young daughters in the house, this poses an opportunity for the father to pursue someone in their own home. In this case, the daughter becomes a filler role for the spouse who is unavailable either emotionally or physically. Though Rice and Harris (2002) found that incest fathers had less deviant sexual tendencies than did other child molesters, it does not seem logical that pursuing sexual relationships in one's family is less deviant that outside, no matter the age group.

As reported in Rice and Harris (2002), many men at some level have some interest in sexually immature girls. When that desire is paired with an available person, despite their status in the less preferred gender-age category, no opportunities exist in the preferred gender-age category, and the person is unlikely to resist, incest is the next likely step in the process. This explanation is much more socially driven and mutually exclusive than the prior two explanations (Rice & Harris, 2002).

Finally, the fourth hypothesis for father-daughter incest is the presence of psychopathy in the father. This hypothesis did not stand up well to the research in that the offenders of father-daughter incest reported lower rates of sexual or violent recidivism as compared to those who molest outside of their family. In addressing psychopathy, the presence of recidivism in sexual or violent crimes is a hallmark.

A similar body of research attempted to also outline the reasons for father-daughter incest (Copps Hartley, 2001). This research posed that the acts of incest occurred, again, for one of four reasons: "a need for sexual gratification, seeking an outlet from the dissatisfaction in their lives, contact as an expression of anger and contact as an inappropriate way to show affection or love" (Copps Hartley, 2001, p. 464). Though some appear similar to that of Rice and Harris's (2002) categories, some distinctions exist.

Those men who endorsed the first reason of seeking sexual gratification were noted to be hypersexualized by their own accounts. They stated that their wives had complained about their extensive needs and over half of the men who reported sex as being extremely important to them also indicated that they were not being sexually active with their partners at the time that the incest began (Copps Hartley, 2001).

Though all men in this study indicated that they were somewhat dissatisfied with their lives, almost half stated that this was a primary motivation for their incest behaviors. Some descriptions were related to wanting to "feel better or to cope with the lack of affection in their lives" (Copps Hartley, 2001, p. 465).

Regarding anger as a motivation, the men reported using their sexual abuse of their daughters as a way to either get back at their wives or at their own personal abusers. This revenge toward spouses was noted to be for either the lack of sexual intimacy within the relationship or as a form of jealousy for a wife's extramarital affair (Copps Hartley, 2001).

Lastly, the fourth motive for father-daughter incest as outlined by Copps Hartley (2001), is inappropriately showing affection. One father was quoted as stating that it was "because I loved her . . . I wanted to have something between us, a bond between us that would last forever" (p. 466). This sort of thinking implies that the boundaries between parents and children were severely blurred and that may be indicative of the father's relationship with his parents being equally enmeshed.

When compared to extrafamilial child molesters, father-daughter offenders "were older, had less serious and disturbed backgrounds, had less criminal and antisocial conduct as adults, and had exhibited better social adjustment" (Rice & Harris, 2002, p. 334). This seems counterintuitive on a few levels: less disturbed backgrounds does not account for their ability to break social norms and molest family members, nor does the proposal that fewer antisocial traits were demonstrated, and finally the element of social adjustment does not logically coincide with one who would opt for a sexual relationship with a daughter versus a member of their age group. (Rice & Harris, 2002).

One body of literature focused on mother-son incest with the mother as the perpetrator. This is seminal because of the understanding that most incestual relationships are propagated by men no matter the age or relation to the victim (whether it be a daughter or sister). Their findings supported that men who had been a victim of an incestual relationship with their mother suffered greater psychiatric trauma than did other sexually abused males (Kelly, Wood, Gonzalez, MacDonald & Waterman, 2002). There is a dearth of information on mother-son incest and that may be a product of social perceptions of mothers as nurturers (Kelly et al., 2002). Mothers are usually granted a greater leniency with physical touching of their children because they tend to be the primary caregiver, are seen as nurturers and generally society refuses to see women as sexually perverted. With this being the case, the incidence of mother-son incest may be much higher than originally thought and has not been widely researched (Kelly et al., 2002).

Abuse perpetrated by a mother to a son may take on a different nature than other forms of incest, according to literature reviewed in Kelly et al. (2002). The leniency discussed previously may lend toward less intrusive sorts of incest such as fondling. Nonetheless, the effects on men who were abused by their mothers appears to be more distressing than when the perpetrator is from outside the family. According to Kelly et al. (2002), the distress manifests itself in interpersonal and sexual problems, aggression and may demonstrate a greater prevalence of dissociation. Many men in therapy for incestual relationships with their mother reported extreme rage, shame, and overwhelming sadness. Such symptoms are not only peculiar to men who have been molested by their mothers but also by other adults including their fathers (Kelly et al., 2002).

The study conducted by Kelly et al. (2002) explored literature on coping strategies and perceptions of abuse among a clinic referred population. In their research, some notable conclusions were drawn regarding perception of the abuse. They described two categories of victims: ones who perceived the abuse as negative and those who described their initial feelings of abuse as positive and/or neutral (Kelly et al., 2002). One potential finding from Kelly et al.'s (2002) study postulates that men who retrospectively labeled their perception of their abuse as positive have a more negative prognosis for adjustment. Those men who reported initially to have positive feelings later stated that they felt more aggression, sometimes sexually, engaged more frequently in self-destructive behavior and generally reported more negative symptoms than did men who initially found the abuse to be negative (Kelly et al., 2002). Such findings may speak to the nature of coping mechanisms used during and after their trauma that were ultimately destructive. This may support the hypothesis that the men later felt the shame and guilt of breaking the social norm with mother-son incest and sublimated that anger and aggression out in their adult lives.

Though origins of sexual orientation are a taboo topic, one finding from Kelly et al. (2002) found that men who had been involved in mother-son incest reported more heterosexual orientations than did men who had been abused by fathers or other males outside their family unit. The question remains whether the abuse led to having a similar orientation later in life or did the young child's already founded orientation lead to a greater vulnerability for molestation from adults with a similar heterosexual or homosexual orientation. (Kelly et al., 2002).

When incest involves brothers and sisters, rather than fathers or stepfathers and stepdaughters, a few distinctions are found (Cyr, Wright, McDuff & Perron, 2002). Brother-sister incest does not get reported as readily as father-daughter incest at a rate of 18 versus 78 percent (of total cases), but that figure may not accurately represent how often it occurs. There is a myth that when any sexual assault occurs between a brother and a sister that it is merely sexual exploration that is harmless and does not represent any underlying assault (Cyr et al., 2002). This mind-set allows such instances of brother-sister incest to go unreported and understudied. This understanding is fostered by the statistics that state that younger sibling incest may include genital exploration while the older, adolescent incest more frequently includes intercourse or attempted intercourse. The occurrence of intercourse is also an element more highly correlated with brother-sister incest than with father/stepfather-daughter incest relationships (Cyr et al., 2002). In reviewing the age differential between brothers and sisters when the brother is the perpetrator, usually the brother is older than the sister and that, paired with the inherent domination given to males by society, serves as a factor to continue the incest relationship (Cyr et al., 2002).

A number of variables were found to correlate with family dynamic where brother-sister incest was present (Cyr et al., 2002). A retrospective view from women found that the households were "dysfunctional in child rearing practices, relational patterns among family members, family rules and response patterns to family stressors" (Cyr et al., 2002, p. 960). The women also reported physical and verbal abuse, a lack of parental supervision, having more siblings in the home and an emotionally absent mother.

Long-term effects of brother-sister incest were found as follows: nearly half the victims of brother-sister incest studied never married, the victims were more likely to be abused physically in later life, most victims reported some sort of problems in the workplace or in social situations, as well as a general dissatisfaction with life (Cyr et al., 2002). Many victims also reported a constant personal search for esteem and a sense of identity. Other similar types of responses to the long-term effects were a mistrust of others, difficulties in sexual responsiveness in consensual relationships, continuous self-blame, and a pattern of being in the victim role in most other relationships. Interestingly, many of these symptoms are also seen in victims of father-daughter incest, indicating that the effects of incest may be independent of the perpetrator-victim relationship.

Overall society has placed a taboo on such intrafamilial relationships but on occasion incestual relationships are consensual. The incest complex refers to situations where the relationship is agreed upon on some level. According to this author's personal communications, this phenomenon may begin with some amount of mild coercion such as providing alcohol or other means of persuasion. Though this is more rare than forced incest, it is portrayed in the media at many different levels. One episode of *Law and Order: SVU* portrayed two elements of psychological disorders when a man was arrested for piquerism and was found in bed with his mother with whom he had an incestual relationship. Another media that is more disturbing is the popular young adolescent series by V. C. Andrews that begins with the book *Flowers in the Attic* which portrays brother-sister consensual incest. What is most unsettling is that these books are targeted at the 13 to 16-year-old age group and yet still address morally and legally charged issues such as consensual incest (author's notes).

"Incest is not a static event," was an exceptional quote by Copps Hartley (2001, p. 461) to illustrate the dynamic nature of the incest relationship. It does not begin one day with a family member approaching another for sexual intercourse. It is a build up of many personal, family and societal factors that the individual channels into destructive means. Factors involved in the offender are not to be used as excuses but rather to look and explore more thoroughly what contributed to the incest. Common features of incest offenders were found to be passive or dependent personality styles, possibly have been the victim of physical or sexual abuse within their family of origin, rejection by one or both of their parents, dissatisfaction with their current marriage, sexual difficulties with adults and subsequent dissatisfaction and problems with empathy and bonding (Copps Hartley, 2001).

Also a factor is the element of low self-esteem (Copps Hartley, 2001); there are a number of empowering feelings children bring about in adults, most of which are purely platonic and focus on the adults ability to be a caregiver and allow the child to fully rely on them for support. When this construct is paired with some of the above mentioned characteristics, the way that power is exhibited is drastically different.

One interesting facet found in the research conducted by Copps Hartley (2001) was that typical incest offenders (if such a label could be designated) generally has not had other molestation contact with children outside of their family; this meaning that the incest offender is not a child molester of only opportunity and would otherwise target extrafamilially if not for the availability of a family member.

EFFECTS OF INCEST

Some long-term effects of incest have been addressed along the way, but it is important to focus on the overarching effects regardless of victim-perpetrator relationship or perception of abuse. Armsworth and Stronck (1999) noted in their examination of the effects of incest that "relational patterns are learned and passed down across generations" (p. 303). With this in mind, some programs are directed at the parent's abusive behaviors in an effort to reduce the likelihood that the behaviors will be passed down along the generations (Armsworth & Stronck, 1999).

Women who were survivors of incest as children were studied for their parenting styles and the conclusions supported the notion that incestual abuse is pervasive and the long-term effects are then funneled into their difficulties as parents. Three major themes were found among the women: unbalanced development, disconnected lives, and disowned dramas (Armsworth & Stronck, 1999). The notion of an unbalanced development is as a result of having too much exposure to one aspect, such as sexual experience, and not enough exposure to another aspect of growing up such as love, nurturing, and acceptance. This leads the victim to have a lesser capacity for empathy and concern for others because it was never fostered in them growing up. Another factor in the unbalanced development is that many abused children are parentified and, therefore, lack the experience of truly being a child. This diminishes the safety and security that most children receive and teach the children that life is uncertain and overwhelming (Armsworth & Stronck, 1999).

The issues surrounding disconnected lives highlight the isolation the victim felt as they carried a horrible secret with them and the feelings of shame and guilt that usually accompany sexual abuse (Armsworth & Stronck, 1999). This disconnect is further fostered by the confusing signals they are receiving; they are wanted in a sexual capacity but possibly not in any other way. Children aim for interpersonal connections and attachment biologically and when those needs are not met in the way they are intended to be met, they must rely on themselves and not their caregivers for the feelings of connectedness they desire (Armsworth & Stronck, 1999; Courtois, 2000).

Finally, the construct of disowned dramas is an abstract reference to the turmoil and disaster faced by young children who are not yet old enough to understand the "drama" of what is happening to them. These dramas were forced to be played out in silence and thus had to exist only within the family context. This forces the victim to "disown" the problems when outside of the home and open them back up when they are with family (Armsworth & Stronck, 1999). These constructs translate into an altered parent; no matter how they would like to raise their children without the traces of turmoil they faced as children, the well worn paths of abuse are still traceable in their interactions with others.

Other factors in the long-term effects center around the accompanying physical and verbal abuse that most children endure along with sexual abuse. This fosters a number of other feelings of inadequacy as well as the guilt and shame associated with the sexual abuse (Courtois, 2000). Some cases may have effects so profound that a diagnosis of post-traumatic stress disorder may be applicable. Some victims may experience recurring, intrusive thoughts, have experienced feelings of helplessness, reliving the trauma based on a particular trigger, and in the end have a blunted, cut-off reaction to other related stimuli (Courtois, 2000).

Another possibility is that the victim may experience dissociation during the offense as touched on earlier when the victim wanted to remove herself emotionally since she was incapable of removing herself physically (Courtois, 2000; Sheinberg &

Fraenkel, 2001). By splitting off from consciousness, the trauma can be put aside. This can be intensely problematic later in life; the capacity to resolve problems has been ultimately crushed and the child's defense against any sort of upset becomes dissociation. This can keep one from experiencing other ways of problem resolution that are more effective and less detrimental to the psyche.

Feelings of betrayal from the one that should be protecting you, feelings of powerlessness, fear of stigmatization and an inappropriate link between sex and abuse are also products of childhood incest trauma (Courtois, 2000). Another important result is a presence of sexual dysfunction. Courtios (2000) stated that women who survived incest reported a lower capacity for sexual arousal or orgasm and reported less sexual satisfaction than did survivors of other molestations including rape. Other dysfunctions found were vaginismus, dyspareunia, desire disorders, and other paraphilic disorders (Courtois, 2000). These are not peculiar to females (except vaginismus); one report states that nine out of ten men experienced similar sexual dysfunction symptoms (Courtois, 2000).

TREATMENT

According to Marotta and Asner (1999), the group setting of psychotherapy may be beneficial in alleviating the isolation and other interpersonal problems that exist in the survivors of incest. In general, some form of therapy, whether it is group or individual, was found to be better than no therapy at all and those who make use of counseling opportunities show more signs of stable mental health than do those who do not engage in counseling of some nature.

In respect to recidivism, incest offenders were found to reoffend sexually at a rate of 6.4 percent 6.5 years after their conviction (Firestone, Bradford, McCoy, Greenberg, Larose, & Curry, 1999). This figure indicates that incest offenders reoffend at a lower rate than do other child molesters who targeted extrafamilially. No matter what criteria used to determine incest offenders and their rates for recidivism, all studies are underrepresentations of the actual rate at which they occur due to sensitive nature of the offense (Firestone et al., 1999). Among the recidivist, a higher propensity for alcoholism was found. When compared to extrafamilial child molesters and rapists, the incest offenders were considered less antisocial. The Firestone et al. (1999) study also found that although penile plethysmograph assessments were not sensitive for recidivism, they were able to distinguish those who had deviant sexual arousal such as incest fantasies.

The first hurdle in treating both the incest offender and victim is to get them to come forward. This may be intensely problematic because of the inherent sense of shame, guilt and secrecy that go along with an incest relationship (Armsworth & Stronck, 1999; Copps Hartley, 2001).

When the offender comes in for treatment, whether it is while they are incarcerated for their crime or in the public sector, the goal in treatment is behaviorally to stop the individual from offending again (Courtois, 1988). Beyond a behavioral context, it is crucial to understand the person's belief system that afforded them the ability to begin an incestual relationship. It is also necessary to treat the incestual behaviors directly as well as the effects such behavior has on the individual's life (Courtois, 1988). There is also a need to stay away from normalizing any activity that is conducted around the incestual behavior. A hallmark of some therapeutic orientations is that the clinician stay neutral in their behavior and responses. When dealing with incest offenders, it must be understood that they have made a practice of normalizing their activities to themselves and to their victims (Courtois, 1988). It is fundamental to address their behavior in a context that does not allow for such deviant behaviors while at the same time being empathetic to the frustration, confusion and other underlying problems that may accompany their incestual motivations.

Treating the incest offender requires one to understand the offender's motives for acting out in such a way (Copps Hartley, 2001). That is the sense of reality that the offender lives and offends under, and until that construct is accepted, therapy will not touch the underlying motives and belief systems that made incestual behavior acceptable to the offender.

There is also a profound need to lead the offender toward accepting responsibility for their actions to the victim and the family as a whole (Sheinberg & Fraenkel, 2001). Another facet of offender treatment is aimed at fostering empathy for others. This is an ability that many offenders lack, which is problematic for relationships in general. A typical approach to treating the behaviors is through a cognitive behavioral modality (Sheinberg & Fraenkel, 2001). It is controversial as to whether therapy can change an offender's partner of choice from children to adults, but through therapy the offender can learn to manage his impulse control (Sheinberg & Fraenkel, 2001).

It is also important to look at reasons and explanations for incest behaviors. Because the practice is not considered the norm, it logically follows that some historical information may help to understand where the deviant sexual desires originate (Sheinberg & Fraenkel, 2001). This is where more dynamically centered therapy can be beneficial, though that modality is controversial among strict behaviorists.

When conducting therapy with juvenile incest offenders, there is a positive notion that because they are young, their tendencies have yet to be solidified and are thus more apt to change. There are also inherent psychosocial problems that exist within both juvenile and adult incest offenders that warrant attention in therapy (Sheinberg & Fraenkel, 2001). Another construct that must be addressed during therapy is learning to treat others as people rather than objects. The persuasion and coercion that began the incestual relationship is indicative of selfish thinking patterns, lack of empathy for the victim, and a general nature of objectifying the other person to justify their needs and actions.

In treating victims of incest, most authors illustrate that the therapeutic relationship is paramount because the lack of support and stability the person endured during their childhood (Courtois, 1988; Maltz & Holman, 1987; Sheinberg & Fraenkel, 2001). It is also important for the treatment to address the incest head-on and not indirectly. Victims have spent the majority of their lives being obtuse about the abuse they have to endure and it would not be therapeutic to continue that pattern. It also supports the notion that the incest they suffered from is intolerable even to the therapist and thus somehow as shameful as they always imagined it to be (Courtois, 1988).

It is also seen as fundamental to address the ways that the victims have continued to be victims in other arenas of their lives. The maladaptive patterns such as fleeing from potential positive intimate relationships, their withdrawal from social situations that further their isolation, and not allowing themselves to validate their own feelings are essential core concepts to address in therapy (Maltz & Holman, 1987).

Self-esteem is usually negatively affected in the victim of incest (Maltz & Holman, 1987). This can be due to the objectification they experience as children, the feelings of helplessness, and the shame they carry because of the incest (Maltz & Holman, 1987).

Usually the therapy will need to facilitate learning about communication skills because the victim has not had a voice for a long time (Maltz & Holman, 1987). They will also need help reframing the abuse to give ownership of the responsibility back to the offender and realize that it is not their own. Another construct is to find the child inside themselves that they lost at such a young age. The victim of incest had to be an adult long before they were biologically or psychologically ready for such a transition and therefore had a void where the inner child should have been (Maltz & Holman, 1987).

To conclude, the nature of the incest relationship is more prevalent, less reported, tends to affect the victims to a greater extent than extrafamilial child molestation and the offender recidivates at lower rates (Cyr et al., 2002; Firestone et al., 1999).

CHAPTER

INCEST COMPLEX

Corey Vitello

38

Incest is the great taboo in Western society. Many incest survivors keep their pain and suffering to themselves because of the fear of humiliation, the shame involved, and revictimization brought on by an ignorant society. Families are torn apart and lives are shattered because of this phenomenon.

Throughout the ages, particularly in literature, incest has been described and proliferated (Deaver, 1996). Incest also plays a rather large role in the roots of psychology. Psychoanalytic theory proclaims that all humans are born with a desire to sexually bond with their parents but most children resolve this conflict without incident. However, simply because there is an "explanation" for the basis of the behavior, this does not make the behavior any less objectionable.

DEFINING INCEST

Deriving an adequate definition of incest is difficult because the phenomenon is complicated (Sholevar & Schwoeri, 1999). According to Sholevar and Schwoeri (1999), incest cannot be sufficiently defined unless numerous factors are considered: "... [One] the nature of the act, 2) the degree of the relationship between the parties, and 3) the ages of the parties involved" (p. 77). A typical definition of incest is simply the sexually motivated genital contact between close relatives. From a paraphilic perspective, incest complex is the desire for sexual relations with a relative; from a legal perspective however, incest is a sex crime—generally classified as a felony throughout the United States (Jackson & Sandberg, 1985).

According to Sholevar and Schwoeri (1999), such minimalist definitions do not include the gamut of incestuous behaviors that might better define the phenomena.

> Openly seductive behavior by a relative may be included in a definition of incest, but unless there is involvement of the genitalia or anus of one of the partners, the act cannot be *legally* defined as incest. Therefore, what constitutes incest in a *legal* definition may be too restrictive clinically, because incestuous behavior can include gestures, looks, and touching of a sexually explicit nature [italics in original] (p. 77).

Arguably, by relying on a legal definition of incest the possibility exists that many instances of inappropriate and damaging familial sexual conduct may be overlooked, be misdiagnosed, and consequently, left unpunished.

Additionally, both the relationship between the partners and the age of the partners makes it difficult to legally define an incestuous relationship. For example, Sholevar and Schwoeri (1999) contend that the definition of incest should be extended to include reconstituted and foster families. Specifically, ". . . children, adult stepchildren, and foster and stepchildren are not uniformly or adequately protected by law in all states" (p. 77). Thus, if legal authorities truly desire to protect children from sexually predatory relatives, there is a dire necessity to broaden the legal definition of incest to include these nontraditional relationships. Further, from a clinical standpoint, a narrow definition of incest poses significant problems, ". . . especially when a stepparent's unconscious or even conscious sexual attraction for a stepchild may have been from the beginning a major factor in the decision to marry" (Sholevar & Schwoeri, 1999, p. 77).

How old do the family members have to be to be considered involved in incestuous conduct? When young children become sexually interested in one another, they often participate in what Sholevar and Schwoeri (1999) call "sexual play" (p. 77). "Sexual play may also occur between an older and younger adolescent as a result of impulsiveness, sexual anxiety, or age-related fears about moving in to the adult world. Sexual play, however, is not characterized by the use of force and is usually entered into with some level of *mutual agreement*" [italics in original] (p. 77). Therefore, it is important to examine the context in which the conduct occurs and if the children are relatively similar in age, defining the relationship as incestuous may be overreaching. Sholevar and Schwoeri suggest the age difference between familial partners should be greater than four or five years before the relationship is labeled incestuous.

A California Supreme Court decision decreed that a minor who has sex with a parent shall not be found guilty of incest and cannot be held accomplice to the crime (Chiang, 2001; *People v. Tobias,* 2001). According to *The San Francisco Chronicle* (Chiang, 2001),

> The court overturned a controversial state appeals court ruling that had found a San Jose teenager [16-year-old] an accomplice to the crime [of incest] when she had a sexual relationship with her [38-year-old] father. The lower court said that the jury should have considered her testimony against the father in that context. But . . . the high court said the burden is on the adult to refrain from having sex with the minor (p. A6).

Thus, legally, age is an important factor in determining responsibility for mutually engaging incestuous behavior. According to Justice Janice Rogers Brown, incest is significantly different from other sex crimes because "the act itself is unlawful, whether or not it is consensual or a minor is involved" (Chiang, 2001, p. A6; *People v. Tobias,* 2001). According to the *Chronicle,*

> When a minor is involved, . . . it doesn't matter who initiates the relationship because the minor will always be the victim and can't be convicted of a crime with an adult. . . . [Further, due to the severe stigma associated with incest,] if a child could be charged, the parent could use that threat to keep the minor from reporting the crime (p. A6).

Because the legal system is often the only resource for incest victims to find remedy, it is important to gauge how judges and lawyers view victims of incest. Jackson and Sandberg (1985) examined how rural lawyers and judges attributed blame in incest cases. They found that incest blame depends on numerous factors such as who the offender is, the social context, the situation, and who the victim is. Moreover, male attorneys tend to blame the victim significantly more than female attorneys. What is most disturbing however, is that as incest blame varied, so did sentencing for the offenders. That is, the sentencing of offenders for this criminal act is subjective; lawyers and judges—those individuals who play critical roles in the prosecution of incest cases—are in the position to potentially make light of the harm caused to incest survivors especially if they place even a modicum of blame upon the victim. Consequently, Jackson and Sandberg's study suggests that the legal system cannot guarantee a therapeutic remedy for victims of incest.

PSYCHOANALYTIC THEORY OF INCEST

Psychoanalysts believe the desire to have sexual relations with family members is inherent in all children. They refer to two categories of the incest complex as the Oedipal complex and the Electra complex. The two concepts are relatively similar; the Oedipal complex is a conflict within young boys, and the Electra complex is a conflict within young girls.

Freud believed that during the Phallic Stage of personality development, children begin to focus on the genital region through genital exploration and sexual fantasies (Drapela, 1995). "Autoerotic behaviors emerges; the child is allured by the pleasure brought about through masturbation" (Drapela, 1995, p. 18). It is during this stage that while the child falls in love with the parent of the opposite sex, the child develops hostile feelings toward the parent of the same sex:

> The boy who maintains erotic feelings toward his mother fears that his father will castrate him [castration anxiety]; the girl who is erotically attracted to her father is frustrated since she lacks part of her father's anatomy—the penis [penis envy] (Drapela, 1995, p. 18).

Freud believed that eventually boys and girls resolve this conflict by identifying with the parent of the same sex, thereby repressing the incestuous desires for the parent (Drapela, 1985). For example, a boy will identify with the aggressor by adopting the morals, goals, and mannerisms of his father. "In an indirect fashion, by identifying with his father he can vicariously possess his mother" (Phares, 1991, pp. 82–83) and thus the child satisfies his incestuous desires.

Freud (1966) believed that as personality develops, the child's sexual desire for the parent of the opposite sex "fall[s] victim to infantile amnesia—the forgetting, which veils our earliest youth from us and makes us strangers to it" (p. 326). As stated by Silberstein (1998), "The oedipal sexual wishes experienced by every child for the parent of the opposite sex are recognized as impossible, are desexualized, and are changed into normal filial tenderness" (p. 213).

However, if this resolution through identifying with the aggressor fails for some reason, it is conceivable that the incestuous desires for one's parents, or the desires of a parent for a child will persist through life.

> Failures to maintain the essential generational boundaries throughout the family affects all its members. This may include the childlike dependency of one parent upon the other, the rivalries between parents for the affection and loyalty of a child, the intense parental jealousy of a child, and incestuous proclivities of a parent for a child, including mothers who rid themselves of a husband's desires by offering a daughter as a substitute (Lidz & Fleck, as cited in Silberstein, 1998).

(Researchers in the field of paraphilias have begun to use the term "Cain Complex" to refer to the sibling rivalry that ensues over the affection of the parents.)

INCEST ON THE INTERNET

Although acts of incest are unlawful, this does not dissuade the emergence of numerous websites dedicated to the tabooed practice. Many websites support incestuous behavior, others post pornographic pictures and comic strips claiming to be scenes of incest, and there are still many others, which seek to provide the social support for incest survivors that is tragically limited in most societies.

The website www.realincest.com/ boasts that they only have pictures and videos of authentic incest. They claim to be the real thing—the *truth,* as they put it: sexual encounters between aunts and nephews, uncles and nieces, twin brothers and twin sisters, moms and sons, brothers and sisters, moms and daughters. They offer over thirty incest chat rooms hosting fifteen thousand participants and a "huge incest database, [where] you can contact real people, into real incest!"

One particularly disturbing case of incest posted on this site demonstrated how a mother was able to coerce her son into a sexual relationship:

> That night was hard. It was weird to talk to my son that way. We ended up drinking a lot, and . . . got really drunk. I guess I took charge and talked my son into coming into my bedroom with me. We fell into bed, and almost fell asleep there, but after a while we started touching each other.
>
> (Retrieved October 21, 2002, from www.realincest.com/ricase/)

Ostensibly, this parent took advantage of her child's trust in her as a guardian, manipulated him into a sexual act, and like many sexual predators, used alcohol as a tool of inhibition and impairment in order to seduce her kin.

Another website, www.incestcartoons.com/ entices surfers with elaborately drawn hard-core pornographic comic depictions of incestuous acts. According to the site, these drawings are legal "by ruling of the U.S. Supreme Court anti-virtual child-porn [sic] ruling of Feb/2002." A child can easily stumble onto this disgusting site searching for cartoons on the WEB. The cartoons mimic those same animations familiar to children who watch television on Saturday mornings. There are Japanese-style animations, there are animations so detailed that a child might easily mistaken the fiction for reality. The illustrations are very graphic, combining incest with two values most people relate to: humor and sex. They do this in order to pair these abominable acts with rewarding stimuli to facilitate the conditioning of viewers to incest. They may even be trying to expose children to incest via cartoons in order to normalize the abusive behaviors early on in the children's lives.

A truly troubling site simply addressed, www.incest.com/ claims to provide a dual purpose: "The Incest Help section are for those of you seeking help. The members only and preview sections contain adult oriented material." What makes this site so disturbing is if victims of incest are searching online for support and referral for treatment, they will be led to this site—a site that trivializes, exploits, and promotes incest through pornographic pictures, videos, and commentaries, while at the very same time, it claims to provide assistance for victims. The last thing vulnerable victims who are looking for help need, are to be directed to a site that encourages the acts they are attempting to escape from. Obviously the operators of this website know this.

Although more difficult to locate on the WEB, there is a site genuinely dedicated to help survivors cope with the trauma of incest. This site is sponsored by Survivors of Incest Anonymous, Inc. (SIA) (www.siawso.org/). SIA started in 1982 is intended to be a resource to incest survivors. The organization models itself after such self-help recovery groups as Alcoholics Anonymous.

> There are many emotional problems emerging from the abuse, including inability to trust, perfectionism, phobias, avoidance of both intimacy and emotional bonding. The denial system that insured her survival as a child prevents the survivor from enjoying an unencumbered adulthood.
>
> (Retrieved October 21, 2002 from, www.siawso.org/effects.htm).

SIA defines incest broadly "as a sexual encounter by a family member, or by an extended family member that damaged the child. By 'extended family' member [they] mean a person that you and/or your family has known over a period of time . . . any family member, a family friend, clergy, another child, or anyone that betrayed the child's innocence and trust." SIA recognizes that most perpetrators of incest are also survivors; therefore, each group decides whether it will allow past perpetrators to attend meetings.

CONCLUSION

Incest is unmentionable in most cultures. Both perpetrators and victims (who are often victims themselves) are often labeled and marginalized by uninformed (i.e., ignorant) societies. The legal and popular definitions of incest fail to provide adequate treatment of the etiology, the perpetrators, the victims, and the process of and blame for acts of incest.

Psychoanalysts believe that as all children develop they confront an intrapsychic conflict to have sexual relations with the parent of the opposite gender. They agree that lacking any prepubescent trauma that might interfere with the natural desexualization of feelings towards one's parents, children will develop infantile amnesia and forget that they had these incestuous impulses. Regardless of the psychoanalytical explanation, incest complex is a traumatizing crime that is unfortunately a mainstay on the Internet and an atrocity that has been promulgated throughout history.

C H A P T E R

HEBEPHILIA

Mila Green McGowan

39

All human sexuality can be best described as existing on a continuum in respect to the objects or person of interest, the desired type of sexual activity or the amount of coercion and/or violence involved. As a result, problems arise with the definition and classification of both typical and atypical sexual behaviors. Wincze (1989) refers to any atypical sexual interests as paraphilias and defines a paraphilia as "an extreme degree of investment in, or consumption by, a sexual behavior that dominates and directs a person's sexual practices" (p. 383). Blasingame (2001) specifies that the "essential feature of a paraphilic disorder is the reoccurring sexual urges and sexually arousing fantasies involving either non-human objects, the suffering or humiliation of oneself or one's partner, or children or other non-consenting partners" (as defined by Abel and Osborn, 1992).

HEBEPHILIA, EPHEBOPHILIA AND PEDERASTY

Hebephilia, an adult's sexual interest and attraction to children and adolescents who have reached puberty (Herek, 2002), can be deemed of the coercive type of paraphilias as victims must be convinced in some way to take part in a sexual exchange with an adult. Such an attraction has been described as both a toxic (to the victim) and unorthodox (as a sexual turn-on) (Wincze, 1989) and reflects a psychological propensity (Herek, 2002). Though this definition is not in dispute, there is no agreement about what age group hebephiles are attracted to. While Wincze (1989) reports it is an attraction to adolescents aged fourteen and older, Freund (1981) suggests it is a preference for pubescents aged eleven to sixteen, and still others maintain the interest is towards any youth under the age of eighteen (www.philianews.org). Regardless of age discrepancy, the key definitional component to hebephilia (and ephebophilia and pederasty) is an attraction to youth who are post-pubertal but pre-adulthood.

The ambiguity in regards to victim age may be rooted in the original concepts used to create the term hebephilia. The etymological meaning for hebephilia comes from the Greek legal term *hebe* meaning "the time before manhood" (before sixteen years of age). In some sources *hebe* also means "the time before fourteen years of age," and a Roman source is quoted as defining *hebe* as "the time before eighteen years of age." Overall, *hebe* has come to mean *youth* after the Grecian deity Hebe, who was the god and protector of adolescents and youth. The ending *philia* means deep love or friendship (www.philianews.org). Hebephilia is also referred to in the literature as ephebophilia as the Greek term *ephebo* translates to "one arrived at adolescence—a youth of eighteen or older who is still not an adult" (www.girlgarden.org).

Regardless of the exact age range of youth that hebephiles or ephebophiles are attracted to, Herek (2002) clarifies that the term hebephile is only a diagnostic label; people do not have to act out towards youth to have such a propensity nor to gain the label. Further, he asserts that hebephiles may have little or no sexual orientation (e.g., heterosexual or homosexual) despite myths about sex offenders to the contrary (for example, homosexuals molest children). Blasingame (2001) reports that a hebephile's actions may not always be criminal and will vary in both frequency and severity, ranging from unacknowledged fantasies to the sole means for erotic arousal. He further asserts hebephilic interest, like other paraphilias, are often part of stress reduction efforts of an individual, and end up being integrated into other aspects of a person's life, lifestyle and identity.

Both men and women can be hebephiles, though one prolific hebephile defines his "type" as usually males that appreciate the beauty of post-pubertal girls aged fourteen to seventeen (www.girlgarden.org). A pederast, on the other hand, is the academic and self-imposed term defining a man whose primary sexual interest is in post-pubescent boys (Gonsioreh, Bera, & LeTourneau, 1994).

TYPOLOGIES IN HEBEPHILIA

Two types of hebephiles have been outlined in the literature: fixated and regressed. Fixated hebephiles are exclusively interested in pubertal adolescents, and are subject to a "permanent or temporary arrest of psychological maturation resulting from unresolved formative issues which persist (into adulthood)" (Groth and Birnhaum, 1978 in Herek, 2002). Regressed hebephiles "once (had) a more mature form of sexual expression but now have either temporarily or permanently returned to an earlier stage of development" (Groth & Birnhaum, 1978 in Herek, 2002). Groth and Birnhaum also believe that certain life circumstances, such as extreme stress, can create the regressed hebephile; stress returns them to a less mature psychological state and leads to their sexual interest in teens.

PREVALENCE AND COURSE OF HEBEPHILIA

As Abel and Osborn (1992) report, "it is nearly impossible to determine the frequency of deviant sexual behavior in the general public because reporting deviant interests could be a socially undesirable response and could, potentially, result in self-incrimination." (p. 677). As such, it is unknown how many people can be referred to or self-identify as hebephiles. If we turn to victim statistics, Freund, Heasman, and Roper (1982) report that in a ten-year period in Minneapolis, approximately 792 sexual abuse cases involved either children or pubescents (as reported by Jaffe et al., 1975). An earlier study found 23 percent of all sex crime victims in a five-year period in Washington, D.C., were aged ten to fourteen years old (Hayman & Lanza, 1971 in Freund et al., 1982). Unfortunately, these and other criminal justice statistics are of no help as they do not tell us who abused these pubescent victims. Further, as the Minneapolis statistics reveal, sexual crimes perpetrated against anyone younger than age eighteen are referred to as child molestation and often misrepresent hebephilic acts by lumping them in with pedophilic acts.

Typically, the onset of hebephilia occurs in adolescence (Blasingame, 2001) as almost all paraphilias have been found to begin prior to the age of 21. Abel and Osborn (1992) found, in their work with pedophiles, pedophilia against boys has an average age of onset of 18.2 years old while against girls, an average age of onset of 21.6 years was found. Mohr (1981, as cited in Freund et al., 1982) reported a trimodal age distribution of sex offenders against youth as three peaks were found clustered around the ages 15 to 19, 34, and 55 years old. Offenders in their 30s, who represented the greatest number in Mohr's (1981) work, are thought to represent true and chronic hebephiles (among other paraphiles).

THE DEVELOPMENT OF HEBEPHILIA

Wincze (1989) believes that the development of paraphilias are related to certain background factors, such as experiencing childhood sexual abuse, the lack of a consistent parental environment, sexual ignorance, poor stress-coping abilities, and low self-esteem. Further, he clarifies that despite initial scientific beliefs, abnormal hormonal or genetic conditions are not found more frequently in people with paraphilias.

Behavioral theorists blame such atypical sexual behaviors as hebephilia on faulty childhood learning environments in which opportunities to cross normative sexual boundaries are experienced and reinforced (either directly by abuse or indirectly by observation). Further, repeated experiences with the actual behavior or fantasies coupled with sexual arousal and orgasm strengthens the paraphilic interest over time (Wincze, 1989).

Cognitive theorists hypothesize that certain attitudes, held either within a society or by an individual, facilitate the development of paraphilias. Such beliefs, like conservative sexual ideas, a rigid adherence to traditional sex roles, and the endorsement of adversarial sexual interactions, have repeatedly been linked to sexually inappropriate or violent sexual behaviors (Wincze, 1989; Prendergast, 1991). Another developmental explanation focuses on anomalies in erotic development: delays or advancements in either physical and/or psychological maturation or the missing of "critic developmental periods." One hebephile agrees with this latter explanation, saying "hebephiles tends to have the emotional and sexual desires on the level of the average teen; are not congruent with people their own chronological age" (www.girlgarden.org).

GENETIC, ENVIRONMENTAL AND FAMILIAL ISSUES AFFECTING HEBEPHILIC DEVELOPMENT

As touched on by Groth and Birnhaum (1978 in Herek) and Blasingame (2001), very specific emotional states, such as anxiety, anger, frustration, desperation, are thought to serve as precursors to acting out paraphilic interests. Miccio-Fonseca (2001) believes these stress reactions may be partly the result of internalized "lovemaps," which are templates that exist in the minds of hebephiles (and other paraphiles), thought to be located in the temporal lobes of the brain. These idiosyncratic maps provide an individual with idealized sexuoerotic activity and lovers. Throughout development, our "map" is influenced by our socialization regarding sexuality, our family's lovemaps and sexual history, individual psychological characteristics, inherited propensities, physical growth, the presence of abuse and our sexual status within the family (Miccio-Fonseca, 2001).

Despite claims that hebephiles often report no sexual orientation, some researchers have asserted that the development of certain types of hebephilia (hetero- versus homosexual) and the resulting sexual offenses and recidivism rates, are associated with differences in mean pubertal age. Mean pubertal age is defined as the physiological and behavioral indicators relating to puberty, and include markers such as the age of first orgasm/ejaculation, of first masturbation, of the onset of sexual feelings, fantasy and arousal, of voice change, and of interpersonal sexual activity. Blanchard and Dickey (1998) studied 69 homosexual hebephiles and 130 heterosexual hebephiles (all male), with reported victims aged twelve to fifteen years old. When comparing them to samples of both androphiles (offenders attracted to adults) and pedophiles of both orientations, they found that the age of puberty onset, at first ejaculation and at first masturbation were all earlier for homosexual hebephiles than for heterosexual hebephiles. However, despite their expectations, mean pubertal age, regardless of sexual orientation, was not significantly different between pedophiles, hebephiles or androphiles. "These results suggest that there is no association between pubertal age and erotic preference for the immature physique per se" (Blanchard & Dickey, 1998, p. 280).

Blanchard and Bogaert (1998) further investigated the effect fraternal birth order (how many older and/or younger brothers the male sex offender has) on the development of hebephilia. They found homosexual hebephiles had a high fraternal birth order while pedophiles, of either orientation, did not evidence this effect, nor any sensitivity to maternal birth order. Interestingly, previous studies undertaken by the same researchers found a fraternal birth order effect in both homo- and hetero-sexual androphiles. Father-son relationships and the effect they have on later hebephilic behavior were reviewed by Freund et al. (1982). According to a study they cite (Gebhard, Gagnon, Pomeroy & Christenson, 1965), hebephiles that target males aged fourteen to seventeen reported very poor relationships with their fathers, poorer than those reported by pedophiles that prefer male victims. This same effect was not found in hebephiles that target female victims.

THE PSYCHOLOGY OF HEBEPHILES AND ENGAGING YOUNG VICTIMS

Prendergast (1991) outlines the key control methods hebephiles employ with their victims in order to not only commit the abuse, but to gain control over other aspects of the victim's life. Their goal is to make the youth dependant on them for love, affection, and support. Most importantly, the hebephile uses seduction to satisfy their own need for acceptance. "Getting a youth to cooperate in their own seduction, no matter how minor, provides [a sense of great] control-produced satisfaction for the offender" (Prendergast, 1991, p. 36). The seduction is related to feelings of inadequacy the hebephile has always harbored.

Consistently, hebephiles show a desperate need for acceptance from their victims, so generally they are gentle and friendly while being persuasive. They use money, gifts, privileges and friendship to accomplish their goals and have great patience to first form a trusting relationship with the youth prior to getting their own sexual needs met. Their goal, when engaging in initial sexual exploration with the victim, is to have the victim sexually satisfied so they will like the hebephile and return for more (Prendergast, 1991). Often the hebephile's choice of sex act totally depends on the hebephile's own early sexual molestation and trauma (Freund, 1981). Overall, hebephiles are characterized as manipulative, cunning, and seductive offenders (hence coercive paraphiles) who try to "psych" their victims into compliance, as physical violence is extremely infrequent. When angered or threatened with the loss of the "relationship," the hebephile may threaten to use compromising photographs of the youth as blackmail (Prendergast, 1991). "Once the victim is hooked, the offender can become more bold and more overtly sexual in his/her behavior" (Prendergast, 1991, p. 34).

Many hebephiles report in therapy the "unrealistic small penis complex" (Prendergast, 1991, p. 88). After years of comparing his penis to other males' of his age, the hebephile feels inadequate (he ignores the idea that flaccid penis size is not a determinant of true prowess). In his distorted value system, a small penis makes him less of a man, unable to satisfy either a grown woman or man. The hebephile rationalizes he must become involved with those younger than him because they will not judge him (because of a lack of sexual experience) or will have organs the same size as his. Many hebephiles also report the cognitive distortion that "sex equals love." They rationalize their offenses with "I'm showing you love, I want you to feel good because I love you." They can then believe they are not harming the youth but loving them.

HEBEPHILIA COMPARED TO PEDOPHILIA

One must clearly distinguish hebephiles from pedophiles. Hebephiles are only interested in post-pubertal youth; youth that are capable of enjoying sex to orgasm. The youth they target tend to be easily led or influenced, and may be of either sex. They look for youth who can be controlled and who pose no physical threat. Hebephiles desire a sexual partner with whom they can have an affair and yet with whom they cannot live (because of society), thereby avoiding the risk of failure in a relationship (Prendergast, 1991). In the informal hierarchy of sex offenders, each paraphilic type judges others' behavior as far worse, not understanding the other's choice of victim or actions (Freund, 1981; Prendergast, 1991). Hebephiles may say, "I can't understand those guys [pedophiles] having sex with six and seven year olds. There's nothing there and they can't really do anything. It just doesn't make sense" (Prendergast, 1991, p. 140).

HEBEPHILIA HISTORICALLY

As Wincze (1989) remarks "all sexual behavior falls on a continuum and is defined by the laws and cultural mores of a society" (p. 383). This is key to any discussion of hebephilia. As one astute hebephile writes, "most adult heterosexual men have a degree of sexual attraction to young teen girls as this was once considered both normal and species adaptive" (for evolutionary reasons) (www.girlgarden.org). Historically, sex with youth who were able to procreate was not a perversion, nor a crime, but required. Towards the end of the nineteenth century, as the lifespan of humans increased, and the infant mortality rate decreased in developed nations, youth under age eighteen became "off-limits" as sexual partners for adults. So at that time, hebephilic attractions became seen as deviant, abhorrent, and pathological.

Today, a conflicting message regarding youth and sexuality still exists in the Western world. Specifically, in North America, age of consent laws vary by state and country; for example, in over 50 percent of the states, a youth of sixteen years old may consent to sex, but they are not recognized as an adult until eighteen years of age (www.girlgarden.org). In a few states and Canada, age of consent is fourteen years old. Worldwide, the average age of consent is also fourteen years old. The resulting disparity between the concepts of sexual consent and legal adulthood causes both legal and conceptual confusion for society; not to mention hebephiles and their victims.

COMMENTARY

Hebephilia, as a paraphilia, is not as easily distinguished as criminal or "perverted" as other paraphilias, such as necrophilia or pedophilia. Our present-day American culture, which pervades much of the rest of the world, has blurred the lines between youth and adulthood. On the one hand, we have legally established age guidelines for voting, driving, drinking, military service, and ability to consent to sex. Yet, on the other hand, these boundaries as often artificial and superfluous in many ways. Adults are repeatedly bombarded with messages of youth and youth culture and encouraged at every turn to act young, think young, and look young. Growing up (and old) is not valued, especially for women. Americans have become obsessed with youth, yet are horrified and disgusted when the obsession with youthfulness becomes a sexual attraction.

The media represents society's values and in doing so reflect what Americans have come to see as acceptable and the "norm." As such, television, movies, magazines, and the like, bombard consumers with images of sexualized and eroticized adolescents and children. Singers like Britney Spears wear next to nothing in public and on stage, yet maintain they are chaste, saying their clothes are part of self-expression. This may be so, but no one chastises the grown man who says such young women are "hot." The same can be said for many male youth in the modeling, sports, or music scene, and their throng of adoring older fans. A young girl doesn't stop to think twice when an adult male only five to six years older than she shows sexual interest; they boast about it to their friends, as he does to his. Conversely, young men are portrayed as fantasizing about having sexual contact with much older and experienced women (e.g., *The Graduate, American Pie*). Entire industries are built on hebephilic tendencies, e.g., Larry Flynt's magazine *Barely Legal* and sexy underwear lines for preteens, and they incur no large public outcry all in the name of capitalism.

Other cultures around the world do not recognize hebephilia as a concern as their religious traditions encourage marriages between much older men and young girls. These unions are based on the paternalistic rationale that women must be chaste before marriage and have only sexual relations with a husband. Interestingly, these same cultures do not encourage marriages between two young people nor do they hold males in their societies up to the same high moral standards as females. Even in America, various cultural and ethnic minorities are not surprised by nor uncomfortable with older male relatives engaging in sexual activity with their adolescent girls.

As for the confusing age of consent issue forwarded by one hebephile earlier (www.girlgarden.com), he fails to acknowledge that, though youth at a certain age can consent to sexual acts, be it fourteen or sixteen, most states have age-span provisions written into their criminal code so that sex between consenting teens and sex between a teen and an adult is distinguished. For example, statutory rape in some states occurs not only when someone under the consent age agrees to sex with someone older but also when someone over the age of consent but more than five years younger than the adult partner does so.

In sum, it appears that understanding the development of and the possible increase in hebephilia in present day American society is no easy task. It clearly involves a critical dismantling of not only various cultural and ethnic influences, but also paying attention to the media and the family's roles in socializing growing sexual beings.

CHAPTER

INFANTILISM
An Exploration and Discovery
Dawn Alley

Infantilism, also known as autonepiophilia (Money, 1986) is a paraphilia characteristic of a masquerade in which an individual is symbolically transformed back to infancy. Males with the average age of thirty-eight, with a bachelor's degree or higher, dutifully employed, and who are either married or are partnered comprise 95 percent of infantilists (Speaker, 1989). However, because of the limited number of studies conducted on infantilism in addition to the lack of women who self-identify, this number is offered with caution. Still, if a partner is involved she treats the infantilist according to the generally accepted roles and scripts of an infant. Emblematically, the individual adorns himself in the dress, characteristics, and products of an infant (e.g., diapers, pacifier, bottle, in fetal stance, etc.). In this role, the infantilist gains pleasure from being helpless and out of control. This paraphilia is believed to begin in childhood, as the individual realizes the pleasure gained from wearing diapers but does not reach culmination until adulthood (Speaker, 1989).

Clarification of the term infantilism as a paraphilia and as a medical condition needs to be made from the onset: the paraphilic infantilist prefers to wear diapers as opposed to someone with incontinence who has a medical need to wear them. Another medical condition also termed sexual infantilism is the failure to develop sexually due to an endocrine disorder wherein the ovaries or testes fail to develop and/or function (Columbia University, 2002).

In the current context, the term psychosexual infantilism refers to a sexual expression wherein an individual regresses to an infantile state and voluntarily surrenders personal control (Steckel, 1952). Unlike Steckel who postulated infantilists were disturbed individuals and constricted in their psychological development a more accurate depiction is formed from recent, albeit scanted studies and from an intimate look into the infantilists' community. What emerges is a general awareness of the individual's involvement, the practice itself, some of the precursory factors, and the reasons for maintaining the practice. Deriving from these accounts is a basic understanding of individuals who seek nurturance, love, and acceptance by reaching back to a time when such care was longed for or willingly given.

CLINICAL PRESENTATION AND DIAGNOSTIC ASSESSMENT

According to the *DSM-IV* the criteria for diagnosing infantilism is categorized within the Sexual Masochism Disorders (American Psychiatric Association [APA], 2000). However, because of the general lack of humiliation or bondage an NOS criteria is applicable (i.e., most infantilists do not use degradation or servility). The practice of the infantilist appears to be consistent and stable over time, however, the incidents typically increase during periods of acute stress (Money, 1986) must be present and reoccurring for six months for diagnosis to be made (APA, 2000). Although Sexual Masochism is usually chronic with frequent occurrences, the practice may continue without elevation in severity (Money, 1986).

Continued exploration reveals infantilism to be expiating acceptance as it stands with other moderately accepted sexually deviant practices (e.g., masturbation) bordering that which is accepted and that which is condemned (e.g., homosexuality and pedophilia respectively). Emerging is an increasing prevalent acceptance of the infantilist activity due to it's benign nature, consensual participation, and general concordance with an ordinary and healthy sexual life (Baumeister & Butler, 1997). Here, infantilism is not viewed as pathologic. Rather pathology would only ensue when the practice became an essential component of sexuality, such that without the practice no sexual pleasure could be achieved. Furthermore, pathology is inevitable if the occurrence of the practice takes precedence over a shared relationship (Thornton & Mann, 1997). Accordingly, when the fantasy dominates the individual's sex life, he or she will internalize and begin to replace a once normal and functioning sexual value system with a hedonistic, impersonal, and isolitory practice that perpetuates irreality. Once a refuge, now the individual may recluse into a self-inflicted barrier from social inclusion and self-acceptance.

Emotional intimacy is inevitably disengaged if the practice is done in isolation wherein a sense of entitlement may be instilled (Baumeister & Butler, 1997). Further, the individuals may feel that others are punitively restrained from engaging similar fantasy due to societal disproval. Therefore, they may feel justified or obliged to impose their fantasy onto others. If emotional loneliness is attributed onto others and is paired with the infantilist's own sexual fantasy and if the fantasy continues in isolation the capacity for violence and the likelihood of offending increases (Thornton & Mann, 1997). However, it would appear the most likely progression is directed to sadism, exhibited into transposing the loss of control onto others who are equally willing (Hallin, 1997). Others maintain that sexual masochism in the form of infantilism is one of the safest and potentially acceptable sexually deviant practices, which simply allows them to breakaway from the daily stresses of self and society (Baumeister & Butler, 1997).

ETIOLOGY

Numerous theories have attempted to explain psychosexual infantilism. Three will be considered here: one emphasizing mental templates of normal sexual development (Money, 1996), the second emphasizing learning theory (Cooper, 1993), and the third emphasizing a conscious escape from reality (Baumeister, 1991).

LOVEMAPS

Money (1986) introduced the concept of lovemaps describing them as schematic templates of nurture and imprinted by social influences. Ideally, the lovemaps help encode normal imagery and ideation of sexuality. With continued unresponsive care or trauma (e.g., sexual abuse) the development of the mental templates are interrupted and distortions may occur. For instance, if the template for sexual development is thwarted during infancy an individual's sexual fruition is likely to remain in an infantile state (Money, 1986). The individual is left alone to make sense of sexuality. Attempts to recapitulate past experiences are often made from broken bits of misguided, neglectful, or abusive information that is often distorted because of the negative impact of the adverse experience (Alley, 2000). Deriving sexual enjoyment is likely to occur from an immature regression back to infancy.

LEARNING THEORY

Learning theory as it relates to behavior has been defined as the capacity for behavioral change due to experiences (Lieberman, 1993). The notion here is that a fixation occurred in development and is later recalled and acted upon in adulthood. In support for this McGuire, Carlie, and Young (1965) reported a case in which a young boy witnessed a girl through a window in only her underwear. Thereafter, the image of the girl was thought of when the boy masturbated. This mental image was recalled frequently with sexual gratification as the rewarding outcome. As an adult then, sexual gratification came from the association of woman's undergarments both on a visual and tactile level. Similarly individuals with infantilism have equivalent conditioned responses. One infantilist named "Baby Jamie" described his own story of association as developing around eight as a result of viewing an advertisement for diapers. The affection that was depicted in this advert sparked an inquiry and eventually a deep desire for the perceived love and affection gained when a mother cared for an infant by changing his diaper (Baby Jamie, 2002). Jamie recalled the feeling of being loved and cared for when being diapered coupled with the soft warm feeling that he gleamed from wearing the diaper, he then associated that sensational feeling with being loved. Drawing on this association he disclosed that around the age of twelve he achieved his first orgasm as a result of wearing diapers. Since then he states that he engages in infantilistic acts for comfort and sexual gratification although his sexuality is not solely driven by the adult-baby role he assumes (Baby Jamie, 2002).

ESCAPE THEORY

The fact that life can be overwhelming, ensued with self-awareness, stressful situations and riddled with responsibility provides the third explanation for infantilism. Baumeister (1991) purposed his theory of self-escape as the process of cognitive deconstruction. In this view there are two levels of thinking, which are connected to an individual's awareness of identity. At the highest level of awareness lies meaningful thoughts, mental constructs, inhibitions, standards, and expectations. At the lowest level of awareness lies concrete thinking, impulsivity, sensation, and immediacy. According to this theory the infantilist returns to a more concrete level of thinking and reasoning whereby the individual avoids sometimes painful self-evaluations and potentially stressful life situations and responsibilities (Baumeister, 1991). If one retreats, or deconstructs as it were, to the lower level of awareness, the individual is able to engage in their practice with a trusted partner without fear or judgment. Indeed, one infantilist described his practice as a place for coping where he could relax and escape from his daily routine (Baby Jamie, 2002).

CHARACTERISTICS AND PRACTICE

Infantilists distinguish within themselves at least two groups: adult babies and diaper lovers (Baby Jamie, 2002). Diaper lovers wear diapers for the sole pleasure and sexual gratification of how the diaper feels, smells, and sounds. Adult babies also gleam pleasure and sexual gratification from the diaper, but they gain fulfillment when engaged in playing the role of the infant. Roles within psychosexual infantilism consist of dominant and submissive characters. Because the male is often identified as the adult baby (Money, 1986), their role is often submissive. The adult baby surrenders control to a dominant role (i.e., the Mommy) whereby this individual provides comfort and nurturance as she plays out the part of mum. Those without a regular partner seek out professionals to fulfill this role (i.e., prostitute or dominatrix) Although some disciplinary fantasies are played out, they are usually playful and nonviolent (Baby Jamie, 2002).

Adult sexual practices are usually separate from the adult-baby play and frequently take place after the role-play has concluded (Baby Jamie, 2002). Contrary to the notion that sexual gratification is only gained by wearing the diapers, those whom are self-proclaimed infantilists clarify that they also gain sexual pleasure outside the adult-baby play (Baby Jamie, 2002). Thus, separating and distinguishing infantilism from fetishism wherein the infantilist receives pleasure apart from the diaper and the role of an infant. Further clarification reveals that the adult-baby play is often used as a means of coping to relax (Baby Jamie, 2002), or as a means to feel love and acceptance (Baumeister & Butler, 1997; Money, 1986). Although predominately fun and playful in nature, one infantilist explained that mild humiliation added an exciting dimension occasionally brought into the adult-baby role (Baby Mako, cited in Money, 1986). Here, Baby Mako described an occurrence when he was put to bed wearing the customary diaper and a bottle while his wife played a game of cards with friends. After having soiled himself he called to his wife, who in turn reproved him in front of her friends, thereafter when the wife had finished entertaining, the two fulfilled his fantasy through coitus (Money, 1986).

Another element not often discussed in either the literature or in the infantilist community is urination or defecation. One unidentified man only referred to as "Big baby" stated that this element was often uncomfortable and messy (cited in Baby Jamie, 2002). Another infantilist, known as Bitter Grey confirmed this notion stating that the process of trying to soil the diaper was difficult because his bladder (or as he referred to it his "shy bladder") would not respond; he went on to explain that this element is pleasantly absent from his practice.

CONCLUSIONS

Initially, when embarking on this examination it was presumed that pathology surrounded the infantilist and most of the paraphilic behavior(s) however, what has been revealed is a fairly innocent type of sexual foreplay that is a distant cry from being deviant and instead could be considered to be simply a variant of sexual behavior. As stated previously, this is generally a harmless, consensual act, typically involving two individuals one in a submissive role and the other in the dominant role where the adult play is symbolically representative of infantile state. Although not all the stories of infantilism are so tender, some have derived as a result of abuse or neglect as a child (Money, 1986), and others revealed personal devastation when a partner rejects them because of their practice (Baby Jamie, 2002). Infantilism does not appear to be an atrocious act of degradation superciliously described by Steckel (1959). Once an arcane practice it would appear that psychosexual infantilism is becoming less of a paraphilia and more of an alternative sexual expression and release. Surrounding the ever increasing and diverse infantilistic community is an equally increasing support system that is working to break the barriers of silence and shame attributed to this practice (e.g., Diaper Pail Fraternity, Adult Baby World, & Infantae Press).

The infantilist is someone who has a deep desire for love and comfort coupled with a need to depart from the stresses inherent in daily activities (Baumeister & Butler, 1997; Money, 1986; Thornton & Mann, 1997). They willingly surrender control and regress back to infancy so that the lovely, accepting, and nurturing feelings once experienced or longed for can be achieved. The fact that they are willing to disclose the potentially incriminating fantasy to a partner and risk rejection and that the partner is willing and supportive may suggest a functional, honest, and courageous relationship. On the other hand, there are extremes in every situation and certainly this has been shown here (Big Baby, 2002; Baby Mako, cited in Money, 1986).

Craving for extra attention or longing to return to a time when there was no deadline, no responsibility, or no obligation is not an obscure deviant desire, instead it appears to be common.

Infantilists take the unspoken desire into a conjoining practice played out with the help of symbolism and the willing surrender of control in a nonviolent and safe environment.

FEMALE SEX OFFENDERS

Breaking the Mold the Hard Way

S TEPHANIE G AUDENTI

PREVALENCE OF OFFENDING

The extent of this phenomenon is difficult to assess given the paucity of the data and the estimated underreporting of female sex offenders (Condy, Templer, Brown, & Veaco, 1987). In 1972, Mathis concluded that sexual offending among females was so rare that it was "of little significance." In 1977, Mohr added that sexual offending was "virtually unknown among women," and in 1984, Freund, Heasman, Racansky, and Glancy declared that pedophilia . . . does not exist in women.

According to the Bureau of Justice statistics, during 1994 there were approximately 234,000 offenders convicted of rape or sexual assault under the care, custody, or control of corrections agencies. Despite common beliefs, modern research suggests that females may account for as many as 13 percent of the abuse of females and 24 percent of the abuse of males (Finkelhor & Russell, 1984) with up to 6 percent of the abuse against females and 14 percent of the abuse of males being done without a male accomplice.

In a news article posted on abcnews.com, the Bureau of Justice stated that 96 percent of sexual assaults reported in 1999 involved male perpetrators. In an unpublished study by Graham it was estimated that over 24% of male sex offenders had a history of sexual abuse by a female. Women accounted for about 16% of all felons convicted in State courts in 1996: 8% of convicted violent felons, 23% of property felons, and 17% of drug felons (Bureau of Justice). A comparative analysis published by the Safer Society Press estimated that approximately 5 percent of sexual offenders are female (Turner & Turner 2001). C. Allen used Census Bureau data to estimate that 1.5 million females may have experienced abuse by females and that possibly 1.6 million males have been abused by females (Turner & Turner 2001).

REASONS FOR UNDERREPORTING

Men are generally believed to be the sex offenders and females are believed to be the traditional victims of sex offenders. Throughout history, the connection between women and any form of sexuality has been a sensitive subject, particularly the idea of women sexually offending against others. When one adds helpless, innocent children as victims, the stage is set for a perfectly taboo situation. Women are thought of as the mothers, the nurturers and protectors of innocence. This may be one reason why there is an underreporting of female sexual offenders, because no one wants to think of women as predators or perverts, although that is often not the case in female sex offenses.

According to Marvasti (1986), society is more comfortable with women touching children than men. It is perceived as nurturing. A transition from a woman's touch being nurturing or caressing to being harmful or abusive may be difficult to envision, whereas men engaging in similar behaviors may be perceived as abusive (Plummer, 1981). Another reason for underreporting by the victims themselves may be the child's attachment to their mother as their primary caretaker and the reluctance to lose the parent on whom they are primarily dependent (Groth, 1979).

Elliot, (1993) notes that mothers often being the accompanying parent to their children's doctor's appointments may be able to prevent the health-care worker from discovering abusive situations as they are there to guide their children's answers to the doctor's questions and serve as a reinforcement of fear if the child begins to allude to the abuse. Wilkins (1990) and Krug (1989) believe that the medical field is only recently beginning to realize that females are not only capable, but do commit sexual offenses. When dealing with male victims, a sexually abusive incident committed by an adult female on an adult male is often minimized, supported by the stereotype that males are not capable of being abused by women, particularly sexually. The media serves as a reinforcer of this myth. The website http://www.breakingthesilence.com addresses attitudes that often endure when an adolescent male is sexually abused by a woman: "He got lucky," "broken in by an older woman," "congratulations," "now you're a man," "tell us all the details." Sexual abuse by women is still considered by much of American society as 'seduction' when it involves a male—not abuse!

Matthew Mendel in his book *The Male Survivor,* explores potential reasons why society refuses to acknowledge female abusers. In his study, he found the following reasons accounting for this phenomenon:

- Self-fulfilling assumption that female perpetration is rare or non-existent
- Denial of female sexuality and aggression
- Belief that sexual interaction with an older female is benign or positive

- Greater leeway given to females than males in their physical interaction
- Greater tendency for female perpetration to be interfamilial
- Greater tendency for female perpetration to be covert
- Assumption that female perpetrators act under the initiation or coercion of male perpetrators
- Overextension of feminist explanation of child sexual abuse as stemming from male violence and power differentials between the sexes
- Politically based avoidance of acknowledgment of female perpetration

Mendel also notes that there is far more publicity surrounding cases involving male on male abuse than there is about females being sex offenders.

There is also the myth that males cannot respond physically by becoming erect or ejaculating when they are being subjected to sexual abuse. Sarrel and Masters (1982) conducted a study of eleven males who were molested by females, and conclude that a male's sexual arousal can occur in a variety of emotional states including anger and terror.

One negative reinforcer for males reporting physical abuse by females is the social consequence that they face after such an event. Elliot and Briere (1994) suggest that this is mainly because of the denial and shame attached to being a male victim in Western societies. These "social consequences" may be perceived or real, but still serve to ensure the underreporting of sexual assault of males by females (Williams, 1995).

CHARACTERISTICS OF FEMALE SEX OFFENDERS

Brown, Hall and Panesis (1984) characterizes the majority of female sexual offenders as being between the ages of seventeen to twenty-four (Mathews, Matthews, & Speltz, 1989) add that they typically come from low socioeconomic status and are poorly educated. Wolfe (1985) states that they also generally deny or minimize their behavior, and have substance abuse problems (Mathews et al., 1989). Mendel's study found that female sexual offenders committed their first offense during their mid-teens. Overall, this does not vary much from research results based on male sexual offenders. While O'Conner (1987) argues that the majority of female sex offenders are psychotic, most researchers adamantly disagree. (Grier, Clark & Stoner, 1993; Marvasti, 1986; Wolfe, 1985).

TYPOLOGIES OF SEXUAL ABUSE

Female sex offenders have been convicted of numerous forms of sexual abuse including physical sexual abuse to nonphysical sexual abuse such as exhibitionism and fetishism. Mathews et al. (1989) created three typologies of female sex offenders:

male-coerced, teacher/lover or predisposed. In a Canadian study of nineteen female sexual offenders, it was found that most women fit the male-coerced category (Mathews et al., 1989; Knopp & Lackey, 1987).

Information on whether the women had co-offenders, was available in eighteen of the nineteen cases. Of these eighteen women, 90 percent (sixteen) had co-offenders and 10 percent (two) did not. "In summary, of the eleven women for whom enough information was available, only one fit the classification of teacher/lover. Four were found to fit the male-coerced typology. However, five of the offenders fit into an older classification scheme developed by Mathews (1987a): male accompanied. One of the five was both predisposed and male-accompanied. Male-accompanied offenders co-offend with a male and are more active participants in the abuse against their victims than male-coerced. The distinction Mathews (1987a) made between male-coerced and male-accompanied is important. The researchers note that additional categories should be added to the existing typologies to best explain the existing patterns of female sexual offenders. They identify these categories as angry-impulsive and male-accompanied familial and non-familial.

Other typologies of female sexual offenders exist, including Faller (1987) who classified female sex offenders as: single-parent, polyincestuous, psychotic, adolescent, and noncustodial abuse. McCarty (1986) categorized female sex offenders as co-offenders, accomplices, or independent offenders. Furthermore, Sarrel and Masters (1982) suggested classifying female sexual offenders as: forced assault, babysitter abuse, incestuous abuse, and dominant woman abuse. Although, Faller (1987), McCarty (1986), and Sarrel and Masters (1982) have classified female sex offenders by offense characteristics, Mathews et al. (1989) developed their female sex offender typologie: teacher/lover, male-coerced, and predisposed, based on offender motivation to commit sexual offenses. Atkinson (1995) agrees that motivational typologies are the most useful in understanding female sex offenders.

Psychiatrist Janet Warren and psychologist Julia Hislop (2001) in their research of female sex offenders, developed the following typologies:

- Facilitators—women who intentionally aid men in gaining access to children for sexual purposes

- Reluctant partners—women in long-term relationships who go along with sexual exploitation of a minor out of fear of being abandoned

- Initiating partner—women who want to sexually offend against a child and who may do it themselves or get a man or another woman to do it while they watch

- Seducers and lovers—women who direct their sexual interest against adolescents and develop an intense attachment

- Pedophiles—women who desire an exclusive and sustained sexual relationship with a child (a very rare occurrence)

- Psychotic—women who suffer from a mental illness and who have inappropriate sexual contact with children as a result

DIFFERENCES BETWEEN MALE VS. FEMALE OFFENDERS

One difference between male and female sex offenders is that female sex offenders are less likely to become physically violent toward their victims (Johnson & Shrier, 1987; Marvasti, 1986;). Mendel (1995) found that female sexual offenders are typically not as predatory as male sexual offenders in that they do not tend to actively seek out their victims, rather let victims come to them. He found that female sexual offenders do not usually have as many victims either. According to Mendel (1995), female offenders often wait longer before reoffending than males and tend to take fewer risks in their offenses by developing relationships with their victims before they abuse them.

Hollida Wakefield, who has worked with sex offenders for more than 20 years, states that female sexual offenders "don't seem to be pedophiles like men" (Robinson, 2001). She questions female sexual offenders sexual interest in young children, claiming that she doubts women are typically sexually attracted to their victims, whereas some men often show a preference for children as opposed to same age partners.

Mendel's (1995) study also revealed that the motivation with female sexual offenders tend to differ from males. He noted that the majority of female sexual offenders that he interviewed claimed that they abused their victims to punish the child when they misbehaved or to make the child feel as bad as they did. They frequently denied that the acts had anything to do with sex. This is much different from male offenders who often claim that they were sexually educating the children or that the children came on to them first. Mendel (1995) believes that the commonality of the two groups is that they are both seeking power and control over a powerless population.

REASONS/FORUMS FOR OFFENDING

According to Katherine Ramsland, women sometimes turn to their male children when there is a lack of a continuous relationship with a male adult. Their child becomes a substitute lover. Loneliness has been found to be a driving force in female sexual offenders (Robinson, 2001). Sometimes, these women sexually abuse their children in an attempt to upset their adult male partners. Ramsland (Robinson, 2001) adds that "these female perpetrators generally come from chaotic homes." Ramsland (Robinson, 2001) addresses another subgroup of the female sexual offender population, those women who seduce adolescent men with gifts, alcohol, or simply with their sex. She references a specific court case in which a forty-two-year-old woman was convicted in Florida of contributing to the delinquency of a minor because she offered a fifteen-year-old boy "gifts of alcohol and drugs in exchange for sex." Also in Florida, a thirty-two-year-old female teacher was convicted of having sex with a fifteen-year-old student. Upon her conviction, she claimed that she "loved him the best way I knew how." In another case presented by Ramsland a twenty-four-year-old female brought eight boys "to her home, got them drunk, removed their clothes, and had sex with them." Listening to these cases, one might think that the victims were old enough, they should have known better, or they probably enjoyed it, but in reality these women exploited these boys, despite the romantic fantasy tone they imposed upon it.

Some researchers note that female sex offenses mostly are committed by adult offenders (Wolfe, 1985; McCarty, 1986), however, other researchers have found that sexual abuse often occurs by female adolescent offenders (Fehrenbach and Monastersky, 1988; Johnson, 1989; Higgs, Canavan, & Meyer, 1992). Wakefield (cited in Robinson, 2001) addresses the population of teenage female sexual offenders, commenting that in her experience, this population typically begins to offend when they are experimenting or discovering their sexuality.

A. J. Cooper, a psychologist who works primarily with sex offenders points out some reasons why females may resort to sexual offenses with children. He postulates that these offenses may "result from a combination of hyper sexuality, associations with early sexual experiences, and imitation of abuse perpetrated on them." Cooper characterizes female sexual offenders as "immature, dependent, and sensitive to rejection, so they tend to gravitate toward younger people who are not their peers." He added that these offenders often gravitate toward children because they are less likely to reject the offender as the offender creates situations in which they can be in control (2001). Despite differences that can be identified between male and female sexual offenders, it is important to also identify the major similarity, which is that sexual abuse is not a gender issue but rather an abuse of power and a need for control.

Barbara Koons-Witt (2002) makes a good point when she says that "chivalry continues to influence our contemporary society, and it is revealed by the way in which appropriate behavior is defined along gender lines" (p. 2).

TREATMENT

Dr. J. Atkinson (1995) concluded that the treatment of female sexual offenders must be designed around the specific details of the offense. Germaine Lawrence Incorporated, a "provider of residential treatment to emotionally disturbed adolescent girls," runs four different programs ranging from short-term to long-term in-patient treatment (http://www.germainelawrence.org/web/fasort.html). The agency admits that it's "reliance on treatment methodologies developed for male juveniles may be problematic since it is not clear that female and male sexual offenders share the same characteristics and/or treatment needs" (Mathews, 1987). They are most likely not the only agency treating female sexual offenders with programs originally designed for male sexual offenders.

Germaine Lawrence Incorporated, found that treatment of female sexual offenders should include "exploration of the trauma, underlying feelings, and confused cognition, and the development of more adequate social skills and more adaptive coping mechanisms." Germaine Lawrence Incorporated note that their findings are similar to earlier research by Gil and Johnson's (1993), which found a concern for service providers in sexual abuse treatment programs that focus on either the victim or offender issues in an exclusionary manner. Germaine Lawrence Incorporated suggest that to better understand female sexual offenders, further studies might focus on "[T]he role of sexual gratification as a motivating factor, the parentified child role as a causal agent, clusters of behavior associated with sexual offending, and the continuation of the behavior into adulthood."

VIII

STALKING, RAPE, AND MURDER

CHAPTER

ETIOLOGY OF STALKING, SEXUAL ASSAULT AND VICTIM IMPACT

42

Tamar Kenworthy

STALKING: LEGISLATIVE DEVELOPMENT AND THE IMPACT ON VICTIMS

The phenomenon of stalking has been around for centuries; however, society has only begun to acknowledge its existence within the last decade. Stalking can be defined as "a pattern of repeated unwanted and unwarranted following and harassing behaviors directed by one individual, the stalker, at another individual, the target" (Schell & Lantiegne, 2000, p. 4). This chapter examines stalking and its legislative development within the United States. How stalking was first declared unlawful is presented including national models of anti-stalking legislation, and other state anti-stalking statutes. Criminal harassment, stalking typologies, fantasy, risk assessment and victim impact are explored including a case of domestic stalking.

LEGISLATIVE DEVELOPMENT

CALIFORNIA PRECEDENCE

The development of anti-stalking legislation can be traced back to 1990 where the state of California first imposed statutes that made stalking unlawful. This statute originated after a highly publicized murder of a celebrity, Rebecca Schaeffer, who had been the victim of a stalker. Before this law was implemented, there were no regulations regarding harassment and intent to harm. Even the 1990 anti-stalking regulation imposed by the state of California did not initially fully protect all victims from their stalkers:

> California's stalking law defines a stalker as one who "willfully, maliciously, and repeatedly follows or harasses another person and who makes a credible threat with the intent to place that person in reasonable fear for his or her safety, or the safety of his or her immediate family. The California statute, like most state statutes that followed it, has two main components: a threat requirement and an intent requirement (Tolhurst, 1994).

At its inception, the California statute, although setting the precedence for awareness and action by other states, had some major flaws. According to the California statute, for a threat to be a "credible threat" it must be made with the intent and ability to carry it out. Therefore, a victim of stalking must not only prove that their perpetrator was a threat, but also that the perpetrator had the ability to carry the threat out. This phrase would then preclude individuals who were physically or mentally incapable of doing harm from being a credible threat to their victim, and these victims would not fall under California's anti-stalking law protection.

Furthermore, the original statute attempted to objectify and specify what constituted "reasonable fear." Reasonable fear was defined as causing substantial emotional distress to the victim. Therefore, if the victim was not fearful of his or her perpetrator, the California statute would not cover the victim's safety under this definition of requirement of emotional distress. Overall, the perpetrator must intend to cause fear and emotional distress, and the perpetrator must actually cause emotional distress in order for the original statute to be upheld in court. It was not until 1995 that California rectified some of these definitional problems and broadened the scope of its anti-stalking regulations to make it currently one of the toughest state on stalking perpetrators.

CHAPTER 438

While California laws against stalking were initially viewed as stringent and appeared to encompass all types of stalking behavior, the definitional problem of credible threat did not provide overarching safety for victims of stalking. Recognizing this flaw, Chapter 438 was developed as an amendment to previous state stalking legislation. This amendment provided that it was unnecessary to prove that the perpetrator had an intent to carry out harm toward his or her victim; "requiring the defendant to intend to carry out the threat would make prosecutions for stalking more difficult, and lessen the intended protection offered by the state" (Kachmar, 1996, p. 15). This chapter amendment also changed the length of restraining orders against perpetrators of stalking. Previous law allowed courts to issue restraining orders valid up to five years, and orders valid up to ten years in extreme cases only. Chapter 438 removed the extreme case requirement for restraining orders exceeding five years. This allowed for broader coverage and protection for victims of stalking. Furthermore, Chapter 438 allows courts to require stalking perpetrators to register as sex offenders if the court determines that their offense is sexual in nature. California also provides for interstate stalking, in that victims from one state who relocate to California can have a restraining order issued against their perpetrator even if the perpetrator resides in another state. The California Chapter 438 amendment provides for the protection as well as the anonymity of victims by prohibiting disclosure of victim identity information (e.g., phone number, address). Overall, the newest developments on the California anti-stalking statute have worked to increase victim safety and offender liability.

OTHER STATES' INITIATIVES

California's proactive stance against stalking encouraged many states to recognize and develop their own anti-stalking regulations. In fact, California anti-stalking laws provided for national regulations against stalking issued by the Department of Justice. The need for anti-stalking legislation became nationally recognized when it was estimated in 1993 that around 200,000 stalkers existed in the United States. Furthermore, approximately 90 percent of all women killed by a significant other was stalked prior to their murder (Tolhurst, 1994). It was statistics such as these, and California's proactive stance, that initiated national concern for victims of stalking and the implementation of anti-stalking laws across the United States. By 1994, "almost every state in the nation had a criminal stalking law" (Tolhurst, 1994, p. 16). While anti-stalking law differences exist across the fifty states, some major commonalities exist in terms of threat and intent requirements.

Many states employ threat or conduct requirements in the definition of their anti-stalking laws. This requirement allows for conduct or behavior that is perceived as threatening to the victim to be considered under the scope of stalking. According to the National Institute of Justice, twenty-five states employed this definition of threat. Other states employ the threat and conduct requirement, which stipulates that a threat must be made as well as conduct that demonstrates this threat. States that endorse this requirement do not adequately allow for the safety of victims who may have had a previous relationship with their stalker, such as domestic violence victims. These individuals may suffer from personal, intentional threats that illicit psychological fear in the victim, but which a court would not deem threatening. The numerous stipulations and definitional problems only cause the victim to feel less powerful and virtually unprotected. Similar definitional problems occur with intent requirements.

Intent refers to the perpetrator purposefully planning on causing fear within his or her victim. Several states require that the stalker must intend to cause as well as actually cause fear within the victim. Other states, such as New Jersey, include within its intent requirement that "the stalker must intend to cause and actually cause alarm or annoyance" (Tolhurst, 1994, p. 17). Therefore, this statute covers victims whose perpetrators intend to annoy him or her with the stipulation that the victim must actually fear for his or her safety. Another way states address the intent requirement is by eliminating it completely. Therefore, states that eliminate the intent requirement stipulate that the stalker's actions must cause reasonable fear within his or her victim. While the lack of an intent requirement would benefit more victims of stalking, it appears to be too broad in that mentally-ill individuals may be prosecuted for acts that cause fear in others, but which there was no intent to harm. Overall, the stalking legislation has evolved over the years, and all states have enacted some form of regulation. However, while many states enacted anti-stalking legislation by 1995, Maine only allowed harassment laws to cover victims of stalking, which gave rise to several complications.

MAINE'S HARASSMENT LAW

In 1993, Maine developed an amendment to its harassment law in response to the societal concern over stalking; however, this law failed to protect many victims of stalking:

> In Maine, law enforcement was unable to effectively intervene in stalking situations because there was no law available to encompass the nuances of stalking. Designating harassment, trespassing and loitering as crimes fails to address the cumulative nature of stalking . . . Prosecutors were unable to find an appropriate charge to protect victims from the continued vigilance of a stalker . . . The failure of the system in Maine to adequately address the problem of stalking had serious consequences. It endangered the life of the victim because there was the ever-present possibility of violent confrontation, which could ultimately result in death (Saxl, 1998, p. 2).

The absence of an anti-stalking law within the state of Maine did not afford adequate protection to victims of stalkers. Furthermore, no consequences were provided for perpetrators of stalking. They could be arrested for things such as loitering, trespassing and harassment, but punishment for these "crimes" did not result in any lengthy prison stay or even more than a fine. Eventually, in 1996, Maine recognized stalking as a crime and enacted proper legislation that accounted for sentencing of stalking offenders, regulations in regards to computer stalking, and interstate protection orders. Overall, Maine legislators recognized the definitional problems involved when including stalking behaviors within a harassment statute.

CRIMINAL HARASSMENT AND STALKING

DEFINITIONAL DIFFERENCES

Stalking has often been included or confused with the definition of sexual harassment. Sexual harassment occurs most frequently within the workplace and laws have been enacted for several decades outlining the various behaviors defined under harassment. Sexual harassment can be classified as unwanted sexual attention, sexually oriented remarks and behaviors, and implied threat or consequence in the form of actual reprisal or denial of an opportunity for failure to comply with a sexual request.

> By legal definition, stalking, unlike prohibited sexual harassment, may not include behaviors such as sexual touching, sexual conduct, sexual verbal innuendos, or sexual assault. However, such behaviors may become part and parcel of the stalker's harassment tactics (Schell & Lanteigne, 2000, p. 6).

In contrast to harassment, stalking involves behaviors, which, when viewed together, form a threatening character to the intended victim. These behaviors may have sexual aspects or behaviors involved, but sex is not typically the driving force behind the stalking behaviors of offenders, especially in domestic violence situations. The difference between stalking and workplace sexual harassment may reside in the individual's safety feeling threatened versus their job position or chance of advancement. However, sexual harassment often occurs outside of a workplace environment, and stalking can even occur within a workplace environment.

WORKPLACE STALKING

Despite current anti-stalking legislation, "many businesses and organizations are failing to identify or are continuing to deny that stalking behavior is present within their firms" (Schell & Lanteigne, 2000, p. 13). While sexual harassment laws within the workplace have become increasingly more recognized, the laws that could protect these victims of stalking within the workplace are not easily recognized nor enforced. This often leads to lawsuits after crimes such as property damage, psychological damage, or physical damage and even death have already occurred. Companies are oftentimes held liable for these crimes, but unfortunately for the victim, many companies do not make efforts to prevent stalking before damage can be done.

One study found that "in 90% of these violence-outcome cases, clear warning signals were apparent to workplace managers and union leaders" (Schell & Lanteigne, 2000, p. 13). Therefore, even though anti-stalking legislation exists, enforcement still appears to be lacking especially when in an atmosphere of diffused responsibility. In order for enforcement of anti-stalking laws to take effect within an organization, efficient training of management staff on early signs to look for that may indicate stalking (e.g., gift-giving, frequent touching, privacy intrusions, or whereabouts questioning of their victim), as well as employee awareness seminars that educate employees on workplace stalking, how to report it to management, and clear company policies related to stalking would be needed. While stalking is typically difficult to identify early on, education of employees and allowing them to feel safe when disclosing that they feel they are being stalked, will help in the incidence of workplace stalking. However, stalking still remains difficult to identify early on, even by the victim, and even more difficulties arise when clients stalk their therapists.

THE STALKING OF THERAPISTS

According to a study by Gentile, Asamen, Harmell, and Weathers (2002), 10 percent of their study's participants reported being stalked by at least one client. Also, the majority of stalkers in this study were reported to be female; whereas, in the general population, males account for the greatest number of stalkers. Another study by Romans, Hays, and White (1996) found a stalking occurrence rate of 5.6 percent within their population of counseling center staff members. While these findings may underrepresent the prevalence of therapist stalking, "the impact of being a target of a stalker mitigates against treating such issues as extremely rare" (Romans, Hays & White, 1996, p. 598). The fact that clients who stalk their therapists do exist raises the question of blame.

Many victims of stalking believe they share some of the blame in the fact that the stalker has targeted them, but realizing that even professionals who are attempting to help people with mental illnesses fall victim to stalkers can change the dynamic of blame. Recognizing that the blame resides within the offender rather than the victim should alleviate some self-blame on the part of the victim of a stalker. However, it appears that even those who deal with mentally disordered individuals on a daily basis still struggle with similar victim issues such as self-blame and lifestyle changes. For example, many psychologists in the Gentile, Asamen, Harmell, and Weathers (2000) study began screening patients differently, changed to an unlisted address or phone number, and even obtained a restraining order.

An important difference between professionals being stalked and victims within the general population occurs with reporting the stalking. Psychologists are mandated to protect the identity of their clients as well as offer them help in times of crisis. When a psychologist reports the stalking behavior of a client, he or she must be willing to assume responsibility of breaking therapist-patient confidentiality. Also, if the client is currently in treatment, reporting stalking behavior to the police will disrupt the therapeutic alliance; however, these risks appear minimal in the presence of the fear that encompasses victims of stalkers. This fear is a common link across many victims of stalkers, but depending on the typology of the stalker, instilling fear in his or her victim may not be the primary motive.

STALKING TYPOLOGIES

OLD TRENDS, RECENT REVISIONS

Four stalking typologies have previously been developed within California, and include: simple obsessional, love obsessional, erotomanic, and false-victimization syndrome. Obsessions are defined by the *Diagnostic and Statistical Manual of Mental*

Disorders-Fourth edition-text revision (DSM-IV-TR) as "persistent ideas, thoughts, impulses, or images that are experienced as intrusive and inappropriate and that cause marked anxiety or distress" (p. 457). The simple obsessional stalker can be defined then as an offender who knows his or her victim and stalks because of feeling mistreated or because of a separation with the victim. Love obsessional typically involves a stranger stalker who wishes to initiate contact with the victim. Celebrities most often experience erotomania in which they have fans that believe the celebrity is in love with them. Finally, false-victimization involves an individual who either purposefully contrives a stalker that turns out to be factitious, or an individual who believes (possibly due to mental illness) that they have a stalker when in fact they do not. While these typologies appear to cover different categories of stalkers they lack the thoroughness and breadth of coverage of other classes of stalkers. Hickey, Margulies, and Oddie conducted a study in 1999 (Hickey, 2006) that outlined three stalking typologies with different subcategories. The three typologies include: domestic, stranger and factitious.

DOMESTIC STALKERS

Within the domestic typology are three subcategories of domestic stalkers: power/anger, obsessional, and nuisance. All stalkers within the domestic typology had a previous relationship with the victim, whether as friends, acquaintances or those who were involved within a romantic relationship. The domestic-power/anger stalker generally "harbors feelings of hatred, revenge, and domination over their victim" (Hickey, 2006, p. 126). This type of domestic stalker is likely to do physical harm to his or her victim, and this type of stalker may even kill their victim as in the case of many domestic violence relationships when the victim attempts to leave his or her abuser. The domestic-obsessional stalker typically fits *DSM-IV-TR* criteria for obsessions, and according to Hickey (2006) this type of offender often suffers from a psychological disorder (e.g., schizophrenia, personality disorders). These offenders believe that the victim wants a relationship with them and their thought processes are often irrational regarding the relationship they have with the victim. This classification may also include the stalking of therapists by their clients. Finally, the domestic-nuisance stalker employs various means of harassment in order to get attention from the victim. Typically, this stalker typology believes that the victim enjoys the harassment and their main goal is to establish a relationship with the victim. This type of stalker rarely uses violence or threats against the victim.

STRANGER STALKERS

The second stalker typology involves a perpetrator who has not had a previous relationship or acquaintance with their victim. The subcategories under this typology include: power/anger, obsessional, nuisance, sexual predator, and erotomania. Individuals falling under the stranger-power/anger typology "are primarily men who look for random victims to control, intimidate, and harm" (Hickey, 2006, p. 127).

These individuals generally send threatening notes; the Internet has become a widely used tool for this stalking typology. This stalker will not usually follow through or persist in his or her threats, but rather just expressing their anger releases enough tension for them to move on to other victims in the future. The stranger-obsessional stalker typically becomes fixated on someone they do not know, and they often suffer from a psychological disorder. This typology of stalkers is deemed dangerous due to their unpredictability as a result of their psychological disorder. The stranger-nuisance stalkers are typically anonymous to their victim and the stalking does not escalate into obsessional, or last for a prolonged period of time. Typically these individuals lack the appropriate social skills to connect with people in a conventional manner, and they enjoy the thrill of instilling a little chaos into someone else's life. The stranger–sexual predator stalker is considered the most dangerous stalker. This typology includes rapists, child molesters, and pedophiles. The level of dangerousness of these offenders resides in their level of harm caused to their victim; sexual assault and psychological damage is common among victims of this stalker typology. Finally, the stranger-erotomanic becomes attached to someone whom they believe is in love with them, and their behaviors are often irrational; celebrity stalkers fit into this category.

FACTITIOUS STALKERS

This final typology includes "victims" who falsely report being stalked. The subcategories include: false victimization and hero fantasy. The individual who falls within the false victimization category reports being stalked in order to satisfy feelings of loneliness and rejection. Contact with the police allows these individuals to get the attention they crave. The hero fantasy individuals act out their desire to "catch" their perpetrator. These individuals also crave attention in the form of acceptance or positive regard from others.

PROBLEMS AND DEFINITIONAL COMPLICATIONS

While these typologies serve as a strong framework from which to classify stalking offenders, several problems exist within the typology system. First, offender typologies in general do not account for all unique differences of the perpetrators. Typologies only serve as a starting place, an information system in which to build upon. However, there are similarities in the motives for many perpetrators, which the stalking typologies attempt to account for when categorizing domestic versus stranger and obsessional versus nuisance or power/anger. While these typologies appear to be broad enough to cover every type of stalker, there is some overlap and some stalkers who may not fit neatly into each category. For example, the domestic-nuisance stalker does not include psychologically disordered individuals and precludes any threat of harm made to the victim. However, domestic-nuisance stalkers who are harshly turned down by their victim may have the potential to turn to violence. Also, the stranger–power/anger stalkers could fall easily into harming their victims. Serial killers many times stalk or purposefully choose their victims, and typically it is the power they feel over their victim that drives them. Finally, the factitious-stalking category does not account for individuals who truly believe they are the victim of a stalker. These individuals may not report the stalking behavior regularly to the police because they genuinely fear their stalker because of a mental illness or other significant rejection or abandonment issues. Overall, the typologies allow for a general categorization of offenders who stalk that serve to aid in the understanding of the different forms of stalking. All of these forms of stalking can have a significant impact on the victim whether in the form of physical harm or psychological harm. In order to truly understand the offender, and how the offender's behavior instills harm in his or her victims it is important to explore character aspects of the stalker.

SEXUAL OFFENDERS WHO STALK

COMMONALITIES

Stalkers are typically viewed as pursuing their victim in order to obtain sexual gratification. This sexual gratification can take the form of fantasy or actual harm to the victim. Offenders who use fantasy are driven to pursue their victim by what they have acted out in their minds. This fantasy can include consensual sex with the victim, rape, or even harming the victim and feeling sexually gratified. However, according to research by Harmon, Rosner, and Owens (1998):

> ... with regard to violence toward the target, there does not appear to be a statistically significant difference between individuals who harass for reasons relating to love and individuals who harass for reasons relating to persecution and anger (p. 247).

Therefore, this fits with the power/anger subcategory typologies of domestic and stranger stalkers.

The primary motivation for these offenders is not sexual in nature, but rather a means to release anger or punish their victim. The contention still remains though that fantasy plays a role in most of the stalking typologies. While the fantasy may not include sexual conduct or contact, the fantasy can include gaining power and control over the victim or even fantasizing about the harm intended for the victim. Fantasy is a powerful tool that drives and perhaps motivates many stalkers into continuing in their behavior whether it causes sexual expectation or feelings of power and control. Other commonalities that stalkers share include gender of the stalker, age of the stalker and criminal history.

While there are many variations within a population of stalkers, generally the "research consistently shows that the vast majority of stalkers are male" (Kropp,

Hart, & Lyon, 2002, p. 593). In fact, statistics collected by Kropp, Hart, and Lyon (2002) from police investigation files and victim surveys indicate that males make up 90 percent of stalking perpetrators. However, this statistic may be affected by self-report and stereotyping; males may be less inclined to see themselves as the "victim" and thus may tend not to report incidents of being stalked. Many celebrity stalkers have tended to be female, and these are reported more often because of their high profile within the media. The age of stalkers has been found to have a mean or median within the mid- to late-thirties's age range. While there is no theory or explanation behind this finding, it appears that stalkers as a whole tend to be older. This might account for more domestic stalkers in that they have been in a previous relationship with their victim, and possibly have had more time to become attached. However, only speculation for the reason behind this finding exists. Furthermore, according to Kropp, Hart, and Lyon (2002):

> Stalking does not appear to be an isolated incident of unlawful conduct committed by otherwise ordinary and law-abiding citizens. Instead, studies of police investigational files and clinical-forensic samples report that the majority of stalkers have existing criminal records . . . Histories of violence also are relatively common. Several investigations found that between 25% and 45% of stalkers had prior charges or convictions for assault and other more serious violent offenses . . . (p. 595).

Therefore, in order to better conceptualize the stalker, it is important to understand his or her personal history, which includes a legal history. Possibly being predisposed to stalking behavior resides in past criminal history, or perhaps one is more inclined to initiate unlawful behavior when it has become a way of life. Whatever the reason behind the criminal activity of stalking, many offenders may be further inclined to take their stalking behavior further (i.e., violence) given their past criminal history.

Another aspect of offenders who stalk is their mental capacity and whether they tend to function in a delusional manner or are clear-headed. While many would argue that one must be mentally ill in order to even consider stalking another person, Harmon, Rosner, and Owens (1998) contend that "nondelusional stalkers also exist" (p. 247). Therefore, some offenders who stalk may fall within the stalking typologies of domestic-power/anger or stranger-power/anger where it is not necessarily a question of mental illness that drives their behavior, but rather a sense of anger or rejection. While others who exhibit no signs of mental illness may use stalking as a tool to qualm feelings of loneliness or social isolation. Whether an offender is mentally ill or not, some delusions can still occur in regards to how they perceive their victim, how their victim's actions affect them, and how they view their own behavior. Similarly, it would seem that almost all offenders who stalk still display some form of malfunctioning whether it resides in their thought patterns, behavior patterns, or justifications for their actions. Studies range in estimates of mental illness among offenders who stalk, but the overwhelming majority have found at least a proportion of those studied exhibit a mental illness or a personality disorder (Harmon, Rosner, & Owens, 1998). Overall, it may not be a matter of whether mental-illness is playing a role in the stalking behavior, but the risk factors associated with whether or not the given offender will be violent or prove to be dangerous to his or her target of unwanted attention.

RISK ASSESSMENT

When determining risk of offending, psychologists do not offer a prediction of whether or not a given offender will be violent. Instead, psychologists look to see whether a given offender shows a probability or risk for becoming violent at some time in the near future. Several risk factors have been created that seem to preclude certain individuals for the possibility of becoming violent. These include: age, sex, race, family history, personality, socioeconomic status and factors relating to the offender's access to weapons, social supports and perception of stress. While many of these factors cannot be altered; and therefore, may not be conducive to treatment, "clinical factors (psychiatric diagnosis, symptoms, functioning, substance abuse) were considered manageable factors, which could be subject to change or treatment" (Harmon, Rosner, & Owens, 1998, p. 248). Taken as a whole, these factors aid in determining how individuals handles themselves during times of stress, how they express and/or manage their feelings, and how they deal with their anger. Also, looking at social context and family history allows for a more conceptualized view of the individual's world. How this individual grew up, what forms of social support were available to him or her, and essentially how this person functioned given his environmental circumstances can assist in determining whether the individual is at risk of becoming a violent offender.

Also, if an offender is deemed mentally-ill this does not always mean that the offender is therefore at risk for violence or is to be considered dangerous. According to Rubin (1975):

> The misconception is that particular psychiatric disorders are per se dangerous which is encouraged by certain mental disorders being characterized by some kind of confused, bizarre, agitated, threatening, frightened, panicked, paranoid, or impulsive behavior (p. 18).

Therefore, mental illness itself does not predispose an offender to be violent or dangerous. Rather, it is a combination of the risk factors for violence along with clinical judgment that ultimately determines whether an offender may become violent in the future. While this method is the most widely used, "criteria remain vague and inaccurate" (Rubin, 1975, p. 18). Several instruments have been developed to further assist clinicians in making these determinations, but overall there is no method, instrument, or criteria that is one hundred percent reliable.

PUNISHMENT

Overall, risk assessment does not provide conclusive evidence of one's risk for violence, but it does allow for the courts to make such determinations. When presenting an offender who stalks before the court and addressing all of the factors that may have influenced their behavior, as well as the factors that may influence their level of future violence may foster some protection, though still minimal, to the victim. Demonstrating that the offender is at risk of future violence may ensure that he or she is sentenced into treatment, which is at least one small step in aiding the victim. However, throughout any type of criminal proceeding, the victim's perspective is not shared for any lengthy portion or time, nor is it given much weight in sentencing decisions. Furthermore, offenders who stalk do not typically receive much in the way of punishment; restraining orders can be broken and jail sentences end. The impact that stalking has on the victim may be one of the greatest tools for understanding the dynamics that occur within the stalking "relationship."

VICTIM IMPACT

PSYCHOLOGICAL IMPLICATIONS

The victims of stalking tend to endure several emotional as well as physical responses to their victimization. Victims of any type of crime suffer from the experience, whether in the form of anger, shock, depression, or even self-blame. According to Symonds (1975), "whenever one is the subject of a sudden, unexpected attack of violence there is the initial response of shock, numbness, and unbelief" (p. 94). While there always exists individual differences, the victims of stalking appear to be at risk of suffering severe psychological implications due in part to the persistent nature of the stalker. The world of the individual who has been the victim of stalking is filled with wariness, confusion, and even some form of posttraumatic stress. This is generally a result of the victim wondering why the stalker chose them as in the case of stranger stalking, or why someone they knew would want to cause them psychological harm as in the case of domestic stalking. Furthermore, the victims of stalking explore aspects of their own behavior that may have triggered the stalking, and they begin a process of self-evaluation that leaves them with feelings of helplessness or even depression. In fact, this self-critical behavior only seems to be encouraged by family members, friends, and acquaintances.

Typically, the victims of crime are attributed with some of the blame for their victimization, whether it is the way they dress, their actions or behaviors, the people they choose to socialize with, or the way the choose to live their life. "This general early response to victims stems from a basic need for all individuals to find a rational explanation of violent crime" (Symonds, 1975, p. 92). The same is true for victims of stalking; family members may question their relationship with the stalker, or may attribute some of the blame to the way the victim leads their life. Either way, victims of stalking not only have to deal with the consequences dealt to them by their stalker, but they often also have to deal with a lack of complete support from those they love.

The psychological impact of being stalked may not be able to be conceptualized due to the variance of reactions among victims. However, one more common element is fear. When the element of fear exists within the victim of stalking, these individuals have learned to be almost hypervigilant to the world around them. Trust becomes difficult, feelings of security and safety are lost and may never be fully recovered, and ultimately their entire lifestyle is altered.

BEHAVIORAL CHANGES

Victims of stalking typically experience a lifestyle change. This change can exist in several forms: unlisted phone numbers, phone call identification devices, relocating to a different address or even state, approaching new people with caution, "screening" of potential dates, changing the route he or she takes home from work, and even installing state of the art security alarms or carrying a firearm in the home, etc. Overall, the fear that has been instilled within a victim's life can create significant changes to their daily activities. They may be more cautious when meeting new people, and they may constantly look over their shoulder or change their daily routine so as not to be followed or tracked. These lifestyle changes provide a sense of security to the person, although this feeling may be short-lived. Stalkers that are persistent always seem to find ways around their victim's new lifestyle changes, and eventually what once made them feel safe loses its sense of security. In order to fully understand how a victim experiences being stalked, it is best to hear it straight from the victim.

CASE EXAMPLE

"Sara" is a thirty-year-old single female who lives on her own. She has been the victim of a stalker for over ten years. Her stalker would be considered a domestic stalker because he and Sara dated for a little over two years. Her stalker has never truly gotten over their breakup even though he is currently married and has children; his wife bears a similar resemblance to Sara. Through these years, Sara has gone through several life changes such as: unlisted telephone numbers, relocating to several different addresses and finally across several states, filing of restraining orders, not answering the telephone when the caller id does not register a name, and being very careful and selective with the people she socializes with, as well as with those she dates. She has experienced numerous intrusions on her privacy that have included being followed, receiving excessive phone calls, receiving unwanted gifts, and having her apartment broken into and several of her intimate clothing items taken. Overall, she has endured a lot of stress, fear, anger, and wariness. Currently, she has not heard from her stalker for over a year after her move across several states. When asked to describe what it was like to be stalked, Sara says:

> The scenario that best evokes the feeling of being stalked would most probably be a nightmare. Think of your worst nightmare, you know the one, where you're being chased and you're trying to run but you're in slow motion and the monster that's chasing you is getting closer and closer, you can feel its breath on the back of your neck and you open your mouth to scream but no sounds are coming out. Now imagine not waking up, imagine that nightmare continuing, always trying to run but never quite getting away.

SUMMARY

When conceptualizing stalkers, it is not only important to understand elements of their character in order to assess for violence. Rather it is important to understand what drives their behavior, what motivates them to instill fear into the lives of their victims. What role does fantasy play in their behavior, and how do the elements of power and control factor into their stalking. Overall, it is especially important to realize that stalking impacts the victim in a very real sense, and understanding this impact may aid in understanding what motivates the stalker.

PERCEPTIONS OF RAPE

Cultural, Gender, and Ethnic Differences

CATHERINE FURTADO

43

Rape has been defined as, "the illicit carnal knowledge of a woman, forcibly and against her will," (Shaw, 1999, p. 8). The term "rape," however, is not recognized across all cultures (Dussich, 2001; Heaven & Connors, 1998; Muir & Lonsway, 1996; Rozee, 1993; Sanday, 1981). Many cultures do not believe that a woman's will matters when sexual relations are concerned. Western societies, namely the United States of America, place more of an importance on whether a woman's will has been violated. However, even industrial, First World countries like the United States often overlook the seriousness of the crime of rape. Research has found significant differences in perceptions of rape as a crime and the victim's role in that crime. These differences have been found between various cultures (Dussich, 2001; Heaven & Connors, 1998; Muir & Lonsway, 1996; Rozee, 1993; Sanday, 1981), various ethnic groups (Lefley, Scott, Llabre, & Hicks, 1993; Scott, Lefley, & Hicks, 1993; Wyatt, 1992), occupations (Feild, 1978), and genders (Krulewitz & Nash, 1979).

A study conducted by Koss, Gidycz, and Wisniewski in 1987, examined the actual scope of rape among college students. It is important to understand how prevalent victimization is among females and perpetration of rape is among males. The prevalence of various forms of sexual assault including rape, attempted rape, sexual coercion, and sexual contact were examined. Koss and colleagues found that 46.3 percent of women reported no experiences with sexual victimization, while 53.7 percent of women reported some form of sexual victimization. In terms of the seriousness of the offense, 14.4 percent of women reported unwanted sexual contact, 11.9

percent reported sexual coercion, 12.1 percent reported attempted rape, and 15.4 percent reported rape as the most serious form of sexual victimization experienced. Seventy-five percent of men reported that they had never engaged in any type of sexual aggression. Twenty-five percent admitted to engaging in some form of sexual aggression. Unwanted sexual contact was reported as the most serious offense perpetrated by 10.2 percent of men, sexual coercion for 7.2 percent, attempted rape for 3.3 percent, and rape for 4.4 percent of men. These statistics seem slightly lopsided. Female college students are reporting much more sexual victimization than male students are admitting to. These females may not always be victimized by other college students, but the percentages still seem underrepresentative (Koss, Gidycz, & Wisniewski, 1987). The high percentages of females sexually victimized call for a greater understanding of what factors may increase a woman's vulnerability to victimization and how these victims are viewed by society.

Dussich (2001) identifies three dominant theories dealing with sexual assault that may explain how various groups view sexual assault. The first theory is the "victim-precipitated," in which the victim is seen as somewhat at fault for the act. The victim is thought to have encouraged the act in some way. The second theory is the "psychopathology of rapists," in which the offender is seen as mentally disturbed. The offender is seen as responsible for the act rather than the victim. However, the offender's psychological disorder should be considered the ultimate source of responsibility. The third theory is the "feminist," in which rape is seen as a result of how our cultures teach us that men should be dominant and aggressive and women should be obedient and submissive. Women and men are socialized to view women as sexual objects (Dussich, 2001). These theories prove prominent among various cultures and clearly affect how various cultures view rape and the victim of rape.

CULTURAL DIFFERENCES

Culture has a significant effect on how rape is perceived by both victims and outside parties. Many cultures classify rape differently than western, industrial societies. In a cross-cultural study conducted by Sanday (1981), the prevalence of rape was examined, as well as how rape was perceived and defined in these cultures. In the majority of societies included in this study rape was defined as, "an act in which male or a group of males sexually assaulted a woman," (Sanday, 1981, p. 6). The study included societies from six regions including Sub-Saharan Africa, Circum-Mediterranean, East Eurasia, Insula Pacific, North America, and South and Central America. Societies were classified as "rape prone" if the incidence of rape was high, rape was considered ceremonial, or if rape was used as punishment against women. Four main hypotheses were included in this study:

1. Sexual repression is related to the incidence of rape.
2. Intergroup and interpersonal violence is enacted in male sexual violence.
3. The character of parent-child relations is enacted in male sexual violence.
4. Rape is an expression of social ideology of male dominance (p. 22).

No correlation between sexual repression and the prevalence of rape was found. Correlations were found between intergroup and interpersonal violence and violence acted out against women. Societies in which large amounts of interpersonal violence was prevalent demonstrated a greater prevalence of rape. The practice of raiding neighboring groups for wives and women to violate was also found to be associated with higher rates of rape. The hypothesis concerning parent-child relations increasing the likelihood for rape was not found to be significant. Interestingly, it was found that when the father-daughter relationship was cold or indifferent the likelihood of rape increased. A significant relationship was found between rape and the social sanctioning of male dominance. Women demonstrated less power and authority in societies classified as rape prone. Women are not allowed to participate in decision making and these societies and may be punished for doing so (Sanday, 1981).

This study suggests that rape is more prevalent in societies in which interpersonal violence, male dominance, and separation of the genders are highly valued. Women, in these societies, are seen as good for only reproduction, whereas men are seen as important and necessary for survival. Sexual aggression and sexual dominance over females serves to bolster men's feelings of dominance and power over women (Sanday, 1981). According to Sanday,

> it is important to understand that violence is socially and not biologically programmed. Rape is not an integral part of male nature, but the means by which men programmed for violence express their sexual selves. Men who are conditioned to respect the female virtues of growth and the sacredness of life, do not violate women (1981, p. 26).

Rozee (1993) conducted a study similar to Sanday's. This study, however, focused more on socially condoned rape. Female choice is the major factor leading this study. Rozee classifies sexual acts in which the female agrees to the act as female sexuality. Female sexuality is defined in this study as, "sexual relations in which the female participates out of her free choice," (Rozee, 1993, p. 502). Those acts in which the female does not give approval or is not given a choice are identified as rape. Lack of choice is assumed to be present when, "there is a use of force, threat of force, or coercion; presence of multiple males; physical pain, loss of consciousness, or death; or when the woman is punished or suffers some other negative outcome if she refuses" (p. 502). These acts are also separated into those which are socially condoned based on societal norms and those which are not (Rozee, 1993).

Sexual acts in which the women have a choice and society condones may include acts such as consensual sexual relations between married couples. Sexual acts in which the woman chooses to participate but are not socially condoned may include premarital sex or sex with an outside party while married. Rape may be present, whether or not the act is considered socially acceptable. If the male is not punished after the rape or if the female is the only individual punished after the rape the rape is considered socially condoned. Rape may also be socially approved of if it is part of a cultural ritual or tradition. Rape that is not socially approved of is present when the perpetrator is punished for his actions and the victim is not punished (Rozee, 1993).

Rozee's study (1993) included thirty-five non-industrial societies. In 97 percent of the societies, socially condoned rape was found. Socially acceptable rape was classified into six categories:

1. Marital rape: unchosen genital contact occurring within the institution of marriage (p. 505).

2. Exchange rape: male use of female genital contact as a bargaining tool, gesture of solidarity, or conciliation (p. 507).

3. Punitive rape: any genital contact that is used in a disciplinary or punitive manner (p. 507).

4. Theft rape: the involuntary abduction of a woman from her place of residence to be used as a sexual or reproductive object (p. 508).

5. Ceremonial rape: unchosen genital contact that occurs within the context of various ceremonies, such as defloration rituals or virginity tests, or where sexual intercourse is part of the ceremony and females are expected to participate, willing or not (p. 509).

6. Status rape: any unchosen genital contact that occurs primarily as a result of acknowledged differences in rank between the individuals involved (p. 510).

Marital rape was present in 40 percent of the societies; exchange rape was present in 71 percent; punitive rape was present in 14 percent; theft rape was present in 63 percent; ceremonial rape was present in 49 percent; and status rape was present in 29 percent (Rozee, 1993). All six classifications of rape included in this study are socially sanctioned in these societies. These acts are not considered rape in the societies in which they occur. Despite the fact that the woman is not given a choice in whether or not she participated in these acts, the society does not consider the act a crime. All thirty-five societies included in this study were non-industrial societies. These views of rape may be quite different when compared to industrial societies that consider men and women equal in status.

Research has also been conducted comparing the differences between perceptions of rape and rape victims among specific cultures. Muir and Lonsway (1996) compared rape myth acceptance and rates of reporting rape between Scottish and American individuals. Muir and Lonsway (1996) report that in 1992, 1,429 sexual assaults were reported in Scotland. This rate of reporting demonstrates that 30 per 100,000 of the Scottish population report sexual assault. In 1991, 42.3 per 100,000 of the population of the United States of America reported sexual assaults. Muir and Lonsway use cultural theory to explain the differences in reporting rates between Scotland and the United States. According to cultural theory, "rape is an expression of power and aggression, rather than of sexuality," (Muir & Lonsway, 1996, p. 261).

Because of the greater prevalence of reporting in the United States, it was hypothesized that Americans may be more accepting of rape myths than Scottish individuals. It was also hypothesized that men would be more accepting of rape myths than women. According to Shaw (1999), "rape myths involve situations in which victims of coerced sex are viewed as seductive and therefore culpable," (Shaw, 1999, p. 138). The Illinois Rape Myth Acceptance Scale was used to measure attitudes towards rape. This scale includes items such as, "when women go around wearing low-cut tops or short skirts, they're just asking for trouble" and "rape accusations are often used as a way of getting back at men," (Muir & Lonsway, 1996, p. 261). Researchers found that male participants demonstrated greater acceptance of rape myths than did females. It was also found that American participants displayed more of an acceptance of rape myths than did Scottish participants. These findings suggest that higher rates of rape myth acceptance may be associated with higher rates of reporting sexual assault (Muir & Lonsway, 1996).

Heaven and Connors (1998) examined differences in attribution of rape blame among Australian and white South African individuals. This study focused on how victim characteristics affect the attribution of rape blame. Heaven and Connors (1998) hypothesized that participants would be more likely to blame women victims who are viewed as less respectable and more attractive. Victims who do not resist their attackers, are thought to gain some enjoyment from the act, and who are attacked by strangers will also have more blame attributed to them. In this study, participants were exposed to two vignettes. The first vignette included a thirty-five-year-old mother who was assaulted in a parking lot. The researchers manipulated victim respectability by having one scenario depicting the mother as the president of a historical society who was visiting a sick friend before the attack. The second version of the vignette depicted the mother as a card dealer at a casino who was leaving a pub after having a few drinks when attacked. In the second vignette, the victim was a student assaulted while walking home to her dorm room. The researchers manipulated the vignette to change victim resistance. In one version, the victim fought her attacker. In the second version, the victim did not resist, although she exhibited great fear. On all versions of the vignettes, the Australian participants were less likely to blame the victim than were the South African participants. The manipulation of victim respectability and victim resistance proved non-significant. The study suggests that victim blame, in this case, is not a function of victim characteristics as hypothesized, but rather of the cultural group of participants (Heaven & Connors, 1998).

Jones and Aronson (1973) also examined how victims' respectability affects how much fault is attributed to the victim. They hypothesized that the more socially respectable a woman is the more fault will be attributed to her after being raped. According to the researchers, "individuals believe in a just world where people deserve what they get, and that the more respectable the victim the greater need to attribute fault to her actions since it is more difficult to attribute fault to her character," (Jones & Aronson, 1973, p. 415). It was predicted that a married victim or a victim who was a virgin before the rape would be seen as more at fault than a divorced woman because virgins and married women are seen by society as more respectable than divorced women. The researchers found that when the female victim was a divorced woman, the fault attributed to her was less than that attributed to either the virgin or the married woman. No significant differences were found between the married and virgin victims. Fault was attributed to both of the "respectable" women. The logic attributed to these findings is that a respectable individual is more responsible for the rape because their character did not warrant the misfortune. Researchers found that women were just as likely to blame the more respectable woman as men were (Jones & Aronson, 1973).

Dussich (2001), rather than compare separate cultures, examined three separate groups all living among the same culture. Dussich compared Japanese, Chinese, Korean, and English-speaking women living in Japan to determine whether differences in perceptions of rape and reporting rates of rape existed. Similar to the findings of Sanday (1981) and Rozee (1993) stating that many non-industrial societies see men as the dominant gender and women as inferior to men, Dussich found that a constant theme throughout Japanese culture is that of female deference to males. Because of this cultural belief, sexual misconduct is not always recognized by society and even victims of the assault. Japanese media seems to play an important role in maintaining the cultural beliefs of females inferiority to men. The media portrays rape as, "the unfortunate plight of women who stray from their traditional roles. Rape becomes the fateful punishment of women who are too assertive, too different, and too modern," (Dussich, 2001, p. 279). Rape, in Japan, is often considered an extension of normal sexual gratification bringing many young men to view rape as normal and acceptable (Dussich, 2001).

The Japanese cultural belief that females are inferior to men also affects women's perceptions of rape. According to Japanese culture women are taught not to complain and to endure abuse, "accepting victimization in silence is a virtue," (Dussich, 2001, p. 279). Because of these teachings, many women surrounded by this culture do not report sexual victimization to the authorities. Of the 748 respondents, 29.1 percent reported having been victims of sexual assault. Of this 29.1 percent, 11.5 percent were for rape, 7.8 percent were for attempted rape, 24.8 percent were for sexual contact with force, and 50.0 percent were for sexual contact without force. Of all types of sexual assault reported only 14.1 percent were reported to the police. Only 20 percent of rapes were reported. Rape was hypothesized to yield the greatest amount of reporting because of the serious nature of the crime. Findings did not support this hypothesis. Attempted rape yielded a higher percentage of reporting. According to Dussich, the reason for this discrepancy is the shocking nature of a completed rape. The victim may be too shocked, stunned, and embarrassed to report the rape, whereas an attempted rape may not create the same reaction. No significant differences were found in reporting rates of sexual assault among the various groups living in Japan. This study may even suggest that those individuals not Japanese by origin may be even less likely to report sexual assaults than Japanese women because they do not want to be stigmatized by a culture to which they do not come from (Dussich, 2001).

ETHNIC DIFFERENCES

Individuals from different ethnicities also appear to have different perceptions of rape and the blame that should be attributed to victims of rape. These differences among various ethnicities may not be easily attributed to cultural differences. Research examining differences in perceptions of rape have looked at three main ethnicities, African-Americans, Hispanics, and non-Hispanic whites (Lefley, Scott, Llabre, & Hicks, 1993; Scott, Lefley, & Hicks, 1993; Wyatt, 1992). The majority of this research has examined these three ethnicities all living in the United States. Culture may be a factor affecting perceptions, but it cannot be the only factor because all three ethnicities are surrounded by American culture.

Scott, Lefley, and Hicks (1993) examined responses to sexual assault among African-American, Hispanic, and non-Hispanic white women. It has been hypothesized that factors, including impaired ability to perceive potential threat and to protect oneself, a history of rape or sexual abuse, and mental illness or mental retardation, may increase some women's vulnerability to sexual assault. Scott and colleagues examined the prevalence of these risk factors among women seeking help from a rape treatment center. The sample included 881 adult female rape victims. Out of these 881 victims 27.5 percent had a history of previous rape or sexual abuse, 14 percent had a history of psychiatric hospitalization, 7 percent were mentally retarded, and 2 percent were homeless. Ten percent of the sample reported more than one risk factor. It was found that African-American women were significantly more likely to have reported previous rape or sexual abuse than Hispanics and non-Hispanic whites. Hispanic victims reported significantly more psychiatric hospitalizations than the other two ethnic groups. No significant differences were found between the ethnic groups in the number of victims who were mentally retarded. Seventy-seven percent of those victims reporting being homeless were non-Hispanic whites. These results may suggest that women who are cognitively or emotionally impaired may be victimized more often, however, they do not suggest that rape victims as a whole are more likely to be cognitively or emotionally impaired (Scott, Lefley, & Hicks, 1993).

In a 1993 study conducted by Lefley, Scott, Llabre, and Hicks, cultural definitions of rape were examined among African-Americans, Hispanics, and non-Hispanic whites who had been raped as well as individuals matching in ethnicity who had never been raped. This study asked four questions:

1. Do rape victims as a group differ from non-victims in their definitions of rape and attributions of culpability in different situations involving forced sex between a man and a woman?
2. Do victims and non-victims differ in definition and attribution from each other, and from other groups, according to ethnicity?
3. Do victims and non-victims differ by ethnicity in their perception of public attitudes, that is, the attributions of most men and most women in their respective ethnic communities?
4. Is there an observable relationship between victims' perceptions of public attitudes and their psychological response to rape? (Lefley et al., 1993, p. 625).

Significant differences were found between victims and non-victims. Hispanic victims tended to display greater psychological distress than the other two ethnic groups, however, ethnicity as a predictor of psychological response was second to degree of victimization. Victims and non-victims of the same ethnicity tended to demonstrate the same attributions. Hispanic victims and non-victims displayed the most punitive attitudes towards themselves or other victims, while white participants displayed the least punitive attitudes. African-American women believed that the men in their community would be more likely to blame the victim. Both Hispanic men and women were more likely to blame the victim, while whites were least likely (Lefley, Scott, Llabre, & Hicks, 1993). This study displays results similar to past research showing Hispanic rape victims as more prone to psychological distress and victim-blaming views, with African-Americans next, and whites lowest.

Wyatt, in a 1992 study, examined factors affecting the disclosure patterns of African-American rape victims in comparison with white rape victims. For the purposes of this study, rape was defined as, "the involuntary penetration of the vagina or anus by the penis or another object," (Wyatt, 1992, p. 82). When asked about the occurrence of possible rape-related situations in their own lives, respondents were often confused about whether a situation constituted rape. This confusion was present regardless of ethnicity. Many of these women were unsure if attempted or even completed rapes were actually rapes because they were committed by acquaintances. Twenty-five percent of African-American women and 20 percent of white women reported having experienced either attempted or completed rape. There was not a significant difference between ethnicities in percentage of reported incidents. African-American women reported more attempted rapes than did white women. The majority of incidents reported by both ethnicities were perpetrated by individuals known to the victim. African-Americans, however, reported more rapes or attempted rapes by strangers (Wyatt, 1992).

Physical effects, negative psychological effects, and problems in women's sex lives were present among both African-American and white women. There were no significant differences between the two ethnicities, however. Physical effects included sleep and appetite disturbances, sexually transmitted diseases, and pregnancy. These effects were found in 39 percent of African-American women and 46 percent of white women. Negative psychological effects included fear, anger, anxiety, depression, and preoccupation with the abuse. These effects were found in 85 percent of African-American women and 86 percent of white women. Problems in the women's sex lives included avoidance of sex, decreased frequency of sexual activity, diminished enjoyment, the development of specific sexual problems, and avoidance of men resembling the perpetrator. These problems were found in 48 percent of African-American women and 55 percent of white women (Wyatt, 1992). These results suggest that African-American women and white women experience similar physical and psychological effects following rape or attempted rape, that these two ethnicities do not significantly differ in their experiences as victims.

GENDER DIFFERENCES

Gender is another factor that appears to color individual's perceptions of rape and victims of rape. Krulewitz and Nash (1979) conducted a study to examine gender differences in perceptions of rape. The study focused on three variables including sex of the observer, victim resistance, and assault outcome. The researchers hypothesized that both women and men would apply sex role stereotypes to the rape situation. Participants were randomly placed by sex into different victim resistance and rape outcome groups. In some cases, the scenario stated the victim strongly resisted, while in other scenarios the women did not resist her attacker. Some scenarios depicted a completed rape while others depicted an attempted but not completed rape. Participants were asked to rate the amount of blame they attributed to both the victim and the assailant in the various scenarios. Four major findings emerged in this study:

1. Subjects were more certain that rape had occurred as the victim resisted more.
2. Subjects attributed greater responsibility to the victim for completed rape than for attempted rape, while the reverse pattern was found for the assailant.
3. Women attributed more responsibility to the assailant than did men.
4. Men attributed less fault and more intelligence, and women attributed more fault and less intelligence to the rape victim as she resisted more forcefully (Krulewitz & Nash, 1979).

Researchers found that some participants, despite the fact that the scenarios clearly stated that a rape either had or had not occurred, were still unsure if the scenario depicted a rape. According to Krulewitz and Nash (1979), participants seemed to believe that if the rape was not completed it was due to the victim's ability to stop the assailant in the act. It seems that an attempted rape, rather than a completed rape, implies that the victim did less to initiate the attack herself. If a rape was completed, the victim is seen as somehow encouraging the crime because she was unable to stop the act (Krulewitz & Nash, 1979).

Gender differences in opinions of the victims of rape were also surprising. Women attributed more blame and responsibility to the female victim than the perpetrator. Women perceived the victim as less intelligent when she fought back against her attacker. One would think that because females are the leading victims of rape, women would attribute less blame to the victim. It is surprising that men would see the female victim as less responsible. It would seem that women would identify more with the victim than men and find them less responsible.

OCCUPATIONAL DIFFERENCES

In a 1978 study, Feild investigated differences in rape attitudes between individuals with varying occupations. Occupations examined in this study included police officers, crisis counselors, citizens, and even actual rapists. Eight factors examined included:

Factor 1: Women's Responsibility in Rape Prevention—"A woman should be responsible for preventing her own rape," (Feild, 1978, p. 161).

Factor 2: Sex as Motivation for Rape—"Rape is the expression of an uncontrollable desire for sex," (p. 161).

Factor 3: Severe Punishment for Rape—"A convicted rapist should be castrated," (p. 161).

Factor 4: Victim Precipitation of Rape—"Women provoke rape by their appearance or behavior," (p. 161).

Factor 5: Normality of Rapists—"All rapists are mentally sick," (p. 161).

Factor 6: Power as Motivation for Rape—"All rape is a male exercise in power over women," (p. 161).

Factor 7: Favorable Perception of Woman After Rape—"A woman should not feel guilty following a rape," (p. 161).

Factor 8: Resistance as Woman's Role During Rape—"During a rape, a woman should do everything she can do to resist," (p. 161).

Rapists demonstrated significant differences from the rape crisis counselors on each of the eight factors. Rapists believed that rape prevention was the victim's responsibility, rape is motivated by sex, punishment should not be severe, victims encourage rape through their appearance and behavior, rapists are mentally disturbed, women should not resist during rape, a woman is less desirable after she has been raped, and rape is not motivated by power. Disturbingly, police officers' attitudes were found to be more similar to that of the rapists than the rape crisis counselors. Citizens also displayed attitudes more similar to rapists than rape counselors (Feild, 1978). These findings are frightening. The individuals who are supposed to protect victims seem to identify more with the criminals than the victims. How are victims supposed to feel safe when police officers share similar attitudes with rapists?

Feild also briefly examined differences in gender and ethnicity among the citizens included in the study. It was found that men tended to believe more than women that it is a woman's responsibility to prevent rape, rapist should be punished harshly, victims are more likely to encourage rape by their behavior or appearance, rapists are mentally stable, a woman should not resist during a rape, and a woman is less attractive after being victimized. When African-Americans were compared to whites, it was found that African-Americans felt that women were responsible for preventing rape, victims are less likely to encourage rape through behavior or appearance, rapists are mentally disturbed, and a woman is less desirable after a rape (Feild, 1978).

CONCLUSION

The prevalence of varying attitudes of rape between different cultures, ethnicities, gender, and occupations is clearly evident based upon the research in the area. Countries such as Japan, as well as many tribal cultures, place a large emphasis on male dominance and female subservience. Women are meant to be quiet and not speak up for themselves in these societies. Rape is either an acceptable practice or it is something meant to keep to oneself. Women are stigmatized or even punished for complaining about rape. This is a large culture shock for Americans. Rape is considered a crime. Women may be stigmatized for reporting rape, but they are not punished for their reports. Despite society's occasional poor treatment of rape victims, the act of raping a woman is not socially condoned.

The differences between ethnicities living in the same culture were interesting. Culture seemed to follow these individuals despite the culture of the country in which they were living. Hispanics were found to attribute more blame to female victims, with African-Americans next most likely to attribute blame to the victim, and whites the least likely to attribute blame to the victim. This is not surprising because Hispanics tend to treat women as more submissive to men than whites or African-Americans. The non-Hispanic whites included in the research have, most likely, been more socialized to see men and women as equal, therefore, attributing less blame to the female victim.

Findings concerning gender differences were probably the most surprising. In the majority of the research women attributed more blame to the victim than the perpetrator. It would seem that because the majority of rape victims are female, females would identify more with victims. These findings may suggest that the women included in these studies are actually identifying with the victims, however. It is possible that the victims blame themselves for the rape and the women included in the studies are identifying with that belief.

Another surprising and disturbing finding was the attitudes concerning rape held by police officers and citizens. Police officers and citizens held attitudes that were incredibly similar to that of rapists. The people sent to protect and support victims hold the same beliefs as the people they are supposed to be protecting them from.

All of these differences in perceptions of rape lead to the same conclusion: people need to be educated about rape and what the victim actually goes through during and following a rape. These perceptions may not be based solely on culture, ethnicity, or gender, but rather ignorance about what a serious crime rape is. This education is especially important for police officers. They absolutely should not be holding the same beliefs about rape, or any crime for that matter, as the perpetrator.

CHAPTER

GANG RAPE

Examining Peer Support and Alcohol in Fraternities

STEPHANIE NEUMANN

The college student population is frequently a target for rape. Gang rape is even more frequent on the college campus. Statistics show that an overwhelming percentage of gang rapes whose victims are college students are engaged in by fraternity members. Statistics show that anywhere from 55 to 70 percent of gang rapes perpetrated by college students were committed by fraternity members (Illinois Coalition Against Sexual Assault; Bohmer and Parrot, 1993; Rothman, 1999). Subsequent research has found that 86 percent of sexual assaults victimizing college students occur off-campus, frequently in a fraternity house or other fraternity member dwelling (George Mason University, 2001).

This chapter addresses rape within fraternities. However, to understand rape and gang rape in fraternities, it is essential to first examine these issues from a broader perspective. This includes a general explanation of gang rape in relation to college fraternities as well as fraternity members' attitudes toward gang rape. A case scenario of a fraternity gang rape is presented including an examination of victims, and strategies to avoid victimization by fraternity gang rape.

GANG RAPE

As defined by Sanday (1990) and Hodge (2002) gang rape is, "a violent act committed by a group of males with a common bond (such as gang, fraternity, or athletic team members) in which each member has sex in turn with a female in the presence of the entire group" (Hodge, 2002, p. 2). Research has found that the woman who is the victim of the gang rape is usually a target because of convenience; she is rarely an individual of significance to any one of the group members (Hodge, 2002).

In gang rape cases, a group is considered to be "three or more men" (O'Sullivan, 1991). Traditional social psychology defines a group to be two or more people, however, with respect to gang rape the group dynamics are not present unless there are three or more perpetrators. O'Sullivan (1991) reports that voluntary sexual practices by women are reported with one and two men, however, no reports of voluntary sexual behavior with more than two men has been reported.

The California Penal Code (2005) does not differentiate between gang rape and rape. Rather, in the case of gang rape, the state of California punishes each individual by charging them with rape. Rape, as defined by the Penal Code of California, is "penetration sufficient . . . any sexual penetration, how slight, is sufficient to complete the crime" (p. 83). Within California, rape is punishable by imprisonment sentences of three, six, or eight years, and a possible fine, which is not to exceed seventy dollars. Despite the California Penal Code's definition of rape, it is difficult to convict or arrest a fraternity member for the crime of rape (Frank, 1994; Hodge, 2002).

The prosecution of acquaintance gang rapes on college campuses is often difficult as a result of three factors: (1) when gang rapes are reported, multiple perpetrators may provide "counter-testimony" to the victim's testimony; (2) a woman may remain silent as a response to fear during the gang rape; the victim's silence can be interpreted as consent because objections were not vocalized; and (3) often the victim is unconscious during the rape and unable to identify the perpetrators in court; the court also protects defendants against self-incrimination therefore a perpetrator may never be identified (O'Sullivan, 1991). Considering the difficulty in the arrest and conviction of fraternity members who act as perpetrators in gang rape, only 19.7 percent of sexual assaults reported on the George Mason University campuses resulted in criminal penalties. Furthermore, only 38.8 percent resulted in punishment imposed by the college administration (George Mason University, 2001).

Statistics regarding gang rape illustrate that 1 to 2 percent of all females on college campuses are involved in gang rape (i.e., raped by two or more perpetrators). Overall on college campuses, 16 percent of all rapes and 10 percent of all attempted rapes engage multiple perpetrators. These gang rapes are most frequently committed by fraternity members or athletes (George Mason University, 2001; O'Sullivan, 1997).

GANG RAPE AND FRATERNITIES

In comparison to other types of rape, gang rape on campus is highly understudied. Much of the literature examining gang rape on campus focuses on incidents documented by legal and university reports. Despite the lack of literature, there are important distinctions among the motivations and characteristics of single-perpetrator rapes and multiple-perpetrator rapes that occur on college campuses and within fraternities (O'Sullivan, 1991). The main distinction is the role of group dynamics and peer influence in gang rapes. A question posed by much of the literature examining the relationship between sexual aggression and fraternities is whether gang rapes committed by fraternity members are a reflection of the personalities of individuals within fraternities or whether rape is a reflection of the group dynamics and organizational structure of fraternities as a whole (Boeringer, Shehan, & Akers, 1991).

Research suggests that peer acceptance is highly correlated with sexual aggression. Furthermore, some situations may have a stronger peer influence (e.g., fraternities encourage their members to "be a brother"), which may be a significant reinforcement of sexually inappropriate behavior (Boeringer, 1999, p. 87). Boeringer (1999) states, "the potential exists that enclaves of support for sexually coercive activities may desensitize others to the reality of rape and may provide social acceptance of coercive behavior to a greater extent than in other social settings" (p. 87).

There are specific features of fraternities that perpetuate the likelihood of sexually aggressive tendencies and behaviors among its members. These features as explained by Boeringer et al. are: (1) the emphasized norm of masculinity in an all-male environment; (2) the pledging process which frequently entails excessive alcohol use and pornographic entertainment; and (3) an environment that fosters "rape myths" and the view of women as sexual objects (Boeringer et al., 1991). Additionally, groups such as fraternities encourage alcohol consumption as a method of decreasing women's "sexual reluctance" which in turn facilitates sexually aggressive behaviors (Boeringer et al., 1991, p. 58; Martin & Hummer, 1989).

A study conducted by Boeringer et al. (1991) found that one of the only independent variables that distinguishes fraternity members from independent college students with respect to sexual coercion is the "actual use of nonphysical force and drugs or alcohol to obtain sex" (p. 61). Fraternity members also tend to have characteristics similar to individuals who are coercive and violent in their sexual activities. This behavior tended to be reinforced by fellow fraternity members (Boeringer et al., 1991).

Research has found that the population most likely to engage in rape in college is college fraternity pledges (Bohmer & Parrot, 1993). Furthermore, sexually coercive acts may be enabled by the desire for "male bonding," which is a substantial component of fraternities (Boumil, Friedman, & Taylor, 1993). Corroborating these perspectives is the research of Schwartz and Nogrady (1996), which found that male peer culture and alcohol are powerful predictors of sexually aggressive behavior in males. The results obtained by Schwartz and Nogrady (1996) lead to the conclusion that fraternity membership may increase the likelihood of sexually coercive tendencies due to the strong peer culture and the increased level of alcohol consumption as compared to control groups not affiliated with fraternities.

Membership in a fraternity that is a more "high-risk" group for rape is not sufficient to increase the likelihood of a member's sexually inappropriate behaviors. In addition to being a member of the "high-risk" organization, an individual must also "identify with the group and see it as a reference group" (Humphrey & Kahn, 2000, p. 1315). Humphrey and Kahn (2000) found that high-risk groups were more likely to have increased sexual aggression and hostility toward females, and peer support for sexual aggression than low-risk groups. A member of a fraternity may not identify with other members in this respect; however, individuals who pledge a fraternity are likely to seek out a fraternity whose members hold values similar to the pledge's values (Humphrey & Kahn, 2000). For example, an individual who enjoys consuming large quantities of alcohol is not going to pledge a dry organization. Rather, the individual is going to make the choice to pledge a fraternity in which excessive alcohol consumption is the norm.

O'Sullivan (1991) explains that the reduction of campus gang rape cases depends on males' attitude change toward female sexuality as well as male sexuality. The act of gang rape suggests a "lack of self-respect and self-integration" (O'Sullivan, 1991, p. 153). A shift in attitudes however is not the only variable in need of change. A transformation of attitudes alone will not affect the influence of group norms and group pressure on fraternity gang rape. Group norms however can only be influenced when influential individuals within the group endorse new principles. If all of the influential members do not support the change in attitude the group norms will remain unchanged.

The most recently implemented tactic for intervention with fraternities that commit gang rapes is to combine alcohol and sexual assault prevention and awareness courses. Prevention programs that would be the most effective however, would begin teaching awareness of these factors during middle school, when dating attitudes and behaviors are forming within each individual.

Boeringer (1999) found in a subsequent study that fraternity men had an increased propensity to have the following perceptions: "(a) women like to be physically 'roughed up,' (b) women want to be forced into sex, (c) women have secret desires to be raped, (d) men should be the controllers of the relationship, and (e) sexually liberated women are promiscuous" (p. 85). Overall, the research conducted by Boeringer (1999) concluded that there is a positive relationship between "rape-supportive attitudes" and fraternity membership (p. 87).

ATTITUDES TOWARD FRATERNITY GANG RAPE

Research supports the notion that American culture endorses attitudes that facilitates sexual aggression toward women. The clear differentiation between sexes and the conception of sex-roles through socialization promotes these attitudes toward sexual aggression (Garrett-Gooding & Senter, 1987). Garrett-Gooding and Senter (1987) state, "men (and women) who subscribe to traditional sex-role conceptions will be likely to judge physical sexual coercion of women as acceptable in various situations" (p. 348). These researchers hypothesized that fraternity members would engage more frequently in sexual coercion than independent students. This hypothesis is based on the perception that fraternities foster the sex-role conceptions mentioned above and therefore a socialization effect is occurring within fraternity members regarding their attitudes toward sexual aggression. Furthermore, it is likely that fraternities select their members based on criteria involving traditional sex-role attitudes. The aforementioned hypothesis posed by Garrett-Gooding and Senter was supported by the findings of their study.

RAPE ON COLLEGE CAMPUSES

Rape on the college campus is highly underreported. Students may report sexual assaults to campus officials however sexual assaults on campus are often not reported to the police. Koss and Harvey (1991) report that less than 5 percent of sexual assaults on students are reported to the police.

Bogal-Allbritten and Allbritten (1992) stated that university campuses generally assume one of three attitudes toward acquaintance rape on campus: (1) the campus criticizes the crime but does not punish the behavior; (2) the offense is discretely resolved and the campus reinforces a stance against rape through the distribution of rape prevention materials and rape prevention classes; or (3) the offense is criminalized through the implementation of rape task forces, rape crisis centers located on campus, and the development of policies and sanctions for students who engage in rape behaviors. In general, these stances toward rape on campus are not punitive toward the offender. Rather, these positions taken by college campuses tend to "save face" for the college rather than appropriately criminalize the behavior.

Bohmer and Parrot (1993) identify eight categories which colleges assume in their management of sexual assault on campus. The eight categories in order from most severe to most lenient are: (1) "victims' rights advocates," (2) "ethical," (3) "concerned," (4) "there but for the grace of God," (5) "barn-door closers," (6) "don't rock the boat," (7) "ostriches" and, (8) "victim blamers" (p. 123). Procedures of the first three categories take into consideration ethical principles and concern for the students. The following two categories amend their policies based on the incident. Universities that practice the last three categories of disciplinary measures base their strategies on the avoidance of negative publicity and financial loss (Bohmer & Parrot, 1993).

College campuses could improve their attitudes toward rape on campus by offering "legal information, support services, medical care, counseling, financial assistance, medical and court advocacy, and protection from harassment" (Illinois Coalition Against Sexual Assault, p. 44). Additional steps that can be taken by universities include, establishing who is responsible for investigation, keeping records, ensuring legal rights for the offender, ensuring that officials are sensitive to the needs of the victim . . . [and] following through on disciplinary action, even if the victim drops the charges. The sanctions for specific offenses should be written in details and should be adequate for a charge of this degree of seriousness. A policy should be made for dealing with an entire fraternity (Illinois Coalition Against Sexual Assault, p. 44)

These implementations however, would show greater discipline for individuals who engage in rape behaviors. Rather than keeping rape charges hidden, these policies may bring into the open that rape is a frequent crime on college campuses, particularly within fraternity organizations. The suggestion to improve attitudes toward rape on college campuses eliminates the theory of "out of sight, out of mind." Rape, particularly on college campuses, is an undesirable behavior to report; therefore if it is brought into the open the consequences may be detrimental to the school as well as organizations such as fraternities that more frequently engage in gang rape.

Sadly, college students' attitudes toward rape do not provide a positive outlook for the future of rape. Studies examining college students' attitudes toward rape found that 51 percent of college students might engage in the rape of a female victim if they were assured to not be penalized (Koss & Harvey, 1991). Given that fraternity members only compose 10 percent of the student population, the statistic mentioned above does not speak highly of either fraternity or non-fraternity members (Rothman, 1999).

FRATERNITY RAPE VIGNETTE AND DISCUSSION

In her book on fraternity gang rape, Sanday (1990) presents several vignettes illustrating the heinousness of gang rape within fraternities. One vignette that Sanday presents explores the gang rape of a female victim, who had a casual sexual relationship with a fraternity member; their relationship eventually transformed into a gang rape situation, (see case 44.1)

This account of a fraternity gang rape demonstrates the danger of extreme alcohol consumption while at fraternity parties. Additionally, the account illustrates how the victim's trusting nature toward Tim, a fraternity member with whom she had a casual sexual relationship, resulted in her victimization. This account, however, is not conveying that fraternity members cannot be trusted. Rather, trust should be limited at a fraternity party, particularly when excessive alcohol consumption is a main factor in the environment.

There are a plethora of psychological variables that come into play in this vignette regarding fraternity gang rape. Underlying many of these variables are the dynamics of the group. As a group, the fraternity members feel more comfortable engaging in a manner in which they would not behave if acting individually. For example, the first fraternity member, Tim, who had consensual sexual intercourse with the victim, was kind and complimenting toward her. Tim did not force himself on the victim rather she was willing to engage in intercourse with him. However in the presence of his other fraternity members, Tim became more sexually aggressive and led

Case 44.1 A Fraternity Gang Rape

Early one morning, after a late night party at the RST house at the beginning of my junior year, I was raped by I don't know how many guys. I had been going to RST parties since I was a freshman, even though I was warned on the first day of orientation never to go to the house alone . . . the RST guys were known to be a rowdy crew, heavy drinkers and 'partyers' . . . the brothers marked women who came to their parties with something called power dots. They were black, red, yellow, white, and blue colored dots that the brothers would stick to a girl's clothing at parties . . . Someone said that they indicated how good a friend you were to RST. The estimate for how good a friend you were was based on how easy you were to pick up . . . the parties were for sex and drinking. People would sort of go back and forth between the bedrooms and the party. I first started sleeping with somebody about maybe three weeks after I started going to RST . . . After I had slept with a brother the first time, brothers would approach me fairly directly and say, 'Do you want to go to my room with me?' As an incentive they would offer grain punch or pot . . . The morning I was raped, I had started drinking at a party we had at our apartment earlier in the evening. It was just after the first day of classes. One of my friends from another university was up. I went to the RST party with this girl. She was really high on drugs. I was really drunk. Earlier in the evening I had blacked out for an hour at about nine-thirty or ten and the next thing I remembered was that we were eating a sandwich on our way to the fraternity. When we got to the frat there was a party in session. They had a nasty purple punch that had grain alcohol in it. I started drinking and lost track of my friend. Some brothers came downstairs where I was and invited me upstairs to the balcony in front of the house . . . Tim asked if I wanted to go to his room. I agreed, I thought that would be fine . . . We went to his room and talked for a while. We ended up sleeping together . . . he kept commenting on how good I looked. His comments made me feel uncomfortable, because he's never really mentioned how I'd looked before. After we had sex I had to use the bathroom. Since he didn't have a robe, I wrapped a bath towel around myself. I didn't feel all that naked. I walked out into the hall. There were probably people in the hall, but I don't really remember. He came to the bathroom with me to watch the door because it didn't lock. When we got to the room there was somebody else in the room. He was lying on the bed and I don't think he had any clothes on at the time. Tim told me to go ahead into the room. I didn't remember seeing the guy before and wanted to know who he was. I was kind of confused. I thought maybe this was another one of those situations where Tim wanted a threesome but he hadn't said anything to me. He hadn't introduced me to this guy, which was kind of weird. I sat down on the edge of the bed where the guy was lying . . . he started kissing me. I was sort of willing . . . Then, Tim left and closed the door behind him. I sat up and said, 'Where did Tim go?' And this guy was like, 'Don't worry about Tim now.' And I'm like, 'I don't understand what's going on.' I'm not even sure what he said. Basically, he said something like, 'You'll understand what's going on,' or 'You'll see.' Next, the door opened and some other guys came

(continued)

Case 44.1 (*con't.*)

in. I think maybe two or three came in at that point. Then, I don't know how, but I went from sitting on the edge of the bed to lying down without the towel wrapped around me. Before, I'd been sitting and wearing the towel on the edge of the bed and then I was lying on the bed without the towel and this guy was on top of me, and there was intercourse going on. Then, the other guys in the room would either come over and one would be like touching me while another was having intercourse or whatever. There was somebody leaning on me most of the time, which made me feel like I was being held down. One person sat on the bed and the other person would sit on my chest with their penis in my mouth or something. It was not like they were saying, 'You can't leave,' but I felt like that's what they were saying . . . All I heard them saying was, 'That doesn't hurt, you like that. You don't want to leave now.' At one point there was some anal penetration, which was really painful . . . After the first twenty minutes or so I passed out and didn't wake up until about six in the morning . . . When I woke up there was some guy sitting on my chest with his knees on both sides of my head. I told him to get the hell off me. I'd seen him earlier in the evening, and he said, 'What are you doing? I haven't come yet.' . . . my eyes were puffy from crying also. My lips were bleeding and my jaws were stiff. I couldn't smile. My mouth hurt and my lips felt raw. My anus and vagina also felt sore . . . I must have blacked out after Tim left the room. For two hours the guys must have been coming in and out. I knew what happened in the beginning and I knew that when I regained contact with reality, there was still somebody sitting on me trying to force his penis in my mouth . . . The next morning I knew I had been the victim of a gang bang . . . sometimes when I was at the house, I had heard the brothers singing a song that went something like, 'When I'm older and turning gray, I'll only gang bang once a day.' (pp. 92–100).

---

the victim into a predicament where gang rape was the end result. In addition to the group dynamics and the encouragement that the group provided to the fraternity members, it was helpful to the perpetrators that the victim was overly intoxicated and frequently blacking out. The victim's intoxication and frequent black outs would help keep the perpetrators anonymous. Not aware of whom the perpetrators were and not having the ability to recall the perpetrators or how many there were, the case would not hold up in court if the victim attempted to prosecute the perpetrators.

The psychological and physical consequences that the victim may suffer are not discussed in the vignette, however they are important to consider. Psychological consequences may include post-traumatic stress, poor self-esteem, self-doubt, poor trust, and future vulnerability to subsequent sexual attacks. The physical repercussions of gang rape that are illustrated in this vignette are the vaginal and anal pain that may be a result of internal injuries, jaw aches, and mouth rawness. Other repercussions that are not evident in the vignette are possible sexually transmitted diseases and other illnesses.

WAYS TO AVOID GANG RAPE VICTIMIZATION ON A COLLEGE CAMPUS

Hodge (2002) states that there are three situations in which fraternity gang rape most frequently occurs. Each of these situations typically occurs during or immediately following a fraternity or sorority party. Generally, in these situations, most of the party-goers have consumed large quantities of alcohol. The three common scenarios for fraternity gang rape are,

> (1) One of the members inviting a girl into his room (or any room) where several of his brothers are waiting and raping her repeatedly. This is most likely to happen if the girl has had too much to drink; she will be more likely in this condition to submit to the request to go alone to the room and less likely to be able to physically resist her offenders; (2) One of the members giving a girl a ride or walk home. He could take her to any number of places where other members are waiting; (3) A member inviting his brothers to have sex with his unconscious girlfriend. This is a situation that usually occurs when the girl has been drinking heavily (Hodge, 2002, p. 3).

In these three scenarios, the female victim is usually blamed for her promiscuous behavior and the behavior of the male fraternity members is excused. Victimization can be avoided by being aware of the three typical scenarios for fraternity gang rape. Monitoring drug and alcohol consumption is also a way to avoid gang rape. Although rape is not the fault of the victim, as many people perceive it to be, the potential victim can take steps toward protecting herself against fraternity gang rape. When an individual is victimized and charges are pressed against the perpetrator, it is likely that the perpetrator will evade the charges. Therefore, it is pertinent to recognize at-risk behavior on the behalf of the victim and perpetrator; the frequency of gang rape will not be affected by the legal system, as most fraternity members charged with rape are unscathed. As stated earlier, it has become increasingly difficult to arrest or convict a fraternity member for rape. Therefore, the maladaptive and antisocial behavior of rape is often condoned in Greek life.

PERSPECTIVES ON FRATERNITY GANG RAPE

An article in the *UCLA Bruin* states that researchers manipulate their data regarding rape and gang rape in order to perpetuate prejudice toward fraternities (Rothman, 1999). Rothman (1999) explains that while gang rape within fraternities should be examined and discussed, it is far less prevalent than acquaintance rape and date rape occurrences on college campuses. A perspective frequently ignored in the literature is the implementation of mandatory seminars focusing on rape, alcohol, and hazing issues (Rothman, 1999). The current Greek system has recognized sexual aggression as a problem within its membership and therefore has taken steps to reduce the occurrence of fraternity rapes and other antisocial behaviors linked to fraternity membership (Rothman, 1999).

An article in the *Los Angeles Times* stated that women who frequent fraternity events such as parties should build a safety plan into their party plan. This plan should include the identification of a support system which can be called upon during a time of need during a party, identify a friend who will stay with you if you are drinking excessively, learn individual limitations on sexual behavior, and learn to adamantly say no and find a way out of the sexually aggressive situation (Japenga, 1987).

Often, researchers make the conclusion that affiliation with a fraternity increases an individual's probability of engaging in sexually aggressive or deviant behavior. Although this conclusion may be valid for some fraternities, it is not the standard for all fraternities. There are fraternities that emphasize community service or academic achievement. These fraternities should be distinguished from those which create more of a "party atmosphere" (Humphrey & Kahn, 2000). Humphrey and Kahn (2000) found that while some fraternities are conducive to sexually aggressive behavior and sexual assault, not all fraternities offer this environment. Therefore, it is not reasonable to assume that all fraternities and all fraternity members regularly engage in behaviors such as gang rape.

While fraternity gang rape is not widely recognized on college campuses there are steps that campus groups are taking to reduce the prevalence (Schwartz, DeKeseredy, Tait, & Alvi, 2001). Mahlstedt, Falcone, and Rice-Spring (1993) state that some campuses participate in the Fraternity Violence Education Project which is aimed at reducing sexually aggressive behavior on campus. The techniques that such projects employ include education, public awareness, and group discussions (Berkowitz, 2001).

Prevention methods often assume that the victim is at fault for the rape. The victim is not the individual to blame in situations of rape. Gang rape by fraternity members is likely to occur whether or not the victim enables the forced assault. Altering the victim's behavior is not the only change that needs to occur. More attention needs to be focused on the perpetrators. Young males who engage in excessive drinking, drug use, and gang rapes are often excused if the behavior is performed in the context of a fraternity setting. Fraternity members have created their own culture and social mores to which society has adapted.

The guidelines that are often given to female college students (as mentioned in a preceding section) to avoid victimization by fraternity gang rape are often impractical. The strategies often offered to potential victims tend to remove and isolate females from mainstream life. These strategies also do not account for acquaintance gang rapes or gang rapes perpetuated by significant others.

CONCLUSION

This chapter has examined several aspects of fraternity gang rape including a broad definition of gang rape, more specifically fraternity gang rape, attitudes toward fraternity gang rape, a vignette illustrating fraternity gang rape, techniques to avoiding fraternity gang rape, and perspectives toward fraternity gang rape. In general, researchers surmise that gang rape within fraternities is prominent yet under-reported and under-examined.

Often, colleges and universities strive for perfection in the public eye. As a means of saving face, colleges often secretly address gang rape within fraternities. Subsequently, it appears less consequential for fraternity members to commit acts of rape than the general public. Rapes, like other criminal offenses, are generally punished through retributive means, such as imprisonment. However, perpetrators of gang rape that occur on college campuses are seldom prosecuted. Rather than imprisonment serving as a deterrent for rapists, the lack of retributive measures abets fraternity rapes.

One main variable in the discussion of fraternity gang rapes is alcohol. Nearly all victims of fraternity gang rape are intoxicated at the time of the rape. Furthermore, the fraternity brothers are intoxicated as well. Alcohol tends to inhibit an individual's self-control and restraint. Therefore, victims are likely to struggle less and offenders are likely to not consider the immorality behind the act of rape, as they would if alcohol was not a variable. As seen in the vignette presented earlier, victims also have the potential to black out from alcohol consumption, causing them to not realize the forcible act against them or the number of perpetrators violating the victim.

Fraternity gang rape is enabled by group dynamics and peer reinforcement. However, these variables are not sufficient to cause a fraternity member to engage in gang rape. Individuals who partake in gang rape are often more aggressive and violent than the norm. Therefore, the combination of peer influence, group dynamics, and predisposed aggression feed into the formation of a fraternity member with a greater propensity to engage in sexually aggressive or violent acts such as rape. Although some fraternities do not focus on parties and drinking, many do. Those which focus on these aspects of fraternity life often draw individuals who enjoy engaging in such behavior. Therefore, it is likely that fraternities draw individuals who are predisposed to aggressive sexual tendencies. Engaging in less appropriate sexual behavior is more accepted by society if the individual is a fraternity member.

Unfortunately, society has given leeway to fraternities and the social mores that fraternity members have developed for themselves. The American public has accepted violence toward women and is often anesthetized to its ramifications. The media has also made a significant contribution to the increasing acceptance of sexual violence in society. For example, many movies portray fraternity life as being filled with alcohol, drugs, parties, and sex. Fraternities may feel the need to live up to this portrayal by the media, increasing their actual engagement in these behaviors. Furthermore, campus rape is often concealed from the media, but when the media is involved the rape becomes glamorized. Often fraternity rape cases that are presented in the media have a favorable outcome for the fraternity member.

Fraternities, like many other influential groups within society, seem to have privileges that facilitate antisocial practices and deviant behaviors. Among these behaviors is gang rape. Although shunned in society, fraternity members seem to be praised within a fraternity when a gang rape occurs. Often, rape is used as an initiation tool for fraternity pledges. Gang rape among some fraternity members seems to be a way of expressing masculinity and power.

C H A P T E R

SEXUAL SADISM IN RAPISTS

JEANNE JOHNSON

45

Rape is one of the fastest-growing crimes and is at least four times, perhaps as high as 10 times underreported by victims (Polsachek, Ward, & Hudson, 1997). However, studies indicate that fewer than ten percent of rapists are considered to be sexually sadistic rapists (Baker, 2001). Not only is there an increasing pressure to find an accurate profile of rapists in order to determine who is at risk with these particular characteristics, the pressure to find an accurate profile increases in order to assist in investigations and could be helpful in identifying and apprehending sadistic rapists (Baker, 2001). A psychological profile should include: background, attitudes, values, motivations, and idiosyncrasies of the offender. Also included should be included any trademark behaviors that the rapist commits during the act (Baker, 2001). There is also a necessary demand to find a reliable and successful treatment plan for incarcerated individuals as well as those who seek help in the community.

THEORIES OF RAPE

Theories abound about why some men commit rape. Possibly the first of these theories is that of the psychoanalytic viewpoint, as derived by Freud. Freud proposed that sexual perversion originated in infant sexuality, that sexual urges were present at birth. These urges continued to develop for a time, but were overtaken by a gradual process of suppression. Normal sexual behavior developed because of the physical inhibitions that were occurring during the course of maturation (Janssen, 1995). Since the origins of deviant sexual behavior were in infantile sexual desires that continued into adulthood, the possibility of change was seen as impossible (Polsachek et al., 1997).

Freud believed that perversion involves a deviation in the aim or object of normal sexual desire. Infantile desires is common to all of us, what makes desires perverse is not their content, but that the desires and subsequent behaviors become the exclusive sexual behavior (Janssen, 1995). Janssen (1995) raises the question of whether or not Freud would see rape as a perversion. For example, a rape offender seeks a normal sexual object, an adult female, and a normal aim, genital intercourse. "The act is criminal, not because it is considered a crime against nature, but because the victim has been forced to submit to the act without consent" (Janssen, 1995, p. 11).

The behavioral theory consists of different models, the trait inhibition of rape arousal, suggests that non-consent accompanied by the woman's displays of pain, fear and discomfort empathically inhibit sexual arousal in most men. Phallometric studies suggest that the ratio of arousal to rape versus consenting sexual interactions is higher in rapists and related to the number of victims and amount of violence inflicted upon them (Polaschek et al., 1997). Studies have found that the sadistic rapist finds the visible pain of the victim to be sexually arousing. The rapist enjoys inflicting physical and psychological pain because of a sadistic connection between violence and sexual gratification (Baker, 2001).

The sadistic rapist has made a connection between aggression and sexual gratification. The behavior can be defined as a paraphilia in which the offender is sexually excited by the psychological or physical suffering of a victim. The sadistic fantasy must be acted out and compulsively repeated in order for the rapist to satisfy himself sexually (Baker, 2001).

The state disinhibition of arousal, depicts the loss of ordinary inhibitions of arousal to rape cues. This involves factors that decreases an offender's prosocial motivation, such as a potential victim who is judged to be responsible for an assault because of wearing "provocative" clothing or being in a remote area. Other circumstances that may generate anger toward a potential victim, such as a woman making a derogatory remark concerning the man's performance, may also be included (Polaschek et al., 1997). The final behavioral model suggests that rapists may be characterized by their relative inability to voluntarily restrain sexual arousal, or by their capacity to be both aggressive and sexually aroused at the same time (Polaschek et al., 1997).

The gender inequality or feminist theory of rape defines rape as a mechanism of social control in patriarchal societies (Baron & Straus, 1987). It is argued that rape is more likely to occur in societies where women are regarded as the sexual and reproductive possessions of men. In these societies, men sustain their power and privilege and enforce their sexual rights through threat and use of force (Baron & Straus, 1987). Growing literature states that unwelcome sexual contact and sexually assaultive behavior is a normative experience for many women, this suggests that rape is supported culturally, especially through portrayals of women in the media (Polaschek et al., 1997). This seems likely considering that sexual scripts are closely related to the development of gender-role identities, in which male sexual behaviors are infused with the traditional masculine traits of dominance and aggression (Baron & Straus, 1987).

Social cognition concerns the study of social knowledge, its structure and content, and cognitive processes, including acquisition, representation and retrieval of information, in an attempt to understand social behavior and its mediating factors. Offenders' expectancies or beliefs about their own sexual behaviors and about victims bias the processing of sex-relevant information (Polaschek et al., 1997).

Rapists often see their victims dress as a "come on" and tend to have difficulty seeing the situation from their victim's perspective. They interpret passivity or frightened compliance of a victim as enjoyment of the rape, they also have complications identifying cues in first date situations, particularly with respect to negative mood states. These types of biased processing tend to process women's sexual communications in a distorted manner that create greater levels of mistrust and hostility towards women, in conclusion this supports sexual aggression (Polsachek et al., 1997).

The theory of sociobiology suggests that unlike women, men maximize their reproductive potential by copulating with numerous sex partners. Therefore, men who are domineering in copulation, may have been favored in the evolutionary ancestry in that they would produce more offspring. This suggests that there exists two unlearned drives, sex and the drive to possess and control, that motivate sexual behavior, including rape. It is proposed that men are favored with a stronger sex drive than women. Contradicting feminist and social learning theories, the sociobiologicial theory proposes that aggressive and domineering behaviors are tactics rather than goals, this supports a pure sexual motivation for rape (Polsachek et al., 1997).

Other theorists use a comprehensive theory for the framework of rape. This purports that in order for sexual aggression to occur several factors must converge. These factors are domain specific but within that domain some generalizations are to be expected, in conclusion the social environment, defined broadly to include unfavorable developmental experiences, acts to increase or decrease the likelihood that a male will coerce a female. There are three general categories of causes: motivation to commit the aggressive act, reductions in internal and external inhibitions that serve to prevent aggression, and finally, opportunity (Polsachek et al., 1997). In developing these categories, six predictor variables were used; sexual arousal to rape, dominance as a motive for sex, hostility towards women, attitudes facilitating aggression against women, antisocial personality characteristics, and sexual experience as a measure of opportunity to aggress (Polsachek et al., 1997).

Detrimental developmental experiences, such as parental violence and physical and sexual abuse can lead to the development of an antisocial outlook on male-female relationships. There are two avenues that lead to sexual aggression; hostile masculinity and sexual promiscuity. The first reflects the belief that the hostile home environment is frequently associated with the development of differing attitudes and personality characteristics which make coercive behavior more likely. It is thought that the first four predictors belong to this path. The second, sexual promiscuity, reflects the overuse of sexuality as a source of self-esteem and potentially leads to not only increased opportunity to use coercive tactics in the pursuit of sexual conquest, but also heightens the likelihood that they will be used (Polsachek et al., 1997). One explanation is that inconsistent and harsh discipline as children, by the parents is in excess while the absence of warmth and accepting support, fails to provide the needed social controls with respect to sex and aggression, and may even fuse these two aspects (Polsachek et al., 1997).

Pornography is thought by many to be a large factor in violence toward women. One assumption is that sexism and male dominance are depicted and eminent in pornography. Such images of women as objects of sexual exploitation tend to promote and legitimate male sexual violence. These theories propose that through the sexual objectification of women, which entails the fragmentation of a woman's body and eroticization of her body parts, pornography dehumanizes and degrades women, glamorizes violence, and legitimates sexism (Baron & Straus, 1987). Violent pornography has become more prevalent and images of women who appear to enjoy or are paid to enjoy being coerced, brutalized, and raped are now commonplace, this amplifies the myth that women want to be dominated and victimized (Baron & Straus, 1987).

TYPOLOGIES OF RAPISTS

Knight, Warren, Reboussin, and Soley (1998) classified rapists into four categories. These four primary motivations for rape appear to be related to enduring behavioral patterns that distinguish particular groups of offenders. The four types are opportunistic, pervasively angry, sexual, and vindictive. These four types are further broken down into six subtypes. The opportunistic type is broken into two subtypes, high and low social competence, which is based on their social competence and the developmental stage at which their high impulsivity first was manifested. The sexual type has two subtypes, sadistic and nonsadistic, while the vindictive type also has two types, low and moderate social competence (Knight et al., 1998).

The most dangerous type of rapist is the sadistic rapist, as their purpose is to hurt the victim both physically and psychologically. Often these offenders will torture, mutilate, and murder their victims for the joy of seeing their victims suffer (Baker, 2001). Sadistic rapists usually contemplate their crime for some time, often stalking their victims to determine their living habits (Petter & Witehill, 1998).

The sexual assaults of the opportunistic type appears to be impulsive, predatory acts, controlled more by situational and contextual factors, such as women present during another crime or, a woman encountered in a bar or at a party, than by sexual fantasy or explicit anger at women. The pervasively angry type is thought to be global and undifferentiated anger that occupies all areas of the offender's life. These offenders are equally likely to express their unmanageable aggression at men as well as women. These men have long histories of antisocial aggressive behavior, of which rape is another form. Their offenses are characterized by high levels of expressive anger, and they inflict large levels of physical pain on their victims (Knight et al., 1998).

For the two vindictive offender types, women are centralized as an exclusive focus of their anger. The sexual assaults of these men are distinguished by behaviors that are explicitly intended to harm the woman physically, as well as to degrade and humiliate her. The sadistic type is marked by the sexual fantasy that influences as well as sustains the rape. This preoccupation with sexual fantasy may be distorted by the fusion of sexual and aggressive feelings or characterized by dominance needs and/or intense feelings of inadequacy. The sadistic type is divided into overt and muted types based on whether their sexual-aggressive fantasies are acted upon in violent attacks or remain as fantasies (Knight et al., 1998).

The Federal Bureau of Investigation has also classified rapists into four categories, these are power-reassurance, exploitative, anger and the violent sadistic type (Baker, 2001). The interaction between the sadistic rapist and a surviving victim often provides essential information in constructing the personality profiles of these rapists (Baker, 2001).

SADISTIC RAPISTS

It is important to have a list of defining characteristics of rapists in order to better understand the rationale behind this crime, it is also a helpful tool in determining a successful treatment plan. Information has been obtained between sexually aggressive activity and the endorsement of traditional sex roles and adversarial attitudes to women, as well as rape myths and acceptance of the use of violence towards women, also an early age of the first sexual experience (Polsachek et al., 1997). Rapists appear to be of low socioeconomic status, they tend to have left high school prematurely, show an unstable employment history in unskilled jobs, have similar levels of general social competency, with the possible exception of assertiveness. Caregiver inconsistency and sexual deviation and abuse in the family were related to the severity of sexual aggression (Polsachek et al., 1997).

Sadistic rapists have, as well as those characteristics mentioned above, more abnormal and sexually deviant commonalties. Many of the characteristics that are common among sadistic rapists are significant history of physical abuse, known cross-dressing, telephone scatalogia and indecent exposure (Gratzer & Bradford, 1995). For a detailed list of sadistic rapists characteristics as composed by Dietz, Hazelwood, and Warren (1990) please refer to Table 45.1.

When discussing the sadistic criminal, many researchers agree that the definition of sadism is an important issue, especially when including incarcerated individuals and their crimes. The most accepted definition that many authors use is:

> the experience of sexual pleasure sensations (including orgasm) produced by acts of cruelty, bodily punishment afflicted on one's person or when witnessed in others, be they animals or human beings. It may also consist of an innate desire to humiliate, hurt, wound, or even destroy others in order thereby to create sexual pleasure in one's self (Grubin, 1994a, p. 5).

Table 45.1   Characteristics of Sexually Sadistic Criminals[1]

Characteristics	n	%
Male	30	100.0
White	29	96.7
Parental infidelity or divorce	14	46.7
Physically abused in childhood	7	23.3
Sexually abused in childhood	6	20.0
Married at time of offense	13	43.3
Incestuous involvement with own child	9	30.0
Known homosexual experience	13	43.3
Known cross-dressing	6	20.0
Known history of peeping, obscene telephone calls, or indecent exposure	6	20.0
Shared sexual partners with other men	6	20.0
Education beyond high school	13	43.3
Military experience	10	33.3
Established reputation as solid citizen	9	30.0
Drug abuse (other than alcohol)	15	50.0
Suicide attempt	4	13.3
Excessive driving	12	40.0
Police "buff"	9	30.0
(excessive interest in police activities and paraphernalia)		

[1]From "The Sexually Sadistic Criminal and His Offenses," by P. E. Dietz, R. R. Hazelwood and J. Warren, 1990, *Bulletin of the American Academy of Psychiatry and Law, 18,* (2), p. 168.

This definition coincides with the description given by Dietz et al. (1990), which was written by a man who kidnapped, kept captive, raped, sodomized, and in some cases murdered his victims in several states over an extended period of time. This man kept audiotapes of his sexual torture of his fourth wife, and one of his stranger victims, his own written plans for building an "S & M play area," cells, as well as other paraphernalia which confirm a long pattern of sexual arousal to the suffering of his sexual partners. He offers this definition of sexual sadism:

Sadism: The wish to inflict pain on others is *not* the essence of sadism. One essential impulse: *to have complete mastery over another person,* to make him/her a helpless object of our will, to become the absolute ruler over her, to become her God, to do with her as one pleases. To humiliate her, to enslave her, *are means to this end,* and the most important radical aim is to make her *suffer* since *there is no greater power over another person than that of inflicting pain on her* to force her to undergo suffering without her being able to defend herself. The pleasure in the complete domination over another person is the very essence of the sadistic drive (Dietz et al., 1990, p. 165). [Italics in original]

Another definition that is along the same lines as the previous two is that of Kocsis, Cooksey, and Irwin (2002) which states, "... the sadistic rapist, who exhibits a combination of both sexual and aggressive components. Aggression is eroticized, and the offender is typically aroused and excited by the victim's maltreatment, torment, and suffering. These assaults often involve bondage, torture, and considerable abuse and injury to the victim" (p. 145). This overwhelming desire for control and the feelings that accompany it, is what make sadistically violent criminals different from nonviolent sadists. Those who fantasize about sexually sadistic acts focus more upon sexual arousal related to pain and humiliation, rather than that of total control and domination (Grubin, 1994a).

Sexually sadistic rapists have been described as introspective and solitary persons who rarely show any signs of open violence. This criminal is likely to offend following a loss of self-esteem, experiencing relief in response to his murder, and behaves "normally" after committing the crime (Warren, Hazelwood, & Dietz, 1996). The wish to control lies at the heart of sadism and can be seen through the crime scenes, which are left "organized," in hopes to avoid detection. This suggests much forethought and planning on the part of the offender (Grubin, 1994b).

Violent sexual fantasy plays a major role in sexual sadism (McCollaum & Lester, 1994). There are commonalties in offense characteristics that relate to the paraphilic fantasies and urges that motivate sadistic behavior. For example, careful planning of the offense, the victim being taken to a preselected location, and intentional torture and beating of the victim (Gratzer & Bradford, 1995). Because such offenders have little control over their personal lives, they compensate this inadequacy by controlling their victims and arrangement of the crime scene which has been rehearsed in their fantasy life (Grubin, 1994b). Each time a sexual act is performed, the crime becomes closer to actually enacting the particular paraphilic fantasy (Johnson & Becker, 1997). Often the rapist will keep souvenirs such as personal items or photographs of the victim so that the rapist can relive fantasies and memories of the victim's anguish and the crime itself (Baker, 2001). For a detailed list of characteristics of offenses as composed by Dietz et al. (1990) please refer to Table 45.2.

As adolescents, violent sexual fantasies are often the predecessor of later violent behaviors (Geberth & Turco, 1997). This is one possible way to detect those adolescents who may be at risk as potential sadistic criminals. The triad of enuresis, fire setting, and animal cruelty have been found to be predictors of youth violence leading to adult criminal activities (Johnson & Becker, 1997). Johnson and Becker (1997) state that youths who demonstrate sadistic fantasies along with criminal behaviors should be "red-flagged," and followed closely. They should also be offered treatment to help control these deviant fantasies before they become reality. Johnson and Becker (1997) studied adolescents with the characteristics of sadistic criminals, many of whom had already performed violent acts. One such case study follows:

H. was an 18-year-old white male who had suffered from AD/HD and chronic depression. He was of below average intelligence with possible learning disabilities. At an early age, he recalled having been severely physically abused by his mother, including beating and whipping.

Table 45.2   Characteristics of Offenses[1]

Characteristics	n	%
A partner assisted in offense	11	36.7
Careful planning of offense	28	93.3
Impersonation of police in commission of offense	7	23.3
Victim taken to preselected location	23	76.7
Victim kept in captivity for 24 hours of more	18	60.0
Victim bound, blindfolded, or gagged	26	86.7
Sexual bondage of victim	23	76.7
Anal rape of victim	22	73.3
Forced victim to perform fellatio	21	70.0
Vaginal rape of victim	17	56.7
Foreign object penetration of victim	12	40.0
Variety of sexual acts with the victim[2]	20	66.7
Sexual dysfunction during offense	13	43.3
Unemotional, detached affect during offense	26	86.6
Told victim what to say during assault	7	23.3
Intentional torture	30	100.0
Murdered victim	22	73.3
Committed serial murders (3 or more victims)	17	56.6
Concealed victim's corpse	20	66.6
Victim beaten (blunt force trauma)	18	60.0
Recorded the offense[3]	16	53.3
Kept personal item belonging to victim	12	40.0

[1]From "The Sexually Sadistic Criminal and His Offenses," by P. E. Dietz, R. R. Hazelwood and J. Warren, 1990, *Bulletin of the American Academy of Psychiatry and Law, 18,* (2), p. 170.
[2]A variety of sexual acts is defined as having subjected the victim to at least three of the following: vaginal rape, forced fellatio, anal rape, foreign object penetration.
[3]Includes recordings through writings, drawings, photographs, audio tapes, or videotapes.

Furthermore, he recalled his mother being very sexually provocative throughout his youth, exposing herself to him or watching him undress and making erotic comments. His parents once engaged in sexual intercourse in front of him, and he recalled his mother moaning in what he felt was a haunting and deathlike manner.

At the age of 14, H. began to fantasize about having sexual intercourse with his mother while listening to her moan, killing her, and continuing to have intercourse with her corpse. He admitted that he was masturbating approximately eight times a day to this fantasy, often using his mother's underwear as an erotic aid.

He expressed confusion as to sexual orientation, but generally preferred heterosexual activities. He had had over 100 female sexual partners, often exchanging money for sex. He had also been sexually abused by a 16-year-old baby sitter at the age of 10. He admitted to fantasies of acts of voyeurism, fetishism, cross-dressing, sadism and rape. He had a significant history of alcohol and drug abuse. He had been diagnosed with a borderline personality disorder. He denied any history of killing animals.

At the age of 17, he committed his first killing of an unknown woman via strangulation and continued to commit necrophilic acts with the corpse for at least three days (Johnson & Becker, 1997, p. 339–340).

TREATMENT

One possible suggestion for treatment is that of cognitive/behavioral and psychopharmacology, however these need to be offered early enough in the development of the sexually sadistic and homicidal fantasy. With the early onset one hopes to decrease or even prevent the outcome of such sadistically criminal acts (Johnson & Becker, 1997).

Many forms of treatment, although still in the experimental stages, have been offered. Four commonly used methods to modify sexual interest are: covert sensitization, olfactory/gustatory aversion, masturbatory satiation, and orgasmic reconditioning. The first three aim to reinforce decreased arousal to sexually sadistic fantasies, whereas the latter seeks to reinforce arousal to nondeviant fantasies. Although the effectiveness of these methods is limited, it offers suggestions on ways to change the sexual arousal patterns of such criminals (Hollin, 1997).

Other possible treatment methods include increasing victim empathy, which is not the sole form of treatment—this is often an addition to more stringent forms of therapy (Hollin, 1997). Victim enjoyment of aggression and rape are less important than the perpetrator's pleasure or gratification (Hucker, 1997). It is important to work on the cognitive aspect of sadistic rape, focusing on modifying sexual fantasies and preferences, as well as the misconception of rape, fantasies about forced sex, and sexual arousal to rape depictions (Hucker, 1997). Also, it is important to help the offender realize the inappropriate sex-related cognitions that are likely to predispose these individuals to sex offenses. Establishing the nature of the offender's beliefs about sexual targets, such as women and children, and working toward their realization that these are false social beliefs, will help the offender in changing these misconceptions (Hudson & Ward, 1997).

Assisting the offender in not minimizing, denying, and justifying rape, as well as more liberal attitudes toward women and sex, toward their own sexuality and adversarial relationships between men and women, as well as toward the use of interpersonal violence to attain desired goals, is a necessary avenue in treatment for offenders. A good procedure for modifying inappropriate attitudes is addressing the dysfunctional attitudes or beliefs, identifying the role these play in offending, providing contradictory evidence and costs to him for hiding them, and finally, role-playing the expression of these beliefs together with presenting prosocial alternatives and the advantages they offer. If part of the desire to hurt another really does come from the ability to perceive them as different from oneself, then part of this aspect of treatment must aim to get rapists to reduce their tendencies to view women as another species (Ward, McCormack, Hudson, & Polaschek, 1997).

Although treatments are still being discovered and modified, cognitive/behavioral therapy show promising signs. Early detection is also necessary for adolescents who show characteristics of violent behavior. Studies indicate that some types of treatment can have an considerable effect on recidivism (Clelland, Studer, & Reddon, 1998). Research continues to be performed on the characteristics as well as treatment plans and the effects on recidivism rates. Many believe that the current treatment plans do not demonstrate enough success, while others believe that this population of offenders is non-treatable. Rape continues to be one of the fastest growing crimes of violence and with overwhelming pressure to find an accurate profile, the number of rapists grows in our prison population (Janssen, 1995).

CHAPTER

COERCED SEX AND RAPE PARAPHILIA

A Psychological and Legal Analysis of Pornography

JAMES ALVARADO

46

In the suburbs of Miami, Florida, Carolyn walks along the road to an unknown destination. A man approaches the young Hispanic woman, who can barely speak English, with a video camera in a tinted van. He asks her to come in for an interview. After a long deliberation coupled with the promise of money, she eventually gives in and enters the van, which speeds off. As Carolyn looks around, she realizes that the driver, the cameraman, a woman sitting next to her and Javier sitting patiently behind her outnumber her. Slowly the occupants encourage her to remove more and more clothing with the promise of money. The occupants convince Carolyn to have sex with Javier in exchange for even more money. Following sex the van pulls over to the side of the road and Carolyn exits with the promise that her money will be given once she leaves the van. As she disembarks, her personal property is handed over to her, the van door slams shut and drives away. Nina is left at the side of the road without her promised money (Bang Bus, 2002).

Somewhere near Miami, a young man, Danny, is approached by a tinted van. A man with a camera greets him. Likewise, two beautiful women greet him from inside the van. Danny is told that the occupants of the van make pornographic movies and, after some bargaining, Danny agrees to enter the van with the promise of sex with one of the women and money. As with the previous story, he finds himself outnumbered:

two women (one is driving), a camera man, and Matt in the back. A woman then begins to get Danny aroused and convinces him to close his eyes as she touches him. When he does, Matt steps in and begins to fondle him. The woman then continues to arouse Danny while explaining that before he can have sex with her he will have to allow Matt to have oral sex with him. His protests are quickly muted by an offer of $3000 for his co-operation. After intercourse, Danny is told he will be given his check when he exits the van. He is dropped off near his home and, when he exits, is handed a check that says "Zero Dollar" for the amount and paid to the order of "Dumbass." The van quickly drives off as the man stands stunned about what has transpired (Bait Bus, 2002).

RAPE PORNOGRAPHY

Violent pornography is generally obtained from one of three sources: magazines, video, and the internet. Research has shown that as one progresses from magazines, to video, to the internet, there is an increase in the levels of violence one can obtain (Barron & Kimmel, 2000). Violent pornography on the Internet is often easily spotted. The stories above came from websites such as Bang Bus, Bait Bus, and Cruise Patrol. Each advertises footage of people who are tricked into having sex for money and then abandoned before payment is made. Whether real or staged, these images cater to people who have an interest in coerced sex. This chapter will argue that such depictions are actually congruent with a rape paraphilia and that both the actors and viewers of the material are actually participating in coercive pornography and a version of rape.

THE PSYCHOLOGY OF PARAPHILIAS

According to the *DSM-IV-Tr,* the most salient feature of a paraphilia is a recurrent, intense sexually arousing fantasy, sexual urge, or behavior which involves either non-human objects, suffering or humiliation of oneself or one's partner, or children or other nonconsenting persons. These need to occur over a period of at least six months to fulfill Category A for the specified paraphilias in the *DSM-IV-Tr* (American Psychiatric Association [APA], 2000).

Some people who have paraphilias require the fantasy or stimuli in order to achieve arousal or sexual gratification. Others periodically require the paraphilia for arousal and gratification, while still others do not require the stimuli at all for normal sexual functioning but just desire it (APA, 2002).

Though there is a wide variety of paraphilia, the *DSM-IV-Tr* recognizes only eight distinct types. The manual provides for a ninth category, Paraphilia Not Otherwise Specified (NOS), to encompass any erotic focus that does not fall within the previous eight types (APA, 2000). A paraphilia NOS diagnosis can come in many forms, involving a multitude of acts and objects which a person finds sexually stimulating, including anthropophagy (eating of victims flesh or slicing off parts of the body), autoeroticism (sexual arousal from self-stimulation, usually involving pornography), coprophilia (gratification from touching or eating excrement or urine), pyromania (sexual gratification from fire setting), and rape (forced sexual intercourse) (Hickey, 2006).

The coercive sex websites introduced above encompass a wide variety of paraphilic interests. To name a few: voyeurism (subscribers can watch others have sex), exhibitionism (participants expose themselves and have sex on camera), and sexual sadism (unwilling participants are victimized, pressured into having sex, abandoned after being used, and then their humiliation is shown on the Internet). Finally, and most importantly, is the paraphilia of rape. Those sexually aroused by the thought or depiction of coerced sexual activity can also rely on such stimuli for arousal.

RAPISTS AND THOSE AROUSED BY RAPE

The current body of work addressing sex offenders indicates that there are several common psychopathological disorders involving deficits in anger management, attachment, empathy, social and sexual deficits. An examination of the literature by Lee, Pattison, Jackson, and Ward (2001) divided such disorders into two broad categories: anger-hostility and social-sexual incompetence. The anger-hostility disorder category associates anger and hostility with the psychopathology of sexual offending while the social-sexual incompetence disorder category is linked to sexual offenses, which stem from social, interpersonal, or sexual inadequacies and incompetencies.

ANGER-HOSTILITY

The anger-hostility category encompasses offenses in which offenders act out due to their inability to manage their anger and hostility (Lee et al., 2001). One theory suggested that states of anger and hostility often occur before sex offending and thus encourage it. In these states, emotions like guilt, anxiety, and empathy are unable to restrain a rapist from harming a victim (Hall & Hirschman, 1991). Marshall and Barbaree (1990) argued that rapists have their sexual and aggressive impulses combined. This causes abusive sexual behavior because of a difficulty of discriminating between the two impulses during sexual situations. Overcontrolled hostility within sexual offenders has been found at higher levels than within murderers and other types of offenders (Gudjonsson, Petursson, & Skulason, 1989). Sexual offenders have also been noted to perpetrate greater indirect hostility than violent non-sexual offenders (Fiqia, Lang, Plutchik, & Holden, 1987).

SOCIAL-SEXUAL INCOMPETENCE

This category is rooted in theories which postulate that sex offenders are incompetent in their social and sexual functioning (Lee et al., 2001). For example, according to a theory by Dietz, Cox, and Wegener (1986), exposure may be a reaction to sexual or social rejection. On the other hand, other social-sexual theories attribute exposure to a desire for interpersonal admiration (Langevin & Lang, 1987). Further, the insecure attachment styles of sex offenders are seen to be the result of abusive or neglectful childhood experiences (Marshall & Barbaree, 1990). These faulty attachments cause offenders to fail in establishing intimate relationships and to seek intimacy needs through sexually inappropriate behavior (Lee et al., 2001).

Lee et al.'s (2001) study found that a sample of rapists showed lower sexual esteem and greater sexual depression than a comparison group. They also found high interpersonal sensitivity, interpersonal reactivity and fear of negative evaluation, negatively predicted rape compared to subjects with nonrape paraphilias. Sexual esteem is the dispositional tendency to evaluate positively one's capacity to relate sexually to others while sexual depression is the chronic tendency to feel depressed about the sexual aspects of one's life (Snell & Papini, 1989). Overall, this study found rapists rated low in their ability to relate sexually to others, they had a tendency to feel depressed about their sex life, and lacked empathy towards their victims.

SEX OBTAINED THROUGH COERCION AND FRAUD

Defining rape has baffled lawmakers, legal scholars, and courts for over a century. Two particularly troubling aspects of rape have been sex by coercion (intercourse achieved by a perpetrator using nonphysical pressures such as use of authority, extortion, or threats) and rape by fraud (sexual intercourse accomplished through any type of fraud, deception, misrepresentation, impersonation, or other stratagem) (Falk, 1998). The use of coercion and fraud to obtain sex has been reviewed in the courts as early as the 1800s.

Cases of rape by coercion and fraud fall into six categories. Rape by coercion is covered by (1) abuse of authority and (2) sexual extortion, while rape by fraud is categorized as (3) a form of fraudulent treatment, (4) fraud as to the defendant's identity, (5) sexual scams, and/or (6) sexual theft (Falk, 1998). The first category, abuse of authority, involves sexual intercourse achieved through the use of authority or manipulation of power within a relationship. Perpetrators of this type hold some form of power or authority over their victims. This included those who hold real power, such as teachers, principals, legal guardians, and officers of the law and those who impersonate authority figures such as police officers (Falk, 1998).

The sexual extortion category refers to cases with elements of both coercion and fraud. Such situations involve perpetrators who also have power over victims. However, the power is obtained through the circumstances surrounding their contact with the victim and not through authority. For example, in *People v. Cassandras* (1948), the defendant used the promise of a good paying job to lure a woman outside an employment office into his car and later into a hotel. Then he used various threats, such as reporting her as a prostitute to the police, to obtain sex from her. The court found that Cassandras applied sufficient pressure to be considered force and to convict him of rape (Falk, 1998).

Fraudulent treatment covers cases in which victims are told that sexual acts are necessary for medical treatment, psychological or psychiatric treatment, spiritual guidance, and educational purposes (Falk, 1998). In *Moran v. People* (1872), the defendant secured sexual compliance by convincing patients that sexual intercourse was an alternative to a painful surgical procedure. Fraud as to the defendant's identity is accomplished through the impersonation of someone who the victim has had or wants to have a sexual intercourse with. This can be accomplished by impersonating people, including victims' husbands, sexual partners, or a desired sexual partner (i.e. someone famous) (Falk, 1998).

Sexual scams differ from both rape by fraudulent treatment and by fraudulent identity as they do not involve false promises or impersonations. Sexual scams are usually comprised of an individual in a business setting who offers a false benefit in exchange for sexual services. The fact patterns of these interactions closely resemble fraudulent commercial transactions, with sex being given in exchange for a benefit which is not delivered (Falk, 1998).

United States v. Condolon (1979) offers an example of a sexual scam as well as the problems associated with the prosecution such perpetrators. Condolon obtained an apartment and a business license, and placed an ad in a newspaper offering to find women acting and modeling jobs. Many of the women who responded to the ad were propositioned by Condolon, and a number of them had intercourse with him. Through his scam, Condolon obtained sex although he never had any real means of assisting his clients in obtaining work. *U.S. v. Condolon* demonstrated the common problem with punishing sexual scammers: Condolon was not punished directly for his sexual activities, instead he was prosecuted because he established a fraudulent business and used his telephone to accomplish his fraudulent intentions (Falk, 1998).

Sexual scams also go beyond the boundaries recognized by fraudulent treatment and partner impersonation cases. Court outcomes of sexual scams cases have been mixed as many courts have been reluctant to extend existing statutes to cover such cases. Prosecution usually centers on the other forms of fraud or property offenses which perpetrators committed during the scam (Falk, 1998).

The last category, sexual theft, involves those who are offered sex in exchange for money but are not paid after services are rendered, such as a prostitute or the individuals depicted in the opening scenarios. Courts have resisted extending legislation to cover such offenses. Legal commentators argue that the law does not recognize rape under such circumstances because society views any form of prostitution as immoral and illegal (Falk, 1998).

A PSYCHOLOGICAL AND LEGAL ANALYSIS OF RAPE PORNOGRAPHY

The Bang Bus, Bait Bus, and Cruise Patrol websites contain images of people who are lured into sexual acts through coercion and fraud. The authenticity of their footage is questionable. The recordings on the websites may contain actors pretending to be victims. This point, however, is irrelevant because at issue is usage of the film as pornography and not its legitimacy as a rape. A person who is aroused by and masturbates to images of a staged rape is still being aroused by and masturbating to images of a rape, regardless of the authenticity of the act. The fantasy these sites provide and sell is that of sexual exploitation and rape. From both a psychological and legal standpoint, such websites offer viewers images of sex obtained through fraud and coercion (acts which have clearly been deemed as illegal).

The videos found on these sexually coercive websites can be analyzed under Lee et al.'s (2001) anger-hostility disorders category. Though the perpetrators anger and hostility are not blatantly obvious within the videos, it can be assumed by their actions. Through luring people into a van, the perpetrators isolate the victim. From these, several coercive factors keep the victim from fleeing; they are outnumbered, they are in a moving vehicle, and they face being stranded on the side of the road if they are able to leave. Already vulnerable, the victims are then offered money in exchange for sex. The films depict people being dehumanized into a sexual object. This objectification allows viewers to feel little empathy for the victims who are later abandoned on the side of the road without their promised money and faced with the reality of being sexually exploited.

Three categories of rape through coercion and fraud apply to such websites: sexual extortion, sexual scams, and sexual theft. Sexual extortions involve the use of power over a victim to obtain sex. The predicament of victims in the websites is similar to that of the victim in *People v. Cassandras* (1948). In that case, the victim faced either submitting to sex or the threat of Cassandras calling the police. In the same vein, the Internet videos depict people faced with a choice of sexual compliance or dealing with a van full of people, getting out of a moving vehicle, and possibly, being stranded at the side of the road. The recordings are also sexual scams. Victims are lured into the vans through various means including a ride, money, or sex with a beautiful woman. After the victims are convinced into having sex on tape, they are released without their promised benefit.

While sexual extortion provides the best description for the circumstance which affect the victims, sexual scams is the best category to describe what draws the victim into the van and then convinces victims into having sexual intercourse. The third category, sexual theft, best describes the overall theme of the recordings. A majority of the victims are offered money in return for sex. After intercourse, they are depicted as being abandoned without payment.

A DISCUSSION OF VIOLENT PORNOGRAPHY

Malmuth, Addison, and Koss (2000) performed a meta-analysis on the effects of exposure to nonviolent and violent pornography on aggressive attitudes and behavior. Their results showed that both nonviolent and violent pornography affects aggressive attitudes and behaviors with violent pornography doing so to a greater degree. They also demonstrated that rapists were more aroused by violent pornography than non-rapists. Rapists were also found to be less aroused by nonviolent pornography than non-rapists. Further, exposure to both nonviolent and violent pornography was associated with the increased chance of some form of sexual act by rapists. Malmuth et al. (2000) concluded there is a consistent association between the use of pornography and sexual aggression. Amongst people who were high at risk for sexual aggression, frequent users of pornography were more likely to act out than infrequent users of pornography.

Rape is a combination of both sexual and aggressive elements (Barbaree & Marshall, 1991). The subtly aggressive coercions depicted within the internet pornography sites contain sexual material which fuel the fantasies of a would-be rapist. Viewers are given images of victims who engage in sex under fraudulent and coercive circumstances. Such images are consistent with anger-hostility disorder category of sexual offenses. Legally, the offenders perform acts congruent with sexual extortions, sexual scams, and sexual theft. Pornography of this nature depicts rape. The nonviolent nature of the offense masks the crime at first glance. Careful scrutiny, however, reveals videos that depict people tricked through coercion and fraud into having sex and being abandoned. Of most concern is that while websites such as Bang Bus, Bait Bus, and Cruise Patrol depict, what they would argue, subtle coercive sex, violent pornography of any kind is one of the many motivating factors for convicted rapists, as well as non-incarcerated sexually aggressive men (Lisak & Roth, 1988).

CHAPTER
FEMALE SERIAL MURDERERS

ANNE MARIE PACLEBAR

Contrary to popular belief, female serial killers do exist. There have been a number of female serial killers throughout history, however the exact documented figure is still in much debate. According to Hickey (2006), the total number of documented female serial killers is 64 or about 15% of his study. About 69% acted alone and 31% with one or more partners. Altogether they murdered between 427–612 victims. Most were white (93%) and the remainder African-American. They ranged in age from 15–69 at the time they first began killing. Most of these cases began after 1950 (see Table 47.1). The stereotypical view of women as nurturers and caregivers is an ideal that is very difficult to alter. Many individuals are in denial of the fact that females can also become and act out in heinous, psychopathic, and methodical ways, let alone be categorized as predators. According to James Fox, author of several books on serial and mass murder, "Murder is primarily a male activity. Ninety percent of murders are committed by men" (Cited in Dahlburg, 2002). As will be discussed in this chapter however, some women are capable of being sexual predators, murderers, bludgeoning individuals to death, strangulation, killing for money, and suffocating their own children and loved ones. In doing so these female predators have been known by various monikers (see Table 47.2).

Typically, when an individual hears the word serial killer, one normally thinks of white, heterosexual, males in their twenties and thirties (Welch, 2002). According to *A Short History on All of the Worst Serial Killers in the World,* a website devoted exclusively to serial killer case summaries, the male serial killer is thought to engage in "methodical rampages," and they are almost always sexually motivated.

Table 47.1 Victim/Female Serial Murderer Comparisons in the United States, 1826–2004

Year	Number of Cases	Number of Cases per Year	Number of Victims	Number of Victims per Case	Number of Victims per Year
Total	61	.34	427–612	7–10	2.4(178 yrs)
1826–1849	1	.04	2–5	2–5	.1–.2 (24 yrs)
1850–1874	1	.04	11–30	11–30	1 (25 yrs)
1875–1899	4	.16	63–125	16–31	3–5 (25 yrs)
1900–1924	8	.38	45–46	6	2 (25 yrs)
1925–1949	7	.28	64–100	9–14	3–4 (25 yrs)
1950–1974	13	.52	62–67	5	2–3 (25 yrs)
1975–2004	27	.9	180–239	7–9	6–8 (30 yrs)

(Hickey, 2006, p. 224).

Table 47.2 Monikers of Selected Female Offenders

Year Killing Began	Number of Victims	Name
1864	12–42 Queen	Poisoner/Borgia of Connecticut
1872	14	The Bloody Benders/The Hell Benders
1881	8+	Borgia of Somerville
1901	27	Sister Amy
1901	16–20	Belle of Indiana/Lady Bluebeard
1913	3–5	Duchess of Death
1914	11+	Mrs. Bluebeard
1920	3+	Old Shoe Box Annie
1925	11–16	Giggling Grandma
1925	3	Borgia of America
1931	15	Beautiful Blonde Killer
1949	3–20	Lonely Hearts Killer
1964	5	Grandma
1975	2+	Black Widow
1984	9–12	Death Angel
1989	7–9	Damsel of Death

(Hickey, 2006, p. 244).

Moreover, their killings tend to be part of an elaborate sexual fantasy that builds up to a climax at the moment of their murderous outburst. They usually kill strangers with cooling off periods between each crime. Many enjoy cannibalism, necrophilia and keep trophy-like body parts as reminders of their work. Their violent behavior is mostly directed towards women and children. However some homosexual killers like to hunt gay men. Prostitutes, drifters, male hustlers, and hitchhikers seem to be their victims of choice. Most serial killers lived in violent households, tortured animals and were bedwetters when they were young. As adults, most killers have some sort of brain damage and are addicted to alcohol or drugs (*A Short History on All . . .*).

TYPOLOGIES AND CLASSIFICATIONS

There are varying typologies assigned to female serial killers. Holmes and Holmes, as discussed by Sheptycki (1999), have noted five typologies of female serial killers. They involve visionary, comfort, hedonistic, power seeker, and disciple. The visionary type is similar to that of her male counterpart. These individuals are driven to kill because they have heard voices or have seen visions which demand that they kill a certain person or a category of persons. "The female 'power seeker' is different in important ways. The illustrative examples used in exploring this type are all from a medical setting. Munchausen syndrome by proxy is mentioned as an explanation. Offenders of this type, usually receive some form of psychological satisfaction, such as praise from superiors or gratitude from the patient and family" (Sheptycki, 1999). The next classification involves that of the "comfort type" or those who are motivated to kill for material gain. Those individuals who fall into the "disciple type," oftentimes have a male accomplice. An example would be that of Lynette Fromme and Leslie Van Hooten, members of Charles Manson's family. The last typology, according to Holmes and Holmes, is the "hedonistic type." This classification "is virtually indistinguishable from the 'disciple,' save perhaps for a greater emphasis on sexualized violence" (Sheptycki, 1999).

Kelleher and Kelleher, in their book entitled, *Murder Most Rare: The Female Serial Killer* (1998), have outlined a separate classification system for female serial killers. These consist of black widows, angels of death, sexual predators, revenge killers, those who murder for profit, and team killers. Black widows are the most lethal types, and are identified as the most organized, successful and prevalent. These women systematically murder their spouses, family members, children, or individuals outside the family with whom they established relationships. The black widow kills for two motives. The first of these is profit. "In fact, the overwhelming majority of 'black widows' are lured into murder by the proceeds of life insurance or the assets of the victim. Usually both the life insurance money and other assets will eventually fall into the possession of the perpetrator after the victim's death. In fact, it is not uncommon for these women to insure the victims themselves shortly before they execute a crime, thus giving substantial proof of how calculating, methodical and devious a female serial killer can be" (Evripidov, 1998).

The next of Kelleher and Kelleher's female serial killer typology is the angel of death. Those women who fall into this category systematically murder individuals who are in their care or who rely on them for medical attention and/or support. Motives for these murders may vary (Kelleher & Kelleher, 1998). The most rare crime committed by a woman falls within the grouping of sexual predators. Granted there is a small population of female sexual offenders and our society should be aware of them.

The next typology is that of women who kill to get even. "The perpetrator holds her victims indirectly responsible for whatever may cause her bitterness and attacks them as a symbolic act of retribution. As a result there is an overwhelming consistency among the revenge serial killer's victims, which are often tragically her own children, murdered in a perverted attempt to hurt her spouse. The revenge serial killer is a victim of her feelings, acting on the spur of the moment, which could explain why she shows great remorse after she is apprehended" (Evripidov, 1998).

Women who fall under the murders-for-profit category kill specifically for profit and target victims outside their families. These women are highly organized. "Like the black widow, she prefers poison. Like the 'angels of death' she has a highly dispassionate approach to murder. Like the 'sexual predator' she is fearsome and vicious, and like the 'revenge serial killer,' she is greatly motivated. But she is unique in that she kills for somebody else, usually abused wives that pay her to free them from their torturing husbands" (Evripidov, 1998).

The last typology of the female serial killer is that of female serial killer teams. According to Evripidov (1998), the second-largest category of team killers is comprised of female-female partners. Although rare, their motives may vary, the killings are usually carried out for profit. "On average, the members of the female-female team are older than the members of the male-female team and are active for a longer period of time. Unlike the male-female teams, and like their female counterparts that act alone, the female-female teams prefer subtle weapons such as poison, lethal injections and suffocation" (Evripidov, 1998).

According to Evripidov (1998), a fine line separates the serial killers of opposite sexes.

> For instance, the average period of active killing for the females is eight years whereas for the males it is only four. Female serial killers rarely torture their victims or commit any atrocities on their victims' bodies. They prefer more subtle ways of killing using weapons that are difficult to discern such as poison, lethal injections and induced accidents. The crimes carried out by female serial killers further exhibit a different victim typology from the male serial murders. The latter, usually acting as sexual predators, tend to target adult female victims. The former on the other hand, rarely choose their prey based on sex. Moreover, the female serial killer usually attacks victims that are familiar to her, such as children, relatives and spouses. In the rare situation when she does turn against a stranger, it is usually one who can be dominated easily, such as an elderly person under her care or a child. The age at which a female serial killer claims her first victim ranges from the age of fourteen to the age of sixty-four. The

average female serial murderer begins killing after the age of twenty-five. The female serial killer is more complex than the male and is oftentimes more difficult to apprehend. Since the initial definition of the serial killer is inadequate in satisfactorily explaining this quiet female killer, classifying her becomes a necessity in fully apprehending both her and the nature of her crimes.

Additionally, women have the capacity to be just as deadly as their male counterparts. The only difference, according to Hickey (2006), is that women offenders utilize different methods to achieve their goals than men (see Table 47.3). They are the "quiet" killers: "[W]e are seldom aware one is in our midst because of the low visibility of their killing" (Hickey, 2006, p. 221). This shared mindset concerning the difficult time in identifying female serial killers creates a general problem in regard to their capture and prosecution.

"Aileen Wuornos, a hitchhiking prostitute who killed six men along Florida's highways more than a decade ago, was executed by injection Wednesday after dropping her appeals and firing her lawyers" ("Florida Executes," 2002). At forty-six, Aileen Wuornos became the tenth woman to be executed in the United States since capital punishment resumed in 1977. According to the *Los Angeles Times* (2002), Oklahoma had already put three women to death, and Florida and Texas executed two each. "She will be only the second woman executed in Florida since the death

Table 47.3 Methods and Motives of Female Serial Murderers in the United States, 1821–2004 (N = 64)

Method		Motive	
Some poison	45%	Money sometimes	47%
Poison only	34	Money only	26
Some shooting	19	Control sometimes	14
Some bludgeoning	16	Enjoyment sometimes	11
Some suffocation	17	Sex sometimes	10
Some stabbing	11	Enjoyment only	3
Suffocation only	11	Sex only	0
Shooting only	8	Combinations of the preceding motives	15
Some drowning	5	Other motives including:	23
Stabbing only	3		
Combinations of the preceding methods	32	(1) drug addiction, (2) cults, (3) cover up other crimes, (4) children become a burden, feelings of being an inadequate parent, and so on	

(Hickey, 2006, p. 237).

Aileen Wuornos: Sexual Predator

The grisly trail left by the ninth-grade dropout, who became known as the "Damsel of Death," began in December 1989, when the remains of a Clearwater, Fla., electronics shop owner were found in a junkyard. It was the first of six male bodies that would turn up in a 13-month period near interstate highways in north-central Florida. Aileen Wuornos was arrested in January 1991 at a Daytona Beach biker bar. At her trial, she said she intended to rob one of her customers because she was afraid she was about to lose her lesbian lover and needed $200 for rent. She shot Richard Mallory, 51, the shop owner, in self-defense after he tied her to a steering wheel and sodomized her, she said. "I'm the innocent victim, not him," Wuornos told the jury, which convicted her anyway. She later pleaded no contest to the murders of five other men, and received six death sentences. She said she killed a seventh man whose body was never found. Wuornos had been abandoned at birth by her parents and reportedly raped at 13. (Dahlburg, 2002)

---

penalty was reinstated. On March 30, 1998, Judi Buenoano of Orlando went to the electric chair for fatally poisoning her husband with arsenic, drowning her partially paralyzed son, and trying to kill her fiancée with a car bomb. It was the first execution of a woman in Florida since a slave named Celia was hanged in 1848 for killing her master (Dahlburg, 2002). According to Dahlburg (2002), nine women have been executed since 1976. Additionally, as of July 2002, there were fifty-two women on death rows in the United States, or 1.4 percent of the total number of condemned killers. Fourteen sit on death row in California.

As discussed earlier, the most rare of all female serial crimes is that of "sexual predator." Wuornos shot to death at least six middle-aged men along Florida highways in 1989 and 1990. "She was like a spider on the side of the road, waiting for prey—men" (Dahlburg, 2002). She battled in court to bring her own end closer, firing her lawyers and dropping her appeals. "At a July, 2002, hearing, Wuornos told a judge that she was 'sick of hearing this 'she's crazy' stuff. I'm competent, sane and I'm telling the truth.' She also told the state Supreme Court that she would kill again" ("Florida Executes," 2002), if she had to live the rest of her life in prison.

"But Wuornos is unique in that she killed in the style of male serial killers," notes James Fox. "She killed strangers selected at random" (Dahlburg, 2002). Hickey (2006) noted in his study of female serial killers that 31 percent had killed one or more strangers (see Table 47.4).

Dana Sue Gray, now forty, is one of the least typical female serial killers (Braidhill, 1998). Gray distinguished herself by her taste in victims, her motive, and the gruesomely intimate method of using her hands and a phone cord to strangle, then a handy tool to bludgeon (Braidhill, 1998). She chose as her victims

Table 47.4 Percentage of Female Offenders Killing Family Members, Acquaintances, and/or Strangers in the United States, 1826–2004 (N = 64)

Relationship	Percentage
Family only	35
At least one family member	48
Acquaintances only	18
At least one acquaintance	34
Strangers only	25
At least one stranger	31

(Hickey, 2006, p. 230).

two strangers and one with only remote family ties: Roberts, whose husband was Gray's father's best friend. The clubbing of one of Gray's victims was so savage that Gray dented the iron used in the attack and left so much splatter that a bloody outline of the victim's body remained on the hallway wall after the body was removed. This would put Gray in the same category as so-called hardwired serial killers like Gacy and Ted Bundy (Braidhill, 1998). These killers could be classified as classic psychopaths, totally lacking in empathy. This trait allowed Gray to alternate between vicious murders and celebratory shopping sprees. "A sociopath will walk away from a step-grandmother with knives sticking out of her throat and not feel anything," says Dr. Patricia Kirby, a criminologist and ex-FBI profiler who has focused her research on male and female serial killers (cited in Braidhill, 1998). Kirby further indicated that Gray took pleasure in the killing, and the shopping provided her with something to do in order to celebrate the killing. Kirby adds. "I think a lot of it is a reluctance to admit that society's nurturers can be killers. Just because you don't hear about them doesn't mean they're not there. I think they're just better and quieter and they get away with it" (cited in Braidhill, 1998).

CASE SUMMARIES OF OTHER DOCUMENTED FEMALE SERIAL KILLERS

Kathleen Mojas, a clinical psychologist specializing in women's violence, believes there's been a historic underacknowledgment of female violence. "We're just beginning to admit that women can do this, just like it used to be impossible to believe that a father could molest a daughter. Now we're beginning to admit that women can be violent and can molest and kill" (cited in Braidhill, 1998).

Dana Sue Gray: A Hardwired Killer

Anyone Lake is built around a meandering golf course and a man-made lake carved from the desert of Riverside County. For retirees like June Roberts, it was just the place to contemplate life in the golfing leisure class from behind 12-foot walls with 24-hour security . . . Early one afternoon in 1994, a Cadillac belonging to one of Roberts's former neighbors nosed through the development's gates and stopped in front of her olive and white house on Big Tee Drive. Leaving her 5-year-old passenger in the front seat, the driver walked up to the front door. What immediately transpired when she opened her door isn't known, but Roberts, 66, was ultimately strapped to a chair, strangled with the cord ripped from her telephone and hammered savagely on the face with a wine bottle. (Her autopsy included the phrases "moderately deep ligature furrow" and "6-x-3-inch purple contusion.")

Less than an hour later the Cadillac was parked in front of Bally's Wine Country Cafe in Temecula, where Roberts's killer puffed cigarettes and frowned at the small boy running around the tables. She charged the crab cake and scampi to Roberts's credit card. It was too much to eat, so the waiter packed the rest to go.

The next stop was an eyebrow wax and a perm for herself and a fashionable cut for the boy. Signing the $164.76 charge "June Roberts," she told the stylist she was on a "shopping spree." She spent $511 on a black suede jacket and several pairs of cowboy boots, $161 on a pair of diamond drop earrings—all charged to Roberts. Heading home, she swung by a drugstore and picked up dog treats and two bottles of Smirnoff. On the way to the checkout counter, she paused in the toy aisle and tossed a $5.99 toy police helicopter into her basket.

Ten days later, Dorinda Hawkins, 57, was strangled while working at an antiques store in Lake Elsinore and left for dead. But she survived and gave officers a description of a blonde, wavy-haired female attacker. Within the week, 87-year-old Dora Beebe in nearby Sun City, another golf mecca for retirees, was strangled and beaten to death with a household iron. The outcry over the murder was enough for Riverside County sheriff Cois Byrd to show up in person at the crime scene, hoping to quell the fear among his older constituents.

Finding the suspect didn't take long. Earlier in the day of the Beebe killing, a police task force, acting on a tip, had been following a woman on what looked like routine errands to the bank, drugstore, and supermarket. The cops were watching her unload shopping bags from the trunk of her Cadillac when they learned of Beebe's death—and suddenly realized they had been following her killer on another of her post–murder spending sprees.

When Dana Sue Gray was arrested later that day, police found Beebe's credit cards in her lingerie drawer; a closetful of new clothes, tags still attached; boxes of Nike Air athletic shoes; a purple boogie board; a $1,000 Trek mountain bike; and unopened bottles of Opium perfume. The items were spread out as if in a post-Christmas quandary of where to store all the presents. "It looked like Bullock's," one officer said. Gray was handcuffed and put into a police cruiser, still wearing the diamond earrings purchased with Roberts's credit card. She talked about her new boogie board all the way to the station (Braidhill, K. 1998).

Delfina and Maria de Jesus Gonzales (ninety-one + victims)   These two deadly sisters ran the bordello from hell in Guanajuato, Mexico. They recruited their prostitutes through help wanted ads and killed them when they stopped pleasing the clientele. Sometimes they even killed the johns who showed up to the brothel with big wads of cash. After too many unexplained disappearances the cops raided the premises where they found the bodies of eleven males, eighty females, and several fetuses. (A Short History on . . .)

Dorothea Puente (eight + victims)   Dorothea operated a boarding house in Sacramento, California where she offered quality lodgings for elderly people on fixed incomes. She also offered poison and a bed of flowers to bury their corpses in. As she offed her boarders she kept cashing their social security checks. In 1988, after too many of her boarders disappeared, cops showed up with shovels and unearthed seven corpses from her garden. Another body discovered in the Sacramento River in 1986 was added to her hit list. It's believed that she might have killed up to twenty-five others. She was arrested in Los Angeles on November 17, 1988 after she inquired about an acquaintance's disability check and offered to fix him a nice Thanksgiving dinner with all the trimmings. (A Short History on . . .)

Belle Gunness (fourteen + victims)   A deadly gold digger, Belle lured wealthy Chicago men to her house with classified ads. The original Lady Bluebeard, Belle's criminal career started with the accidental deaths of her first two husbands and two of her children. Coincidentally, with each death she collected insurance money, which kept her afloat until her next rash of bad luck. Once she settled in La Porte, Indiana, she started with her deadly "lonely-hearts" venture. On April 28, 1908, her house was leveled by fire. Ray, her farm hand and presumed lover, was arrested and accused of arson and the murder of Belle and her children. Ray said that the female body found in the embers was not Belle. The body was missing a skull but next to it they found Belle's dentures. Apparently she had faked her own death and escaped with a bag full of money. As investigators started digging up the ranch they found plenty of human bones and dismembered bodies wrapped in gunny sacks and doused with lye. Many of Belle's suitors had been fed to the pigs accounting for the numerous bone fragments found in and around the pig pen. Estimates of her murderous habits put her at fifty to a hundred hits. We've chosen to count only her proven kills. After disappearing, Belle was spotted many times throughout the country. Authorities believe that she was last seen in a bordello in Ohio in 1935. (A Short History on . . .)

Theresa Cross aka Jimmie Knorr (three victims). A mother of three sons and two daughters, she wounded one daughter with a gun, and when the daughter wasn't dead after a few weeks, she tried to remove the bullet. The attempted surgery left the daughter near death. So the kind mother put the girl in a closet and told the other children not to feed her. Eventually, the child died. Another daughter was beaten to death, and the two corpses were taken up to the mountains and, with the help of her teenage sons, burned with a pile of trash. During her trial it came out that she was acquitted in the murder of her former husband years before. (A Short History on. . .)

AFRICAN-AMERICAN SERIAL MURDERERS

48

Behind the Anonymity

Toyia McWilliams

Since the 1980s, society has been intrigued by the phenomena of serial murder (Hickey, 2006; Holmes & Holmes, 2000). Films such as *Silence of the Lambs* and *The Red Dragon* contribute to the growing fascination, which is further illustrated by the great number of books that have surfaced in bookstores throughout the country. Despite the increasing social concern, serial killing has been an intricate part of the U.S. history in addition to other industrialized countries. Names such as David Berkowitz, Ted Bundy, and Jeffrey Dahmer will continue to intrigue criminologists, psychologists, sociologists, and laymen alike. Provided that, there has been a surge in literature that focuses on the psychological make-up and characteristics of a serial killer, which in turn, assists the FBI in constructing typologies and profiles that eventually aid in catching violent criminals. These profiles, however, tend to disregard the African-American experience with regard to serial homicide (Jenkins, 1993). In fact, it is widely assumed that African-American serial killers constitute a small percentage of this specific population. Although the number of African-American serial killers is greater than it is perceived Hickey (2006), scholars and profilers continue to base their typologies and profiles on white males.

THE PHENOMENON OF SERIAL MURDER

Before delving into the nature of African-American serial killers, it is important to define *serial homicide* as well as offer a brief description of the profile that is frequently used by law enforcement agencies and FBI profilers in attempting to identify a serial killer. First, the mere concept of serial killing is difficult in itself. Because of the distortions and differences of opinion as to what constitutes a *serial killer,* a classification table was formed in order to eliminate the confusion.

Classification Table

	Mass Murder	Spree Murder	Serial Murder
# of Victims	3+	3+	3+
# of Events	1	3+	3+
# of Locations	1	3+	3+
Cooling-Off Period	No	No	Yes

For the purpose of this chapter, the definition of serial homicide to be used, defines it as "the killing of three or more people over a period of more than 30 days, with a significant cooling-off period between the murders" (Holmes & Holmes, 1998, p.1).

With regard to the basic profile of serial killers, Holmes and Holmes (1998) reported that approximately 73 percent of all serial killers are white males in their thirties or forties. Furthermore, it is suggested that white male serial killers tend to come from dysfunctional family environments, which in turn creates a great deal of repressed rage. Given that, they have the propensity to commit sexually motivated murders against women, men, and children.

Despite the murders by the Washington, D.C., snipers, scholars and FBI profilers continue to allege that the common profile for serial killers is somewhat universal in terms of motivation and methodology without regard to racial factors and how that may affect the nature of serial homicide. That being said, the media tends to uphold these stereotypes, which is virtually implicit in the number of films depicting serial killers. In doing so, the black component of serial homicide remains essentially ignored in the American pop-culture.

Most films in the true-crime genre portray white males who generally fit the classic stereotype of a serial killer. In addition, "slasher" films have the inclination to depict their monstrous characters as deeply psychotic white males who are categorized as prolific serial killers in the fictional world of movies (e.g., Freddy Krueger, Michael Myers, & Jason Voorhies). Even in the movies, African-American serial killers were practically non-existent. However, a new serial killer, *The Candyman,* came to the silver screen in the early 1990s. In many ways, his revenge crimes could easily be seen as racially motivated.

AFRICAN-AMERICAN SERIAL MURDERERS

According to Jenkins (1993), African-Americans have been an integral part of serial homicide in the U.S. history, including the mid-twentieth century. For the most part, scholars and researchers do not investigate the experience of African-American serial killers despite the similarities they share with white serial killers. Although there are several theories offered to explain this observable fact, it appears that the media and law enforcement have little interest in African-American serial killers because they do not fit the classic profile.

In the mid-1980s, two prolific serial killers were operating in Philadelphia, PA: Gary Heidnik and Harrison "Marty" Graham. In both of these cases, the media reported the gruesome details of these two serial killers in which they both murdered several people in poverty-stricken areas. Eventually, Heidnik found himself in the media spotlight; thus, becoming the focus of a network television interview as well as the subject of a book. In addition, his story became part of a character that was introduced in the book and film of *Silence of the Lambs,* as portrayed by the fictional character of "Buffalo Bill." In contrast, Graham received minimal attention from the media despite the fact that he was convicted of seven murders as opposed to Heidnik's conviction of three murders. As indicated by Jenkins (1993), there appears to be no other reason why Graham was ignored except for the fact that he did not match the widely accepted stereotypes simply because he was African-American.

Although there is not a large amount of literature that concentrates on the racial component of serial killers, the few studies that do exist report that approximately 13 to 22 percent of American serial killers are indeed African-American (Hickey, 2006; Jenkins, 1993). Provided that African-Americans comprise approximately 13 percent of the U.S. population, these findings suggest that the number of black serial killers is slightly disproportioned from the overall percentage. Given those statistics, black serial killers are extremely underrepresented in this cultural phenomenon (see Table 48.1). As reported by Jenkins (1993), when black multiple killers are mentioned in the literature, it is usually in the context of politically motivated or terrorist activity, as in the Zebra murders of the early 1970s. In other words, the media tends to pay attention to black serial murderers when they appear to be politically (or even racially) motivated. The lack of media coverage, however, means serial murder is basically seen as unfamiliar within the black community. Interestingly enough, between 1995 and 2004 nearly half of all new cases of serial murder in the United States involved black offenders (Hickey, 2006).

BLACK VS. WHITE SERIAL MURDERERS

When exploring issues related to serial homicide, it is necessary to distinguish between the typologies. According to Holmes & DeBurger (1998), there are four "core characteristics" used to identify the different types of serial killers—visionary, mission-oriented, hedonistic, and power/control-oriented. In brief, the serial killer who is operating as a visionary type typically murders in response to commands,

Table 48.1   African-American Serial Killers

Offender	Where Active	Dates	# of Victims[1]
Benjamin Atkins	MI	1991–92	11
Jake Bird	WA	1947	44
Eugene Britt	IN	1995	11+
John Brooks	Unknown	Unknown	9
Debra Brown	OH/MI/IN/IL	1984	8
Jarvis Catoe		1935–41	9
Nathaniel R. Code	LA	1984–87	8
Alton Coleman	OH/MI/IN/IL	1984	8
Jerome Dennis	Unknown	Unknown	8
Colin Ferguson	Long Island	1993	6
Carlton Gary	GA	1970–78	7+
Harrison "Marty" Graham	PA	1987–88	7+
Vincent Groves	Unknown	Unknown	14
Kevin Haley & Reginald Haley	CA	1979–84	8
Monroe Hickson	Unknown	Unknown	Unknown
Clarence Hill	PA	1935–41	6
Waneta Hoyt	NY	1965–71	5
Calvin Jackson	NY	1973–74	9+
Richard Jameswhite	Unknown	Unknown	15
Milton Johnson	IL	1983	5
Sidney Jones	Unknown	Unknown	13
Devernon LeGrand	NY	1968–75	Unknown
Michael Player	CA	1986	10
John Lee Malvo (accomplice: John Muhammad)	Washington D.C./VA	2002	10+
Bobby Joe Maxwell	CA	1978–79	10
John Allen Muhammad (accomplice: John Malvo)	Washington D.C./VA	2002	10+
Christopher Peterson	IN	Unknown	Unknown
James Pough	FL	1990	11
Cleophus Prince Jr.	CA	1990	6
Richard Tipton	Unknown	Unknown	11
Debra Tuggle	Unknown	Unknown	4
Henry Louis Wallace	NC	1992–94	9–20
Coral E. Watts	MI/TX	1979–83	10+
Wayne Williams	GA	1979–81	23–28

[1]Approximate number.
*This list is not complete.

which is usually in the form of a voice or a vision stemming from the forces of good and evil (Hickey, 2006). As one can imagine, this offender is often seen as psychotic by FBI profilers and psychologists. Offenders who are mission-oriented, however, believe that they have some type of mission to fulfill in which a particular racial and/or ethnic group may be targeted as well as a specific population such as the elderly, children, or prostitutes. Wayne Williams was believed to be in this category, as scholars alleged that he murdered children in an effort to prevent future generations of African-Americans. The hedonistic type derives pleasure from committing murders, as they tend to be "thrill seekers." Lust murderers also fall into this category because the offender usually becomes sexually involved with their victims, including performing postmortem mutilations (Hickey, 2006). Finally, the power/control-oriented type receives pleasure from achieving power and control over their victims. These offenders enjoy watching their victims cry or beg for mercy (Hickey, 2006).

In relation to African-American serial murderers, it is speculated that these "core characteristics" are widespread. Although this may be the case, it appears that many white serial killers primarily commit sexually motivated crimes. However, it is theorized by some scholars that the majority of serial murders committed by African-Americans do not fall into this category.

Assuming that African-American serial killers are comparable to their white counterparts, scholars tend to discount the impact of racism in terms of how it may contribute to this phenomenon. According to Jenkins (1993), many of the murders committed by African-American serial killers were perceived as typical of the black experience, especially, within the context of a predominantly white society. Given that, there is an underlying assumption that many of the crimes committed by African-American serial killers are racially motivated.

Despite these differences, there are similarities between white and black serial killers. For the most part, African-American serial murderers have the propensity to kill within their own ethnic group (Holmes, 2002; Hickey, 2006). These findings support the theory that most crime tends to be intraracial in nature. The media typically ignores intraracial crime, particularly when African-American serial killers are involved. There also appears to be a common thread between black and white serial killers with respect to victim selection.

PUBLICITY FOR AFRICAN-AMERICAN SERIAL KILLERS

There appears to be bias from the media and law enforcement with regard to African-American serial killers (Hickey, 2006). Factors such as victim selection and racial bias in law enforcement, establishing an unambiguous definition for *serial homicide* and race/ethnicity as well as the possibility of promoting negative stereotypes, have all been implicated in this bias (Jenkins, 1993).

As previously indicated, violent crimes tend to be intraracial in nature despite the popular belief that suggests otherwise. African-American serial killers often go undetected because their victims tend to be poor blacks from impoverished communities (Jenkins, 1993; Hickey, 2006).

Secondly, the definition of *serial homicide* has proven to be a difficult undertaking in that researchers and law enforcement personnel continue to modify this definition to their benefit. Consequently, the actual count for African-American serial killers is quite controversial (Jenkins, 1993). Sometimes it is difficult to distinguish between blacks (non-Hispanics) and Hispanics. As a result, researchers believe that there may be cases in which the race/ethnicity of the serial killer was incorrectly classified (Jenkins, 1993).

Finally, it is hypothesized by Jenkins (1993) that African-American serial killers tend not to be publicized because of the fear of promoting negative stereotypes. Historically, the dominant culture has used stereotypes to encourage separation, which ultimately contributed to the notion of racism. In turn, racism tends to fuel prejudicial attitudes and stereotypes. It is possible that some serial murders are improperly labeled as an "urban homicide" because it is considered expected behavior in underprivileged black communities (Jenkins, 1993). In turn this labeling could impact the scope and depth of the investigation.

THE STEADY INCREASE OF AFRICAN-AMERICAN SERIAL KILLERS

Although African-American serial killers have been present in the United States for quite some time, the overall percentage has greatly increased over the past few years. Jenkins (1993), reported that approximately 13 to 16 percent of American serial killers to be African-American. However, other scholars propose that this number has significantly increased within the past decade. In fact, Hickey (2006) found that the percentage of black serial killers has increased to approximately 22 percent.

There are a few explanations for the increase. As mentioned before, homicide is considered a predominantly intraracial crime. Given that, it is fairly simple for some African-American serial killers to essentially "get away with murder" (Jenkins, 1993). In addition, scholars, investigators, and laymen imply that the increase of black serial killers is a consequence of assimilation (Douglas and Olshaker, 1997). According to Long (2002), "Just as there are now black doctors and lawyers and accountants and golf pros and everything else, now there are even black psycho killers," which further exemplifies the fact that African-Americans are gradually becoming a part of mainstream American culture.

PROLIFIC AFRICAN-AMERICAN SERIAL KILLERS

The following cases involve some of America's prolific African-American serial killers including team killers Alton Coleman and Debra Brown, Jake Bird (1947), Wayne Williams (1979–1981), Coral Watts (1979–1982), and Henry Louis Wallace (1992–1994).

TEAM KILLERS: ALTON COLEMAN AND DEBRA BROWN (1984)

In the mid-1970s, Alton Coleman and his girlfriend Debra Brown participated in a string of murders across five states. In less than two months, the couple managed to commit eight murders, approximately seven sexual assaults, three kidnappings, and fourteen armed robberies. Eventually the couple was arrested, convicted, and sentenced to death for their crimes.

Although very little information is available about their childhoods, both Alton Coleman and Debra Brown developed psychological problems. As a child, Alton Coleman was nicknamed "Pissy" because he had the tendency to wet his bed. According to his relatives, he "always knew" that he was different from his peers in that he had an insatiable appetite for sex, as he was willing to engage in sexual activity at any time. Furthermore, he had a strange desire to dress in women's clothing and participate in rough sex. Coleman often engaged in deviant sexual behavior, as menacing acts sexually aroused him.

In addition, Coleman was fascinated with fire, and had a history of destroying other's property via arson. During his trial, Coleman attempted to manipulate the jury by appealing to their sensitivities. He reportedly told the court and jurors that he suffered from a disturbing childhood, personality disorder, and a brain dysfunction.

Alton Coleman "fits" the F.B.I. description for "disorganized serial killer"; however, an additional component should be considered when examining an offender who is African-American. Coleman was believed to harbor an "intense hatred for blacks" (Gribben, 2001) mainly because the majority of their victims were African-Americans. Of course, there is a difference in opinion, as many people believe that their victim selection was more opportunistic than it was racially motivated. As reported by his friends, "they [their victims] were in the wrong place at the wrong time" (Gribben, 2001).

Another possible motivation for Coleman, as speculated by a friend of the family, was that he was unable to adequately deal with his homosexual tendencies. Coleman openly admitted that he was bisexual, and admitted that he had issues related to sexuality; however, Coleman never offered an opinion as to his motivation for his crimes. Coleman appeared to have established a pattern of justifying his actions and attempting to "get away with murder," as he had always been able to do since he was an adolescent. Debra Brown was equally as aggressive and brutal as her boyfriend. When confronted, Brown made an effort to justify her involvement with the violent crimes by stating that she was "retarded" and essentially intimidated by her boyfriend.

JAKE BIRD (1947)

Jake Bird is one of the first African-American serial killers to operate in this country. Since he lived in a time era in which blacks were devalued, very little information is known about him in terms of the nature of his childhood or his violent crimes as well.

In 1947, Jake Bird was arrested for murder while leaving the scene of a crime. Initially, he denied the charges; however, brain tissue was found in his trousers, which directly linked him to the murder. Known as the "Tacoma Ax Murderer," Jake Bird's victims were white women. He reportedly liked to see his victims tremble in fear. Although Bird did not sexually assault his victims, he preferred to remove all of his clothing prior to committing his violent crimes. Law enforcement speculate that he is responsible for at least forty-four murders in several states including Illinois, Kentucky, Nebraska, Kansas, South Dakota, Ohio, Florida, and Wisconsin.

WAYNE WILLIAMS (1979–1981)

The case of Wayne Williams was considered to be the most controversial event in U.S. history with respect to serial killing (Ferrall, 1999; Grattet, 2000; Bell & Bards Ley, 2000). Many citizens from the black community did not believe that Williams was responsible for the Atlanta Child Murders, and believed that members of a white supremacist group were actually responsible for the murders. Williams' victims allegedly included twenty-eight young boys/men and two young girls. Despite witness testimony he was ultimately convicted on two counts of murder and sentenced to a double term of life in prison.

The Atlanta Child Murders began in the summer of 1979. Young boys from the black community randomly started disappearing. In many of these cases, law enforcement was unable to link these crimes to a single serial killer and ultimately mislabeled the crimes as a "regular" homicide. In fact, law enforcement rarely investigated these crimes, and postmortem examinations were often incomplete.

Although there was a distinct pattern among Williams's victims, law enforcement was unable to connect the victims. There was no single method that Williams preferred, as his victims were either shot, strangled, stabbed, bludgeoned, or suffocated. Furthermore, Williams's murders of the young males did not appear to be sexually motivated, although he reportedly sexually assaulted his two female victims prior to strangling them to death.

Some believe that Williams suffered from internalized racism in that he reportedly hated his race and murdered African-Americans because they reminded him of his status (Hickey, 2006). Provided that, it was theorized that Williams wanted to eradicate future generations of blacks by murdering black children in order to prevent breeding. Furthermore, it was also believed that Williams had latent homosexual urges and killed young black boys in an attempt to overcompensate for these desires.

CORAL WATTS (1979–1982)

Although he admitted to murdering thirteen women, Watts was convicted and sentenced for aggravated burglary with intent to commit murder. Consequently, Watts was sentenced to sixty years without a chance for parole, but later his sentence was reduced to 40 years with the possibility of parole.

Although Watts confessed to thirteen murders, he was suspected of killing many more. Watts began his serial killing at age of 15. According to records (Coral Watts, n.d.), he was delivering newspapers in an apartment building and allegedly assaulted a young woman. It became evident that Watts enjoyed engaging in such behavior and had no remorse. Watts admitted to doctors that he often dreamed of physically assaulting women. Furthermore, he asserted that he felt calmed by these dreams, as they appeared to provide stress relief.

Upon his release, Watts continued to assault young women. He returned to high school and excelled in athletics such as football and boxing. After his high school graduation in 1972, he attended Lain College in Jackson, TN for a few months on a football scholarship; however, he later returned home with a minor leg injury. By the time he enrolled in Western Michigan University in Kalamazoo, he purportedly was averaging approximately one attack every two weeks. In 1974, he attacked two women and murdered another on the campus.

Eventually, Watts was convicted on the assault cases and began serving prison time. While incarcerated, police asked him about the murder but he refused to respond. Watts soon began complaining about depression and was sent to Kalamazoo State Hospital where he attempted to hang himself. A few months later, he was released and returned to his mother in Detroit, MI.

For two years, Watts managed to avoid arrest. In 1979, he married but the relationship lasted for only six months. His wife described their marriage as "bizarre." Between October of 1979 and November of 1980, Watts continued to assault and murder young women in the Detroit area, Ann Arbor, and Windsor, Ontario. Simultaneously, his marriage was deteriorating and his wife divorced him. Watts moved back in with his mother in Inkster and the assaults continued.

Dubbed the "Sunday Morning Slasher," Watts primary means of assault was to beat, strangle, stab, hang, or drown his victims. In 1982, he was arrested and confessed to thirteen murders asserting that he was "releasing the spirit" and vowed that he saw "evil" in the eyes of his victims (Coral Watts, n.d.).

Although is it unknown as to what truly motivated this serial murderer, Watts assaulted and/or murdered many of these women after he had sexual relations with his wife. According to Valerie Goodwill (Watts' ex-wife), she reported that he frequently "went out" after they had sex. At the same time, his murders were not considered sexually motivated crimes because he did not rape any of his victims. However, Watts displayed extreme anger, resentment, and deep-seated hatred for women.

HENRY LOUIS WALLACE (1992–1994)

When Henry Louis Wallace was arrested in 1994 in North Carolina, he had been suspected of raping and strangling five young black women (Lapeyre, 2002). Interestingly, each of the victims was associated with Wallace in some way. In fact, his victims were either a friend of his girlfriend or worked in the fast-food industry with him. Despite the common link, the police department was not able to make a connection between Wallace and the victims nor were they able to see a distinct pattern in the killings.

Wallace was born in 1965 in South Carolina to an unwed mother and a father he never knew. Wallace lived in a very impecunious environment with a mother who allegedly forced Wallace and his sister to beat each other with a switch when they misbehaved. In addition, his mother and sister would sometimes make him wear dresses in order to humiliate him. Furthermore, he witnessed a gang rape at the age of seven. Wallace learned to associate aggression with sex at an early age.

Wallace began stealing at an early age that later resulted in many job terminations. He joined the Navy but was discharged after breaking and entering near a naval base. At this time, he moved back in with his mother and sister in South Carolina. He acquired a job at Taco Bell and began smoking crack cocaine in 1992. During this time, Wallace's crimes escalated from burglary and drug use to serial murder.

Wallace typically targeted young black women that he knew from work or through his girlfriend. He would charm his way into their apartments and waited until their guard was down before he attacked them. His pattern was to strangle, sexually assault, and then wash down the corpses in the shower. As a disorganized killer, he used items from the victims such as a curling iron cord, or towel to strangle his victims. After he raped his victims, he would steal money or valuables so he could get enough money to buy crack. In some instances, he asked victims for their PIN numbers to credit cards and ATM cards, as well as safe combinations.

According to the police, they felt there was no pattern to the killings. In one case, one of the murdered victims was ruled an "accidental death" caused by thermal burns because Wallace burned the victim in order to destroy evidence. However, the victim actually died of strangulation.

Although it is not quite known what motivated Wallace to commit these violent crimes, the fact that he was addicted to crack cocaine contributed a great deal to the murders. It is highly conceivable that Wallace developed some degree of resentment towards women and wanted to "punish" them for unknown reasons. The fact that he stole money and valuables from his victims was secondary to the murder itself. Wallace stole to support his habit. When Wallace was arrested in March of 1994, he confessed to the nine murders and disclosed that he killed several women while he was in the Navy which brings his victim total to approximately twenty young women.

In comparing Wallace with the classic typologies used by FBI profilers and law enforcement personnel to identify serial killers, it is evident that Wallace did not meet the profile. For the most part, serial killers tend to target strangers; however, Wallace's victims were those he knew. Police departments consequently had difficulty linking the crimes despite the patterns. In addition, many serial killers like to take souveniers or trophys (e.g., hair, an article of clothing, and even digest flesh or bodily fluids) in order to remember their victims. Wallace, on the other hand, primarily stole from his victims in order to buy drugs. Although he was viewed as a sexually motivated predator, his crimes were easily misidentified as "regular" homicides.

CONCLUSION

It is very difficult for the black community to accept the fact that African-Americans can be serial killers, as evident by the reactions to the Washington, D.C., snipers when their identity was revealed. It is likely that America will begin to pay more attention to African-American serial killers.

It may also be believed that the media and law enforcement agencies do not want to publicize African-American serial killers because some people fear that white Americans will somehow use this information to essentially reinforce the stereotype that blacks have a greater propensity for criminal activity. As reported by Pouissant (Fears & Thomas-Lester, 2002), "For a long time, there were a lot of black people who felt that anything one black person did would reflect on the entire race." In regards to African-American serial killers, this cultural phenomenon affects the black community in that the percentage of black serial killers is gradually increasing.

PART

TREATING SEX OFFENDERS AND COMMUNITY ATTITUDES

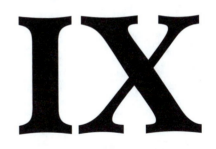

CURING SEXUALLY DEVIANT BEHAVIOR

49

An Exploration of Approaches

FELICIA BLOEM

When considering sexual deviancy the following question arises: Is a person cured of sexual deviate behavior when the behavior stops or when the thinking about the behavior stops? Typically one may concede that a sexual offender would be cured when the thoughts stop. However, some may believe that sexual offenders may never be cured.

As one might expect there are multiple opinions regarding treatment of sexual offenders. Along with thinking patterns and behavior modification, there are also biological based cures for sexual deviate behaviors that focus on controlling sexual impulses. Considering the implications of treating sexual offenders, it became evident that treatment is contingent on the theoretical assumptions that drive each professionals treatment objectives. For example, if a particular professional field believes that treatment of sexual offenders is based on stopping the illegal behaviors, efforts may focus on changing the sexual offenders behaviors to specifically tackle the illegal actions of the offender.

Despite society's expectation on treatment for offenders, there is always some level of recidivism and recidivism itself is hard to measure (Rosen, 1996, p. 392). This difficulty in measuring effective treatment becomes a concern for the public and the judicial system as they both seek continued safety for the community. Correspondingly, the public places pressure on the legal system to find answers and treat offenders before release back into the public. However, the costs to measure rates of recidivism are enormous and diverse. Costs may include that of the emotional and physical health of victims, engendered fear, and investigation costs surrounding sex crimes. Additional costs surround the conviction, incarceration, and treatment of sex offenders (Heilbrun, Nezu, Keeney, Chung, & Wasserman, 1998).

Many questions must be considered regarding the various approaches available for treatment of sex offenders. For instance, what is the most effective treatment for sexual offenders? What is societies main objective in treatment of sexual offenders? Is the goal to cure sexual deviation biologically, cognitively, or to end the acting-out of illegal sexual behaviors? From the law enforcement view, the goal is to stop the behavior or the illegal actions. Societies resolve is much more complicated.

At this point, there are many approaches to the treatment of sexual offenders focusing on biological factors, thinking patterns, and acting out behaviors, but unfortunately there is minimal research to back up efficacy of one treatment over another. In this discussion, various approaches, research, and recidivism rates will be discussed, in an effort to understand where progress in treatment of sexual offenders currently stands.

DEFINITIONS

Currently there is no recorded "cure" for sexual deviate behaviors. Cure meaning, restore to health and eliminate disease, evil, etc. (*Oxford,* 2001). Although there are several treatment alternatives that intend to cure sexual deviations, there are no reliable approaches that have withstood the rigor of research. Research indicates that all treatment approaches demonstrate some level of recidivism. Recidivism is broadly defined as a relapse and reengagement of previous criminal activity (*Oxford,* 2001). One author states, "the purpose of treatment of sex offenders is to stop sexual violence and victimization. No system of treatment or theoretical orientation has achieved 100 percent success in the treatment of sex offenders" (Rosen, 1996, p. 392).

TREATMENT

For the purpose of this discussion, regarding treatment approaches, the terms sexual offenders, sexual deviate behaviors, and sexual dysfunction will be used throughout. These terms will define a person who has been involved in a sexual crime, as defined by the law, and who participates in sexual treatment as a volunteer or mandated service.

Additionally, the majority of the research is based on a male sample of sexual offenders. There are female sexual offenders, but for this discussion the research and dialogue is based on the male population of sexual offenders (Rosen, 1996).

COGNITIVE-BEHAVIORAL TREATMENT

To start the discussion, the following description of one of the more popular treatments for sexual offenders is offered (Becker & Murphy, 1998). This treatment approach is called cognitive-behavioral and is primarily conducted within sex offender groups. This approach focuses on the thinking and behaviors of the offender and implements an educational model to restructure the offender's cognitive dysfunctions. Becker and Murphy state, "the theories that currently predominate the sex offender treatment field have been the behavioral theories, which focus on conditioning of deviant sexual arousal and on the development of cognitions that justify and maintain deviant sexual behavior" (Becker & Murphy, 1998). This particular model is quite comprehensive in the area of sexual deviance because it combines several different strategies.

One of these strategies is the relapse prevention model (RPM). The entire protocol for treatment groups using RPM is constructed to alter dysfunctional beliefs, cognitions, and behaviors. "The theoretical model is based in the concept that sexual offenses are not committed on impulse and there are offense precursors that can be identified and addressed" (Shaw, 1999, p. 279). These offense precursors are identified and examined, and this initiates the process of restructuring thoughts and behavioral patterns of each offender.

In the initial session of treatment, the participants are required to communicate accountability to the various community social networks they are connected within (e.g., probation, CPS, family, neighborhood). This provides accountability and changes any secrecy of the offender's lifestyle in which they were accustomed to. Then instructions and boundaries of group behavior are explained to the offenders. This clear, direct communicative format teaches the sex offenders, from the start, the need to take responsibility for their crime. The group develops into a place of trust that models good communications skills to the offenders. Additionally, the group enforces a simple rule stating there must be a male and female therapist as co-leaders. This sets a standard of conduct that again models appropriate conduct between genders.

The RPM is an accurate representation of the cycle of offence. This model educates the offender on the very addictive behaviors they may initiate without thought. The process of educating the offender on this cycle confronts the denial and rationalization they experience. Confronting the defenses and educating them makes them familiar with their patterns. As the offenders become observant of negative patterns (awareness) and personal triggers, they can learn to prevent situations of increased temptation or weakness. Knowing this cycle in advance and being aware of the progressions warns the offender of habitual behavior. The next phase is educating the offender on vulnerabilities and preparing them for strategies to change the patterns and prevent relapse.

Another aspect of RPM is to uncover the reality of the crimes each offender commits. Openly communicating the crimes and confronting cognitive distortions in a group setting slowly dismantles the perception of normalcy the offender rationalizes. The group is a powerful resource, uniting men with similar destructive behaviors, experiencing various levels of insight, and exploring personal change. The combination of accountability, personal responsibility, education, and cognitive restructuring, challenges the offender to move forward to a positive behavior change. After treatment and good education the change is ultimately their responsibility to maintain.

Another strategy utilized is called arousal reconditioning (Shaw, 1999, p.283). Arousal reconditioning is used in behavioral therapies in efforts to control or modify sexual arousal. Sexual offenders often have sexual responses to inappropriate or socially unacceptable images or objects. In orgasmic reconditioning, the orgasm is viewed as the conditioning factor or contingency that intensifies the inappropriate behavior (Shaw, 1999, p. 283). The fantasy, or thought pattern then evokes arousal and leads to the orgasm. In the reconditioning aspect, the participant would begin using the image that elicits arousal (imagined inappropriate image first) then just before the orgasm the image is changed to a socially appropriate image. As arousal increases towards the socially appropriate image, it would replace the inappropriate image. Additional methods of reconditioning include the use of shock, chemical odors, and aversive stimuli paired with the arousal of inappropriate images (Shaw, 1999, p. 284).

One component of this model is education. Sexual offenders are taught social skills or communication, healthy sexuality, anger management, and methods of coping (Shaw, 1999, 286–287). These are taught on the premise that the sexual offender is naïve and insecure about various personal aspects of sexual conduct. The education is utilized to build the offender's confidence and ability to make reasonable decisions based on further education and self-awareness.

Cognitive-behavior treatments combine many strategies to provide a comprehensive approach for treating sex offenders. In Becker and Murphy's article addressing the knowledge of assessing and treating sex offenders, they state the following: "Although behavioral and cognitive theories have mixed support, they clearly have had significant heuristic value and have driven the development of what appears to be more successful treatment programs" (Becker & Murphy, 1998).

RELIGION/SPIRITUALITY RECOVERY

In correctional settings, offenders often turn to religion and clearly, spirituality is one approach that provides treatment to sexual offenders. Regardless of one spiritual affinity, people can and do stop committing sins and crimes. According to Hickey, the turn to religious belief may illicit an attempt to "... correct the wrong that was done and to become productive members of society. Prisons seem to breed religious conversions, which sometimes do appear to effect a change in attitude and behavior" (Hickey, 2006, p. 50).

In addressing the topic of spirituality in regards to a treatment alternative, it is important to mention that all methods of treatment can be used as an educational device to manipulate another for some secondary gain. For example, some offenders use religion to convince family or legal professionals that they are healed to gain early release or trust. Religion at times can be a particularly vulnerable area used for ill purposes. However, the essence of spirituality is a very healing form of intervention to many offenders. According to Twerski and Nakken (1997), much like animals humans have physical urges and desires and also possess the desire for spiritual fulfillment. It is suggested that humans experience a vague unrest when their spiritual needs are unmet. Twerski and Nakken believe that "while hunger, thirst, or the sex drive are easily identified, spiritual craving is harder to recognize and fulfill. People may feel that something is missing, but not know what that something is" (p. 113). A religious experience can often provide a renewed purpose or meaning in an offender's life filling a void of emptiness.

Despite religions useful interventions, it remains one aspect of treatment that cannot be measured or tested in determining effects of recidivism. This can be an added disadvantage to professionals who are trying to develop empirically based treatment programs. To be sure, spirituality can provide many therapeutic advantages and benefits. The benefits include some of the following: a sense of forgiveness, sense of purpose, dependence on a higher power for strength and confidence, community with others who share similar beliefs, reason to change offensive acts or thoughts, and sense of direction or peace. The positive aspect of religiosity, as treatment, cannot be denied although more research is needed to explain recidivism among the offenders who have claimed religion yet continue to offend.

CASTRATION

Another approach to treatment is castration. It is defined as "an irreversible procedure for controlling the serum level of testosterone in the body, ultimately resulting in the reduction of sexual arousal" (Heilbrun, Nezu, Keeney, Chung, & Wasserman, 1998). This method represents a severe form of dealing with sexually unacceptable behaviors and is often thought to be a definitive cure. Interestingly, research on this approach, indicates it is not a full proof alternative to treat sexual deviance. In Europe, several research studies analyzed the recidivism rates of castrated sexual offenders in comparison to noncastrated offenders (e.g., Rosen, 1996). In their findings, castration was found to decrease recidivism as compared to non-castrated groups, although there was still reported recidivism among castrated participants (1996). One article reported that on several occasions, sexual offenders have requested castration as an alternative to incarceration (Miller, 1998). Although reports indicate that the courts have denied these requests for various reasons, including legal and ethical obligations of the state, "There have been continued attempts to use surgical castration to reduce inappropriate sexual behavior; however because the procedure is irreversible, because the clinical evidence demonstrates that it is not always effective, and because irreversible medications are now widely available, it has largely fallen into disfavor" (Miller, 1998, p. 443).

Another term related to this alternative treatment is chemical castration. This method is associated with drug intervention, although it involves the use of hormones to decrease abnormal sexual arousal, orgasm, and fantasies (Miller, 1998). Cyproterone acetate (CPS) and Medroxyprogesterone acetate (MPA) are two hormone treatments that have been used and tested in research, MPA is the only hormone that is FDA approved in the United States (Miller, 1998). There are numerous side effects in hormone usage despite some researchers claiming that hormone treatments appear to be the most effective (Noffsinger & Resnick, 2000).

PHARMACOLOGICAL INTERVENTIONS

The biological basis of behavior is another factor that poses a possible cure for sexual deviation. There are many reasons that a sexual offender would require medication. Some of these reasons include the following: control sexual impulses, aid mental illnesses that are underlying the sexual dysfunction, or to control sexual offenders that are dangerous and out of societies control (Miller, 1998; Noffsinger & Resnick, 2000). In the book, *Sexual Aggression,* Shaw states, "Psychopharmacological treatment for sex offenders may be used as the main treatment modality in offenders who are high risk to offend and are unresponsive to other interventions or as an adjunct to other forms of treatment" (Shaw, 1999, p. 320). These other forms of treatment include diagnosable mental disorders. Curing mental illness or suppressing the symptoms of the mental illness through drug intervention can provide compliance for alternate treatment programs such as psychotherapy, group therapy, or community accountability. Research indicates positive effects on sex addicts or sexual offenders with antidepressants such as Paxil and Prozac (Slater, 2000; Zohar, Kaplan, & Benjamin, 1994; Miller, 1998). This begs the question whether there is an underlying depressive disorder, obsessive-compulsive tendency, or just hyperactive sexual impulse in those who are sexually deviant. There is no easy answer for the complexity of each individual's case. However, drug intervention can help to contribute to the rehabilitation of sex offenders.

There are risks involved in drug treatment, as Shaw states, "The use of pharmacological treatments for sex offenders raises a number of legal and ethical concerns. Because these drugs may alter sexual attitudes and beliefs, they have been viewed by their opponents as mind controlling" (Shaw, 1999, p. 319). This raises the question of the rights of sexual offenders and also the ethical obligation in treating them. With drug treatment there is the risk of noncompliance to self-administered medications, side effects of the medications, and also long-term implications of drug use not treating the underlying symptoms.

A concern for society and the courts lies in weighing the risks of placing someone in society that may/or may not be at risk to reoffend. The majority of sex offenders will at some point be released back into a community. Society is seemingly pacified with the drug treatments and the hope that the offender is cured and thus, no longer a threat. However, without assurances from reliable studies that drug treatments stop the sexual offender, the drugs serve as merely a band-aid for society's concerns of safety.

OTHER PSYCHOTHERAPIES

Psychotherapy can include numerous theoretical approaches of treatment. Often individual psychotherapy utilizes psychoanalytic, psychodynamic and object relational styles to understand the psychosexual developmental stages or intra-psychic characteristics of the offender. These can be helpful considering that some offenders have prior victimization and abuse issues. There are also cognitive-behavioral, cognitive affective, rational emotive, and solution-focused therapies. These focus on the beliefs, thoughts, and behaviors of the offender. Additionally, there are psychoeducational individual sessions and family systems therapies. Psychoeducational individual therapy focuses on educating the offender and family systems focuses on understanding the offender's family connections. Social support, communication, healthy sexuality classes, and stress or anger management are also alternate methods for treatment. These methods are used in professional and correctional settings depending on the type of offender, and mental health facility rendering service.

SOLITUDE OR CONFINEMENT

One of the inevitable consequences to sexual deviate behavior is interaction with the legal system. There are varying legal implications for the numerous types of sexual offenses. As public outrage grows concerning the release of sexual offenders, there becomes added pressure on the judicial system to lengthen the charges on convicted sex criminals. Certainly, for those convicted of severe sex crimes involving murders there is the chance of a life sentence, which eliminates re-offences. Parole and community accountability is dependent on the particular regulations of the state involved in legislation.

RECOMMENDATIONS

One recommended strategy for intervention and treatment of sexual offenders is a thorough clinical assessment. The main objective in assessing sex offenders is to receive an accurate picture of their risk to society, whether the offender would be receptive to treatment, and what type of treatment would be appropriate. The following quote identifies some essential factors for conducting comprehensive assessments.

> Guidelines for assessing sex offenders strongly advise that the clinician collect collateral material as part of the assessment process before evaluation. Because of the problem of denial among offenders, it is very important that an assessor attempt to gather information from more than just the offender. Generally, sources of data are victim statements, police reports, previous mental health and medical records, juvenile and adult criminal records, and probation or parole reports when available. The key part of any assessment of an offender is the collection of a detailed psychosocial and psychosexual history. The psychosocial history includes family, medical, criminal, and mental health history in addition to history of substance abuse. The sexual history focuses on both deviant and non-deviant behaviors in addition to the individual's ability to develop relationships. (Becker & Murphy, 1998, p. 220)

The assessment is vital in determining treatment indicators and identifying risk factors. A proper assessment like the one explained above, can give insight and direction in recommending appropriate treatment services.

Concerning treatment, the most comprehensive style of therapy is the multi-modal approach. Under this approach, each person in treatment receives thorough assessments and individualized treatments according to specific symptoms. The treatment goal is to block the offender's interest in deviant sexual behavior (Noffsinger, Resnick, 2000). The multimodal approach combines many types of treatment intervention as available and recommended by the initial assessment. This approach would include cognitive behavioral groups with relapse prevention, psychotherapy, education, drug interventions, and community based accountability. Research indicates that sexual offenders, that complete treatment or show motivation to comply with required treatment programs have lower levels of recidivism (Heilburn, Nezu, Keeney, Chung, & Wasserman, 1998; Noffsinger & Resnick, 2000). Most recidivism rates are measured by follow up measuring violations of parole or new arrests, which could neglect undetected acts of recidivism. However, recidivism is difficult to access thus qualifying treatments are often ambiguous.

CLOSING REMARKS

In the introduction, the question of a cure for deviant sexual behavior was put forth and throughout this chapter, many approaches to cure sexual offenders have been addressed. Currently, there is no cure for sexual deviate behavior because there is not a clear understanding of the origin of sexual deviance in a human being. This origin or reason for the deviate thoughts and behaviors of sex criminals eludes those who work among them. These professionals, who work with sex offenders, believe in their treatment programs theoretical orientation and apply various strategies to treat offenders. These treatment programs focus on the beliefs, cognitions, behaviors, and biological factors influencing the offender in hope to eliminate relapse. Relapse is an inevitable factor in all treatment programs. To prevent relapse and treat offenders effectively, a good assessment is necessary to assign appropriate interventions. Effective intervention will often use a multimodal treatment approach that applies a variety of strategies that best fits the offender's psychological needs. Although, with assessments and treatment interventions one component is still missing: the offender's choice to engage in sexually deviant behavior. In addition to focusing on individual needs, offenders' personal accountability and decisions need to be carefully analyzed.

With the growing unrest of the victims of sexual offences, to see justice to their cases, along with the judicial system and prisons dealing with sexual offenders, there is an urgent need to understand effective treatment interventions. So the question again is asked: Can a sexual offender be treated and cured of reoffending? The answer includes an assessment of the individual's unique characteristics, several strategies of treatment, compliance from the sexual offender, more research to back up efficacy, and offender personal accountability.

ASSESSMENT OF ADULT MALE SEX OFFENDERS

50

Clinical Interviewing and Assessment Instruments

ELIZABETH JONES

Psychology from its inception has been in a neverending search for the mysteries embedded in human nature and behavior. One of the mysteries lies in the violent behaviors humans inflict on other humans. To answer the questions posed by these behaviors, psychologists have been charged with examining various methods of violence perpetrated by individuals in society. Sex offenders is one of the many groups that are assessed by psychologists in an attempt to better understand the individual who perpetrates these crimes, as well as to assist professionals in various fields with the aftermath of these crimes and the prevention of future sex crimes. This chapter explores two main areas of assessment specific to adult male sex offenders: interview technique and self-report instruments.

INTERVIEW TECHNIQUE AND CONTENT

The importance of understanding technique in terms of what and how to ask a sex offender to provide information cannot be understated. Not only is the psychologist asking the offender to relay information regarding the instant offense, he is also required to obtain sensitive information regarding the offender's history (Seligman & Hardenburg, 2000). The goal of an interview with a sex offender, Perry and Orchard (1992) suggest the following four areas:

1. Determining the diagnosis for the offender

This is especially important when more than one diagnosis is appropriate for the offender, such as the determination of the presence of and Axis I and Axis II diagnosis as well as differential diagnosis. The psychologist who conducts an assessment of a sex offender should be knowledgeable of the various known paraphilias as defined by the American Psychiatric Association, as well as others that may not be recognized, but are noted by professionals who work with sex offenders. The psychologist should pay special attention to the existence of more than one paraphila, as those with a paraphila are often found to have three or more (Hickey, 2006; Seligman and Hardenburg, 2000). Proper diagnosis of the presence of paraphilas including clinical diagnosis of Axis II personality disorders as well as Axis I disorders such as depression, anxiety, obsessive compulsive, substance abuse, and psychotic disorders assist treatment by clinicians as well as other professionals in various other forensic arenas.

2. Treatment Plan Development

The goal of the sex offender assessment can be two-fold. Information gathering by conducting a through clinical interview can assist in determining the most appropriate treatment selection for the individual offender. It can help in development or revision of treatment plans as well as evaluation of the effectiveness of current treatment programs (Porter, Fairweather, Drugge, & Herve, 2000).

3. Providing Information for Other Professionals

The interview will provide needed information for the psychologist to diagnosis and assess amenability for treatment of the offender, but several other professionals may also use the information. Judges use assessments to determine an offender's length of sentence, type of placement within a forensic facility, and parole or probation requirements (Hanson & Harris, 2000). Lawyers may use the interview information to build a stronger case for or against the offender or find new information the offender may not have revealed to the lawyer. Prison and jail mental health professionals may use the information to evaluate for special needs of the offender as the offender enters the institution.

4. Providing Information for the Client

Finally, the interview information can be used with the offender to assist in the offender understanding the nature of the offense. It can be used to highlight treatment areas for the offender as well as to evaluate progress within a treatment program (Hudson & Ward, 2000).

Marshall (1999) also suggests there are eight areas of importance in the assessment of sexual offenders:

1. Sexual behaviors
2. Social Functioning
3. Life History
4. Cognitive Processes

5. Personality Patterns

6. History of Substance Abuse and Substance Abuse at the Time of the Instant Offense

7. Physical/Health-Related Problems

8. Relapse Related Issues

Marshall's as well as Perry and Orchard's recommendations for focusing the interview of the sex offender may prove helpful for the psychologist in designing and implementing an effective and efficient interview.

BACKGROUND INFORMATION

Gathering a detailed account of a client's history is an important component of any psychological assessment. The ability to appropriately obtain this information is equally, if not more important when conducting a sex offender assessment interview.

Several areas should be explored during the interview. Questions that may be asked to obtain this information can be broken down into several smaller areas, which may assist in organizing the plethora of information provided by the offender.

Prenatal, Infancy, and Early Childhood History

- Was the pregnancy of the offender's mother planned?
- Were the parents of the offender married or otherwise committed to each other at the time of the offender's birth?
- Was the offender's mother actively using alcohol or other substances at the time of pregnancy and/or breast-feeding?
- Were there any complications during pregnancy or delivery?
- What is the birth order of the offender?
- Were there any childhood illnesses, high fevers or head trauma suffered by the offender?
- Was there any early childhood losses of a primary caretaker or other important relationship?
- Were developmental milestones (toilet training, walking, talking) met within expected time frames?
- Is there evidence of preverbal trauma as a result of physical, sexual, emotional abuse or neglect?

Childhood History

- When did the offender first attend school?
- Were there any behavioral problems either at home or school?

- Was the offender ever evaluated for a learning disability? If yes, what was done by the school to address the needs of the offender? Were these efforts successful?

- Was the offender ever placed into a special class because of disruptive or aggressive behavior?

- How able was the offender to establish and maintain peer and other interpersonal relationships?

- How did the offender perform academically during primary school?

- Was the offender's family stable or transient in terms of housing?

- Did the offender's family have a history of using public assistance/welfare?

- Were the parent's employed? If yes, what type of employment? Was this stable or frequently changed?

- Was there alcohol or substance abuse in the home?

- Did the offender have access to inappropriate materials (pornographic magazines, reading material, and access to Internet material)?

- Was there a history of domestic violence in the home?

- How did the parents express or repress sexuality within the home? Were their opportunities for the offender to witness sexual contact between adults?

- How did the offender interact with siblings?

- Was there a history of family contact with the criminal justice system?

Adolescent History

Many of the same questions posed in the childhood section can be restated in the adolescent portion of the interview. What becomes more important to focus on in this section of the interview is the offender's sexual development. Questions may arise in the childhood section regarding sexuality, especially if there is a history of sexual abuse. Kafka and Prentky (1994) found that 25 to 30 percent of individuals with a paraphila had a history of physical and/or sexual abuse. It should also be noted that paraphilias often develop during childhood and early adolescence (Hanson & Harris, 2000; Levine, Risen, & Althof, 1994). During adolescence, an individual becomes increasingly aware of sexual feelings and sensations. This can be an especially difficult section of the interview to complete for the novice psychologist, as the questions become sexually graphic in nature. It is imperative for the psychologist to understand that asking detailed questions regarding the offenders sexual development provides essential information for the assessment. Questions in this interview section can include:

- When did the offender first become aware of his sexuality? What beliefs did the offender establish based upon this awareness?

- How did the offender learn about sexuality (school, home, peers)?

- How did the family respond to adolescent sexuality within the home (shame, open, repressed)?
- At what age did the offender have his first romantic relationship?
- At what age did the offender first start to masturbate?
- What was the content of masturbatory fantasies used by the offender during adolescence?
- How frequently did the offender masturbate and where did he masturbate?
- At what age did the offender first have sexual contact with another individual? Was this contact consensual? Did it occur within an established romantic relationship or was it experimental?
- Who did the offender find sexually attractive? If it was outside the norm, how did the offender's family respond?
- Were there any large discrepancies in the age of whom the offender found sexually attractive or whom the offender engaged in sexual activity?
- Did the offender have an increase in aggressive and/or violent behavior?
- Did the offender have any contact with the juvenile justice system?

Prior to moving into the final interview section, which will explore in detail specific areas of importance for the psychologist conducting a sex offender assessment, it would prove helpful to provide what was found by Perry and Orchard (1992) to be a common family constellation for sex offenders. In this dynamic, it was found that the father is emotionally distant, indifferent, and uninvolved with the family. The mother is unaffectionate, demanding, intrusive, and belittling. With the introduction and perpetuation of this parenting and relationship style, a child may have difficulties with social skills, distorted ideas of sexual intimacy and lowered self-esteem. These are common factors identified in adult sex offenders (Hudson & Ward, 2000). It is often useful to have an understanding of attachment theory to further flush out aspects of the offender's relationship with his parents as well as their understanding, or lack thereof, of mutually agreed-upon and rewarding interpersonal relationships (Perry & Orchard, 1992).

ADULTHOOD ASPECTS OF SEXUAL OFFENDING

The final section of the assessment interview explores the offender's adulthood experiences. Several pieces come together in this section of the interview, including reasons for and the course of the offending behavior and his/her current lifestyle (Porter, Fairweather, Drugge, & Herve, 2000; Seligman & Hardenburg, 2000).

Course of conduct possibly provides some of the most vital information regarding the offender's behavior. Before this section of the interview, it is suggested (Fisher, Beech, and Browne, 1999; Marshall, 1999; Tierney and McCabe; 2001) that the psychologist takes the opportunity to review the various pieces of collateral information provided prior to the assessment commencing. These can include the police report from the arresting incident, hospital records, victim statement(s), and probation and/or parole records and reviews. This can again be an area of difficulty for psychologists as the material is graphic and can at times be visual if and when pictures are provided within the collateral information. Important areas to obtain information during the interview are numerous, but should include several key areas.

The nature of the behavior focuses on the actual act of the offending behavior. Questions should be asked that will facilitate the psychologist in understanding the physical act of the offense, offender's beliefs and reactions to the physical act.

Time of onset of offending behavior may be based in adulthood, but it is helpful for the psychologist to keep in mind that often sexually offending behaviors start in adolescence (Kafka & Prentky, 1994). Often it is the psychologist who will uncover the progression of offending behavior from adolescent through adulthood. This is also the case with frequency of sexually inappropriate and offending behaviors (Goodman, 1993; Marshall, 1999).

Reasons for the offender's behavior can include many variations and assist the psychologist in deriving an evaluation of level of violence and threat of re-offense. Some sex offenders derive a sense of self, power, direction or meaning of life from the perpetration of offences (Hanson & Harris, 2000). For other offenders, sexually aggressive behaviors can alleviate symptoms of anxiety, depression, and loneliness, or to express rage (Levine, Risen, & Althof, 1994). Other offenders gain relief from the demands of everyday life. While other offenders perpetrate their crimes to recreate feelings associated with childhood sexual or physical abuse (Levine et al., 1994).

Current Lifestyle

Sex offenders can provide information for the psychologist through relaying information in connection with current or past consensual sexual relationships experienced. It has been frequently found that sex offenders lack sexual knowledge. This can be seen in adolescent offenders who will often not be able to identify specific genitalia of either gender, will often use immature language to identify genitalia and sexual behaviors, immature ideas and beliefs in regard to consent of a partner in sexual activities and understanding of the sexual act being pleasurable, emotionally as well as physically, for both involved in the sexual act (Porter, Fairweather, Drugge, & Herve, 2000). This can be seen in adult offenders as well, although these offenders may have acquired a mature vocabulary, the understanding of mutual intimate relationships may still be sorely lacking in these offenders.

Sex offenders may lack the self confidence in adulthood that is needed in order to establish mutually rewarding intimate relationships (Levine, Risen, and Althof, 1994). Many have been found to have sexual dysfunction in "conventional partner sexual behavior" (Levine et al.). This may be a result in the increase in frequency and intensity of deviant sexual fantasy and behavior as an outlet for sexual energy and urges.

COMMON PATTERNS FOR SEXUAL OFFENDING BEHAVIORS

Several behaviors have been found in sex offenders that provide information regarding the level and intensity of offending behaviors currently as well as providing some level of insight into assessment of future risk for reoffense. Although not all of these are found in every sexual offender, they have been found frequently enough to establish as common patterns of behavior among sexually offending adult males (Hudson & Ward, 2000).

Solitary behaviors may include frequent masturbation in conjunction with paraphilic fantasy. This often is seen as a progression from "victimless" (voyeurism), to exhibitionism, allowing for limited inclusion of others to progression to more intrusive, aggressive and violent sexual behaviors.

Fantasy is often the springboard into paraphilic and sexual offending behaviors. As are solitary activities as discussed above, this is a progression. Fantasies, while being able to sexually excite the offender, will become less satisfying. The offender may then move to explore the sexual urges and perhaps even create practice scenarios as a method of increasing sexual excitement that the fantasy alone may no longer provide. Finally, the offender may chose to act out the fantasy, once fantasy and planning no longer provide enough sexual satisfaction for the offender. This too can often been seen as a progression, as with many other types of offenders. The behavior may be less violent initially, but given time and continued sexual gratification from acting out the fantasy and urges, behavior will frequently progress into more violent acts against the victim (Prentky & Knight, 1991).

PERSONALITY PATTERNS OF SEX OFFENDERS

Several researchers (Fisher & Howells, 1993; Goodman, 1993; Marshall, 1999; Perry & Orchard, 1992) have offered several personality patterns that have been seen in male adult sex offenders. Again, as stated in the previous section, all of these patterns may not be present in every sexual offender.

Marshall (1999) suggested that vulnerability, impaired self-esteem, little empathy and insight, poor social skills, and inadequate attachment to parents or primary caretakers frequently characterize sex offenders. Fisher and Howells (1993) indicated that sex offenders tend to be angry, lonely, and lacking in successful interpersonal relationships, especially intimate in nature. These researchers also suggest that sex offenders are often found to be self-centered.

Goodman's (1993) findings suggest sex offenders lack a clear sense of self. These offenders may vacillate between devaluing and idealizing the self, and often are diagnosed with narcissistic personality disorder or are found to have narcissistic personality features. Also found was that sex offenders switch between punishing themselves and feeling entitled. These features are also found in individuals with narcissistic personality disorder or features of this disorder. Perry and Orchard

(1992) found that sex offenders are easily overwhelmed by strong emotions. They tend to be well defended and guarded in their presentation to others. Perry and Orchard also suggest sex offenders possess a diminished sense of responsibility or remorse for the offending behavior.

All of the above findings assist the psychologist in understanding sex offenders and should be kept in mind while conducting the interview section of the assessment. In understanding the personality underpinnings, the psychologist can more effectively evaluate the specific personality patterns of these offenders.

ASSESSMENT INSTRUMENTS FOR SEX OFFENDERS

When a psychologist conducts an effective and through clinical interview, selection of appropriate instruments can be made easier. From the information provided by the offender in the interview, the psychologist is better able to select instruments that will highlight or clarify various areas of the offender's personality, motivations, level of insight and empathy, amenability to treatment as well as risk for reoffense.

Every psychological assessment should begin with a general clinical assessment instrument. The Minnesota Multiphasic Personality Inventory-II (MMPI-II) is a strong instrument in that it provides a myriad of Axis I diagnostic and clinical information. While Axis I diagnostic information is exceedingly important to have during the assessment process, especially when attempting to differentiate diagnosis, the more pervasive areas of personality need to be examined just as closely. The Millon Clinical Multiaxial Inventory-Third Edition (MCMI-III) is a valuable tool when exploring adult personality patterns. Since the instrument is designed to closely resemble the *DSM-IV* diagnostic criteria for personality disorders, results may provide a more developed picture of the pervasive personality patterns of sex offenders (Chantry & Craig, 1994; Marshall, 1999). Using both these instruments together can often give the psychologist both a complete Axis I and Axis II clinical picture, which proves helpful in evaluating sex offenders.

Self-report measures have also proven helpful in assessing sex offenders, but often the results of some of these tests need to be evaluated with an eye for malingering on the part of the individual being evaluated. Specifically, instruments such as the Beck Inventories (Beck Depression Inventory-II, Beck Anxiety Inventory and Beck Hopelessness Scale) are extremely face valid, and as a result, an individual, sex offender or not, can easily "fake bad" on these instruments. It should be stated that using the Beck inventories in conjunction with a less face valid instrument, such as the MMPI-2 or MCMI-III can assist in assessing levels of current depressive and/or anxiety symptoms as well as suicidal ideation (Marshall, 1999; Seligman and Hardenburg, 2000).

Although instruments designed for sex offenders exist, there is no current consensus on which instruments provide the most useful information. What has been indicated by these instruments is there appears to be three areas that most instruments share when examining sex offenders: Assertiveness, sexual discomfort and expressed and repressed aggression and violence (Seligman & Hardenburg, 2000). Further research in these area, as well as development of a more standardized battery of assessment instruments to use in conjunction with the clinical interview, would prove exceedingly helpful in the progression of assessment of sexual offenders.

AREAS OF FUTURE RESEARCH

As with all psychological assessment, there are two components of the process: the interviews and psychological testing. Both of these areas could be further explored in an effort to make assessment of sex offenders more productive and useful for all involved.

One area that should be examined is the attitude of psychologists who conduct the assessments for sex offenders. Often, psychologists who do not actively pursue their career in a forensic arena, have difficulty viewing offenders in at least a glimmer of a positive light. This negative view of offenders, specifically sex offenders, proves detrimental to the offender being evaluated as well as the profession of psychology. In order to provide appropriate and effective assessments for these offenders, psychologists need to examine their ability to conduct such assessments in a fair and nonjudgmental manner.

In terms of assessment instruments, there is a wide range of research that would prove beneficial for psychologists. Although there will most likely never be a "sex offender assessment battery" developed, certainly continued refinement of the tools currently in use would be helpful for those conducting sex offender assessment. Specifically, tools that examine specific types of sex offenders and differences between sex offenders would prove exceedingly useful not only to those psychologists who conduct assessments, but for professionals who provide treatment for sex offenders.

CONCLUSION

This chapter has examined the importance of the clinical interview when conducting a sex offender evaluation as well as briefly examining some of the psychological instruments that can be used during these assessments. With continued research by psychologists and other mental health professionals, perhaps one day a more full understanding of the motivation behind sexual offending can be unveiled and treatment modified and improved. And, although many may believe it an impossibility, perhaps there will come about an understanding of sex offenders that could evolve into an effective treatment plan for sexually offending individuals, that would both protect society from further victimization, as well as allow the sex offender to learn a new way of relating to others around them as well as themselves.

C H A P T E R

SEX OFFENDER RECIDIVISM MEASURES

51

A Comparison of Popular Risk Assessment Instruments

KATHERINE NICKCHEN

Webster's Collegiate Dictionary, 10th edition, defines recidivism as the "tendency to relapse into a previous condition or mode of behavior (e.g., criminal behavior relapse)." Multiple arrests for repeat offenses is an issue of major concern for the American justice system and for all American citizens. The media's portrayal of sex offenders has increased the attention on policies, rehabilitation, and the ability to protect the public from these individuals. Thus, predicting who will and will not recidivate has increased dramatically in importance. Violence risk assessment, predicting who may or may not act violently in the future, is an expanding part of the mental health field. The question remains, how does one go about assessing the risk of future violent behavior?

Over the past decade research has focused on methods of prediction, variables predictive of future behavior, and the implementation of these tools. The methods of prediction include clinical and actuarial approaches. The clinical approach to risk assessment relies on subjective conclusions reached by a clinician. The clinician explores risk level through interviews with the suspect and review of medical, police, etc. records. Research has shown that "psychiatrists and psychologists are accurate in no more than one out of three predictions of violent behavior . . ." (Monahan, 2000, para. 7).

Hall (1988) looked at 342 sexual offenders for a comparison of predictive abilities between actuarial variables and clinical judgment. Psychologists and psychiatrists attempted to predict recidivism based on their judgments pertaining to completion of treatment programs. The actuarial prediction used an equation based on past sexual and non-sexual offenses, age, IQ, and MMPI data. The actuarial predictions outperformed the clinical predictions with clinical predictions only slightly better than chance.

The actuarial approach isolates specific risk factors and statistically associates them with violent behavior. Actuarial predictions consistently surpass clinical judgment in accuracy making this the preferred method of prediction (Byrne, Byrne, Hillman, & Stanley, 2001; Borum, 1996; Hall, 1988; Gardner, Lidz, Mulvey & Shaw, 1996; Monahan, 2000; Mossman, 1994; Quist & Matshazi, 2000). "Literature indicates that actuarial prediction is more accurate than clinical prediction, but in practice actuarial methods seem to be used rarely" (Gardner et al., 1996, p. 35). These authors (Gardner et al., 1996) suggest that this results from clinicians' adverse reactions to the calculations, level of difficulty, length of time required, and limited funding to purchase measures actuarial methods require. Furthermore, implementation of actuarial instruments may be too costly due to length of time required to score and calculate each test by hand or the computer programs required to obtain the scores and calculations. Researchers are currently attempting to develop measures that reduce these concerns (Gardner et al., 1996).

Most clinicians are faced with the need to assess violent risk of a patient and currently no explicit national professional standard exists for this assessment or management of risk. Borum (1996) examined recent research developments on violence risk. Progress is addressed through: (a) research on predictive ability, (b) the relationship between mental disorders and violence, (c) base rates of violence, and (d) risk factors for violent behavior. This information is used to develop reliable and more efficient assessment tools. Borum outlines recommendations for improving risk assessment within clinical practice. The first recommendation goes back to improved risk assessment technology. New tests are being developed and researched including the Dangerous Behavior Rating Scheme, Violence Prediction Scheme, HCR-20, Spousal Assault Risk Assessment Guide, etc. The second recommendation attempts to establish guidelines that will help the clinician establish risk based on scientifically grounded principles for assessment and treatment. The third recommendation is that more extensive training is needed for students and clinicians in the basic concepts of risk assessment research.

By using actuarial methods, variables can be statistically identified to correlate with violent behavior. "Several risk factors for violent behavior are well documented; male gender, young age, previous violence, substance abuse, psychopathy, childhood abuse and maladjustment, positive psychotic symptoms, suicidality, impulsivity, anger, treatment noncompliance, lack of community support or supervision, poor family relations, and stress" (Douglas, Ogloff, & Nicholls, 1999, p. 917–918). Further variables can be reviewed in the following articles: Jones et al., 2001; Hall and Proctor 1987; Hanson & Bussiere, 1998; Hanson & Harris, 2000; Monahan et al., 2000; Malamuth, 1986; Silver et al., 2000 and Steadman et al., 2000. Byrne et al. (2001) distinguish between static (non-changeable—age of first offense, current age of offender) and dynamic factors (changeable—skills deficits, current behaviors, personality dispositions). Dynamic factors are further categorized into stable dynamic (personality disorders and deviant attitudes) and acute dynamic (negative mood or alcohol intoxication) risk factors. Variables chosen for instruments are based on these factors. Stable dynamic risk factors were the most predictive of recidivism. Functional analysis incorporates both actuarial and clinical measures that identify static, stable dynamic, and acute dynamic risk variables. Tustin (1995) defines functional analysis as "a process of identifying possible functions of a response by gathering objective information about the environmental events immediately surrounding it, especially the antecedents and consequences of the response." Results indicate that inclusion of dynamic variables may help in predicting future risk. A recommended solution to complications of recidivism measurements is the development of a measure that is in two parts: a screening tool for static variables to establish a background for an offense and a tool to measure dynamic variables to establish a current likelihood of offense.

Hanson and Harris (2000) looked at dynamic (changeable) risk factors for recidivism through file reviews and interviews of 208 recidivists and 201 nonrecidivists: "[D]ynamic risk factors continued to be strongly associated with recidivism, even after controlling for preexisting differences in static risk factors" (p. 6). Examples of risk factors that were researched include social influences, problems evident during supervision, sexual offense history, lifetime total number of victims, sexual deviance, treatment history, and antisocial personality disorder. The three best static predictors of this study were the Violence Risk Appraisal Guide (VRAG), IQ, and sexual deviance producing a combined multiple correlation of $R = .40$. The three best stable dynamic predictors (factors that can remain unchanged for months) of this study were sees self as no risk, poor social influences, and sexual entitlement producing a combined multiple regression of $R = .53$. The three best acute dynamic predictors (factors that can change rapidly; days, hours, or minutes) were access to victims, no cooperation with supervision, and anger producing a combined correlation of $R = .32$. The static, stable, and acute predictors together increased the correlation to $R = .60$. Only two dynamic factors, anger and sexual preoccupation, contributed unique variance in stepwise regression ($R = .21$). "The results suggest that offenders are most at risk for re-offending when they become sexually preoccupied, have access to victims, fail to acknowledge their recidivism risk, and show sharp increases in dysphonic moods, such as anger" (Hanson & Harris, 2000, last paragraph).

Predicting degrees of risk is important in predicting recidivism. The level of risk for an individual has the potential to determine the possibility of parole, type or degree of treatment, or the environment to which they are released (inpatient, outpatient, or independent care). Level of risk is determined based on scores received on risk assessment instruments (actuarial data).

As of 1996, Nevada began using the State of Nevada Community Notification Sex Offender Assessment Scale (SONCNSOAS) in "making decisions regarding community notification of the parole of sex offenders" (Schofield, 1999). The measure was developed by a committee composed of the Nevada Department of Prisons, Nevada Department of Parole and Probations, and the Nevada Department of Mental Hygiene and Mental Retardation. It followed the format of a New Jersey measure, the Registrant Risk Assessment Scale. Schofield (1999) achieved reliability and validity scores on the SONCNSOAS that indicated scores should be interpreted cautiously ($\alpha = .68, r = .62$, respectively). As a result, its effectiveness in predicting recidivism rates was weak. The study attempted to differentiate between two groups of incarcerated prisoners: those with multiple convictions and those with a single conviction. The hypothesis was that multiple-conviction offenders would score higher on the SONCNSOAS than the single-conviction offenders. The mean sum for first-time sexual offenders ($M = 59.00, SD = 16.14$) was greater than that of multiple offenders ($M = 53.90, SD = 20.00, p < .05$). This result contradicted the hypothesis. Sixteen of the total twenty items were used to assess reliability. Of these sixteen variables, only eight significantly differentiated between the two groups. Five of eight variables indicated first-time offenders were at higher risk than were multiple offenders. This finding also contradicted the hypothesis. This measure was chosen because the participants are sex offenders currently serving sentences in the Nevada Department of Prisons System.

The HCR-20 was constructed to be applicable in predicting violence in a variety of populations, including civil and forensic psychiatric patients (Douglas, Ogloff, and Nicholls (1999) and corrections offenders (Douglas & Webster, 1999). "The promise of this instrument lies in its foundation on a conceptual model or scheme for assessing dangerousness, its basis in the empirical literature, and its operationally defined coding system" (Borum, 1996, p. 950.). The variables chosen for this measure were based on previous research (Hall et al., 1987; Hanson & Bussiere, 1998; Hanson & Harris, 2000; Jones et al., 2001; Gendreau et al., 1996; Langstrom & Grann, 2000; Monahan et al., 2000; Malamuth, 1986; Silver et al., 2000; Steadman et al., 2000). The measure includes 10 questions pertaining to historical factors, five to dynamic (changeable) clinical factors, and five to situation risk management factors.

The Static-99 is based on static factors and was first published in 1999. It is a combination of the Rapid Risk Assessment for Sex Offense Recidivism (RRASOR) and the Structured Anchored Clinical Judgment Minimum scale (SACJ-min). Hanson (1997) reports the RRASOR was designed to predict sex offense recidivism using a small number of easily scored variables (male victims, unrelated victims, prior sex offenses, and age ranging from 18 to 24.99). The SACJ uses a stepwise approach. "The first step classifies offenders into three risk categories (low, medium, high) based on their official convictions. In the next steps, offenders can be reclassified (up or down) based on protective or aggravating factors" (Hanson & Thornton, 2000, p. 121). Completing a treatment program would be considered a protective factor and would lower the initial risk level. An aggravating factor would be two or more of the following: any stranger victims, any male victims, never married, convictions for non-contact sex offenses, substance abuse, placement in residential care as a child, deviant sexual arousal, and psychopathy. This would result in the initial risk level being increased one category. When compared, analysis suggested the RRASOR and SACJ-Min were assessing "related but not identical constructs" (Hanson & Thornton, 2000, p.122). It was demonstrated that the new scale predicted future violent behavior better than either original scale. Hanson and Thornton's (1999) study compared the relative predictive accuracy across samples of the RRASOR, SACJ-Min, and Static-99 for both sexual recidivism and any violent recidivism. This scale has been validated across many studies and in many different settings.

Barbaree, Seto, Langton and Peacock (2001) compared five actuarial instruments and one guided clinical instrument across 215 sex offenders released from prison for an average of 4.5 years. The instruments evaluated include the VRAG (Violence Risk Appraisal Guide), SORAG (Sex Offender Risk Appraisal Guide), RRASOR (Rapid Risk Assessment of Sexual Offense Recidivism), Static-99, MnSost-R (Minnesota Sex Offender Screening Tool-Revised), and a guided clinical assessment tool, MASORR (Multifactorial Assessment of Sex Offender Risk of Recidivism). The authors expected that the VRAG and SORAG would accurately predict violent recidivism, whereas the RRASOR, Static-99, and MnSOST-R would accurately predict sexual recidivism. Results indicated that the VRAG, SORAG, RRASOR, and Static-99 were successful in predicting general, serious, and sexual recidivism. The MnSOST-R failed to meet statistical significance in the prediction of serious and sexual recidivism, although it did predict general recidivism. The MASORR had not been empirically evaluated prior to this study but research indicates that pretreatment was a significant predictor in the positive direction of any recidivism. No instrument was found to be superior in predicting recidivism. Sixty-two sexual offenses committed by twenty-three male repeat offenders were evaluated to explore if patterns of behavior ("fixed emotional propensity") developed, and remained relatively stable, across time. With the assumption that past behaviors can predict future behaviors, the authors attempted to discern: (a) one offender from another offender, and (b) if type of offense is related to recidivism. This study distinguished between an aggressive and non-aggressive sexual offender style. The differences between the two were found to be related to psychological characteristics and historical patterns of deviant behavior. The results indicated that the "fixed emotional propensity" of an offender may help in determining recidivism. The established patterns of the offenders may be useful in predicting future offenses and nature of the offense.

Dempster (1995) examined the predictive validity of five risk assessment measures for recidivism. The instruments used included the Psychopathy Checklist-Revised (PCL-R), Violence Risk Appraisal Guide (VRAG), Sexual Offender Risk Appraisal Guide (SORAG), Raid Risk Assessment for Sexual Offense Recidivism (RRASOR), and the Sexual Violence Risk–20 (SVR-20). The SVR-20 was a structured clinical interview while all other instruments were actuarial in nature. Four types of outcomes were analyzed: 1) nonrecidivists vs. nonviolent recidivists vs. sexually violent recidivists, 2) all violent recidivists vs. nonrecidivists, 3) sexually violent recidivists vs. all other participants, and 4) sexually violent vs. generally violent recidivists. Files of 120 male sexual offenders released from federal correctional institutions in British Columbia between January 1, 1988 and December 31, 1992 were included in this study. Findings indicated that predictions of violent recidivism maintained a relatively high level of accuracy across all instruments. Results indicate the SORAG is superior in detecting violent recidivism in sex offenders. The instruments' correlations to violent recidivism are as follows: PCL-R, $r = .45$; VRAG, $r = .56$; SORAG, $r = .64$; RRASOR, $r = .40$; SVR-20 Actuarial, $r = .52$; SVR-20 Clinical, $r = .43$. Instruments in the study displayed moderate predictive validity with respect to sexual recidivism with relatively no differentiation between measures. The RRASOR provided higher predictive accuracy with sexually violent recidivism than with violence in general. Most instruments did not distinguish sexually violent recidivism from general, nonsexual violent recidivism.

Douglas, Ogloff, and Nicholls (1999) evaluated the predictive validity of the HCR-20 (Historical, Clinical, and Risk Management) and the PCL:SV (Psychopathy Checklist: Screening Version). The HCR-20 was developed based on empirical literature. It has the potential to be applicable in a variety of settings and can be coded from archival data for research purposes. The dynamic and situational factors enable the measure to be used repeatedly over the course of therapy for one individual. The PCL:SV measures characteristics of psychopathy. The sample was made up of 193 involuntarily hospitalized inpatients from a large psychiatric hospital in western Canada. The measures were coded retrospectively and were based on the participants' case files. Results indicate both instruments are related to violence with moderate to large effect sizes. The HCR-20 "possessed incremental validity over the PCL:SV and tended to be more strongly and consistently related to violence." The HCR-20 adds predictive accuracy above and beyond that of the PCL:SV, but the PCL:SV does not add to the predictive accuracy of the HCR-20. Douglas and Webster (1999) looked at the concurrent validity of the HCR-20 through comparison to other risk assessment measures. The Psychopathy Checklist-Revised (PCL-R) and the Violence Risk Appraisal Guide (VRAG) were used as comparison measures. Both the VRAG and the PCL-R have been used in forensic and correctional settings and are recognized as displaying a relationship with violent behavior. The HCR-20 was "constructed to be applicable to a variety of populations, including civil and forensic psychiatric patients and correctional offenders." This study was coded on seventy-five Canadian male, federally sentenced, maximum-security offenders. The authors conducted a retrospective chart review. This study was done to find the relationship of the HCR-20 to existing criminal charges and other risk measures, not predictive validity. The results indicate the HCR-20 correlates to incarcerated violent offenders as well as or better than the VRAG and PCL-R.

Silver, Smith, and Bankes (2000) examines actuarial devices used for predicting recidivism. The authors assess the generalizability of the new "iterative classification" procedure and compare it with more traditional recidivism devices. The placement of cases into groups was random and consisted of over 5,800 cases per category. When data are used in the iterative classification procedure, they are separated into three initial categories on the basis of predicted risk: low-risk (predicted probabilities below a prespecified score), high-risk (predicted probabilities above a prespecified score), and an intermediate risk (predicted probabilities that fall in between the prespecified scores). The intermediate-risk category is then submitted to additional statistical analyses resulting in placing items into one of the two remaining categories. This procedure can be done repeatedly until no further scores are affected statistically and the cases cannot be placed into either low- or high-risk categories. This procedure affects scores on reanalysis because as cases are eliminated, the new group has a different distribution of risk factor characteristics. This provides new information for the statistical procedures. The results obtained from this study found the iterative classification procedure was able to classify a higher percentage of cases into low-risk and high-risk categories compared to other measures. It was also determined that shrinkage was no more apparent in iterative classification than in other devices. Shrinkage means that the more the data are relied on during the construction, the greater the opportunities to capitalize on chance variation in the data. Each measure was designed for a specific job. As long as the job requirements fit the qualifications of the measure then the measure will perform accurately. The iterative classification procedure was designed to classify cases into three levels of risk. If the objective is to predict "risky" cases then the measure is beneficial.

Steadman et al. (2000) studied differences between a main effects regression approach and a classification tree approach to violence risk assessment. The main effects regression approach implies that a single set of questions will fit all people whose violence is being evaluated. A classification tree approach employs different combinations of questions depending on the answers to prior questions. The classification tree also employs dichotomous thresholds. There are both low and high thresholds that are determined prior to analysis. Based on the scores, the participants are placed into categories. The scores below the low threshold are considered low-risk and the scores above the high threshold are considered high-risk. The remaining scores are then placed into the midrange, labeled "unclassified." The unclassified scores are pooled together, reanalyzed, and distributed accordingly. This step is repeated until no further scores can be distributed into the low or high-risk group. The repeated classification steps are labeled iterative classification trees (ICT). Of the 939 participants tested using both measures, 76.5 percent were classified into either low or high-risk categories using the ICT method and 57.1 percent for the main effects method. While the initial results for the ICT method appear positive, more research is needed.

Hall and Proctor's study from 1987, involving 342 nonpsychotic male sexual offenders, analyzed the utility of criminological variables as predictors of recidivism. Using FBI records, arrests and rearrests of the subjects were categorized as (a) sexual felonies against adults (rape, sodomy); (b) sexual felonies against children (statutory rape, incest); (c) nonsexual violent felonies against persons that involved actual or threatened harm (robbery, assault); (d) nonsexual nonviolent felonies against property or the public order (possession of illegal drugs). A multivariate regression analysis indicated that arrests for sexual offenses against adults were associated with arrests for sexual reoffenses against adults and with non-sexual violent re-arrests. Of the variables used, the best predictor of rearrests is prior arrest history.

Monahan et al. (2000) attempted to develop a version of the Iterative Classification Tree (ICT) that was appropriate for clinical use. Previous versions were cumbersome and time-consuming. This version uses risk factors that are commonly available in records or can be routinely assessed. A classification tree approach employs different combinations of questions depending on the answers to prior questions, like a decision tree. Using this approach risk assessment of violence is predicated on many combinations of risk factors. Answers to questions determine the next question asked. This approach also employs two thresholds: one for identifying high-risk cases and one for identifying low-risk cases. The research consisted of 939 male and female psychiatric patients between eighteen and forty years old. The chi-squared automatic interaction detector (CHAID) was used to "identify groups of cases that shared the same risk factors and that also shared the same values on the outcome measure of violence." After several iterations, 72.6 percent of the participants were able to be placed in either the low-risk (50.9 percent) or high-risk (21.7 percent) categories. This tool is specifically designed for assessing the risk of violence. Efforts to manage the risk of violence "will require additional data." The major limitation of this study is that it was normed on individuals hospitalized for mental disorders, so generalizability across other settings is in question.

Quist and Matshazi (2000) consisted of nineteen males and sixteen females residing at a juvenile group home. The Child and Adolescent Functional Assessment Scale (CAFAS) was empirically tested to determine the degree to which it predicted recidivism among juvenile offenders. Stable factors (age, sex, ethnicity) were compared to dynamic factors (attitudes, personal relationships, and education). The CAFAS is made up of several subscales: Role Performance, Behavior Toward Others, Moods/Self-Harm, Substance Use, and Thinking. Within the study, the CAFAS was found to be significantly related to recidivism. Higher CAFAS scores were indicative of greater risk for future offenses.

Monahan (2000) is a review of violence risk assessment and how it pertains to the admissibility of clinical risk assessments of violent behavior as scientific evidence in courts. The author contrasted the clinical approach with the actuarial approach. Actuarial assessments have repeatedly outperformed the clinical approach in predicting recidivism. Research indicates that actuarial measures and statistical procedures have improved greatly in the past decade. The actuarial devices discussed included the Violence Risk Appraisal Guide (VRAG), HCR-20, and the Iterative Classification Tree (ICT). Factors in determining admissibility *(Daubert v. Merrell Dow Pharmaceuticals Inc.)* include: 1) the extent to which the theory has been or can be tested, 2) the extent to which the test relies upon the subjective interpretation of the expert, 3) whether the theory has been subjected to peer review and/or publication, 4) the technique's potential rate of error, 5) whether the underlying theory or technique has been generally accepted as valid by the relevant scientific community, and 6) the nonjudicial uses that have been made of the theory or technique. As of this article, admissibility of expert testimony in violence assessment had yet to be evaluated. In cases preceding the *Daubert* decision, the court endorsed the admissibility of expert testimony in violence assessment. The author encourages courts to recognize the proper role and limitations of expert evidence and testimony in the courtroom.

Based on the research indicated there is clear evidence that actuarial instruments are better predictors than clinical judgment. The difficulty is to choose which instrument to use and what type of offense is the evaluator trying to predict. Instruments may predict general recidivism, violent recidivism, sexual recidivism, or sexually violent recidivism. Research indicates the most validated instruments include the PCL-R, Static-99, VRAG, and the HCR-20.

CHAPTER

SEX OFFENDER ATTITUDES, STEREOTYPES, AND THEIR IMPLICATIONS

52

MILA GREEN MCGOWAN

As most people have very little direct experience with offenders of any kind they are likely to base their impressions of them on information gleaned from popular culture, the media, or informal conversations (Filkins, 1996; Stalans & Lurigio, 1990; Stalans, 1993). For example, an ABC News survey conducted with 1,013 American adults in 2000 found over 80 percent of respondents believed crime to be a problem in our country based solely on what they have seen or read in the news. Only 17 percent reported any personal experience with incidents of crime. But Roberts and Stalans (1997) warned, while news programs and fictional crime dramas often make for good television viewing, they seldom "reflect the true nature of crime" and often "present a distorted view of the reality" of the criminal justice system (p. 3). Though much psychological and criminological research exists on crime causation and punishment, very little of it is transmitted to the public through the media (Roberts & Stalans, 1997). As a result, people form inaccurate criminal stereotypes by retrieving biased information from memory (called "accessibility bias") or by calling up their own images of criminal acts and evaluating salient environmental cues (called "simulation heuristic") (Stalans & Diamond, 1990).

Attribution theory tells us that people are far more likely to attribute negative behavior (like criminal actions) to the person rather than to the environment. This tendency to underestimate the role of situational factors in explaining others' behaviors, called the fundamental attributional error, is key to understanding how people see offenders and make judgments about the root causes of their antisocial actions and their future behavior (Roberts & White, 1986). Research has established a link between certain attitudes, beliefs and emotions and the ideas and expectations people have about justice (Redondo, Luque, & Funes, 1996), the volume of crime and criminal recidivism. Research has also shown that very diverse groups of people hold stereotypical beliefs about criminals partly because offenders are easily stereotyped as a socially acceptable out-group (Reed & Reed, as cited by Roberts & White, 1986). While many professionals in the criminal justice system have direct contact with offenders that provides them with detailed information about certain offenses and offenders, the public must rely on often biased personal conversation or sensationalized media depictions of crime to form their impressions (Stalans & Lurigio, 1990). As a result, the public compared to professionals are more likely to "recall more severe attributes or create more severe impressions about criminal cases" (Stalans & Lurigio, 1990, p. 336).

The effect of criminal stereotypes on our informational and decision-making processes has been demonstrated in studies of the verdicts and sentencing decisions of mock juries. Other inquiries have evaluated public support for various criminal justice policies, and looked at how both criminal justice professionals and laypersons form their impressions of the harm done by crime and offender recidivism risk.

While "[T]he criminal justice system specifies a set of definable features which comprise the concept of the specific crime" (Filkins, 1996, p. 16), these are not used as they should be. Lawyers, judges and jurors are all directed to use these concepts to make decisions about criminal acts and those who are alleged to have carried them out. However, research has shown that many people's crime prototypes do not follow the language of the law as they are presumed to. Instead, their representations are based on their own stereotypes about others. Smith (as cited in Filkins, 1996) concluded our mental representations of certain crimes are often inaccurate. She found subjects were more apt to find a defendant guilty of an alleged crime if the scenario she presented contained more features judged typical of that crime. That is, regardless of the legal criminal elements prescribed by law as necessary for guilt, mock jurors assigned guilt to defendants based on all the behaviors they engaged in or the traits they exhibited rather than on just the relevant evidence. Defendants were found guilty in typical crime scenarios 93 percent of the time compared to only 63 percent of the time in atypical crime scenarios, regardless of the criminal act (Smith, as cited in Filkins, 1996).

In their study of mock jury sentencing decisions, Bodenhausen and Wyer (1985) asserted people rely on criminal stereotypes to infer the reasons for a criminal's actions and then punish based on those inferences, rather than on the factors set forth during the trial or by law. Subjects recommended more severe punishments for offenses that were stereotypic of the transgressor's ethnic group and racial stereotype-consistent criminal behavior (e.g., a Hispanic committing an assault or a Caucasian committing forgery) yielded stiffer sentences. In addition, stereotypic-consistent behavior lead subjects to perceive criminals as more likely to repeat the offense. This finding supports an earlier assertion (see Deaux; Taylor & Jaggi; as cited in Bodenhausen & Wyer, 1985) that stereotype-consistent behavior is seen as more stable and more likely due to the actor's disposition and not to situational circumstances.

Bodenhausen (1988) surmised that jurors only consider other relevant information in sentencing decisions, such as mitigating factors, if a stereotyped-based explanation for the criminal behavior is not available. He found subjects sought out and recalled information confirming their existing stereotypic beliefs more readily than any other evidence presented.

It has long been assumed that one's belief about crime causation will inform one's decisions about how criminals should be treated (Stalans & Diamond, 1990). Research has supported this link as Cullen, Clark, Cullen and Mathers (as cited by Roberts & Stalans, 1997) found people who attributed crime causation to the environment favored rehabilitation while those that looked to individual causes supported punishment more readily. This dichotomy of attitudes held up among samples of law students, criminology students, and probation officers. Other studies have revealed peoples' underlying theories of crime causation help them to distinguish between crime types. For example, a public sample blamed property crimes on environmental factors, such as poor parenting, but blamed sex crimes on individual factors, i.e. mental instability (see Hollins & Howells, as cited by Roberts & Stalans, 1997).

Additional research has focused on relating public perceptions of crime to recidivism rates in an effort to uncover criminal stereotypes. These inquires (see Graber; Quinney; as cited by Roberts & White, 1986) demonstrated, while members of the public hold exaggerated views of crime rates and criminal recidivism, some citizens are able to estimate more realistically certain aspects of crime, such as particular offense rates and gender ratios of offenders (McPherson; Warr; as cited by Roberts & White, 1986). Roberts and White (1986) reported their work on public estimates of recidivism revealed the majority of respondents surveyed overestimated recidivism rates by an excess of anywhere from 24 to 40 percent depending on the crime category. Further, they found evidence of the attitude that offenders convicted of a particular crime would in fact be reconvicted of the same crime (e.g., a property crime versus a person crime) and at similar rates the next time. This attitude existed despite the fact that criminal justice data clearly demonstrates property crimes are the most likely second offense of any recidivist, regardless of the nature of the first conviction, and that recidivism rates for crime categories do vary significantly (Roberts & White, 1986).

In a second study, the same researchers found that people attach a stable probability of the chance of offense repetition over any number of subsequent offenses, even though reoffense rates increase significantly as criminal records grow. Roberts and White (1986) believed such errors stem from both the media's overreporting of crimes committed by recidivists and from the presence of negative public attitudes about offenders, e.g., viewing all offenders alike regardless of personal differences. Demographic offender variables, such as age, level of education, income, gender, marital status, and employment status, were not found to be related to the public's beliefs about criminal recidivism, despite that fact that increasing age, for example, has been shown to be a protective factor for future recidivism (Roberts & White, 1986).

SEX OFFENDER ATTITUDES AND STEREOTYPES

Hogue (1993) reported "[A]necdotal evidence suggests that while some individuals may hold positive attitudes towards prisoners in general they are very negative in their attitudes towards sexual offenders" (p. 28). Many believe this increased negativity is due to the strong and often-conflicting emotions that sex offenses raise in all of us. Berliner (1998) agreed and reported "[S]ex offenders engender an especially strong public response and are the subject of unusual legislative remedies compared to other criminals" (p. 1203) as a result. Ironically, though more severe criminal sanctions, such as longer sentences, mandatory minimums and "strike" laws, have been explicitly directed at sex offenders, so too have special considerations for leniency in which felony sex offenders remain in the community and avoid incarceration if they comply with court-ordered therapy and supervision (Berliner, 1998).

In our country's history, various groups have advanced different ways of thinking about sex offenders and their crimes. Late in the 1930s, the FBI began to publicly characterize sex offenders as 'degenerates' who were sick individuals going about the country harming innocent women and children. In response, sexual psychopathy legislation arose offering treatment for sex offenders in hospitals and release when they were cured (Lieb, Quinsey, & Berliner, 1998). Psychiatrists and the medical community played a key role in helping define the problem and advance solutions.

By the 1970s, the women's movement took over the fight against sexual offending and victimization. They advocated for a change in social mores and called for an increased awareness of the oppression of women and girls through sex offenses (Lieb et al., 1998). The victims became the focus of sexual crimes and stronger criminal penalties resulted as a form of retribution for the devastating effects of sexual victimization. Instead of hospitalization, offenders now went to prison and treated with specialized programs while incarcerated.

In the 1990s, public and legislative attention on sex offenses and their perpetrators shifted once again. Now only the most heinous sex crimes and most violent and incorrigible offenders are of apparent concern. Holmes and Holmes (2002) reported today's "victimization of children is such an unexplainable phenomenon that its etiology and practice is most difficult to explain and understand. Consequently, we view those who prey on children to be truly perverted or dastardly ill" (p. 158). Generally, society relies on the label of "sexual predator" to refer to sex offenders as a group in its legislative, legal and everyday language. But this label describes only the most serious offenders who target strangers, have multiple victims or commit especially violent offenses (Lieb et al., 1998). It fails to adequately conceptualize offenders who commit other sexual crimes and only creates unnecessary panic in the general public about the chance of sexual victimization. Jenkins (1998) believed this misconception leads to "fact creation," as well-known and stereotypical beliefs become reframed as truths. As a result, many citizens will assert sexual abuse is pervasive, a problem of vast scope; abusers are compulsive individuals who commit their crimes frequently, ones whose pathologies resist rehabilitation or cure; and sexually deviant behavior often escalates to violence and murder (Jenkins, 1998). But, he asserted, ideas such as these were not social facts twenty-five years ago.

Many believe the most recent shift in sex offender conceptualization is dependent on four issues (Lieb et al., 1998). One, political consensus is more easily obtained on crimes that cause serious physical injury; two, intrafamilial offenses do not threaten the stability of society as a whole; three, intrafamilial offenders are easier to watch and prevent from accessing victims in the future; and four, extrafamilial offenders are known to have more victims and be most persistent. Because of this last "truth" regarding extrafamilial offenders being most difficult to address, they have become the focus of sex offender legislation and public reactions.

Recent surveys of both the general public and law enforcement agencies (see Matson; Leib & Phillips, as cited by Berliner, 1998) reveal that sexual violent predator laws are popular and well-received. Jenkins (1998) believed this general acceptance is due to the proliferation of the predator model, allowing society to view sex offenders as "being little removed from the worst multiple killers and torturers" (p. 2).

ATTITUDES EXPRESSED BY THE GENERAL PUBLIC

... About Sex Offenders

General public attitudes towards sex offenders appear to be becoming less accepting and more hardened; victims are also becoming far less willing to keep silent about past or present sexual victimization. Men convicted of sex offenses are often labeled and treated as monsters or deviants and cast out from their communities. "Although a very small percentage of sex crimes against children involve violence or death, the tragic loss of a child has led many victims' families to demand . . . better management of sex offenders." (Trivits & Reppucci, 2002, p. 691). For example, since the 1990s, significant changes in criminal and civil law policies regarding sex offenders have been seen in every state reflecting a change in public opinion. Not only have sentences been lengthened, but sex offender registration requirements are in place in all fifty states, and in forty-six of those states, public officials have been given permission to release information regarding released sex offenders to the public (Lieb et al., 1998).

General public dissatisfaction with sex offender punishment has also been expressed as "tabloid newspapers and many of the public appear to believe that the Courts should "lock them up and throw away the key." (Clark, 1993, p. 3). Ironically, though citizens often complain that the justice system is too lenient on offenders, when given more details about a particular crime or offender, the public supports sentences that are similar to or lighter than those the judges have given in actual cases (Lieb et al., 1998). Recently, the California Department of Corrections reported the average time served by 2,307 sex offenders in the state as of 2001 was 3.5 years. Rapists and sodomists served the longest sentences, with an average of nearly 6 years in prison (CDC, 2001d).

A 1997 public opinion poll was conducted in Washington state to assess public attitudes regarding community notification policies (cited in Phillips & Troyano,

1998). The poll found 82 percent of respondents felt the public should be notified of released sex offenders residing in their area. Further, 75 percent of respondents felt they had learned more about sex offenses in general and how sex offenders operate because of existing notification laws. A similar poll, conducted in Georgia the same year, found 79 percent of adult respondents felt the public has a right to know about a convicted sex offender's past and that this right superceded the offender's right to privacy. Sixty percent agreed with the statement "sex offenders are different from other types of criminals" (cited in Hansen, 1997).

In a recent study by Green McGowan (2003), members of the public were found to express attitudes towards sex offenders that were significantly more negative that those expressed by mental health providers (both forensic and nonforensically trained) and as negative as those expressed by law enforcement officers. While race, educational level and being a parent were significant covariates for all respondents, a person's vocation (i.e. subject group) was still found to be the most important factor underlying how positive or negative the expressed attitudes were.

...About Rape

Various researchers have attempted to ascertain the views held about particular sexual crimes and sex offenders by the public. Many of these efforts have focused on rape. Unfortunately, "some people continue to misunderstand the tragic consequences of rape and trivialize its horror and pervasiveness" (Anderson, Cooper, & Okamura, 1997, p. 296). Anderson and colleagues (1997) report certain key attitude clusters have been found to relate to attitudes regarding rape, such as attitudes towards women and attitudes towards violence. Their meta-analysis of numerous rape studies found a number of demographic and individual variables contributed to significant differences in rape attitudes among the public. For example, men expressed more accepting attitudes towards rape than women and older subjects expressed slightly more accepting attitudes than younger subjects. Also, respondents from lower socioeconomic backgrounds expressed more accepting rape attitudes. Interestingly, among both genders, when subjects ascribed to traditional gender role beliefs, they more strongly endorsed rape myths.

Kershner (1996) asked 122 adolescents to indicate their level of agreement with 24 rape myths. She chose to sample adolescents as statistics have shown that this age group comprises at least 18 percent of single-offender and 30 percent of multiple offender rapes. Further, approximately 36 percent of rape victims are aged twelve to nineteen years old (U.S. Dept. of Justice, as cited by Kershner, 1996). Kershner found students did not view a rapist as necessarily having a prior criminal history. Subjects also endorsed the view that women cannot effectively fight off an attacker. In a sample of over 1,000 citizens, Feild (1978) also found the public, rapists and police officers agreed that women should not resist during a rape. Kershner's (1996) study found teens thought stranger rape was more serious than date rape, some girls either encourage rape by the way they dress or provoke a man into raping them, and most women fantasize about being raped. Further, the adolescents reported most men who are raped are gay and rapists have a greater need for sex than other people.

In a Canadian survey, Roberts, Grossman and Gebotys (1996) asked 1,522 citizens about recent national rape reform legislation. Only 16 percent of respondents correctly identified sexual assault as the new term for rape or indecent assault. However, 83 percent recognized that a man can be charged with the sexual assault of his spouse and 84 percent also understood a sexual assault can take place without any lasting physical injury to the victim or use of a weapon. Over 75 percent of the sample correctly believed sexual assault does not necessitate sexual intercourse. As to the incidence of sexual assaults, while women believed many such crimes occur, men thought the numbers were lower. Both genders consistently agreed that underreporting of rape was a problem. Men were slightly more confident that the perpetrators of sexual assault are caught, however, the majority of respondents felt sexual assault perpetrators remain largely unpunished for their acts.

...About Child Sexual Abuse and Incest

In a random survey of the public's knowledge about child abuse, Dhooper, Royse and Wolfe (1991) asked, among other things, if the stepfather of a fifteen-year old girl has sex with the girl several times while her mother was out constituted child abuse. Ninety-nine percent of the 742 respondents identified this behavior as abusive and inappropriate. Subjects were also asked about the characteristics of people who abuse children. At least 50 percent of the sample endorsed each of the following beliefs about abusers: they are mentally ill, under a lot of stress and pressure, abused as children, emotionally immature and ashamed of their behavior.

Maynard and Wiederman (1997) surveyed 404 undergraduate students on their attitudes towards child sexual abuse. Using vignettes, they varied the age and sex of the child victim and the sex of the adult perpetrator to investigate how these specific factors, as well as the subjects' view on gender roles, would affect their attitudes towards child molest. Interestingly, when an older child was the victim of child abuse, significantly less respondents thought the occurrence as abusive and the adult was seen as less responsible for the act. Further, significantly fewer respondents felt the event was as abusive if the child and perpetrator were of the opposite sex. Adults were assigned the least amount of blame when the children in the vignettes were in their teens and of the opposite sex. Despite expectations, students with traditional sex role attitudes did not see the abuse of male children or teens as less harmful than that of women. Unfortunately, when women abused children, lack of overt victim resistance led subjects to assume the interaction was less abusive.

Calvert and Munsie-Benson (1999) surveyed 246 members of the public on their beliefs about child sexual abuse. They found women who were married and a parent, as well as Caucasian and had a higher education, reported the most accurate information about child sexual abuse in general. Further, 86 percent of all those surveyed believed children usually tell the truth about being sexually abused and 71 percent felt parents would most likely know if their child had been victimized, mostly due to presumed behavioral changes in the victim. In addition, the researchers were able to identify some common misperceptions among their respondents. For example, while many were aware that a trusted adult was the most likely person to perpetrate child sexual abuse, very few thought another child would perpetrate a sexually abusive act, and "a significant minority thought that strangers would be the most likely perpetrator" of such crimes (p. 679).

...About Sexual Recidivism

Roberts and White (1986) found subjects estimated, "of those first-time sex offenders who were re-convicted, 80 percent will commit a similar sex related offense" to the first crime (p. 233). In a second study, the same researchers found another sample overestimated the second- and third-reoffense rates of sex offenders consistently by 62 percent. They concluded that "[N]ot only do people overestimate the proportion of first-time sex offenders who repeat, (but they also) see little change in the probability of reconviction for second and third-time sex offenders. Members of the public discern more consistency in the pattern of criminal recidivism than is reflected in the official statistics" (Roberts & White, 1986, p. 236). That is, first-time sexual recidivists were thought to reoffend at average rate of 62 percent, while second-time recidivists were thought to reoffend at a rate of 59 percent. A national opinion poll, conducted with over 1,100 American adults, found 87 percent of the respondents either agreed or strongly agreed with the statement 'most sex offenders continue to repeat their crimes no matter what the punishment' (*Star Tribune,* 1991).

SEX OFFENDER ATTITUDES EXPRESSED BY PROFESSIONALS

Lea, Auburn, and Kibblewhite (1999) lament the dearth of research into sex offender attitudes among professionals. They surmised the few studies in this area tell us "[P]rofessional attitudes towards sex offenders differ depending on the nature of the relationship (and the degree of contact) between sex offender and professional" (p. 106). Their research on attitudes towards sex offenders among certain professionals, e.g., police, psychologists, probation officers and correctional officers, produced a attitudinal continuum from highly positive to highly negative with most subjects expressing attitudes on both sides of the continuum depending on the aspect of sex offending discussed. Earlier inquiries investigating the attitudes of professionals towards sex offenders have also found this continuum of stereotypical responses among various groups of professionals.

Another study, by Saunders (1988), found no significant differences between five subject groups (police, social workers, public defenders, district attorneys, and judges) on their judgements of offender or victim culpability in sexual offenses. Subjects in all five professional groups equally agreed that the crime of child sexual abuse is a serious one in their communities. Kelley (1990) surveyed three groups of professionals (police officers, child protective workers and nurses) on their attributions of responsibility for child sexual abuse and how it relates to sex offender punishment. As expected, the offender was assigned the greatest amount of responsibility, but only 12 percent of the 228 subjects assigned complete responsibility to the offender. Instead, the victim's mother and society, as well as the child victim, were also assigned some degree of responsibility. All participants endorsed court involvement for the offender, but only half supported incarceration. Interestingly, 30 percent of respondents predicted the child would grow up to be a sex offender, and 5 percent predicted the child would grow up to be homosexual.

Green McGowan (2003) found significant difference in attitudes about offenders and the behaviors they engage in when surveying samples of law enforcement, non-forensic mental health and forensic mental health. Even when significant between group differences in race were controlled for, professional subject group was found to significantly related to expressed scores.

Redondo and colleagues (1996) addressed professional estimations of sex offender recidivism, comparing their findings to the earlier findings of Roberts and White (1986) regarding public estimates of recidivism. Redondo et al. (1996) found their sample estimated initial sex offender recidivism at 31 percent with subsequent recidivism percentages ranging anywhere from 45 to 52 percent after reading true case vignettes in which no actual recidivism had been recorded. Though the professionals' estimates were in fact lower than those made by the public sample (the public estimated 57, 53 and 55 percent, respectively—see Roberts & White, 1986), no further analysis for statistical significance was discussed. However, unlike the public sample, professionals correctly estimated sexual recidivism risk declined with age and increased as the number of previous convictions rose. Also unlike the public sample, the professionals took notice of the effect of certain "social reinstatement factors" (Redondo et al., 1996) when estimating sexual reoffense. For example, offenders with jobs, not dependant on drugs, returning to a non-deprived community, and having the help of social services were all estimated to be less likely to reoffend than those experiencing the opposite conditions (i.e. no job, drug-dependant, deprived or without support). However, Redondo and colleagues concluded that both professionals and academicians tend to, like the general public, incorrectly consider criminal and sexual offense recidivism as a "phenomenon of vast magnitude" (Redondo et al., 1996, p. 399). This misperception serves only to further distort the reality of reoffense likelihood and in turn, affects the attitudes held by such professionals hold towards sex offenders.

The Attitudes of Law Enforcement Officers

Numerous inquiries into the attitudes held by law enforcement personnel towards criminals, and specifically, sex offenders, have been undertaken in the Unites States, Canada and the United Kingdom. Using Hogue's (1993) Attitude Towards Sexual Offenders Scale (ATS), police officers were found to evidence the most stereotyped attitudes towards sex offenders, especially if they indicated they had had no training or experience with sex offenders on the job, according to a study by Lea et al. (1999). Hogue (1993) originally found, using the ATS, police officers indicated significantly more negative attitudes towards sex offenders and sexual offending when he compared their responses to those of prison officers, probation officers, and psychologists. Police officers evidenced a mean score of 62, while mean scores ranging from 72 to 80 were found among prison officers and a mean score of 91 was found among probation officers and psychologists. According to Hogue (1993), lower ATS scores indicate a more negative attitude and the presence of stereotypical beliefs about sex offenders, while higher ATS scores indicate more positive attitudes and less stereotypical beliefs. In 2003, Green McGowan found, again using the ATS, that a sample of 50 law enforcement officers evidenced a mean score of 59.

Trute, Adkins, and MacDonald (1992) found a sample of 80 police officers viewed the issue of child sexual abuse and its impact on victims as less serious than the 35 child welfare workers and 21 community mental health professionals. Further, officers tended to view sex offender treatment as less effective, highlighting instead punishment, when compared to the other two groups. Saunders (1988) also found police officers were the most punitive when sentencing of sex offenders, even more than criminal court judges. Kelley (1990) reported police officers attributed proportionally more responsibility to the offender in child sexual abuse instances than either nurses or child protective workers. As such, these officers recommended more severe punishment for sex offenders than the other two groups.

Most importantly, unlike the child welfare and mental health workers, the police were likely to believe that child sexual abuse occurs only in a certain type of family and is perpetrated by a select type of individual (Trute et al., 1992). In Feild's (1978) study of attitudes towards rape among various groups, police officers were found to hold rape attitudes more similar to a sample of rapists than to those expressed by crisis counselors. Both the officers and rapists expressed the same attitudes about the basic motivations for rape (power and sex), the normality of rapists (rapists are not mentally normal) and the attractiveness of a rape victim after a rape (a raped women is less desirable).

The Attitudes of Social/Child Welfare Workers
Only a few studies to date have investigated the attitudes held by social workers, child protective workers or welfare workers towards sexual offending and sex offenders. In Trute et al.'s (1992) Canadian study, child welfare workers correctly reported that child sexual abuse occurs in a variety of situations and is committed by various types of perpetrators. Thus, the researchers surmised, the sample did not endorse the stereotype that child sexual abuse is rare and committed only by socially deviant individuals. Saunders (1988) found social workers generally evidenced the second-most-lenient attitudes towards the need to punish sex offenders (after public defenders), instead displaying compassionate attitudes that supported rehabilitation efforts. Kelley (1990) found child protective workers assigned more responsibility to society and to a victim's mother after a child had been molested than police officers did. Further, the workers recommended family and individual therapy for both the victim and the perpetrator more often than police and medical professionals.

Ward, Connolly, McCormick, and Hudson (1996) found both Australian social workers and social work students appropriately attributed sexual offending to the various reasons endorsed by the literature, such as personal inadequacy, developmental issues, cognitive/emotional deficits and power and control issues. Interestingly, their sample attributed sex offending very infrequently to sexual motivations while incarcerated sex offenders cited this reason most frequently.

The Attitudes of Lawyers and Judges

Only one study (see Saunders, 1988) has addressed the attitudes held by various legal personnel towards sex offenders. This work found significant differences in the willingness to punish sex offenders among groups of district attorneys, public defenders and judges. Nevertheless, all the groups' scores fell in the middle range of the punishment-treatment continuum, suggesting that respondents were conflicted over the rehabilitation-retribution debate. Public defenders were found to be the least punitive, as opposed to judges who proved to be the most punitive.

The Attitudes of Correctional Administrators and Officers, Probation and Parole Officers

A number of research endeavors have focused on the attitudes and stereotypes held by prison or correctional officers, and probation and parole officers. Each employed the ATS (Hogue, 1993) to assess these attitudes, as it is the first and only sex offender attitudinal measure designed for and tested on such populations of professionals. Hogue (1993) asserted he focused on these populations initially because he believes, even in prisons where everyone is criminal, sex offenders are singled out by staff and other inmates as being the worst of the worst. Despite this belief, a sample of correctional officers exhibited a range of attitudes towards sex offenders when surveyed by Hogue (1993) with the ATS. A significant difference was found in attitudes between correctional officers who were selected and presently taking part in a sex offender treatment program compared to correctional officers who were not in such a program, a mean score of 80 versus 72. Those officers not involved in the treatment program expressed negative attitudes akin to those expressed by the most negative group overall, police officers, while those officers involved in the treatment milieu expressed more positive attitudes, much like the responses given by psychologists and probation officers (Hogue, 1993).

A later study using the ATS (see Hogue & Peebles, 1997) found that prison officers expressed the most negative attitudes when compared to probation/parole officers, social workers, mental health managers, and therapists. Radley (2001) attempted to replicate Hogue's (1993) findings with the ATS by giving the questionnaire to 40 respondents, half of which were prison officers working in sex offender prison wings. She found all officers reported more positive attitudes toward sex offenders than Hogue had previously found, a mean score of 97 compared to Hogue's mean score of 72. However, Radley (2001) found, just as Hogue had, prison officers evidenced significantly lower ATS scores in comparison to the probation and psychology staff members surveyed.

Weekes, Pelletier, and Beaudette (1995) surveyed 82 correctional officers, comparing their perceptions of sex offenders who victimize children or women their perceptions of non–sex offenders. Significant differences were found on 14 of the 19 perception scales between sex offenders as whole (both victim groups combined) and the non-sex offenders. These differences were evidenced in judgments made on safe/dangerous, harmless/harmful, good/bad, predictable/unpredictable, strong/weak, moral/immoral, and mentally ill/mentally normal perception scales, among others. Higher scores, indicating more negative perceptions, were given to both groups of sex offenders on all 19 perception scales. Surprisingly, sex offenders were not seen to differ significantly in any way from other offenders in regards to their sex drive, level of self-control, intelligence, or efforts at manipulation.

Within the prison environment, many negative attitudes are reported to exist towards sex offenders, not just those expressed by prison staff, but also those expressed by other prisoners; "[T]raditionally, prisoners convicted of sexual offenses have been the outcasts of the prison system." (Hogue, 1993, p. 27). Specific derogatory labels are used to describe these offenders and often they become the targets of aggression by other prisoners. "It is not uncommon for prisoners convicted of a sex offense to hide their conviction from other prisoners as a way of preventing victimization" (Radley, 2001, p. 1). Boechler (1998) found that sex offenders are the most common inmates to be beaten, raped or murdered by other inmates as well as by staff. A study by Ireland and Archer (as cited in Radley, 2001) found both men and women prisoners reported sex offenders were among the most frequently bullied in prisons with over 30% of respondents reporting them as potential targets.

Some forensic professional attitudinal inquiries have investigated the proposed link between degrees of sex offender criminal responsibility and sentencing judgments. Researchers have proposed (see Hanson & Slater, 1993) that it is possible "professionals working with child molesters have sufficiently well developed views concerning the causes of child molesting" (p. 45) so that offenders' accounts have little influence on the attributions made about offender responsibility. In Hanson and Slater's (1993) study, it was expected that offenders who were judged to have very little control over their sexual deviancy (and thus be less responsible) would engender more lenient and sympathetic responses in certain forensic professionals. Interestingly, while membership in a certain professional group (e.g., probation/parole officer vs. forensic therapist) did not affect sentencing recommendation, offender account did. Significantly harsher sentences were meted out to offenders claiming "I can do what I want, the law is wrong" compared to the other eight accounts, such as "I did not touch her, I was possessed by the devil, or I was abused as a child." Overall, the probation/parole officers found all nine accounts more believable than the therapists did.

The Attitudes of Non–Forensic Mental Health Providers

Saunders (1988) reported mental health professionals have struggled to make sense of the various theories of causation underlying deviant criminal behavior. Many mental health professionals believe, based on their expertise, that sex offenders have psychological disorders that, in some sense, excuse their behavior and make them good candidates for psychological intervention. But as Ward et al. (1996) cautioned, mental health workers are subject to the same social stereotypes and inappropriate cultural messages about sex and violence that we all are. As such, the possibility that either abuse-supportive or offender-damning attitudes exist among mental health workers is high. Frighteningly, Stermac and Segal (1989) found some clinicians view adult sexual contact with children to be of partial benefit to the child. However, in Feild's (1978) study of attitudes towards rape, crisis counselors as a group (compared to samples of the public, rapists and police officers) reported the most negative view of rape.

Kalichman, Craig, and Follingstad, as cited by Reidy and Hochstadt (1993), studied the patterns of blame attribution among psychiatrists, psychologists and counselors in regards to incest. They found that the younger the child, the more blame was attributed to the father, while the older the child, the less blame was placed on the offender. All the professionals allotted some amount of blame in incest cases on the mother. Male clinicians consistently placed more blame for the abuse on the child and mother than female therapists.

In 1993, Reidy and Hochstadt undertook a similar study of mental health professionals' attitudes toward father-daughter incest. Surveying 100 California professionals, they found participants allocated similar percentages of blame to the victim, to society, and the life situation of the offender, regardless of the child's age. Most assigned the majority of blame to the father while the mother was consistently assigned 10 percent of the blame for the incest. Only when the victim was an adolescent did about one-third of the sample assign a small amount of blame to the daughter, rather than judging her as totally blameless. Overall women blamed the victim the least regardless of her age.

The Attitudes of Sex Offender Therapists, Prison Psychologists, and Other Forensic Mental Health Providers

Lea and colleagues (1999) found most of the forensic professionals in their study realized sex offenders were a diverse group, but still asserted they showed universal traits. While some subjects said there was no such thing as a typical sex offender, most sketched two types of offenders: rapists and pedophiles. On the whole, subjects drew distinctions between the behaviors of these two groups in terms of violence, aggression and personal variables. Rapists were reportedly driven by the need to dominate and control while pedophiles were viewed as wanting company and affection from their victims. Subjects described sex offenders generally with the following adjectives: articulate and intelligent, subnormal, socially inadequate, egocentric and selfish, and scheming and manipulative (Lea et al., 1999). Seventy percent (70 percent) of the sample endorsed the idea that sex offenders are created not born, while 57 percent believed sex offenders are incapable of establishing normal relationships. Thirty percent (30 percent) embraced the notion that sex crimes are the result of some form of mental deviancy or an inherent biological abnormality in offenders. Of concern to the researchers were the 13 percent of respondents who failed to find a difference between rape and consensual sex. These participants opined many sexual offenses occur because of sexual "misunderstandings."

Prison or forensic psychologists are thought to hold the least negative attitudes about sex offenders. Hogue (1993) found, with a sample of 11 prison psychologists, a mean score of 91 on the ATS. This mean was the highest (indicating the most positive attitudes) for any group among samples of police officers, prison officers and other therapeutic personnel. Radley (2001) also found the highest ATS scores resulted from the 20 psychologists and probation officers she surveyed, compared to prison officers and other non-discipline staff. In a more recent study (personal communication, 2003), Hogue found a sample of secure forensic hospital mental health staff produced a mean ATS score of 74.53. Green McGowan (2003) reported a sample of 50 forensic mental health professionals evidenced a significantly higher mean ATS score (87.88) than non-forensic mental health professionals (mean ATS score = 75.64).

In another study, forensic therapists were found to attribute more responsibility to sex offenders regardless of the type of account offenders gave for their behavior (e.g., abuse as sex education, the victim enjoyed the sex, etc.) over probation/parole officers (Hanson & Slater, 1993). Still, both groups considered offenders personally responsible for their inappropriate actions. The greater attribution of responsibility made by forensic therapists was suggested by the authors, to be grounded in an appropriate level of skepticism that should follow from good therapeutic training and past work with victims. Despite the difference in causality beliefs, respondents from both groups did not sentence offenders differently. The researchers concluded the more believable the account the offender gave for his behavior, the less responsible the offender was held for the abuse and thus, the less harshly sanctioned.

SPECIFIC STEREOTYPICAL BELIEFS

In Green McGowan's (2003) survey of the public, the police, nonforensic mental health providers, and forensic mental health providers, respondents were asked to depict their ideas about specific facets regarding sex offenders, offenses and their victims. Some significant differences were found between the four groups. For example, participants were asked how they would allocate $1 million among sex offender or victim treatment, sexual abuse prevention/education or offender incarceration. Law enforcement officers assigned significantly more weight to incarceration and less weight to offender treatment than the other three groups.

A comparison of the sample's other responses indicated, forensic mental health providers believed significantly more sex offenders are 'innocent' of what they are accused of than both law enforcement and members of the public. At the same time, non-forensic mental health providers assigned significantly more weight than the other three groups to the idea that sex offenders are guilty of 1 to 10 previous offenses when finally caught.

While all 200 respondents reported men as the most likely perpetrators of sex crimes, forensic mental health professionals most strongly endorsed adolescent boys as perpetrators than both the law enforcement sample and the public sample. Unsurprisingly, police officers and the public felt differently about offenders in treatment than the mental health professionals did (e.g., the public and police were more apt to feel treatment would not stop reoffense). Despite expectations, significantly more forensic clinicians felt these offenders were "unwilling to go" to treatment. When considering child molester arousal, while the public and law enforcement predominantly endorsed the idea that molesters are only attracted to/aroused by children, both mental health groups instead supported the idea that attraction and arousal to both adults and children in molesters is most common. As for mental illness, analysis found the public assigned significantly more weight to the possibility of psychosis than the other three groups. The public also erroneously assigned significantly less weight to the idea that offenders might have drug or alcohol problems than the two mental health samples. All respondents agreed both women and girls are the most common victims of sexual offenses.

THE IMPLICATIONS OF EXPRESSED SEX OFFENDER ATTITUDES AND STEREOTYPES

Gabor (as cited by Roberts & Stalans, 1997) observed, "[F]actually incorrect and rigid views of criminals, if held by many, can lead us seriously astray in our attempts both to understand crime and to control it" (p. 6). Further, even though some stereotypes have a small amount of accuracy to them, psychologists agree that applying generalized ideas and beliefs about a group of people as a whole to one person is not correct or just (Baron & Byrne, 1991). As such, attempts to assess sex offender stereotypes and their impact, can direct later educational efforts so that a more accurate picture of such criminal behavior informs crime control strategies; i.e., punishment versus rehabilitation. While many believe the majority of sex offenders are caught, convicted and in prison, the reality is "only a fraction of those who commit sexual assault are apprehended and convicted for their crimes. Most convicted sex offenders eventually are released to the community under probation or parole supervision" (CSOM, 2000, p. 2). As such, it is imperative that we understand sex offender stereotypes and how they impact every aspect of the community.

THE IMPACT ON SEX OFFENDERS, THEIR VICTIMS AND TREATMENT

Studies have found that stereotypes can affect the self-evaluation of those targeted. Someone who is the focus of negative societal beliefs may become a self-fulfilling prophecy, acting in ways that reinforce the negative judgments put upon them (Lott & Saxon, 2002). Steele (cited by Lott & Saxon, 2002) coined this effect as "stereotype threat" in which a person, the target of a stereotype, realizes that widely held, negative group stereotypes applies to them in a given situation, regardless of their actions. The person surmises that their behavior will be subject to the idiosyncratic interpretations and misperceptions of others regardless of what they do. As a result, they act according to what they believe is thought or expected of them, either out of fear, hopelessness or an unconscious desire to comply. Thus, if a sex offender is expected to reoffended and treated as such by society and the criminal justice system, he may be destined to do so, according to Steele's explanation. Fedoroff and Moran (1997) surmise that sex offenders already have difficulty establishing lasting relationships, and after conviction, finding gainful employment because they are ex-convicts. Add to this the stereotypes they encounter and their fear of vigilantism once their community is notified about their presence, it is no surprise offenders often fail to register with local law enforcement when they relocate to new areas, further encouraging a situation of even fewer community ties and exacerbating the chance of reoffense.

Garfinkel (as cited by Younglove & Vitello, 2003) believed "labeling people as violent sexual predators and thereby communicating to them the message that they are mentally abnormal in ways, prevents them from controlling their antisocial conduct and undermines the potential of the treatment they are offered" (p. 32). Theorist Edwin Lemert explained how this "secondary deviance" becomes the driving force behind sexual recidivism. That is, once an offender accepts the label they are given into their self-image, they allow it to become the underlying force behind their societal interactions. So instead of their criminal behavior being the result of various biological, psychological, or social influences, it is generated directly from the offender's criminal self-image (see Younglove & Vitello, 2003).

The stereotypes held by forensic professionals have also been found to affect the services employed and the amount of interprofessional consultation relied upon in instances of sexual crimes. How individuals within a profession, or a group of professionals as a whole, view the meaning underlying sexual assault and abuse, affects their choice of treatment regime, investigative approaches and inter-agency collaboration efforts. Further, Ward et al. (1996) concluded that "professional attitudes towards sexual offenders impact social service delivery and in particular, the nature and quality of services provided" (p. 39). Kalichman, Craig, and Follingstad (as cited by Reidy & Hochstadt, 1993) asserted professionals' attitudes can have a profound effect on decisions to report abuse and the vehemency with which victim credibility is investigated. Finkelhor, Gomez-Schwartz, and Horowitz (1984) found while child protective workers prefer a wide range of resources (e.g., medical, mental health, school), mental health professionals less frequently engage other disciplines. Unfortunately, forensic mental health professionals evidenced the least effort in connecting to other professional groups.

The Colorado Department of Corrections undertook a study in 2000 investigating the status of state correctional sex offender treatment programs. They asked each of the states if they provided sexual offenders with formal sex offender treatment during incarceration. Seventy-three percent of the states reported the existence of such a program, 16 percent had no program and the rest were considering or developing a program at the time of inquiry. Interestingly, the two states with existing Sexual Violent Predator statutes (California and Florida), allowing post-release civil commitment, did not have any in-prison treatment programs.

THE IMPACT ON SEX CRIME INVESTIGATIONS AND PROSECUTIONS

Even though many in the criminal justice system agree that sexual crimes are a societal concern, there is "some disagreement as to whether (these crimes) require intense treatment or harsh punishment; professionals cannot agree whether sexual assault is a sickness, a crime or a family problem" (Trute et al., 1992, p. 367). Further "[I]t has been suggested that criminal stereotypes may affect judgments at all stages of the legal process" (Macrae & Shephard, 1989, p. 189), including suspect identification and pursuit, witness identification of perpetrators, criminal prosecution and sentencing. For example, Feild (1978) reported attitudes towards rape have been demonstrated to affect people's behaviors concerning the reporting of rape, the treatment of rape victims in court, and the processing and investigation of rape allegations.

A survey of new policemen found many reported an ability to smell or feel a criminal, to have a sixth sense about a person (Robinson, as cited in Bull & Green, 1980), but they denied this ability was based on any criminal stereotypes they might hold. Additionally, whether or not a witness selects a particular person from a line-up and identifies that person as the perpetrator, may be influenced by the degree to which the person resembles the commonly-held stereotype for the specific type of crime (Bull & Green, 1980). Research has added that a defendant's appearance at trial influences jury decision-making. Physically unattractive defendants are more likely to be found guilty and awarded harsher sentences than attractive ones (Sigall & Ostrove, 1975).

THE IMPACT ON FORENSIC SERVICE PROVIDERS

The general attitude towards prisoners held by correctional officials and workers is important, "because it is likely to influence the way prisoners respond to the (correctional) regime and the effectiveness of attempts to help prisoners change their offending behavior" (Hogue, 1993, p. 27). As such, Epps (1993) warned that those working therapeutically with sex offenders must not only be aware of their biases towards their clients but must also acquire a variety of specific counseling skills while remaining realistic about the nature of sexual offending. Additionally, Radley (2001) concluded it becomes important to assess not only the attitudes staff hold towards sex offender clients prior to their exposure to such individuals, but to also determine their ability to model appropriate attitudes to others. Ward et al. (1996) opined "professional attitudes towards sexual offenders, and other deviant populations, impact services" provided for the "victims of abuse and those associated with them, since such attitudes can become part of the framework of expert knowledge" (p. 39).

Fedoroff and Moran (1997) clarified, "for psychological conditions, the belief of the therapist that the condition is curable is one of the most robust predictors of whether the condition will be [cured]" (citing Frank, p. 174). In the case of sex offenders, asserting this group of offenders is incurable is counterproductive to those in treatment, those providing the treatment and those developing new methods of intervention. As the majority of these offenders are eventually released, asserting they are incurable is not only an unproven assumption but a dangerous one, according to Fedoroff and Moran (1997).

For forensic mental health professionals, Epps (1993) remarked, "[W]orking with perpetrators and victims of sexual offending is exceptionally stressful and demanding" (p. 26) both personally and professionally. The stress of working in an environment, which is judged by outsiders and many within the correctional system to be unproductive and useless, can only serve to frustrate and exhaust even those with the best training and intentions. Lea et al. (1999) found nearly one-quarter of their sample of professionals working with sex offenders "articulated the view they continually have to work around the stereotyping of sex offenders by both professionals and lay persons alike and that this hampers their practice" (p. 111). As Lea et al. (1999) state, "[T]hose who work with sex offenders are vulnerable to attracting a courtesy stigma" (p. 113) because they are judged to have sympathy for sex offenders.

THE IMPACT ON LEGISLATION AND SOCIETY

Prentky, Lee, Knight, and Cerce (1997) opined "[S]ex offenders constitute a subsample of dangerous criminals who both elicit a disproportionate number of special statutes involving legal proceedings for commitments to segregated units of prisons or mental health facilities, and require an inordinate number of ad hoc discretionary and dispositional decisions" (p. 654). As a result, all states now require convicted sex offenders to register with law enforcement upon release from incarceration (Lieb et al., 1998). California was the first state to pass legislation requiring sex offender registration in 1944 (see CA Penal Code, § 290, 2001) and over the next 52 years, every other state followed suit. By 1996, Lieb et al. (1998) estimated over 185,000 sex offenders were registered under such provisions. Efforts to track released sex offenders and protect society were further enhanced with the advent of Community Notification statutes, beginning in 1990 in Washington state. These new statutes made it legal for authorities to inform citizens and schools in a community of the presence of a high-risk sexual offender and clarified that convicted sex offenders in these locales were to register with local police annually on their birthdays (Jenkins, 1998). By mid-1996, this registration and notification practice became legislation in 35 states. However, Zevitz and Farkas (2000) explained "[T]he basic dilemma associated with community notification is balancing the public's right to be informed with the need to successfully reintegrate offenders into the community" (p. 8).

Today, the actual level of community notification varies state to state, as different institutions, organizations or agencies are given confidential sex offender information based on various discretionary decisions made by local law enforcement. For example, no discretion is exercised in Alabama, Louisiana, or Texas and information is given out to the public on all sex offenders convicted of specific crimes. However, in Indiana, Georgia, and Pennsylvania only limited information on the same type of offenders is provided to childcare facilities, children's service organizations, and state licensing agencies (Lieb et al., 1998). In California, where over 100,000 registered sex offenders are now posted on-line for public viewing, Penal Code § 290(m)(1), 2001 provides that

> When a peace officer reasonably suspects, based upon information that has come to the officer's attention, that a child or other person may be at risk of a sex offender convicted of an offense listed in paragraph 1 of sub-division 290.4, a law enforcement agency may provide information that the agency deems relevant and necessary to protect the public, agencies and organizations the offender is likely to encounter.

In some states, considered passive notification states, private citizens must take the initiative to seek information about offenders while in active notification states, the police notify all relevant groups deemed to be at risk from a particular offender (Jenkins, 1998). Zevitz and Farkas (2000) outlined that notification can be accomplished by way of news media releases, internet postings, targeted notification to various agencies and organizations, or through community meetings arranged to notify residents about sex offenders. Other states have tiered systems in which the risk an offender poses is matched to one of many levels of appropriate disclosure, dictating who is notified by authorities about an offender's presence. By the end of the 1990s, Congress passed a bill creating the National Sex Offender Registry so that police agencies throughout the country could gain access to information about all convicted and registered sex offenders regardless of the agency's jurisdiction (Jenkins, 1998).

In addition to registration, certain incarcerated sex offenders face involuntary civil commitment upon their release from custody. In various states, including California, a Sex Offender Commitment Program (SOCP) or Sexually Violent Predator (SVP) statutes exist. These "[P]redator laws were enacted to extend the confinement of sex offenders considered dangerous who could no longer be held in the criminal justice system" (La Fond, 2003, p. 178).

In California, as of 1996, a person is deemed a SVP if they have been previously convicted of certain sexual offenses against two or more victims and are determined to have a diagnosed mental disorder that makes it likely they will engage in sexually violent predatory behavior upon community release (see CA W.I.C. § 6600, 1993). Once hospitalized as a SVP, after being deemed as such in a criminal court, treatment is given for two years. Commitment can only be extended if the court grants a new petition (CA Dept. of Mental Health, 2003). As of May 2003, 4,838 Californian sex offenders had been referred for SVP consideration and commitment since the statue's inception. Of these, only 23 percent met the criteria for the SVP label. In court, 237 sex offenders were found to not be sexually violent predators and released, 422 were civilly committed and in 259 cases, the trial is pending (CA DMH, 2003). In comparison, as of the Spring of 2002, 2209 offenders nationwide have been detained or committed under SVP laws (La Fond, 2003, citing Lieb).

Despite the belief that such legislative and enforcement efforts as mandatory registration and community notification should prevent future victimization, few have endeavored to assess the effect they have had on sex offenders and their behavior. "Despite the extensive attention and public support that notification laws have generated, empirical research on their impact is nearly nonexistent (Zevitz & Farkas, 2000, p. 10). Only one study has addressed whether notification does in fact affect sex offender recidivism rates. Schram and Milloy (as cited in Trivits & Reppucci, 2002) found comparable rearrest rates between offenders subject to community notification and a matched group with no notification. The only difference noted was those in the notification group were rearrested twice as quickly after their reoffense that those in the matched no-notification group.

The media often portrays sex offenders in a negative light, feeding into prevailing public opinions about such offenders. For example in the "Name and Shame campaign" of the *News of the World,* the pictures and identities of convicted sex offenders were released to the public (Radley, 2001). Unfortunately, in some instances this campaign led to the forced eviction of people from their homes by organized mobs. In a study by Zevitz and Farkas (2000), various parole agents reported numerous problems with finding residences for released sex offenders. One respondent noted "[T]he person who agreed to house the sex offender received death threats and decided not to house him," while another reported "[S]hortly after the offender was placed, he was evicted from his apartment. There was a media onslaught, with most information being negative . . . All landlords subsequently contacted denied residence, most out of fear for media attention" (Zevitz & Farkas, 2000, p. 15). Lieb et al. (1998) and Trivits and Reppucci (2002) both reported that the potential for citizens to harass released sex offenders following notification is a real concern, despite law enforcement efforts advising the public that legal action will be taken against those engaging in vigilantism. Younglove and Vitello (2003) asserted "notifying neighbors about the presence of a registered sex offender very often results not in [the] sense of safety and wellbeing [intended], but rather just the opposite—panic and vigilantism" (p. 32). As such, the American Civil Liberties Union (ACLU) has criticized notification laws as "simply raising the level of fear, anxiety and anger (of the public) and fostering a climate that can lead to vigilantism" (Ritter, 1995, p. 7A).

To address these concerns, incidents of sex offender harassment have been tracked in various states. In 1995, Oregon reported that 10 percent of the 237 sex offenders revealed through community notification had experienced harassment. In 1996, New Jersey reported only 5 recorded instances of physical or verbal assaults against publicized sex offenders, while Washington state recalled 33 instances out of a total 942 notifications (Lieb et al., 1998). Acts of vigilantism have included car bombing, arson, physical assault, property damage, threats and picketing outside offenders' residences (Trivits & Reppucci, 2002). However, though the rates of reported harassment appear low, underreporting plays a role in these numbers (as discussed by Lieb et al., 1998). We can assume that other instances of harassment, as well as discrimination and exclusion, do go on after communities are told a sex offender's history, but these incidents are not reported to law enforcement for a variety of reasons, the least of which is sex offenders do not expect to receive protection from law enforcement agencies.

Clark (1993) expressed his concern that the existence of attitudes of intolerance and disdain, especially in the public, towards sex offenders obscures the reality that most sex offenders are serving finite sentences and will eventually be returned to society, unsupervised, sometime in the future. Even those deemed to be SVPs will eventually be released. However, because "these [few] individuals have been demonized by terms like 'sexually violent predators' or 'the worst of the worst'" (La Fond, 2003, p. 180), the public is so frightened by their release that almost insurmountable political and psychological barriers to reasonable release planning abound. As such, many SVPs do not believe they will ever be released which creates a greater disincentive to participate in treatment (La Fond, 2003).

Peebles (1999) pointed out "many people hold onto the myth that men who commit sexual offenses are few and easily identified by their abnormal behavior and menacing appearance" (p. 287). These and other stereotypes neither protect the public nor help prevent future sex offenses. In part, as a effort to combat the beliefs of the uneducated and intolerant, Berliner (1998) suggests that social policies regarding sexual offenses should allow for a range of sentencing options that recognizes all sex crimes victims do not desire the same prosecution outcomes and sex offenders are a diverse group of criminals.

REFERENCES

Abbey, E. C. 1882. *The sexual system and its derangements*. Retrieved October 23, 2002, from *http://www.mum.org/abbey14.htm*.

ABC News Survey on Crime, 2000. Retrieved December 15, 2002 at *http://www.publicagenda.org/issues/images/crime*.

Abel Screening, Inc. 1995. *The Abel assessment for sexual interest*. Atlanta, GA: Author.

Abel, G. G., & Harlow, N. 2001. *Stop child molestation*. Philadelphia, PA: Xlibris.

Abel, G. G., & Osborn, C. 1992. The paraphilias: The extent and nature of sexually deviant and criminal behavior. *Clinical Forensic Psychiatry,* 15(3): 675–687.

Abel, G. G., Becker, J. V., Cunningham, R. J., Mittleman, M., & Rouleau, J. L. 1988. Multiple paraphilia diagnoses among sex offenders. *Bulletin of the American Academy of Psychiatry and the Law,* 16: 153–168.

Abel, G. G., Becker, J. V., Mittelman, M., Cunningham-Rathner, J., Rouleau, J. L., & Murphy, W. D. 1987. Self-reported sex crimes of nonincarcerated paraphilics. *Journal of Interpersonal Violence,* 2(1): 3–25.

Abouesh, A., & Clayton, A. 1999. Compulsive voyeurism and exhibitionism: A clinical response to paroxetine. *Archives of Sexual Behavior,* 28(1): ProQuest 1–4.

Abrahamsen, D. 1960. *The psychology of crime*. New York: Columbia Press.

Adshead, G. 1997. Transvestic fetishism: Assessment and treatment. In D. R. Laws & W. O'Donohue (Eds.), *Sexual deviance: Theory, assessment and treatment* (pp. 280–296). New York: The Guilford Press.

Agnes, M. 1996. Webster's New World College Dictionary.

Agnew, J. 1982. Klismaphilia: A physiological perspective. *American Journal of Psychotherapy,* 36(4): 554–566.

———. 1986. Hazards associated with anal erotic activity. *Archives of Sexual Behavior,* 15(4): 307–314.

Ainsworth, M. 1967. *Infancy in Uganda*. Baltimore: Johns Hopkins University Press.

Ainsworth, M., Blehar, M., Waters, E., & Wall, S. 1978. *Patterns of attachment*. Hillsdale, NJ: Erlbaum.

Alexander, P. C. 1992. Application of attachment theory to the study of sexual abuse. *Journal of Consulting and Clinical Psychology,* 60: 185–195.

Alford, G., Webster, J., & Sanders, S. 1980. Covert aversion of two interrelated deviant sexual practices: Obscene phone calling and exhibitionism. A single case analysis. *Behavior Therapy,* 11: 15–25.

Alison, L., Santtila, P., Sandnabba, N. K., & Nordling, N. 2001. Sadomasochistically oriented behavior: Diversity in practice and meaning. *Archives of Sexual Behavior,* 30(1): 1–12.

Allen, D. W. 1974. *The fear of looking.* Charlottesville, VA: The University Press of Virginia.

Alley, D. 2000. *Separation anxiety and psychopathology.* Unpublished Masters thesis, Pepperdine University, California.

Alvin, P., & Rivera, J. 1995. Sexual pathology and dangerousness from a Thematic Apperception Test protocol. *Psychological Assessment and Clinical Practice,* 26(1): 72–77.

American Psychiatric Association. 1994. *Diagnostic and Statistical Manual of Mental Disorders* (4th ed.). Washington, DC: American Psychiatric Association.

———. 2000. *Diagnostic and Statistical Manual of Mental Disorders,* (4th, text-revision.) Washington, DC: American Psychiatric Association.

Americans for a Society Free from Age Restrictions. 2003. *www.asfar.org.*

Ames, M. A., & Houston, D. A. 1990. Legal, social, and biological definitions of pedophilia. *Archives of Sexual Behavior,* 19: 333–342.

Anderson, K. B., Cooper, H., & Okamura, L. 1997. Individual differences and attitudes towards rape: A meta-analytic review. *Personality and Social Psychology Bulletin,* 23(3): 295–316.

Anonymous author 2000. Sentencing-federal guidelines-vulnerable victim enhancement-sleeping victims. *Criminal Law Reporter,* 66(25): 588–589.

———. 2002. VICAP alert: Serial rapist/killer. *FBI Law Enforcement Bulletin,* 71(6): 25.

———. 2002. *What does the consensual partner of a vampire get from this?* Retrieved from *http://www.geocities.com/area51/station/8655/contents.html.*

———. n.d. *A short history on all of the worst serial killers in the world!* Retrieved December 2, 2000 from *http://members.tripod.com/ahrens/serial/.*

———. n.d. *Glossary.Sex.Com.* Retrieved, September 25, 2002 from *http://www.glossary.sex.com.*

———. n.d. *Ally Farson case summary.* Retrieved December 2, 2002 from *http://www.allyfarson.com/html/casesummary.html.*

———. n.d. *Anal ecstasy.* 2002. Retrieved 9/29/02 from *http://www.anal-ecstasy.com/enema/topics.htm.*

———. n.d. *Auto-erotic asphyxiation syndrome.* Retrieved October 12, 2002 from *www.studioja.com/aboutaas.htm.*

———. n.d. *Coral Watts: Serial killer.* Retrieved December 3, 2002 from *http://www.murdervictims.com/watts.htm.*

———. n.d. *Hebephiles.* Retrieved September 22, 2002 from *http://www.girlgarden.org.*

———. n.d. *Hebephilia.* Retrieved September 22, 2002 from *http://www.philianew.org.*

———. n.d. *Sexual deviancy.* Retrieved September 25, 2002 from *http://www.sexualdeviancy.com/New_Folder/Frotteurism.htm.*

———. n.d. *The auto-erotic asphyxiation syndrome in adolescent and young adult males.* Retrieved October 31, 2002 from *www.silentvictims.org.*

———. n.d. *The wacky world of murder: Jake Bird.* Retrieved on December 11, 2002 from *http://www.geocities.com/Area51/Shadowlands/4077/bird.html.*

———. n.d. *Wayne Williams.* Retrieved December 3, 2002 from *http://www.angelfire.com/oh/yodaspage/williams.html.*

———. 1998. *Mental health and psychology directory.* Retrieved September 25, 2002 from *http://www.psychnet-uk.com.*

———. 2001. *Peter Kurten.* Retrieved December 1, 2002 from: *http://home.cfl.rr.com/hagar/kurten.htm.*

————. n.d. There's a word for illicit touching: Frotteurism. (2002, October 20). *Pittsburgh Post-Gazette*, p. A21.

————. n.d. *Making love with a sleeping partner.* Retrieved September 26, 2002,' from *http://burknet.com/robsfantasy/section3.html.*

————. n.d. *Nymphomania.* Retrieved November 1, 2002 from *http://ensexlopedia.com/Sex_Education/nymphomania.htm.*

————. n.d. *Society for human sexuality.* Retrieved 9/29/02 from *http://www.sexuality.org/l/fetish/enemafaq.html.*

————. n.d. *Speculum Pages.* Retrieved 10/14/02 from *http://www.speculumpages.com/index1.html.*

————. 2002. *Surgical questions.* Retrieved from *http://abcnews.go.com/sections/world/DailyNews/amputate.html.*

————. 2002. Internet porn sweep breaks up massive global network of pedophiles. *Juvenile Justice Digest,* 29: 22, 1.

Araji, S. K. 1997. Sexually Aggressive Children. London: Sage.

Armsworth, M. W., & Stronck, K. 1999, Summer. Intergenerational effects of incest on parenting: Skills, abilities and attitudes. *Journal of Counseling & Development* 77: 303–314.

Arndt, W. B., Hietpas, T., & Kim, J. 2005. Critical characteristics of male serial murderers. *American Journal of Criminal Justice.* Vol 1.

Arrigo, B., & Purcell, C. 2001. Explaining paraphilias and lust murder: Toward an integrated model. *International Journal of Offender Therapy and Comparative Criminology,* 45(1): 6–31.

Atkinson, J. 1995. *The assessment of female sex offenders.* Correctional Service Canada.

Atkinson, M., & Young, K. 2001. Flesh journeys: Neo primitives and the contemporary rediscovery of radical body modification. *Deviant Behavior,* 22: 117–146.

Awad, G., Saunders, E., & Levene, J. 1984. "A clinical study of male adolescent sex offenders." *International Journal of Offender Therapy and Comparative Criminology,* 28(2).

Baby Jamie 2002. *Psychosexual infantilism.* [On-line]. Retrieved from *http://www.babyjamie.com.*

Baer, J. 1999. Family relationships, parenting behavior, and adolescent deviance in three ethnic groups. *Families in Society,* 80: 279–285.

Bait Bus. n.d. Retrieved September 15, 2002 from *http://www.baitbus.com.*

Baker, T. 2001. Investigations: Serial rapists. *Law & Order,* 49(10): 229–233.

Bang Bus. n.d. Retrieved September 15, 2002 from *http://www.bangbus.com.*

Barbaree, H. E., & Marshall, W. L. 1991. The role of male sexual arousal in rape: Six models. *Journal of Consulting and Clinical Psychology,* 59(5): 621–630

Barbaree, H. E., Seto, M. C., Langton, C. M., & Peacock, E. J. 2001. Evaluating the predictive accuracy of six risk assessment instruments for adult sex offenders. *Criminal Justice and Behavior,* 28(4): 490–521.

Bardsley, M. 2002. *Serial killer profile: Charles Starkweather.* Retrieved December 2, 2002 from *http://www.courttv.com/hannibal/stark1.html.*

Baron, L., & Straus, M. A. 1987. Four theories of rape: A macrosociological analysis. *Social Problems,* 34(5): 467–489.

Barron, M., & Kimmel, M. May 2000. Sexual violence in three pornographic media: towards a sociological explanation. *The Journal of Sex Research,* 37(2): 161–168.

Bassarath, L. 2001. Conduct disorder: A biolpsychosocial review. *Canadian Journal of Psychiatry,* 46: 609–616.

Baumeister, R. F. 1989. *Masochism and the self.* Hillsdale, NJ: Lawrence Erlbaum Associates.

————. 1991. *Escaping the self: Alcoholism, spirituality, masochism, and other flights from the burden of selfhood.* New York: Basic Books.

Baumeister, R. F., & Butler, J. L. 1997. Sexual masochism: Deviance without pathology. In D. R. Laws & W. O'Donohue (Eds.), *Sexual deviance: Theory, assessment, and treatment* (pp. 225–239). New York: The Guilford Press.

Becker, J., & Murphy, W. 1998. What we know and do not know about assessing and treating sex offenders. *Psychology, Public Policy, and Law,* 4(1–2): 116–137. Retrieved from PsycArticles on November 26, 2002.

BehaviorNet. 2002. Clinical Capsule: DSM-IV & DSM-IV-TR Paraphilia. *http://www.behaviornet .com/capsules/disorders/paraphilia.htm.*

———. 2002. Clinical Capsule: DSM-IV-TR Voyeurism. *http://www.behaviornet.com/capsules/ disorders/voyeurismTR.htm.*

Bell, R. S., & Bardsley, M. 2000. *The Atlanta child murders.* Retrieved on December 10, 2002 from *http://www.crimelibrary.com/serial/atlanta/.*

Bemporad, J., Dunton, H., & Spady, F. 1976. The treatment of a child foot fetishist. *American Journal of Psychotherapy,* 30(2): 303–316.

Benezech, M., Bourgeois, M., Boukhabza, D., & Yesavage, J. 1981. Cannibalism and vampirism in paranoid schizophrenia. *Journal of Clinical Psychiatry,* 42: 7, 290.

Bergman, A. S. 1997, May 7. *The meaning of the breast.* Retrieved from *http://www .paweekly.com/PAW/morgue/monthly/1997_May_7.BREAST.html.*

Berkowitz, A. D. 2001. Critical elements of sexual assault prevention and risk reduction programs. In C. Kilmartin (Ed.), *Sexual assault in context: Teaching college men about gender* (pp. 77–98). Holmes Beach, FL: Learning Publications.

Berliner, L. 1998. Sex offenders: Policy and practice. *Northwestern University Law Review,* 92: 1203–1229.

Bhugra, D. 2000. Disturbances in objects of desire: Cross-cultural issues. *Sexual and Relationship Therapy,* 15(1): 67.

Bickley, J., & Beech, A. R. 2001. Classifying child abusers: Its relevance to theory and clinical practice. *International Journal of Offender Therapy and Comparative Criminology,* 45(1): 51–69.

Blanchard, R., & Bogaert, A. F. 1998. Birth order in homosexual versus heterosexual sex offenders against children, pubescents and adults. *Archives of Sexual Behavior,* 27(6): 595–603.

Blanchard, R., & Dickey, R. 1998. Pubertal age in homosexual and heterosexual offenders against children, pubescents and adults. *Sexual abuse: A journal of research and treatment,* 10(4): 273–283.

Blasingame, J. May, 2001. *Sexual paraphilias.* Symposium conducted at the annual training conference of the California Coalition on Sexual Offending, Irvine, California.

Bmezine 2002. Retrieved from *http://www.bmezine.com.*

Bodenhausen, G. V. 1988. Stereotypic biases in social decision making and memory: Testing process models of stereotype use. *Journal of Personality and Social Psychology,* 55: 726–737.

Bodenhausen, G. V., & Wyer, R. S., Jr. 1985. Effects of stereotypes on decision making and information processing strategies: The impact of task complexity. *Journal of Personality and Social Psychology,* 48: 307–324.

Boechler, S. V. (1998, June). *Sex offenders as other: The distancing of offenders, the benefits and the impact.* Paper presented at the 59th Annual Convention for the Canadian Psychological Association; Edmonton, Alberta.

Boeringer, S.B. 1999. Associations of rape-supportive attitudes with fraternal and athletic participation. *Violence Against Women,* 5(1): 81–90.

Boeringer, S. B., Shehan, C. L., & Akers, R. L. 1991. Social contexts and social learning in sexual coercion and aggression: Assessing the contribution of fraternity membership. *Family Relations,* 40: 58–64.

Bogaert, A. F., & Sadava, S. 2002. Adult attachment and sexual behavior. *Personal Relationships,* 9: 191–204.

Bogaert, A. F., Bezeau, S., Kuban, M., & Blanchard, R. 1997. Pedophilia, sexual orientation, and birth order. *Journal of Abnormal Psychology,* 106: 331–335.

Bogal-Allbritten, R., & Allbritten, W. 1992. An examination of institutional response to rape on college campuses. *Family Violence Bulletin,* Fall 1992.

Bohmer, C., & Parrot, A. (Eds.). 1993. *Sexual assault on campus.* New York: Maxwell Macmillan International.

Book, R. G., & Perumal, G. 1993. Sexual asphyxia: A lesser epidemic. *Medicine & Law,* 12(6–8): 687–698.

Borum, R. 1996. Improving the clinical practice of violence risk assessment: Technology, guidelines, and training. *American Psychologist,* 51: 945–956.

Boumil, M. M., Friedman, J., & Taylor, G. E. 1993. *Date rape: The secret epidemic.* Deerfield Beach, FL: Health Communications.

Bourguignon, A. 1983. Vampirism and auto-vampirism. In L. B. Schlesinger & E. Revitch (Eds.) *Sexual dynamics of anti-social behavior* (pp. 278–302). Springfield, IL: Charles C Thomas Publishing.

Bowlby, J. 1969. *Attachment and loss: Vol. 1 Attachment.* New York: Basic Books.

———. 1973. *Attachment and loss: Vol. 2 Separation.* New York: Basic Books.

Bradford, J. M. W. 1996. The role of serotonin in the future of forensic psychiatry. *Bulletin of American Academy of Psychiatry and the Law,* 24: 57–72.

Bradford, J. M., Boulet, J., & Pawlak, A. 1992. The paraphilias: A multiplicity of deviant behaviors. *Canadian Journal of Psychiatry,* 37: 104–108.

Braidhill, K. 1998, December. To die for. *Los Angeles Magazine,* 48, 124–131.

Brewis, J., & Linstead, S. 2000. The worst thing is the screwing (2): Context and career in sex work. *Gender, Work and Organization,* 7(3): 168–180.

Bronswick, A. L. 2001. Using sexually related crime scene characteristics to profile male serial killers: A question of motivation. Unpublished dissertation, Alliant International University, Fresno, CA.

Brown, C. J. 1983. Paraphilias: Sadomasochism, fetishism, transvestism and transsexuality. *British Journal of Psychiatry,* 143: 227–231.

Brown, G. R. 1994. Women in relationships with cross-dressing men: A descriptive study from a non-clinical setting. *Archives of Sexual Behavior,* 23(5): 515–530.

Brown, M. 2002. Fire expertise often root of arson. Retrieved December 1, 2002 from: *http://www.sacbee.com/content/news/story/3276537p-4302970c.html.*

Brown, M. E., Hull, L. A., & Panesis, L. K. 1984. *Women who rape.* Boston, MA: Massachusetts Trial Court.

Bruce, C. 2002. *The thrill of the killer.* Retrieved November 23, 2002 from *http://erosnoir.com/ articles/103002-killer.htm.*

Bruno, R. L. 1997. *Devotees, pretenders and wannabes: Two cases of factitious disability disorder.* Retrieved from *http://www.amputee-online.com/amputee/bruno_art.html.*

Buhrich, N. 1983. The association of erotic piercing with homosexuality, sadomasochism, bondage, fetishism, and tattoos. *Archives of Sexual Behavior,* 12: 167–171.

Buhrich, N., & McConaghy, N. 1977. The discrete syndromes of transvestism and transsexualism. *Archives of Sexual Behavior,* 6(6): 483–495.

———. 1979. Three clinically discrete categories of fetishistic transvestism. *Archives of Sexual Behavior,* 8(2): 151–157.

Bull, R. H. C., & Green, J. 1980. The relationship between physical appearance and criminality. *Medicine, Science and the Law,* 20(2): 79–93.

Bullough, B., & Bullough, V. 1997. Are transvestites necessarily heterosexual? *Archives of Sexual Behavior,* 26(1): 1–12.

Bureau of Justice Statistics. Retrieved November 30, 2002 from *http://www.ojp.usdoj.gov/bjs/ crimoff.htm#sex.*

Burg, B. R. 1982. The sick and the dead: The development of psychological theory on necrophilia from Krafft-Ebing to the present. *Journal of the History of the Behavioral Sciences,* 18(3): 242–254.

Byrne, M. K., Byrne, S., Hillman, K., & Stanley, E. 2001. Offender risk and needs assessment: Some current issues and suggestions. *Behaviour Change,* 18(1): 18–28.

Cal. Penal Code. Section 290. (2001).

Cal. Welfare and Inst. Code (WIC), Section 6600, et seq. (1993).

Calef, V., & Weinshel, E. M. 1972. On certain neurotic equivalents of necrophilia. *International Journal of Psychoanalysis,* 53(1): 67–75.

California Crime Rates, 1960–2000. Retrieved December 17, 2002 at *http//:www.disastercenter .com.crime.*

California Department of Corrections. (2000). California sex offenders. Retrieved May 15, 2003 from *http://www.doc.state.co.us/admin_reg/PDFs/SO-report-send2.pdf.*

———. (CDC, 2001a): *Felony parolee population, December 2001.* Retrieved December 17, 2002 at *http//:www.cdc.state.us.*

———. (CDC, 2001b): *Parole violators returned to California prisons, 2001.* Retrieved December 17, 2002 at *http//:www.cdc.state.us.*

———. (CDC, 2001c): *Recidivism rate for felons paroled in California with 1 and 2 years, 2001.* Retrieved December 17, 2002 at *http//:www.cdc.state.edu.*

———. (CDC, 2001d): *Time served in prison upon first release, 2001.* Retrieved December 17, 2002 at *http//:www.cdc.state.us.*

———. (CDC, 2002a): *Characteristics of admissions to california prisons, 2002.* Retrieved December 17, 2002 at *http//:www.cdc.state.us.*

———. (CDC, 2002b): *Prison census data, June 2002.* Retrieved December 17, 2002 at *http//:www.cdc.state.us.*

———. (CDC, 2002c): *Second and third strikers, September 2002.* Retrieved December 17, 2002 at *http//:www.cdc.state.us.*

California Department of Mental Health. 2003. *Sex Offender Commitment Program (SOCP).* Retrieved May 6, 2003 from *http://www.dmh.ca.gov/socp.*

California Penal Code. 2005. *Penal Code Handbook of California with Related Statutes,* Longwood, FL: Gould Publications.

Calvert, J. F., Jr., & Munsie-Benson, M. 1999. Public opinion and knowledge about childhood sexual abuse in a rural community. *Child Abuse and Neglect,* 23(7): 671–682.

Carlisle, A. C. 2000. The dark side of the serial-killer personality. In L. Gerdes (Ed.), *Serial killers* (pp. 106–118). San Diego, CA: Greenhaven Press.

Carrera, M. 1981. *Sex—the facts, the acts, and your feelings.* New York: Crown Publishers.

Carroll, L., & Gilroy, P. 2002. Transgender issues in counselor preparation. *Counselor Education & Supervision,* 41: 233–242.

Carroll, S. T., Riffenburgh, R. H., Roberts, T. A., & Myhre, E. 2002. Tattoos and body piercings as indicators of adolescent risk-taking behaviors. *Pediatrics,* 109: 1021–1027.

Carstens, C. 1982. Application of a work penalty threat in the treatment of a case of juvenile firesetting. *Journal of Behavior Therapy and Experimental Psychiatry,* 13: 159–161.

Casey, T. S. 2000. *Traditional frequently asked questions for alt. vampires.* Retrieved September 30, 2002, from *www.altvampyres.net/newsgroup/faq/traditional.shtml.*

Cassidy, J. 1995. Attachment and generalized anxiety disorder. In D. Cicchetti & S. Toth (Eds.), *Rochester symposium on developmental psychopathology:* Vol. 6. Emotion, cognition, and representation (pp. 343–370). Rochester, NY: University of Rochester Press.

Cassidy, J., & Shaver, P. 1999. *Handbook of attachment: Theory, research, and clinical application.* New York: The Guilford Press.

Cauffman, E., Woolard, J., & Reppucci, N. D. 1999. Justice for juveniles: New perspectives on adolescent's competence and culpability. *Quinnipiac Law Review,* 18: 403–419.

Cautela, J. 1986. Behavioral analysis of a fetish: First interview. *Journal of Behavior Therapy and Experimental Psychiatry,* 17(3): 161–165.

Center for Sex Offender Management (CSOM). (2000, August). *Myths and facts about sex offenders.* Washington, DC: Author.

Cesnik, J. A., & Coleman, E. 1989. Use of lithium carbonate in the treatment of auto-erotic asphyxia. *American Journal of Psychotherapy,* 43(2): 277.

Chantry, K., & Craig, R. 1994. Psychological screening of sexually violent offenders with the MCMI. *Journal of Clinical Psychology,* 50: 430–435.

Chapl, T. C., Rice, M. E., & Harris, G. T. 1995. Salient victim suffering and the sexual responses of child molesters. *Journal of Consulting and Clinical Psychology,* 163: 249–255.

Chasseguet-Smirgel, J. 1981. Loss of reality in perversions—with special reference to fetishism. *Journal of the American Psychiatric Association,* 29: 511–534.

Cheaney, J. B. 2001. The real me: Self-obsessed madness is becoming more and more extreme. *World,* 16.

Check, J., Perlman, D., & Malamuth, N. 1985. Loneliness and aggressive behavior. *Journal of Social and Personal Relationships,* 2: 243–252.

Chiang, H. (2001, April 27). Child in incest is always the victim, state high court says; Minor can't be held complicit even if sex act consensual. *The San Francisco Chronicle,* p. A6.

Chidley, J. (1996, June 3). Death in the dark streets. *Maclean's,* 109(23): 48.

Clark, M. 1996. The auto-erotic asphyxiation syndrome in adolescent and young males. Retrieved October 12, 2002 from *www.silentvictims.org.*

Clark, N. E. 1993. Sexual offenders: An overview. In Clark, N. E. & Stephenson, G. M. (Eds.), *Sexual offenders: Context, assessment and treatment* (pp. 2–8). Leicester, U.K.: The British Criminological Society.

Cleaver, H. Jan. 18, 2002. Satanic killers tell of blood sucking rituals. *The Daily Telegraph.* London, U.K.

Clelland, S. R., Studer, L. H., & Reddon, J. R. 1998. Follow-up of rapists treated in a forensic psychiatric hospital. *Violence and Victims,* 13(1): 79–86.

Cohen, M., Seghorn, T., & Clamas, W. 1969. Sociometric study of the sex offender. *Journal of Abnormal Psychology,* 74: 249–255.

Coleman, E. 2001. *What sexual scientists know about . . . compulsive sexual behavior.* Society for the Scientific Study of Sexuality. Retrieved from Web search on Yahoo on October 30, 2002. *http://open-mind.org/News/SLA/8htm.*

Colin, C. (July 8, 1999). Sometimes it's ok to wake them. *Health and Body.* Retrieved October 27, 2002 from: *http://www.salon.com.*

Colorado Department of Corrections. (2000, August). State Sex Offender Treatment Programs. Retrieved May 6, 2003 from *http://www.doc.state.co.us/admin_reg/PDFs/SO-report-send2.pdf.*

Columbia University. (2002). *Abnormalities of sexual development.* [Online]. Retrieved from *www.cpmcnet.columiba.edu.*

Condy, S. R., Templer, D. I., Brown, R., & Veaco, L. 1987. Parameters of sexual contact of boys with women. *Archives of Sexual Behaviour,* 16(5): 379–394.

Cooper, A. J. 2000. "Female Serial Offenders," in Louis B. Schlesinger (Ed.), *Serial offenders: Current thought, recent findings.* Boca Raton, FL: CRC Press.

Cooper, A. M. 1993. Psychotherapeutic approaches to masochism. *Journal of Psychotherapy Practices and Research,* 2: 51–63.

Cooper, A., Morahan-Martin, J., Mathy, R. M., & Maheu, M. 2002. Toward an increased understanding of user demographics in online sexual activities. *Journal of Sex and Marital Therapy,* 28: 105–129.

Copps Hartley, C. 2001. Incest offenders' perceptions of their motives to sexually offend within their past and current life context. *Journal of Interpersonal Violence,* 16(5): 459–475.

Corsini, R. J. 1999. *The dictionary of psychology.* Philadelphia, PA: Brunner/Mazel.

Courtois, C. A. 1988. *Healing the incest wound.* New York: W. W. Norton Company.

———. 2000. The sexual after-effects of incest/child sexual abuse. *Siecus Report,* 29(1): 11–16.

Cramer, J. 1990, September 22. Transvestite prostitutes ply streets in fear. *The Los Angeles Times,* 1.

Creager, H. 2003, May. United States Probation and Parole: Supervision of Sex Offenders. In T. Tobin (Chair), *California and its sex offenders.* Symposium conducted at the annual meeting of the California Consortium of Sexual Offending, San Diego, CA.

Crittenden, P. M., Partridge, M. F., & Claussen, A. H. 1991. Family patterns of relationship in normative and dysfunctional families. *Development and Psychopathology,* 3: 491–512.

Cross, W. E., Parham, T. A., & Helms, J. E. 1991. The stages of black identity development: Nigrescence models. In R. L. Jones (Ed.), *Black psychology* (3rd ed., pp. 319–338). Berkeley, CA: Cobb & Henry.

Cruise Patrol (n.d.). Retrieved September 15, 2002, from *http://www.cruisepatrol.com.*

Curnoe, S., & Langevin, R. 2002. Personality and deviant sexual fantasies: An examination of the MMPI's of sex offenders. *Journal of Clinical Psychology,* 58(7): 803–815.

Cyr, M., Wright, J., McDuff, P., & Perron, A. 2002. Intrafamilial sexual abuse: Brother-sister incest does not differ from father-daughter and stepfather-stepdaughter incest. *Child Abuse and Neglect,* 26: 957–973.

Dahlburg, J. T. 2002, October 9. The nation; serial killer's life still intrigues on the eve of her death; crime: Today, Aileen Wuornos may be only second woman executed in Florida since 1976. *The Los Angeles Times,* A10.

Dalla, R. L. 2000. Exposing the "pretty woman" myth: A qualitative examination of the lives of female streetwalking prostitutes. *Journal of Sex Research,* 37(4): 344–353.

Davis, S. F., & Palladino, J. J. 2000. *Psychology* (3rd ed.). Upper Saddle River, NJ: Prentice Hall, Inc.

de Ruiter, C. & van Izendoorn, M. J. 1992. Agoraphobia and anxious-ambivalent attachment: An integrative review. *Journal of Anxiety Disorders,* 6: 365–381.

de Silva, W. P. 1999. ABC of sexual health: Sexual variations. *British Medical Journal,* 318(7184): 654–656.

Deaver, D. 1996, March 28. Columbia professor speaks about incest in Middle Ages. *Old Gold and Black,* 79(4).

DeFrancis, V. 1969. *Protecting the child victim of sex crimes committed by adults.* Denver: American Humane Society Association.

Dekkers, M. 1994, July 1. A little oink. Dearest pet: On bestiality. *New Statesman & Society,* 37.

Dempster, R. J. 1995. *Prediction of sexually violent recidivism: A comparison of risk assessment measurements.* Unpublished master's thesis, Simon Fraser University, Canada.

Denko, J. D. 1973. Klismaphilia: Enema as a sexual preference. *American Journal of Psychotherapy,* 27(2): 232–250.

———. 1976. Klismaphilia: Amplification of the erotic enema deviance. *American Journal of Psychotherapy,* 30(2): 236–255.

Denny, D. 1999. Transgender in the United States: A brief discussion. *SIECUS Report,* 28(1): 8–13.

Densen-Gerber, J. 1993. Preface. In C. L. Linedecker (Author), *Prison groupies: The shocking true story of the women who love America's deadliest criminals* (pp. 9–14). New York: Windsor Publishing.

Department of Justice—Bureau of Justice Offender Statistics. Retrieved December 17, 2002 at *http//:www.ojp.usdoj.gov.*

Dhooper, S. S., Royse, D. D., & Wolfe, L. C. 1991. A statewide study of the public attitudes toward child abuse. *Child Abuse & Neglect,* 15: 37–44.

Diagnostic and Statistical Manual for Mental Disorders (DSM-IV-Tr). 2000. Fourth Edition—text revision. Washington, DC: American Psychological Association.

Diamant, L., & Windholz, G. 1981. Loneliness in college students: Some theoretical, empirical, and therapeutic considerations. *Journal of College Student Development,* 22: 515–522.

Dietz, P. E., Cox, D. J., & Wegener, S. 1986. Male genital exhibitionism. In W. J. Curran, A. L. McGarry & S. A. Shah (Eds.), *Forensic psychiatry and psychology* (pp. 365–385). Philadelphia, PA: F.A. Davies.

Dietz, P. E., Hazelwood, R. R., & Warren, J. 1990. The sexually sadistic criminal and his offenses. *Bulletin of the American Academy of Psychiatry and Law,* 18(2): 163–178.

Dingwall, E. J. 1925. *Male infibulation.* Bale Publishers.

Dixon, D. 1983. An erotic attraction to amputees. *Sexuality and Disability,* 6: 3–19.

Docter, R. F., & Fleming, J. S. 2001. Measures of transgender behavior. *Archives of Sexual Behavior,* 30: 255–271.

Docter, R. F., & Prince, V. 1997. Transvestism: A survey of 1032 cross-dressers. *Archives of Sexual Behavior,* 26(6): 589–605.

Doermann, D. J. 1999. Gale encyclopedia of medicine: Sexual perversions. Retrieved September 25, 2002 from *http:www.findarticles.com.*

Doniger, W. 1995. The mythology of masquerading animals, or, bestiality. *Social Research,* 62(3): 751–764.

Donnelly, D., & Fraser J. 1998. Gender differences in sado-masochistic arousal among college students. *Sex Roles,* 39: 391–407.

Dotinga, R. 1999. *Murder case centers on amputation fetish.* Retrieved from *http://www.APBnews.com.*

———. 2000 *Out on a limb.* Retrieved from *http://dir.salon.com/health.feature/2000/08/29/ amputations/index.html.*

———. n.d. *Bizarre—People who want healthy arms and legs removed. http://www.rense.com/ general11/arms.htm.*

Douglas, J. E., & Munn, C. M. 1992. Violent crime scene analysis: Modus operandi, signature, and staging. *FBI Law Enforcement Bulletin,* 61(2): 1–10.

Douglas, J. E., & Olshaker, M. 1997. *Journey into darkness.* New York: A Lisa Drew Book/Scribner.

Douglas, J. E., Burgess, A. W., Burgess, A. G, & Ressler, R. K. 1992. *Crime classification manual.* San Francisco, CA: Jossey-Bass.

———. 1997. *Crime classification manual.* San Francisco, CA: Jossey-Bass Publishers.

Douglas, K. S., & Webster, C. D. 1999. The HCR-20 violence risk assessment scheme: Concurrent validity in a sample of incarcerated offenders. *Criminal Justice and Behavior,* 26(1): 3–19.

Douglas, K. S., Ogloff, J. R. P., & Nicholls, T. L. 1999. Assessing risk for violence among psychiatric patients: The HCR-20 violence risk assessment scheme and the Psychopathy Checklist: screening version. *Journal of Consulting and Clinical Psychology,* 67(6): 917–930.

Drapela, V. J. 1995. *Review of personality theories* (2nd ed.). Springfield, IL: Charles C Thomas.

Dube, R., & Hebert, M. 1988. Sexual abuse of children under 12 years of age: A review of 511 cases. *Child Abuse and Neglect,* 12: 321–330.

Dussich, J. P. 2001. Decisions not to report sexual assault: A comparative study among women living in Japan who are Japanese, Korean, Chinese, and English-speaking. *International Journal of Offender Therapy and Comparative Criminology,* 45(3): 278–301.

Dyer, C. 2000. Surgeon amputated healthy legs. *British Medical Journal,* 320(7231): 332–333. ProQuest, 1–2.

Elliott C. 2000. A new way to be mad. *The Atlantic Monthly,* 286(6): ProQuest, 1–14.

Elliott, D., & Briere, J. 1994. Forensic sexual abuse evaluations of older children—Disclosures and symptomology. *Behavioural Sciences and the Law,* 12(3): 261–277.

Elliott, D. S. 1993. Health-enhancing and health-compromising lifestyles. In S. G. Millstein, A. C. Petersen & E. O. Nightingale (Eds.), *Promoting the health of adolescents: New directions for the twenty-first century* (pp. 119–145). New York: Oxford University Press.

Ellis, A., & Sagarin, E. 1964. *Nymphomania: A study of the oversexed woman.* New York: Gramercy Publishing Company.

Elman, R. A. 1997. Disability pornography: The fetishization of women's vulnerabilities. *Violence against Women,* 3: 257–270.

Elysa, 2002. *www.elysa.uquam.ca.*

Engels, R. M., Dekovic, M., & Meeus, W. 2002. Parenting practices, social skills and peer relationships in adolescence. *Social Behavior and Personality,* 30: 3–17.

English, D. J., & Ray, J. A. 1991. *Children with sexual behavior problems: A behavioral comparison.* Olympia, WA: Department of Social and Health Sciences.

Epps, K. 1993. A survey of experience, training and working practices among staff working with adolescent sex offenders in secure units. In N. K. Clark & G. M. Stephenson (Eds.). *Sexual offenders: Context, assessment and treatment* (pp. 19–26). Leicester, U.K.: The British Psychological Society.

Erickson, W. D., Walbeck, N. H., & Seely, R. K. 1988. Behavior patterns of child molesters. *Archives of Sexual Behavior,* 17: 77–86.

Erlbaum, J. 1999, September/October. Sick Chicks: CindyLea Hendy is a rapist. *Popsmear Magazine,* 22. Retrieved November 30, 2002, from *http://www.popsmear.com/popculture/features/22/sickchicks.html.*

Ernulf, K. E., & Innala, S. M. 1995. Sexual bondage: A review and unobtrusive investigation. *Archives of Sexual Behavior,* 24: 631–657.

Everaerd, W. 1983. A case of apotemnophilia: A handicap as sexual preferences. *American Journal of Psychotherapy,* 37: 285–293.

Evripidov, C. 1998. *Female Serial Killers.* Retreived December 2, 2002 from *http://www.people .virginia.edu/~ce4b/jack.html.*

Falk, P. J. 1998, Spring. Rape by fraud and rape by coercion. *Brooklyn Law Review,* 64(1): 39.

Faller, K. C. 1987. Women who sexually abuse children. *Violence and Victims* 2(4): 263–276.

Farley, M., & Barkan, H. 1998. Prostitution, violence and posttraumatic stress disorder. *Women and Health,* 27(3): 37–49.

Favazza, A. 1996. *Bodies under siege: Self-mutilation and body modification in culture and psychiatry* (2nd ed.). Baltimore: The Johns Hopkins University Press.

Fears, D., & Thomas-Lester, A. 2002, October 26. Blacks express shock at suspects' identity; most say they expect a serial killer to be white. *The Washington Post.* Retrieved on December 1, 2002, from *http:// www.northernlight.com.*

Federal Bureau of Investigation 1982. *Uniform crime reports.* Washington, DC: U.S. Government Printing Office.

Federal Bureau of Prisons 2001. *Quick facts: Type of offenses as of May* 2002. Retrieved December 15, 2002 from *http//:www.bop.gov.*

———. 2003 *Quick Facts.* Retrieved November 18, 2002 from *http//:www.bop.gov.*

Fedoroff, J. P., & Moran, B. 1997. Myths and misconceptions about sex offenders. *Canadian Journal of Human Sexuality,* 6(4): 263–176.

Fedoroff, J. P., Brunet, A., Woods, V., Granger, C., Chow, E., Collins, P., & Shapiro, C., 1997. A case-controlled study on men who sexually assault sleeping victims. In C.Shapiro & A. McCall-Smith (Eds.), *Forensic Aspects of Sleep.* New York: John Wiley & Sons.

Fedoroff, J. P., Fishell, A., & Fedoroff, B. 1999. A case series of women evaluated for paraphilic sexual disorders. *Canadian Journal of Human Sexuality,* 8(2): 127–140.

Fedoroff, J. P., Hanson, A., McGuire, M., Malin, M., & Berlin, F. S. 1992. Simulated paraphilias: A preliminary study of patients who imitate or exaggerate paraphilic symptoms and behaviors. *Journal of Forensic Sciences,* 3(7): 902–911.

Feeney, J. A. 1995. Adult attachment, coping style and health locus of control as predictors of health behaviour. *Australian Journal of Psychology,* 47: 171–177.

Fehrenbach, P. A., & Monastersky, C. 1988. Characteristics of female adolescent sexual offenders. *American Journal of Orthopsychiatry* 58(1): 148–151.

Feild, H. S. 1978. Attitudes toward rape: A comparative analysis of police, rapists, crisis counselors, and citizens. *Journal of Personality and Social Psychology,* 36(2): 156–179.

Ferrall, B. R. 1999. Murder: United States, Atlanta. *Journal of Criminal Law and Criminology,* 89(4). Retrieved on December 1, 2002, from ProQuest.

Fetish Information Exchange, Bestiality—ZooSexuality. 2002, November 3. *http://www.fetishclub .com/exchange/bestiality.shtml.*

Feyerabend, P. 1995. *Killing Time.* University of Chicago Press: Chicago, IL.

Filkins, J. W. 1996. *Interactive effects of crime prototype and criminal stereotype on juridical decisions.* Unpublished dissertation. Loyola University of Chicago.

Fineman, K. R. 1980. Firesetting in childhood and adolescence. *Psychiatric Clinics of North America,* 3: 483–500.

Finkelhor D., & Russell, D. 1984. Women as perpetrators: Review of the evidence. In D. Finkelhor, (ed.). *Child sexual abuse: New theory and research* (pp. 171–187). New York: Free Press.

Finkelhor, D., Gomez-Schwartz, G., & Horowitz, J. 1984. Professionals' responses. In D. Finkelhor (Ed.). *Child sexual abuse: New theory and research* (pp. 200–215). New York: Free Press.

Finkelhor, D., Hotaling, G., Lewis, I. A., & Smith, C. 1990. Sexual abuse in a national survey of adult men and women: Prevalence, characteristics and risk factors. *Child Abuse and Neglect,* 14: 19–25.

Finkelhor, D., Williams, L. M., & Burns, N. 1989. *Sexual abuse in day care.* Newbury Park, CA: Sage.

Fiqia, N. A., Lang, R. A., Plutchik, R., & Holden, R. 1987. Personality differences between sex and violent offenders. *International Journal of Offender Therapy and Cooperative Criminology,* 31: 211–266.

Firestone, P., Bradford, J. M., Greenberg, D. M., & Nunes, K. L. 2000. Differentiation of homicidal child molesters, nonhomicidal child molesters, and nonoffenders by phallometery. *The American Journal of Psychiatry,* 157(11): 1847–1850.

Firestone, P., Bradford, J. M., McCoy, M., Greenberg, D. M., Larose, M. R., & Curry, S. 1999. Prediction of recidivism in incest offenders. *Journal of Interpersonal Violence,* 14(5): 511–531.

Fisher, D., & Howells, K. 1993. Social relationships in sexual offenders. *Journal of Sex and Marital Therapy,* 8(2): 225–251.

Fisher, D., Beech, A., & Browne, K. 1999. Comparison of sex offenders to nonoffenders on selected psychological measures. *International Journal of Offender Therapy and Comparative Criminology,* 43(4): 473–491.

Flinker, J., Englund, M., & Sroufe, A. 1992. Predicting peer competence in childhood from early parent-child relationships. In R. Parke & G. W. Ladd (Eds.), *Family and peer relationships: Modes of linkages* (pp. 77–106). Hillsdale, NJ: Erlbaum.

Florida executes female serial killer. 2002, October 10 *The Los Angeles Times,* p. A33.

Fontana-Rosa, J. C. 2001. Legal competency in a case of pedophilia: Advertising on the Internet. *International Journal of Offender Therapy and Comparative Criminology,* 45(1): 118–128.

Ford, M. E., & Linney, J. A. 1995. Comparative analysis of juvenile sexual offenders, violent nonsexual offenders, and status offenders. *Journal of Interpersonal Violence,* 10: 56–71.

Fox, J. A., & Levin, J. 1998, November. Multiple homicide: Patterns of serial and mass murder. *Crime and Justice,* 23: 407–418.

———. 2000. Identifying serial killers. In L. Gerdes (Ed.), *Serial killers* (pp. 29–37). San Diego, CA: Greenhaven Press.

Frank, T. 1994. *Fraternity rape bibliography.* Retrieved November 22, 2002 from *http://kates feminist.info/rape/info/fratrape.html.*

Freud, S. 1932. The acquisition of power over fire. *International Journal of Psychoanalysis,* 13: 405–410.

———. 1934. *Civilization and its contents.* Cited in Slovenko (1965).

———. 1953. *Collected papers.* E. Jones (Ed.). London: Hogarth Press.

———. 1966. *The complete introductory lectures on psychoanalysis.* New York: Norton.

Freund, K. 1981. Assessment of pedophilia. In M. Cook & K. Howells (Eds). *Adult Sexual Interest in Children.* New York: Academic Press.

Freund, K., Heasman, G. A., & Roper, V. 1982. Results of the main studies on sexual offenses against children and pubescents: A review. *Canadian Journal of Criminology,* 24(4): 387–397.

Freund, K., Scher, H., & Hucker, S. 1983. The courtship disorders. *Archives of Sexual Behavior,* 12(5): 369–379.

———. 1984. The courtship disorders: A further investigation. *Archives of Sexual Behavior,* 13: 133–139.

Freund, K., Seto, M. C., & Kuban, M. 1996. Two types of Fetishism. *Behavioral Research Therapy,* 34: 687–694.

Freund, K., Steiner, B. W., & Chan, S. 1982. Two types of cross-gender behavior. *Archives of Sexual Behavior,* 11: 49–63.

Freund, K., Watson, R., & Dickey, R. 1990. Does sexual abuse in childhood cause pedophilia? An exploratory study. *Archives of Sexual Behavior,* 19: 557–569.

Frost, K. 2002. Case notes and comments: The constitutionality of an internet execution: Lappin v. Entertainment Network, Inc. *Journal of Art and Entertainment Law,* 22: 173.

Fudge, E. 2000. Monstrous acts: Bestiality in early modern England. *History Today,* August: 20–25.

Furnham, A., & Haraldsen, E. 1998. Lay theories of etiology and "cure" for four types of paraphilia: Fetishism, pedophilia, sexual sadism, and voyeurism. *Journal of Clinical Psychology,* 54: 689–700.

Gagnon, J. H. 1990. The explicit and implicit use of the scripting perspective in sex research. *Annual Review of Sex Research,* 1: 1–43.

Gardner, R. A. 1993. *A theory about the variety of human sexual behavior.* Institute for Psychological Therapies, 5. Retrieved November 1, 2002, from *http://www.ipt-forensics.com/journal/volume5/j5_2_8.htm.*

Gardner, W., Lidz, C. W., Mulvey, E. P., & Shaw, E. C. 1996. A comparison of actuarial methods for identifying repetitively violent patients with mental illnesses. *Law and Human Behavior,* 20(1): 35–48.

Garrett-Gooding, J., & Senter, R., Jr. 1987. Attitudes and acts of sexual aggression on a university campus. *Sociological Inquiry,* 59: 348–371.

Gaynor, J., & Hatcher, C. 1987. *The psychology of firesetting: Detection and intervention.* New York: Brunner/Mazel.

Geberth, V. J. 1996. *Practical homicide investigation: Tactics, procedures, and forensic techniques* (3rd ed.) Boca Raton, FL: CRC Press, Inc.

Geberth, V. J., & Turco, R. N. 1997. Antisocial personality disorder, sexual sadism, malignant narcissism, and serial murder. *Journal of Forensic Sciences,* 42(1): 49–60.

Gebhard, P. 1965. Situational factors affecting human sexual behavior. In F. Beach (Ed.), *Sex and Behavior* (pp. 483–495). New York: John Wiley.

Gebhard, P. H., Gagnon, J. H., Pomeroy, W. B., Christenson C. V. 1965. *Sex Offenders: An Analysis of Types.* New York: Harper & Row.

Gentile, S. R., Asamen, J. K., Harmell, P. H., & Weathers, R. 2002. The stalking of psychologists by their clients. *Professional Psychology: Research and Practice,* 33: 490–494.

George Mason University 2001. *National Statistics.* Retrieved November 22, 2002 from *http://www.gmu.edu/facstaff/sexual/ffnational.html.*

Gijis, L., & Gooren, L. 1996. Hormonal and psychopharmacological interventions in the treatment of paraphilias: An update. *The Journal of Sex Research,* 33: 273–290.

Gil, E., and Cavanagh Johnson, T. 1993. *Sexualized children: assessment and treatment of sexualized children and children who molest.* Rockville, MD.: Launch Press.

Gilmartin, B. G. 1975. That swinging couple down the block. *Psychology Today,* 8: 54–58.

Gleitman, H. 1996. *Basic Psychology,* (4th ed.) New York: W. W. Norton & Company.

Gold, L. 1962. Psychiatric profile of a firesetter. *Journal of Forensic Sciences,* 7: 404–417.

Gold, S. N., & Heffner, C. L. 1998. Sexual addiction: Many conceptions, minimal data. *Clinical Psychology Review,* 18: 367–381.

Goldberg, R., & Wise, T. 1985. Psychodynamic treatment for telephone scatologia. *The American Journal of Psychoanalysis,* 45: 291–297.

Goldstein, M. (n.d.). *Sadomasochism raises civil rights issues.* Retrieved September 21, 2002 from *http://www.leatherquest.com/News/ma7.html.*

Gomez, A. J. 1998. Rabies: A possible explanation for the vampire legend. *Neurology,* 51(3): 856–859.

Gonsioreh, J. C., Bera, W. H., & LeTourneau, D. 1994. *Male sexual abuse: A trilogy of intervention strategies.* Thousand Oaks, CA: Sage.

Goodman, A. 1993. Diagnosis and treatment of sexual addictions. *Journal of Sex and Marital Therapy,* 19(3): 123–136, 225–251.

Gosselin, C. 1979. Personality characteristics of the average rubber fetishist. In Cook M. & G. Wilson (Eds.), *Love and attraction: Proceedings of an international conference* (pp. 395–399). Oxford: Pergamon.

Grattet, R. 2000. The Atlanta youth murders and the politics of race. *Contemporary Sociology,* 29(3): Retrieved on December 1, 2002 from ProQuest.

Gratzer, T., & Bradford, M. W. 1995. Offender and offense characteristics of sexual sadists: A comparative study. *Journal of Forensic Sciences,* 40(3): 450–455.

Green, M. 2003. *Who is the predator? How law enforcement, mental health professionals (forensic and non-forensic), and the general public stereotypes sex offenders.* Unpublished doctoral dissertation. Alliant International University, Fresno, California.

Green, R. 2001. (Serious) sadomasochism: A protected right of privacy? *Archives of Sexual Behavior,* 30: 543–550.

Greenberg, D. M., Bradford, J., & Curry, S. 1995. Infantophilia: A new subcategory of pedophiles? A preliminary study. *Bulletin of the American Academy of Psychiatry and Law,* 23: 63–71.

Gregson, I. 2002 *Naked amputees.* Retrieved from *http://www.nakedamputees.com/apotemnophilia -erotica.htm.*

Gribben, M. 2001. *Alton Coleman and Debra Brown: Odyssey of mayhem.* Retrieved on December 10, 2002 from *http://www.crimelibrary.com/serial8/coleman-brown/index.htm.*

Grier, P. E., Clark, M., & Stoner, S. B. 1993. Comparative study of personality traits of female sex offenders. *Psychological Reports,* 73: 1378.

Griffiths, M. 2001. Sex on the Internet: Observations and implications for Internet sex addiction. *The Journal of Sex Research,* 38(4): 333–342.

Grohol, J. 2002. Pyromania: Symptoms. *http://psychcentral.com/disorders/sx88.htm.*

Groneman, C. 1994. Nymphomania: The historical construction of female sexuality. *Signs: Journal of Women in Culture and Society,* 19: 337–367.

Groneman, C. 2000. *Nymphomania: A history.* New York: W. W. Norton and Company.

Groth, A. N. 1979. *Men who rape.* New York: Plenum Press.

Grubin, D. 1994a. Sexual sadism. *Criminal Behavior and Mental Health,* 4: 3–9.

———. 1994b. Sexual murder. *British Journal of Psychiatry,* 165: 624–629.

Guay, J. P., Proulx, J., Cusson, M., & Quimet, M. 2001. Victim-choice polymorphia among serious sex offenders. *Archives of Sexual Behavior,* 30(5): 521–533.

Gudjonsson, G. H., Petursson, H., & Skulason, S. 1989. Psychiatric evidence: A study of psychological issues. *Acta Psychiatric Scandinavia,* 80: 165–169.

Gutheil, T. G., Price, M., Commons, M. L., Kafka, M. P., & Dodd-Kimmey, S. 2001. Redefining telephone scatologia: Treatment and classification. *Psychiatric Annals,* 31(5): 282.

Gwennifer 2000. *The history of vampirism.* Retrieved September 30, 2002, from *http://www .gwennifer.freeservers.com/history/html.*

Hall, G. C. 1988. Criminal behavior as a function of clinical and actuarial variables in a sexual offender population. *Journal of Consulting and Clinical Psychology,* 56: 773–775.

Hall, G. C., & Proctor, W. C. 1987. Criminological predictors of recidivism in a sexual offender population. *Journal of Consulting and Clinical Psychology,* 55: 111–112.

Hall, G. C. N., & Hirschman, R. 1991. Toward a theory of sexual aggression: A quadripartite model. *Journal of Consulting and Clinical Psychology,* 59: 643–669.

Hall, J. R., Jr. 1998. The truth about arson. *NFPA Journal,* November/December: 58–67.

Hallin, C. R. 1997. Sexual sadism: Assessment and treatment. In D. R. Laws & W. O'Donohue (Eds.), *Sexual Deviance: Theory, assessment, and treatment* (pp. 225–239). New York: The Guilford Press.

Hansen, J. O. 1997, June 10. Sexual predators: Why Megan's Law is not enough. *Atlanta Journal-Constitution,* p. D11.

Hanson, R. K., & Slater, S. 1993. Reactions to motivational accounts of child molesters. *Journal of Child Sexual Abuse,* 2(4): 43–59.

Hanson, R. K., & Bussiere, M. T. 1998. Predicting relapse: A meta-analysis of sexual offender recidivism studies. *Journal of Consulting and Clinical Psychology,* 66(2): 1–15.

Hanson, R. K., & Harris, A. J. 2000. Where should we intervene?: Dynamic predictors of sexual offense recidivism. *Criminal Justice and Behavior,* 27(1): 6–35.

Hanson, R. K. 2002. Evaluation of Manitoba's Secondary Risk Assessment. Unpublished Manuscript.

Hanson, R. K., & Thornton, D. 1999. Static-99: Improving actuarial risk assessments for sex offenders. *Department of the Solicitor General of Canada,* User's Report, 1–23.

———. 2000. Improving risk assessments for sex offenders: A comparison of three actuarial scales. *Law and Human Behavior,* 24(1): 119–136.

Hanson, R. K., Scott, H., & Steffy, R. A. 1995. A comparison of child molesters and nonsexual criminals: Risk predictors and long-term recidivism. *Journal of Research in Crime and Delinquency,* 32: 325–337.

Hare, R. 1993. *Without conscience.* New York: The Guilford Press.

Harmon, R. B., Rosner, R., & Owens, H. 1998. Sex and violence in a forensic population of obsessional harassers. *Psychology, Public Policy, and Law,* 4: 236–249.

Hazan, C., & Shaver, P. 1987. Romantic love conceptualized as an attachment process. *Journal of Personality and Social Psychology,* 52: 511–524.

HBO & Company. 1998. Health Information: Pyromania. *http://www.westsub.com/encyclopedia _reference_display.cfm?rid=657.*

Heaven, P. G., & Connors, J. 1998. Victim characteristics and attribution of rape blame in Australia and South Africa. *Journal of Social Psychology,* 138(1): 131.

Heilbrun, K., Nezu, C., Keeney, M., Chung, S., & Wasserman, A. 1998. Sexual offending: Linking assessment, intervention, and decision making. *Psychology, Public Policy, and Law,* 4(1–2): 138–174. Received from PsychArticles on November 26, 2002.

Hekma, G. 2001. Saints, spikes, stripping. *Gay-News, 119.* Retrieved November 3, 2002 from *http://www.gay-news.com/article.php?sid=211.*

Hemphill, R. E., & Zabow, T. 1992. Clinical vampirism: A presentation of 3 cases and a reevaluation of Haigh, the "Acid-Bath Murderer." In R. Noll (Ed.). *Vampires, werewolves and demons: Twentieth century reports in the psychiatric literature* (pp. 61–73). New York: Brunner/Mazel.

Herek, G. M. 2002. *Hebephilia.* Retrieved September 22, 2002 from University of California-Davis website: *http:// www.psychology.ucdavis.edu.*

Hickey, E. W. 2001. *Serial murderers and their victims.* Belmont, CA: Wadsworth.

———. 2002. *Serial murderers and their victims* (3rd ed.). Belmont, CA: Wadsworth.

———. 2006. *Serial murderers and their victims.* (4th ed.) Belmont, CA: Wadsworth.

Higgs, D. C., Canavan, M. M., & Meyer, W. J. 1992. Moving from defense to offence: The development of an adolescent female sex offender. *The Journal of Sex Research,* 29(1): 131–139.

Hill, J. P., & Holmbeck, G. N. 1986. Attachment and autonomy during adolescence. In G. Whitehurst (Ed.). *Annals of Child Development,* 3: 145–189.

Hill, S. W. 1994. *Nurture-born killers: The motivation and personality development of the serial killer,* Retrieved December 2, 2002 from *http://members.telocity.com/~snyderboy/femvio/serial _murder.htm.*

Hirschi, T. 1969. *Causes of delinquency.* Berkeley, CA: University of California Press.

Hodge, J. 2002. Gang rape on campus. *Sexual victimization.* Retrieved November 22, 2002 from *http://cfs.he.utk.edu/240class/victim.htm.*

Hogue, T. E. 1993. Attitudes towards prisoners and sexual offenders. In N. K. Clark, & G. M. Stephenson (Eds.). *Sexual offenders: Context, assessment and treatment* (pp. 27–32). Leicester, U.K.: The British Psychological Society.

Hogue, T. E., & Peebles, J. 1997. The influence of remorse, intent and attitudes toward sex offenders on judgments of a rapist. *Psychology, Crime, and Law,* 3: 249–259.

Hollin, C. R. 1997. Sexual sadism: Assessment and treatment. In D. R. Laws, and W. T. O'Donohue (Eds.), *Sexual deviance: Theory, assessment, and treatment* (210–224). New York: The Guilford Press.

Holmes, R. M., and Deburger, J. 1988. *Serial murder.* New Bury Park, CA: Sage Publishers.

Holmes, R. M., and Holmes, S. T. 2000. *Mass murder in the United States.* Upper Saddle River, NJ: Prentice Hall Publishers.

———. 2002. *Profiling violent crimes: An investigative tool.* (3rd ed.). Thousand Oaks, CA: Sage.

Holmes, S. A. 2002, October 25. Many voice surprise arrested men are black. *New York Times.* Retrieved December 1, 2002, from ProQuest.

Hopkins, P. D. 1994. Rethinking sadomasochism: Feminism, interpretation, and simulation. *Hypatia,* 9: 116–139.

Horley, J. 2001. Frotteurism: A term in search of an underlying disorder? *The Journal of Sexual Aggression,* 7: 51–55.

Hosken, F. 1978. The epidemiology of female genital mutilations. *Tropical Doctor,* 8: 150–156.

Howitt, D. 1999. *Paedophiles and sexual offences against children.* London, U.K.: Plenum Publishing Corporation.

Hoyek, C. 1951. Criminal incendiarism. *Journal of Law and Criminology,* 41: 836–845.

Hucker, S. J. 1997. Sexual sadism: Psychopathology and theory. In D. R. Laws & W. O'Donohue (Eds.), *Sexual deviance: Theory, assessment and treatment* (pp. 194–209). New York: Guilford Press.

Hucker, S. J., & Stermac, L. 1992. The evaluation and treatment of sexual violence, necrophilia and asphyxiophilia. *Psychiatric Clinics of North America,* 15(3): 703–719.

Hudson, S. M., & Ward, T. 1997a. Intimacy, loneliness, and attachment style in sexual offenders. *Journal of Interpersonal Violence,* 12: 323–339.

———. 1997b. Rape: Psychopathology and theory. In D. R. Laws and W. T. O'Donohue (Eds.), *Sexual deviance: Theory, assessment, and treatment* (332–355). New York: Guilford Press.

———. 2000. Interpersonal competency in sex offenders. *Behavior Modification,* 24(4): 494–527.

Humphrey, S. E., & Kahn, A. S. 2000. Fraternities, athletic teams, and rape: Importance of identification with a risk group. *Journal of Interpersonal Violence,* 15(12): 1313–1322.

Hunter, J. A., Jr, & Figueredo, A. J. 2000. The influence of personality and history of sexual victimization in the prediction of juvenile perpetrated child molestation. *Behavior Modification,* 24(2): 241–263.

Illinois Coalition Against Sexual Assault. (n.d.). *Acquaintance rape.* Retrieved November 22, 2002 from *http://www.icasa.org/Uploads/acquaintance_rape-final.pdf.*

Inciardi, J. A. 1970. The adult fire setter: A typology. *Criminology,* 8, 145–155.

Innala, S. M., Goeteborgs, S. U., & Ernulf, K. E. 1989. Asphyxiophilia in Scandinavia. *Archives of Sexual Behavior,* 18(3): 181–189.

International Pediatrics (2001). Annual Publication: *Adolescent Sex Offenders.* v. 16, 2.

Isenschmid, D. S., Cassin, B. J., Bradford, R. H., and Sawait, K. 1998. Tetrachloroethylene intoxication in an auto-erotic fatality. *Journal of Forensic Sciences,* 43(1): 231–234.

Jackson, T. L., & Sandberg, G. 1985. Attribution of incest blame among rural attorneys and judges. *Women & Therapy,* 4(3): 39–52.

Jaffe, P. D., & DiCataldo, F. 1994. Clinical vampirism: Blending of myth and reality. *Bulletin of the American Academy of Psychiatry and Law,* 22(4): 533–544.

James, J., & Meyerding, J. 1997. Early sexual experiences and prostitution. *American Journal of Psychiatry,* 134: 1381–1385.

Janssen, E. 1995. Understanding the rapist's mind. *Perspectives in Psychiatric Care,* 31(4): 9–13.

Japenga, A. 1987, May 13. New strategies proposed to fight gang rape on campus [Electronic version]. *The Los Angeles Times,* p. 1.

Jenkins, P. 1988. Myth and murder: The serial killer panic of 1983–85, *Criminal Justice Research Bulletin,* 3(11): 1–7.

———. 1993. African-Americans and serial homicide. In R. M Holmes & S. T. Holmes (Eds.), *Contemporary perspectives on serial murder* (pp. 17–32). Thousand Oaks, CA: Sage Publications.

———. 1998. *Moral panic: Changing concepts of the child molester in modern America.* Birmingham, NY: Yale University Press.

Jenks, R. J. 1998. Swinging: A review of the literature. *Archives of Sexual Behavior,* 27(5): ProQuest, 1–10.

Jensen, H. M., & Poulsen, H. D. 2002. Auto-vampirism in schizophrenia. *Nordic Journal of Psychiatry,* 56(1): 47–48.

Johnson, B. 2002. The vampire lectures. *Literature and Psychology,* 48: 125–128.

Johnson, B. R., & Becker, J. V. 1997. Natural born killers? : The development of the sexually sadistic serial killer. *Journal of the American Academy of Psychiatry and Law,* 25(3): 335–348.

Johnson, R. L., & Shrier, D. 1987. Past sexual victimization by females of male patients in an adolescent medicine clinic population. *American Journal of Psychiatry* 144(5): 650–652.

Johnson, T. C. 1989. Female child perpetrators: Children who molest other children. *Child Abuse and Neglect,* 13: 571–585.

Jones, C., & Aronson, E. 1973. Attribution of fault to a rape victim as a function of respectability of the victim. *Journal of Personality and Social Psychology,* 26(3): 415–419.

Jones, F. 1981. Therapy for firesetters [Letter to the Editor]. *American Journal of Psychiatry,* 138: 261–262.

Jones, K. L., Shainberg, L. W., & Byer, C. O. 1985. *Dimensions of human sexuality.* Dubuque, Iowa: Wm. C. Brown Publishers.

Jones, P. B., Harris, P. W., Fader, J., & Grubstein, L. 2001. Identifying chronic juvenile offenders. *Justice Quarterly,* 18(3): 479–507.

Joy. 2002. *www.weaselwerks.com/peebits.html.*

Jynxed's Realm. Retrieved September 24, 2002 from *http://jynxedrealm.tripod.com/stuff/death5.html.*

Kachmar, A. J. 1996. Review of selected 1995 California legislation: Crimes, stalking. *Pacific Law Journal,* 27: 589.

Kafka, M. P. 1994. Sertraline pharmacotherapy for paraphilias and paraphilia-related disorders: An open trial. *Annals of Clinical Psychiatry,* 6: 189–195.

———. (1997a). A monoamine hypothesis for the pathophysiology of paraphilic disorders. *Archives of Sexual Behavior,* 26: 343–358.

———. (1997b). Hypersexual desires in males: An operational definition and clinical implications for males with paraphilias and paraphilia-related disorders. *Archives of Sexual Behavior,* 26: 505–526.

———. (1994a). Preliminary observations of DSM-IIIR axis I comorbidity in men with paraphilia and paraphilia-related disorders. *Journal of Clinical Psychiatry,* 55(11): 481–487.

Kaplan, H. S. 1996. Erotic obsession: Relationship to hypoactive sexual desire disorder and paraphilia. *The American Journal of Psychiatry,* 153(7): 30–47.

Karr, G. 1996 September 9. *Union, SC lake takes seven more lives.* Retrieved December 2, 2002 from *http://www.familyofmen.com/female_serial_killers.htm.*

Kaufman, I., Heins, L., & Reiser, D. 1961. A re-evaluation of the psychodynamics of firesetting. *American Journal of Orthopsychiatry,* 31: 123–136.

Kear-Colwell, J., & Boer, D. P. 2000. The treatment of pedophiles: Clinical experience and the implications of recent research. *International Journal of Offender Therapy and Comparative Criminology,* 44(5): 593–605.

Kear-Colwell, J., & Sawle, G. 2001. Coping strategies and attachment in pedophiles: Implications for treatment. *International Journal of Offender Therapy and Comparative Criminology,* 45: 171–182.

Kelleher, M., & Kelleher, C. 1998. *Murder most rare: The female serial killer.* London, U.K. Praeger.

Kelley, S. J. 1990. Responsibility and management strategies in child sexual abuse: A comparison of child protective workers, nurses and police officers. *Child Welfare,* 69: 43–51.

Kelly, R. J., Wood, J. J., Gonzalez, L. S., MacDonald, V., & Waterman, J. 2002. Effects of mother-son incest and positive perceptions of sexual abuse experience on the psychosocial adjustment of clinic-referred men. *Child Abuse and Neglect,* 26: 425–441.

Keppel, R., & Birnes, W. 1997. *Signature killers-interpreting the calling cards of the serial murderer.* New York: Pocket Books-Simon Schuster.

Kershner, R. 1996. Adolescent attitudes about rape. *Adolescence,* 31(121): 29–34.

Kippen, C. 2002. *The history of footwear: Foot fetish and shoe retifism.* Retrieved 3/10/03 from *http://podiatry.curtin.edu.au/fetish.html#naughty.* Curtin University of Technology, Department of Podiatry.

Kippen, C. n.d. *Paraphilia and paraphilia-related disorders.* Retrieved October 28, 2002 from *http://www.curtin.eu.au/curtin/dept/physio/podiatry/footsex.html.*

Kirby, P. 2003. Signature killers. In E. Hickey (Ed.) *Encyclopedia of Murder and Violent Crime* (pp. 436–438). Thousand Oaks, CA: Sage Publishers.

Kirk, P. L. 1969. *Fire investigation.* New York: Wiley.

Klaf, F. S., & Brown, W. 1958. Necrophilia, brief review and case report. *Psychiatric Quarterly,* 32: 645–652.

Klein, R. G. 1994. Anxiety disorders. In M. Ruttler, E. Taylor & L. Hersov (Eds.), *Child and adolescent psychiatry* (pp. 242–261). Oxford: Blackwell.

Knight, R. A., Warren, J. I., Reboussin, R., & Soley, B. J. 1998. Predicting rapist type from crime-scene variables. *Criminal Justice and Behavior,* 25(1): 46–80.

Knopp, F. H., & Lackey, L. B. 1987. *Female sexual abusers: A summary of data from 44 treatment providers.* The Safer Society Program of the New York State Council of Churches, Orwell, VT.

Koa, A. 2001 *The difficult appendage.* Retrieved from *http://www.ama-assn.org/ama/pub/category/6262.html.*

Kocsis, R. N., Cooksey, R. W., & Irwin, H. J. 2002. Psychological profiling of offender characteristics from crime behaviors in serial rape offences. *International Journal of Offender Therapy and Comparative Criminology,* 46(2): 144–169.

Kolko, D. 1985. Juvenile firesetting: A review and methodological critique. *Clinical Psychology Review,* 5: 345–376.

———. 1988. Community interventions for juvenile firesetters: A survey of two national programs. *Hospital and Community Psychiatry,* 39: 973–979.

Koons-Witt, Barbara A. 2002. The effects of gender on the decision to incarcerate before and after the introduction of sentencing guidelines. *Criminology,* 40: 297–327.

Koss, M. P., & Harvey, M. R. 1991. *The rape victim: Clinical and community interventions.* Thousand Oaks, CA: Sage Library of Social Research.

Koss, M. P., Gidycz, C. A., & Wisniewski, N. 1987. The scope of rape: Incidence and prevalence of sexual aggression and victimization in a national sample of higher education students. *Journal of Consulting and Clinical Psychology,* 55(2): 162–170.

Krafft-Ebing, R. 1906. *Psychopathia sexualis.* Brooklyn, NY: Physicians and Surgeons Book Company.

Kropp, P. R., Hart, S. D., & Lyon, D. R. 2002. Risk assessment of stalkers: Some problems and possible solutions. *Criminal Justice and Behavior,* 29: 590–616.

Krueger, R. B. & Kaplan. M. S. 1997. Frotteurism: Assessment and treatment. In D. R. Laws & W. O'Donohue (Eds.). *Sexual deviance: Theory, assessment, and treatment* (pp. 131–151). New York: The Guilford Press.

Krug, R. S. 1989. Adult male reports of childhood sexual abuse by mothers: Case descriptions, motivations and long-term consequences. *Child Abuse and Neglect* 13: 111–119.

Krulewitz, J. E., & Nash, J. E. 1979. Effects of rape victim resistance, assault outcome, and sex of observer on attributions about rape. *Journal of Personality,* 47: 557–574.

La Fond, J. Q. 2003. Outpatient commitment's next frontier: Sexual predators. *Psychology, Public Policy and Law,* 9(1/2): 159–182.

Labuschagne, G. 2003. Multi-murder: The challenges facing psychological investigators. Unpublished paper. Commander of the Investigative Psychology Unit, Serious and Violent Crime Component, Detective Service Head Office, South African Police Service.

Landlord jailed for raping sleepwalking tenant. 2001 October 24. Retrieved October 22, 2002 from: *http://www.crime .about.com/library/weekly/aa1z1100a.htm.*

Langevin, R., & Lang, R.A. 1987. The courtship disorders. In G. D. Wilson (Ed.), *Variant sexuality: Research and theory* (pp. 202–228). London: Croom Helm.

Langevin, R., Lang, R. A. & Curnoe, S. 1998. The prevalence of sex offenders with deviant fantasies. *Journal of Interpersonal Violence,* 13: 315–327.

Langstrom, N. & Grann, M. 2000. Risk for criminal recidivism among young sex offenders. *Journal of Interpersonal Violence,* 15(8): 855–871.

Lapeyre, J. 1998–2002. *The serial killer the cops ignored: The Henry Louis Wallace murders.* Retrieved on December 1, 2002 from *http://crimemagazine.com/Henrylouiswallacemurders.htm.*

Larratt, S. 2002 *MODCON: The secret world of extreme body modification, BMEZINE.com,* Kanada.

Lasser, M. 1999. *One man's stuggle.* Retrieved from Web search on October 30, 2002 from *http://www.pureintimacy.org/online1/essays/a0000018.html*

Laws, D. R. & O'Donahue, W. 1997 *Sexual deviance: Theory, assessment, and treatment.* New York: The Guilford Press.

Lea, S., Auburn, T., & Kibblewhite, K. 1999. Working with sex offenders: The perceptions and experiences of professionals and paraprofessionals. *International Journal of Offender Therapy and Comparative Criminology,* 43(1): 103–119.

Leach, C. 1998. Rape in antiquity: Sexual violence in the Greek and Roman worlds. *Notes and Queries,* 45(1): 154.

Lee, J. K. P, Pattison, P., Jackson H. J., & Ward, T. 2001. The general, common, and specific features of psychopathology for different types of paraphilias. *Criminal Justice and Behavior,* 28(2): 227–256

Lefley, H. P., Scott, C. S., Llabre, M., & Hicks, D. 1993. Cultural beliefs about rape and victims' response in three ethnic groups. *American Journal of Orthopsychiatry,* 63(4): 623–632.

Leitenberg, H., & Henning, K.. 1995. Sexual fantasy. *Psychological Bulletin.* Vol. 117, 469–496. Retrieved from PsycARTICLES on October 17, 2002.

Leo, J. 2001. The sex-change boom: Is politics the appropriate arena for this discussion? *U.S. News & World Report,* 130(10): ProQuest, 1–2.

LeVay, S. 2000. The science of sex: Breathless. Retrieved October 12, 2002 from *www.nerve.com/Regulars/Scienceofsex/10-31-00.*

Levine, S., Risen, C., & Althof, A. 1997. Paraphilic characteristics. In B. Strong, & C. De Vault (Eds.), *Human sexuality: Diversity in contemporary America* (pp. 329–330). Mountain View, CA: Mayfield Publishing.

Levine, S. B., Risen, C. B., & Althof, S. E. 1990. Essay on the diagnosis and nature of paraphilia. *Journal of Sex and Marital Therapy,* 16(2): 89–102.

———. 1994. Professionals who sexually offend: Evaluation procedures and preliminary findings. *Journal of Sex and Marital Therapy,* 20(4): 288–302.

Levitt, E. E., Moser, C., & Jamison, K. V. 1994. The prevalence and some attributes of females in the sadomasochistic subculture: A second report. *Archives of Sexual Behavior,* 23: 465–473.

Lewis, N. D. C. 1965. Pathological fire setting and sexual motivation. In R. Slovenko (Ed.), *Sexual behavior and the law.* Springfield, IL: Charles C Thomas.

Lewis, N. D., & Yarnell, H. 1951. Pathological fire setting (pyromania). *Nervous and Mental Disease Monographs,* 82.

Lewis, N. D. C., & Yarnell, H. 1951. *Pathological firesetting (pyromania).* New York: Coolidge Foundation Publishers.

Lidz, T., & Fleck, S. 1963. *The family and the human adaptation.* New York: Brunner/Mazel.

Lieb, R., Quinsey, V., & Berliner, L. 1998. Sexual predators and social policy. *Crime and Justice,* 23: 43.

Lieberman, D. A. 1993. *Learning behaviour and cognition* (2nd ed.). Sterling, CA: Brooks/Cole.

Linedecker, C. L. 1993. *Prison groupies: The shocking true story of the women who love America's deadliest criminals.* New York: Windsor Publishing.

———. 1998. *The vampire killers.* New York: St. Martin's Press.

Linzey, A. 2000. On zoophilia. *The Animals' Agenda,* 20(3): 29.

Lipsitz, J. D., Martin, L. Y., Mannuzza, S., Chapman, T. F., Liebowitz, M. R., Klien, D. F., & Fryer, A. J. 1994. Childhood separation anxiety disorder in patients with adult anxiety disorders. *American Journal of Psychiatry,* 151: 927–929.

Lisak, D., & Roth, S. 1988. Motivational factors in nonincarcerated sexually aggressive men. *Journal of Personality and Social Psychology,* 55(5): 795–802

Litman, L. C. 1999. *A case of pyrophilia.* Canadian Psychiatric Association. Retrieved December 1, 2002 from: *http://www.cpa-apc.org/publications/archives/bulletin/1999/feb/clinical_review.htm.*

Livingstone, T. 2002, August 3. *Face of a killer vampire.* The Western Mail. Calgary, Canada.

Lo, V., & Wei, R. 2002. Third-person effect, gender pornography on the Internet. *Journal of Broadcasting & Electronic Media,* 46: 13–28.

Long, R. 2002, November 25. The color of killing. *National Review.* Retrieved December 1, 2002 from ProQuest.

Lothstein, L. M. 2001. Treatment of non-incarcerated sexually compulsive/addictive offenders in an integrated, multimodal, and psychodynamic group therapy model. *International Journal of Group Psychotherapy,* 51: 553.

Lotke, E. 1996. Sex offenders: Does treatment work?, *Corrections Compendium,* 21: 1.

Lott, B., & Saxon, S. 2002. The influence of ethnicity, social class, and context on judgments about U.S. women. *The Journal of Social Psychology,* 142(2): 481–499.

Lussier, P., Proulx, J., & McKibben, A. 2001. Personality characteristics and adaptive strategies to cope with negative emotional states and deviant sexual fantasies in sexual aggressors. *International Journal of Offender Therapy and Comparative Criminology,* 45(2): 159–170.

Maccaskill, J. 2001, June 23. What do you want, blood?: Fangs are really looking up for vampires. *The Scottish Daily Record.* Edinburgh, Scotland.

MacLean, P. 1990. *The triune brain in evolution.* New York: Plenum Press.

Macrae, C. N., & Shephard, J. W. 1989. Do criminal stereotypes mediate juridic judgments? *British Journal of Social Psychology,* 28: 189–191.

Mahler, M. S., Pine, F., & Bergman, A. 1975. *The psychological birth of the human being.* New York: Basic Books.

Mahlstedt, D., Falcone, D., & Rice-Spring, L. 1993. Dating violence education: What do students learn? *Journal of Human Justice,* 4: 101–117.

Main, M., & Solomon, J. 1990. Procedures for identifying infants as disorganized/disoriented during the Ainsworth Strange Situation. In M. T. Greenberg, D. Cicchetti, & E. M. Cummings (Eds.), *Attachment in the preschool years* (pp. 121–182). Chicago: The University of Chicago Press.

Malamuth, N. M. 1986. Predictors of naturalist sexual aggression. *Journal of Personality and Social Psychology,* 50: 953–962.

Malamuth, N. M., & Donnerstein. E. 1984. *Pornography and sexual aggression.* Orlando: Academic Press.

Malamuth, N., Addison, T., & Koss, M. 2000. Pornography and sexual aggression: Are there reliable effects and can we understand them? *Annual Review of Sex Research.* Mount Vernon: Society for the Scientific Study of Sex. Retrieved from PsycARTICLES on October 17, 2002.

Male serial killers: Serial killers A–Z. (n.d.). Retrieved October 31, 2002 from: *http://darkday.tripod.com/a-h/cole/html.*

Maletzky, B. M. 2002. The paraphilias: Research and treatment. In N. Gorman (Ed.), *A guide to treatments that work* (pp. 525–557). New York: Oxford University Press.

Maltz, W., & Holman, B. 1987. *Incest and sexuality: A guide to understanding and healing.* Lexington, MA: Lexington Books.

Manassis, K., & Bradley, S. J. 1994. The development of childhood anxiety disorders: Toward an integrated model. *Journal of Applied Developmental Psychology,* 15: 345–366.

Mangan, M. 2002. *Sleepsex.org Newsletter.* Retrieved October 24, 2002 from: *http://www.sleepsex.org/text/newsletter%50archive/may2002.html.*

Marie-Josephe & Chopin-Marce 2001. Exhibitionism and psychotherapy: A case study. *International Journal of Offender Therapy and Comparative Criminology,* 45: 626–633.

Marotta, S. W., & Asner, K. K. 1999, Summer. Group psychotherapy for women with a history of incest: The research base. *Journal of Counseling Development,* 77: 315–323.

Marriage made in prison: What leads a woman to marry a convicted killer? (2002, September 27). Retrieved December 7, 2002 from *http://abcnews.go.com/sections/2020/DailyNews/2020 _menendez020927.html.*

Marshall, W. L. 1989. Intimacy, loneliness and sexual offenders. *Behaviour Research and Therapy,* 27: 491–503.

———. 1999. Current status of North American assessment and treatment programs for sexual offenders. *Journal of Interpersonal Violence,* 14(3): 221–239.

Marshall, W. L., & Barbaree, H. E. 1990. An integrated theory of the etiology of sexual offending. In W. L. Marshall, D. R. Laws, & H. E. Barbaree (Eds.), *Handbook of sexual assault: Issue, theories, and treatment of the offender* (pp. 257–275). New York: Plenum

Marshall, W. L., & Christie, M. M. 1981. Pedophilia and aggression. *Criminal Justice and Behavior,* 8: 145–158.

Marshall, W. L., & Williams, S. 2001. The assessment and treatment of sexual offenders. In *Compendium 2000 on Effective Correctional Programming* (pp. 135–145). Ottawa, Canada: Correctional Service Canada.

Martin, P. Y., & Hummer, R. 1989. Fraternities and rape on campus. *Gender and Society,* 3: 457–473.

Marvasti, J. M. 1986. Incestuous mothers. *American Journal of Forensic Psychology,* 7(4): 63–69.

Masters, W., Johnson, V., & Kolodny, R. 1982. *Human sexuality.* Boston: Little Brown.

Mathews, R. 1987. *Preliminary typology of female sex offenders.* MN: PHASE and Genesis II for Women.

Mathews, R., Matthews, J. K., & Speltz, K. 1989. *Female sexual offenders: An exploratory study.* Orwell, VT: The Safer Society Press.

Mathis, J. L. 1972. *Clear thinking about sexual deviation.* Chicago: Nelson Hall.

Mawhinney, V. T. 1998. Behavioral maladaption contagion in America: An applied theoretical analysis. *Behavior and Social Issues,* 8(2): 159–185.

Maxwell, S. R., & Maxwell, C. D. 2000. Examining the "criminal careers" of prostitutes within the nexus of drug use, drug selling and other illicit activities. *Criminology,* 38(3): 787–810.

Maynard, C., & Wiederman, M. 1997. Undergraduate students' perceptions of child sexual abuse: Effects of age, sex and gender-role attitudes. *Child Abuse & Neglect,* 21(9): 833–844.

Mayseless, O., Danieli, R., & Sharabany, R. 1996. Adults' attachment patterns and coping with separation. *Journal of Youth and Adolescence,* 25: 667–690.

McCammon, S., Knox, D., & Schacht, C. 1993. *Choices in sexuality.* Minneapolis, MN: West.

McCarthy, B. W. 1994. Sexually compulsive men and inhibited sexual desire. *Journal of Sex and Marital Therapy,* 20: 200–209.

McCarty, L. M. 1986. Mother-child incest: Characteristics of the offender. *Child Welfare,* 65(5): 447–458.

McCollaum, B., & Lester, D. 1994. Violent sexual fantasies and sexual behavior. *Psychological Reports,* 75: 742.

McCully, R. S. 1992. Vampirism: A historical perspective and underlying process in relation to a case of auto-vampirism. In R. Noll (Ed.). *Vampires, werewolves and demons: Twentieth century reports in the psychiatric literature* (pp. 37–56). New York: Brunner/Mazel.

McDonald, J., & Bradford, W. 2000. The treatment of sexual deviation using a pharmacological approach. *The Journal of Sex Research,* 37(3): 248–257.

McGrath, P., Marshall, P., & Prior, P. 1979. A comprehensive treatment program for a firesetting child. *Journal of Behavioral Therapy and Experimental Psychiatry,* 10: 69–72.

McGuire, R. J., Carlisle, J. M., & Young, B. G. 1965. Sexual deviations as conditioned behavior: A hypothesis. *Behavior Research and Therapy,* 2: 185–190.

McKenacher, D. W., & Dacre, J. I. 1966. A study of arsonists in a special security hospital. *British Journal of Psychiatry,* 112: 1151–1154.

McNally, R. T., & Florescu, R. 1994. *In search of Dracula: The history of Dracula & vampires.* New York: Houghton Mifflin.

McNamara, J. J. & Morton, R. J. 2004. Frequency of serial sexual homicide victimization in Virginia for a ten-year period. *Journal of Forensic Sciences,* May, 49(3).

Mead, B. T. 1975. Coping with obscene phone calls. *Medical Aspects of Human Sexuality,* 9: 127–128.

Meigs, A., & Barlow, K. 2002. Beyond the taboo: Imagining incest. *American Anthropologist,* 104(1): 38–49.

Mendel, M. P. 1995. *The Male survivor; the impact of sexual abuse.* Thousand Oaks, CA: Sage Publications.

Meston, C. M., Heiman, J. R., & Trapnell, P. D. 1999. The relation between early abuse and adult sexuality. *The Journal of Sex Research,* 36: 385–395.

Miccio-Fonseca, L. C. (2001, May). *Sexual deviancy.* Symposium conducted at the annual training conference of the California Coalition on Sexual Offending, Irvine, California.

Miller, R. 1998. Forced administration of sex-drive reducing medications to sex offenders: treatment or punishment? *Psychology, Public Policy, and Law,* 4(1–2): 175–199. Retrieved from PsycArticles on November 26, 2002.

Milner, J. S., & Dopke, C. A. 1997. Paraphilia not otherwise specified: Psychopathology and theory. In D. R. Laws, & W. O'Donohue. *Sexual deviance: Theory, assessment and treatment* (pp. 394–423). New York: The Guilford Press.

Minaar, A. 2001. Witch purging and muti murder in South Africa: The legislative and legal challenges to combating these practices with specific reference to the Witchcraft Suppression Act (No. 3 of 1957, amended by Act No. 50 of 1970). *African Legal Studies,* 2: 1–21.

Mitchell, S. A., & Black, M. J. 1995. *Freud and beyond: A history of modern psychoanalytic thought.* New York: Basic Books.

Moergen, S., Merkel, W., & Brown, S. 1991. The use of covert sensitization and social skills training in the treatment of an obscene telephone caller. *The Journal of Behavior, Therapy, & Experimental Psychiatry,* 21: 269–275.

Mohandie, K. 2000. "Playing God": Case study of a modern day vampire. Presentation for a training of Los Angeles Criminal Investigators (LAPD).

Mohr, J. 1977. *The paedophilias: Their clinical, legal and social implications.* In B. Schlesinger (Ed.), *Sexual behaviour in Canada: Patterns and problems.* Toronto: University of Toronto Press.

Mohr, J. W., Turner, R. E., & Jerry, M. B. 1964. *Pedophilia and exhibitionism.* Toronto, Canada: University of Toronto Press.

Monahan, J. 2000. Violence risk assessment: Scientific validity and evidentiary admissibility. *Washington and Lee Law Review,* 57(3): 901–909.

Monahan, J., Steadman, H. J., Appelbaum, P. S., Robbins, P. C., Mulvey, E. P., Silver, E., Roth, L. H., & Grisso, T. 2000. Developing a clinically useful actuarial tool for assessing violence risk. *British Journal of Psychiatry,* 176: 312–319.

Money, J. 1981. *Love and love sickness: The science of sex, gender difference and pair-bonding.* Baltimore: Johns Hopkins University Press

Money, J. 1984. Paraphilias: Phenomenology and classification. *American Journal of Psychotherapy,* 38: 164–179.

———. 1986. *Lovemaps: Clinical concepts of sexual/erotic health and psychology, paraphilias, and gender transposition in childhood, adolescence, and maturity.* New York: Irvington.

———. 1988. *Gay, straight and in between.* New York: Oxford Press.

———. 1989. *Lovemaps: Clinical concepts of sexual/erotic health and pathology.* Buffalo, NY: Prometheus Books.

———. 1990. Paraphilia in females: Fixation on amputation and lameness: Two personal accounts. *Journal of Psychology and Human Sexuality,* 3: 165–172.

———. 1999. *The Lovemap Guidebook: A Definitive Statement.* New York: Continuum.

Moran v. People, 25 Mich. 356 (1872).

Morgan, R., & Steinem, G. 1980. The international crime of genital mutilation. *Archives of General Psychiatry,* 32: 1409–1013.

Morneau, R. H., Jr. & Rockwell, R. 1980. *Sex, motivation and the criminal offender.* Springfield, IL: Charles C Thomas.

Morse, D. R. 1993. The stressful kiss: A biopsychosocial evaluation of the origins, evolution, and societal significance of vampirism. *Stress Medicine,* 9: 181–199.

Morton, J. 1990. *The unrepentant necrophile.* Retrieved September 26, 2002 from California State University at Berkeley website: *http://csua.berkeley.edu/~aspolito.*

Mosher, D., & Anderson, R. 1986. Macho personality, sexual aggression, and reactions to guided imagery of realistic rape. *Journal of Research in Personality,* 20: 77–94.

Mossman, D. 1994. Assessing predictions of violence: Being accurate about accuracy. *Journal of Consulting and Clinical Psychology,* 62(4): 783–792.

Muir, G., & Lonsway, K. A. 1996. Rape myth acceptance among Scottish and American students. *Journal of Social Psychology,* 136(2): 261.

Munroe, R. L., & Gauvain, M. 2001. Why the paraphilias? Domesticating strange sex. *Cross-Cultural Research,* 35: 44–61.

Murray, J. B. 2000. Psychological profile of pedophiles and child molesters. *The Journal of Psychology,* 134(2): 211–224.

Myers, W. A. 1991. A case history of a man who made obscene telephone calls and practiced frotteurism. In G. I. Fogel & W. A. Myers (Eds.). *Perversions and near-perversions in clinical practice.* New York: Vail-Ballou Press.

———. 1995. Addictive sexual behavior. *American Journal of Psychotherapy,* 49: 473–480.

Nagler, S. 1957. Fetishism: A review and a case study. *Psychiatric Quarterly,* 31: 713–741.

Nandon, S. M., Koverola, C., & Schulderman, E. H. 1998. Antecedents to prostitution: Childhood victimization. *Journal of Interpersonal Violence,* 13: 206–221.

Neil, W. 2000. A psychoanalytic contribution to psychic vampirism: A case vignette. *The American Journal of Psychoanalysis,* 60(2): 177–186.

Neuwirth, W., & Eher, R. 2003. What differentiates between anal rapists and vaginal rapists. *International Journal of Offender Therapy and Comparative Criminology,* 47(4): 482–488.

Nobus, D. 2002. Over my dead body: On the histories and cultures of necrophilia. In R. Goodwin & D. Cramer (Eds.), *Inappropriate relationships: The unconventional, the disapproved, and the forbidden* (pp. 171–189). Mahwah, NJ: Lawrence Erlbaum Associates, Inc.

Noffsinger, S. G., & Resnick, P. J. 2000. Sexual predator laws and offenders with addictions. *Psychiatric Annals,* 30, 1–9. Retrieved September 27, 2002, from the ProQuest database.

———. 2000. Sexual predator laws and offenders with addictions. *Psychiatric Annals,* 30: 602.

———. 2000. Sexual predator laws and offenders with addictions. *Psychiatric Annals.* Retrieved from ProQuest on October 17, 2002.

Noll, R. 1992. *Vampires, werewolves and demons: Twentieth century reports in the psychiatric literature.* New York: Brunner/Mazel.

North American Man-Boy Love Association (2003). *www.nambla1.com.*

Noyes, J. K. 1997. *The mastery of submission: Inventories of masochism.* Ithaca & London: Cornell University Press. *http://www.ensexlopedia.com/Sex/Education/paraphilia.htm.*

O'Brien, M. J. & Bera, W. H. 1985. Adolescent sexual offenders: A descriptive typology. *Preventing Sexual Abuse,* 1: 1–4.

O'Connor, A. A. 1987. Female sex offenders. *British Journal of Psychiatry,* 150: 615–620.

O'Connor, T. 2001. *Characteristics of fire setters.* Retrieved December 1, 2002 from: *http://faculty.ncwc.edu/toconnor/401/401lect20.htm.*

O'Rourke, T. 2002. How to seek pleasure in public places. *Cosmopolitan,* 233: 156.

O'Sullivan, C. (Ed.). 1997. The commonwealth fund survey of the health of adolescent girls. *The Commonwealth Fund.* New York: Commission on Women's Health.

O'Sullivan, C. S. 1991. Acquaintance gang rape on campus. In A. Parrot & L. Bechhofer (Eds.), *Acquaintance rape: The hidden crime* (pp. 140–156). New York: John Wiley & Sons.

Oberholser, J. C., & Beck, J. 1986. Multimethod assessment of rapists, child molesters, and three control groups on behavioral and psychological measures. *Journal of Consulting and Clinical Psychology,* 54: 682–687.

Observant. The Official Homepage of the First Church of Zoophilia. (2002, October 27). *http://www.thoughtshop.com/fcz/.*

Open Love Christian Community. (2000). *Advanced topics in human sexuality.* Retrieved September 30, 2002 from *http://www.geocities.com/openlcc/se601.html.*

Pa, M. 2001. Beyond the pleasure principle: The criminalization of consensual sadomasochistic sex. *Texas Journal of Women and the Law,* 11: 51–92.

Palermo, G. B. 2001. Editorial: The dilemma of sexual offenders. *International Journal of Offender Therapy and Comparative Criminology,* 45(1): 3–5.

Palermo, G. B., & Farkas, M. A. 2001. *The dilemma of the sexual offender.* Springfield, IL: Charles C Thomas.

Peabody, G. A., Rowe, A. T., & Wall, J. H. 1954. Fetishism and transvestitism. *Journal of Nervous and Mental Disease,* 153: 339–350.

Pedophile Liberation Front (2003). *www.childlove.org.*

Peebles, J. E. 1999. Therapeutic jurisprudence and the sentencing of sexual offenders in Canada. *International Journal of Offender Therapy and Comparative Criminology,* 43(3): 275–290.

Pellegrino, C. 1994. *Return to Sodom and Gomorrah.* New York: Avon Books.

Penrose, V. 1970. *The bloody countess: The crimes of Erzebet Bathory.* London: Creation Books.

People v. Cassandras, 83 Cal. App. 2d 272 (1948)

People v. Tobias, 25 Cal. 4th 327 (2001).

Perry, G. P., & Orchard, J. 1992. *Assessment and treatment of adolescent sex offenders.* Sarasota, FL: Professional Resource Press.

Person, E., & Ovesey, L. 1978. Transvestism: New perspectives. *Journal of the American Academy of Psychoanalysis,* 6(3): 301–323.

Petter, L. M., & Witehill, D. L. 1998. Management of female sexual assault. *American Family Physician,* 58(4): 920–926.

Phares, E. J. 1991. *Introduction to personality* (3rd ed.). New York: HarperCollins.

Phillips, A. 1998. *A defense of masochism.* New York: St. Martin's Press.

Phillips, D. M., & Troyano, R. 1998. *Community notification as viewed by Washington's citizens.* Olympia, WA: Washington State Institute for Public Policy.

Pithers, W., & Gray, A. 1997. Personal communication cited in Araji, S.K. 1997. *Sexually aggressive children.* London: Sage

Plante, T. G. 1999. *Contemporary Clinical Psychology.* New York: John Wiley & Sons, Inc.

Polaschek, D. L. L., Ward, T., & Hudson, S. M. 1997. Rape and rapists: Theory and treatment. *Clinical Psychology Review,* 17(2): 117–144.

Pollock, N. L., & Hashmall, J. M. 1991. The excuses of child molesters. *Behavioral Science and the Law,* 9: 53–69.

Porter, S., Fairweather, D., Drugge, J., & Herve, H. 2000. Profiles of psychopathy in incarcerated sexual offenders. *Criminal Justice and Behavior,* 27(2): 216–233.

Prendergast, W. E. 1991. *Treating sex offenders in correctional institutions and outpatient clinics.* New York: Haworth Press.

Prentky, R. A., & Burgess, A. W. 2000. Diagnosis and classification. In R. A. Prentky, & A. W. Burgess (Eds.). *Forensic management of sexual offenders* (pp. 24–69). New York: Kluwer Academic/ Plenum Publishers.

Prentky, R. A., & Knight, R. A. 1991. Identifying critical dimensions for discriminating among rapists. *Journal of Counsulting and Clinical Psychology,* 59: 643–661.

Prentky, R. A., Knight, R. A., Sims-Knight, J. E., & Straus, F. 1989. Developmental antecedents of sexual aggression. *Development and Psychopathology,* 1: 153–169.

Prentky, R. A., Lee, A. F. S., Knight, R. A., & Cerce, D. 1997. Recidivism rates among child molesters and rapists: A methodological analysis. *Law and Human Behavior,* 21(6): 635–659.

Price, M., Gutheil, T. G., Commons, M. L., Kafka, M. P., & Dodd-Kimmey, S. 2001. Telephone scatologia: Comorbidity and theories of etiology. *Psychiatric Annals,* 31: 226–232.

Price, M., Gutheil, T., Commons, M., Kafka, M., & Dodd-Kimmey, S. 2001. Redefining telephone scatologia: Treatment and classification. *Psychiatric Annals,* 31: 282–289.

Price, M., Kafka, M., Commons, M., Gutheil, T., & Simpson, W. 2002. Telephone scatologia comorbidity with other paraphilias and paraphilia-related disorders. *International Journal of Law and Psychiatry,* 25: 37–49.

Prins, H. 1985. Vampirism, a clinical condition. *British Journal of Psychiatry,* 146: 666–668.

Purcell, C. 2000. *An investigation of paraphilias, lust murder and the case of Jeffrey Dahmer: An investigative model.* Fresno, CA: Doctoral Dissertation.

Pyromania. 2000. *http://jhhs.client.web-health.com/web-health/topics/GeneralHealth/generalhealth-sub/generalhealth/psychological/pyromania.html.*

Pyromania. 2001. *http://healthinmind.com/english/pyrom.html.*

Quinn, J., & Twomey, P. 1998. A case of auto-erotic asphyxia in a long-term psychiatric setting. *Psychopathology,* 31(4): 169–173.

Quinsey, V. L. 1986. Men who have sex with children. In D. Weisstub. (Ed.), *Law and Mental Health: International Perspectives* (Vol. 2) pp. (140–172). New York: Pergamon Press.

Quinsey, V. L., Chaplin, T. C., & Upfold, D. 1989. Arsonists and sexual arousal to firesetting: Correlation unsupported. *Journal of Behavior Therapy and Experimental Psychiatry,* 20: 203–209.

Quist, R. M., & Matshazi, D. G. M. 2000. The child and adolescent functional assessment scale (CAFAS): A dynamic predictor of juvenile recidivism. *Adolescence,* 35: 181–192.

Rachman, S., & Hodgson, R. J. 1968. Experimentally induced "sexual fetishism": Replication and development. *Psychological Record,* 18: 25–27.

Radley, L. 2001, July. Attitudes towards sex offenders. *Forensic Update,* 66.

Rajs, J., Lundstrom, M., Broberg, M., Lidberg, L., & Linquist, O. 1998. Criminal mutilation of the human body in Sweden—a thirty year medico-legal and forensic psychiatric study. *Journal of Forensic Sciences,* 43(3): 580–653.

Ramsland, K. 1998. *Piercing the darkness: Undercover with vampires in America today.* New York: Harper Collins.

Raptor, Y. 2002, November 4. *http://us.vclart.net/vcl/Artists/Yiffy-Raptor/Zoophilia_Report.rtf.*

Raymond, N. C., Coleman, E., Ohlerking, F., Christenson, G. A., & Miner, M. 1999. Psychiatric comorbidity in pedophilic sex offenders. *The American Journal of Psychiatry,* 156(5): 786–788.

Redding, R. E. 1997. Juveniles transferred to criminal court: Legal reform proposals based on social science research. *Utah Law Review,* 709–763.

Redondo, S., Luque, E., & Funes, J. 1996. Social beliefs about recidivism in crime. In G. Davies, S. Lloyd-Bostock, M. McMurran & C. Wilson. (Eds.), *Psychology, law and criminal justice: International developments in research and practice* (pp. 394–400). New York: Walter de Gruyter.

Reidy, T. J., & Hochstadt, N. J. 1993. Attribution of blame in incest cases: A comparison of mental health professionals. *Child Abuse & Neglect,* 17: 371–381.

Reinhardt, J. M. 1957. *Sex perversions and sex crimes.* Springfield, IL: Charles C Thomas.

Reiss, A. J., & J. A. Roth (Eds.) 1993. *Understanding and preventing violence.* Washington, DC: National Academy Press.

Renshaw, K. 1997. Infant sexuality. In B. Strong & C. DeVault (Eds.), *Human sexuality: Diversity in contemporary America* (pp. 158–9). Mountain View, CA: Mayfield Publishing Company.

Resnick, H. L. P. 1983. Eroticized repetitive hangings. In L. B. Schlesinger & E. Revitch (Eds.) *Sexual dynamics of anti-social behavior* (pp. 228–245). Springfield, IL: Charles C Thomas.

Ressler, R., Burgess, A., & Douglas, J. 1988. *Sexual homicide: Patterns and motives.* Lexington MA: Lexington Books.

Ressler, R. K., Burgess, A. W., Hartman, C. R., Douglas, J. E. & McCormick, A. 1986. Murderers who rape and mutilate. *Journal of Interpersonal Violence,* 1(3): 273–287.

Rice, M. E., & Harris, G. T. 2002. Men who molest their sexually immature daughters: Is a special explanation required? *Journal of Abnormal Psychology,* 111(2): 329–339.

Rickles, N. K. 1950. *Exhibitionism* (1st ed.). Philadelphia, PA: J.B. Lippincott Company.

Rinehart, N. J., & McCabe, M. P. 1998. An empirical investigation of hypersexuality. *Sexual and Marital Therapy,* 13(4): 369.

Ritter, J. 1995, January 12. Sex offender notices: Public safety vs. rights. *USA Today,* p. 7A.

Roberts, J. V., & Stalans, L. J. 1997. *Public opinion, crime and criminal justice.* Boulder, CO: Westview Press.

Roberts, J. V., & White, N. R. 1986. Public estimates of recidivism rates: Consequences of a criminal stereotype. *Canadian Journal of Criminology,* 28: 229–241.

Roberts, J. V., Grossman, M. G., & Gebotys, R. J. 1996. Rape reform in Canada: Public knowledge and opinion. *Journal of Family Violence,* 11(2): 133–147.

Robinson, B. 2001 *The unusual suspects; Female sex offenders are rare, driven by more than sex.* Retrieved November 30, 2002 from *http://abcnews.go.com/sections/us/DailyNews/female_sex offenders0101015.html.*

Roche, T. 2000, March 20. The joy of sex with the dead. *San Francisco Bay Guardian.* Retrieved November 3, 2002 from: *http://www.burknet.com/robsfantasy/secadd05.html.*

Roheim, G. 1932. Psychoanalysis of primitive cultural types. *International Journal of Psychoanalysis* 13: 1–224.

Romans, J. S. C., Hays, J. R., & White, T. K. 1996. Stalking and related behaviors experienced by counseling center staff members from current or former clients. *Professional Psychology: Research and Practice,* 27: 595–599.

Rosen, I. 1996. *Sexual deviation* (3rd ed.). Oxford, NY: Oxford University Press.

Rosenfeld, D. S., & Elhajjar, A. J. 1998. Sleepsex: A variant of sleepwalking. *Archives of Sexual Behavior,* 27(3): 269–278.

Rösler, A., & Witztum, E. 2000. Pharmacotherapy of paraphilias in the next millennium. *Behavioral Sciences and the Law,* 18(1): 43–56.

Rothenberg, J. 2002. *The role of fantasy.* Retrieved December 1, 2002 from: *http://www.courttv.com/onair/shows/profiler/column_1023.html.*

Rothman, G. 1999, October 14. Assumptions about Greeks unfairly based on stereotypes [Electronic version]. *Daily Bruin.* Retrieved November 22, 2002 from *http://www.dailybruin.ucla.edu/db/issues/99/10.14/view.rothman.html.*

Rozee, P. D. 1993. Forbidden or forgiven? Rape in cross-cultural perspective. *Psychology of Women Quarterly,* 17: 499–514.

Rubin, B. 1975. Prediction of dangerousness in mentally ill criminals. In S. A. Pasternack (Ed.), *Violence and victims* (pp. 15–40). New York: Spectrum Publications, Ltd.

Rucki, E. 1997. *Essay: The sexual motivation behind the vampire.* Retrieved September 27, 2002 from *http://members.aol.com/RAVEN2DOVE/sexualmotive.html.*

Safarik, M. E., Jarvis, J. P., & Nussbaum, K. E. 2002. Sexual homicide of elderly females: Linking offender characteristics to victim and crime scene attributes. *Journal of Interpersonal Violence,* 17(5).

Sanday, P. R. 1981. The socio-cultural context of rape: A cross-cultural study. *Journal of Social Issues, 37*(4): 5–27.

———. 1990. Fraternity gang rape: Sex brotherhood, and privilege on campus. New York: New York University Press.

Sandnabba, N. K., Santtila, P., & Nordling, N. 1999. Sexual behavior and social adaptation among sadomasochistically oriented males. *The Journal of Sex Research, 36*(3): 282.

Santtila, P., Sandnabba, N. K., Alison, L., & Nordling, N. 2002. Investigating the underlying structure in sadomasochistically oriented behavior. *Archives of Sexual Behavior, 31*(2): 185–196.

Sarrel, P. M., & Masters, W. H. 1982. Sexual molestation of men by women. *Archives of Sexual Behaviour, 11*(2): 117–131.

Saunders, E. J. 1988. A comparative study of attitudes towards child sexual abuse among social work and judicial system professionals. *Child Abuse and Neglect, 12*: 83–90.

Sawle, G. A., & Kear-Colwell, J. 2001. Adult attachment style and pedophilia: A developmental perspective. *International Journal of Offender Therapy and Comparative Criminology, 45*(1): 32–50.

Saxl, M. V. 1998. The struggle to make stalking a crime: A legislative road map of how to develop effective stalking legislation in Maine. *Seton Hall Legislative Journal, 23*: 57.

Schell, B. H., & Lanteigne, N. M. 2000. *Stalking, harassment, and murder in the workplace: Guidelines for protection and prevention.* Westport, CT: Quorum Books.

Schmid, E. 1914. Zur Psychologie der Brandstifter; *Psychologische abhandlungen, band I,* pp. 80–179, cited in Slovenko (1965).

Schofield, R. L. 1999. *Sex offender recidivism: An evaluation of the state of Nevada community notification sex offender assessment scale.* Unpublished doctoral dissertation, California School of Professional Psychology.

Schott, R. L. 1995. The childhood and family dynamics of transvestites. *Archives of Sexual Behavior, 24*(3): 309–327.

Schwartz, M. D., & Nogrady, C. A. 1996. Fraternity membership, rape myths, and sexual aggression on a college campus. *Violence Against Women, 2*(2): 148–162.

Schwartz, M. D., DeKeseredy, W. S., Tait, D., & Alvi, S. 2001. Male peer support and a feminist routine activities theory: Understanding sexual assault on the college campus. *Justice Quarterly, 18*(3): 623–649.

Scott, C. S., Lefley, H. P., Hicks, D. 1993. Potential risk factors for rape in three ethnic groups. *Community Mental Health Journal, 29*(2): 133–141.

Scott, J. E., & Curvelier, F. 1993. Violence and sexual violence in pornography: Is it really increasing? *Archives of Sexual Behavior, 22*(4): 357–372.

Seidman, B. T., Marshall, W. L., Hudson, S. M., & Robertson, P. J. 1994. An examination of intimacy and lonliness in sex offenders. *Journal of Interpersonal Violence, 9*(4): 518–534.

Seligman, L., & Hardenburg, S. A. 2000. Assessment and treatment of paraphilias. *Journal of Counseling and Development, 78*: 107–113.

Serber, M. 1970. Shame aversion therapy. *Journal of Behavioral Therapy and Experimental Psychiatry, 1*(3): 213–215.

Shapiro, C. M., Fedoroff, J. P., & Trajanovic, N. N. 1996. Sexual behavior in sleep: A newly described parasomnia. *Sleep Research, 25*: 367.

Sharp, D. 1993, October 5. 'Granny Killer' stalks Fla. County. *USA Today*, A6.

Shaw, J. 1999. *Sexual aggression.* Washington, DC: American Psychiatric Press, Inc.

Shear, K. M. 1996. Factors in the etiology and pathogenesis of panic disorder: Revisiting the attachment-separation paradigm. *American Journal of Psychiatry, 153*: 125–136.

Sheinber, M., & Fraenkel, P. 2001. The relational trauma of incest: A family based approach to treatment. New York: The Guilford Press.

Sheptycki, J. W. E. 1999. Contemporary perspectives on serial murder/Serial murder. *The British Journal of Criminology, 39*: 323–329.

Sholevar, G. P., & Schwoeri, L. D. 1999. Sexual aggression in the family. In J. A. Shaw (Ed.), *Sexual aggression* (pp. 75–106). Washington, DC: American Psychiatric Press.

Shortes, C. 1998. "Cleaning up a sewer": The containment of S/M pornography. *Journal of Popular Film & Television, 26*: 72–79.

Sigall, H., & Ostrove, N. 1975. Beautiful but dangerous: Effects of offender attractiveness and nature of crime of juridic judgment. *Journal of Personality and Social Psychology, 31*: 410–441.

Sigusch, V. 1998. The neosexual behavior. *Archives of Sexual Behavior, 27*(4): 331–359.

Silberstein, J. A. 1998. Matricide: A paradigmatic case in family violence. *International Journal of Offender Therapy and Comparative Criminology, 42*(3): 210–223.

Silver, E., Smith, W. R., & Bankes, S. 2000. Constructing actuarial devices for predicting recidivism: A comparison of methods. *Criminal Justice and Behavior, 27*(6): 733–764.

Silverstein, J. L. 1996. Exhibitionism as countershame. *Sexual Addiction & Compulsivity, 3*(1): 33–42.

Simon, W., & Gagnon, J. H. 1986. Sexual scripts: Permanence and change. *Archives of Sexual Behavior, 15*: 97–120.

Simpson, G., Tate, R., Ferry, K., Hodgkinson, A., & Blaszczynski, A. 2001. Social, neuroradiologic, medical, and neuropsychological correlates of sexually aberrant behavior after traumatic brain injury: A controlled study. *The Journal of Head Trauma Rehabilitation, 16*: 556–569.

Slater, L. 2000. How do you cure a sex addict? *New York Times Magazine.* Retrieved from ProQuest on October 17, 2002.

Slobogin, C. 2002. Modern studies in privacy law: Searching for the meaning of Fourth Amendment privacy after Kyllo v. United States: Peeping techno-Toms and the Fourth Amendment: Seeing through Kyllo's rules governing technological surveillance. *Minnesota Law Review, 86*: 1393.

Slovenko, R. 1965. *Sexual behavior and the law.* Springfield, IL: Charles C Thomas.

Smallbone, S. W., & Dadds, M. R. 2001. Further evidence for a relationship between attachment insecurity and coercive sexual behavior in non-offenders. *Journal of Interpersonal Violence, 16*: 22–35.

Smith, M. D., & Morra, N. N. 1994. Obscene and threatening telephone calls to women: Data from a Canadian national survey. *Gender & Society, 8*(4): 584–596.

Snell, W. E., Jr., & Papini, D. R. 1989. The sexuality scale: An instrument to measure sexual-esteem, sexual-depression and sexual-preoccupation. *Journal of Sex Research, 26*: 256–263.

Society for Human Sexuality. 2002. Retrieved 11/04/02 from *http://www.sexuality.org/l/fetish/asffeeet.html.*

Soltys, S. M. 1992. Pyromania and fire setting behaviors. *Psychiatric Annals, 22*(2): 79–83.

Speaker, J. T. 1989. *A review of psychosexual infantilism in adults: The eroticisation of regression.* [Online]. Retrieved from *http://www.sexuality.org*

Sroufe, L. A. 1996. *Emotional development.* New York: Cambridge University Press.

Stadolnik, R. J. 1999. Child and juvenile firesetting behavior: Psychological moves from myth to facts. *Massachusetts Psychological Association Quarterly, 42*: 8–16.

———. 2000. *Drawn to the flame: Assessment and treatment of juvenile firesetting behavior.* Sarasota, FL: Professional Resource Press.

Stalans, L.J. 1993. Citizens' crime stereotypes, biased recall, and punishment preferences in abstract cases: The educative role of interpersonal sources. *Law and Human Behavior, 17*(4): 451–470.

Stalans, L. J., & Diamond, S. S. 1990. Formation and change in lay evaluations of criminal sentencing. *Law and Human Behavior, 14*(3): 199–214.

Stalans L. J., & Lurigio, A. J. 1990. Lay and professionals' beliefs about crime and criminal sentencing: A need for theory, perhaps schema theory. *Criminal Justice and Behavior, 17*(3): 333–349.

Star Tribune National Poll. 1991. Storrs, CT: Roper Center Public Opinion Online.

State v. Dionne, 814 So. 2d 1087 (2002).

State v. Vines, 487 SE2nd 521 (GA App 1997).

Steadman, H. J., Silver, E., Monahan, J., Appelbaum, P. S., Robbins, P. C., Mulvey, E. P., Grisso, T., Roth, L. H., & Banks, S. 2000. A Classification Tree approach to the development of actuarial violence risk assessment tools. *Law and Human Behavior, 24*(1): 83–100.

Steck, R. N. 1992. The American dream 1992: A long trek. *Dun and Bradstreet, Inc. D & B Reports,* 40(4): 26.

Steckel, W. 1952. *Patterns of psychosexual infantilism.* New York: Grove Press.

Stein, D., Black, D., Shapira, N., & Spitzer, R., 2001. Hypersexual disorder and preoccupation with Internet pornography. *The Journal of Psychiatry.* Washington: Americian Psychiatric Association. Retrieved from PsycARTICLES on October 17, 2002.

Stein, M. L. 1996. Sex with animals story stirs uproar. *Editor & Publisher,* 129(4): 10.

Stekel, W. 1943. *Peculiarities of behavior: Wandering mania, dipsomania, kleptomania, pyromania, and allied impulsive acts* (Vol. 2). New York: Liveright Publishing Corporation.

Stermac, L. E., & Segal, Z. V. 1989. Adult sexual contact with children: An examination of cognitive factors. *Behaviour Therapy,* 20: 573–584.

Stermac, L., Du Mont, J., & Dunn, S. 1998. Violence in known-assailant sexual assaults. *Journal of Interpersonal Violence,* 13(3): 398–412.

Stermac, L., Hall, K., & Henskens, M. 1989. Violence among child molesters. *The Journal of Sex Research,* 26: 450–459.

Stewart, M. A., & Culver, K. W. 1982. Children who set fires: The clinical picture and a follow-up. *British Journal of Psychiatry,* 140: 357–363.

Steyn, M. 2001 Animal lovers: Life, liberty and the pursuit of . . . brute creatures. *The Spectator,* 20–21.

Stone, M. H. 2001. Serial sexual homicide: Biological, psychological and sociological aspects. *Journal of Personality Disorders,* 15(1): 1–14.

Storr, A. 1964. *Sexual deviation.* Baltimore: Penguin Books.

Stroller, R. J. 1991. *Pain & passion: A pyschoanalyst explores the world of S & M.* New York and London: Plenum Press.

Strong, B., & DeVault, C. 1997. *Human sexuality: Diversity in contemporary America.* Mountain View, CA: Mayfield Publishing.

Stryker, J. 1999, July 8. Sleepstabbing. *Health and Body.* Retrieved October 27, 2002 from: *http://www.salon.com/health/feature/1999/07/08/sleepwalking.*

Studer, L. H., Clelland, S. R., Aylwin, A. S., Reddon, J. R., & Monro, A. 2000. Rethinking risk assessment for incest offenders. *International Journal of Law and Psychiatry,* 23(1): 15–22.

Symonds, M. 1975. The accidental victim of violent crime. In S. A. Pasternack (Ed.), *Violence and victims* (pp. 91–99). New York: Spectrum Publications, Ltd.

Taormino, T. 2002. I like to watch. *The Village Voice,* 47(37): 144.

Tennent, T. G., McQuaid, A., Loughnane, T., & Hands, A. J. 1971. Female arsonists. *British Journal of Psychiatry,* 119: 497–502.

Texas Commission on Law Enforcement Officer Standards and Education. 2001. *Pyromania.* Retrieved December 1, 2002 from: *http://www.utexas.edu/cee/dec/tcleose/index.html.*

The exclusive Menendez prison interview. 2002, September 27. Retrieved November 23, 2002, from *http://www.etonline.com/celebrity/a12478.htm.*

The Oxford American Desk Dictionary and Thesaurus (2nd ed.) 2001. New York: Berkley Books.

The Virtual Psychology Classroom. 2002. *Psychiatric disorders: Voyeurism.* Retrieved November 4, 2002, from *http://allpsych.com/disorders/paraphilias/Voyeurism.html.*

Theodorides, J. 1998. Origin of the myth of vampirism. *Journal of the Royal Society of Medicine,* 91: 2, 114.

Thornton, D., & Mann, R. 1997. Sexual masochism: Assessment and treatment. In D. R. Laws & W. O'Donohue (Eds.), *Sexual deviance: Theory, assessment, and treatment* (pp. 225–252). New York: The Guilford Press.

Tierney, D. W., & McCabe, M. P. 2001. An evaluation of self-report measures of cognitive distortions and empathy among Australian sex offenders. *Archives of Sexual Behavior,* 30(5): 495–519.

Tobin, T. 2003, May. *California and its sex offenders.* Symposium conducted at the annual meeting of the California Consortium of Sexual Offending, San Diego, CA.

Tolhurst, K. A. 1994. Comment: A search for solutions: Evaluating the latest anti-stalking developments and the national institute of justice model stalking code. *William & Mary Journal of Women & Law,* 1: 269.

Tollison, C. D., & Adams, H. E., 1979. *Sexual disorders: Treatment, theory, and research* (1st ed.). New York: Gardner Press, Inc.

Trivits, L. C., & Reppucci, N. D. 2002. Application of Megan's Law to juveniles. *American Psychologist,* 57(9): 690–704.

Trute, B., Adkins, B., & Macdonald, G. 1992. Professional attitudes regarding the sexual abuse of children: Comparing police, child welfare and community mental health. *Child Abuse and Neglect,* 16: 359–368.

Turner, M. T., & Turner T. N. 2001. *Female Adolescent Sexual Abusers.* Brandon, VT: Safer Society Press.

Turner, S. M., Beidel, D. C., & Epstein, S. H. 1991. Vulnerability and risk for anxiety disorder. *Journal of Anxiety Disorders,* 5: 2.

Turvey, B. 1995. An objective overview of auto-erotic fatalities. Retrieved October 12, 2002 from *www.corpus-delicti.com/auto.html.*

Tustin, R. D. 1995. The effects of advance notice of activity transitions on stereotypic behavior. *Journal of Applied Behavior Analysis,* 28: 91–92.

Twerski, A. J., & Nakken, C. 1997. *Addictive thinking and the addictive personality* (2nd ed.). New York: MJF Books.

United States Department of Justice 1997. Retrieved from *http://www.us.gov*.

United States v. Conlodon, 600 F. 2d 7 1979.

United States v. Lambey, No. 90-5619, 974 F. 2d 1389, 1992 U.S. App. LEXIS 20651.

United States v. Schmeltzer, No. 91-8338, 960 F. 2d 405, 1992 U.S. App. LEXIS 7726.

Updegraff, K. A., Madden-Derdich, D. A., Estrada, A. U., Sales, L. J., & Leonard, S. A. 2002. Young adolescents' experiences with parents and friends: Exploring the connections. *Family Relations,* 51: 72–80.

Vaillant, P. M., & Blasutti, B. 1992. Personality differences of sex offenders referred for treatment. *Psychological Reports,* 71: 1067–1074.

van Ijzendoorn, M. H. 1997. Attachment, emergent morality, and aggression: Toward a developmental socioemotional model of antisocial behavior. *International Journal of Behavioral Development,* 21: 703–727.

Vandenbergh, R. L., & Kelly, J. F. 1992 Vampirism: A review with new observations. In R. Noll, (Ed.). *Vampires, werewolves and demons: Twentieth century reports in the psychiatric literature* (pp. 27–36). New York: Brunner/Mazel.

Vold, G., Bernard, T., & Snipes, J. 1998. *Theoretical criminology.* New York: Oxford University Press.

Walsh, B., & Rosen, P. 1988. *Self-mutilation: Theory, research & treatment.* New York: The Guilford Press.

Ward, T., Connolly, M., McCormick, J., & Hudson, S. M. 1996. Social workers' attributions for sexually offending against children. *Journal of Child Sexual Abuse,* 5(3): 39–55.

———. 1995. Cognitive and affective deficits in sex offenders. *Sexual Abuse: A Journal of Research and Treatment,* 7: 67–83.

Ward, T., Hudson, S. M., & Marshal, W. L. 1996. Attachment style in sex offenders: A preliminary Study. *The Journal of Sex Research,* 33: 17–26.

Ward, T., McCormick, J., Hudson, S. M., & Polaschek, D. 1997. Rape: Assessment and treatment. In D. R. Laws, and W. T. O'Donohue (Eds.), *Sexual deviance: Theory, assessment, and treatment* (356–393). New York: The Guilford Press.

Warren, J. I., Hazelwood, R. R., & Dietz, P. E. 1996. The sexually sadistic serial killer. *Journal of Forensic Sciences,* 41(6): 970–974.

Warren, J., & Hislop, J. 2001. Female sex offenders: A typological and etiological overview. In *Practical Aspects of Rape Investigation: A Multidisciplinary Approach,* 3rd ed., New York: Elsevier Publishers.

Warren, S. L., Huston, L., Egeland, B., & Sroufe, L. A. 1997. Child and adolescent anxiety disorders and early attachment. *Journal of the American Academy of Child and Adolescent Psychiatry,* 36: 637–644.

Weekes, J. R., Pelletier, G., & Beaudette, D. 1995. Correctional officers: How do they perceive sex offenders? *International Journal of Offender Therapy and Comparative Criminology,* 39(1): 55–61.

Weinberg, M. S., Williams, C. J. & Calhan, C. 1994. Homosexual foot fetishism. *Archives of Sexual Behavior,* 23(6): 611–626.

———. 1995. "If the shoe fits . . .": Exploring male homosexual foot fetishism. *The Journal of Sex Research,* 32(1): 17–27.

Weinberg, M. S., Williams, C. J., & Moser, C. 1984. The social constituents of sadomasochism. *Social Problems,* 31: 379–389.

Weiner, A. 1996. Understanding the social needs of streetwalking prostitutes. *Social Work,* 41(1): 97–99.

Welch, L. 2002, November. Could you be a predator's next target? *Cosmopolitan,* 253: 143.

Wenig, H. G. 2002. *Amputism: A little known paraphilia.* Retrieved from *http://home.t-online.de/home/Amelo-Forum.hintergrund/theorie2/wenig-engl.htm.*

Wikipedia 2002. Paraphilia. *http://www.wikipedia.com/wiki/Paraphilia.*

Wilkins, R. 1990. Women who sexually abuse children: Doctors need to become sensitised to the possibility. *British Medical Journal* 300: 1153–1154.

Williams, C. L. 2002. Sexual harassment and sadomasochism. *Hypatia,* 17: 99–117.

Williams, S. 1995. *Female sex offenders.* Addendum to Risk Assessment Training Manual (pp. 38–46). Correctional Service Canada.

Wilson, C. 2000. *The mammoth book of the history of murder.* New York: Carroll & Graf.

Wilson, G. 1978. *Secrets of sexual fantsay.* Toronto: J. M. Dent & Sons.

Wilson, N. 2000. A psychoanalytic contribution to psychic vampirism: A case vignette. *American Journal of Psychoanalysis,* 60: 177–186.

Wincze, J. P. 1989. Assessment and treatment of atypical sexual behavior. In S. R. Leiblum, & R. C. Rosen (Eds.) *Principles and practice of sex therapy: An update for the 1990's* (2nd ed) (pp. 382–403). New York: The Guilford Press.

Winick, B. J. 1995. Ambiguities in the legal meaning and significance of mental illness. *Psychology, Public Policy and Law,* 1: 534.

Wise, T. N., & Goldberg, R. L. 1995. Escalation of a fetish: Coprophagia in a nonpsychotic adult of normal intelligence. *Journal of Sex and Marital Therapy,* 21: 272–275.

Wolfe, F. A. 1985. *Twelve female sexual offenders.* Presented at "Next steps in research on the assessment and treatment of sexually aggressive persons (Paraphiliacs)." March, 1985, St. Louis, MO.

Wolff, J. 1999. Vamping with vampires: The sexy, scary new cult. *Cosmopolitan,* 226(1): 150–153.

Wolford, K. R. 1980. Some attitudinal, psychological and sociological characteristics of incarcerated arsonists. *Fire and Arson Investigator,* 22: 1–30.

Wrightsman, L. S. 2001. *Forensic psychology.* Belmont, CA: Wadsworth.

Wrightsman, L., Nietzel, M. T., & Fortune, W. H. 1998. *Psychology and the legal system.* Pacific Grove, CA: Brooks/Cole Publishers.

Wyatt, G. E. 1992. The sociocultural context of African American and White American women's rape. *Journal of Social Issues,* 48(1): 77–91.

Young, A. M., Boyd, C., & Hubbell, A. 2000. Prostitution, drug use, and coping with psychological distress. *Journal of Drug Issues,* 30(4): 789–800.

Younglove, J. A., & Vitello, C. J. 2003. Community notification provisions of "Megan's Law" from a therapeutic jurisprudence perspective: A case study. *American Journal of Forensic Psychology,* 21(1): 25–38.

Zatz, N. 1997. Sex work/sex act: Law, labor, and desire in construction of prostitution. *Signs,* 22(2): 277.

Zavitzianos, G. 1971. Fetishism and exhibitionism in the female and their relationship to psychopathy and kleptomania. *International Journal of Psycho-Analysis,* 52: 297–305.

Zevitz, R. G., & Farkas, M. A. 2000. The impact of sex-offender community notification on parole/probation in Wisconsin. *International Journal of Offender Therapy and Comparative Criminology,* 44(1): 8–21.

Zohar, J., Kaplan, Z., & Benjamin, J. 1994. Compulsive exhibitionism successfully treated with Fluvoxamine: A controlled case study. *Journal of Clinical Psychology,* 55.

Zolondek, S. C., Abel, G. G., Northey, W. F., Jr., & Jordan, A. D. 2001. The self-reported behaviors of juvenile sexual offenders. *Journal of Interpersonal Violence,* 16(1): 73–85. Retrieved on September 27, 2002, from the ProQuest database.

Zoophilia for Beginners. 2002, October 27. *http://www.beastlinks.net/stories/html/beginners.htm.*

Zucker, K. J., & Blanchard 1997. Transvestic fetishism: Psychopathology and theory. In D. R. Laws & W. O'Donohue (Eds.), *Sexual deviance: Theory, assessment and treatment* (pp. 253–279). New York: The Guilford Press.

INDEX

C

California Department of Corrections, 10, 12, 483. *See also* CDC

California Penal Code, 398

Canchus, 123

castration, 210–11, 455–56

CDC, 10, 12. *See also* California Department of Corrections

Center for Sex Offender Management, 4

Chase, Richard Trenton, 116

Chiang-Shih, 123

child abuse, 18, 37

Child Abuse and Trauma Scale (CAT), 311

child sexual abuse/molestation, 4–5, 6–7, 8, 9, 42, 135, 200, 253, 301, 329–39, 485–86, 488

  categorization of, 4

  molesters, 27, 28, 310–11, 314, 319–27, 337

  typologies, 8

circumcision, female, 212

Clarke Institute of Psychiatry, 321–22

Cluster B personality disorders, 276

cognitive-behavioral techniques, 141, 256, 453–54

Cole, Carroll "Eddie", 269

Commonwealth of Massachusetts v. Appleby, 225

comorbidity, 20, 313, 314

compulsive sexual behavior (CSB), 49

conduct disorder, 15

coprophilia, 137–42, 149, 310

covert sensitization, 255

Creager, Helen, 10

crime rates, 62

cross-dressing, 35–37, 38, 39, 40, 43, 66, 171–72, 174–75, 176, 221, 413. *See also* transvestism

cyesolagnia, 66

D

Dahmer, Jeffrey, 98, 101, 273, 274, 281, 437

decapitation, 99

defense mechanisms, 42, 44

Department of Justice, 15, 373

depression, 30, 49, 139, 141, 142, 148. *See also* sex offenders, depression in

Diagnostic and Statistical Manual for Mental Disorders (DSM-IV), 5, 36, 40, 41, 49, 58, 69, 71, 73, 140, 147, 156, 165; 171, 186, 188, 238, 244, 257, 275, 276, 279, 282, 293, 294, 301, 309, 310, 313, 315, 319, 356, 420

Dichotomous Paraphiliac Model, 58

DNA, 102, 270

Dodd, Westley Allan, 100

Dracula, 123

drugs, 42, 63, 64, 97, 99, 112, 263, 268, 365, 405

  abuse of, 42

  illicit manufacturing of, 102

  problems, 493

  residential treatment services, 42

  treatment programs, 42, 456

DSM-IV. See Diagnostic and Statistical Manual for Mental Disorders

dynamic-behavioral theory, 296

E

erotophonophilia, 61. *See also* murder, lust

exhibitionism, 4, 5, 60, 71, 72, 73, 86, 98, 99, 147, 234, 238, 239, 252, 253, 254, 256, 257–65, 310, 363

exhibitionists, 12, 71, 100, 250, 252